COVER PHOTO:
Joffre Lakes Provincial Park

MW00597919

Official Partners:

  ATVBC  BC Forest Safety *Unsafe is Unacceptable* BCFROA BCParks BCWF CAMPING & RV IN BC

I

THE TEAM

DIRECTORS
Russell Mussio
Wesley Mussio

VICE PRESIDENT
Chris Taylor

EDITOR IN CHIEF
Russell Mussio

GIS & CARTOGRAPHY

MANAGER
Andrew Allen

GIS SPECIALISTS
Farah Aghdam
David Mancini

CARTOGRAPHERS
Aaron Dixon
Graeme Fahy
Oliver Herz
Dale Tober

MARKETING & CREATIVE SERVICES

MANAGER
Nazli Faghihi

GRAPHIC & LAYOUT DESIGN
Elisa Codazzi
Farnaz Faghihi
Nicky Forshaw

SOCIAL MEDIA
Carly Watson

CONTENT WRITERS
Sean Anderson
Leslie Bryant MacLean
Trent Ernst
Brian Harris
Jay Hoare
Colin Hughes
Mike Manyk
Jason Marleau
Russell Mussio
Stepan Soroka

SALES
Basilio Bagnato
Chris Taylor

ADMINISTRATION
Shaun Filipenko
Jo-ana Maki

TECH SUPPORT
Sal Kahila
Matthew Steblyna

ACKNOWLEDGEMENTS

This book could not have been compiled without the dedicated and talented people at Backroad Mapbooks. Thanks to Sean Anderson, Leslie Bryant MacLean, Lorne Collicutt, Jay Hoare, Colin Hughes and Mike Manyk who continued with the work of Trent Ernst, Brian Harris, Jason Marleau and others before of shifting through the incredible amount of recreational opportunities in Southwestern BC. Combined with the talented efforts of Farah Aghdam, Andrew Allen, Basilio Bagnato, Elisa Codazzi, Aaron Dixon, Farnaz Faghihi, Nazli Faghihi, Shaun Filipenko, Nicky Forshaw, Oliver Herz, Sal Kahila, Jo-ana Maki, David Mancini, Stepan Soroka, Matthew Steblyna, Chris Taylor, Dale Tober and Carly Watson we are able to produce the most comprehensive guidebook for a truly spectacular region of British Columbia.

Each edition we consult a variety of people and resources to help ensure our information is as up to date as possible. These sources range from the very helpful Recreation Sites and Trails personnel, including John Crooks and Alistair McCrone, to Katie Lemire BC Park Ranger for Thompson Western Mountain Area. We would also like to thank Craig Morrison of the Mountain Resorts Branch and Marie Fournier-Beck and Allison MacDonald from Squamish - Lillooet Regional District. And, as always, we turn to many other resources such as Clubtread, Bivouac and the various other backcountry trail and hut information sources out there to dig up more information on those many hidden treasures in the area.

Another incredible resource for our updates is our readers many of who have taken advantage of our GPS Track Submission Program. From here, we have many notable contributors that include Arnold Grimm, Russell Grosser, Colleen MacDonald, Steve McAbee, Meredith Twaites and Andrew Wallwork. This is by no means a complete list; so please continue to send your tracks and updates our way!

These maps are a synthesis of a variety of sources, mostly Federal, Provincial and Municipal Government. We would like to express our gratitude to the helpful map providers © Department of Natural Resources Canada also the maps contains information licensed under the Open Government License – British Columbia as well as the Open Government Licence - North Vancouver and Vancouver.

Finally we would like to thank Allison, Devon, Jasper, Madison, Nancy and Penny Mussio for their continued support of the Backroad Mapbook Series. As our family grows, it is becoming more and more challenging to break away from it all to explore our beautiful country.

Sincerely,
Russell and Wesley Mussio

Library and Archives Canada Cataloguing in Publication

Mussio, Russell, 1969
Backroad Mapbook, Vancouver, Coast & Mountains BC
[cartographic material] / Russell Mussio. -- 4th ed.

ISBN 978-1-926806-51-8

1. Recreation areas--British Columbia--Lower Mainland--Maps. 2. Recreation areas--British Columbia--Squamish-Lillooet--Maps. 3. Recreation areas--British Columbia--Fraser River Valley--Maps. 4. Outdoor recreation--British Columbia--Lower Mainland--Guidebooks. 5. Outdoor recreation--British Columbia--Squamish-Lillooet--Guidebooks. 6. Outdoor recreation--British Columbia--Fraser River Valley--Guidebooks. 7. Lower Mainland (B.C.)--Maps. 8. Squamish-Lillooet (B.C.)--Maps. 9. Fraser River Valley (B.C.)--Maps. 10. Lower Mainland (B.C.)--Guidebooks. 11. Squamish-Lillooet (B.C.)--Guidebooks. 12. Fraser River Valley (B.C.)--Guidebooks. I. Ernst, Trent. Backroad mapbook, Vancouver, Coast & Mountains BC. II. Mussio Ventures Ltd. III. Title.

G1172.S68E63M87 2013   796.509711'3   C2013-900515-3

DISCLAIMER

Backroad Mapbooks does not warrant that the backroads, paddling routes and trails indicated in this Mapbook are passable nor does it claim that the Mapbook is completely accurate. Therefore, please be careful when using this or any source to plan and carry out your outdoor recreation activity.

Please note that traveling on logging roads, river routes and trails is inherently dangerous, and without limiting the generality of the foregoing, you may encounter poor road conditions, unexpected traffic, poor visibility, and low or no road/trail maintenance. Please use extreme caution when traveling logging roads and trails.

Please refer to the Fishing and Hunting Regulations for closures and restrictions. It is your responsibility to know when and where closures and restrictions apply.

HELP US HELP YOU

A comprehensive resource such as Backroad Mapbooks for Vancouver, Coast and Mountains BC could not be put together without a great deal of help and support. Despite our best efforts to ensure that everything is accurate, errors do occur. If you see any errors or omissions, please continue to let us know.

* ALL UPDATES WILL BE POSTED ON OUR WEBSITE

CONTACT US

☎ 604-521-6277
toll free 1-877-520-5670

✉ updates@backroadmapbooks.com

📠 604-521-6260

📍 Unit 106- 1500 Hartley Ave
Coquitlam, BC, V3K 7A1

🌐 backroadmapbooks.com

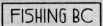

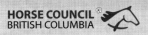

INTRODUCTION

Garibaldi Provincial Park
© Aaron Dixon

WELCOME

Welcome to the 4th edition of the Vancouver, Coast and Mountains Backroad Mapbook.

Originally titled Southwestern BC, this mapbook was the very first in our series, and the start of a very popular run of outdoor recreation mapbooks. We now have over two million books in circulation across Canada and are extremely proud to be Canada's most trusted source for outdoor adventure planning!

▶ **THE AREA:** This book covers the southwest corner of beautiful British Columbia, Canada. Vancouver, Gibsons, and Powell River mark the western edge of this area, with Hope, Manning Park, Boston Bar and Lillooet to the east. Chilliwack, Maple Ridge, Squamish, Whistler and Gold Bridge are some of the prominent communities in between. These towns and cities are surrounded by diverse terrain, including lush rainforests, coastal fjords, powerful rivers and deep, dark lakes. Rugged mountains literally rise from the ocean floor, their snow-capped peaks reaching majestically towards the sky. This area's natural beauty is unparalleled, and the verdant landscape teems with life of all kinds.

▶ **THE ACTIVITIES:** The Vancouver, Coast and Mountains region is an outdoor recreation paradise. There are not many other places in the world where you can go ocean kayaking and alpine skiing in the same day. No matter the season, outdoor enthusiasts have an expansive variety of opportunities. Rich fisheries are just as active in winter as in summer. An expansive trails network can be explored on foot, bike, ski or snowshoe. Kayakers will have just as much fun on the inland rivers as they will exploring the endless ocean coastline. The opportunities for outdoor recreation in southwestern BC are endless.

▶ **THE BOOK:** As always, we have spent hundreds of hours updating the maps to provide you with the most comprehensive coverage possible. We have added countless roads, trails and recreation sites. New colouring and easier to read text will keep you navigating smoothly. We have gone to new lengths to better define motorized and long distance trails, as well as to classify paved and unpaved road systems.

The writing has also been expanded and updated, including many new entries and countless updates. Thanks again to all of the people who have submitted tracks and way-points as well as general updates to the book. We are also indebted to the various retailers and people at Recreation Sites and Trails and BC Parks for helping ensure we are up to date on the many improvements in those facilities.

This Backroad Mapbook is much more than a set of maps; it is your guide to adventure and a key to endless possibilities. The maps and writing will transport you to another place, even from the comfort of your armchair. Enjoy!

BACKROAD HISTORY

The Backroad Mapbook idea came into existence when Wesley and Russell Mussio were out exploring. They had several books and a few maps to try to find their way through the maze of logging roads around southern BC. The brothers were getting very frustrated trying to find their way and eventually gave up. Not to be outdone, the two ambitious brothers started brainstorming. Eventually the Backroad Mapbook idea was born.

They published their first book in January 1994 and it quickly sold out. Rather than simply reprinting it, they listened to the feedback of customers and made several alterations that helped improve the book. This formula of continuing to make the product better continues today and has helped establish the Backroad Mapbook series as the top selling outdoor recreation guidebook series in the country. From the tiny beginnings in that Vancouver apartment with maps strewn all over the walls, to one of the most sought-after outdoor products in the country, the Backroad Mapbook series has truly come a long way.

RESOURCE ROADS ARE PLANNED AND CONSTRUCTED TO DEVELOP AND PROTECT BC'S NATURAL RESOURCES; WHILE PRIMARILY USED BY FORESTRY, AGRICULTURE, MINING, AND OIL AND GAS THEY ALSO PROVIDE ACCESS TO RECREATIONAL OPPORTUNITIES.

WHAT TO EXPECT

Resource roads are gravel or dirt and they may be single lane with sharp turns, soft shoulders, narrow bridges, poor alignment and grades steeper than on highways. Not all hazards will be marked and there might not be protective barriers at dangerous or steep sections; roadside brush may limit visibility.

APPLY THE SAME RULES OF THE ROAD AS USED ON HIGHWAYS

Drive on the right hand side. Wear your seatbelt. Don't drink and drive. Take your license and insurance. Obey the speed limit – unless posted otherwise, it's up to 80 km/hr. but many roads are designed and built for 60 km/hr. or less.

DRIVE ACCORDING TO ROAD CONDITIONS

Travel a speed that allows you to stop within half of your line of sight (other vehicles need room to stop too). If dusty or slippery, slow down so you can react to oncoming traffic, potholes, wildlife, changing road conditions and unexpected hazards; large industrial vehicles can't manoeuver as quickly as passenger vehicles.

FOCUS ON YOUR DRIVING; EXERCISE CAUTION, PATIENCE AND COURTESY

Keep your headlights and taillights on. Industrial drivers are familiar with the road; let them go ahead and give them room to do their job. It might be advantageous for you to follow industrial vehicles, watch for brake lights and make sure you find a turn out when they do (to clear oncoming traffic).

OBSERVE AND OBEY THE SIGNS

Signs communicate information about the road, traffic you can expect, active worksites or hazardous conditions; take time to read and understand signs at the start of the road and along the way.

STOP IN THE RIGHT SPOT

If you must stop along the road find a pull out or straight section that provides good visibility from both directions and is wide enough for traffic to pass. Pull over onto the shoulder; avoid stopping in a curve or on the crest of a hill.

BE PREPARED

Plan your trip before you go! Beware of road conditions and traffic; share trip information with a reliable contact, bring a map and GPS. Carry extra clothing, footwear, food, water and fuel. Have an emergency first aid kit. Make sure your vehicle is ready for the trip – good tires, a spare, chains in winter, tools including a shovel and a fire extinguisher.

BC Forest Safety Council
1-877-741-1060
VINBC.CA

KEEP AN EYE OUT FOR THE PROGRAM

BC Forest Safety
Unsafe is Unacceptable

REPORT A CONCERN OR COMPLIMENT ABOUT A VEHICLE AT 1 877 741 1060 OR VINBC.CA

VISITOR CENTRES

Watch for the Visitor Centre signs located thoughout the Vancouver, Coast and Mountains Region.
Visitor Centres can help with:

- Hotel and activity/attraction bookings
- Maps and directions
- Travel advice and free guides
- In-depth knowledge of the community and region
- National and BC parks information
- Many other travel-related services

VANCOUVER, COAST & MOUNTAINS BC

Visitor Centre

Abbotsford
Visitor Centre
(Year Round)   See Map 3/E7

Nestled in the shadow of majestic Mt. Baker, in the heart of the Fraser Valley, you will find Abbotsford, British Columbia, Canada. Visiting Abbotsford introduces you to an eclectic blend of modern urban style and friendly country living.

34561 Delair Rd
Abbotsford, BC V2S 2E1
1-888-332-2229
604-859-1721
info@tourismabbotsford.ca
f /TourismAbbotsford
@TourismAbby
www.TourismAbbotsford.ca

Chilliwack
Visitor Centre
(Year Round)   See Map 4/C4

Visit beautiful Chilliwack for wilderness camping, paragliding, golfing, fishing, paddle boarding, kayaking, ATVing, Mountain biking, river rafting, and so much more! Pick up a copy of the Chilliwack Hiking and Outdoor Adventure Guide.

44150 Luckakuck Way
Chilliwack, BC V2R 4A7
1-800-567-9535
604-858-8121
info@tourismchilliwack.com
f /TourismChilliwack
@greatoutside
www.TourismChilliwack.com

Hope
Visitor Centre
(Year Round)   See Map 15/F6

Embrace the Journey!
*Fishing *Bouldering *Gold Panning
*60km of Trails *Biking *Othello Tunnels
Pick up your free Hope Visitor Guide
& Trails of Hope map to maximize your adventure!

919 Water Avenue
Hope, BC V0X 1L0
604-869-2021
vc@hopebc.ca
f /TourismHope
@TourismHope
www.HopeBC.ca

Peace Arch
Visitor Centre
(Year Round)   See Map 2/C7

Courteous, knowledgeable staff provide professional visitor counselling and itinerary planning, accommodation reservations plus attraction and transportation ticketing, and helpful travel information including transportation and community information on all areas of British Columbia.

289 Hwy 99
Surrey, BC V3S 9N7
604-541-4555
BCVCPeaceArch@destinationbc.ca
f /HelloBC
@HelloBC #exploreBC
www.hellobc.com

Pemberton
Visitor Centre
(Seasonal: May to September)   See Map 33/C1

Summer activities, golf, fishing, cycling, 2 Provincial Parks, winter sports, water sports, horseback riding, historic Museum, BMX & Stock Car Tracks, Airport.

Hwy 99 & Pemberton Portage Rd
Pemberton, BC V0N 2L0
604-894-6175
info@pembertonchamber.com
f /Pemberton.VisitorCentre
@PembertonBC
www.TourismPembertonBC.com

Squamish
Visitor Centre
(Year Round)   See Map 22/C6

Visit our Provincial Parks and explore the extensive trail system. Hike, bike, climb, windsurf or kiteboard. Visit the Sea to Sky Gondola, Britannia Mine Museum & the West Coast Railway Heritage Park..

#104-38551 Loggers Lane
Squamish, BC V8B 0H2
1-877-815-5084
604-815-4994
info@tourismsquamish.com
f /TourismSquamish
@TourismSquamish
www.ExploreSquamish.com

Whistler
Visitor Centre
(Year Round)   See Map 32/F5

Located in the spectacular Coast Mountains of British Columbia, Whistler is Canada's premier, year-rounddestination for adventure.

4230 Gateway Dr
Whistler, BC V0N 1B4
1-877-991-9988
604-935-3357
activity@tourismwhistler.com
f /GoWhistler
@GoWhistler
www.whistler.com

NAVIGATING

Each of our Backroad Mapbooks is filled with amazing experiences that show you how to enjoy the outdoors and create unforgettable memories. Visit backroadmapbooks.com for our other great products, tips & tutorials, features and updates to further enhance your outdoor experiences.

INTRODUCTION

After a brief introduction to the region, you can find valuable planning tools such as information on Travel/Tourism and Visitor Centres, and the ever-so-important Map Legend.

ADVENTURES

Exclusive to Backroad Mapbooks, this section is filled with adventure write-ups, put together by our team of outdoor researchers and with the help of local residents & communities. From backroad attractions to fishing hotspots and winter adventures, you have access to the most comprehensive backcountry planning tool available on the market.

COMMUNITY PROFILES

This section features detailed overviews and photos provided by community locals, providing insight into major towns and cities within the region and what each community has to offer, as you trek into the backcountry.

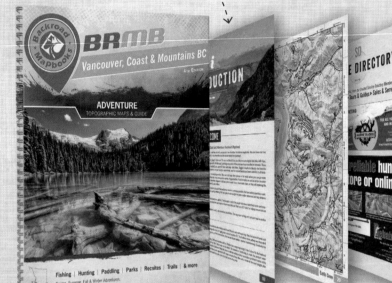

TOPO MAPS

Containing the core foundation of our Mapbooks, this section begins with a regional map key and leads into our nationally-acclaimed topographic maps, with hundreds of thousands of kilometers of backroads, backcountry trails and points of interest.

SERVICE DIRECTORY

Another essential trip planning resource, the Service directory allows you to find details on some of the best Accommodations, Sales /Services and Tours/Guides in the area.

MAP & ADVENTURES INDEXES

A full map and adventures index of the guide's contents is included with page numbers and map coordinates for easy reference.

TRIP PLANNING

Everything you need to know before heading into the outdoors, including important contact information for general services, parks, wildlife, club & association contacts, distance chart, alongside a list of advertisers featured in the mapbook. We also have included handy pages for making general notes or reservations.

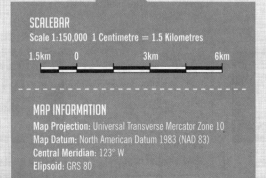

SCALEBAR
Scale 1:150,000 1 Centimetre = 1.5 Kilometres

1.5km   0   3km   6km

MAP INFORMATION
Map Projection: Universal Transverse Mercator Zone 10
Map Datum: North American Datum 1983 (NAD 83)
Central Meridian: 123° W
Elipsoid: GRS 80

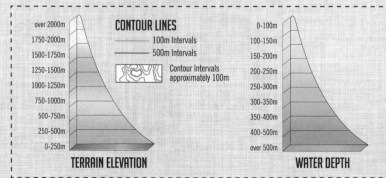

TERRAIN ELEVATION	CONTOUR LINES	WATER DEPTH
over 2000m	——— 100m Intervals	0-100m
1750-2000m	——— 500m Intervals	100-150m
1500-1750m	Contour Intervals approximately 100m	150-200m
1250-1500m		200-250m
1000-1250m		250-300m
750-1000m		300-350m
500-750m		350-400m
250-500m		400-500m
0-250m		over 500m

MAP LEGEND

 National / Provincial Parks

 Community Forests / Interpretive Forests / Recreation Sites / Regional Parks

 Conservancy / Ecological Reserve / Protected Area / Wildlife Area

 Canadian Forces Base / Mining / Restricted Area / Motorized Closures

City

First Nations

Glacier

 Water

 Swamps

 WMU (Wildlife Management Units)

 TFL (Tree Farm Licence Area)

Municiple / Regional District

LINE CLASSIFICATIONS

Freeways

Highways

Secondary Highways

Arterial Paved Roads

Rural Paved Roads

Local Paved Roads

Railways

Unpaved Secondary Highways

Forest Service & Main Industry Roads

Active Industry Roads (2wd)

Other Industry Roads (2wd / 4wd)

Unclassified & 4wd Roads

Deactivated Roads

Ferry Routes

Trans Canada Trail

Long Distance Trails

Snowmobile Trails

Motorized Trails ATV/OHV & Snowmobile

Developed Trails

Routes (Undeveloped Trails)

Saltwater Fishing Area

Portage Routes

Lake Paddling Routes

River Paddling Routes

Transmission Lines

Pipelines

Cut / Seismic Lines

MAP SYMBOLS

ON THE TRAIL

- ATV / OHV / Motorbiking
- BC Recreation Site (Camping)
- BC Recreation Site (Camping-RV)
- Big Tree
- Cabin / Chalet / Hut / Shelter
- Campsite (back country / water access only)
- Campsite / Limited Facilities
- Caving / Spelunking
- Cross Country Skiing / Back Country Ski Touring
- Cycling / Mountain Biking
- Hiking
- Horseback Riding
- Interpretive Trail
- Picnic Site
- Ranger Station / Patrol Cabin
- Rock Climbing
- RV Campsite / Trailer Park
- Ski Area
- Snowmobiling
- Snowshoeing
- Trailhead
- Viewpoint / Forestry Lookout (abandoned)
- Wildlife Viewing

ON THE WATER

- Anchorage
- Beach
- Beacon
- Boat Launch
- Canoe Access Put-in / Take-out
- Dam
- Diving
- Ferry
- Float Plane Landing
- Fish Hatchery
- Fish Spawning / Ladder
- Hotspring
- Lighthouse
- Marsh
- Paddling (canoe-kayak)
- Portage
- Portage Distance
- Sunken Ship
- Waterfall

ON THE ROAD

- Airport
- Airstrip
- Gate
- Highway: Trans Canada
- Highway Interchange
- Information Centre
- Parking
- Visitor Centre

OTHER

- Arrow / Location Pointer
- BRMB Geocache
- City, Town, Village Indicator
- Customs
- Golf Course
- Gondola
- Hang-gliding
- Microwave Tower
- Mine Site
- National Historic Site
- Pictograph
- Point of Interest
- Resort
- Resort (BCFROA)
- Wilderness Area / Wildlife Area / Wildlife Reserve
- Winery

Visit **backroadmapbook.com** to see tutorials on how to use different elements of our legend

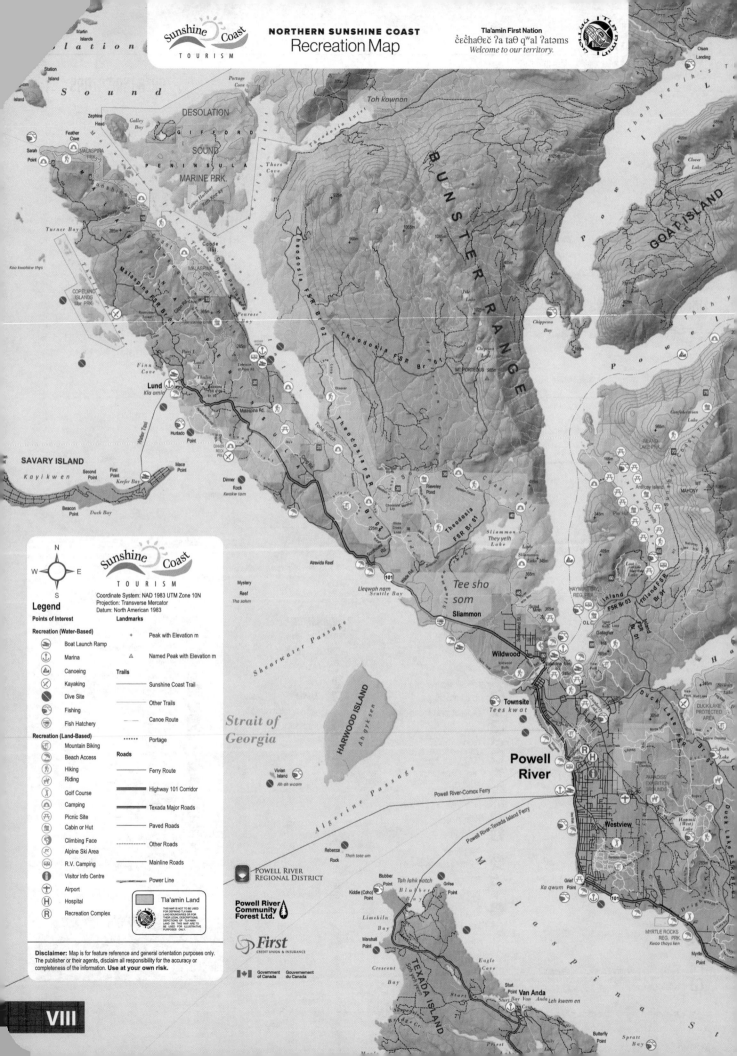

NORTHERN SUNSHINE COAST
Recreation Map

Sunshine Coast TOURISM

Tla'amin First Nation
čɛčhaθɛč ʔa taθ qʷal ʔatəms
Welcome to our territory.

Legend

N W E S

Sunshine Coast TOURISM

Coordinate System: NAD 1983 UTM Zone 10N
Projection: Transverse Mercator
Datum: North American 1983

Points of Interest

Recreation (Water-Based)
- Boat Launch Ramp
- Marina
- Canoeing
- Kayaking
- Dive Site
- Fishing
- Fish Hatchery

Recreation (Land-Based)
- Mountain Biking
- Beach Access
- Hiking
- Riding
- Golf Course
- Camping
- Picnic Site
- Cabin or Hut
- Climbing Face
- Alpine Ski Area
- R.V. Camping
- Visitor Info Centre
- Airport
- Hospital
- Recreation Complex

Landmarks
- + Peak with Elevation m
- △ Named Peak with Elevation m

Trails
- —— Sunshine Coast Trail
- —— Other Trails
- — · — Canoe Route
- ······ Portage

Roads
- ═══ Ferry Route
- ═══ Highway 101 Corridor
- ═══ Texada Major Roads
- —— Paved Roads
- ----- Other Roads
- —— Mainline Roads
- —— Power Line

Tla'amin Land

THIS MAP IS NOT TO BE USED FOR DEFINING TLA'AMIN LAND BOUNDARIES OR FOR THEIR LEGAL DESCRIPTIONS. DEPICTIONS OF TLA'AMIN LAND ON THIS MAP ARE TO BE USED FOR ILLUSTRATIVE PURPOSES ONLY.

POWELL RIVER REGIONAL DISTRICT

Powell River Community Forest Ltd.

First CREDIT UNION & INSURANCE

Government of Canada Gouvernement du Canada

Disclaimer: Map is for feature reference and general orientation purposes only. The publisher or their agents, disclaim all responsibility for the accuracy or completeness of the information. **Use at your own risk.**

VIII

Map Labels

D E S O L A T I O N S o u n d

DESOLATION SOUND

GIFFORD PENINSULA

MARINE PRK.

Martin Islands

Station Island

Feather Cove

Sarah Point

Zephine Head

Galley Bay

MALASPINA PRK.

Portage Cove

Toh kownon

Theodosia Inlet

B U N S T E R   R A N G E

GOAT ISLAND

Cochrane Isl.

Thors Cove

Grace Harbour

Koh kee ky

Turner Bay

285m

Koo kwohkw thys

COPELAND ISLANDS Mar. PRK.

MALASPINA PRK.

Okeover Arm

Penrose Bay

MT PORTEOUS 985m

Isle Lake

1025m

Chippewa Lake

Chippewa Bay

Finn Cove

Thulin

Lund
Kla amin

Hurtado Point

Malaspina Rd.

Toh kaca

Theodosia FSR Br 01

Theodosia FSR Br 02

Theodosia FSR

Rieveley Pond

Coast Trail

Theodosia FSR Br 01

Sliammon They yelh Lake

Confederation Lake

MT MAHONY

SAVARY ISLAND
K a y i k w e n

Second Point

First Point

Keefer Bay

Mace Point

Dinner Rock PRK.

Dinner Rock
Kwakw tam

Chocolate Lily

Wilde Creek Lake

225m

Little Sliammon Lake

Beacon Point

Duck Bay

Abrevida Reef

Mystery Reef
Tha sahm

Llegwah nam
Scuttle Bay

Tee sho som

Sliammon

HAYWIRE BAY REG. PRK.

Inland FSR Br 03

Inland FSR

Gallagher

S h e a r w a t e r   P a s s a g e

Wildwood

Townsite
Tees kwat

DUCKLAKE PROTECTED AREA

Strait of Georgia

HARWOOD ISLAND
A h g y t sen

Powell River

Vivian Island
Ah ah woom

Westview

Duck Lake

PARADISE EXHIBITION GROUNDS

A l g e r i n e   P a s s a g e

Powell River-Comox Ferry

Rebecca Rock
Thah tote um

Powell River-Texada Island Ferry

Hammil (West) Lake

Blubber Point

Toh lahk natch

Grise Point

Grief Point
Ka qwum

Kiddie (Coho) Point

B l u b b e r   B a y

M a l a s p i n a   P e n i n s u l a

MYRTLE ROCKS REG. PRK.
Kwoo thays ken

Limekiln Bay

Marshall Point

Eagle Cove

Crescent Bay

TEXADA ISLAND
Sah yah nuh

Stut Point Van Anda
Sturt Bay Van Anda Leh kwem en

Butterfly Point

Spratt Bay

Priest

TOPOGRAPHIC MAPS

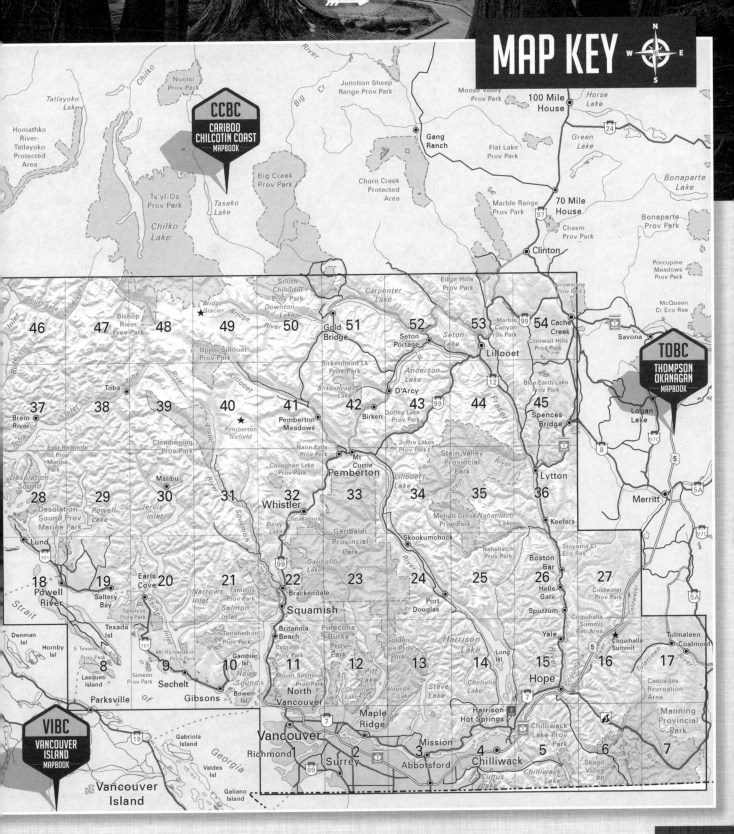

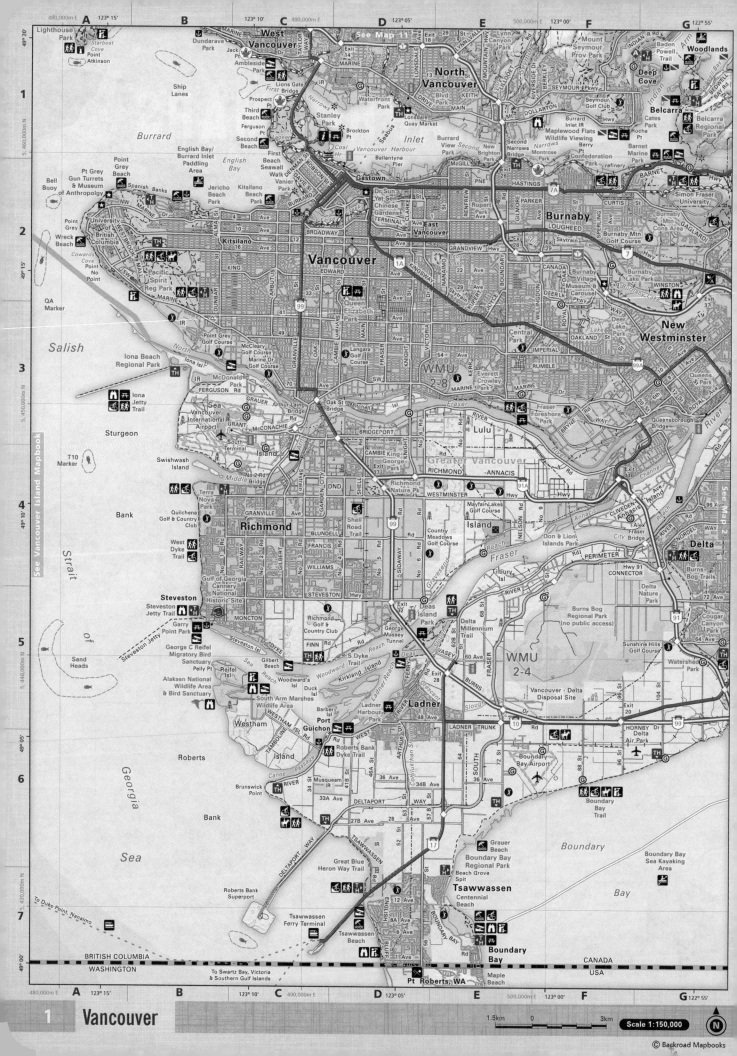

Scale 1:150,000

© Backroad Mapbooks

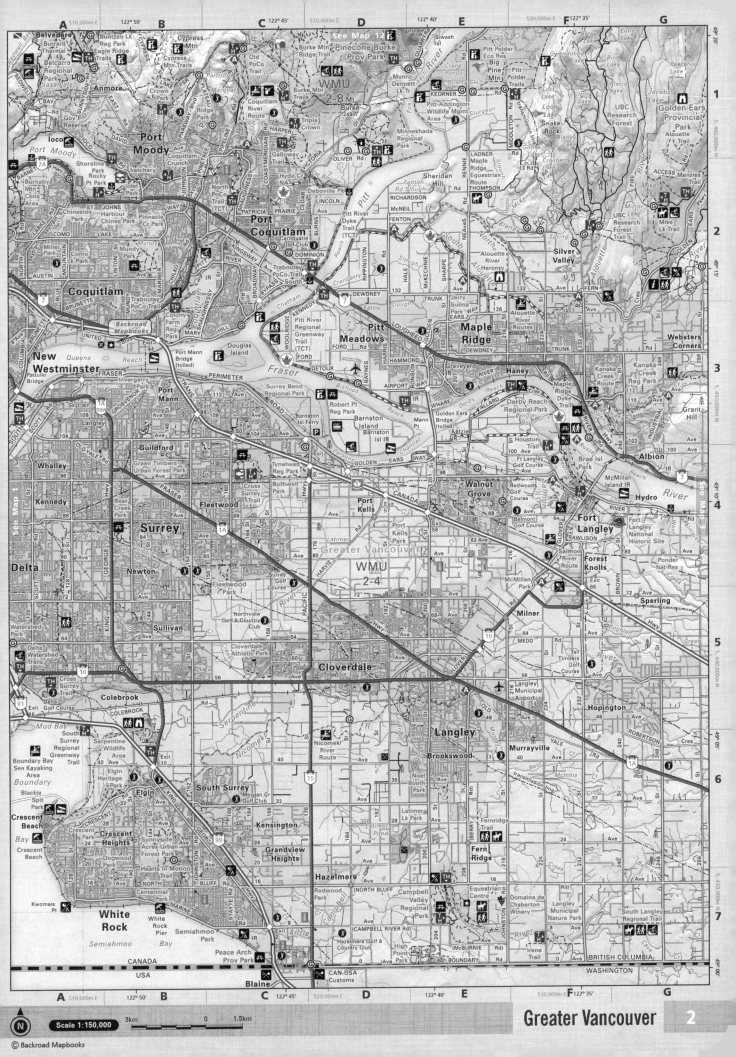

Greater Vancouver

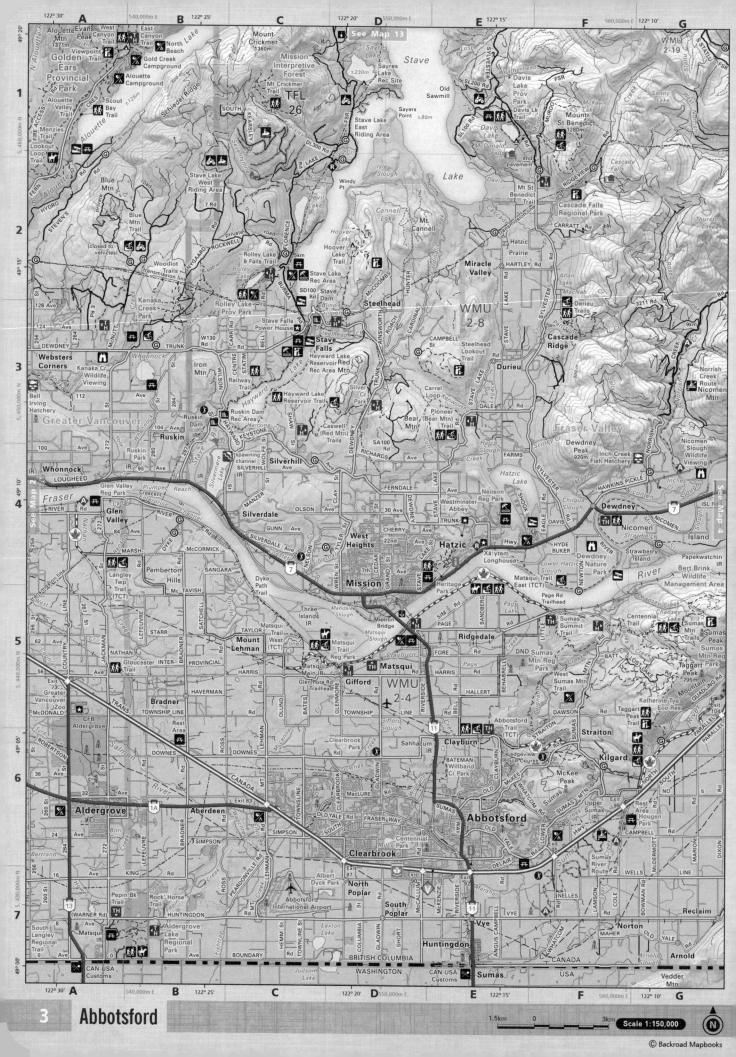

Scale 1:150,000

© Backroad Mapbooks

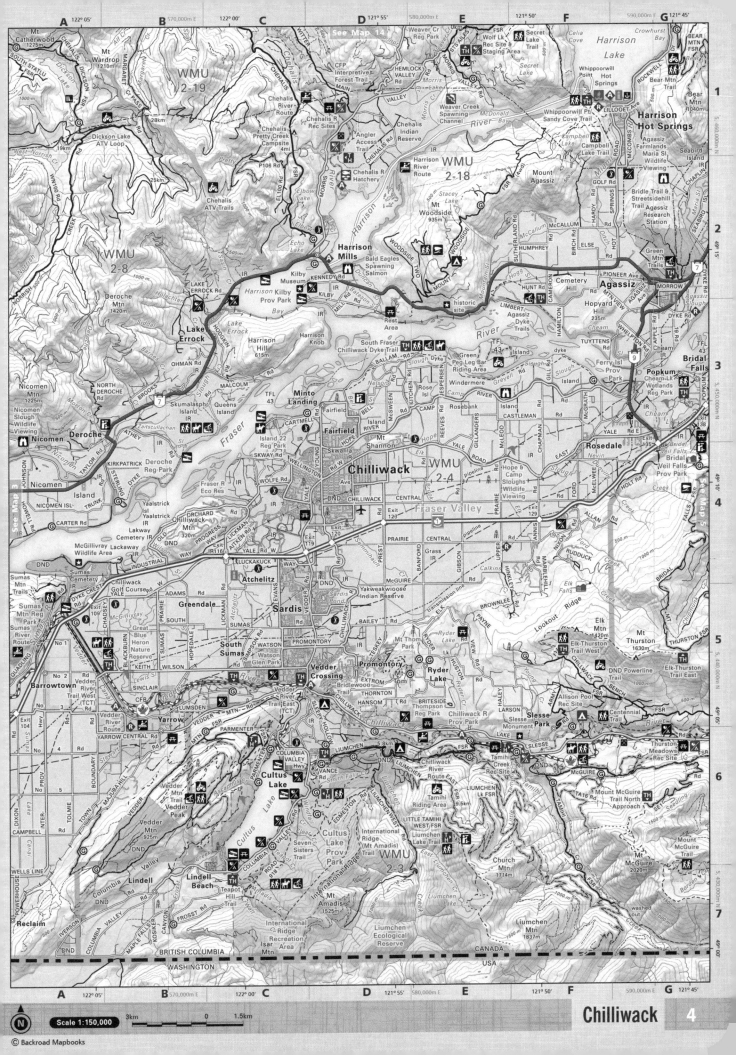

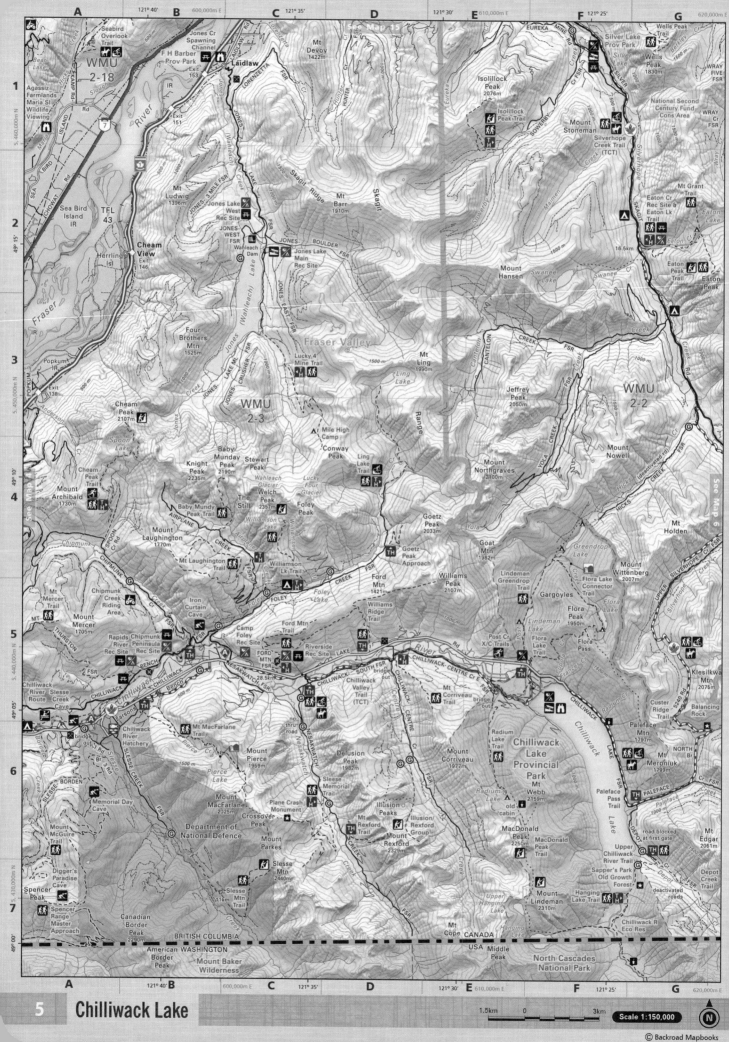

Scale 1:150,000

© Backroad Mapbooks

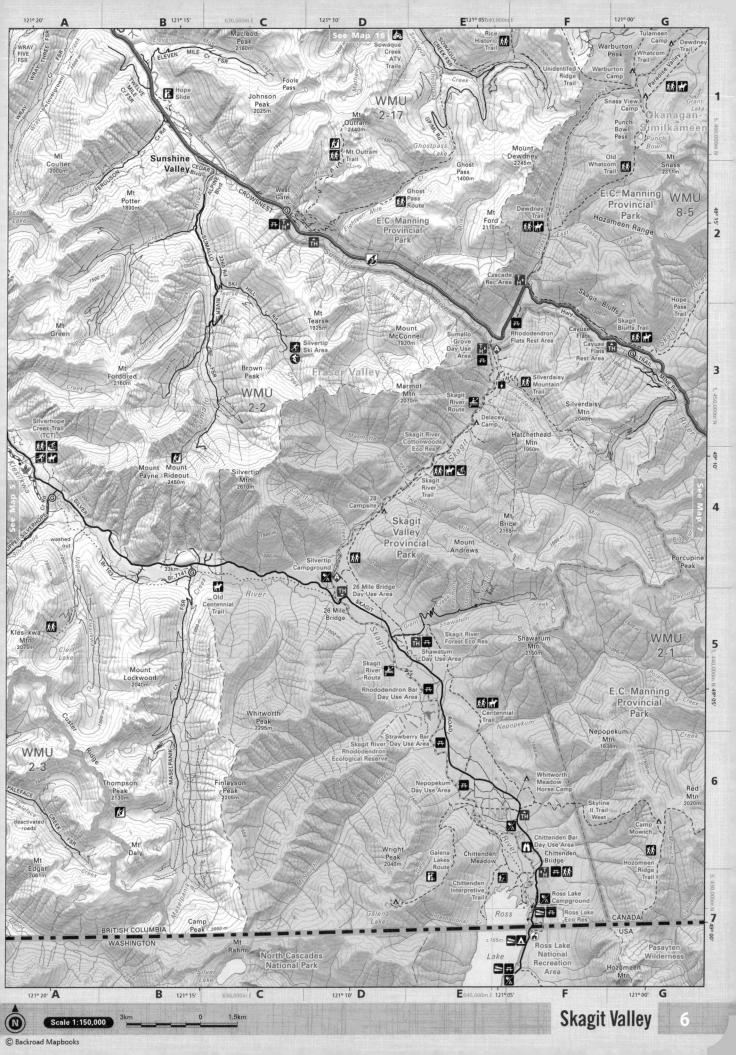

Skagit Valley **6**

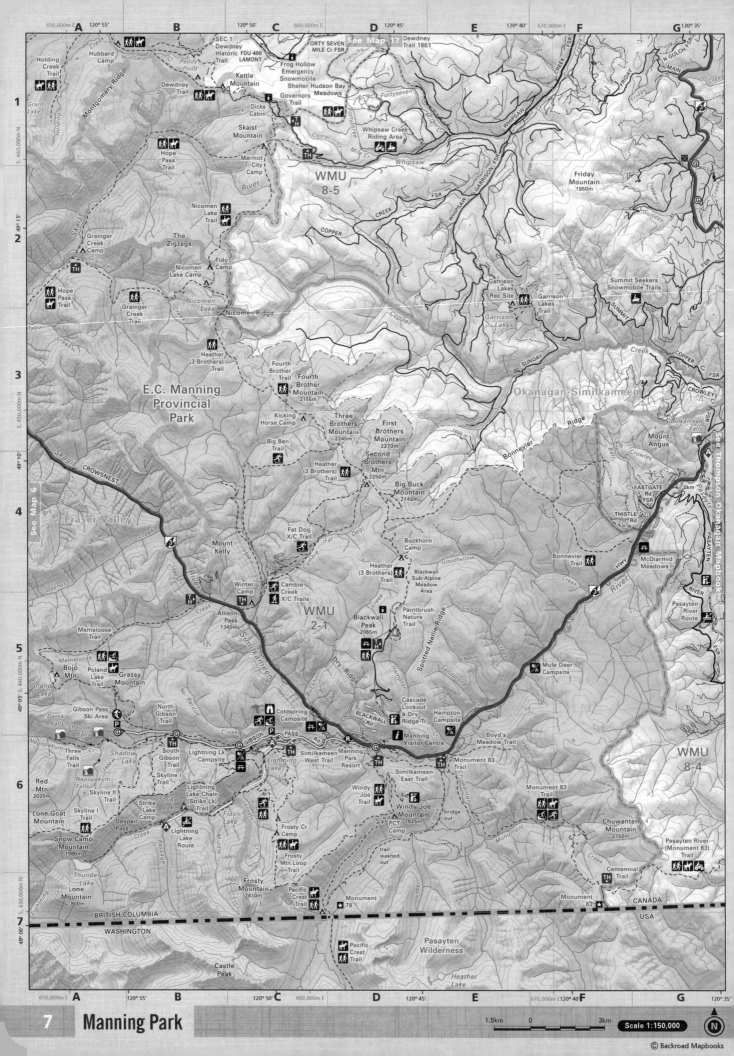

Scale 1:150,000

© Backroad Mapbooks

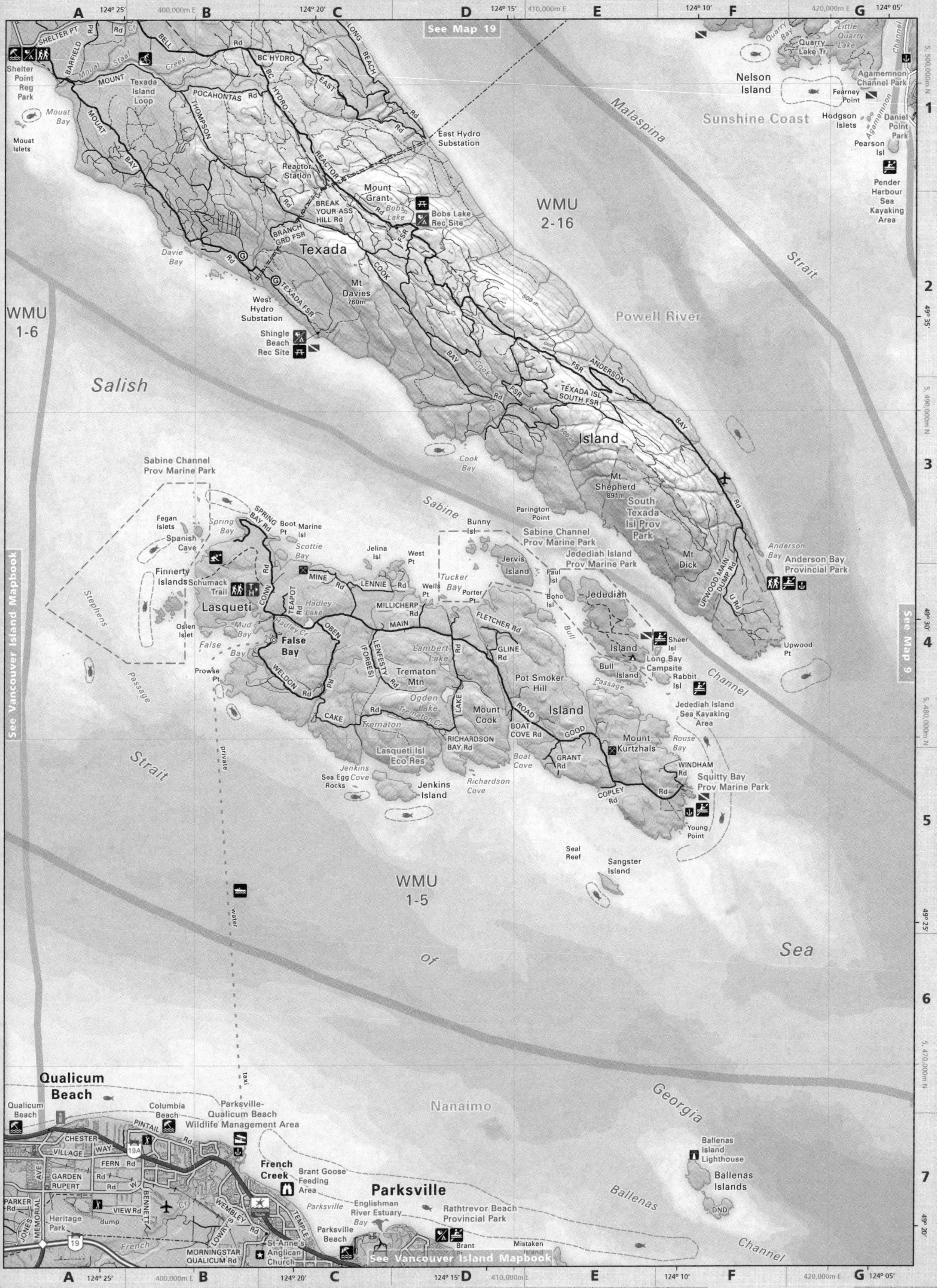
See Map 19
Shelter Point Reg Park
SHELTER PT Rd
BARFIELD Rd
Mouat Bay
Mouat Islets
MOUNT
Texada Island Loop
MOUAT BAY
BELL
Stab Creek
BC HYDRO
POCAHONTAS Rd
THOMPSON
LONG BEACH
EAST Rd
East Hydro Substation
Reactor Station
REACTOR Rd
Mount Grant
BREAK YOUR ASS HILL Rd
Bobs Lake
Bobs Lake Rec Site
BRANCH GRD FSR
Texada
Davie Bay
Mt Davies 760m
TEXADA FSR
West Hydro Substation
Shingle Beach Rec Site
WMU 2-16
Malaspina
Strait
Powell River
Sunshine Coast
Nelson Island
Quarry Bay
Quarry Lake Tr
Little Quarry Lake
Agamemnon Channel Park
Fearney Point
Hodgson Islets
Daniel Point Park
Pearson Isl
Pender Harbour Sea Kayaking Area
WMU 1-6
Salish
COOK BAY Rd
Cook Cr
FSR
ANDERSON
TEXADA ISL SOUTH FSR
Island
BAY Rd
Cook Bay
Mt Shepherd 891m
South Texada Isl Prov Park
Mt Dick
UPWOOD MAIN
DUMP Rd
U Rd
Anderson Bay
Anderson Bay Provincial Park
Upwood Pt
Paringon Point
Sabine
Sabine Channel Prov Marine Park
Fegan Islets
Spring Bay
SPRING BAY Rd
Boot Pt
Marine Isl
Scottie Bay
Spanish Cave
Finnerty Islands
Schumack Trail
Stephens
Lasqueti
Jelina Isl
West Pt
MINE Rd
LENNIE Rd
TEAPOT Rd
CONN Rd
Hadley Lake
Bunny Isl
Tucker Bay
Wells Pt
Porter Pt
Jervis Island
Sabine Channel Prov Marine Park
Jedediah Island Prov Marine Park
Paul Isl
Boho Isl
Jedediah
MILLICHERP Rd
MAIN
FLETCHER Rd
Mud Bay
Olsen Islet
Hadley Cr
False Bay
OBEN
LENFESTY (FORBES) Rd
Lambert Lake
GLINE Rd
Bull
Island
Sheer Isl
Long Bay Campsite
Rabbit Isl
Bull Island
Passage
Channel
Prowse Pt
WELDON Rd
Trematon Mtn
Pot Smoker Hill
Island
Ogden Lake
Trematon Cr
LAKE Rd
Mount Cook
ROAD
BOAT COVE Rd
CAKE
Trematon L
RICHARDSON BAY Rd
GOOD
Jedediah Island Sea Kayaking Area
Rouse Bay
Mount Kurtzhals
GRANT Rd
Lasqueti Isl Eco Res
Boat Cove
WINDHAM Rd
Squitty Bay Prov Marine Park
COPLEY Rd
Jenkins Cove
Sea Egg Rocks
Jenkins Island
Richardson Cove
Young Point
Seal Reef
Sangster Island
Passage
Strait
private
water taxi
WMU 1-5
of
Sea
Georgia
Nanaimo
Ballenas
Channel
Ballenas Island Lighthouse
Ballenas Islands
DND
Qualicum Beach
Columbia Beach
Parksville-Qualicum Beach Wildlife Management Area
PINTAIL
CHESTER
VILLAGE WAY
FERN Rd
GARDEN Rd
RUPERT Rd
W
BENNETT
PARKER Rd
MEMORIAL AVE
JONES
Heritage Park
dump
VIEW Rd
WEMBLEY
LOWRY'S Rd
French Cr
MORNINGSTAR QUALICUM Rd
French Creek
Brant Goose Feeding Area
Parksville
Englishman River Estuary
Parksville Bay
Parksville Beach
St Anne's Anglican Church
Rathtrevor Beach Provincial Park
TEMPLE
Brant
Mistaken Island
See Vancouver Island Mapbook
See Map 9
See Vancouver Island Mapbook
19
19A
A B C D E F G
1 2 3 4 5 6 7
124° 25' 124° 20' 124° 15' 124° 10' 124° 05'
400,000m E 410,000m E 420,000m E
49° 35' 49° 30' 49° 25' 49° 20'
5,500,000m N 5,490,000m N 5,480,000m N 5,470,000m N
500 m

Scale 1:150,000

3km 0 1.5km

© Backroad Mapbooks

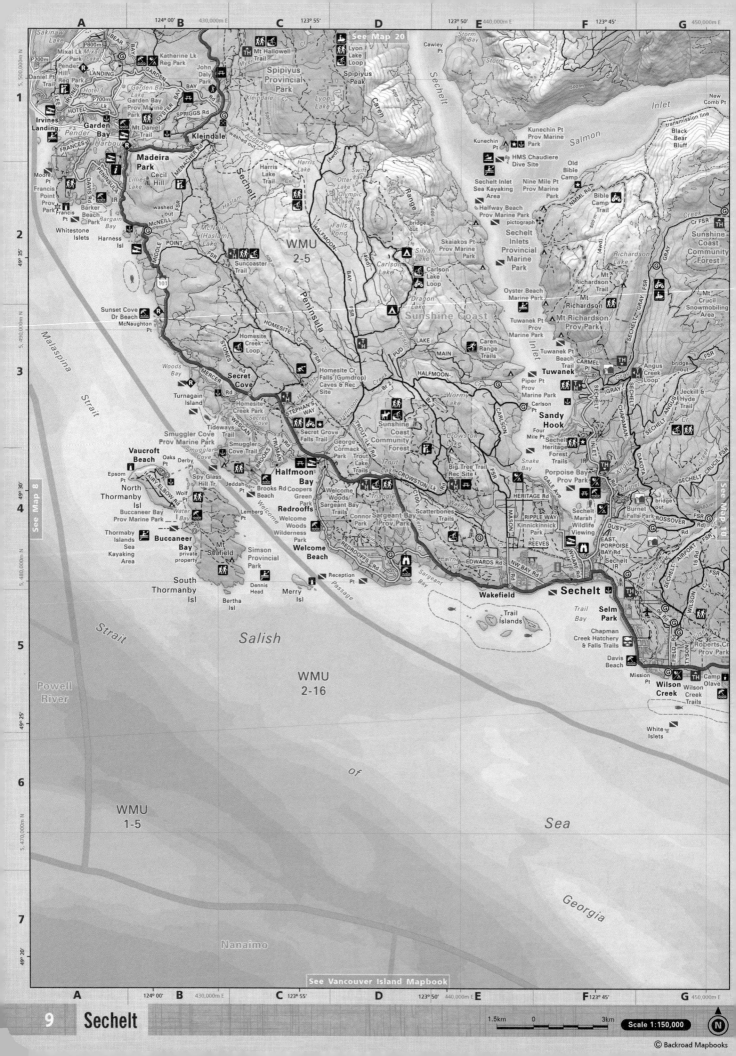

Scale 1:150,000

1.5km   0   3km

© Backroad Mapbooks

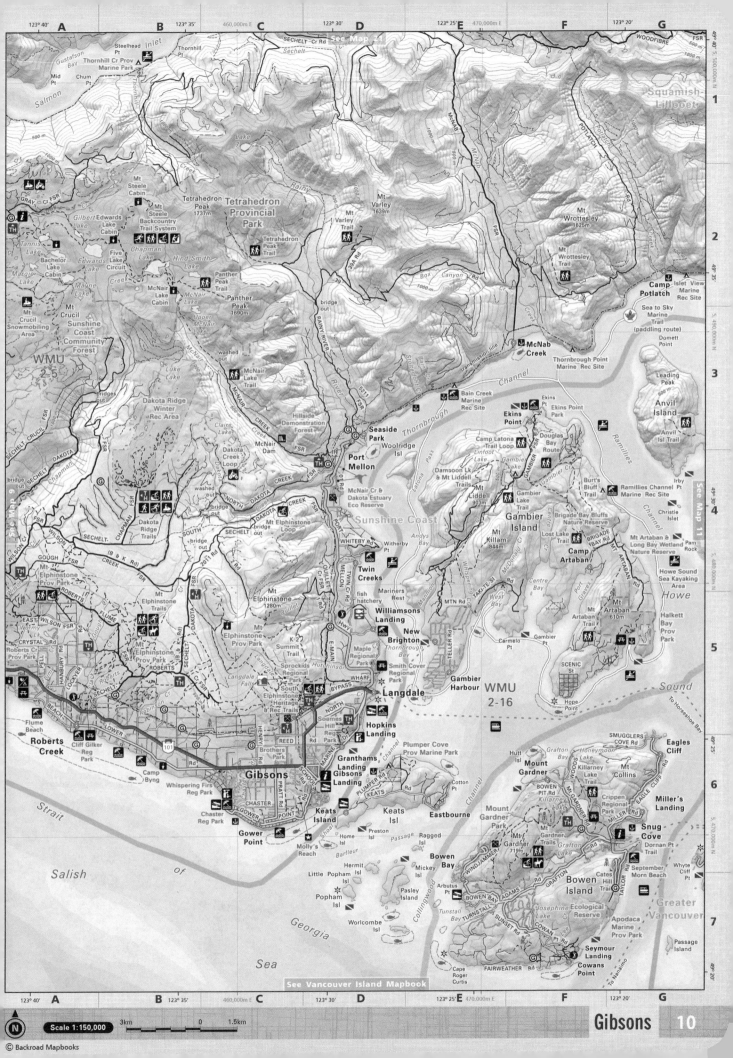

Scale 1:150,000

3km 0 1.5km

© Backroad Mapbooks

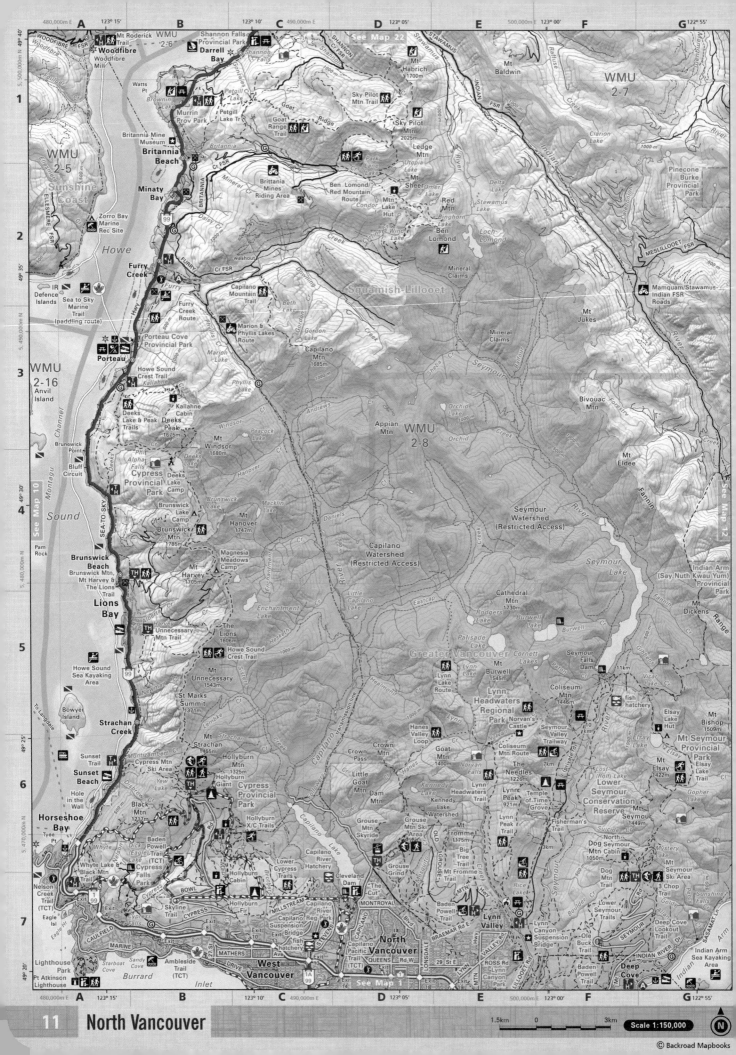

Scale 1:150,000

1.5km   0   3km

© Backroad Mapbooks

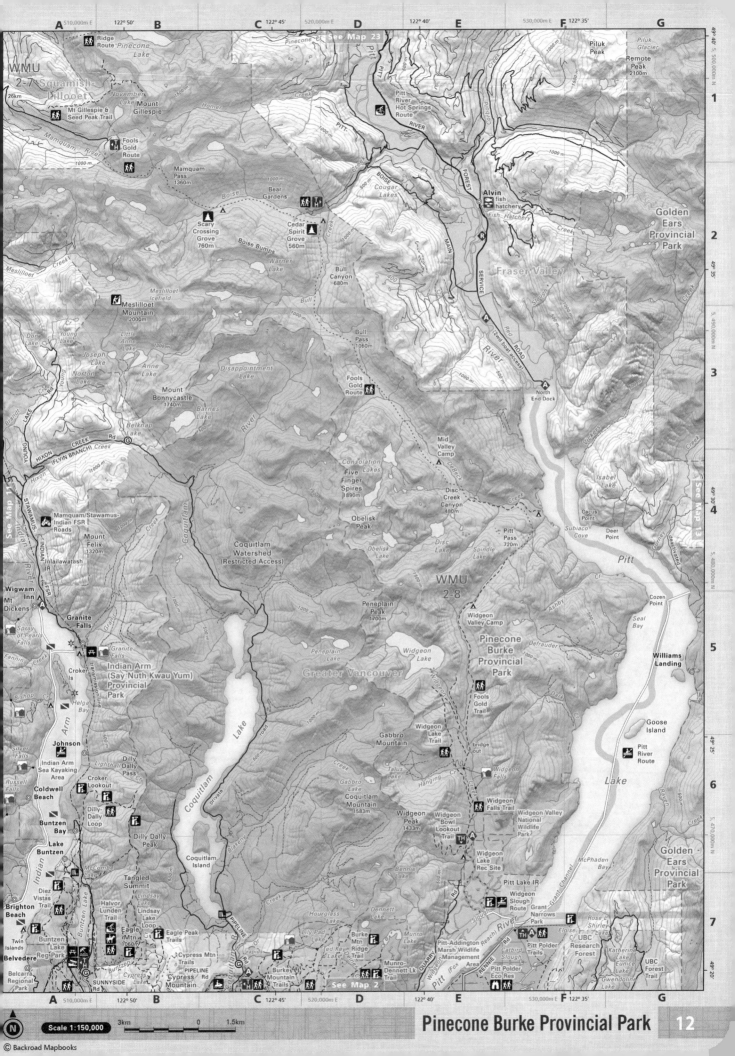

Pinecone Burke Provincial Park 12

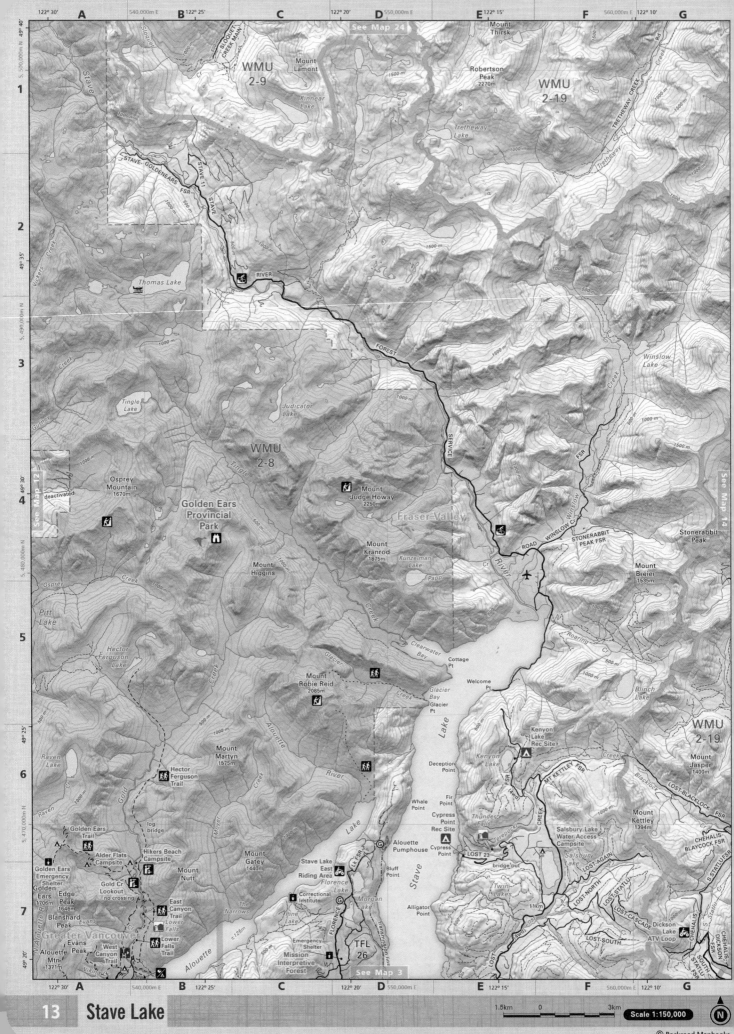

Scale 1:150,000

© Backroad Mapbooks

See Map 3

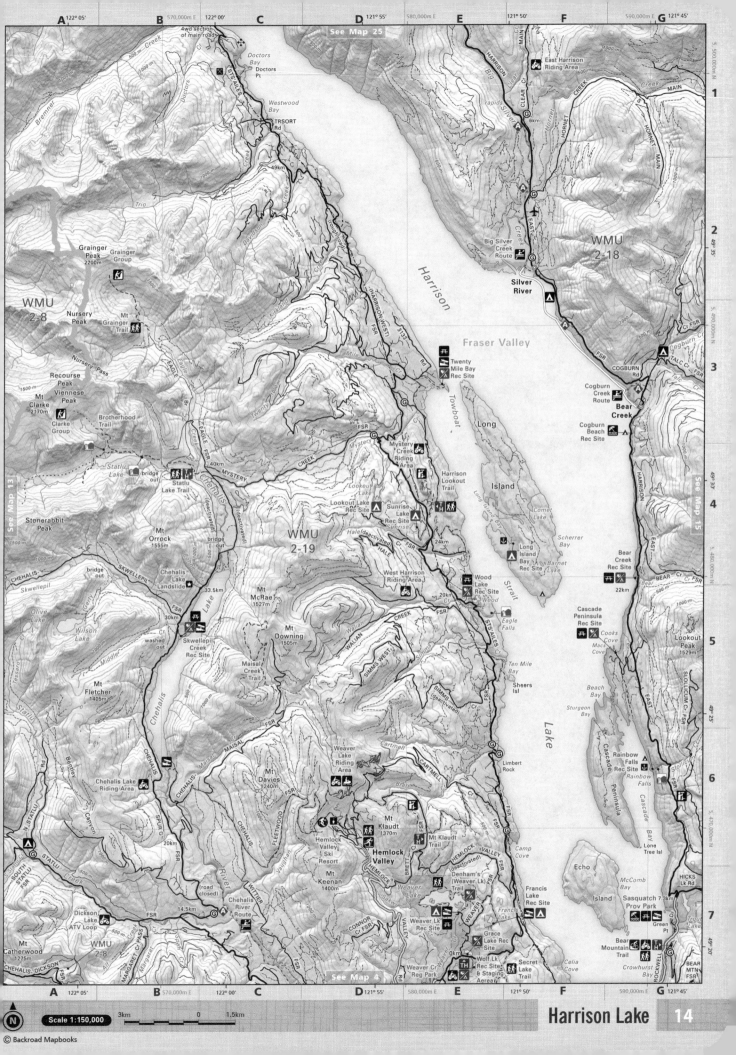

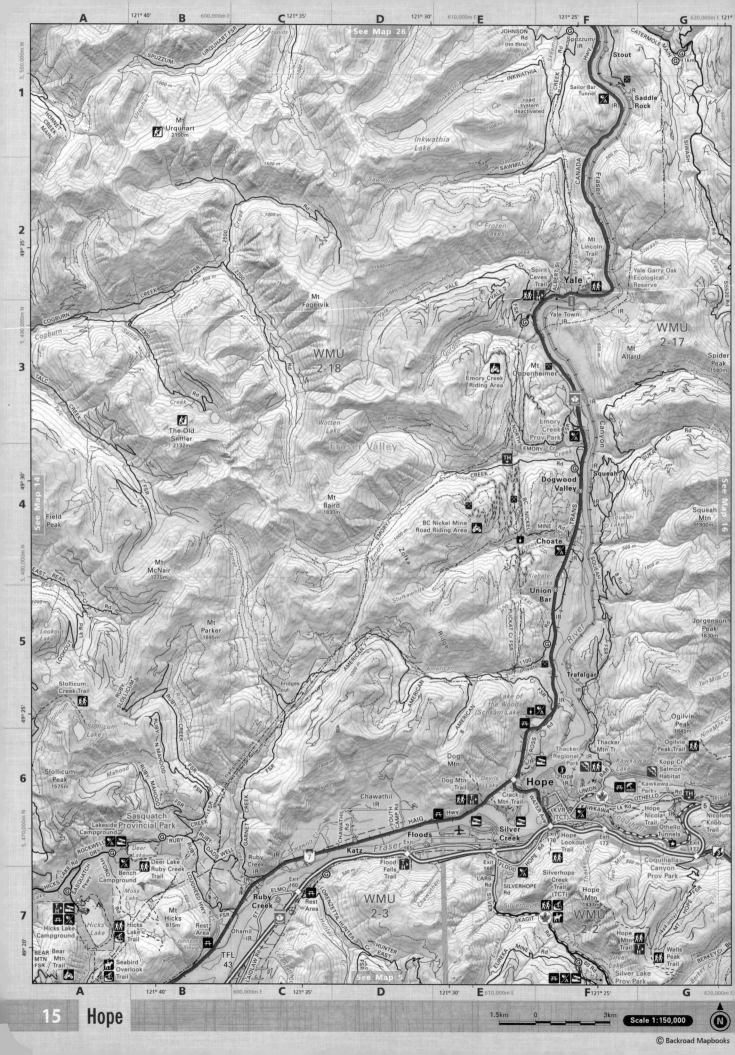

Scale 1:150,000

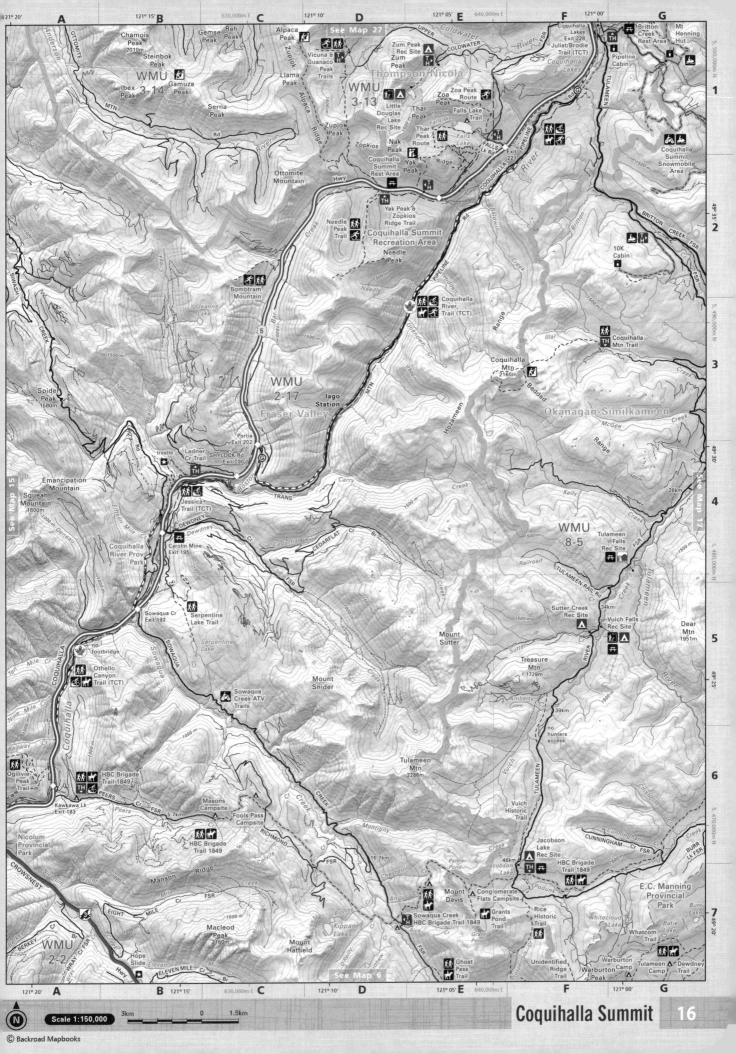

Coquihalla Summit

© Backroad Mapbooks

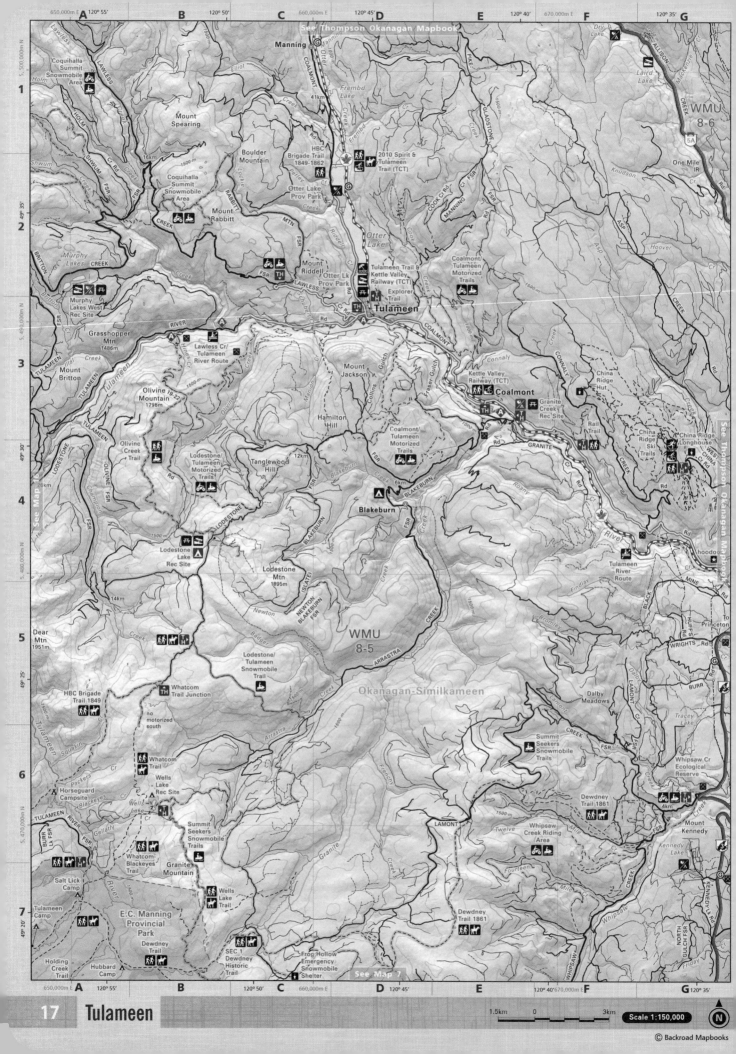

Scale 1:150,000

1.5km   0   3km

© Backroad Mapbooks

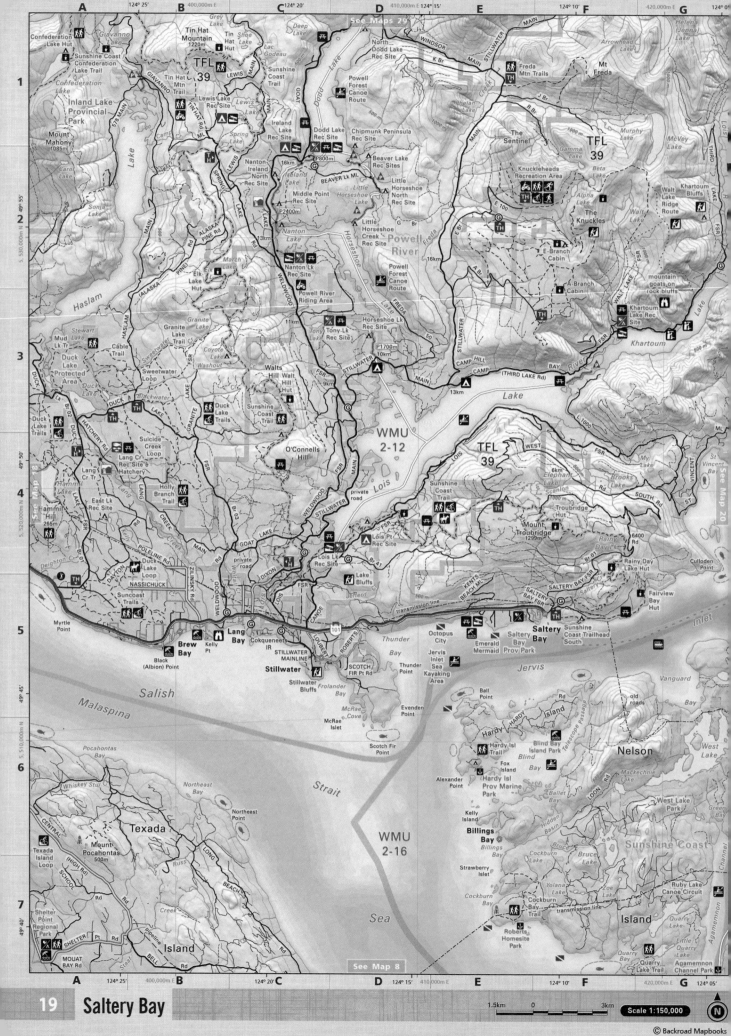

Scale 1:150,000

© Backroad Mapbooks

Scale 1:150,000

3km   0   1.5km

© Backroad Mapbooks

Scale 1:150,000

© Backroad Mapbooks

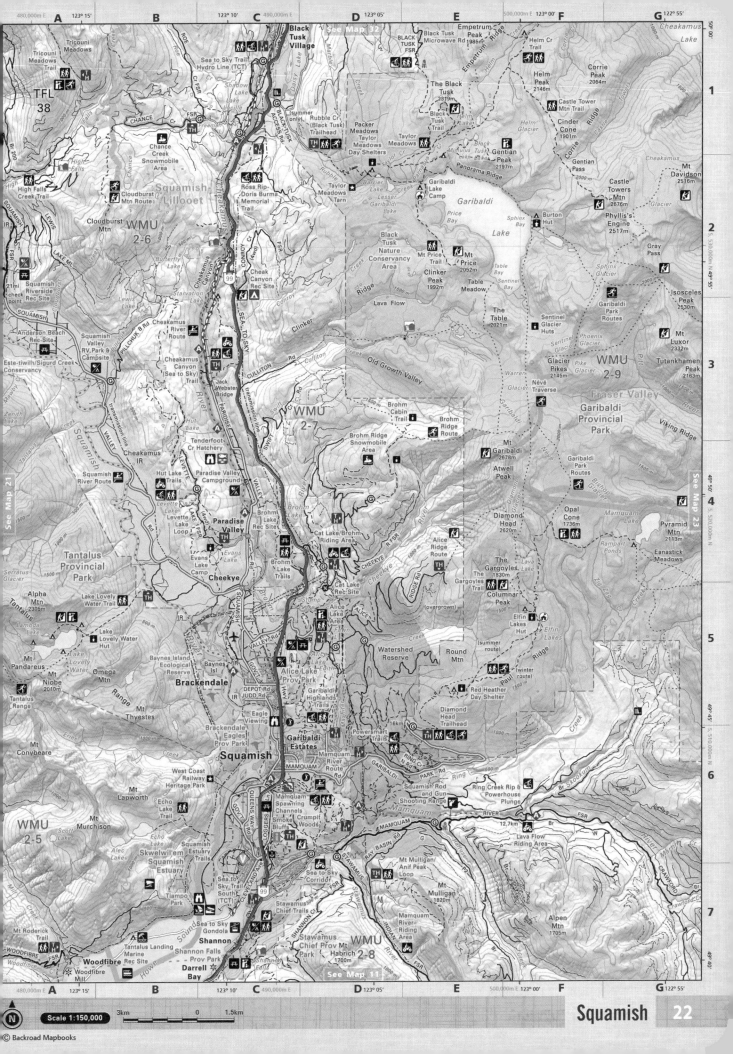

23 Garibaldi Provincial Park

Scale 1:150,000

1.5km   0   3km

N

© Backroad Mapbooks

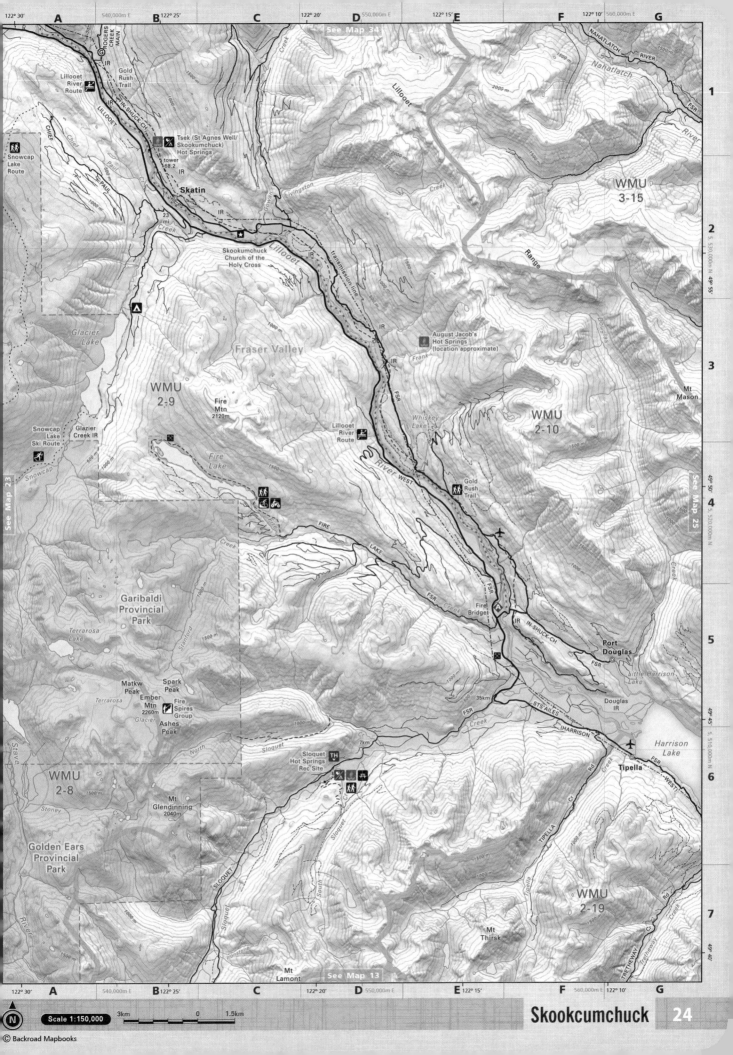

WMU
3-15

Nahatlatch

Nahatlatch River

Lillooet

Range

Douglas

Mt
Mason

WMU
2-10

Whiskey
Lake

Gold
Rush
Trail

August Jacob's
Hot Springs
(location approximate)

Frank

Lillooet
River
Route

River WEST

FSR

FSR

FSR

IR   IN-SHUCK-CH

Fire
Bridge

Port
Douglas

little Harrison
Lake

Douglas
IR

STS'AILES

HARRISON

Harrison
Lake

Tipella

FSR WEST

WMU
2-19

Mt
Thirsk

TIPELLA

See Map 13

Mt
Lamont

ROGERS
CREEK
MAIN

IR

Gold
Rush
Trail

LILLOOET

IN-SHUCK-CH

PAUL

Lillooet
River
Route

CHIEF

Snowcap
Lake
Route

Tsek (St'Agnes Well/
Skookumchuck)
Hot Springs

tower
168.2

Skatin

23
mi
Creek

Skookumchuck
Church of the
Holy Cross

Lillooet

transmission line

IR

IR

IR

IR

Cowan

Livingston
Creek

Glacier
Lake

Fraser Valley

WMU
2-9

Fire
Mtn
2120m

Snowcap
Lake
Ski Route

Glazier
Creek IR

Snowcap

Fire
Lake

Fire

Creek

FIRE

LAKE

Garibaldi
Provincial
Park

Terrarosa
Lake

Terrarosa

Stanford

Matkw
Peak
Ember
Mtn
2260m

Spark
Peak

Fire
Spires
Group

Ashes
Peak

Glacier

North

Stave
River

WMU
2-8

Steney

Mt
Glendinning
2040m

Golden Ears
Provincial
Park

Sloquet

Sloquet

SLOQUET

Ironstone Cr

Sloquet
Hot Springs
Rec Site

TH

7km

South

Sloquet

Creek

35km

FSR

Creek

N

Scale 1:150,000

3km   0   1.5km

© Backroad Mapbooks

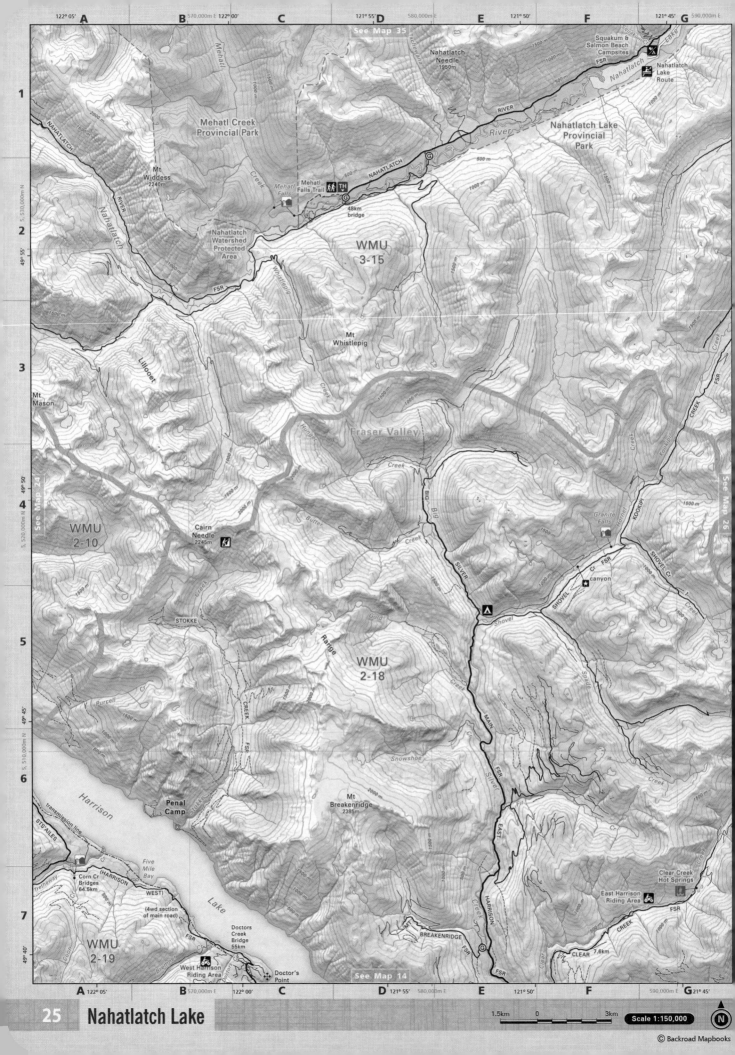

Mehatl Creek
Provincial Park

Mt
Widdess
2240m

Nahatlatch
Watershed
Protected
Area

WMU
3-15

Nahatlatch
Needle
1950m

Squakum &
Salmon Beach
Campsites

Nahatlatch
Lake Route

Nahatlatch Lake
Provincial
Park

Mehatl
Falls

Mehatl Falls Trail

48km
bridge

Mt
Whistlepig

Fraser Valley

Mt
Mason

WMU
2-10

Cairn
Needle
2245m

Granite
Falls

canyon

STOKKE

WMU
2-18

Range

Snowshoe

Harrison

Penal
Camp

Mt
Breakenridge
2385m

Clear Creek
Hot Springs

East Harrison
Riding Area

Corn Cr
Bridges
64.5km

Five
Mile
Bay

(HARRISON

WEST)

(4wd section
of main road)

Doctors
Creek
Bridge
55km

BREAKENRIDGE

CLEAR   7.6km

WMU
2-19

West Harrison
Riding Area

Doctor's
Point

25   Nahatlatch Lake

1.5km   0   3km   Scale 1:150,000

N

© Backroad Mapbooks

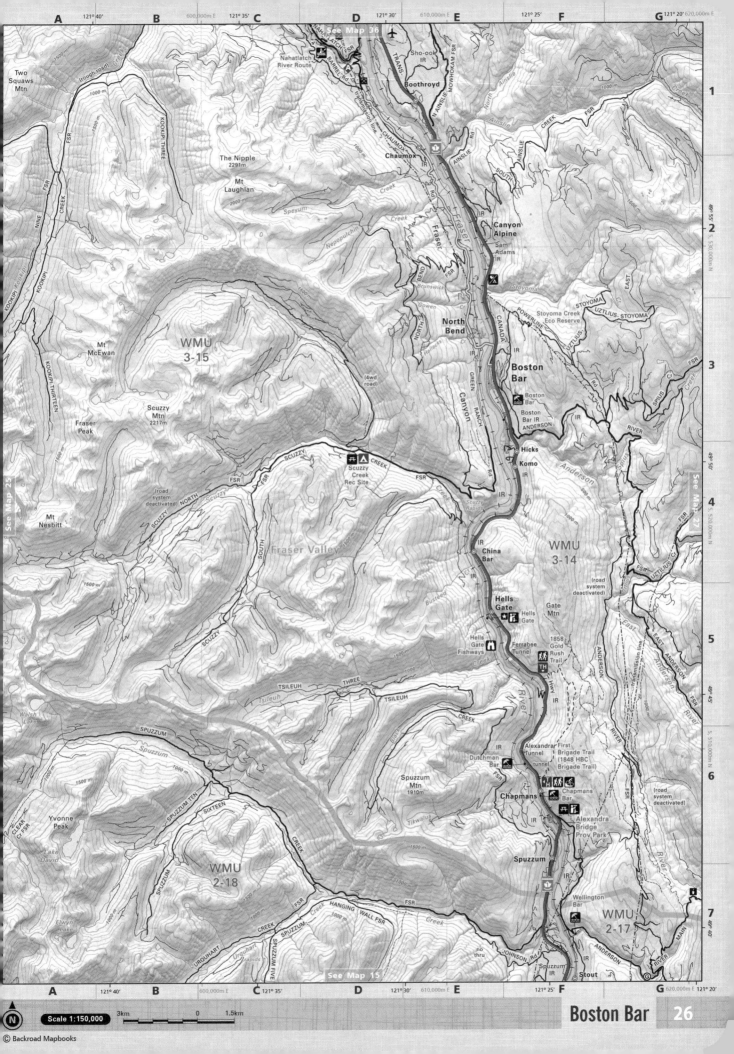

Scale 1:150,000

3km · 0 · 1.5km

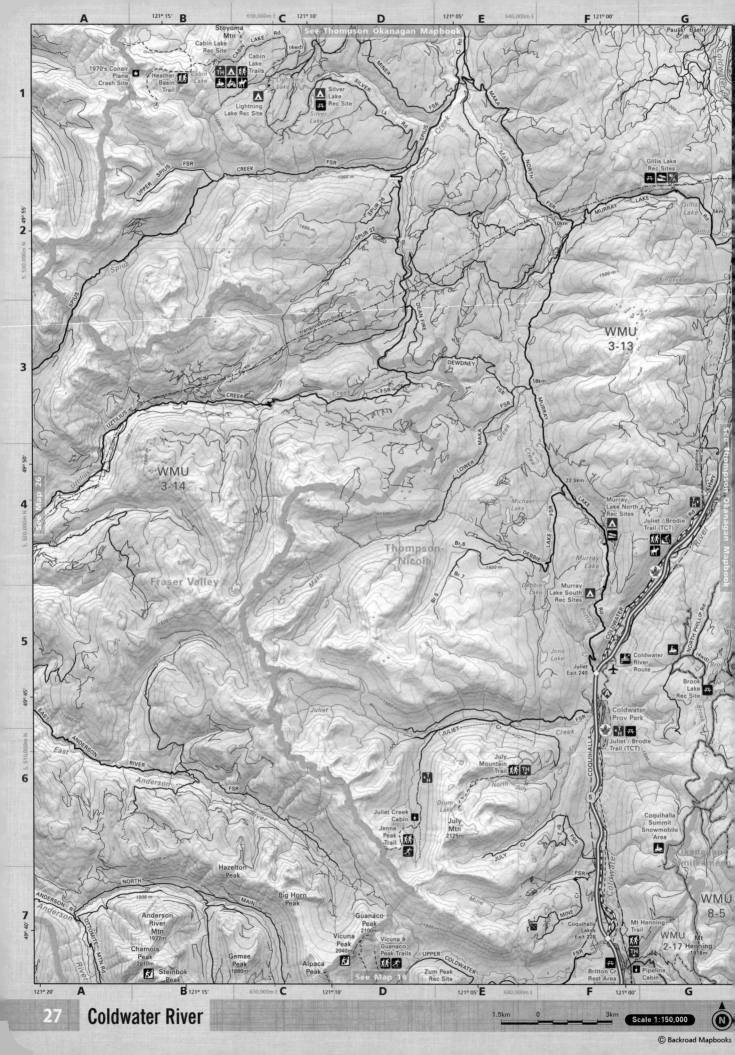

Stoyoma Mtn

Cabin Lake Rec Site

Cabin Lake Trails

Lightning Lake Rec Site

Silver Lake Rec Site

1970's Conair Plane Crash Site

Heather Basin Trail

WMU 3-13

WMU 3-14

Fraser Valley

Thompson-Nicola

Gillis Lake Rec Sites

Murray Lake North Rec Sites

Juliet / Brodie Trail (TCT)

Murray Lake South Rec Sites

Coldwater River Route

Brook Lake Rec Site

Coldwater Prov Park

Juliet / Brodie Trail (TCT)

Juliet Exit 240

July Mountain Trail

Juliet Creek Cabin

Jenna Peak Trail

July Mtn 2125m

Coquihalla Summit Snowmobile Area

Hazelton Peak

Anderson River Mtn 1977m

Chamois Peak 2010m

Gemse Peak 1880m

Steinbok Peak

Big Horn Peak

Guanaco Peak 2100m

Vicuna Peak 2040m

Alpaca Peak

Vicuna & Guanaco Peak Trails

Zum Peak Rec Site

UPPER COLDWATER

WMU 8-5

Mt Henning Trail

Coquihalla Lakes Exit 228

Mt Henning 1818m

WMU 2-17

Britton Cr Rest Area

Pipeline Cabin

See Map 16

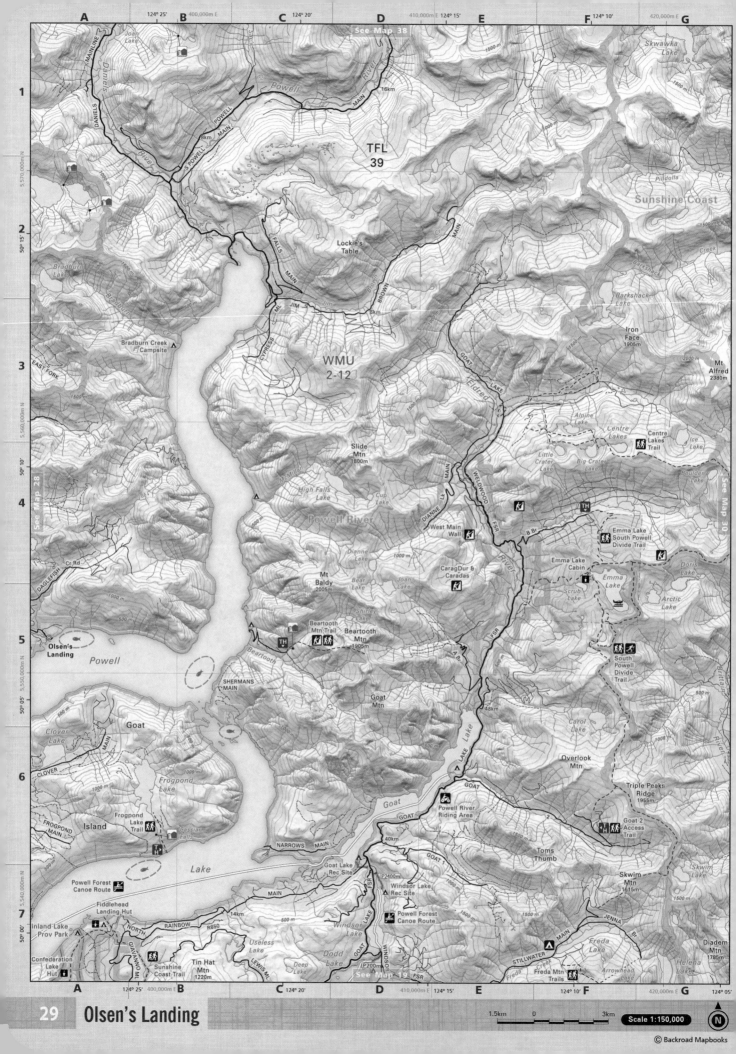

Scale 1:150,000

© Backroad Mapbooks

Princess Louisa Inlet

30

Scale 1:150,000   1.5km   0   3km

© Backroad Mapbooks

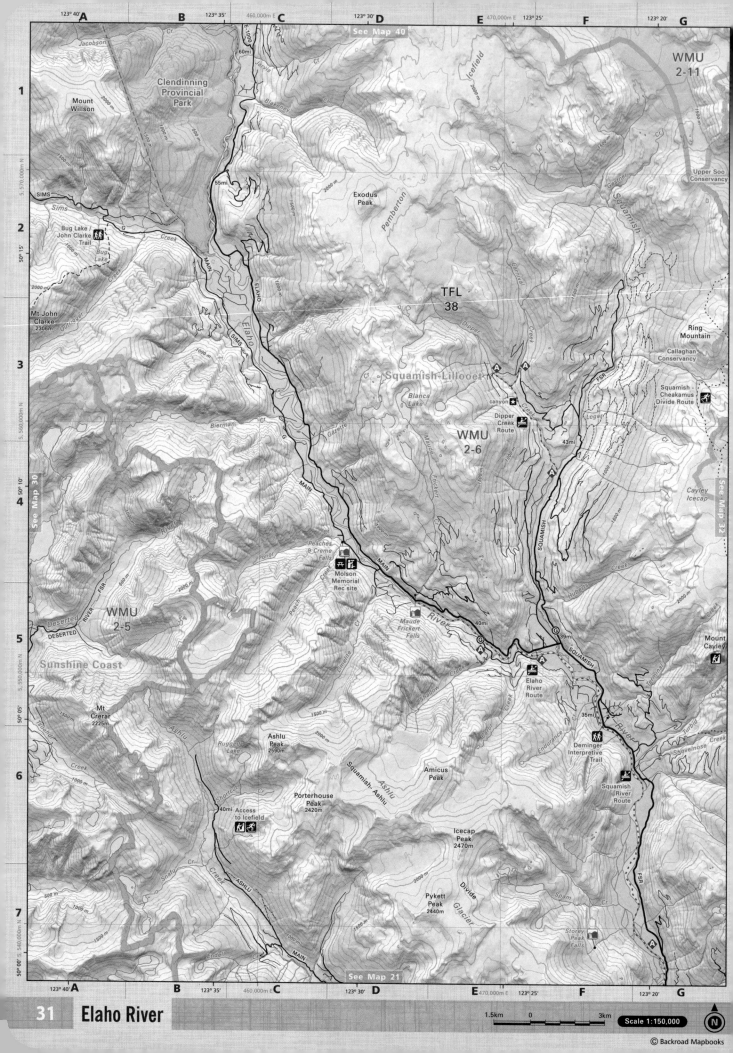

WMU
2-11

Upper Soo
Conservancy

Mount
Willson

Clendinning
Provincial
Park

Jacobson

Exodus
Peak

TFL
38

Ring
Mountain

Bug Lake /
John Clarke
Trail

Bug
Lake

Squamish-Lillooet

Callaghan
Conservancy

Squamish -
Cheakamus
Divide Route

Mt John
Clarke
2306m

Blanca
Lake

canyon

Dipper
Creek
Route

WMU
2-6

SIMS

Bierman

Cayley
Icecap

See Map 30

Gazette

Maude
Frickert

WMU
2-5

Deserted

Peaches
& Creme
Falls

Molson
Memorial
Rec site

Sunshine Coast

DESERTED

RIVER

FSR

Maude
Frickert Falls

Elaho
River
Route

Mount
Cayley

Mt Crerar
2225m

Ashlu

Deminger
Interpretive
Trail

Rugged
Lake

Ashlu
Peak
2590m

Squamish-Ashlu

Amicus
Peak

Squamish
River
Route

Porterhouse
Peak
2420m

Access
to Icefield

Icecap
Peak
2470m

Divide
Glacier

Pykett
Peak
2440m

Shovelnose

Storey
Peak
Falls

FSR

MAIN

ASHLU

31 Elaho River

1.5km 0 3km Scale 1:150,000

© Backroad Mapbooks

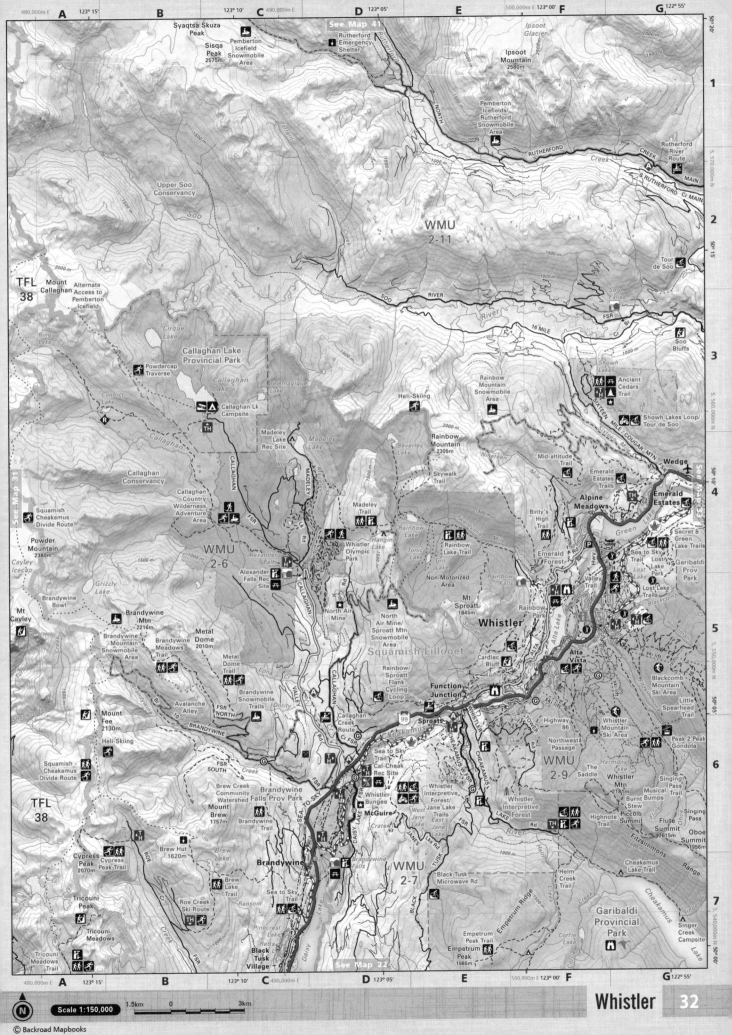

Scale 1:150,000
1.5km   0   3km

© Backroad Mapbooks

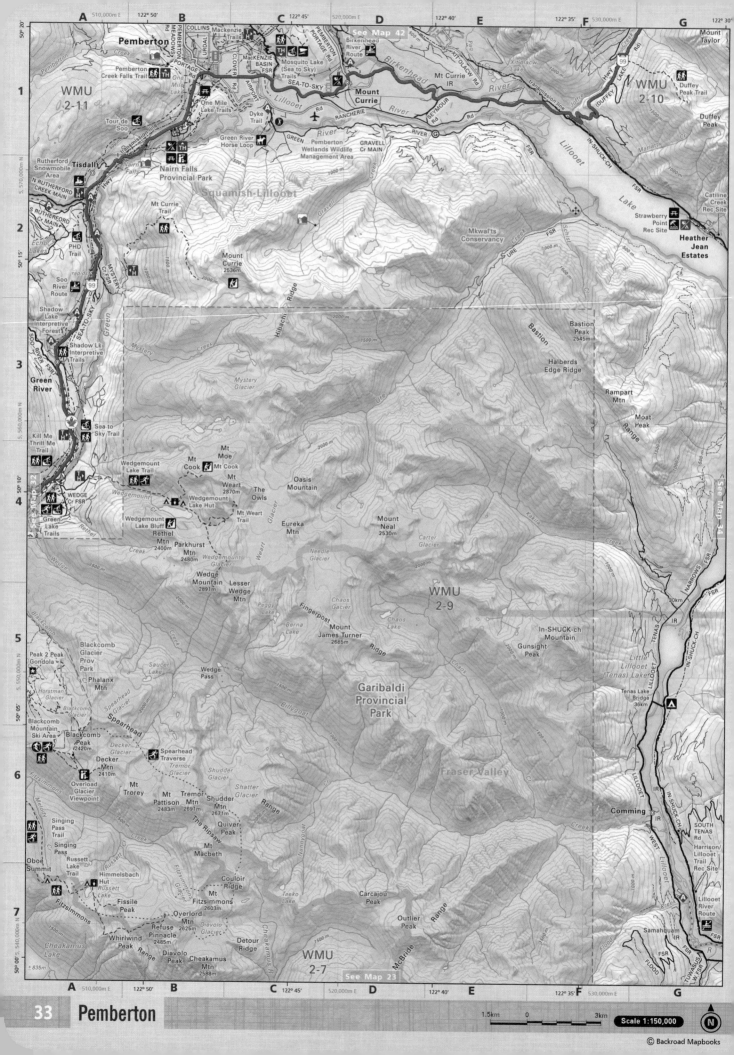

Scale 1:150,000

© Backroad Mapbooks

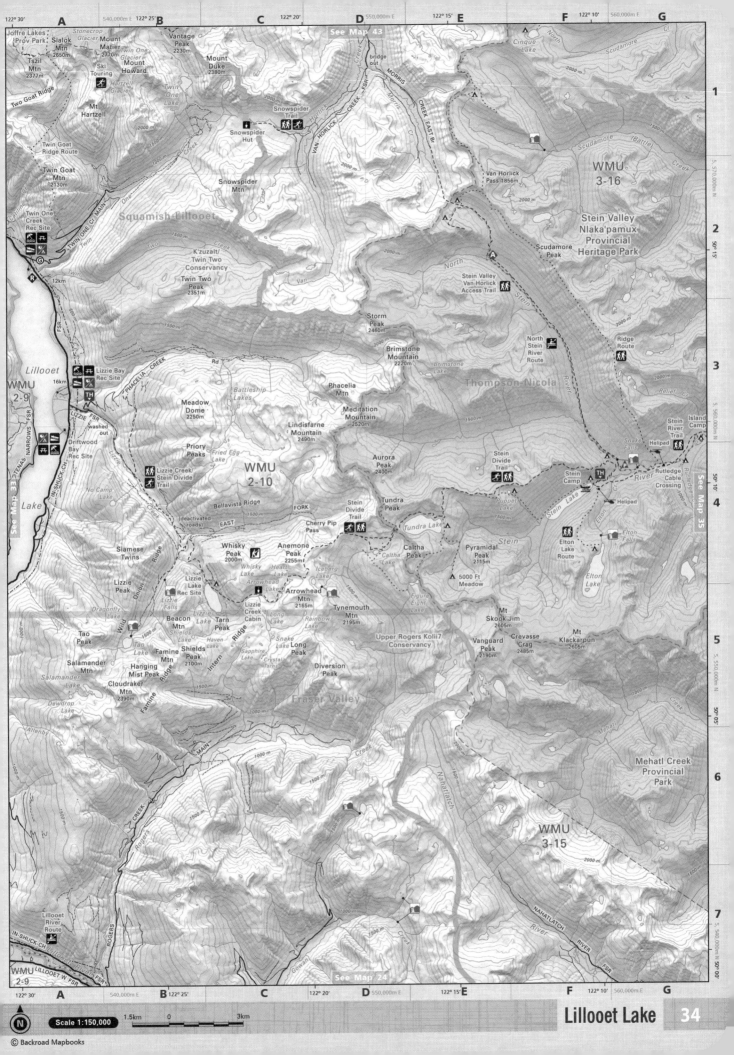

Lillooet Lake

34

Scale 1:150,000 1.5km 0 3km

© Backroad Mapbooks

N

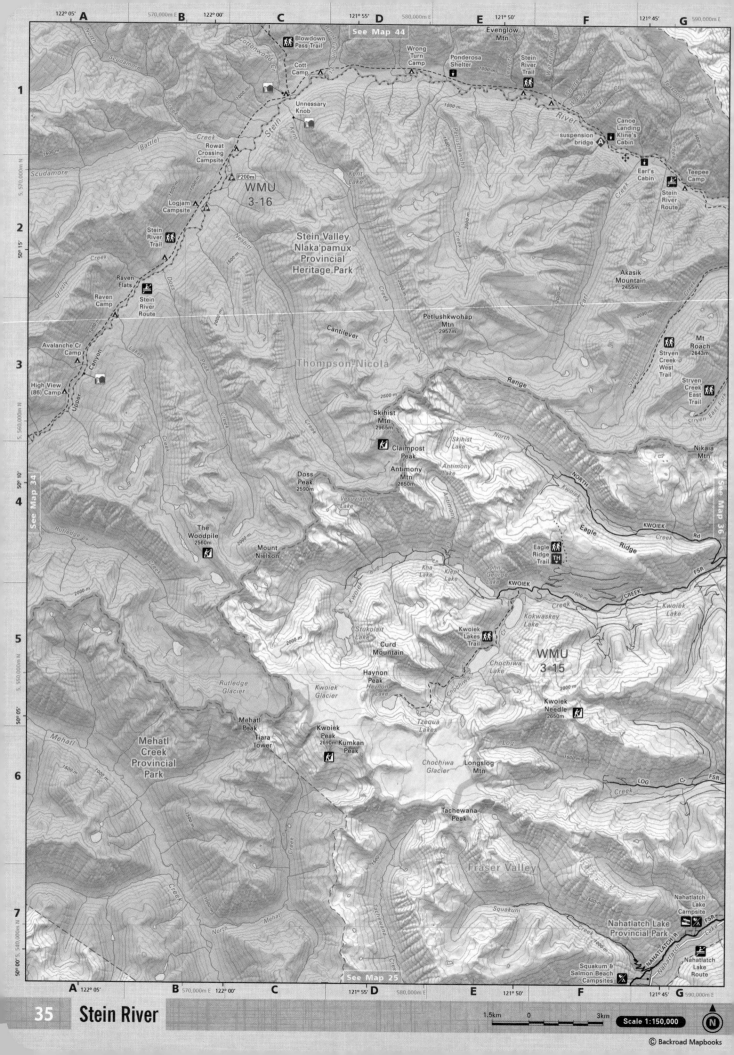

Scale 1:150,000

© Backroad Mapbooks

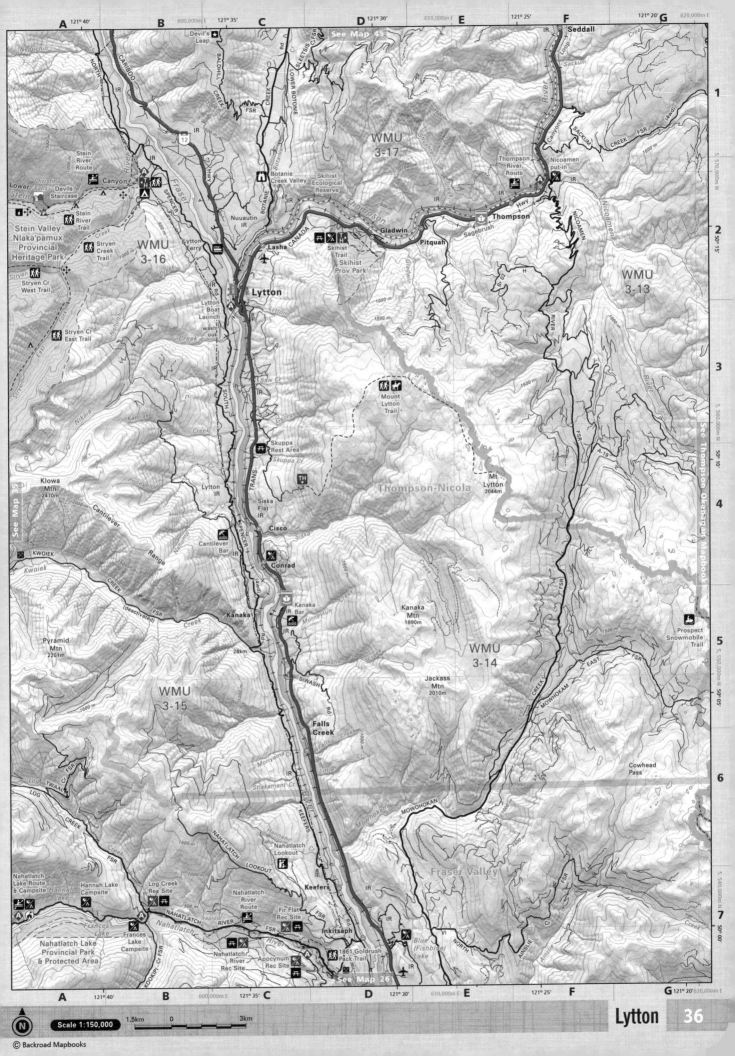

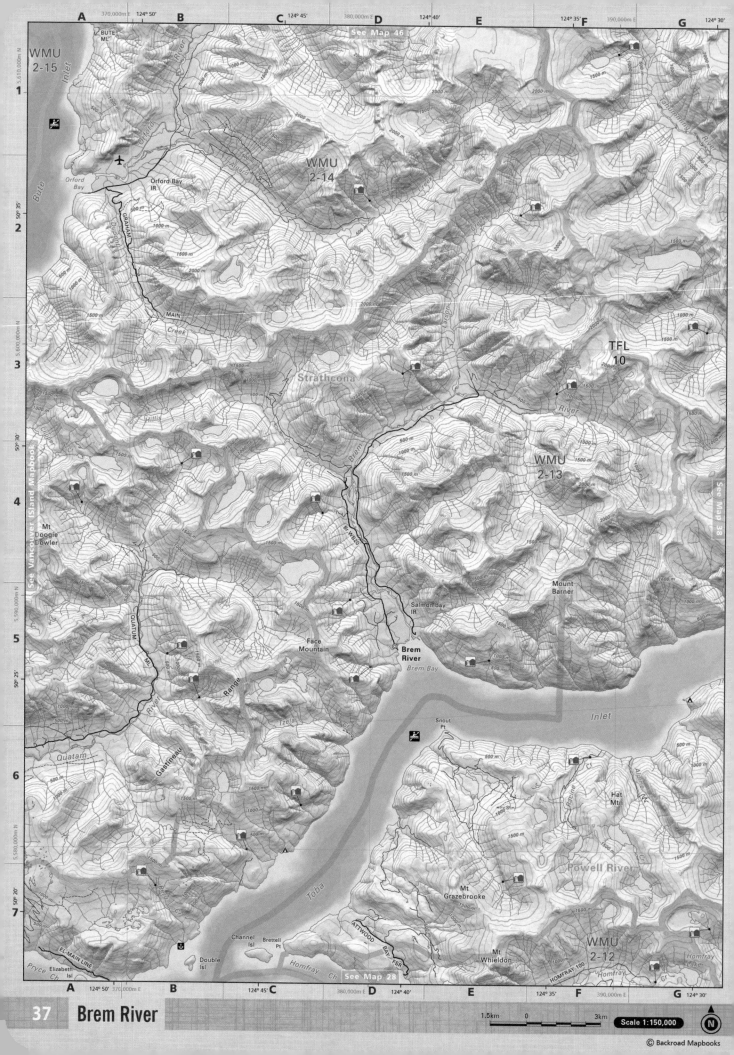

Brem River

Scale 1:150,000

© Backroad Mapbooks

A   124° 25'   B   400,000m E   C   124° 20'   D   410,000m E   124° 15'   E   F   124° 10'   420,000m E   G

Tahumming Glacier

2000 m

Tahumming

WMU
2-13

River

Powell River

Klahoose
IR

Toba

Quaniwsom
IR

RIVER
MAIN
River

Montrose
Cr. Falls

Montrose

Eller

Creek

River

Blackfin
Glacier

Toba

Lunar Cr

MACK
ML

CHUSAN
FSR

Julian
Peak
2000 m

Boyle
Lake

Creek

Little

Inlet

Toba

Daniels
Lake

Well
Lake

Leo
Lake

TFL
39

Raindrop
Lake

River

MAIN
Daniels

Marika
Lake

Sac's
Lake

27km

POWELL MAIN

WMU
2-12

Powell

River

Skwawka
Lake

Sunshine
Coast

Joan
Lake

P121

A   124° 35'   B   400,000m E   C   124° 30'   D   410,000m E   124° 25'   E   F   124° 20'   420,000m E   G

50° 35'   50° 30'   50° 25'   50° 20'

5,610,000m N   5,600,000m N   5,590,000m N   5,580,000m N

N

Scale 1:150,000   1.5km   0   3km

Julian Peak   38

© Backroad Mapbooks

WMU 2-11

Upper Lillooet Provincial Park

Manatee Group

Obelia Peak

Marlin Peak

Bonito Peak

Albacore Peak

Mermaid Peak

Dolphin Peak

Sirenia Mtn

Wahoo Tower

Remora Peak

Manatee Peak

Dugong Peak

Manatee Glacier

Sirenia Glacier

Meager Glacier

Toba

Albino Dome

Ballpeen Mtn

Albino Glacier

Belinda Mtn

Plateau

Elaho

Swede Saw Mtn

Berm Peak

Berm Lake

Belinda Lake

Jointed Mtn

Racoon Mtn

Racoon Lakes

Teeter Peak

Icefield

Mittelberg Mtn

WMU 2-13

Blackfin Peak

Wave Glacier

Beach Mtn

Totter Peak

Havoc Glacier

Elaho Mtn

TFL 38

Blackfin Glacier

Procyon Lake

Clendinning Provincial Park

Elaho Range

Limpet Ridge

Comber Peak

Breaker Peak

Lunar Pass

Doolittle Glacier

Clendinning Lake

Frontline Mtn

Clendinning

Clendinning

Mt Doolittle

Mt Clendinning

Windige Mtn

Mt Boardman

Boardman Glacier

Squamish-Lillooet

Howitzer Peak

Mt Thomas

Bottiger Peak

Sergeant Mtn

TFL 38

Mt Perkins

WMU 2-6

TFL 10

Pivotal Mtn

Corporal Mtn

Mt Whiting

Whiting Glacier

Mt Oswald

Blümlisalp Mtn

Ross Ridge

Mt Vanstone

Range

Mt Pollock

See Map 38

See Map 40

WMU 2-12

Sunshine Coast

WMU 2-5

Tinniswood Glacier

See Map 30

39 Toba

1.5km   0   3km   Scale 1:150,000

© Backroad Mapbooks

N

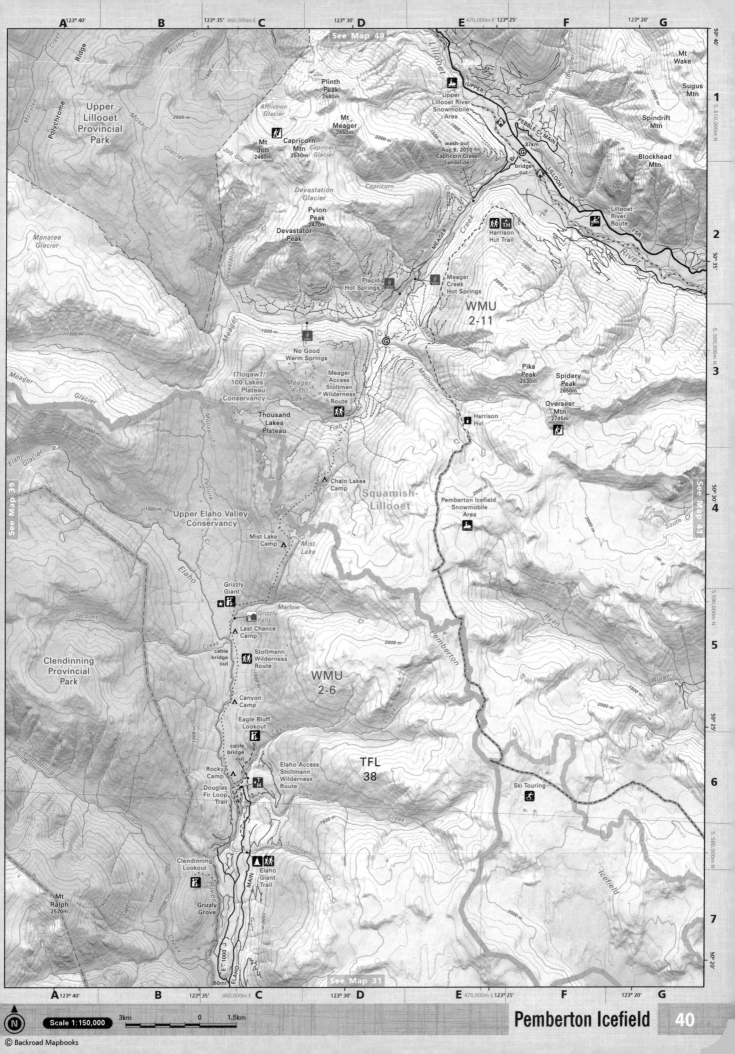

Map labels

Ridge

Upper Lillooet Provincial Park

Polychrome

Manatee Glacier

Mosaic Glacier

Plinth Peak 2680m

Affliction Glacier

Mt Job 2480m

Capricorn Mtn 2570m

Capricorn Glacier

Mt Meager 2650m

Job Glacier

Devastation Glacier

Pylon Peak 2470m

Devastator Peak

Meager Creek

Mt Wake

Sugus Mtn

Spindrift Mtn

Blockhead Mtn

Upper Lillooet River Snowmobile Area

37km

wash-out Aug 6, 2010 Capricorn Creek Landslide

bridge out

PEBBLE CR MAIN

Lillooet

Lillooet River Route FSR

Harrison Hut Trail

WMU 2-11

Placid Hot Springs

Meager Creek Hot Springs

No Good Warm Springs

I7loqaw7/ 100 Lakes Plateau Conservancy

Meager (Fish) Lake

Meager Access Stoltman Wilderness Route

Thousand Lakes Plateau

Pika Peak 2530m

Spidery Peak 2650m

Overseer Mtn 2745m

Harrison Hut

Chain Lakes Camp

Squamish-Lillooet

Pemberton Icefield Snowmobile Area

Upper Elaho Valley Conservancy

Mist Lake Camp

Mist Lake

Grizzly Giant

Grizzly Falls

Last Chance Camp

Stoltmann Wilderness Route

cable bridge out

Canyon Camp

Eagle Bluff Lookout

cable bridge out

Rocky Camp

Douglas Fir Loop Trail

Elaho Access Stoltmann Wilderness Route

WMU 2-6

TFL 38

Ski Touring

Clendinning Provincial Park

Mt Ralph 2520m

Clendinning Lookout

Elaho Giant Trail

Grizzly Grove

See Map 39

See Map 41

N

Scale 1:150,000   3km   0   1.5km

© Backroad Mapbooks

Pemberton Icefield   40

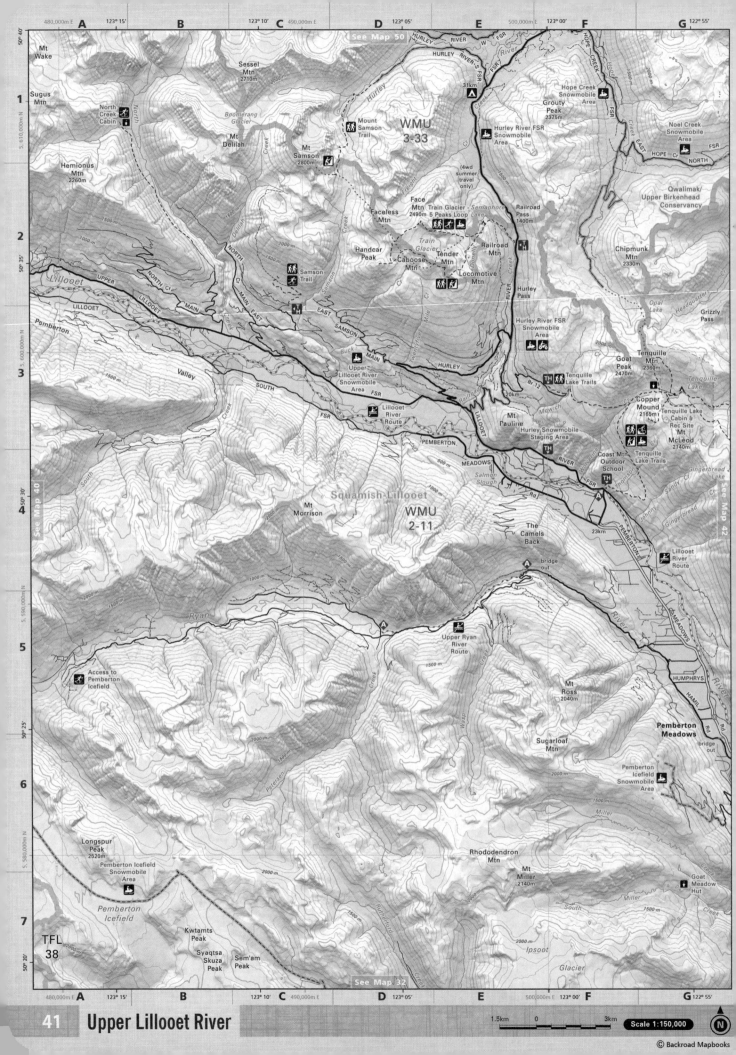

Scale 1:150,000

© Backroad Mapbooks

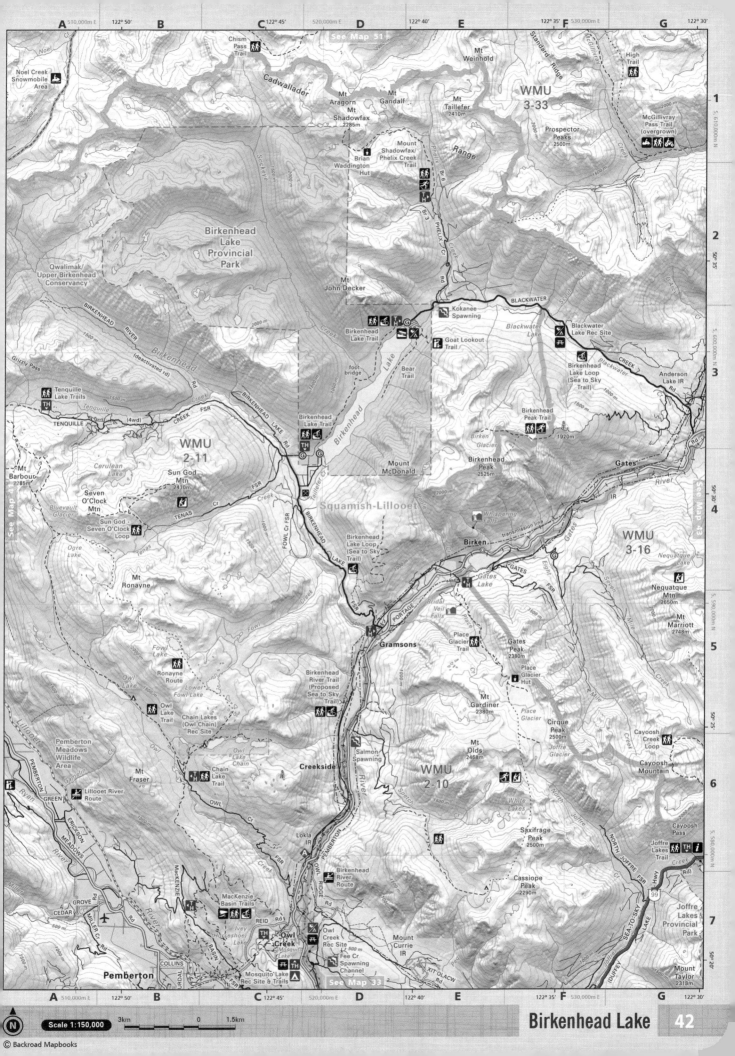

Birkenhead Lake

42

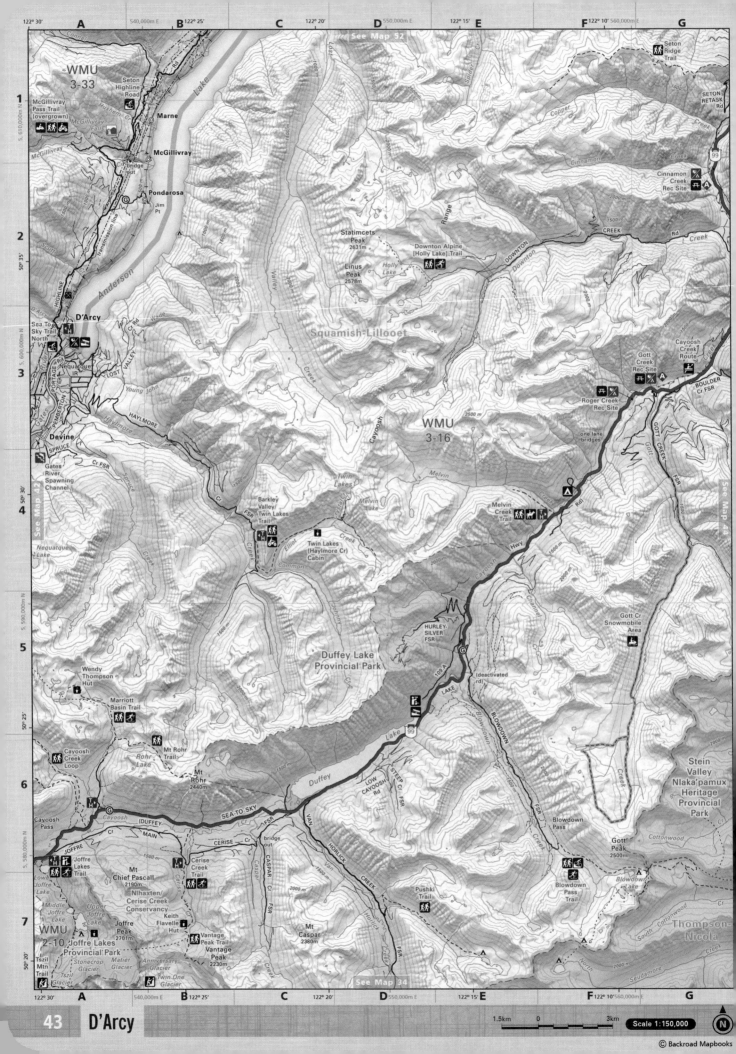

WMU
3-33

Seton
Highline Road

McGillivray
Pass Trail
(overgrown)

McGillivray
Falls

Marne

McGillivray

bridge
out

Pondarosa

Jim
Pt

Seton
Ridge
Trail

SETON
RETASK
Rd

Cinnamon
Creek
Rec Site

Statimcets
Peak
2631m

Downton Alpine
[Holly Lake] Trail

Linus
Peak
2578m

Holly
Lake

Range

Squamish-Lillooet

Sea To
Sky Trail
North

D'Arcy

Gott Creek
Rec Site

Cayoosh
Creek
Route

Nequatque
IR

Devine

HAYLMORE

Roger Creek
Rec Site

one lane
bridges

BOULDER
Cr FSR

WMU
3-16

Gates
River
Spawning
Channel

Barkley
Valley/
Twin Lakes
Trail

Twin Lakes
(Haylmore Cr)
Cabin

Melvin
Lake

Melvin
Creek
Trail

Gott Cr
Snowmobile
Area

Nequatque
Lake

Twin
Lakes

Duffey Lake
Provincial Park

HURLEY-
SILVER
FSR

(deactivated
rd)

Wendy
Thompson
Hut

Marriott
Basin Trail

Cayoosh
Creek Loop

Rohr
Lake

Mt Rohr
Trails

Mt
Rohr
2440m

Duffey

LOW
CAYOOSH
Rd

Stein
Valley
Nlaka'pamux
Heritage
Provincial
Park

Blowdown
Pass

Gott
Peak
2500m

Cayoosh
Pass

JOFFRE

SEA-TO-SKY

MAIN

CERISE

bridge
out

STEEP Cr
FSR

Blowdown
Pass Trail

Blowdown
Lake

Joffre Lakes
Trail

Mt
Chief Pascall
2190m

Cerise
Creek
Trail

Nlhaxten/
Cerise Creek
Conservancy

Keith
Flavelle Hut

Pushki
Trail

Lower
Joffre
Lake

Upper
Joffre
Lake

Joffre
Peak
2701m

Vantage
Peak Trail

Vantage
Peak
2230m

Mt
Caspar
2380m

WMU
2-10

Joffre Lakes
Provincial Park

Tszil
Mtn
Trail

Tszil
Glacier

Stonecrop
Glacier

Matier
Glacier

Middle
Joffre
Lake

Anniversary
Glacier

Twin One
Glacier

Thompson-
Nicola

1.5km 0 3km   Scale 1:150,000

© Backroad Mapbooks

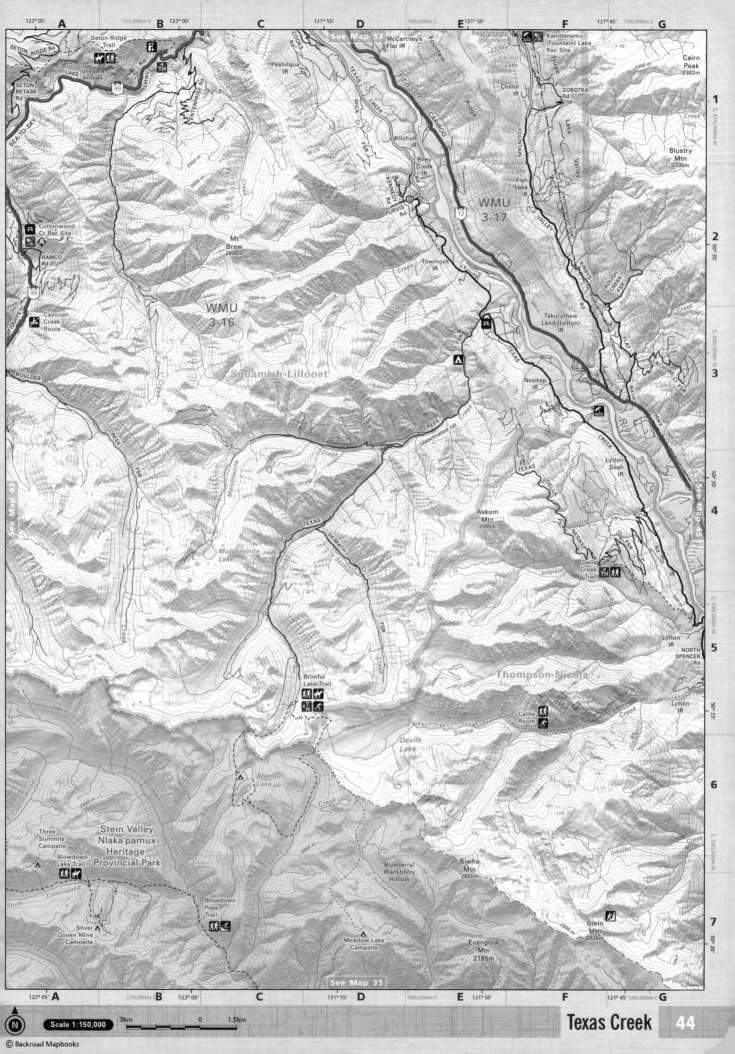

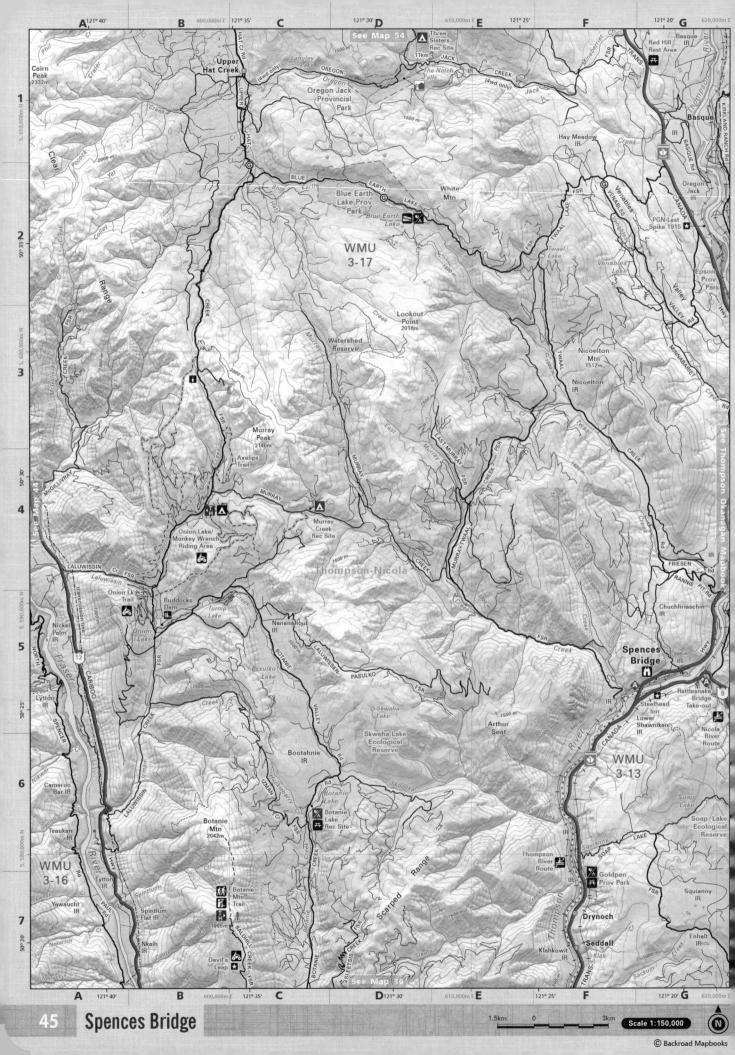

Scale 1:150,000

© Backroad Mapbooks

A 370,000mE **124° 50'** **B** 124° 45' **C** **D** 124° 40' **E** 124° 35' **F** 390,000mE **G**

Homathko

Gargoyle
Glacier

Gargoyle
Creek

Incisor
Peak

Homathko

Mt
Grenville
3109m

Icefield

Galleon
Peak

Bute

WMU
2-15

Gunsight
Peak

1

Teaquahan

Galleon Creek

2500 m

South
Grenville
Glacier

50° 55'

5,640,000m N

Homalco
IR

Homathko Estuary
Provincial Park

Mt
Bute

Glacier

2

TFL
43

River

SPUD ML

Potato
Point
IR

Waddington
Harbour

Southgate
Peak

Elliott

House
Mtn

Hamilton
Pt

Inlet

SOUTHGATE

Southgate

MAIN

3

50° 50'

5,630,000m N

Pigeon Valley

Ward
Pt

Creek

SOUTHGATE

River

MAIN

Mt
Rodney

See Vancouver Island Mapbook

Bute

Strathcona

4

Superb
Mtn
2469m

Mount Sir
Francis Drake

WMU
2-14

50° 45'

5,620,000m N

5

Boyd
Pt

Inlet

Needle
Peaks

Parabola
Glacier

Tolo
Mtn

6

River

7

Hovel
Bay

Orford

HOVEL
BAY ML

River

WMU
2-13

50° 40'

BUTE
ML

Powell River

A 370,000mE **124° 50'** **B** 124° 45' **C** 124° 45' **D** 380,000mE **E** 124° 40' **F** 124° 35' **G** 124° 30'

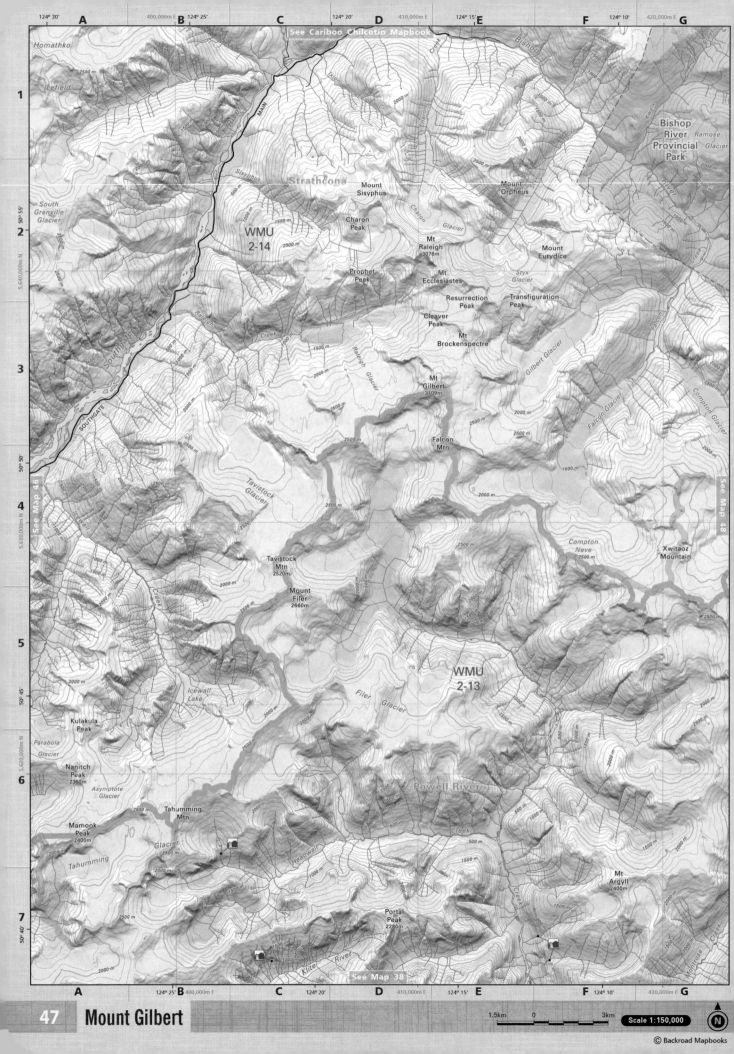

A   B   124° 25'   400,000m E   C   124° 20'   410,000m E   D   124° 15'   E   F   124° 10'   420,000m E   G

Homathko
Icefield
2500 m

South
Grenville
Glacier

Bishop
River
Provincial
Park

Ramose
Glacier

Sisyphus

Strathcona

Mount
Sisyphus

Mount
Orpheus

WMU
2-14

Charon
Peak

Mt
Raleigh
3078m

Mount
Eurydice

Prophet
Peak

Mt
Ecclesiastes

Styx
Glacier

Raleigh

Resurrection
Peak

Transfiguration
Peak

Cleaver
Peak

SOUTHGATE

Creek

Raleigh Glacier

Mt
Brockenspectre

Gilbert Glacier

Mt
Gilbert
3109m

Falcon
Mtn

Falcon Glacier

Compton Glacier

Tavistock
Glacier

Compton
Neve

Xwitaoz
Mountain

Icewall
Lake

Tavistock
Mtn
2520m

Mount
Filer
2660m

Kulakula
Peak

WMU
2-13

Parabola
Glacier

Nanitch
Peak
2360m

Filer Glacier

Asymptote
Glacier

Filer

Powell River

Mamook
Peak
2400m

Tahumming
Mtn

Creek

Tahumming

Glacier

Headwall

Mt
Argyll
2400m

Portal
Peak
2280m

Klite River

Melrose Creek

See Map 46
See Map 48
See Map 38

A   B   124° 25'   400,000m E   C   124° 20'   410,000m E   D   124° 15'   E   F   124° 10'   420,000m E   G

1.5km   0   3km   Scale 1:150,000   N

© Backroad Mapbooks

WMU 5-5

WMU 5-4
Cariboo

Ts'yl-Os Provincial Park

Monmouth Mtn 3194m

Fluted Mtn

Chapman Glacier

Mt Taylor

Edmond Glacier

Transition Peak

Ramose

Mixala Glacier

Clao Peak

Skmalts Naxwexnt Glacier

Sxwitaoz Glacier

Mt Fowler

Stalhalam Glacier

Bishop River Provincial Park

Mt Tsunamen

Mt Appalus

Mt Sawt

Mt Binkert

Frank Smith Glacier

Mt Porter

Stanley

Smith

Donar Glacier

Mt Donar

Mt Fulgora

Mt Mills

WMU 2-14
Strathcona

Glacier

WMU 3-32

Mt Chloe

Mt Daphnis

WMU 3-33

Stanley Peak

Compton Glacier

Compton Mtn

Toba Peak 2896m

Magaera Glacier

Mt Magaera

Bridge Glacier

Metslaka Keta

Ring Glacier

Mt Alecto

Bridge Peak

Toba Glacier

WMU 2-11
Squamish-Lillooet

Bishop Glacier

Lillooet Glacier

Montrose Glacier

Mount Tisiphone

Lillooet Mountain

Montrose Peak

Powell River

WMU 2-13

Dalgleish Glacier

Delta Peak

Mu Peak

Silt Lake

Upper Lillooet Prov Park

Mount Dalgleish

Obelia Peak

See Map 47
See Map 49
See Map 39

N
Scale 1:150,000
1.5km   0   3km

© Backroad Mapbooks

Mount Dalgleish 48

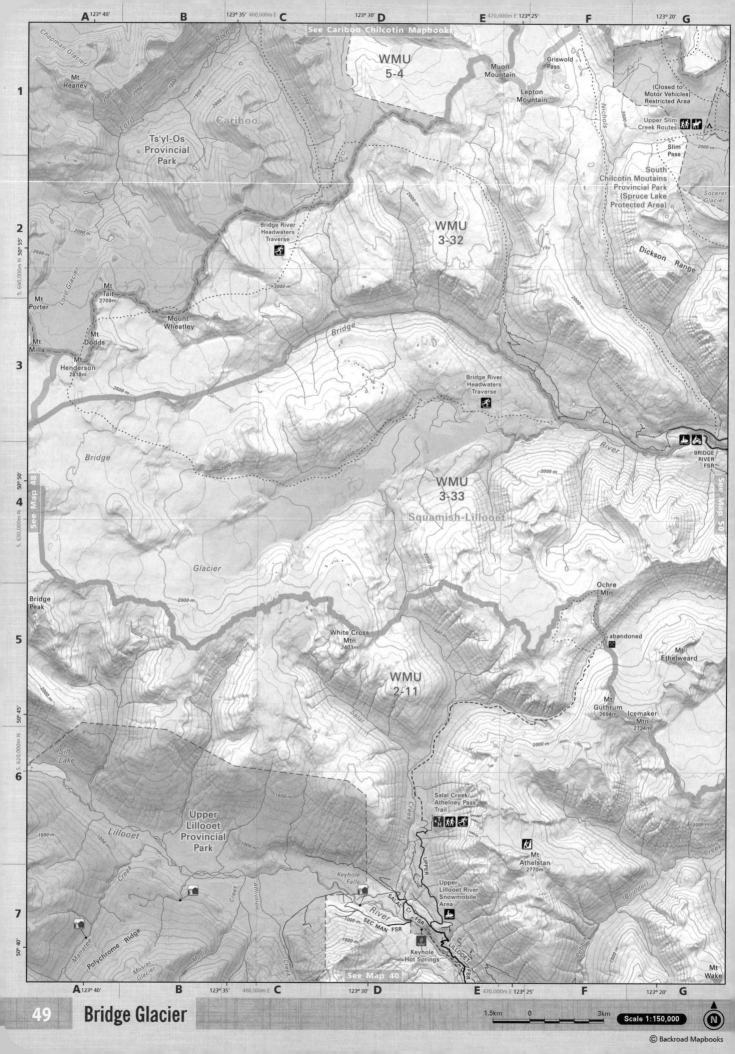

Scale 1:150,000

© Backroad Mapbooks

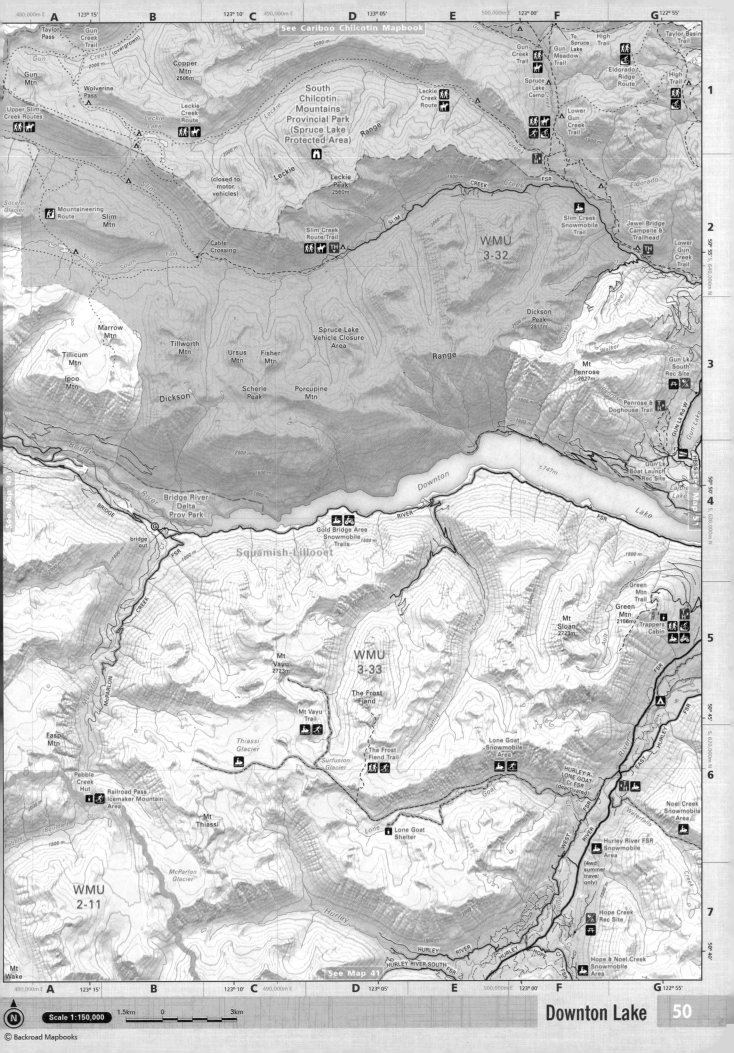

A 123° 15' B 123° 10' C 490,000m E D 123° 05' E 500,000m E 123° 00' F G 122° 55'

Taylor Pass

Gun Creek Trail (overgrown)

Gun Mtn

Gun Creek

Gun Mtn

Wolverine Pass

Copper Mtn
2606m

Upper Slim Creek Routes

Leckie Lake

Leckie Creek Route

Socter Glacier

South Chilcotin Mountains Provincial Park (Spruce Lake Protected Area)

Leckie Creek Route

Leckie Range

Leckie Peak
2560m

Gun Creek Trail

Gun Creek

Spruce Lake Camp

To Spruce Lake

Gun Meadow Trail

High Trail

Taylor Basin Trail

Eldorado Ridge Route

High Trail

1

Mountaineering Route

Slim Mtn

(closed to motor vehicles)

Leckie

Slim Creek Route/Trail

TH

Slim Gl

South Fork

Cable Crossing

SLIM

CREEK

Slim Creek Snowmobile Trail

Creek

FSR

Jewel Bridge Campsite & Trailhead

TH

Lower Gun Creek Trail

Lower Gun Creek Trail

50° 55' 5,640,000m N

2

WMU 3-32

Dickson Peak
2811m

Jewel

Hoxel

Walker

Mt Penrose
2627m

Gun Lk South Rec Site

3

Marrow Mtn

Tillicum Mtn

Tillworth Mtn

Ursus Mtn

Fisher Mtn

Spruce Lake Vehicle Closure Area

Range

Ipoo Mtn

Dickson

Scherle Peak

Porcupine Mtn

Penrose & Doghouse Trail

TH

Gun Lx Rd W

HESS LK Map 51

50° 50' 5,630,000m N

Bridge

River

Downton

±747m

Gun'Lk Boat Launch Rec Site

Lajoie Lake

4

See Map 49

BRIDGE

bridge out

G

FSR

Bridge River Delta Prov Park

Squamish-Lillooet

RIVER

Gold Bridge Area Snowmobile Trails

Lake

FSR

Green Mtn Trail

Green Mtn
2156m

Trappers Cabin

5

McParlon

CREEK

Mt Vayu
2723m

WMU 3-33

Mt Sloan
2723m

Alut

Jamie Creek

FSR

50° 45' 5,620,000m N

Fasp Mtn

Mt Vayu Trail

Thiassi Glacier

The Frost Fiend

The Frost Fiend Trail

Surfusion Glacier

Lone Goat Snowmobile Area

Goat

HURLEY R. LONE GOAT Cr FSR (deactivated)

River

WEST

FSR

East

Hurley

Noel Creek Snowmobile Area

6

Pebble Creek Hut

Railroad Pass · Icemaker Mountain Area

Mt Thiassi

Lone

Lone Goat Shelter

Pebble (Boulder) Cr

McParlon Glacier

WMU 2-11

Hurley

Hope Creek Rec Site

Hurley River FSR Snowmobile Area

(4wd summer travel only)

Hope & Noel Creek Snowmobile Area

7

Mt Wake

HURLEY RIVER-SOUTH FSR

HURLEY RIVER

HOPE Cr

50° 40'

See Map 41

A 123° 15' B 123° 10' C 490,000m E D 123° 05' E 500,000m E 123° 00' F G 122° 55'

N

Scale 1:150,000

1.5km 0 3km

Downton Lake 50

© Backroad Mapbooks

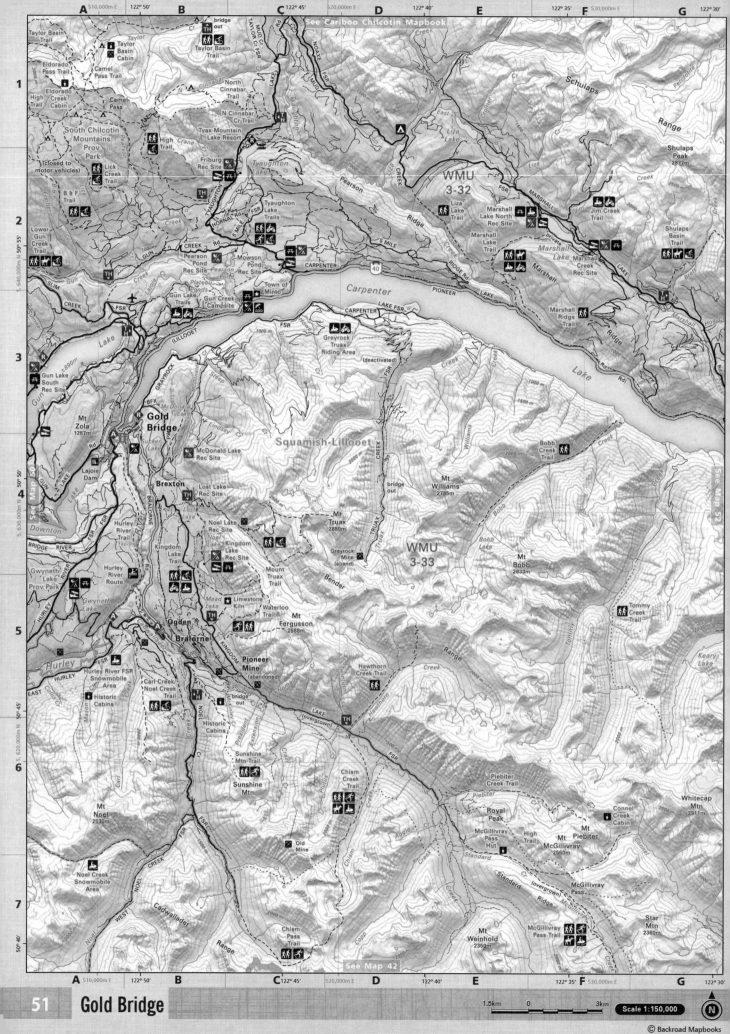

Scale 1:150,000

© Backroad Mapbooks

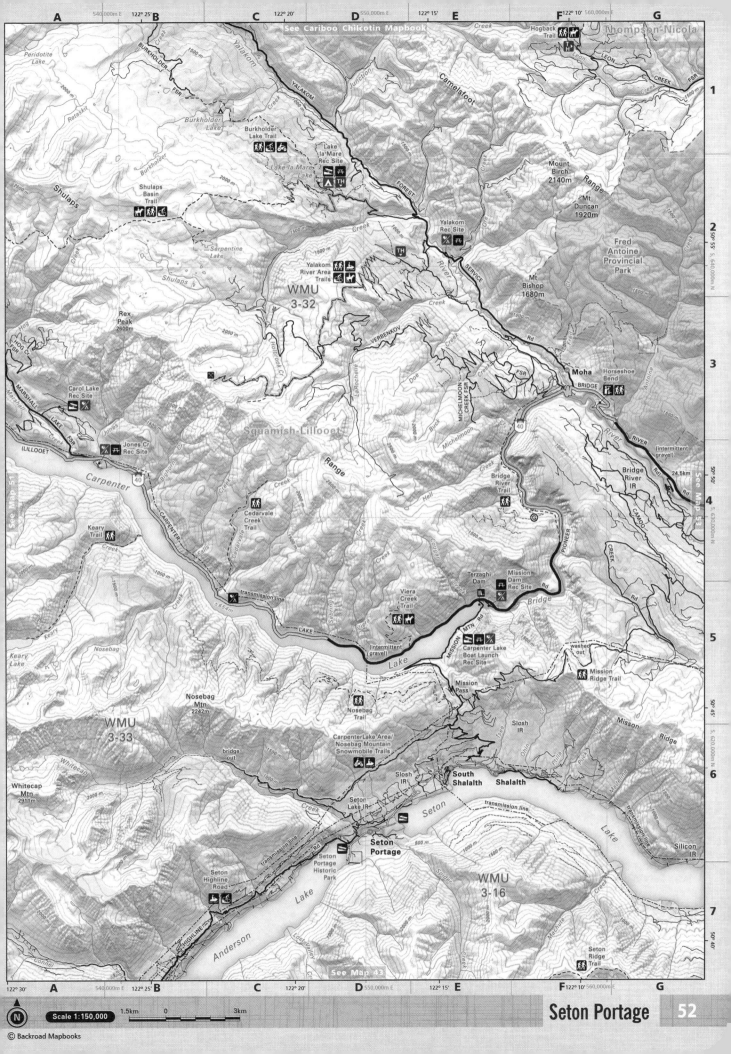

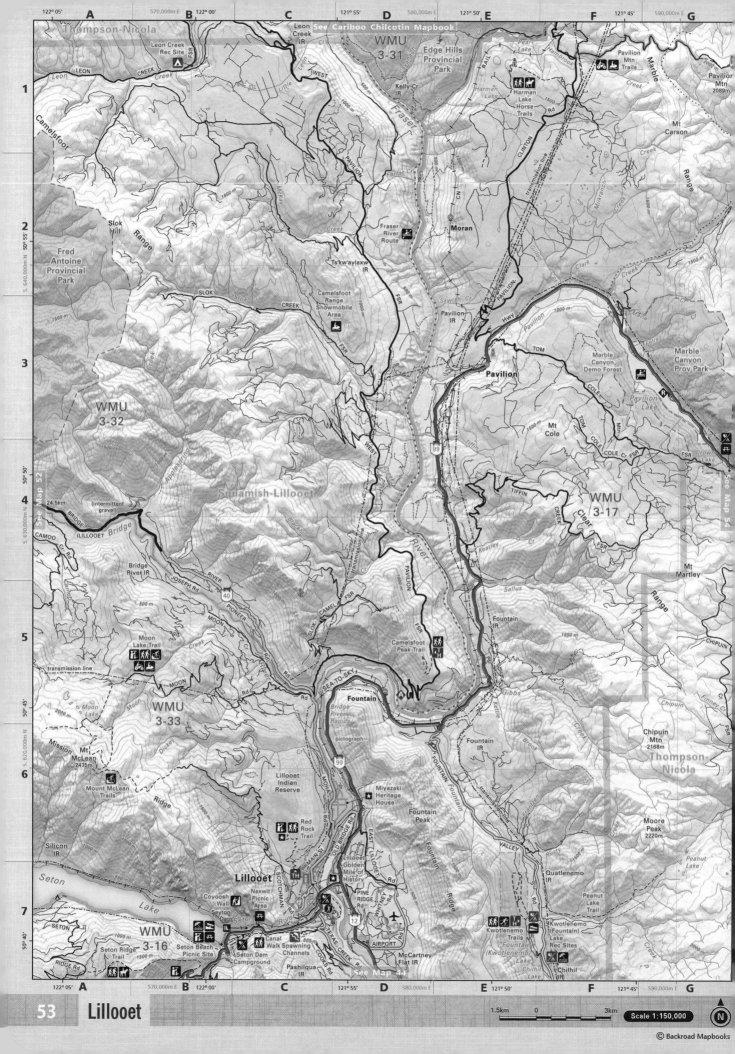

Scale 1:150,000

© Backroad Mapbooks

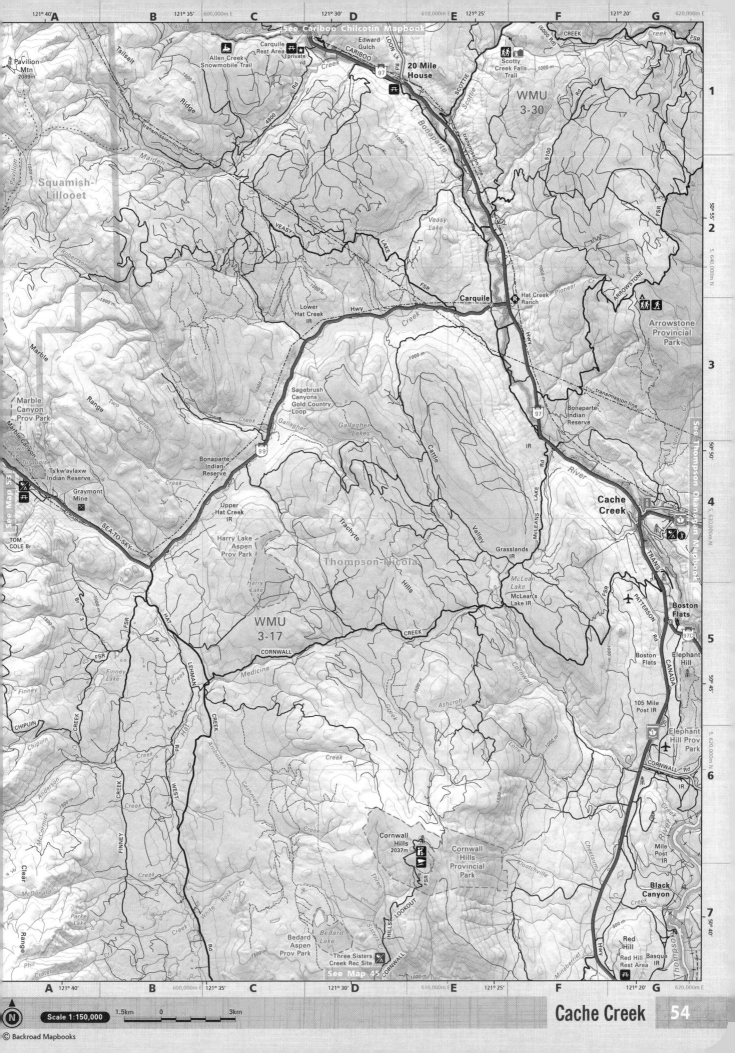

British Columbia's backyard provides campers and RVers with numerous choices of camping sweet spots. Search Camping and RV BC's mapping tool to locate over 1,500 campgrounds, offering four unique camping experiences:

- **Privately operated campgrounds and RV parks** (including municipal campgrounds)
- **Provincial campgrounds** (BC Parks)
- **National campgrounds** (Parks Canada)
- **Recreation Sites and Trails BC** (operated by the provincial government)

Plan to gear up and get on the road!

SCAN ME!

RVCAMPINGBC.COM
Your one stop for campgrounds and RV parks in British Columbia

CONNECT WITH US f y p •• You Tube

Reservations:

SD

SERVICE DIRECTORY

Find what you are looking for, from our trusted Service Directory Members.

▶**Accommodations** ▶ **Tours & Guides** ▶ **Sales & Services**

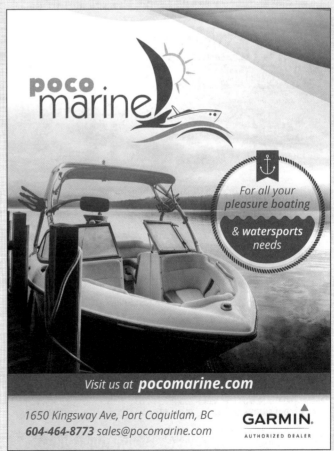

SERVICE DIRECTORY

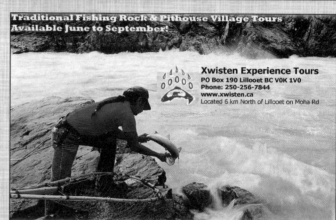

BACKROAD GPS MAPS
ADVENTURE TOPOGRAPHIC MAPS & GUIDE

ACTIVITY POI'S
Thousands of SEARCHABLE points-of-interest with descriptions, including campsites, recreation sites, boat launches and canoe access, fish species, trailheads, scenic viewpoints, and more.

COMPATIBILITY
GARMIN GPS and GARMIN Basecamp compatible.

PADDLE ON
PADDLING ROUTES - Clearly marked canoe and kayak routes including portage distances, access points and more.

1,000s OF TRAILS
Thousands of clearly marked multi-use and motorized trail systems (ATV, hiking, mountain biking, horseback riding, cross-country skiing, snowshoeing, snowmobile, and more).

3D VIEW
3D terrain shading on compatible devices and in Basecamp.

SCALE |⟷|
10,000, 20,000 or 50,000 base scale maps (depending on the province/area).

GETTING THERE
ROUTABLE ROADS - Contains routable roads, including forest service, industry and city roads, as well as highways, to make getting to your destination easy by creating point-to-point routes on compatible devices.

RESOURCE DETAILS
From BC to Manitoba we provide resource information like no other. Oil & Gas facility points, LSD Grids, Townships, cutlines, pipelines and more.

UNPARALLELED DETAILS
SHADED RELIEF - Detailed topography highlighting the area's terrain using industry leading contour lines and relief shading.

ALL TERRAIN
1000s of kilometres of ATV and snowmobile trails including trailheads, length, difficulty, and more.

TOWNSHIP & RANGE SECTION
Available in Alberta, Manitoba, and Saskatchewan.

CROWN AND PRIVATE / RESTRICTED LAND
Identified in BC, Ontario, Nova Scotia and New Brunswick.

ON THE HUNT
WILDLIFE MANAGEMENT AREAS
Smart background and searchable Wildlife Management Units (WMUs) or Zones for anglers and hunters.

PARK ACCESS
National, provincial and urban parks, picnic areas, huts and cabins, campsites, and more.

ADDRESS SEARCH
Available in Alberta, Manitoba, Ontario, New Brunswick, Nova Scotia, PEI, Newfoundland & Labrador, and Yukon.

CO-OPERATION
Updated regularly and developed in cooperation with local agencies (government, parks, fisheries, forestry and tourism organizations, local municipalities, non-profit outdoor groups and clubs, consumers, and more) to ensure accuracy.

THE ANGLING EDGE
Hot spots, stocking, tips and techniques, regulations and more.
LAKE BATHYMETRY - Depth contour lines for fishing lakes, rivers and streams. Available in BC, Alberta, Saskatchewan, and Ontario.

MISCELLANEOUS
Landmarks, caves, hot springs, waterfalls, glaciers, lighthouses, and more.

ORDER ONLINE NOW!

backroadmapbooks.com

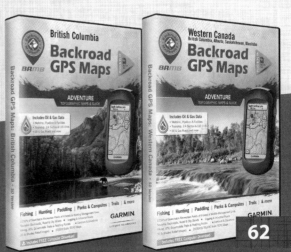

62

WE'VE GOT YOUR BACK IN THE BACKCOUNTRY!

HORSE COUNCIL BRITISH COLUMBIA

Did You Know? Since 2011, Horse Council BC, through our BC Equestrian Trails Fund, has provided over $175,000 to member clubs and affiliates in support of preservation, construction and improvements to trails, trailheads and horse camping areas all over BC.

Nearly all of this enhancement to backcountry access is available to **all** trail users. The fund is made up of membership dollars, plus individual and corporate donations.

In addition, Horse Council BC provides excellent third party liability and ADD coverage from Capri Insurance with our yearly membership.

Become a member today, and help HCBC continue to provide support and funding for BC's extraordinary trails! To learn more about Horse Council BC, visit us at **hcbc.ca**

Trip Planning Notes:

ADVENTURES

FISHING
HUNTING
PADDLING
BACKROAD
PARK
RECSITE
WINTER
TRAIL
WILDLIFE
ATV [OHV]
SNOWMOBILE

Awaken the adventurer within as you explore the thousands of backcountry adventures we have put together for you in the following section. With no shortage of year-round recreational opportunities in the Vancouver Coast and Mountains region of BC, our adventure section can guide you through alpine skiing and ocean kayaking in the same day. Or, choose to spend the day hiking through old growth forests, going on a hunting expedition, driving along scenic backcountry roads or fishing one of the hundreds of lakes and rivers. Hardcore adventurers will enjoy trekking to some of Canada's highest waterfalls, biking down single-track trails through the rainforest or experiencing the thrill of snowmobiling among massive snow-capped mountain peaks. No matter what your ideal adventure may be, from hunting to fishing, wildlife viewing to camping, ATVing to horseback riding, the following 11 adventure sections will have you outdoors and exploring in no time. Make sure to read through the adventure Summary at the beginning of each section, for a quick overview summary of that activity as it pertains to the region. Each Adventure section is made up of countless listings and descriptions of different activities offering endless possibilities when it comes to planning your next adventure. Make sure to check out the symbols beside each listing, showcasing the numerous nearby activities. Once you find the perfect adventure listing, use the map reference to locate and explore your next excursion on our maps. We hope you enjoy exploring these adventures, as much as we enjoyed bringing them to you!

BACKROAD
ADVENTURES

The Lower Mainland of BC is the most populated area in Western Canada. That being said, the opportunities to travel short distances and be alone in nature abound. You really enjoy the best of both worlds as you explore this area of Canada.

While there are destinations throughout the area that require a four-wheel drive vehicle and a winch for emergencies, many remote logging roads can be enjoyed in a reliable two-wheel drive automobile. Just be aware of logging trucks moving along at high speeds and be prepared to get quickly out of the way.

For example, the Hurley River Road is one of the most popular routes into the area north of Pemberton. While the road is gravel and can be bumpy, it is easily passable by two-wheel drive vehicles and is an incredibly scenic route. For the adventurous, many great four-wheel drive routes head off from here. The offshoots of logging roads offer hours of exploration. For the four-wheel drive adventurer, the Whipsaw Trail southwest of Princeton offers challenging driving, and the Lawless-Britton Forest Service Road between Tulameen and the Coquihalla Highway offers amazing scenery and wildlife viewing opportunities.

Another popular route, the West Harrison Lake Forest Service Road, has recently been renamed the Sts'ailes Forest Service Road, a tribute to the First Nations community who have lived along the west side of Harrison Lake for generations. This 70 km (44 mile) route is subject to washouts and avalanches. Unfortunately backroads change; bridges wash out, roads are deactivated and gates pop up. We do our best to keep you posted (visit the update page at www.backroadmapbooks.com before setting out), but if in doubt it might be worth calling the local forest district office (numbers at the back of the book) to find out current road conditions. However, if you come across a change that we need to know about, please send an email to updates@backroadmapbooks.com.

Not everyone has an interest in getting off the beaten path, and the Vancouver Coast and Mountains area offers so much to see without leaving the pavement. There is no end to the amazing selection of spots to visit; museums, gardens, historical sites, etc. Plan a day trip to one of these locations or a round trip to take in any number of the great spots you can visit. In southwestern BC, you are only limited by your imagination.

Alexander Falls (Map 32/C5)

Similar to most of the sights in the Callaghan Valley, Alexander Falls has seen several improvements including an upgraded viewing platform, more parking and added outhouses. The 43 metre (140 ft) high falls is found about 8 km up the paved Callaghan Valley Road leading to the Whistler Olympic Park Nordic Area. The area is open year-round, but the access road to Whistler Olympic Park is blocked by a security gate after hours. The area is very wild; bears, both black and grizzly, are often seen. Dogs are allowed but because of the bears, it is wise to keep your pet on a leash at all times.

August Jacob's Hot Springs (Map 24/E3)

These hot springs do exist, but are extremely difficult to find. A fair bit of bushwhacking on Frank Creek is required to get to the springs. There are no soaking pools here as the water flows down a rock face approximately 4 metres (13 ft) to the creek below. The water is very hot at 49°C (120°F) at the top of the waterfall and source of the spring.

Black Tusk (Map 22/E1)

Black Tusk gets its name from its deep black colour and its sharp, tooth-like appearance. The 2,319 metre (7,608 ft) peak is visible from points along the Sea to Sky Highway (Hwy 99), as well as from the hiking trail to its peak. The distinct peak is one of the most recognizable in the Coast Mountains. Although no technical skills are required, the hike is moderately strenuous with a difficult final ascent. The route gains 1,735 m (5,690 ft) of elevation in 13.5 km (8.4 mi) and hikers should plan for an 8-10 hour return hike.

Brandywine Falls (Map 32/D7)

One of the most photographed waterfalls in the province, Brandywine Falls is an impressive 66 metre (215 ft) cascade that freefalls over the lip of a cliff into a deep bowl. Found next to the Sea to Sky Highway (Hwy 99), the falls are easily accessible at the top, but difficult to access from the base. The park is open for the 2 km return hike to the falls from April until November; it is gated in the evening and during the winter months.

Bridal Veil Falls (Map 4/G4)

There is a very short trail to the base of Bridal Veil Falls, found east of Chilliwack off of the Trans-Canada Highway (Hwy 1). The 60 metre (195 ft) falls don't really fall; they get their name from the fact that the water runs down the face of the cliff, spreading out thinly like a veil.

Britannia Mine Museum (Map 11/B1)

Found alongside the Sea to Sky Highway (Hwy 99) between Whistler and Vancouver, the former Britannia Mines were once one of the world's largest copper mines. Mining artefacts and original blueprints of Mill 3 (a National Historic Site) are available for viewing. Board an authentic mining train and descend underground into a 1910 tunnel; wait for the lights to go off (briefly) to see how miners would have worked. Activities involving fossils, minerals and gold panning are also on site. The museum is open year-round from 9:30 am to 5:30 pm with 45 minutes guided tours offered throughout the day. For additional details, visit the museum website at www.britanniaminemuseum.ca.

Bungee Bridge (Map 32/D6)

Located south of Whistler on the Calcheak Forest Service Road, the bungee bridge is worth a visit even if you don't plan on jumping. The bridge is part of the Sea to Sky Trail and although you can drive to it, a more scenic way to get there is to hike or bike from Brandywine Falls Provincial Park. There are great views from the bridge down into the gorge and out over the mountains.

Burnaby Village Museum & Carousel (Map 1/F3)

Found on Deer Lake Avenue off Canada Way, the Burnaby Village Museum allows visitors to stroll down the streets of a 1920s village, exploring heritage and replica buildings and interacting with period costumed interpreters who welcome visitors and give demonstrations in many of the homes, businesses and shops. Highlights of the museum include an Interban tram car, a 1912 carousel and more. Check out the museum website at www.burnabyvillagemuseum.ca for full details.

Capilano Suspension Bridge (Map 11/D6)

Originally built in 1889, the Capilano Suspension Bridge stretches 135 metres (450 ft) across and 70 metres (230 ft) above the Capilano River. It is at the heart of a series of adventures here, including the Treetops Adventure, which links a series of giant Douglas firs via elevated suspension bridges as well as the Cliff Walk, where visitors can visit previously unexplored parts of the park on cantilevered and suspended walkways jutting out from the granite cliff face. The popular tourist area is found at 3735 Capilano Road. Additional details can be found at www.capbridge.com.

Cascade Falls (Map 3/F2)

Located outside of Mission, there is a pair of falls here. The upper falls are 28 metres (91 ft) high and the lower falls are about half that. The lower falls are no longer readily accessible as the trail has been re-routed. The hike to the falls is a short 750 metre jaunt with an elevation gain of 40 metres (130 ft). The trail to the falls is open April through November. The regional park and falls are found off Ridgeview Road to the east of Sylvester Road on the way to Davis Lake.

Cascade Lookout (Map 7/D5)

Manning Provincial Park sits in the heart of the Cascade Mountains. The turnoff to the Cascade Lookout and Sub-Alpine Meadows is located across the highway from Manning Park Resort. The 16 km drive ascends a steep and winding road right into the mountains. At the 8 km mark, the Cascade Lookout provides spectacular must-see vistas of valleys, lakes and rivers. Visitors who drive the remaining 8 km will be treated to a myriad of flower-clad meadows. If you experience the sensation of being on top of the world, it's because you are! The road is open June to September, weather permitting.

Chatterbox Falls (Map 30/F3)

The remote access to this hidden inlet discourages most visitors from ever venturing to Princess Louisa Park. What a shame; the spectacular fjord-like setting and world famous Chatterbox Falls (only a ten minute excursion from the ocean) are certainly worth the visit. The falls drop 40 metres (120 ft) almost directly into the ocean.

Chehalis Lake Landslide (Map 14/B5)

In December 2007, a massive landslide about 200 meters (655 ft) wide and 500 metres (1,640 ft) long occurred around the 33.5 km mark of the Chehalis Forest Service Road. The force of the material (approximately half a million cubic metres of rock and sediment) entering Chehalis Lake generated a wave that was estimated to be 15 metres (50 ft) high in some places. The wave scoured much of the shoreline destroying all three recreation sites along the lake edge. The area is still very unstable and sightseeing is not recommended.

Chilliwack Lake Provincial Park (Map 5/F6)

Besides its main attraction, Chilliwack Lake, this 9,122 hectare (22,530 ac) park also encompasses several pristine lakes and rugged mountain peaks. Several trails can be followed while exploring this area. At the southeast end of the lake, the old growth forest at the former Sapper's Park also features a rare old growth fir and balsam tree forest. Those exploring by water are advised to stay clear of the outflow of Chilliwack Lake as dangerous currents exist both here and for several kilometres downstream.

Christ Church (Anglican) National Historic Site (Map 15/F6)

A National Historic Site, the Christ Church (Anglican) is the oldest continuously operating church on the BC mainland. The church was designed by Captain Grant of the British Royal Engineers in 1861 at the height of the Fraser Gold Rush. It is found at 681 Fraser Avenue in Hope.

Clear Creek Hot Springs (Map 25/G6)

Clear Creek is often packed on summer weekends. The soaking pools are located just off the Clear Creek Forest Service Road, about 13 km from its junction with the Harrison East Forest Service Road. Access changes frequently, so be prepared to hike or bike in. Even at the best of times, the springs are only accessible by four-wheel drive or ATV. There are four soaking pools ranging from an old cedar-box to a porcelain bathtub, the hottest of which is 43°C (109°F). Be sure to watch out for two great waterfalls along the road in at around the 7 km mark.

Coquihalla Summit Recreation Area (Map 16/D2)

The Boston Bar Summit Rest Area sits near the summit of the Coquihalla Highway (Hwy 5) and provides a scenic picnic area for highway travellers. Here you can marvel at the incredible views of Zopkius Ridge and Needle Peak or embark on the challenging trails that climb to the various peaks in the area.

Cypress Falls Park (Map 11/A7)

In addition to the falls, this tiny, out of the way park has one of the largest stands of remaining old growth trees in the Lower Mainland. Access is found off Woodgreen Drive, which is accessed from Exit 4 of the Upper Levels Highway (Hwy 99) in West Vancouver. The trail in is an easy 3 km (1.9 mi) hike which takes about an hour to complete.

BACKROAD ADVENTURES

Domaine de Chaberton Winery/Fraser Valley Wine Tours (Map 2/E7)
One of Langley's oldest and largest wineries, Domaine de Chaberton hosts free public tours year-round, at 2:00 and 4:00 pm from February to November and at 3:00 pm in December and January, weather permitting. It is one of the most popular stops on the Fraser Valley Winery Tour. Visitors can take a guided tour of the rest of the wineries or stop and pick up a map at a local visitor information centre. Domaine de Chaberton Estate Winery is found at 1064 216 Street in Langley. Visit www.chabertonwinery.com for more information.

Dr Sun Yat Sen Chinese Gardens (Map 1/D2)
Vancouver's Chinatown is the second largest in North America, while the Sun Yat Sen Chinese Gardens is the largest Chinese garden outside of China. Built in 1986, the garden is the first full-scale Scholar garden built outside of China using traditional techniques. This style of garden was typically for China's ancient elite. It features covered walkways and traditional architecture, making it a delight in any weather. The gardens are located at 578 Carrall Street, a short walk from downtown Vancouver or shorter walk from the Stadium-Chinatown Skytrain station. Opening hours, entrance fees and more can be found at the Garden's website www.vancouverchinesegarden.com.

Elaho Giant (Map 40/C7)
A rather hard to find but easy to follow 10 minute trail leads to a 1,400 year old fir tree. Access is found on the western side of Elaho Main just before the Sundance Creek Bridge; the trailhead is not well marked so you might have to park near the bridge and hike along the road to find it. Without the quick response of firefighters, the tree would have been lost in a June 2015 fire. Although the base was blackened, it appears the tree will live to see a few more years.

Fort Langley National Historic Site (Map 2/F4)
Fort Langley is called "the birthplace of BC." In 1827, the Hudson's Bay Company established a fur trading post here. As the post grew, so did its influence. Furs were shipped to Europe via Cape Horn, produce was traded to the Russians in Alaska, local cranberries found their way to California, and Fraser River salmon were shipped to Hawaii! In 1858 rumours of gold on the Fraser River caused a massive influx of Americans to the area. Worried that the Americans might annex the area, British Columbia was proclaimed a Crown Colony on this site by James Douglas on November 19, 1858. These days, visitors can see beaver pelts, Hudson Bay Company blankets and other historical artefacts and watch demonstrations of blacksmithing and barrel-making by costumed interpretive staff.

Gastown (Map 1/D2)
Surrounded by the towering buildings of downtown Vancouver, the historic district of Gastown is Vancouver's oldest neighbourhood, featuring cobblestone streets and beautiful redbrick architecture around Water Street. Gastown is home to the world's first steam-powered clock and the old Canadian Pacific Railway Station, built in 1912. Here you will get a sense of the design sensibilities of the era.

George C. Reifel Migratory Bird Sanctuary (Map 1/B5)
Situated on Westham Island, the sanctuary consists of 344 hectares (850 ac) of managed wetlands, natural marshes and low dykes. Although there are great opportunities to view birds year-round, the fall season (October to early December) offers visitors the chance to view the snow geese on their migration and spring is the perfect time to view eagles, hawks and seals. Winter visitors often encounter the small Saw-Whet Owl roosting, and the sanctuary provides winter shelter for many types of eagles, hawks and owls. The sanctuary is open from 9:00 am to 4:00 pm daily. Additional details can be found on their website at www.reifelbirdsanctuary.com.

Grouse Grind (Map 11/D7)
The Grouse Grind is a 2.9 km trail up the face of Grouse Mountain. It is commonly referred to as "Mother Nature's Stairmaster." This is a very challenging hike and you will need to be prepared for changing weather conditions. Do not be fooled by the Grind's proximity to and view of Vancouver. Starting from the end of Nancy Greene Way in North Vancouver, the elevation gain is 853 meters (2,800 ft) and the summit is at 1,127 meters (3,700 ft). It takes an average of 1.5-2 hours to complete the climb and once at the top, relax and take the Skyride back down. The Grind is closed during winter and a couple hours before dusk at other times of the year.

Grouse Mountain Skyride (Map 11/D6)
The Grouse Mountain Skyride is North America's largest aerial tram system and offers panoramic views over Vancouver and the Coast Mountains. Found at 6400 Nancy Greene Way in North Vancouver, it takes visitors to the top (well, almost top) of Grouse Mountain, high above the city. Once there, take in the sites and visit the Refuge for Endangered Wildlife, where two orphaned grizzly bears and three timber wolves live in a protected sanctuary. Or take in the view from an eagle's perspective at Theatre in the Sky, a high definition tour over the land and sea of Southwestern BC. In summer, enjoy lumberjack shows, hiking trails, guided eco walks, paragliding, falconry demonstrations, scenic chairlift rides and helicopter tours, just to name a few activities. In winter, Grouse Mountain offers the finest in local skiing and snowboarding, as well as snowshoeing, ice-skating and sleigh rides. Full details, webcams and more can be found at www.grousemountain.com.

Gulf of Georgia Cannery (Map 1/B5)
Built in 1894, the Gulf of Georgia Cannery is one of BC's last remaining intact canneries. Found in Steveston village at 12138 Fourth Avenue, the collection of buildings includes the main cannery, icehouse, drum storage shed and others that sit atop wood pilings. There are also 10,000 well-preserved artefacts at the cannery to browse through. Visit their website, www.gulfofgeorgiacannery.org, for more information.

> Never feed wild animals – this can alter their natural behaviour and be dangerous for both of you.

Harrison Hot Springs (Map 4/F1)
While the humble (well, it never was really humble) hotel at Harrison Hot Springs has morphed into a destination resort complete with a marina and a golf course, at its heart remain the hot springs. The springs in no way retain any of their natural character, but coming here is the easiest way to have a soak in a hot springs in western BC. There are five separate pools here, at a variety of temperatures, two indoor and three outdoor, with temperatures varying from 38°C to 65°C (100-150°F) at the source.

Hell's Gate (Map 26/E5)
Found next to the Trans-Canada Highway (Hwy 1) between Hope and Cache Creek, Hell's Gate is a 35 metre (115 ft) wide gorge that restricts the river. Flowing at a rate of over 200 million gallons of water per minute during spring runoff, the best way to see Hell's Gate is via the Airtram. The Airtram brings travellers 150 metres (500 ft) from the highway down to near river level and operates from late April until mid-October. Rates and dates can be found on their website, www.hellsgateairtram.com. As you watch the raging river, think back to Simon Fraser's trip through here in 1808, the first European exploration of the region. The falls were named after Fraser's comment, "We had to travel where no human being should venture, for surely we have encountered the gates of hell."

High Falls (Map 22/A2)
The father of trail building in the Lower Mainland, Halvor Lunden, discovered these falls while working on a nearby power station. He is the one to blame for the steep, sometimes perilous trail to a viewpoint over the falls. The trail gains 622 metres (2,040 ft) in just over 4 km (2.5 mi) and there are some short chain assisted areas to climb. The impressive falls cascade into a narrow canyon, over 100 metres (325 ft) high and sometimes less than 2 metres (6 ft) wide. Unfortunately, due to the narrow, winding canyon, it is impossible to see the falls from top to bottom.

Hollyburn Giant (Map 11/C7)
At the junction of the Old Brewis Trail and the Crossover Trail (both in the Brother's Creek area), you will find this giant fir, standing 43.7 metres (143 ft) high, with a diameter of 2.96 metres (9.7 ft). The tree is well over 1,100 years old. Access is found from the west side of Lawson Creek Bridge on Pinecrest Drive or Eyremount, Crestwell and Millstream Roads.

BACKROAD ADVENTURES

Homesite Creek [Gumdrop] Caves (Map 9/C3)

The trailhead is found on the Homesite Forest Service Road just north of the powerline and is usually signed as long as vandals have not removed the sign. The trail leads half an hour (one-way) in a southeast direction from the road to a series of twelve limestone caverns, the largest one being 10 m (35 ft) deep.

H.R. MacMillan Space Centre (Map 1/C2)

Discover the wonders of the cosmos at the H.R. MacMillan Space Centre. Located across English Bay from downtown Vancouver in Vanier Park, the Space Centre offers space-related knowledge and resources for kids and adults. One of the major events is the Laser Light shows, from Laser Pink Floyd to Laser Radiohead. Also extremely popular is the planetarium, where visitors can see projections of the night sky, as well as multimedia presentations on the past, present and future of space. Full details about the centre including programs, hours, admission fees and more can be found on the Centre's website, www.spacecentre.ca.

Hat Creek Ranch (Map 54/E3)

The Historic Hat Creek Ranch was a roadhouse, built in the 1860s, which catered to miners, stagecoaches and wagon trains along the Cariboo Waggon Road. The ranch was in operation until 1916, when automobiles were introduced to the Cariboo. These days, visitors can take a tour of the Roadhouse, visit a Native Village, take a stagecoach ride or go gold panning. Camping is available as well in various forms including tent and RV, miners' tents, covered wagons, teepees, cabins and more. The tourist attraction is found off Highway 99 near its junction with Highway 97. Visit the ranch website at www.hatcreekranch.ca for full details.

Iona Jetty (Map 1/B3)

Located in Richmond, just north of the airport, the Iona Jetty is a 24 km (15 mi) return bike trail that is a combination of a dyke, road and a 4 km (2.5 mi) jetty into the ocean. There are views of jets taking off and landing, multiple water birds to see and a beach with picnic tables. Those with a limited amount of time can just visit the Iona Jetty with an 8 km (5 mi) return ride starting and returning to Iona Beach Park. The Jetty is also a great spot for stargazing at night.

Keyhole [Pebble Creek] Hot Springs (Map 40/E1)

These wild hot springs are located about 5.4 km past the Meager Creek Road, just before the Upper Lillooet Forest Service Road leaves the river and climbs steeply east. It is a 1.5 km steep scramble along the banks of the Lillooet River to the springs that bubble out onto the sand about 15 metres (40 ft) above the river on the north bank. The springs are inaccessible in times of high water and chances are you will have to dig your own soaking pool. Temperatures at the source range from 51° to 60°C (124-140°F).

Kilby Museum (Map 4/C3)

Located between Mission and Agassiz off of the Lougheed Highway (Hwy 7), Kilby is a reminder of the once thriving community of Harrison Mills, which is now a ghost town. Goods from the 1900s are stocked at the General Store Museum, while it is possible to discover what it was like to live in the rural 1920s at the Manchester House Hotel or even explore the adjacent farm. The museum is open from early April until mid-December and there is a campground on site. Full details can be found on the museum website, www.kilby.ca.

Lillooet Golden Mile of History (Map 53/D6)

Not one, not two, but 14 historic locations are found along the main street of Lillooet. From the Bridge of 23 Camels to the Old Bridge, a steel cable and wood bridge built in 1913; there is no shortage of sites from the Cariboo Gold Rush days. Highlights include the Miyazaki Heritage House, the Lillooet Museum and the CNR Station.

Lynn Canyon Suspension Bridge (Map 11/E7)

Much more humble than the nearby Capilano Suspension Bridge, the Lynn Canyon Park and Suspension Bridge are a nice hiking destination. Built in 1912, the bridge is suspended 50 metres (164 ft) above the creek and leads to a series of waterfalls to view and trails to explore. The large pool below the bridge is a popular destination for locals and tourists as it features a beautiful, but extremely cold, swimming hole. The park is found east of Lynn Valley Road by following Peters Road to Park Road.

Maplewood Farm (Map 1/E1)

This all-weather farm attraction gives visitors a hands-on up close experience with over 200 animals and birds. There are opportunities to feed animals, ride a pony and the new picnic shelters allow guests to make it a full day of adventure. The farm is found in North Vancouver off of Seymour River Place, which is found north of the Old Dollarton Road after crossing over the Seymour River. Visit the farm website, www.maplewoodfarm.bc.ca, for full details.

Meager Creek Hot Springs (Map 40/D3)

Officially closed due to a massive landslide in 2010, Meager Creek Hot Springs rest in a spectacular, remote and sometimes dangerous area. The geologically active area is prone to landslides, floods and avalanches. At its height of popularity, the springs had 30,000 yearly visitors and were beautifully developed with gorgeous pools and a caretaker. Today, it is still possible to access the site via a 7 km (4.3 mi) hike from the washed out bridge over the Lillooet River. This crossing can be challenging during high water and a rope is recommended. Closer to the springs, another crossing of Capricorn Creek required. A new route was created to access the VOC Harrison Hut by the UBC Varsity Outdoor Club in 2014. It has created a good, but long and challenging access trail to the hot springs as well. Temperatures in the pools at the hot springs range from 47° to 59°C (117-138°F).

Molly's Reach (Map 10/C6)

Inspired by the hit TV show The Beachcombers, which aired from 1972 until 1990, no visit to Gibsons on the Sunshine Coast of BC would be complete without visiting Molly's Reach. Today, the recently converted restaurant sits at the end of School Road with the famous tugboat used in the show, the Persephone, resting nearby.

MSA Museum/Trethewey House on Mill Lake (Map 3/D6)

The MSA Museum Society's mission is to offer the history and heritage of Abbotsford and surrounding areas. Featuring the Trethewey House, the museum is situated next to lovely Mill Lake and its wonderful walking paths. The arts-and-crafts style bungalow was built in 1920 by J.O. Trethewey, who was co-owner of the Abbotsford Lumber & Mining Company (once BC's 3rd largest employer). Trethewey House's unique "touch and feel" museum house has been restored back to its 1920s state, featuring original woodwork, light fixtures, fireplaces, some original décor and is filled with interesting stories to be discovered.

Museum of Anthropology (Map 1/A2)

The University of British Columbia's Museum of Anthropology boasts a vast collection of Indigenous art and artefacts from BC and around the world. See traditional canoes, masks, jewellery, carvings, longhouse replicas and totem poles – including the world's smallest, which measures just 4.4 cm (1.7 inches). The museum is found at 6393 Northwest Marine Drive. Full details, current exhibits and more can be found at the museum website, www.moa.ubc.ca.

Nairn Falls (Map 33/B1)

Another of the many waterfalls around Whistler, Nairn Falls Park is open from March through December. The 2.4 km (1.5 mi) return hike along the Green River is easy and follows a well-worn trail. The total drop of the falls is 60 metres (200 ft) but it is made up of a series of 10 to 20 metre falls.

Northair Mine (Map 32/D5)

As Monty Python would say, now for something completely different! Northair Mine is an area of abandoned cement foundations which are covered in graffiti art. The mine here operated from 1976 until 1982 when it was abandoned. Although you can hike, if you choose to drive, a four-wheel drive vehicle is recommended. The road to the mine is accessed from Callaghan Valley Road, which leads to Whistler Olympic Park, 7.7 km from where the road meets Highway 99.

Norvan's Castle (Map 11/E6)

Found along the Coliseum Trail, this is the largest of a number of big trees that have been discovered in this area. It is located along Norvan Creek. It is the fourth largest western hemlock (by volume) in the world and the widest, at 2.9 metres (9.5 ft). If you are going to see the tree, plan for an 8+ hour hike to explore the entire 24 km (15 mi) return trail. Although this is not a developed trail, the first 7 km is relatively easy. However, the last 5 km is a lot more challenging. The views are great and Norvan Falls makes a fine destination as well.

Othello Tunnels (Map 15/G6)

Othello Tunnels are a 1900s engineering feat. They were constructed by slicing through solid granite, almost entirely by hand, to link the Kootenay region of BC to the coast by rail. Named for the engineer's love of Shakespeare, visitors (and

Shakespeare buffs) can now trek through the tunnels found east of Hope on the Trans Canada Trail in the Coquihalla Canyon Provincial Park.

Peak 2 Peak Gondola (Map 32/F5)
The Peak 2 Peak Gondola travels 4.4 km (2.7 mi) in just 11 minutes between Whistler's Roundhouse Lodge and the Rendezvous Lodge on Blackcomb Mountain. Summer visitors can enjoy spectacular views of glaciers and peaks and the gondola offers access to an expanded hiking trail network on both Whistler and Blackcomb Mountains. Winter enthusiasts can enjoy the world class skiing on both hills if they wish.

Pitt River Hot Springs (Map 23/D7)
Tucked into a nook between the cliffs of the Pitt River Canyon and the Pitt River, these hot springs are one of the most scenic hot spring destinations in southern BC. Unfortunately (or fortunately, depending on your perspective), the 30 km paddle/boat ride up Pitt Lake, the long bike ride/hike in along the Pitt River Forest Service Road and precarious scramble down to the pools from the top of the cliff (ropes are provided) make them a challenge to get to. For the less adventurous, there are also tour operators that will run you up to the hot springs. The springs' source temperature is approximately 57°C (135°F). As the pools are covered by the Pitt River for the better part of the year, late winter and late summer into fall are the best times to visit.

If you plan to travel through remote areas it is imperative that you leave a detailed itinerary with friends or family.

Place Creek Falls (Map 42/E5)
Place Creek Falls is one of the most impressive waterfalls in British Columbia, although few people know it. The 412 metre (1,375 ft) high waterfalls cannot be seen all at once, but the parts that can be seen are very impressive. The falls are accessed by the Place Creek Trail, a steep, difficult trail to the Place Glacier. Access to the area is across private land.

Placid Hot Springs (Map 40/D3)
These hot springs can be found by staying on the Upper Lillooet River Forest Service Road past the old turn off to Meager Hot Springs. As the name suggest, these springs are small and not very hot, with the temperature varying between 40 and 60°C (104-140°F).

Point Atkinson Lighthouse (Map 11/A7)
The lighthouse at Point Atkinson gives Lighthouse Park its name and can be seen from several viewpoints in the park. It was named in 1792 when Captain George Vancouver charted and named the land where the lighthouse sits. It later became the site of one of Canada's first manned light stations in 1874, although the lighthouse that currently occupies the point was built in 1912. While the original building no longer exists, old military buildings can be found here, remnants of the site's military moment in the sun during World War II.

Point Grey Gun Turrets (Map 1/A2)
The only military force to ever invade Canada actually came from the USA. But during World War II, there was a serious fear of attacks by Japanese forces, particularly after Pearl Harbour. As a result, places like Point Grey had gun turrets built to defend against invaders. Fortunately, no attack came and the two gun turrets at tower beach serve only as a reminder of those times. The concrete turrets also serve as canvases for some rather creative graffiti artist and are found off Northwest Marine Drive at the edge of the University of BC campus.

Powell River Historic District (Map 18/F4)
The Powell River townsite is the only declared National Historic District in western Canada and only one of seven in Canada. The city was first constructed in 1910, and is surprisingly intact, with over 400 original buildings remaining, including the Patricia Theatre — the oldest continuously running theatre in Canada. The town, while a company town built by the Powell River Company, was pre-planned as a direct response to the excesses of the industrialism of the late 19th Century and designed as a place where families could flourish. Full details regarding the historic district can be found at www.powellrivertownsite.com.

Queen Elizabeth Park (Map 1/D2)
Located in the geographic centre of Vancouver, built out of the largest rock quarry in the city, and surrounded by steep cliffs, Queen Elizabeth Park features panoramic views of the Vancouver skyline. It also offers beautiful flower gardens. In addition to the Quarry Gardens, Arboretum and Rose Gardens, there is public art spread around the grounds.

Rainbow Falls (Map 32/F5)
One of the largest falls in southwestern BC, Rainbow Falls is also one of the most disappointing for waterfall baggers. Despite their height, viewing them is extremely difficult; only about a quarter of the falls can be seen at one time. The falls are estimated to be 380 metres (1,250 ft) high, although the creek drops over 660 metres (2,165 ft) in the space of less than a kilometre. Some would argue that these falls should be considered a single unit, which would make it one of the tallest falls in North America. Access is by trail off the Alta Lake Road west of Whistler. The 1.4 km return hike is relatively easy with a few steep sections. The trail is open from March through December, but dogs are not permitted.

Sea to Sky Gondola (Map 22/C7)
Providing a new vantage point of two of the areas great attractions, Shannon Falls and the Squamish Chief, the ten minute gondola also offers great views of the Howe Sound fjord and surrounding mountains. The gondola rises to an 885 metre (2,900 ft) summit, where further adventure awaits. There are several trails to explore, including two different interpretive loops with cantilevered viewing platforms, the spectacular Sky Pilot Suspension Bridge, rock climbing, and access to extended backcountry hiking routes.

Science World (Map 1/D2)
One of Vancouver's most recognizable structures, the geodesic dome is just the shiny shell that holds a variety of hands-on interactive displays. Kids big and small can spend hours and even days exploring the inspirational feature exhibitions and shows in the Science Theatre. Found at 1455 Quebec Street, Science World is easily accessed from the Skytrain or even the Aquabus and False Creek Ferries. Details on current exhibits, hours and admission fees can be found at www.scienceworld.ca.

Sechelt Heritage Forest Trails (Map 9/F3)
This second growth-forest contains some ancient cedar tree specimens ranging from 600 to 1,000 years old. A network of community built hiking trails provides easy access to this majestic area, while several viewpoints provide fine views of Sechelt Inlet. Access the Heritage Forest from Sechelt Inlet Road – the parking area is marked as "Hidden Grove."

Secret Grove Falls Trail (Map 9/C3)
This short trail leads to scenic waterfalls on Homesite Creek, a great spot for a picnic. The area is also popular for motorized trail riding. To access this area head north from Halfmoon Bay along Highway 101. Watch for the trailhead sign about 500 metres past Brooks Road.

Seymour Valley Trailway (Map 11/F7)
Located behind Capilano University, the Seymour Valley Bikeway is a 10 km (6 mi) one-way paved trail that travels deep into the Seymour Valley. Although the elevation gain is minimal, the trail is a rolling track so you will gain and lose much more elevation than you might imagine over the trip. The trail offers great views of the Fannin Range, Lynn Ridge Peaks, the Needles and cliffs of Jack's Burn and Paton's Lookout. At the end of the trail, there are boardwalks and a salmon hatchery.

Shannon Falls (Map 22/C7)
On the official list of big waterfalls in BC, Shannon Falls places a respectable third. While there are many unofficial waterfalls that are taller, this one wins the popularity contest. Not only are they very easy to access, and open year-round, they are also one of the prettiest falls in the province. The falls tumble 337 metres (1,105 ft) before they come crashing to the ground next to the Sea to Sky Highway (Hwy 99) south of Squamish. Those looking to extend the hike can take the Stawamus Chief Trail to the Upper Shannon Falls Trail (now called the Sea to Summit Trail). The 3.5 km (2.2 mi) hike from the parking area is a moderate hike due to the 450 metres (1,475 ft) elevation gain over a short distance. The hike is worth it, not just to view the falls but for hilltop and rock outcrops at the end of the trail as well as views from Squamish to Howe Sound.

Showh Lakes Ancient Cedars (Map 32/F3)

One of two main stands of ancient trees near Whistler, there is a mix of old growth yellow and red cedar and Douglas fir here. The western red cedars are estimated at over 1,000 years old, with a diameter of over 3 metres (10 ft). The Douglas fir trees are over 650 years old. Access is found 4 km up the recently improved Cougar Mountain Forest Service Road, which is found about 2 km past Crazy Canuck Drive on Highway 99. The upgraded Ancient Cedars Trail is now signed and the other trails in the area are also being maintained. At only 5 km (3 mi) return, the hike should take less than two hours; this allows time to hike the Showh Lakes Trail, a loop that rejoins the Ancient Cedars Trail.

Skookumchuck Narrows (Map 20/D6)

On a 3 metre (9.8 ft) tide, 757 billion litres (200 billion gallons) of water race through the narrows connecting Sechelt Inlet to Jervis Inlet. The result is a crescendo of turbulent rapids renowned for their astounding whirlpools and whitewater. It is an easy 8 km (5 mi) round trip to the viewing point at Roland Point from Egmont Road. You will want to arrive here when the tidal surge is at its strongest. Check with the Sechelt Visitor Centre for best time to view.

Sloquet Hot Springs (Map 24/D6)

Despite the long drive and fairly rough access road, this site remains quite popular. The campsite is maintained by the Douglas First Nation and there is a camping fee and donations are requested to help maintain the pools. The parking area lays 8.5 km up the Sloquet Forest Service Road, which is found around the 76.5 km mark of the In-shuck-ch Forest Service Road. From here is a steep walk leads down to the meadow and springs. The springs flow over a 9 metre (30 ft) cliff into several progressively cooler pools built out of stones before emptying into the frigid waters of Sloquet Creek. At its source, the water is an extremely hot 68°C (154°F) and is known to have a fairly strong sulphurous odour. Please respect the pools and do not bring any pets to the hot springs or food into the pools.

Spanish Banks (Map 1/B2)

Spanish Banks, on the south side of English Bay, are a great place to visit at low tide. With the water out, the sand flats leave crabs exposed and attract eagles looking for an easy meal. When the tide is below a metre (3 ft), you can walk nearly halfway into English Bay. You will often find skimboarders playing out on the sand as well.

Spipiyus Provincial Park (Map 9/C1–20/C7)

The Caren Range has an old growth forest of yellow cedar, hemlock and balsam. A ring count on a yellow cedar stump, found in a section of the forest that was logged outside the park, showed the tree was over 1,835 years old when logged, making it the oldest known yellow cedar in Canada. Another western hemlock stump showed the tree to be over 1,200 years old, again, the oldest known tree of its species. While some of the old growth has been logged, much of it is still standing, protected in this provincial park. Another unique attraction to the area is the restored fire tower, one of the last remaining in the province, which is located at the top of Mount Hallowell.

Squamish Lil'wat Cultural Centre (Map 32/F5)

Located in Whistler at 4584 Blackcomb Way, this cultural centre was created to celebrate the history of the local Squamish and Lil'wat First Nations. The centre showcases these cultures through art, exhibits, a museum, food, film and live performances. There is also a gallery dedicated to modern Aboriginal art, where visitors can make their own crafts. The gallery is open daily and details regarding current exhibits, etc. can be found on the centre's website at www.slcc.ca.

Stanley Park (Map 1/C1)

Tucked away in Stanley Park in Vancouver are two of BC's largest red alders, six of BC's biggest Bigleaf Maples (including the tallest) and a whole mess of other big trees. They are among the easiest big trees to access in the region. But even if big trees are not your thing, Stanley Park is the green heart that beats within the breast of Vancouver, a verdant isthmus surrounded on three sides by water. The park offers a little bit for everyone, from man-made attractions like the Vancouver Aquarium to plenty of trails that pass through lush rainforest, past large trees (and even larger tree stumps) and into places where the noise and rush of the city fade away, if only for a moment.

Stawamus Chief (Map 22/C7)

A granite monolith towering 700 metres (2,297 ft) over Squamish, the Chief is one of the most popular climbing destinations in Canada. The 3 km² (1.9 mi²)

granite monolith is thought to be the second largest such geological feature in the world, after Yosemite's El Capitan. The Chief can be viewed from a variety of angles: from Squamish looking up, from the end of a hiking trail looking down or from up close and personal by experienced rock climbers. The most notable features of the Chief are named, including the Grand Wall and a trio of gullies that separate the Chief into three distinct peaks. A moderately difficult hike taking 2 to 3 hours accesses the first peak. The trail has numerous stairs and pull chains as it climbs 540 (1,770 ft) over its 1.5 km distance. Many include the Upper Shannon Falls (Sea to Summit) Trail to extend the outing.

Stave Falls Power House (Map 3/C3)

The Power House at Stave Falls in Mission tells the story of BC's power industry. Interactive games and informative displays explain how electricity is created. See turbines and generators, as well as a Detroit model electric car, all from 1912!

Storey Peak Falls (Map 21/G1)

One of the largest falls in the Squamish area, these falls cascade around 450 metres (1,500 ft) down a cliff in the Squamish River Valley. In periods of high rainfall or spring melt, these are impressive falls, but in the dog days of summer, the flow is very slow. The waterfall is located on an unnamed creek on the far side of the river and accessing the base of the falls is difficult. They can be seen from the Squamish River Main near "The Bayou," around the 29 mile marker from the open staging area on the river side of the road.

Temple of Time Grove (Map 11/F6)

A grove of 100 metre (300 ft) tall Douglas Fir trees found in the Lower Seymour Conservation Reserve became the impetus behind a push by a number of local environmental groups to see the Conservation Reserve turned into a park. That hasn't happened, but the grove has developed somewhat of a cult following. A rough flagged route climbs steeply to these trees and it is about 3 km (1.9 mi) return to the Hydraulic Creek bridge starting point. These trees can be hard to find, but are worth the effort.

Take care of the areas we love by taking all garbage with you and leaving only footprints.

Tsek (St Agnes Well/Skookumchuck) Hot Springs (Map 24/B2)

Located on private land, there is now a fee to camp and use the springs, which are open year-round. An A-Frame bathhouse covers the main soaking pool, which is made from half of a fibreglass septic tank, but there are several other soaking tubs outside the bathhouse. The water is hot, 54°C (130°F), but a second pipe brings in cold water, so bathers can adjust the temperature to their liking. The springs are located below the Pemberton-Douglas Forest Service Road, near BC Hydro tower #682, next to the rushing Lillooet River. Access here can be rough in wet weather.

Vancouver Aquarium (Map 1/C1)

There are over 70,000 creatures housed at Canada's largest aquarium in Stanley Park. From the beautiful white beluga whales to dolphins and sea otters right down to starfish and anomies, there is plenty to see here. For those looking for a unique experience, the Aquarium offers Animal Encounter sessions, where you can help feed and train the animals or get up close with the beluga whales. Full details regarding exhibits, hours and admission fees can be found at www.vanaqua.org.

Vancouver Art Gallery (Map 1/C2)

From Canada's largest collection of West Coast artist Emily Carr's work, to ever-changing world-class exhibitions in a stunning neo-classical heritage building, the Vancouver Art Gallery offers one of the city's top cultural experiences. Found in downtown Vancouver at 750 Hornby Street, the gallery is open every day of the year except Christmas and New Year's Day and offers unique products in the Gallery Store. Visit the gallery website at www.vanartgallery.bc.ca for full details.

Vancouver Maritime Museum (Map 1/C2)
Featuring more than 170,000 objects including 35,000 artifacts, 20,000 books, 262 original paintings/artwork and 114,000 photographs, the Vancouver Maritime Museum interprets the story of Canada's great Pacific port and its links with the Pacific Rim. Noted as being one of the largest maritime museums on the West Coast of North America, the museum is found in Vanier Park to the west of the Burrard Street Bridge at 1905 Ogden Avenue. Hours change from summer to winter. Visit the museum website at www.vancouvermaritimemuseum.com for more information.

VanDusen Botanical Garden (Map 1/C2)
The VanDusen Botanical Garden is a 22 hectare (55 ac) garden in the heart of Vancouver that features plant species from many different types of ecosystems. These include plants from the Himalayas to the Mediterranean through to the Louisiana swamps and the Pacific Northwest. The garden also features an amazing orchid inspired Visitor Centre. It is found at 5251 Oak Street; visit www.vandusen.org for more information.

West Coast Railway Heritage Park (Map 22/C6)
Found in downtown Squamish, the West Coast Railway Heritage Park is home to BC's most famous train, the Royal Hudson. It is also Western Canada's largest collection of heritage Railway equipment, including Canada's only authentic railway post-office car, as well as cabooses, snowploughs, cranes and other artefacts from the eras of steam, diesel and electric trains. Additional information about the park, including details of the "Polar Express" can be found at www.wcra.org.

Westminster Abby (Map 3/E4)
Peek into the life of a Benedictine Monk at the Westminster Abbey Monastery in Mission. On site are the abbey grounds, seminary campus and the monks' farm (which supports their self-sufficient lifestyle). Admire the beautiful stained glass windows and hear the chimes of the 10-bell tower. Visitors are welcome for services. Visit www.westminsterabbey.ca for more information.

Whistler Gondolas (Map 32/F5)
In winter, the gondolas at Whistler Blackcomb are mainly the domain of skiers and snowboarders, but in summer, visitors can explore the mountains, aided by the most extensive high-speed lift system in the world. Two gondolas from Whistler Village (Excalibur and Whistler Village), four-person chairlifts at the base of Blackcomb and Whistler mountains and a gondola at the Creekside base, 4 km south of Whistler Village, virtually eliminate line-ups. Relatively new is the Peak 2 Peak Gondola, which connects the top of Whistler to the top of Blackcomb.

Wreck Beach (Map 1/A2)
Considered by many to be one of the best clothing optional beaches in the world, Wreck Beach is one of Vancouver's top beach destinations. The combination of natural beauty and hippie-esque, anything-goes vibe makes this a popular destination…even if you don't want to take your clothes off. In the summer, Wreck Beach plays host to a number of fun, nude beach events, including the annual Bare Buns Run and the "world-record" skinny dipping event. The steep, difficult access trails can be found near UBC's Museum of Anthropology on Marine Drive. Be sure to check the tides, when the tides are high (often by late afternoon), most of the beach is underwater.

Xa:ytem Longhouse Interpretive Centre (Map 3/E4)
This 9,000 year old ancient Aboriginal village site features a sacred transformer stone and one of BC's oldest houses. The house offers visitors a chance to learn about Sto:lo history, culture, archaeology and spirituality. Look for the longhouse off the Lougheed Highway (Hwy 7) to the east of Hatzic and the Dewdney Trunk Road.

Yale (Map 15/F2)
One of the Gold Rush boomtowns was Yale. In its heyday it was hailed as the largest city north of San Francisco and west of Chicago. Now much smaller, historic Yale still evokes the spirit of the Gold Rush. Explore one of the oldest churches in BC – St. John the Divine – or walk through Pioneer Cemetery with headstones dating from 1862. Want to re-live history? Don a period costume, visit the Saloon and chat with some of Yale's historical characters in the interactive exhibit, "Yale: A Living History." Additional details and an event calendar can be found at www.historicyale.ca.

TRAVEL ESSENTIALS FOR BACKCOUNTRY TRAVEL

Listed below are a few essential items to take on any hiking or backpacking trip, or when travelling any backroad. These items will fit into a small backpack/hip pack and can be used in case of emergency. Pre-pack these items in their own bag to make bringing them along convenient, and to decrease the likelihood of forgetting these survival items.

Communication Devices
Whistle, signal mirror and cell phone (but never rely on electronic devices in the backcountry).

Food & Water
Carry high energy food bars along with water and Gatorade or similar drink.

Extra Clothing
Include an extra layer including toque, gloves and rain gear.

Flashlight or Headlamp
Bring spare batteries.

Fire Starter
Waterproof matches and/or lighter with candles or other accelerant (cotton balls mixed with Vaseline).

Shelter
A light weight tarp or bivy bag/space blanket along with string.

Pocket Knife and Repair Kit
Knife, needle and thread, webbing, shoelaces, old bicycle inner tube, buckles and/or heavy duty carbineer, and other items that might be needed.

First Aid Kit
Gauze, adhesive tape, bandages, scissors, tweezers, gloves, antiseptics, antibiotics, etc.

Navigational Aid
Map & compass and GPS with spare batteries.

Sun Protection & Bug Spray
Sunglasses and sunscreen and bug spray during bug season.

North Shore SAR has a nice list along with imagery that is easy to read… www.northshorerescue.com/education/what-to-bring/

We make fishing even better.
When you buy a fishing licence, you help us stock more than 800 lakes a year and create more fishing spots close to home. You also help fund important research, conservation and education programs. To learn more and purchase your licence visit gofishbc.com.

Freshwater Fisheries
Society of BC

FISHING
ADVENTURES

The fishing in Southwestern BC is simply outstanding. The breadth and variety is unparalleled, the scenery is amazing and there is good fishing throughout the entire year. From winter steelhead to summer trout and char; from spring cutthroat to fall salmon — there is always an active fishery to entice you. There are also some pretty impressive fish that roam in the lakes, streams and ocean around the area.

We have divided the fishing opportunities into three sections: Lake, River and Ocean Fishing. The Lake section covers a tremendous variety of waterbodies that range from easily accessible urban lakes to remote boat access or hike-in lakes. The Sunshine Coast to Powell River area is the self-proclaimed cutthroat capital of the world, while fishing around Whistler and in the Fraser Valley is equally promising. Each write up contains the resident species and a few other important tidbits, such as stocking information, to help you pick a lake that will suit your wishes.

The River (or stream) section is a collection of all the major rivers and a selection of creeks in the area. If you cannot find the stream of interest, look for the major tributary it feeds. Most creeks have similar characteristics. River fishing is easily the most popular fishery in the region since there always seems to be a good run of salmon, steelhead or sea-run cutthroat. Add in the resident trout and char and you will see why anglers come from around the world to test these waters.

The final section is for Ocean Fishing. Once again we are not able to cover every hole, but we have done our best to include the more popular and productive salmon hot spots. By listing the popular fishing holes and when the fish are running, you should be able to pinpoint a place to start.

Combining this information with our detailed maps should help you get out and enjoy a few hours, days or even weeks of fishing. But if you want even more details on the better lakes and streams in the region, we recommend picking up the Southwestern BC Fishing Mapbook, which is loaded with fishing tips, depth charts and hot spot maps and includes even more alternatives than this book. It is the perfect complement to this mapbook.

Remember, it is essential to review the fishing regulations before heading out. In particular, the regulations for steelhead and salmon change frequently; visit the recreational fishing section at www.pac.dfo-mpo.gc.ca for up-to-date information.

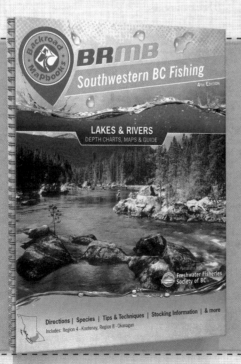

DID YOU KNOW?

OUR FISHING MAPBOOKS INCLUDE EVERYTHING YOU NEED TO REEL IN THAT CATCH OF THE DAY!

LAKES & RIVERS

Each fishing lake and river receives a full-page description with bathymetric (depth) lake charts, river maps, descriptions, species, stocking info directions and access points.

TIPS & TECHNIQUES

From trolling to ice fishing, to fly fishing and jigging, we provide you with some of the best fishing tips and techniques, including information on baits, lures and equipment.

 backroadmapbooks.com/fishing-maps

Lake Fishing

Alice Lake (Map 22/D5) ◧

This is a popular recreation lake with a large, grassy picnic site and two sandy beaches. It is a good place to bring a family to try to catch small trout in the spring or swim and sunbath in the summer. The lake has Dolly Varden as well as rainbow and cutthroat. The fish, particularly the stocked rainbow, remain small (a 30 cm/12 in fish would be a good-sized catch) but numerous. The best time to fly fish is during the black ant hatch in May. A man-made wharf at the east end is a good spot to try. There are no powerboats allowed on the lake.

Alouette Lake (Map 3/A1–13/D7) ◧

This popular recreational lake is stocked occasionally with rainbow and has benefited from a fertilization program that has helped the kokanee numbers which, in turn, has increased the size of the cutthroat, rainbow, Dolly Varden and lake trout. Some of the lake trout can grow to over 10 kg (22 lbs) and are often caught by trolling a plug below the 60 ft (18 m) level. The other species can be found by trolling along the drop-offs at one of the creek estuaries or in one of the many bays. The lake is very deep (up to 130 m/425 ft deep) and the fish can be scattered. Bull trout can also be found in the lake, but must be released. Check the regulations for other restrictions.

Alpha Lake (Map 32/E5) ◧

This lake is found in Whistler, to the south of the larger Alta Lake. It is home to substantial development on its shores. The main public access points are from the Valley Trail and Alpha Lake Park, which are both found on the east side of the lake. The lake still offers some good fly-fishing in June and early July for fair sized stocked rainbow, while trolling (electric motors only) can produce a few small kokanee and Dolly Varden.

Alta Lake (Map 32/E5) ◧

Alta Lake is the biggest of a chain of lakes found in Whistler and produces the best fishing in the valley. Recent reports boast of cutthroat to 60 cm (24 in) that are being caught on sinking lines around the weed beds, near docks and around the drop-offs using minnow imitation flies. Cutthroat continue to be supplemented with a stocking program. Rainbow to 30 cm (12 in) are also fairly active, while kokanee and dollies also roam the lake in smaller numbers. The lake is glacier fed and the fishing is best in June to early July, particularly near the inflow and outflow creeks (south and north ends of the lake). Fishing is much more effective from a boat or float tube, but be wary of sudden winds. Check the regulations for special restrictions.

Anderson Lake (Map 43/A3–52/D7)

This large lake is accessed from D'Arcy or Seton Portage. The lake offers good fishing for rainbow and dollies mainly by trolling. There are a number of private residences that line the lake.

Anne Lakes (Map 12/B3)

Located in Pinecone Burke Provincial Park, Anne Lake and its little sister to the north are a challenge to reach now that the Stawamus-Indian Forest Service Road south of Squamish has been gated. The lakes are not ice free until early May. At this time, the small rainbow are quite aggressive. Fishing should remain steady through the summer and into the fall for those willing to walk or bike in from the Indian Arm.

Belknap Lake (Map 12/B3)

This small lake is the first lake on the trail to Anne and Joseph Lakes. The remote access allows for some good fishing for generally small rainbow, especially after the lake opens up in spring.

Birkenhead Lake (Map 42/D3)

Birkenhead Lake is home to a provincial park complete with a beach, boat launch and camping facilities. The lake contains fair numbers of rainbow, dollies, kokanee and whitefish. Trolling is the mainstay of the lake with the best time to fish being in the early summer or fall. The water is surprisingly clear, making fly-fishing exciting when you see a fish rise. Private cabins are found along the northwest shore of the bigger lake. While there is a trail along the western shore, there are very few places that are open enough to fish from. Bull trout can also be found here, but must be released if caught.

Black Lake (Map 28/B4)

This lake is located on West Redonda Island and receives very little fishing pressure. To reach the lake, you must boat to Roscoe Bay Marine Park and then bushwhack your way in. Once you reach the lake, try trolling or fly-fishing for the cutthroat that reach 2 kg (4.5 lbs). There is a tenting site in the marine park.

Blackwater Lake (Map 42/F3) ◧

Blackwater Lake is a dark coloured but clear lake located off the Blackwater Creek Road. It is stocked annually with rainbow to offset the winterkill potential in the lake. Fishing is reported to be steady for fairly small fish by fly fishing or spincasting from a boat or a float tube during the spring or fall. There is a recreation site with camping on the northeast end of the lake.

Blue Earth Lake (Map 45/D2)

Protected by parkland, this lake is located south of Upper Hat Creek on the Earth Lake Road. The lake is not overly popular despite its scenic surroundings, crystal-clear water and prominent shoals. It offers a good fishery for rainbow trout up to 1 kg (2 lbs) by fly-fishing or trolling. There is rustic camping and a place to launch small boats at the lake.

Blue [Fishblue] Lake (Map 36/D7) ◧

Located in the Fraser Canyon, north of Boston Bar, Blue Lake is more nutrient rich than lakes farther south and west. The fishing starts in late April and tails off in early July for rainbow, which are stocked annually. By September, the fishing picks up again in this low elevation lake and continues into November. This is a decent fly-fishing lake with a resort to base your activities.

Bob's Lake (Map 8/D2)

This small Texada Island lake is home to a recreation site and small rainbow trout. The lake is best fished in the spring and fall as shallow waters warm significantly during summer.

Botanie Lake (Map 45/D6)

This lake is accessed by the Botanie Valley Road north of Lytton. It provides decent fishing for rainbow, but access is limited as the lake lies on an Indian Reserve (private property).

Brohm Lake (Map 22/C4) ◧

Brohm Lake is located next to Highway 99 and receives heavy fishing pressure throughout the year. The lake contains lots of Gammarus shrimp and chironomids, which feed the stocked rainbow, and the resident cutthroat and dollies. You can take advantage of the small hand launch, though it is possible to fish from shore.

Brown Lake (Map 20/C6)

This small lake is found next to the trail leading to Skookumchuck Narrows and has been stocked with cutthroat in the past. Rumour has it that some of these fast growing fish top the scales at 7 kg (17 lbs). That is a big fish for such a small lake and more likely than not just an angler's tale. More recent reports indicate the fish average 25-30 cm (10-12 in) in size.

Browning Lake (Map 11/B1) ◧

Located in Murrin Provincial Park next to Highway 99, this small (no powerboats) lake is stocked frequently with 20-25 cm (8-10 in) rainbow. It is not uncommon to see several anglers lining the shores as you drive past on the way to (or from) Squamish. The lake is stocked with catchable-sized rainbow, which are usually fished out by the end of the year. The lake has a nice day-use area.

Buntzen Lake (Map 12/A7) ◧

Buntzen Lake is a BC Hydro Reservoir and is subject to dramatic and sudden changes in water level, although at 200 m (650 ft) deep, you won't have to worry about them draining the lake dry. The lake is easily accessed from Coquitlam and is a very popular recreational area. Anglers will find heavily stocked rainbow along with resident cutthroat, dollies and kokanee, all averaging about 30 cm (12 in) in size. Since there is a powerboat restriction, it is best to bring a float tube or canoe and try spincasting or fly-fishing from the edges of the lake. The lake has steep drop-offs and a trail circles the lake making shore fishing quite easy.

Burnaby Lake (Map 1/G2)

Surrounded by parkland off Kensington Avenue or Gaglardi Way in central Burnaby, this lake has a few fish to tease ardent anglers. It is not a destination type lake, but if you are out paddling with the family why not bring a fishing rod along and try for carp. No powerboats are allowed.

Burkholder Lake (52/C1)

Located to the west of Yalakom River, this small lake receives light fishing pressure. As a result, it offers some good fly-fishing for small rainbow.

Butterfly Lake (Map 22/B2)

Difficult access makes this small lake a very good fly-fishing destination. Rainbow average 25 cm (10 in) in size and are best caught in the spring and fall.

Callaghan Lake (Map 32/B3)
Accessed by the Callaghan Forest Service Road southwest of Whistler, this bigger lake provides decent fishing for rainbow up to 1 kg (2 lbs). Given the high elevation, the fishing starts in early summer and continues through to the fall. Trolling is the primary method of fishing. The scenic lake is now part of a provincial park complete with a rustic camping area and boat launch. The lake was once stocked, but the rainbow trout have established a self-sustaining population.

Campbell Lake (Map 4/F1)
Campbell Lake is a small, shallow lake, found in the mountains west of Harrison Hot Springs. The lake can be accessed by a rough four-wheel drive road, then a short hike in. Alternately, you can access it via a long hike from Harrison Hot Springs. The lake contains a few small rainbow best caught in the early spring or late fall.

Carlson and Dragon Lakes (Map 9/D3)
These two lakes are accessed off the Halfmoon Forest Service Road (four-wheel drive recommended) on the Sunshine Coast. Despite the size difference, both lakes have fair numbers of cutthroat up to 30 cm (12 in). Due to the elevation, fishing is best in the early spring or fall.

Carpenter Lake (Maps 51, 52)
Carpenter Lake is a long, narrow man-made lake, which provides reasonably good fishing for dollies, rainbow and kokanee that can reach 2 kg (4 lb) in size. Trolling is the mainstay of the lake, although it is possible to shore fish at the creek mouths. Boaters should be wary of deadheads and draw down on the lake.

Cat Lake (Map 22/D5)
This tiny, low elevation lake is one of the first lakes to be fishable in spring and sees heavy pressure throughout the year, though the fish are usually quite small. Despite the low elevation, the fishing remains good through summer as the lake is deep and the thick trees shelter the lake from too much direct sunlight. The lake has been stocked in the past with rainbow, which are still reported in fair numbers here. The scenic lake is quite popular and sports a walk in recreation site with wharf to cast from for those who do not have a floatation device.

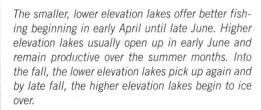

The smaller, lower elevation lakes offer better fishing beginning in early April until late June. Higher elevation lakes usually open up in early June and remain productive over the summer months. Into the fall, the lower elevation lakes pick up again and by late fall, the higher elevation lakes begin to ice over.

Cerulean Lake (Map 42/B4)
Nestled below Sun God Mountain, Cerulean Lake is seldom fished, as the only access is via helicopter or bushwhacking up a creek draw from the Birkenhead Lake Forest Service Road. The best fishing is around the northern and western shores where the lake drops off steeply. This high elevation lake is deep, cold and contains a fair number of rainbow in the 15-30 cm (6-12 in) range.

Chadsey Lake (Map 3/G5)
Chadsey Lake is found within Sumas Mountain Park and is accessed by trail. The illegal introduction of largemouth bass has all but wiped out the rainbow fishery. Bass anglers can expect fair fishing for average size largemouth. Since the small lake is hard to shore fish, bringing a float tube or pontoon boat is recommended.

Cheakamus Lake (Map 32/G7–23/A1)
Cheakamus Lake is the easiest lake in Garibaldi Provincial Park to access and the earliest to open up (in May). The lake is accessed by a gentle 3 km trail from the end of the Cheakamus Lake Road that allows anglers to haul in a float tube or canoe. The scenic lake contains rainbow in the 20-30 cm (8-12 in) range, as well as a few larger dollies. The lakeshore is heavily forested, limiting access for shore fishing.

Chehalis Lake (Map 14/B5)
North of Harrison Bay on the Chehalis Forest Service Road, this lake is 10 km long and has historically provided spotty fishing throughout the year for cutthroat,

rainbow or dollies, averaging 20-30 cm (8-12 in). The lake was hit by a giant mudslide in 2009 leaving a lot of debris and destroying the campsites and boat launches. However, the Skwellepil Creek Recreation Site on the west side has recently been reopened for camping and fishing enthusiasts.

Chilliwack Lake (Map 5/F6)
This popular lake features a number of camping areas and former recreation sites, which have now been consolidated as part of the provincial park. While the former Paleface and Depot Creek recreation sites and Sappers Provincial Park still grant access to the lake, camping is not allowed. The lake contains rainbow, cutthroat, dollies and kokanee, all growing up to 2 kg (4.5 lbs). Since the lake is glacier fed, the waters remain cold throughout the summer, while the fishing remains steady. The fish here are notoriously difficult to catch, with trolling being your best bet. Any wild trout over 50 cm (20 in) must be released.

Clerf Lake (Map 6/A5)
Clerf Lake is a small high elevation lake located to the south of the Silver Skagit Road. It is reached by a long trail off the deactivated Upper Klesilkwa Creek Road. Due to the high frequency of winterkill, it is unconfirmed whether there is still a rainbow fishery.

Clowhom Lake (Map 21/D6)
This remote lake is found at the north end of the Salmon Inlet and requires boat access. From there, it is advised to pack a canoe into the lake and paddle to the north end where the Clowhom River enters the lake. Because of the difficult access, the lake provides very good fishing during the fall (September–early October) for cutthroat up to 2 kg (4.5 lbs) in size, as well as a few large dollies. It is possible to fish from shore, although using a floatation device is better.

Como Lake (Map 2/A2) 🔲
An urban lake in the heart of Coquitlam, Como Lake is well stocked with rainbow to offset the heavy fishing pressure. The lake also holds brown catfish and carp and there are rumours that people still pull out cutthroat and brook trout. During the spring and fall, the fishing is usually pretty good, but in summer the lake warms up and the fishing slows down. Most people spincast or fly fish from shore (there is no fishing on the lake's northern shore) or from the two docks. No motors are allowed on the urban lake.

Coquihalla Lakes (Map 16/F1)
The Coquihalla Lakes receives little fishing pressure, despite the fact that they lie alongside a major highway (Hwy 5) and are home to a resort with a campground. Even more surprising, the lake offers good fishing for rainbow trout up to 1 kg (2 lbs) by trolling. The fishing season, given the high elevation, begins in early summer and lasts until fall.

Cranberry Lake (Map 18/G3)
Cranberry Lake is located just east of Powell River and provides marginal fishing for cutthroat up to 40 cm (16 in) in size throughout the spring and early summer. There is a beach and boat launch at the lake, which is easily accessed by paved road. No powerboats are allowed on the lake.

Crown Lake (Map 53/G4) 🔲
Crown Lake lies in Marble Canyon Provincial Park and is home to the park campsite. The lake offers heavily stocked rainbow that can grow to 1 kg (2 lbs). Pavilion and Turquoise Lakes are found nearby in the park and offer similar fishing to Crown Lake.

Crowston Lake (Map 9/E4) 🔲
A rough logging road leads from Highway 101 just south of Trout Lake to this small lake. The lake is best fished in the spring and fall as the waters warm significantly in the summer. Since the shore is lined with weeds, fly-fishing or spincasting from a small boat or float tube for the cutthroat is your best option. The fish average 20-40 cm (8-16 in) in size. Crowston gets stocked with small numbers of cutthroat each year.

Cultus Lake (Map 4/C6)
Accessed by paved road south of Chilliwack, this popular recreational lake is noted more for its boating and jet skiing than fishing, although trolling in the early spring or late fall can produce small rainbow and the odd larger cutthroat and Dolly Varden. Steelhead and all five varieties of salmon also run through the lake, but there is no fishery for these. The large lake remains relatively cool in the summer and while fishing does slow a bit, it does not suffer the doldrums to the same extent as smaller, shallower lakes in the area. Shore anglers can try working around one of the five main inflow creeks, around the Main Beach, or in Maple Bay. Provincial parks, stores, resorts, water slides and all manner of tourist traps are available at this popular summer retreat. Check for special boating restrictions and retention limits.

Davis Lake (Map 3/E1)

To the east of Stave Lake, Davis Lake is home to a provincial park complete with a campground, beach and boat launch. The lake provides an opportunity to catch small cutthroat (up to 30 cm/12 in) primarily in the spring. This is a low elevation lake and is stocked regularly with cutthroat. You will need to carry a boat or canoe in since the access road is gated. No powerboats are allowed on the lake.

Deeks Lake (Map 11/B4)

Located at the north end of Cypress Provincial Park, this lake is reached along the Howe Sound Crest Trail from the south or the Deeks Lake Trail from the northwest. Either way, it is a strenuous hike to the lake. To save your back hauling a float tube, you can produce by casting from shore at the inflow and outflow creeks. Given the elevation, fishing for the small cutthroat begins in late spring and extends into the summer.

Deer Lake: Burnaby (Map 1/F3)

Deer Lake is not a great fishing lake, but it is easily accessible off Deer Lake Parkway or Canada Way in Burnaby. The lake is regularly stocked with rainbow and has cutthroat, but these fish are usually muddy and do not make good table fair. Alternatively, visitors can have a lot of fun fishing for black crappie, which become much more active in the summer. Also, whitefish are found here and can make for some exciting action on light gear. The lake can be fished from the shore, or by float tube or canoe/small boat, which are available to rent in summer. No powerboats are allowed here and be sure to check the regulations on retention limits.

Deer Lake: Sasquatch Park (Map 15/B7)

Located in Sasquatch Provincial Park, Deer Lake is stocked with rainbow. It was also previously stocked with cutthroat and both species can be found in the 20-35 cm (8-14 in) range. The lake is best fished by boat, although shore fishing along the road is possible. Since the fish are plentiful, they are easily caught using a number of methods. Note that electric motors only are allowed on the lake.

Dennett Lake (Map 12/D7)

A small lake located in Pinecone Burke Provincial Park. Reports are mixed on this lake. Some say there are no fish; some say you will find cutthroat and brook trout. If you want to find out for yourself, you will have to hike a steep 4 km (2.5 mi) one-way trail to find out. Nearby Munro Lake is all but a distant memory since the dam let go.

Devil's Lake (Map 3/C2)

A short trail leading downhill from the 4.9 km mark on the Florence Lake Forest Service Road accesses the popular lake. It is a definite advantage to pack in a canoe or float tube as the western shore is very brushy and the deeper, more productive area is off the northeastern shoreline. The low elevation means better fishing for the cutthroat occurs in the early spring or fall.

Dodd Lake (Map 19/C2–D1)

Dodd Lake is one of the larger lakes in the Powell Forest Canoe Circuit that can also be accessed by vehicle along the Goat Lake Main. It holds cutthroat that can reach 3 kg (6.6 lbs) and some small kokanee. Trolling is the preferred method of fishing although casting a fly or a lure in one of the small bays can be productive. There are a few recreation sites on the low elevation lake, with the main (Dodd Lake) site sporting a boat launch.

Duck Lake (Map 19/A3)

Duck Lake is a low elevation lake, easily accessed on the Duck Lake Forest Service Road east of Powell River. It provides fair fishing for cutthroat in the 25-30 cm (10-12 in) range as well as some small kokanee. Trolling is the preferred method at this lake.

Duffey Lake (Map 43/D6)

This large, beautiful lake is accessed by Highway 99 northeast of Pemberton. The lake has rainbow and dollies (up to 2 kg/4.5 lbs), which are best caught by trolling. There is a campsite and a boat launch at the north end of the lake.

Eaton Lake (Map 5/G2)

Located on a steep trail off the Silver Skagit Road, Eaton Lake holds many small rainbow and cutthroat, averaging 20-30 cm (8-12 in). This is a high mountain lake that is noted for its cold water and limited shore fishing opportunities.

Echo Lake (Map 22/B6)

This mountain lake is located west of Squamish. The difficult access should ensure a peaceful fishing experience for anglers.

Edith Lake (Map 22/D5)

Found in Alice Lake Park, Edith Lake contains stocked rainbow (to 30 cm/12 in) and a few wild cutthroat. Fly-fishing is very difficult from shore due to the encroaching vegetation and the expansive muddy shallows. Bait anglers are able to pick their

spots and cast a bobber out far enough to get some action. There are some nice submerged logs, which can be seen in the murky water. Sink a wet fly next to one of the logs and you have a good chance for success.

Elbow Lake (Map 4/C2)

Found along the Chehalis Forest Service Road north of Harrison Mills, Elbow Lake is a small, steep-sided lake that is stocked regularly with rainbow. Access is found at the south end of the lake. The road runs along the lake's west side, creating a clearing where shoreline anglers can fish.

Elsay Lake (Map 11/G6)

This high elevation lake is found towards the north end of Mount Seymour Park. A long challenging trail passes beneath Mount Seymour and Mount Elsay before reaching the lake. Elsay Lake has good numbers of small rainbow for the brave angler willing to venture in during the late summer.

Emily Lake (Map 18/F6)

Like other lakes on Texada Island, Emily Lake is a very nutrient rich lake, which leads to vibrant insect and aquatic vegetation growth. This means plenty of food for the fast growing cutthroat. The lake is found at the north end of the island by a short trail that leads through private property (permission necessary to access the lake).

Evans Lake (Map 22/C4)

Evans Lake is surrounded by private property, making for limited access. But ardent anglers can take advantage of the trail system found near Evans Lake Camp. The lake opens up early in the year and offers small rainbow. The lake is suffering from a white worm infestation and it is not recommended that you keep any fish caught here.

Falls Lake (Map 16/E1)

Falls Lake is accessed by a gentle 2 km trail from the Falls Lake Road exit (Exit 221) on Highway 5. Not many anglers venture into this scenic mountain lake, which can provide fast action for small rainbow during the summer.

Fire Lake (Map 24/C4)

This long, narrow lake has many small rainbow up to 30 cm (12 in). The remote, high elevation lake is found just outside the Garibaldi Provincial Park boundary. The final kilometre or so to the lake is along a hiking trail. The rainbow here come readily to a fly or lure in the summer through fall.

Flash Lake (Map 7/C6)

Located southwest of Lightning Lake along the Lightening Lake Chain Trail, Flash Lake holds a good number of rainbow averaging 20-25 cm (8-10 in).

Flora Lake (Map 5/F5)

A most difficult hike reaches Flora Lake. Given this, fishing pressure is not heavy. For those willing to carry a float tube 7 km (4.5 mi) to the lake, the fishing can be fairly good for small rainbow in the 20-25 cm (8-10 in) range, primarily by fly-fishing.

Foley Lake (Map 5/D4)

This scenic, low elevation lake is quite unique. It has crystal clear, cold waters that are more common in high elevation lakes. The lake makes a good family destination due to the relatively easy access off the Foley Creek Forest Service Road. In addition to stocked rainbow, the lake has Dolly Varden, which can grow to about 35 cm (14 in) or 2 kg (4 lbs). There is an electric motor restriction on the lake.

Fountain [Kwotlenemo] Lake (Map 53/E7)

Fountain Lake is the most popular of the lakes in the Three Valley Chain. It is home to several popular recreation sites complete with boat launches. The fishing is fairly good for stocked rainbow up to 2 kg (4.5 lbs), particularly by trolling slowly (electric motors only). If fishing is slow, nearby Chilhil and Cinquefoil Lakes are worth a try.

Fowl Lakes (Map 42/B5)

Those that can make it to these remote lakes should expect some good fishing through the summer for generally small rainbow. Access is by rustic trail north of the Owl Lake Chain.

Frances Lakes (Map 36/B7)

The first of a series of scenic lakes in Nahatlatch Provincial Park, Frances Lake also sports a campsite and good road access. Unfortunately, the fishing here is hit and miss for rainbow, Dolly Varden and cutthroat.

Francis Lake (Map 14/E7)

Accessed by a rough four-wheel drive road off the Sts'ailes (formerly Harrison West) Forest Service Road, this small lake is home a small recreation site. The stocked rainbow are best caught in the spring and fall. The lake can be fished from the

shore, though expansive shoals make it a bit difficult. It is best to bring a float tube or canoe to this lake as no powered boats are allowed.

Freda Lake (Map 29/F7)
Located on the Stillwater Main, this fair sized lake has a fair number of cutthroat trout in the 25-35 cm (10-14 in) range. The lake provides decent trolling throughout the spring and fall.

Garden Bay Lake (Map 9/B1)
Found next to Pender Harbour, Garden Bay Lake sees more attention from paddlers since most of the anglers devote their attention to the saltwater fishery. This is a shame. The pretty lake has cutthroat up to 35 cm (14 in) best caught in the spring or the fall. There is an electric motor only restriction here.

Garibaldi Lakes (Map 22/E2)
Located in Garibaldi Provincial Park, these two spectacular sub-alpine lakes are accessed by the steep Black Tusk Trail. The lakes are fairly high in elevation and fishing is possible from June through the summer and fall. Garibaldi Lake provides excellent fishing for small rainbow that can reach the 45-55 cm (18-22 in) range. Shore fishing is possible. Lesser Garibaldi Lake holds rainbow that are smaller (25-30 cm/10-12 in) and fewer in number.

Fishing pressure in the urban areas can be heavy. You will often find better luck with the stocked lakes (look for the symbol).

Garrison Lakes (Map 7/E2)
These two scenic sub-alpine lakes are accessed by trail only off the Sunday Summit Forest Service Road. The lakes produce rainbow up to 2 kg (4.5 lbs), best caught by fly-fishing. Given the elevation, fishing is best left to the early summer through fall. The remote access limits fishing pressure.

Gates Lake (Map 42/E4)
Also known as Birken Lake, Gates Lake is located along the road to D'Arcy and holds rainbow and dollies up to 2 kg (4.5lbs), as well as smaller kokanee and cutthroat. Given the easy access and the private residences that line the lake, this lake receives heavy fishing pressure. A resort is located at the lake.

Gillis Lake (Map 27/G2)
This popular lake is easily accessed off the Coquihalla Highway (Hwy 5). As a result, the recreation site with a cartop boat launch can be busy on weekends. Fishing for rainbow trout up to 1.5 kg (3 lbs) in size remains steady due in part to the stocking program. The best time for fishing is during the spring and fall using a fly or by trolling.

Glacier Lake (Map 24/B3)
A rough four-wheel drive road leads to this remote lake on the boundary of Garibaldi Provincial Park. The difficult access means that there is fairly good fishing for rainbow trout, kokanee and Dolly Varden throughout the spring and fall. Trolling is your best bet, although sampling the shoreline with a fly or small lure can be effective.

Goat Lake (Map 29/D7–E6)
Goat Lake is a low elevation lake containing small kokanee, cutthroat up to 2 kg (4.5 lbs) and rainbow trout. The big lake offers excellent fly-fishing and spincasting for rainbow when they congregate near the mouth of Eldred River in late April to mid-May in preparation for spawning. The rest of the year, rainbow and kokanee are best caught by trolling. There is a pair of rustic campsites along the southeast shore of the lake, which is part of the Powell Forest Canoe Circuit. No fishing is allowed between November 1st and March 31st.

Grace Lake (Map 14/E7)
Grace Lake is a small, marshy lake that is too small and shallow to troll effectively. Anglers wishing to chase the stocked rainbow (up to 35 cm/14 in) should use a float tube or a small boat in the spring and fall. Found next to the Sts'ailes (formerly Harrison West) Forest Service Road, the lake and recreation site are busy places. Check the regulations for special restrictions.

Green Lake (Map 32/G4)
Located just north of the Whistler along Highway 99, this emerald coloured lake has rainbow up to 1 kg (2 lbs), dollies up to 3 kg (6.6 lbs) and some smaller kokanee.

The lake is best trolled, but fly anglers will find good fishing at many places around the lake, including the River of Golden Dreams Inlet. Check the regulations for special restrictions.

Greendrop Lake (Map 5/F4)
Greendrop Lake has fair numbers of small rainbow that can reach 30 cm (12 in) in size. These trout are best taken on the fly from a float tube. The deep water and high elevation ensures that the water temperature remains cold throughout the summer and the 6 km (3.6 mi hike) keeps out all but the most avid angler. The lake makes a fine overnight destination for those willing to make the hike in.

Green Timbers Lake (Map 2/B4)
Found in the heart of Surrey off of 96th Avenue, most people would be shocked to know that this small lake produces some trophy trout. Rumours are that a 4.5 kg (10 lb) rainbow was caught here. The lake is stocked annually with catchable sized rainbow trout and is only accessible on foot. There is good shore access allowing fly anglers to practice their craft. Note the 2 trout daily retention limit.

Gun Lake (Map 50/G4–51/A3)
Gun Lake is a popular recreational lake to the west of Gold Bridge. The big lake is lined with cabins, has a resort, a boat launch and even a recreation site on the west side of the lake. The lake offers fair fishing for rainbow up to 1 kg (2 lb), small kokanee and dollies up to 4 kg (9 lbs). Trolling is the mainstay of the lake.

Gwyneth Lake (Map 51/A5)
Located next to the Hurley River Forest Service Road, Gwyneth Lake is a shallow lake that can be fished using a dry fly or by spincasting.

Hammil [West] Lake (Map 19/A4)
Hammil Lake is a medium sized water body found east of Powell River. Given the low elevation, it provides decent fishing for cutthroat in the spring and fall. There is a boat launch as well as a good trail system to provide access for shore anglers.

Hanging Lake (Map 5/E7)
Located high up in the mountains on the border between Canada and the USA, this lake is reached by a steep trail from the south end of Chilliwack Lake. The lake holds rainbow that grow over 45 cm (18 in) in size. Fly-fishing and spincasting can be a lot of fun on this lake.

Hannah Lake (Map 36/A7)
Easily accessed off the Nahatlatch River Forest Service Road, Hannah Lake is scenic but does not have exceptional fishing. Anglers can find rainbow, Dolly Varden and cutthroat by trolling.

Harrison Lake (Maps 4, 14, 24, 25)
Harrison Lake is a huge lake that is 55 km long and averages a couple kilometres wide. The best boat access is from Harrison Hot Springs or Green Point. The town also provides full facilities including hotels and camping. Although mainline logging roads run up each side of the lake, there are few access points. You can find cutthroat up to 40 cm (16 in) and rainbow up to 1.5 kg (3 lb) by trolling. The best locations to fish near the south end of the lake are at the mouth of Cascade Bay or along the shores north of the Harrison River outflow. The lake is very deep (up to 200 m/650 ft) and is known for its hostile winds. Check for special restrictions.

Haslam Lake (Map 19/A3–B1)
This big lake is easily accessed northeast of Powell River. The lake provides fairly good trolling for cutthroat, rainbow and kokanee that average 30 cm (12 in) in size. The odd fish can grow up to 2 kg (4.5 lbs). Despite its size, the low elevation lake has an electric motor only restriction.

Hatzic Lake & Slough (Map 3/E4)
Hatzic can easily be found by travelling 6 km east of the town of Mission on Highway 7. Not known as a great fishing lake, Hatzic Lake does support rainbow, cutthroat, black crappie, carp, juvenile Coho and sturgeon. Rainbow are the most numerous and will reach up to 0.5 kg (1 lb). You might also try your luck in the Hatzic Slough, which features similar fishing to the lake.

Hayward Lake (Map 3/C3)
Hayward Lake is a manmade lake easily accessed to the west of Mission off of the Dewdney Trunk Road. The lake has been extensively stocked with steelhead and rainbow in the past but the fish population has not really grown. The lake is best fished by boat for small rainbow (up to 35 cm/14 in) towards the south end, near the Ruskin Dam where there is a deep hole. Shore fishing is possible along the western shores or at the north end where the Stave River empties into the lake. There are day-use facilities at the lake together with a concrete boat launch.

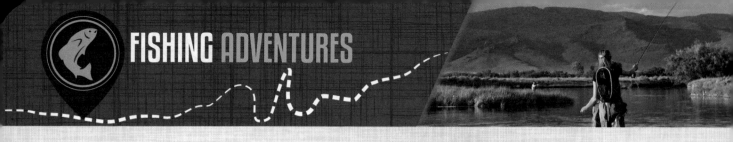
Hicks Lake (Map 15/A7)

Forming the hub of Sasquatch Provincial Park, Hicks Lake contains fairly good numbers of stocked rainbow as well as resident kokanee and cutthroat. Good fishing is found around the small island or at the mouth of one of the four bays in the spring or fall. When the water warms in the summer, the sandy beach may be more appealingthan the fishing. At this time, it is best to try trolling deep near the centre of the lake. The nearby Beaver Pond (found to the north) produces surprisingly well. It is not unusual to catch rainbow or cutthroat up to 40 cm (16 in), if you can get beyond the logs and vegetation. There is a 10 horsepower motor restriction here.

Hoover Lake (Map 3/D2)

This small trail access lake is set in a thick forest and is rarely visited, with a nearly 4 km (2.5 mi) hike from the Dewdney Trunk Road, east of Stave Falls to the lake. The lake warms up in the summer. In the spring and fall you can expect good fishing from a float tube for rainbow and cutthroat averaging 20-30 cm (8-12 in) in size. Shore fishing is difficult due to debris except for a few spots along the east shore.

Horseshoe Lake (Map 19/D2)

Most anglers access this lake from the recreation site on Nanton Lake. Horseshoe has many small cutthroat, rainbow and kokanee that are best caught by fly-fishing or trolling. The cutthroat are known to grow up to 2 kg (4.5 lbs) in size, although catching a fish this size is rare. It is best to concentrate your fishing efforts in the channel between Horseshoe Lake and Nanton Lake or in one of the many bays or weed beds that line the western shore of the lake. There are a couple of rustic (and quite lovely) camping spots, developed for canoeists on the Powell Forest Canoe Circuit.

Hotel Lake (Map 9/A1)

Hotel Lake has cutthroat up to 35 cm (14 in), best caught in the spring or fall by fly-fishing or spincasting. The low elevation lake is found north of Pender Harbour and is an electric motor only lake. The cutthroat are supplemented with a small stocking program every year. Note the electric motor restriction.

Hut Lake (Map 22/B4)

This small lake has numerous small rainbow that come readily to a fly, bait or small lure. The road up to this lake is very rough and overgrown and you may have to walk or bike in from Levette Lake.

Inkwathia Lake (Map 15/D1)

A high elevation lake northwest of Yale accessed along the Inkwathia Forest Service Road. If you have a high clearance four-wheel drive vehicle, you'll only need to walk about 2 km to the lake, which is home to plenty of rainbow.

Inland [Loon] Lake (Map 18/G2)

A popular recreational destination, this pretty lake is located northeast of Powell Lake. Given the low elevation, it is best to troll in the spring or early summer (there is no boat launch, but a short carry with a cartopper will bring you to the lake). The lake provides good fishing for cutthroat up to 50 cm (20 in) in size as well as for a few small kokanee. A well maintained, wheelchair accessible trail circles the lake allowing shore fishing. The lake is heavily regulated to help protect the vulnerable cutthroat.

Ireland Lake (Map 19/C2)

Ireland Lake is one of the smaller lakes along the Powell Forest Canoe Route. There is no vehicle access to the lake but you can bushwhack from the Goat Lake Main, or hike along either of the portage trails to the lake. The lake offers good fishing for small cutthroat and kokanee throughout the spring and into the early summer. It is best to fish near the creek inlet leading to Dodd Lake or at the outlet to Nanton Lake.

Isabel Lake (Map 12/G4)

Isabel Lake is worth a try if you want a multi-day excursion into rarely visited country. The lake is accessed by an unmarked trail from the shores of Pitt Lake, which, in turn, is only accessed by boat. Once you reach the lake, you will be rewarded with very good fishing for rainbow on a fly or by spincasting. Given the elevation, the fish remain active throughout the summer months.

Ivey [Horseshoe] Lake (Map 42/C7)

It is catch and release only in this small lake, which can be heartbreaking if you happen to land one of the monster rainbow that inhabit this trophy lake. The stocked rainbow trout, which grow up to 4 kg (9 lbs), are cagey. There are also some small cutthroat in this lake found northwest of Pemberton off Reid Road. Check the regulations for other restrictions.

Jane Lakes (Map 32/E6)

The main access route to the Jane Lakes (a series of three mountain lakes) is now blocked by a fence built by BC Rail. You can still venture in by bike or foot along the old washed out road. The lakes provide good fishing throughout the spring and fall since they are stocked regularly. There are rumours of rainbow up to 50 cm (18 in) and 2 kg (4.5 lbs).

Joffre Lakes (Map 43/A7)

Off the Duffey Lake Road near Cayoosh Pass, a trail leads past three sub-alpine lakes. Upper Joffre Lake is the highest of these high elevation lakes and has the best fishing for small rainbow beginning in July and running to October. Middle and Lower Joffre Lakes also have small rainbow but the fish are not as plentiful. Rustic camping is possible at each lake.

Jones [Wahleach] Lake (Map 5/C2)

This man-made, high elevation lake is found tucked in at the base of Mount Cheam. The Jones Lake Forest Service Road rises sharply from the valley bottom to the lake, where you will find fair fishing for small rainbow and big stocked cutthroat trout, and excellent fishing for small kokanee that can reach 1 kg (2 lbs) in size. Trolling is the mainstay of the fishery. Visitors will find a nice campsite, day-use area and boat launch near the north end of the lake. Check the regulations for special restrictions.

Joseph Lake (Map 12/B3)

Found by a trail leading past Anne and Little Anne Lakes, this lake also has fair numbers of small rainbow. Unfortunately, the northern road access into this area has been gated making the best access from the south. It is a long hike or bike in from the Indian Arm.

Katherine Lake (Map 9/B1)

Katherine Lake is located in Katherine Lake Park to the north of Garden Bay Lake. The smaller lake offers cutthroat up to 35 cm (14 in) in size. The lake is best fished in April and May and again in the fall. Katherine Lake Park has a beach and camping.

Kawkawa Lake (Map 15/F6)

Found just east of Hope, this lake and park are a popular place for locals. In addition to a boat launch, the park offers picnicking facilities and a beach. Most of the fishing action comes from the kokanee, which can grow to fairly large sizes (up to 40 cm/16 in). Cutthroat and dollies are the other main species, although there are rumours that people are pulling smallmouth bass out of this lake. Shore fishing is limited so it is best to bring a boat and try some trolling. The lake is closed to fishing in the winter and has special retention levels for the kokanee.

Khartoum Lake (Map 19/G3)

Khartoum Lake does not receive heavy fishing pressure and provides good fishing for cutthroat up to 2 kg (4.5 lbs). Concentrate your efforts at the inflow of Lois River or in the channel between Lois and Khartoum Lake. Most anglers access the lake via the Camp Bay/Third Lake Road, at the recreation site that sports a boat launch. Check the regulations for special restrictions.

Killarney Lake (Map 10/F6)

Killarney Lake is a small lake on Bowen Island, about 2 km from the Snug Cove Ferry Terminal in Crippen Regional Park. This low level lake warms up in summer, so spring and fall are the best times to come here for rainbow and cutthroat.

Kingdom [King] Lake (Map 51/B5)

Kingdom Lake is a pretty lake, sporting a nice recreation site with small boat launch. The lake contains many small rainbow.

Klein Lake (Map 20/B6)

Klein Lake is accessed off the North Lake Road, to the east of Earl's Cove. The small but deep lake has many small cutthroat easily caught by trolling, fly-fishing and spincasting. Its scenic surroundings and good fishing make it a popular destination for locals. A recreation site on the north end of the lake provides camping and cartop boat launch facilities. This lake is wheelchair accessible and has an electric motor only restriction.

Kokomo Lake (Map 20/A7)

Kokomo is reached by portaging from Sakinaw Lake. Given the difficult access, fishing for small cutthroat can be quite good. The lake has an electric motor only restriction.

Lafarge Lake (Map 2/C2)

Also known as the Coquitlam Pit, this former gravel pit has been dammed to create an urban fishing hole and picnic site. The small, low elevation lake is located between Pinetree Way and Pipeline Road in Port Coquitlam. The lake contains rainbow (the odd one up to 35 cm/14 in) and carp. The lake is intensively stocked with rainbow. A great place to fish from is along the western shore. There is a two trout retention limit here.

Lajoie [Little Gun] Lake (Map 50/G4)
Located just south of Gun Lake, this lake provides good fishing for stocked rainbow trout and a few dollies that both reach up to 1 kg (2 lbs). There is a cartop boat launch here, but an electric motor only restriction.

Lake Errock [Squakum Lake] (Map 4/B3)
Lake Errock is located alongside Highway 7 and is known more as a recreation lake than a fishing lake. It does have small cutthroat and rainbow best caught in the spring or fall, as well as course fish like catfish and bullheads. The lake has been stocked in the past.

Lake Lovely Water (Map 22/A5)
To reach this scenic sub-alpine lake, you will have to somehow cross the Squamish River. Then you will have to endure a perilously steep 5 km (3 mi) hike along a poorly maintained trail. The reward is great views and good fishing for rainbow. Shore fishing is possible.

Lake Lucille (Map 22/C1)
Lucille Lake is located west of Highway 99 across the Cheakamus River Bridge. The lake requires a short hike when you reach the powerline crossing (the road is blocked by the railway tracks). The lake has an electric motor only restriction and produces brook trout and the occasional rainbow in the 30-40 cm (12-16 in) range. There are reports of fish as large as 2.5 kg (5.5 lbs).

Lake of the Woods [Schkam Lake] (Map 15/F5)
Off Highway 1 north of Hope, this lake is stocked annually with rainbow, which can grow to 35 cm (14 in). Spring and fall are the best times to fish here. The Lake of the Woods Resort offers accommodation and a boat launch (electric motor only).

Latimer Pond (Map 2/D6)
Also known as Stokes Pit or Surrey Pond, this man-made waterbody offers fishing for cutthroat and rainbow trout. As with most urban ponds, pressure can be heavy and fishing slow. Last stocked in 2006, the lake is found off 28th Avenue to the west of 200th Street.

Levette Lake (Map 22/B4)
The steep road may deter anglers without a four-wheel drive vehicle, but the number of small rainbow that grow to 30 cm (12 in) should make the drive worthwhile. There are a few private cabins along with a steep cartop boat launch at the south end of the lake. Although fishing from the shore is possible, you may wish to bring a float tube or small boat in order to get away from the trees and debris around the shoreline. The lake has an electric motor only restriction.

Lewis Lake (Map 19/C1)
Located off the rough Tin Hat Road, you will need a four-wheel drive to get to Lewis Lake. The lake provides good fishing for cutthroat up to 2 kg (4.5 lbs) in summer and early fall. A small recreation site is found on the lake.

Lewis Lake (Map 22/B3)
An old gated four-wheel drive road leads along Pillchuck Creek up to this small lake. Due to the difficult access, anglers can expect a good fly-fishing lake during the spring and fall. The stocked rainbow average 25 cm (10 in) in size.

Lightning Lake (Map 7/C6)
Lightning Lake is the most popular lake of the Lightning Lake chain, due in no small part to the good access, nice campsite, boat launch and trail system. It is slightly higher in elevation than the others and fishing is steady throughout the summer. The lake contains many small cutthroat and rainbow. No powerboats are allowed here.

Lillooet Lakes (Maps 33, 34)
By May, spring run-off causes these lakes to murk up and the water does not begin to clear until late August. The best time to fish for the rainbow, cutthroat and dollies in these poor producing lakes is in April. Work the narrows between the two lakes, or at the creek mouths. There are several recreation sites offering boat launches and camping along the bigger lake. No wild trout over 50 cm (20 in) may be retained.

Lindeman Lake (Map 5/F5)
Lindeman Lake is a cold, emerald green lake that is reached by a fairly steep 3 km (2 mi) trail. The moody lake has good numbers of rainbow trout that average 20-30 cm (8-12 in) in size and are best caught on the fly. Although it is possible to fish from shore, a float tube is more effective.

Ling Lake (Map 5/D3)
It is a long hike from Foley Lake to Ling Lake along a washed-out road, then a trail. Once you reach the high elevation lake, you will be rewarded with good fishing for rainbow up to 1 kg (2 lbs) throughout the summer months and into the fall. The lake is best fished using a float tube and casting a fly or small lure.

Liumchen Lake (Map 4/E7)
You will need a four-wheel drive vehicle or, better yet, an ATV to access the trail into this small lake. Due to the difficult access and the high elevation, the fishing is quite good for trout into the summer. Some nice trout (up to 35 cm/14 in) are caught here annually.

Liza Lake (Map 51/E1)
Liza Lake is located off the Marshall Lake Forest Service Road and offers good fishing for small rainbow that are best caught by fly-fishing.

Lizzie Lake (Map 34/C5)
The road up to this scenic sub-alpine lake is water barred and/or washed out making access a challenge. However, the lake does offer good fishing for small rainbow best caught by fly-fishing or spincasting. Despite the good trail system along the northern end, shore fishing is difficult.

Lodestone Lake (Map 17/B4)
Lodestone is a lovely little lake located at the end of the Lodestone Forest Service Road. The high elevation lake offers fair fishing for small rainbow beginning in early July through to October. A recreation site at the lake provides a cartop boat launch and camping, while ATV and snowmobile trails, and the historic Hudson Bay Brigade Trail offer endless exploring in the surrounding mountains.

Life jackets and personal flotation devices are known to save lives; they only work when they are worn and fitted correctly.

Loggers Lake (Map 32/E6)
Found in the Whistler Interpretive Forest, Loggers Lake can only be accessed by foot or bike. The small, scenic lake offers reasonable fishing for stocked rainbow that are rumoured to grow to 45 cm (18 in) in size.

Lois Lake (Map 19/D4–F3)
Lois Lake is one of the larger lakes in the Powell River area. Most people doing the Powell Forest Canoe Circuit start here. The lake is home to cutthroat up to 2 kg (4.5 lbs), as well as small kokanee. It is best fished by trolling, but you can also try spincasting or fly-fishing at the inflow and outflow of the lake, around the islands or in one of the sheltered bays. Check the regulations for special restrictions.

Lookout Lake (Map 14/D4)
Located off the Sts'ailes Forest Service Road, a four-wheel drive vehicle is recommended to access the lake. The lake contains a good number of stocked rainbow and resident cutthroat up to 35 cm (14 in). Try working the bays at the south end of the lake. Shore fishing is difficult, but not impossible.

Lost Lake (Map 32/G5)
Found at the north end of Whistler, this tiny lake is a popular year-round destination with a picnic area and beach as well as an excellent trail system that includes part of the Valley Trail. The lake is stocked with catchable-sized rainbow that can reach 30 cm (12 in) but are usually quickly fished out. There are bull trout in the lake as well. The lake has an electric motor only restriction.

Lyon Lake (Map 9/C1)
Follow the Halfmoon Forest Service Road north from Highway 101 to this small lake. The road deteriorates significantly as you approach the lake making a four-wheel drive vehicle a must. There are stocked cutthroat in the 20-40 cm (8-16 in) range as well as a few larger fish. Fly-fishing and spincasting in the spring or fall are your best bets. There is a recreation site at the south end of the lake providing camping.

Mackechnie Lake (Map 19/F6)
Located on Nelson Island, this small, low elevation lake provides fairly good fishing for cutthroat up to 1 kg (2 lbs) in the spring and fall. Old logging roads from Hidden Basin reach the lake.

McDonald Lake (Map 51/B4)
Home to rainbow, most prefer to troll this small lake east of Gold Bridge. The difficult access may deter some from bringing in a boat.

Madeley Lake (Map 32/C3)
Found to the northwest of Whistler on the Madeley Lake Road (four-wheel drive/bike access), this lake produces very well for rainbow up to 30 cm (12 in). There is a small campground at the north end of the lake with a rough cartop boat launch. It is highly recommended that you bring a float tube or a boat you can pack-in as the lake is difficult to shore fish except at the south end.

Mamquam Lake (Map 22/G4)
Located well inside Garibaldi Provincial Park, this lake is accessed by a 22 km (13.5 mi) hike along the Diamond Head Trail. The lake is seldom fished so it offers good fishing for generally small rainbow from shore. If you can get out on the water, there are rumours of nice trout as large as 50 cm (20 in). This is a high elevation lake and the water doesn't open up until early summer.

Marion/Phyllis Lakes (Map 11/B3)
To reach these two mountain lakes, you must walk or bike a gated road from Highway 99 just north of Furry Creek. The lakes do not receive heavy fishing pressure, so you can do quite well for small cutthroat and dollies, particularly in the spring and fall. It is possible to fish from the shore, but it is recommended to bring a float tube.

Marshall Lake (Map 51/F2)
Marshall Lake has good fishing for stocked rainbow up to 1 kg (2 lbs) primarily by trolling. There are two recreation sites, one at the south end of the lake, the other at the north.

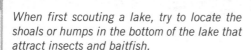

When first scouting a lake, try to locate the shoals or humps in the bottom of the lake that attract insects and baitfish.

Mead Lake (Map 51/B5)
Just south of Kingdom Lake, this small lake is accessed by a four-wheel drive vehicle or by a hike. It provides good fishing for small rainbow throughout the spring and fall.

Mike Lake (Map 2/G2)
This tiny lake is found in Golden Ears Park and has stocked rainbow and wild cutthroat that grow up to 30 cm (12 in), best caught in the spring. Fishing from a canoe or float tube is your best bet as the shoreline is shallow and marshy. There is a fishing dock for people without watercraft. No powerboats are allowed here.

Mill Lake (Map 3/D6)
Located in the heart of Abbotsford, next to the Seven Oaks Shopping Centre, this urban lake is heavily stocked with rainbow. The marshy lake also contains bullheads, crappies and largemouth bass. You will need a boat or tube to get to the deepest hole. The best place to fish from shore is off the dock or from the beach. This lake is a designated wheelchair access lake, with a good paved path and rails on the dock. No powerboats are allowed on the lake.

Mixal Lake (Map 9/A1)
Mixal Lake is another of the series of lakes north of Garden Bay and Pender Harbour. The low elevation lake offers fishing for small cutthroat mainly in the spring and Coho in the fall. The lake has an electric motor only restriction.

Moon Lake (Map 53/A6)
This tiny lake is noted for having large rainbow that can reach 2 kg (4.5 lb) in size. The remote lake has poor access and requires hiking or quading in from a four-wheel drive logging road.

Morgan Lake (Map 13/D7)
Morgan Lake is a catch and release and fly-fishing only lake that sports brook trout and cutthroat up to 2 kg (4.5 lbs). For best results, bring a float tube as shore fishing is very difficult and the lake is quite deep in the middle. Access is off the Florence Lake Forest Service Road north of Stave Falls. Check the regulations for special restrictions.

Morris Lake (Map 4/E1)
Morris Lake is connected to the Harrison River just east of the Weaver Creek spawning channel by a rather large channel. Accessed of the Morris Valley Road, the last portion is quite rough and most people walk in. The fishing is not great here, but you can catch cutthroat up to 50 cm (20 in). Check the regulations for special restrictions.

Mosquito Lake (Map 42/C7)
Located just east of Ivey Lake near Pemberton, Mosquito Lake has a recreation site with a picnicking area. The small lake has stocked rainbow and resident cutthroat up to 30 cm (12 in), but the fishing is usually slow.

Moss Lake (Map 15/A7)
If you want to get to Moss Lake, you will have to hike at least 1.5 km and you will want to pack a float tube with you. If you don't have a four-wheel drive vehicle, the hike will be longer, but these obstacles have kept this small lake a viable fishing destination bordering Sasquatch Provincial Park. The lake features rainbow in the 25-35 cm (10-14 in) range that were last stocked in 2006.

Mowson Pond (Map 51/C3)
This lake used to offer very good fishing for stocked rainbow. Unfortunately, the Tyaughton Lake Fire burned the landscape surrounding this former fishing hot spot, adversely affecting the water levels and fishing. Hopefully the fishing will return back to the glory days when trout up to 36 cm (14 in) were a real joy to catch on the fly.

Murphy Lakes (Map 17/A2)
Off the Lawson-Britton Creek Forest Service Road, these popular mountain lakes contain rainbow and brook trout that can grow up to 1.5 kg (3+ lbs) in size. The eastern lake has larger fish. The lakes are home to rainbow that somehow withstand some fairly heavy fishing pressure. There is a recreation site on the western lake.

Murray Lake (Map 27/F4)
Murray Lake is accessed off a steep bumpy road north of the Coquihalla Highway (Hwy 5). Nonetheless, the two recreation sites and boat launch get frequent use. Trolling and fly-fishing are your best bet to catch the rainbow that reside here. There are a few private cabins on the lake.

Nahatlatch Lake (Map 25/F1–36/A7)
Wonderfully scenic, the lake holds limited numbers of rainbow, dollies and cutthroat. If you are going to make a serious effort to catch something, your best bet is to go trolling in the spring or fall. Former recreation sites along the Nahatlatch River Forest Service Road provide camping for the paddlers and anglers that frequent the area.

Nanton Lake (Map 19/C2)
Nanton Lake is accessed off the Goat Lake Main and is really an extension of HorseshoeLake. In addition to kokanee, the lake has developed a reputation for holding some cutthroat as large as 3 kg (6.5 lbs). Try fly-fishing or trolling near the channel from Horseshoe Lake or at one of the inflow creeks. There is camping on its western shores.

Nicomen Lake (Map 7/B3)
As the crow flies, Nicomen Lake is 10 km from the nearest road, but the hike in is nearly double that, along the Hope Pass Trail/Grainger Creek Trail. Given the tough access, you can usually expect some good fishing for rainbow that average 20-30 cm (8-12 in) in size. A small, scenic tenting site is located at the lake.

Nita Lake (Map 32/E5)
The smallest in a chain of three lakes in Whistler, Nita is a deep, cold lake that offers fairly good fishing even in the warm weather of summer. Nita Lake has an electric motor only restriction and offers good fishing for small stocked rainbow and some kokanee.

North Lake (Map 20/B6)
North Lake is a well-developed lake, and is the highest elevation lake on the north end of the Sechelt Peninsula. The lake provides slow fishing for cutthroat averaging 25-30 cm (10-12 in) in length. April and May or October are the best times to fish. Accessed of Egmont Road, the lake has full facilities and has an electric motor only restriction.

Norton Lake (Map 12/A3)
Norton Lake is noted for having the largest rainbow of all the lakes in the Hixon Creek area, getting up to 2 kg (4.5 lbs). Unfortunately, the northern road access into this area has been gated making the best access from the south. It is a long hike or bike in from the Indian Arm.

Olive Lake (Map 14/A5)
You will have to bushwhack your way to Olive Lake from the end of the North Statlu Forest Service Road, a distance of about 3 km (2 mi). The lake contains cutthroat up to 25 cm (10 in) as well as some rainbow.

Onion Lake [Ruddocks Dam] (Map 45/B5)
You would not expect to find a private catch and release lake this far from the city, but that is what is here. Anglers willing to pay can enjoy fishing for wild trout here.

Ogre Lake (Map 42/A4)
A long and rugged trail leads to Ogre Lake. Due to the remote sub-alpine setting, fishing with most small lures and flies is good through the summer for generally small rainbow.

Owl Lake Chain (Map 42/B6)
From the Owl Creek Forest Service Road (four-wheel drive access), a steep trail leads to Owl Lake as well as several other lakes in the watershed. These lakes have small rainbow (up to 30 cm/12 in) that rarely see a lure. Owl Lake sees most of the action and casting from shore is possible.

One Mile Lake (Map 33/B1)
South of Pemberton and right next to Highway 99, One Mile Lake sees more than its share of anglers. There are a few rainbow and cutthroat (up to 30 cm/12 in) that are best caught by spincasting or fly-fishing from a small boat or float tube throughout the spring and fall. This is an age restricted waterbody reserved for children, seniors, or disabled resident of BC only.

Otter Lake (Map 17/D2)
This popular recreation lake has private cabins and camping, as well as a boat launch and a beach at the Otter Lake Provincial Park. The Coalmont Road skirts the west side of the lake, while the Kettle Valley Railway runs along the east side. Despite stocking of rainbow and brook trout in the lake, fishing still remains fairly spotty. There are also some lake trout, kokanee and whitefish available. The best method of fishing is trolling during the early spring or late fall as the lake warms due to the low elevation.

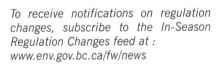

To receive notifications on regulation changes, subscribe to the In-Season Regulation Changes feed at : www.env.gov.bc.ca/fw/news

Pavilion Lake (Map 53/G3)
Pavilion Lake, the largest lake in the Marble Canyon Area, has fair fishing for stocked rainbow up to 1.5 kg (3.5 lbs), primarily caught by trolling. The lake also offers good ice fishing a cartop boat launch as well as camping and a resort.

Paxton Lake (Map 18/F6)
This small lake can be accessed by a four-wheel drive vehicle off the Gillies Bay Road on Texada Island. The lake contains cutthroat up to 2kg (4.5 lbs), which can be caught in the early summer by spincasting or fly-fishing.

Pearson Pond (Map 51/B2)
The fishing at Pearson Pond was adversely affected as a result of a fire, which blazed through the area in 2009. Hopefully the fishing will improve in the near future. For now, the fishing is very slow for stocked brook trout that can reach decent sizes. The lake also makes a fine ice fishing destination.

Petgill Lake (Map 11/C1)
This lake is accessed by a steep 11.5 km (7 mi) return trail leading from Highway 99. Since the lake is no longer stocked, it is unclear whether the small trout have survived. Shore fishing is possible for those still willing to haul up fishing gear.

Pierce Lake (Map 5/B6)
This lake is reached by a steep, difficult trail leading from the Chilliwack Lake Road. The hike is worth the effort given the beautiful mountain scenery, but the fishing can be hit and miss. Some report good fly-fishing or spincasting for larger trout (over 50 cm/20 in), while others say it is slow and only has small trout in the 20-30 cm (8-12 in) range. Regardless, the lake is quite deep and allows for decent shore fishing.

Pitt Lake (Map 12/E3–F7)
At the south end of Pitt Lake, Grant Narrows Park provides the main boat launch onto this large lake. The lake contains resident rainbow, dollies, sturgeon and whitefish but the action really picks up when the salmon species and steelhead migrate through the lake. In particular, in the spring (April through May) sea-run cutthroat cruise to the north end of the lake looking for salmon fry returning to the ocean. When boating, watch for the sandbars, deadheads and sudden winds. Check the regulations for special restrictions.

Plateau Ponds (Map 51/B3)
Found by trail to the east of Gun Lake, these small waterbodies are stocked with eastern brook trout. During the spring and fall, fishing can be quite steady here.

Poland Lake (Map 7/A5)
This high elevation lake is accessed by the Poland Lake Trail in Manning Provincial Park. The small lake contains many small rainbow up to 20 cm (8 in). There is a rustic campground next to the lake.

Powell Lake (Map 18/F3–29/C2)
Powell Lake is a big lake that resembles an inlet or a fjord, running narrow and deep into the heart of the Coast Mountains. The lake is notoriously difficult to fish and is subject to strong winds. If you are lucky, you might manage to catch one of the cutthroat or rainbow that can reach up to 4 kg (9 lbs). Your best bet is trolling around Goat Island, near Olsen's landing, or near Haywire Bay. Check the regulations for special restrictions.

Priest Lake (Map 18/F6)
Priest Lake is the biggest lake on Texada Island, found south of Van Anda off the Gillies Bay Road. As a result, trolling is the preferred method for cutthroat up to 2 kg (4.5 lbs) in late spring or early summer.

Rice Lake (Map 11/E7)
Found in the Seymour Demonstration Forest, Rice Lake is best accessed by trail from the end of Lillooet Road. The irregularly shaped lake is stocked annually with catchable sized rainbow to help maintain the fishery. There is good wheelchair access here. There is a two trout retention limit.

Richardson Lake (Map 9/F2)
Surrounded by a provincial park, this picturesque lake is best accessed by four-wheel drive vehicle or ATV. A former recreation site provides camping at the west end of the lake. Angling here is for cutthroat, which grow up to 30 cm (12 in), with trolling being the preferred method of fishing.

Rolley Lake (Map 3/C2)
Rolley Lake is home to a popular provincial park complete with camping, a boat launch and a beach. The lake has stocked rainbow (up to 30 cm/12 in) as well as a few larger dollies and cutthroat. It is best fished near the north end where there is a deep hole. No powerboats are allowed in this low elevation lake, which is accessed off Bell Street to the north of the Dewdney Trunk Road.

Ross Lake (Map 6/F7)
At the end of the Silver Skagit Road, Ross Lake sits on the border between Canada and the USA. The lake is quite shallow on the BC side of the border during draw down, when the lake is little more than a mud flat. Earlier in the year, the lake is best trolled for rainbow and Dolly Varden that average 30-45 cm (12-18 in). Around mid-August the dollies are preparing to spawn and can be found near the snag infested estuary. There is camping, a boat launch and a beach at the provincial park. Be wary of stumps and debris as well as special regulations.

Ruby Lake (Map 20/B6)
Ruby Lake is a popular recreation lake, and many private residences line the shores. The lake also has a resort, boat launch and camping. Despite the heavy fishing pressure (check the regulations for special restrictions), the lake produces well for cutthroat, usually around 25-35 cm (10-14 in), and small kokanee, mainly by trolling. In the summer, the waters in this low elevation lake warm up, making water sports more popular than fishing.

Sakinaw Lake (Map 20/A7)
Sakinaw is a large, deep lake lined with private residences and summer cottages. Salmon and sea-run cutthroat can be caught in the fall near the channel flowing into the ocean at the southwest end of the lake. With patience, it is also possible to catch large cutthroat (up to 60 cm/24 in) and some small kokanee in the spring. Check the regulations for special restrictions.

Salsbury Lake (Map 13/E7)

Salsbury Lake is found north of Davis Lake off the Lost Creek Forest Service Road and offers small, rainbow and kokanee to 30 cm (12 in). Shore fishing is difficult due to the debris, while trollers should stick with shallow presentations. Former recreation sites provide access and a gravel boat launch to the lake.

Sanctuary Pond (Map 1/E2)

This tiny pond in Hastings Park in the centre of Vancouver offers a great little urban fishery. Anglers here will find a fishing pier, washrooms and a trail around the lake. Catchable sized rainbow are stocked here in the thousands. Check the regulations for special restrictions before heading here.

Sardis Pond (Map 4/D5)

Located in Sardis Park on Vedder Road south of Chilliwack, this pond is open year-round to residents of BC who are disabled, under the age of 16, or seniors. This has both cutthroat and rainbow trout that were last stocked in 2006. The shallow nature of the lake does result in slow fishing during warmer months.

Sasamat Lake (Map 2/A1)

Sasamat Lake is located within Belcarra Regional Park off Bedwell Bay Road and is better known for its great beach and picnic facilities than its fishing. In the early spring and late fall it is possible to catch wild cutthroat or stocked rainbow that can grow up to 45 cm (18 in). Powerboats are restricted on the lake from May to September (electric motors only the rest of the year), however it is best to fish near the middle of the lake, where there is a deep hole, or along the western shoreline. For shore anglers, a 200 m (650 ft) long floating dock at the south end of the lake or two docks at the outflow are excellent spots.

Sayres Lake (Map 3/D1)

This low elevation lake is accessed by short trail from the Florence Lake Forest Service Road. Visitors will still find a dock where you can launch a small boat or canoe, but the fishing is not what it once was. The lake can be fished from shore but it is better to fish with a float tube or small boat (electric motor only) in order to cast/troll towards the centre of the lake. The average rainbow tends to be quite small (less than 30cm/12in) and there are also some small dollies and brook trout. Check the regulations for special restrictions including the electric motors only restriction.

Seton Lake (Map 52/D6– 53/B7)

Seton Lake holds large rainbow (up to 2 kg/4.5 lbs), lake trout (up to 5 kg/11 lbs) and dollies up to 6 kg (13 lbs) along with kokanee and mountain whitefish. Trolling a large spoon at the drop-off of one of the creek estuaries such as Madeleine, Tsee or Machute Creeks is particularly effective. Casting a large spoon off the Seton Lake Canal Dock just east of Lillooet can also be very effective. Steelhead anglers will find Seton Portage, the short river between Anderson Lake and Seton Lake, fairly productive. Rainbow and dollies up to 2 kg (4.5 lbs) are also found in the river.

Showh Lakes (Map 32/F3)

Despite the difficult four-wheel drive/trail access off the Sixteen Mile Creek Forest Service Road, this catch and release fishery has really increased in popularity recently. Both lakes used to be stocked with cutthroat that now reproduce naturally. Also, both lakes are present and they reach some impressive sizes. In fact, 50 cm (20 in) rainbow are not uncommon. Due to the elevation, this fishery heats up in the early summer and maintains through the fall.

Silver Lake (Map 5/F1)

Easily accessed off the Silver Skagit Road, this lake is home to a provincial park complete with camping, a boat launch and picnic facilities. The lake has small rainbow, cutthroat and kokanee as well as a few larger dollies (up to 2 kg/4.5 lbs). Small steelhead come into the lake in the winter and Coho come through in the fall. For best results, you can cast a float with bait from the southern shoreline, fly fish at the creek outflow, or troll the shallow lake. Check the regulations for special restrictions.

Silvermere Lake (Map 3/C4)

This manmade lake next to the Lower Stave River is easily accessed off Highway 7. The lake is very marshy and shallow making it better for water skiing or catching catfish and bullheads than rainbow. More recently, the lake has become a popular largemouth bass fishery. The best place to fish is near the highway, either from shore or by boat. Private residents line the east side of the lake, making access difficult.

Sliammon Lake (Map 18/F2)

Found close to Powell River off the Theodosia Forest Service Road, this lake provides fair fishing for cutthroat up to 2.5 kg (5.5 lbs) and for small kokanee. Trolling is the preferred method although it is possible to catch fish by fly-fishing or spincasting in the many bays.

Slollicum Lake (Map 15/A6)

Reached by a 3 km (2 mi) trail off a four-wheel drive road on the east side of Harrison Lake, this lake has numerous small rainbow. Try fishing at the north end of the lake where the fish tend to congregate.

Stacey Lake (Map 4/E2)

Found west of Agassiz, watch for a spur road to this lake after kilometre 7 off the rough Mount Woodside Forest Service Road. The lake is stocked with rainbow and the fishing here is decent in late spring and again in fall. The lake is subject to winterkill.

Statlu Lake (Map 14/B4)

Statlu Lake is located to the north of Chehalis and is reached by a rough four-wheel drive road and then a short hike. Rainbow tend to be small but plentiful in this scenic lake set below some majestic peaks.

Starvation Lake (Map 22/C3)

Starvation Lake is a tiny lake that is reached by trail on an old road leading from the very end of the Paradise Valley Road. The spring-fed lake produces rainbow as large as 2 kg (4.5 lbs) in the spring. Rustic camping is available at the lake.

Practicing catch and release will greatly help ensure the future viability of sport fisheries.

Stave Lake (Maps 3, 13)

Stave Lake is a large lake, stretching 27 km through the mountains north of Mission. Despite its size, access is limited. Most boaters launch near the Stave Falls Dam. There are also a few places to get to the water from logging roads on either side of the lake. The low elevation lake has been damned by BC Hydro resulting in fluctuating water levels and spotty fishing. There are a few rainbow, cutthroat, kokanee, Dolly Varden and whitefish in the lake. Most of the trout remain small, but the odd 50 cm (20 in) cutthroat is reported, while dollies up to 5 kg (11 lbs) also roam the lake. Trolling is preferred because the fish are scattered but watch for debris and high winds that can make boating treacherous at times.

Strike Lake (Map 7/B6)

Strike Lake is one of the trail accessed Lightning Lakes in Manning Park. Found a short jaunt past Flash Lake, the smaller Strike Lake contains many small rainbow (up to 20 cm/8 in) best caught by spincasting, bait fishing or fly-fishing.

Stump Lake (Map 22/D5)

Stump Lake is nestled in a thick, second growth hemlock/cedar forest in Alice Lake Provincial Park. A trail circles the lake, offering access for shore anglers, though is difficult to cast from shore except in a few limited areas. However, the lake has a muddy bottom, murky water and shallows that extend far out from shore making it best to have a float tube. The lake was previously stocked with rainbow and they can still be caught (up to 30 cm/12 in). Cutthroat are currently being stocked. In addition, the lake also holds pumpkinseed sunfish.

Sunrise Lake (Map 14/E4)

Sunrise Lake is another in a series of small lakes found in the hills above Harrison Lake off the Sts'ailes (formerly Harrison West) Forest Service Road. The lake is quite deep and cold and can provide good shore fishing or trolling (electric motors only). There is a recreation site and a boat launch that is maintained by the local four-wheel drive club. Access to the lake itself is by very high clearance four-wheel drive vehicles or by foot.

Swanee Lake (Map 5/F2)

This lake is accessed off a long, rough, bushwhack from the Silver Skagit Road near where it crosses the Silverhope Creek just south of the Eaton Lake Forest Service Site. The lake has fair fishing for small rainbow from June to early fall.

Tannis Lake (Map 10/A2)

Located along the Mount Steele Backcountry Trail System, this small lake is one of a series of small mountain lakes in the area. It provides good fishing for rainbow in the 20-30 cm (8-12 in) range, in fall or early summer by trolling.

Tenquille Lake (Map 41/G3)

This scenic sub-alpine lake is found beneath Tenquille Mountain. It is reached by any one of three trails leading from surrounding logging roads. The lake is a popular hiking and mountaineering destination, but it also has good fishing for rainbow in the 20-30 cm (8-12 in) range. Fly-fishing with a dry fly can be a lot of fun. There is a lakeshore camping area as well as a cabin in the area.

Thomas Lake (Map 13/B3)

Located well and truly back in Golden Ears Provincial Park, Thomas Lake is a fly-in lake. The fact that few anglers ever make it into this lake, which has been stocked in the past with rainbow, means fishing should be excellent.

Thunder Lake (Map 7/A7)

Thunder Lake is the farthest lake along the Lightning Lake Chain Trail and sees a lot less action than the other lakes in the chain. The lake also contains many small rainbow (up to 20 cm/8 in) best caught by bait or fly-fishing.

Trout Lake (Map 1/D2)

Looking at this urban lake found off the Grandview Highway (12th Avenue) in East Vancouver, you wouldn't figure there would be good fishing here. The lake was heavily stocked with rainbow in the past, but don't expect anything big and you will need to fish this one in the spring or fall before it heats up.

Trout [Halfmoon Bay] Lake (Map 9/D4)

This small, productive lake is located next to Highway 101 just to the east of Halfmoon Bay on the Sunshine Coast. Despite its easy access, the lake has lots of stocked cutthroat up to 2 kg (4.5 lbs). The lake is best fished by casting towards the weeds on the north end of the lake. An electric motor only restriction is in place.

Trout Lake (Map 15/A7)

Fishing from the bushy, marshy shoreline of this shallow lake is not an appealing proposition. Instead, bring a float tube or a small boat. The lake is in Sasquatch Provincial Park and contains many small rainbow that easily take to flies. The lake gets quite warm in summer and has a no powerboat restriction on it.

Turquoise Lake (Map 54/A4)

This small lake has good fishing for stocked rainbow growing up to 1 kg (2 lbs). Kokanee have also been stocked recently and are present in small numbers as well. The lake sports a cartop boat launch.

Twenty Minute Lake (Map 7/C6)

This tiny lake is located right along the Gibson Pass Road just east of Lightning Lake. Fishing is slow for small rainbow.

Tyaughton Lake (Map 51/C2)

Tyaughton is native for flying fish. The lake is quite deep and clear making fly-fishing difficult, but casting towards shore with a fly or small lure can be very effective for the stocked rainbow. There are also unconfirmed reports of dollies in the lake, which hosts a recreation site and fine resort.

Unwin Lake (Map 28/D5)

Unwin Lake is located in Desolation Sound Marine Park via a short trail. It is possible to portage a canoe or small boat in. The lake, as well as the lake further upstream, is rarely fished and provide excellent fishing for cutthroat up to 30 cm (12 in). The lakes are best fished in late fall or early summer with bait.

Venables Lake (Map 45/G2)

This lake supports rainbow that can reach 1 kg (2 lbs). Trolling in the spring or fall is your best bet. A cartop boat launch is at the lake, which is accessed via the Venables Valley Road (two-wheel drive access).

Waugh Lake (Map 20/C6)

Waugh Lake is found on the Egmont Road and is frequently fished for cutthroat and rainbow up to 40 cm (16 in). The cutthroat are a little more abundant as they are stocked regularly. An electric motor only restriction applies at the lake.

Weaver Lake (Map 14/E7)

Weaver Lake has good numbers of stocked rainbow and resident cutthroat that can reach 50 cm (20 in). The lake receives heavy pressure during the summer, due in no small part to the scenic recreation site complete with a beach, boat launch and trail around the lake. Trolling is popular although the lake, given its numerous bays and undulating shoreline, is well suited to spincasting or fly-fishing. Fishing is best on the western side because the water is deeper. Better fishing is found in May and June or in September and October.

Welcome Lake (Map 2/A2)

This small lake is located in the city of Coquitlam on Gatensbury Street. The lake is stocked with rainbow and cutthroat.

Wells Lake (Map 17/B6)

Reaching this tiny mountain lake requires a long hike along the Whatcom Trail or an ATV ride. When you reach the lake, you will be rewarded with good fishing for small rainbow that holds steady through the summer and early fall. A very rustic recreation site offers camping at the lake.

West Lake (Map 19/G6–20/A6)

Located on Nelson Island, West Lake is reached along a network of old logging roads from Hidden Basin. It is a big lake for the island. The low elevation lake has some surprisingly large cutthroat, growing up to 3 kg (6.5 lbs) as well as rainbow. The lake is best fished in the spring or early summer using a boat. There is a resort on the lake. Note that there is a 12 kmh (7.5 mph) speed restriction on the lake.

Whonnock Lake (Map 3/B3)

Whonnock Lake is an urban lake located northwest of Mission off of 276th Street. It is a marshy lake that is very shallow and has notably dark but clean water. The lake has cutthroat, crappies, carp and stocked rainbow which all grow up to 25 cm (10 in). The marshy shoreline makes shore fishing very difficult so bring a canoe or float tube (no powerboats). There are day-use facilities at the lake making it a popular summer lake.

Widgeon Lake (Map 12/E5)

Widgeon Lake is a tough lake to access, but it provides good fishing for rainbow trout up to 2 kg (4.5 lbs). The lake is very deep and cold. Anyone making the long hike up should carry a float tube, as casting a line from the shore is difficult, if not impossible.

Wilson Lake (Map 14/A5)

Wilson Lake is west of Chehalis Lake along a long series of rough backroads that may need to be walked due to washouts. Trolling seems to be the preferred fishing method for the rainbow that reside here.

Windsor Lake (Map 29/D7)

Windsor Lake can be reached either along the Goat Lake Main or by boat from Dodd Lake (there is a short portage trail). The cutthroat in this lake are very small but the numbers allow fast fishing, particularly in the spring.

Wood Lake (Map 14/E5)

Access into Wood Lake, off the Sts'ailes (formerly Harrison West) Forest Service Road, is gated when the campsite is not open. This small lake, not much more than a pond, contains good numbers of stocked rainbow up to 40 cm (16 in) best caught in the spring or fall. No powerboats are allowed here.

Wormy Lake (Map 9/E3)

Wormy Lake is accessed by four-wheel drive road off the Honeymoon Forest Service Road on the Sunshine Coast. The cutthroat in the lake average 35-45 cm (14-18 in) and are usually difficult to catch. The best time to fish is during spring.

Wotten Lake (Map 15/D3)

Wotten Lake is a remote lake, containing rainbow. The lake receives very little fishing pressure and can offer exceptional fly-fishing and spincasting for rainbow.

Young Lake (Map 12/A3)

Young Lake is a small, remote lake that offers small rainbow that usually come readily to most flies and small lures after the lake opens up in spring. Unfortunately, the northern road access into this area has been gated making the best access from the south. It is a long hike or bike in from the Indian Arm.

DID YOU KNOW?

Our Fishing Mapbook Series contain hundreds of bathymetric (depth) lake charts and river maps, each with a full page description including facilities, directions, access points, fish species, stocking info, fishing hot spots and so much more!

River & Stream Fishing

Alouette River (Map 2/D2–3/A1; 13/C6) ⬛
This urban river flows from the Alouette Lake into the Pitt River. All five species of salmon return to the system, however current regulations only allow the harvest of Chinook and Coho at certain times. There is also a small run of stocked steelhead in December through March and cutthroat in the spring and fall. Cutthroat area also stocked on the system. Look for Coho in late September and October and Chinook in October and November. Given its easy access, pressure is heavy and the fishing is marginal. Check the regulations before fishing.

American Creek (Map 15/E5)
American Creek is accessed by Highway 1 and the American Creek Road. It has small resident rainbow best caught in July and August after spring runoff. In early summer (June to early July), the odd salmon can be caught near the mouth of the creek.

Anderson River (Map 26/E4–16/B1)
Anderson River flows into the Fraser River north of Hell's Gate. The river has resident dollies and rainbow, which can be caught by bait fishing or spincasting. There is also a small run of steelhead in the late winter to early summer. Check the regulations before heading out.

Ashlu Creek (Map 21/G2–31/B6)
Most of this stream's length can be accessed by two-wheel drive vehicle except the upper reaches, which are best left for four-wheel drive. Due to the falls, the migratory fish are only found in the lower 3 km of the river. Steelhead and dollies can be caught here from March through May. There is also a Coho run in October. Resident rainbow and dollies can be caught above the falls. There is a bait ban and other restrictions here.

Big Silver Creek (Map 14/F2–25/D4)
This creek flows into Harrison Lake near the Silver Creek Camp. It is easily accessed by an extensive network of logging roads. The creek is only fishable below the falls, 7 km upstream. Steelhead can be caught in the winter months and resident cutthroat throughout the year. Check the regulations for special restrictions.

Birkenhead River (Map 33/D1–42/A2)
The Birkenhead River flows into the northwest end of Lillooet Lake and is accessed by the road to D'Arcy or the Birkenhead Forest Service Road. Sockeye and Chinook salmon enter the river in good numbers in the fall, as do some large rainbow trout that follow the salmon upstream. Glacial silt entering the river during spring runoff restricts fishing in May through July. There is no fishing for salmon from August 1st to September 15th to protect spawning Chinook and there is a year-round bait ban.

Brem River (Map 37/D5–F4)
This remote river is fly or boat in only. Logging roads (which can be hiked or biked) provide access to upper reaches of the river. The river is best known for its winter steelhead, but also has resident cutthroat, a Chinook run in summer and a Coho run in fall. Note that there is a bait ban and a no fishing area below the falls, 1.5 km from the mouth of the river.

Bridge River (Map 49/C3–50/B4; 52/E5–53/C5)
This small river flows into the Fraser River to the north of Lillooet. Outside of the upper reaches, good access is found along most of the river. Steelhead, Coho and Chinook in the fall as well as resident rainbow offer a good variety of fishing.

Brittain River (Map 30/B7–29/G6)
Brittain River is a remote river in Jervis Inlet, which is accessed by boat. Due to its limited access, the river is very good for steelhead from November through March as well as resident cutthroat in the spring and fall. The farther you walk/bike up the river the better the fishing becomes.

Brunette River (Map 1/G2–2/A3)
The Brunette is a dark river that drains Burnaby Lake. Efforts to clean the river up have resulted in cutthroat and stocked steelhead taking up residence here again. The green space protecting the river also provides good access for anglers from Cariboo Road and North Road. When fishing for trout, no fishing is allowed from Cariboo Dam to Cariboo Road and it is catch and release on all steelhead. The stream is closed to salmon fishing. Check the regulations for retention limits and closed areas.

Capilano River (Map 1/C1–11/C7; 11/C5) ⬛
The Capilano is perhaps the most popular fishing river on the North Shore. Hundreds of anglers gather here during the prime fishing months. The river has a small summer steelhead run and a small winter run from December to April. The steelhead are stocked. The real action begins in August when the Coho start to return to the Capilano Hatchery. There is a bait ban restriction from August 1st to October 31st and you must release all steelhead. Check the regulations for other restrictions.

Chapman Creek (Map 9/G5–10/B2) ⬛
Chapman Creek is located west of Sechelt and flows into the ocean at Wilson Creek. The creek is accessed by the West Road along most of its length and provides fishing for steelhead in February to April, Coho in the fall and resident cutthroat year-round. Every once and awhile steelhead are stocked into the creek. Check the regulations for closed areas.

Cheakamus River (Map 22/C5–C1; 29/D7–F7)
The upper reaches of the Cheakamus River flow beside Highway 99 and provide fishing for small resident rainbow, which are best fished using artificial bait since there is a bait ban on the river. Beyond the canyon, most of the upper reaches are impassable. Even below the canyon, fishing should be restricted to when the river is not swollen with spring runoff (September to May). The lower Cheakamus, between Fergie's Lodge and up the Paradise Valley Road, offers a fairly good spring steelhead run (April through May) which must all be released. There is no retention of pink, Chinook and chum and only hatchery Coho may be retained. Coho enter the river in October and can be caught throughout the winter. Resident dollies and cutthroat are also present year-round.

Chehalis River (Map 4/D2–14/B6) ⬛
This river flows from Chehalis Lake southward into the Harrison River and is considered one of the best local steelhead rivers. There is a good run of winter steelhead beginning in December until March as well as a few steelhead in June and July. Both fisheries are enhanced by hatchery stock. Sea-run cutthroat are also stocked annually. Chinook run in July through August, while a good Coho run (up to 7 kg/15 lbs) can be found in October through early December so long as there are fall rains. Since the river is mostly walled in by a steep canyon, most anglers are usually found along the gravel bars near the Morris Road Bridge. Those that make it into the canyon will find it less crowded, but difficult to fly-fish. Water levels affect the quality of fishing, so check the local fishing websites for fishing reports on this river. Also be sure to check the regulations for restrictions.

Chilliwack River (Map 4/C6–5/E5)
This river is known as the Chilliwack River above the Vedder Bridge and the Vedder River below the bridge. The total fishing length is about 36 km, all the way to Slesse Creek. The Chilliwack is easily accessed along the Chilliwack Lake Road and receives heavy fishing pressure. The best place to fish the river is above the bridge. The river has an excellent steelhead run from December through March as well as a few steelheads in the summer months. Chum and Coho fishing can be very good in September to October due to hatchery enhancement. Cutthroat fishing can be very good beginning in July until October and Chinook fishing can be decent in July through September. Check the regulations for special restrictions.

Clowham River (Map 21/D3–E5)
Clowham River is a remote stretch of water that flows southward into the northeast end of Clowham Lake. It provides sea-run cutthroat fishing in the spring and fall as well as Coho fishing in the fall. There are also resident cutthroat and dollies available.

Cogburn Creek (Map 14/G3–15/C2)
Cogburn Creek flows into the Harrison River just north of the Bear Creek Camp. It has steelhead in January to April as well as some resident cutthroat throughout the year. A set of impassable falls limits fishing to the first 3 km of the creek. There is no fishing from May 1st to June 30th.

Copper Creek (Map 7/C2–G3)
Copper Creek crosses Highway 3 about 10 km north of the Manning Park East Gate. The creek contains small rainbow.

Coquihalla River (Map 15/F6–16/F1)
The Coquihalla is a medium sized river flowing into the Fraser River at Hope. Access to lower reaches is via Kawakawa Lake Road east of Hope; further upstream access is found off Highway 5. Dolly Varden are available all year and a small run of winter steelhead are present in the lower reaches from February through March. A bigger run of summer steelhead occurs from June through September, while a few Coho also show up in the lower reaches in October and November. Check the regulations for restrictions, including closures around the railway tunnels.

Coquitlam River (Map 2/B3–12/C7; 12/C4)
Flowing from Coquitlam Lake into the Pitt River, this shallow urban river has a small run of steelhead in December to April, Coho in November and December and chum in the fall. There are a few small cutthroat and dollies that reside in the river year-round. The Coquitlam River Trail provides good access to the various holes. There is no fishing above the Mary Hill Bypass bridge from May 1st to June 30th; note the other special restrictions.

Deserted River (Map 30/G5– 31/B4)
Deserted River is a remote river flowing into the Jervis Inlet that can only be reached by boat and then bushwhacking up the river. Given its difficult access, there is a good run of steelhead in the winter as well as Coho in the fall.

Elaho River (Map 31/F5–40/A4)
The Elaho River flows into the Squamish River and is easily accessed along most of its length by the Elaho Road. A few steelhead are found in March to May as well as a few Coho in September and October. The river is noted more for its resident Dolly Varden, which can reach 2 kg (4.5 lbs), as well as smaller rainbow. There is a bait ban restriction in place year-round and all steelhead must be released.

Emory Creek (Map 15/E4)
Emory Creek crosses Highway 1 about 18 km north of Hope where a provincial campsite provides good access. The best fishing is during late spring and fall for dollies or in the summer for rainbow trout. The creek also has Chinook salmon, which are best caught near the mouth in June and July, and a fall run of Coho. A few steelhead are known to show up in late winter.

Fraser River (Maps 1–5, 15, 26, 36, 44, 45, 53)
The Fraser River, between Coquitlam and American Creek, offers excellent fishing for salmon and sturgeon, which can exceed 450 kg (1000 lbs). Most of the fishing occurs off one of the many gravel bars that line the river. Having a boat to access the quieter bars for salmon and the back eddies for sturgeon is helpful. Perhaps the busiest time on the river is during the sockeye run from mid-July to late September, but the Chinook fishery beginning in June and lasting until October is also popular. Coho enter the river in late September and run until December. Chum are caught in October and pink in August and September. Sea-run cutthroat are caught throughout the fall until early spring and steelhead from November to March. The cutthroat fishery is supplemented with stocking. Anglers need to be wary of in season changes to the regulations.

Gold Creek (Map 3/B1–13/B6)
This creek is found in the Golden Ears Provincial Park and flows southward into the Alouette Lake. The creek is accessed by a series of trails and can be fished for small cutthroat, rainbow and dollies, which reside in the creek year-round. After spring runoff is the best time to fish.

Gray Creek (Map 9/G3–10/A2)
Gray Creek flows from a series of mountain lakes into the Sechelt Inlet south of Tuwanek. The creek has cutthroat in the spring and fall and Coho in the fall.

Green River (Map 32/G4–33/C1)
Green River flows northwest from Green Lake and enters the Lillooet River to the east of Pemberton. Most of the length of the river is easily accessed off Highway 99. Glacial silt entering the river makes it difficult to fish. It is possible to catch a few larger dollies (up to 1.5 kg/3 lbs) and a few small rainbow.

Harrison River (Map 4/D2–F1)
This is a popular and productive river. In addition to casting from shore around the Highway 7 Bridge near Harrison Mills, anglers often launch a boat at Kilby Park off Highway 7. Sockeye start their annual migration in July, while Pink run every other year between August and October. Chinook and Coho are caught during the fall, with the best time being in late October. Chum also offer an excellent fishery in late October and November. Cutthroat fishing can be particularly effective from December through March, although during spring runoff (May through June) the fishing tails off because the waters are quite murky. A stocking program helps the cutthroat fishery here. The river also offers decent steelhead fishing in December and January as well as whitefish in June. There are different regulations for fishing above and below the Highway 7 Bridge so please check the government websites noted above.

Hope Slough (Map 4/F4)
Hope Slough is a slow moving, meandering waterway near Chilliwack that is surrounded by private property. The slough can be accessed by a canoe and contains cutthroat, which can be best caught in spring and fall, as well as a run of Coho in fall.

Hunter Creek (Map 5/D1–15/D7)
Hunter Creek is a small creek that flows northward into the Fraser River to the west of Hope. Chinook are available at the mouth of the creek in June and July whereas cutthroat and steelhead frequent the estuary in the winter.

Indian River (Map 11/F2–12/A5)
Indian River is a beautiful, clear river that flows into the north end of the Indian Arm. Anglers access the river near the estuary by boat. There are also resident cutthroat and Dolly Varden that are best caught in the spring when they follow the salmon fry migration. However, the best time to visit this river is in late summer and fall when pink and chum run. The pink run every odd year and enter the river in large schools from August until September, while the chum enter the system in October and November. There is non-retention of any salmon year-round and a bait ban on the river from December 1st through September 30th.

Kanaka Creek (Map 2/F3–3/B2)
This is a small urban creek in Maple Ridge which has a few steelhead in January to March, cutthroat in September to April and a few Coho in the fall. Most of the creek can be easily accessed by paved roads and a good trail system. Note that there is no fishing for salmon upstream of the 112th Street Bridge and no fishing from May 1st to June 30th.

Lang Creek (Map 19/B4)
Lang Creek flows from Duck Lake into the ocean just southeast of Powell River. There are steelhead in January to March as well as cutthroat in the spring and fall in the river. However, the best fishing is now in the shallow estuary for hatchery Chinook averaging 20 kg (44 lbs). They are fished in mid-September to late October, while the occasional Coho and chum can also be caught.

> *The streams are heavily regulated and the regulations for steelhead and salmon change frequently, visit www.pac.dfo-mpo.gc.ca for salmon regulations and www.env.gov.bc.ca/fw/fish/regulations for non-salmon information.*

Lawless Creek (Map 17/A1–B3)
Lawless Creek drains the slopes of Mount Thynne towards Tulameen where it flows into the Tulameen River. Lawless Creek Forest Service Road accesses most of the lower reaches, but access to the upper reaches is by bushwhacking. Small rainbow trout are found here.

Lillooet River (Map 33/E1–49/A6; 24/G6–33/G6)
The Upper Lillooet River is a slow meandering stream that is easily accessed from Pemberton. South of Little Lillooet Lake, the Lower Lillooet River is a much faster flowing stream that extends all the way to Harrison Lake. It contains steelhead (March to May), resident dollies, Coho (October) and Chinook (April to May). However, the river is very silty during spring runoff and fishing is poor during May through October, although the estuaries such as Rogers Creek offer cleaner water at this time. Chinook are closed from July 30th to September 30th; check the regulations before fishing.

Little Campbell River (Map 2/C7–F7)
This river flows into Georgia Straight near Mud Bay and, given its urban setting, does not offer great fishing opportunities. There is a very small run of winter steelhead as well as Coho, Chinook and cutthroat entering the river in late fall (October to November). It is possible to catch the cutthroat until the spring as they often winter within the river system to spawn. The river has been extensively rehabilitated by the community hatchery, which has helped the returns somewhat. Access to the river is where 16th Avenue crosses the river near the Peace Portal and Hazelmere Golf Courses.

Lynn Creek (Map 1/E1–11/E6)
Lynn Creek is a difficult river to access and only has 5 km of fishable waters. There are a couple trails that bring you to some nice holes that hold a small run of winter steelhead in December to April and small runs of Coho and Chinook in the fall. There is a bait ban restriction year-round and a closed section; check the regulations before heading out.

Mamquam River (Map 22/C6–12/A1)

Mamquam River flows westward into the Squamish River just south of Brackendale. The best places to try are at the mouth of the river where it enters the Squamish River or at the estuary of Mashiter Creek. The Mamquam contains fair numbers of steelhead in March to May with April being the best time to fish. Coho and dollies are also present in October to early November, while all four species of salmon return to the Mamquam. There is a bait ban and special retention limits.

Maria Slough (Map 4/G2–5/A1)

This water body is an extension of the Fraser River near Agassiz. The Seabird Island Road provides access along most of its 10 km length. The slough offers some very good fishing for sea-run cutthroat (up to 2.5 kg/5 lbs) in October through March along with resident cutthroat and dollies throughout the year. There is also a good run of Coho beginning in late October until mid-December.

McNab Creek (Map 10/E2)

Flowing into the Thornbrough Canal near Port Mellon, McNab Creek is accessed by boat. Look for cutthroat in the spring and fall, Coho in October and November and steelhead in the winter.

McNair Creek (Map 10/C3)

Flowing into the Thornbrough Canal at Port Mellon, McNair Creek is accessed by Highway 101 and logging roads. Look for cutthroat in the spring and fall, Coho in October and November and steelhead in the winter.

Miami River (Map 4/G1)

This stream runs into Harrison Lake at Harrison Hot Springs. In the summer months anglers will find rainbow and in late October cutthroat and Coho. Although the mouth of the creek is the most popular spot, some of the larger pools upstream can be particularly good for Coho and cutthroat in late November when the waters have risen due to rainfall.

Nahatlach River (Map 26/D1–36/A7; 25/F1–34/E6)

The Nahatlach flows into the Fraser River south of Lytton. The fast flowing stream contains resident rainbow and dollies, as well as steelhead in the winter, Chinook in the late summer and Coho in the fall.

Nikomekl River (Map 2/A6–F5)

This river flows into Georgia Straight near Mud Bay and, given its urban setting, does not offer great fishing opportunities and is heavily regulated. There is a very small run of winter steelhead as well as Coho and sea-run cutthroat that enter the river in late fall. Check the regulations for several special restrictions.

Nicomen Slough (Map 3/F4–4/C3)

This slough attaches to the Fraser and provides access for Coho up into Norrish Creek in October and November and chum in October and November. The slough is also a good place to go looking for cutthroat in spring and fall. Watch for speed restrictions on parts of the slough.

Norrish [Suicide] Creek (Map 3/G3)

A falls at 7.5 km restricts fishing to the lower reaches. There are steelhead in December to March, cutthroat in the spring and fall and Coho in fall. Small resident rainbow trout are available year-round; however, there is no fishing permitted from May 1st to June 30th.

Pasayten River (Map 7/G4)

Easily accessed along the Pasayten River Forest Service Road, this river is home to small rainbow, which can be caught by fly-fishing or spincasting.

Pitt River (Map 2/C3–12/E7; 12/E3–23/A3)

While it is possible to fish in the Lower Pitt River, the Upper Pitt offers some of the best fishing in the Lower Mainland and is basically one 65 km long fishing hole. The bottom 24 km or so of the Upper Pitt is where most of the action takes place. The river is home to rainbow trout, bull trout, steelhead (in spring), sockeye (in August) and Coho (in October). Unfortunately, there is no way to the Upper Pitt other than boat or plane. There is a lodge on the river, but note the bait ban and closed sections. Catch and release fishing is encouraged.

Potlatch Creek (Map 10/G2)

A boat access only river north of Anvil Island in Howe Sound, Potlatch River is a good cutthroat stream in spring.

Rainy River (Map 10/C2–D3)

Rainy River is accessed by Highway 101 to Port Melon and then along a deteriorating logging road. The river has steelhead in February to March, cutthroat year-round and Coho in October and November.

Roberts Creek (Map 10/B6–C4)

Roberts Creek is found west of Gibson and contains steelhead and cutthroat. Those fish are best caught near the estuary.

Ruby Creek (Map 15/B6)

Ruby Creek flows southward into the Fraser River east of Agassiz. The creek has resident rainbow and cutthroat as well as steelhead in the winter and Coho in the fall. Most of the creek can be accessed by gated logging roads that may or may not be drivable. Check for closures.

Salmon River (Map 2/F4–3/B6)

A slow, meandering river that flows into the Fraser near Fort Langley, the Salmon River is closed to fishing above 232nd Street. Resident cutthroat and Dolly Varden along with a good run of Coho in fall and winter steelhead draw anglers.

Sawmill [Five Mile] Creek (Map 15/E2)

This small creek crosses Highway 1 approximately 6 km north of Yale. You will find Chinook salmon near the mouth of the river in June and July.

Scuzzy Creek (Map 26/B4–E4)

Scuzzy Creek flows eastward into the Fraser River south of Boston Bar. An extensive logging road network provides access along most of the creek length. There are small resident cutthroat in the creek that are best caught by bait fishing.

Sechelt Creek (Map 21/C7–E7)

Sechelt Creek is a remote creek located towards the north end of the Salmon Inlet. The creek is accessed by boat and then along a logging road, preferably with a bike. Anglers will find resident cutthroat as well as Coho in the fall and steelhead in the winter.

Serpentine River (Map 2/B6–C5)

This river flows into Georgia Straight near Mud Bay and, given its urban setting, does not offer great fishing opportunities and is heavily regulated. There is a very small run of winter steelhead as well as Coho and sea-run cutthroat that enter the river in late fall.

Seton River (Map 53/C7)

Below the lake, the lower river is a dam controlled river that connects Seton Lake with the Fraser River. It is easily accessed from the Duffey Lake Road (Hwy 99) at Lillooet. There is a fish hatchery on this section of the river, which offers a variety of species. Trout (brook, bull, cutthroat and rainbow), Dolly Varden and whitefish offer year-round fishing opportunities, while salmon (Chinook, Coho, pink and sockeye) and steelhead run in the river in the fall and winter.

Seton Portage (Map 52/D6)

The short river between Anderson Lake and Seton Lake called Seton Portage offers steelhead as well as rainbow and dollies (up to 2 kg/4.5 lbs). Steelhead anglers should try near the inflow and outflow, while the rainbow and dollies are caught at the mouth of Whitecap Creek.

Seymour River (Map 1/E1–11/F5)

The Seymour River is the easiest of the North Shore rivers to fish since a trail system extends north along the river to the Seymour Dam. Anglers will find a small run of winter steelhead from late December to early April and a small summer steelhead run in June until late July. Although stocked, all steelhead (and resident trout) must be released. In fall, Coho and some Chinook head up the river. Check the regulations for other restrictions.

Silverhope Creek (Map 5/G3–15/E7)

This large, fast flowing creek reaches the Fraser River just west of Hope. It has a small steelhead run in the summer (June to August) and again in the winter (January to April). There are also a few salmon that enter the river in the fall and there are some resident cutthroat and dollies. For best success, fish at the mouth of the creek or try some of the deep holes along the creek. Check the regulations for special restrictions.

Similkameen River (Map 7/B3–G4)

The Similkameen River begins near Allison Pass in Manning Park and flows in an easterly direction some 160 km before entering the United States near Osoyoos. Most of the river length is accessed by Highway 3. The river produces well for rainbow on a (dry) fly. There is a bait ban from April 1st to October 31st as well as a catch and release fishery for rainbow between the Highway 3 bridge at Princeton and 31 km south of Princeton. A good whitefish fishery is offered in the winter season.

Skagit River (Map 6/F7–7/B5)
Offering some of the best rainbow trout fishing in southwestern BC, the Skagit is a slow meandering river. Anglers either walk along the Skagit River Trail from Sumallo Grove or float down the river to sample some of the more remote pools. Other access is through the Skagit Valley just west of Hope. Day-use and camp-ground facilitiesexist close to fishing access points. Fishing is restricted until July with the best fishing being towards August and September, after the runoff has subsided. The rainbow in the Skagit River average 20-30 cm (8-12 in), but can grow as large as 50 cm (20 in). Dollies enter the Skagit from Ross Lake and can grow as large as 5 kg (10 lbs). These fish are in the river in the fall, but some remain year-round. Currently, all fish must be released and there is a bait ban on the river year-round. There is no fishing from November 1st to June 30th.

Skwanka River (Map 30/B3–39/A7)
The Skwanka is another remote river with a logging road that follows the river valley. The river contains Chinook, Coho, cutthroat and a small run of winter steelhead.

Sloquet Creek (Map 13/B1–24/F6)
Sloquet Creek flows northeast into the Lillooet River. A deteriorating logging road accesses the lower portions of the creek. There are steelhead in January to April, resident dollies and Coho in the fall. While in the area, why not visit the hot springs for a relaxing après fishing soak?

Spuzzum Creek (Map 26/A6–F7)
Spuzzum Creek is a small creek that crosses Highway 1, 25 km north of Yale. Like most of the small creeks that flow into the Fraser, the closer you get to the Fraser, the better the fishing is. The creek has a steelhead fishery from January to April, Chinook salmon in June and July and rainbow throughout the year.

Squamish River (Map 22/C7–31/G2)
This large river flows southward into Howe Sound at Squamish. It has a total of 60 km of fishable water. Due to glacial silt and spring runoff, the Squamish is very difficult to fish from early May to the end of July. Also, the lower reaches of the river below Brackendale are very unproductive. The best time to fish is in the fall to early spring from the Ashulu Creek estuary to below the Cheakamus River. The river offers steelhead beginning in January with the best time being in late March. Four species of salmon return to the Squamish: pink, Coho, Chinook and chum. The Coho are present in October and November, while dollies are available year-round. Note the regulations as there is a bait ban and restrictions as to what you can keep.

Stave River (Map 3/B4; 13/F5–24/A6) 🖼
The Stave has two distinct sections. The Lower Stave River is a short, broad river that flows out of Hayward Lake, which in turn falls out of Stave Lake. The lower section offers the typical migratory species including pink (odd years), summer Chinook, fall Coho and chum and winter steelhead. The Upper Stave River flows into the north end of Stave Lake and can only be reached by boat and then biking or hiking up the Stave River Forest Service Road. There are resident cutthroat and dollies in the river. Given the remote access, the upper river can be very productive, particularly in the late fall. Both steelhead and cutthroat are stocked heavily into the river system. Check the regulations for a closed area.

Stawamus River (Map 11/E2–22/D7)
Stawamus River is a small stream that flows into Howe Sound at Squamish. It provides slow fishing for steelhead in April and May and Coho in the fall. There are also resident cutthroat and dollies. Access is limited to the lower reaches and there is a bait ban here most of the year.

Stein River (Map 34/E4–36/B2)
Although the Stein offers very good fishing for steelhead in the winter, Chinook and Coho in the fall and rainbow year-round, few visitors to the valley bring along fishing rods. This makes the fishing all that better.

Sumas River (Map 3/F7–4/A5)
This river parallels Highway 1 for a good stretch and provides a few cutthroat in the spring and fall, resident dollies year-round, Coho in the fall (mid-September to December)and steelhead in the winter. There are even carp in the canal. A boat launch is available at the Sumas Pumping Station. There is a special retention limit on steelhead.

Sumallo River (Map 6/B3–E3)
The upper reaches of the Sumallo River are easily accessed from the Sumallo River Forest Service Road. The lower reaches parallel Highway 3 east of Sunshine Valley. The river offers good fishing for rainbow and dollies in summer. Although small, the rainbow trout receive most of the attention. There is a bait ban and other restrictions here.

Texas Creek (Map 44/C5–E3)
Texas Creek is found south of Lillooet and flows to the northeast into the Fraser River. Texas Creek Road provides access, but if you want to reach the upper portion of the creek you will need a four-wheel drive vehicle and a lot of patience (due to water bars). The creek provides excellent fishing for small rainbow.

Theodosia River (Map 28/D5–G3)
This remote river flows into the Theodosia Inlet near Desolation Sound. The river is accessed by boat and then by following the Theodosia Main logging road up the river. The river provides steelhead and cutthroat in the spring and fall as well as Coho in September and October.

Thompson River (Map 36/C2–45/G5)
This large river is renowned for its excellent steelhead fishery, but in recent times the fishing has declined. Regardless, anglers come from around the world to try to hook into one of these mighty trout (some reach 13 kg/30 lbs) during the late fall (October–December). The pools around Spences Bridge are legendary. Other species in the river include several salmon runs, rainbow trout, sturgeon, Dolly Varden and whitefish. Check the regulations for special restrictions.

Tingle Creek (Map 13/B3–D5)
This small, remote creek flows into Clearwater Bay on Stave Lake. Accessed by boat, it provides resident rainbow, dollies and cutthroat.

Tulameen River (Map 17/A7–G5)
The Tulameen flows from the Cascade Mountains before arcing past the town of Tulameen and spilling into the Similkameen River at Princeton. The 81 km long river contains a number of species, most notably rainbow and brook trout and mountain whitefish. Although most sections of the river are easily accessed, there are some remote, wild sections that offer excellent fishing.

Tzoonie River (Map 20/G5–21/B3)
Tzoonie River is a remote river flowing southward into Narrows Inlet. It is accessed by boat and then by following the Tzoonie River Road, preferably by mountain bike. The river provides steelhead fishing in December to March as well as Coho fishing in the fall. There are also resident Dolly Varden and cutthroat in the river system.

Vancouver River (Map 20/D2–21/A2)
The Vancouver River is yet another remote river that flows into Jervis Inlet. A mountain bike can be used to access the length of the river along an old rail line/road from Vancouver Bay. The river has steelhead in January to May, cutthroat in October and November and Coho in the fall. There are also resident dollies available.

Vedder River (Map 4/A5–C5) 🖼
The Chilliwack River becomes the Vedder River below the Vedder Bridge, as it slowly flows into the Vedder Canal. This section of the river is the most popular stream to fish in the Fraser Valley. It is not uncommon to see hundreds of anglers lined up shoulder-to-shoulder trying for the winter steelhead, chum and Coho fishing in September to October as well as Chinook in July through September. The steelhead are stocked. Some anglers will launch a boat at the Sumas Pumping Station to avoid the crowds. Water levels definitely affect the quality of fishing so be sure to watch the weekly fishing reports on the local fishing websites. Also be sure to check the current restrictions before heading out.

Weaver Creek (Map 4/E1–14/E7)
Home to the Weaver Creek Spawning Channel, this small creek has a good run of steelhead in December to March and cutthroat all year. Sections of the creek are closed to fishing.

Whonnock Creek (Map 3/B3)
Whonnock Creek crosses Highway 7 between 272nd Street and 280th Street. The river contains cutthroat, has a small run of Coho in fall and a small run of winter steelhead.

Widgeon Creek (Map 12/E6)
This creek drains Widgeon Lake southward into Pitt River. It is accessed by canoe from Grant Narrows and has resident cutthroat as well as steelhead in the winter and Coho in the fall. Powered boats are not allowed here.

Whipsaw Creek (Map 7/D1–17/G6)
Whipsaw Creek crosses Highway 3 south of Princeton and is a rainbow stream. You can access the northwest banks of the river from the Whipsaw Creek Forest Service Road or you can access the southeastern shore from the Friday Main.

Yale Creek (Map 15/E2)
This small creek is off Highway 1 just north of Yale. The creek offers Chinook in June through July at the mouth of the Fraser River.

Ocean Fishing

Bowen Island (Map 10/F7)
Due to its proximity to Vancouver, Bowen Island is a popular fishing destination. The southern end of the island gets most of the attention but there are many areas to drop a line in. Collingwood Channel produces very well for winter Chinook from December to April, while Cowan Point to Cape Roger Curtis is another good area for wintering Chinook on a deep troll. Cowan Point also produces well for Chinook in May through July, Coho in late August to October, pinks in late August to September (odd years) and sockeye in September with trolling being your best bet. Snug Cove is often trolled southward to the Copper Mine for Chinook from December to March and from June to August. Coho can be found from July to September. Watch out for heavy traffic in the area, especially ferries. If you are fishing the Collingwood Channel, be mindful of the Rockfish Conservation Area that is located south of Keats Island.

Burrard Inlet Shore Casting (Map 1/B1–G1)
In addition to the hot spots off shore, there are some select shore fishing areas and good crabbing opportunities here. Try off of Stanley Park for crab during flood tides. To catch larger crab, use fresh salmon heads and scraps. Just remember, you cannot leave your crab traps set up overnight here. Shore fishing for perch and other small fish can be found at the Jericho Sailing Club, Ambleside Park in North Vancouver, and Cates Park near Deep Cove. The last two spots are also good for salmon during the spawning season from July to September. The mouth of the Seymour River is another good spot for salmon.

Capilano River (Map 1/C1)
The mouth of the Capilano is an incredibly popular area to fish, especially for the Coho that congregate at the river mouth. Casting from shore at the gravel bar is a good bet for Coho beginning in June until November, but you will have to do it at lower tides as it is submerged at high tides. You can also anchor a boat near the lighthouse and mooch on a tide change. A number of Chinook in the 10-15 kg (30-40 lb) range also come into the area in late summer until mid-October. These fish are best caught by trolling during flood tides. In December through April, winter Chinook frequent the mouth and can be caught by mooching 60-80 m (200-265 ft) offshore. Care must be taken to ensure you are not fishing in the navigational channel.

As with all coastal areas of BC, there are seemingly endless areas to fish for Pacific salmon, as well as sea-run cutthroat, shellfish and groundfish. You will need to confirm openings with the Department of Fisheries and Oceans (visit www.pac.dfo-mpo.gc.ca or call 1-866-431-3474). You should also note the many rockfish conservation areas.

Copeland Islands (Map 28/A7)
The Copeland Islands, north of Lund, offer some good fishing for Chinook and Coho. The best location to fish is on the inside passage (Thulin Passage) by trolling a plug or by fishing from shore. Chinook can be caught from mid-April until July. Check the regulations as most of the islands are in a Rockfish Conservation Area, although the mainland side of Thulin Passage is still open.

Earls Cove (Map 20/B5)
From May to August, Earls Cove is a good destination for Coho and Chinook. It is sheltered from the winds of Jervis Inlet so it makes a good place for smaller crafts. If you are fishing for Chinook, it is best to try a deep mooch (20-45 m/65-100 ft). Smaller Coho (bluebacks) come into the area in May and you can catch mature Coho until August.

Egmont Area (Map 20/C5)
In order to get into the Sechelt Inlet, fish must first pass Egmont Point. Fishing can be quite good year-round for Chinook and Coho. Moochers tend to stay close to Earls Cove, while trollers tend to troll toward Egmont. Do not go too far south or you will be in the Rockfish Conservation Area that starts near the Skookumchuck Rapids and extends to the south.

Fraser River Estuary (Map 1/A2–C7)
The Fraser River is the pathway for millions of migrating salmon, and the river mouth can provide some of the best fishing anywhere. Between Point Grey Bell Buoy and the QA marker off the North Arm, the T-10 marker off the Middle Arm, around the Sand Heads off the end of the Steveston Jetty in the tide lines and from Roberts Bank to the Tsawwassen Ferry Terminal all produce at particular times (just follow the crowds). The Chinook fishery (from mid spring until the end of September) gets most of the attention. The waters of the Fraser are murky, making it necessary to attract the fish. Other salmon species include pinks every odd year in August and September, sockeye in July and August and hatchery Coho from August to October, while chum are present in October to November.

Gibsons Area Shore Casting (Map 10/A5–D5)
Those in the Gibsons area without a boat can try for salmon and sea-run cutthroat along the beaches. Try along the Gibsons waterfront, Chaster Beach or near Angus Creek. Or you can head north to try the Roberts Creek area. The best time for shore casting for salmon is from July to September. Look for a decent drop off and incoming tides. Typically, the larger the tidal difference the better the fishing. Look for jumping salmon and try casting into those waters.

Grant Reefs (Map 18/A2)
Finding Grant Reefs is half the fun as they are submerged but marked by a series of kelp beds. The reefs provide good fishing for Coho from May to July and Chinook in July and August.

Gower Point/Gibsons Gap (Map 10/C6)
Gower Point is considered one of the premier Coho areas on the Sunshine Coast. Locals fishing the area usually anchor near the drop-off at the south end of the point and try mooching or strip casting. The Gap is a shallow rock shelf that extends from the south end of Keats Island to Cape Byng west of Gibsons. The water on either side of the shelf drops off rapidly to 45 m (150 ft) and it is at the drop-off where the fish hold. Coho are caught from June to September and the occasional Chinook is caught here in May to September. There are also good numbers of pinks caught during late July and early August in odd years.

Halfmoon Bay (Map 9/C4)
This bay is one of the best fishing areas on the Sunshine Coast, producing Chinook from November through March as well as in June and July and again in September. Coho are present in July through September. Both species are best caught by trolling around the points leading into the bay. But watch for the Rockfish Conservation Area around Jeddah Point.

Harmony Island/Granville Bay (Map 20/B3)
This area is popular for Chinook in April through early June as well as Coho later in summer (July and August). As of 2015, you can only fish south of the Harmony Islands as the area north of the islands in Hotham Sound is a Rockfish Conservation Area. Your best bet is to try mooching near the estuary of Freil Lake. Check the regulations for specifics on the closed area before heading out.

Harwood Island (Map 18/D3)
To the east of Powell River, Harwood Island marks a good area for salmon fishing. The best spots to fish for Coho and Chinook are off the east and southwest sides of the island using a deep troll.

Hole in the Wall (Map 11/A6)
This is a very popular fishing spot just north of Horseshoe Bay named for a mining test hole on the granite cliff rising above the ocean. The area is notoriously fickle with mooching near the cliffs where you will find the 150 m (490 ft) ledge. The best bet for Chinook is November through March and again in July through September. Troll deep (25-35 m/80-120 ft) in the winter months. The occasional Coho is caught in the area between July and September.

Indian Arm (Map 1/A1–12/A5)
Indian Arm produces an excellent fishery for pinks in late August to early September during odd numbered years. These fish congregate just south of the Vancouver Yacht Club against the rock cliff. It is best to drift fish and cast into the school of fish. Another good fishery occurs in late October when chum enter the arm.

Keats Island (Map 10/E6)
This small island to the west of Bowen Island is best fished for wintering Chinook in November through April off Cotton Point. The point can also produce well for Chinook and Coho in June to October. Nearby Home Island is a small rock outcrop also known as Salmon Rock. This area receives heavy fishing pressure because it is a constant producer for Chinook in March and April and Chinook and Coho in June to September. There is a Rockfish Conservation Area that extends from the southern shoreline to a group of island to the south.

Lasqueti Island (Map 8/B3–E5)
By far the best location to fish around Lasqueti Island is off Young Point, which attracts many moochers. Trollers can circle the point or work their way up along the northeastern shoreline. Coho are the most common fish here, especially in July. Off the northeastern end of Lasqueti Island, from Fegen Islets to False Bay, anglers can try for Coho and Chinook, primarily by a shallow troll. Try trolling for Coho in June through October with the bigger northerns coming through in September to October. The occasional Chinook can be caught in July and August. Watch for large Rockfish Conservation Areas all around the island.

Mystery Reef (Map 18/C2)
Mystery Reef is situated to the northwest of Harwood Island. It produces good numbers of Coho in May through June as well as a few Chinook in July and August. If the bait is near the reefs, anchor off the north or south end of the reef and try some mooching or jigging. Otherwise, try trolling around the reef as the fish are likely scattered. Remember to keep out of the Rockfish Conservations Area to the northeast.

Nelson Island (Maps 8, 19)
Nelson Island is the large island at the northwest end of Sechelt Peninsula. Ackland Reef, which is several hundred yards off the mouth of Quarry Bay, provides one of the best fisheries for Coho throughout July and August. Anchor at the edge of the reef and try jigging or mooching. Chinook are around in May through August. Fearney Point provides a popular fishery for Chinook, pink and Coho. Green Bay is located in Agamemnon Channel on the southeast side of the island. This area offers good fishing for Chinook as well as Coho. Moochers do well by concentrating in the inlet to the bay or on the point to the north of the bay. For trollers, it is best to troll around the point. Quarry Bay is a good area to troll for Coho in July and August or for Chinook in April to July. There are large Rockfish Conservation Areas along the northwestern shoreline.

Pender Harbour (Map 9/A1)
The number of resorts and guides in the area is proof of the fine fishing around Pender Harbour. Francis Point is a good location for trolling for both Chinook and Coho from May through September. The Gap leading into Pender Harbour is extremely popular with anglers and is a good place to mooch with live herring for Chinook throughout the year. Lee's Bay is located between Daniel Point and Irvines Landing and is another popular mooching area for Chinook throughout the year. A bit further north, Sakinaw Estuary, or the A-Frame, is best trolled or mooched near the point south of the actual estuary. The best fishing for the Chinook is in December through March and for the Coho in July and August. Watch for a narrow Rockfish Conservation Area south of the harbour.

Point Atkinson (Map 1/A1)
The lighthouse in Lighthouse Park marks Point Atkinson. A rock shelf extends off the point to the 18-25 m (60-90 ft) level before dropping off to 60 metres or more. It is at this drop-off that trolling is most effective for Chinook in the winter and July to September as well as for a few Coho and pinks in August through September. Due to strong currents, it is best to troll in a circular manner around the point. If fishing is slow, trolling along the West Vancouver Waterfront, about 300 metres (1,000 ft) offshore, can be effective all the way to the Ambleside boat launch.

Powell River Area (Map 18/F3–19/B5)
The old boat breakwater, known as The Hulks, marks the location of some good Chinook fishing in May through August. Most anglers begin trolling near the Hulks at dawn and then work their way outward throughout the morning. Another area to try is the Westview Waterfront. The occasional wintering Chinook can be caught in December to April on a deep troll. However, the better fishing is in May through July for Chinook and Coho. Grief Point is located south of Powell River and can be good year-round, although from May to August is when the Chinook are found off the point in good numbers. Myrtle Point/Rocks are found between Powell River and Brew Bay and offer good fishing for Chinook from May to July and for Coho in July. Trolling along the shoreline from Myrtle Rock all the way to the point is the most common method of catching fish. Shore casting is possible in the area, but the best bet is to head south to Lang Bay and try the estuary there for returning salmon in September and October.

Roberts Creek Area (Map 10/A6–C7)
The shoreline extending from Wilson Creek all the way to Gower Point can be a very productive trolling area for Coho from June to October and for Chinook in June and again in September to October. It is also possible to catch wintering Chinook in December to March. Moochers tend to focus their efforts approximately 200 m (650 ft) from the wharf at Roberts Creek where there is a noticeable drop-off. The area is subject to large swells.

Saint Vincent Bay (Map 19/G4–20/A4)
Saint Vincent Bay has a number of fishing holes all the way out to Elephant Point and Culloden Point. Both points are best for Coho (bluebacks beginning in April until May and then mature Coho throughout the summer) whereas Saint Vincent Bay is best for Chinook. This area can be extremely busy during the summer months.

Sarah Point (Map 28/A6)
Sarah Point marks the northern tip of Malaspina Peninsula and fish entering Desolation Sound must pass by here. There are some wintering Chinook but the main fishery is from May and June for Chinook and late August to early September for Coho. Trolling around the point seems to work the best.

Generally speaking, it is best to fish shallower at first light and work deeper as morning progresses. The opposite is true in the evening.

Savary Island (Map 18/A1)
In July and August, the south side of Savary Island can be trolled using a typical Coho lure. The Coho can be found in good numbers along the south side of the island and northward to Hernando Island. Jigging or casting along the kelp beds on the south side of the island can also be effective.

Scotch Fir Point (Map 19/D6)
This point marks the beginning of Jervis Inlet and migratory salmon must pass here to get into its system of creeks and rivers. As a result, it offers good fishing throughout the summer months for Coho in December through March and May for Chinook. Do not go too far to the south or you will be in the Sinclair Bank Rockfish Conservation Area.

Sechelt Shore Casting (Map 9/D5–F5)
From July to September salmon fishing from shore can be productive. Try just to the south of Sechelt around the Chapman River and Mission Point area, to the north in Sargent Bay, or the northern shore line in Porpoise Bay. It is best to time shore casting for the flood tides after very low tides (in the 3 m/10 ft range).

Sechelt Inlet (Map 9/F4–20/D6)
This long narrow inlet leads all the way from Egmont south to Sechelt. Porpoise Bay sees the most pressure, as it butts up against Sechelt. Coho start running through this area in July and Chinook in August. In odd years the inlet sees a good fishery for pinks, too. Some areas to try include Snake Bay, Tillicum Bay, Carlson Point and Highland Point. Note the two Rockfish Conservation Areas; one is located from Skookumchuck Rapids south along the western side of the inlet, the other is at the eastern end of Salmon Inlet.

Texada Island (Maps 8, 18, 19)
Texada Island is a popular destination with several different hot spots to sample. Anderson Bay is located on the southeast side of Texada and offers some good trolling and mooching for Chinook in April to July and Coho beginning in May until August. Just north of the bay, the series of pilings mark another good mooching area for Chinook throughout the year and Coho. Blubber Bay to Davis Bay provides a good trolling area for Coho and Chinook in May through September. Grilse (Coho) Point is located at the northern tip of Texada and is considered a premier Coho area in August. Mouat Bay is known primarily as a trolling area for Coho. Sturt Bay is found near Van Anda and provides a holding area for Chinook in the summer months when bait is present in the bay. Given the confined area, mooching and jigging are your better choices. Outside the bay, Coho can be caught from July to September by trolling in the tide lines. Upwood Point is the southernmost point of land on Texada and Coho can be found from July to October, while Chinook cruise the area year-round. The area is best trolled. Be wary of the many Rockfish Conservation Areas around the island.

Vivian Islands (Map 18/C4)
West of the bigger Harwood Island, Vivian Island offers Chinook in July and August primarily by trolling. There are also Coho in June through August.

#SAVEBCWILDLIFE
Join, Donate, Volunteer

To protect, enchance and promote the wise use of the environment for the benefit of present and future generations.

www.bcwf.bc.ca

BCWF
BC WILDLIFE FEDERATION

HUNTING ADVENTURES

BC hunters enjoy some of the widest variety of game animals anywhere on the continent. This diversity of wildlife is made possible by the range of habitats: from riverbank to alpine and desert to rainforest. Regardless of habitat, though, winter is normally the bottleneck for survival of wild animals.

The Coastal area of BC is blessed with a temperate climate that usually ensures a lower than average winter mortality rate for animals. As a result, the coast has the largest population of overwintering waterfowl and raptors in the country. However, the farther inland you go, the colder the winters get.

Hunters can currently expect some of the best big game hunting this region has ever had, due to many recent mild winters, easier backcountry access and a decline in the number of hunters.

Ducks and geese don't do well in mountainous terrain and much of the low-lying wetland areas are protected by parks. While Canada geese have reached nuisance numbers in urban areas, many of the best hunting areas are closed by municipal bylaws. Still, the birds are there and the seasons are long.

There are also few upland game species in this region. These bird species prefer the drier climes of the interior, as opposed to the wet coastal weather.

To hunt in BC you need a Hunter Number, which you can get after completing the Conservation and Outdoor Recreation Education course (see http://www.bcwf.bc.ca/programs/core/index.html). You then need a hunting license and a species tag for each big game animal you intend to hunt. More details on licensing are at http://www.env.gov.bc.ca/fw/wildlife/hunting/regulations/. Some game animals are controlled though Limited Entry Hunting (http://www.env.gov.bc.ca/fw/wildlife/hunting/resident/leh.html), while non-resident hunters must be accompanied by a licensed guide. Licenses can be picked up at many sporting good stores, as well as Service BC locations.

Because Wildlife Management Units (WMU) 2-4 and portions of 2-8 overlap with the most heavily populated area in the province, hunters in these areas need a Fraser Valley Special Area Hunting License in addition to the other hunting licenses. Further, hunters need to carry at least $1,000,000 in Public Liability and Property Damage Insurance.

Big and Small Game Species

Bighorn Sheep

Bighorn rams have large, spiral horns and are generally brown or grayish brown in colour, with lighter undersides and rump. They have soft hooves with hard outer rims that give them good footing in mountainous terrain. They have incredible eyesight and are able to detect movement over a kilometre away. This, coupled with their mountainous habitat, makes them some of the most difficult and most challenging species to hunt. Many people who hunt bighorn come away disappointed.

Bighorns are the largest wild sheep in North America, with rams weighing up to 135 kg (300 lbs). Ewes average around 70 kg (150 lbs). They spend their summer high in the alpine, while in winter they migrate to south facing slopes where snow cover is minimal. They are often found around mineral or salt licks.

California Bighorn are found on the eastern facing slopes of the Coast Range and into the interior. There is Limited Entry Hunting in all the Thompson (Region 3) Management Units found in this book, but there are no openings in the Lower Mainland Region.

Black Bear

Black bears are the most common predator in the Lower Mainland and can be found in good numbers in almost any habitat. Adult male bears weigh up to 300 kg (660 lbs) and females about 200 kg (440 lbs). They get to that size by eating almost anything, from grass, roots and berries to freshly killed meat and rotting fish.

"Black" is the name, and black is the most common colour, but this animal's pelage can vary from jet black through various shades of red and brown to bluish or pure white. There are both spring and fall hunting seasons for bear. In spring, the right habitat is just about anywhere where there is new green growth. Logged openings, recent wildfires and utility corridors are good areas to start. The south facing slopes of major river valleys are a prime choice to hunt bear in the early season. By fall, bears are working hard to fatten up for winter and can be found anywhere where there is an abundance of food. Good places to start a fall bear hunt are wild berry patches or along streams, particularly those with spawning salmon.

Bobcat

Bobcats are tawny coloured (grayer in winter) with indistinct black spotting. They have short stubby tails with black tips and white undersides, and large pointed ears with telltale black tufts at the tips. The male cats average between 9 and 14 kg (20-30 lbs), with females weighing about two thirds as much. Bobcats prefer warmer, drier climates and generally stick to the southern parts of BC, with the Lower Mainland home to about 18 percent of the province's bobcat population. They prefer scrubby country and not-too-dense forests for hunting. A bobcat track loosely resembles that of a coyote or dog, and is about twice the size of a housecat's.

Bobcats are often hunted in the winter when their tracks are easily visible. A good strategy is to head out early in the morning, after a plow, and look for fresh tracks crossing the road. A bobcat's feeding range can vary between the size of a city block (when there are plenty of small rodents) to up to 350 km² (220 mi²) when prey is larger and more spread out.

Cougar

This largest member of the cat family in North America is tawny coloured with lighter coloured hair under the chin, throat and belly. An adult male cougar is about the same size as an adult human although an adult female is usually less than 40 kg (90 lbs). Both sexes have a muscular tail, about as thick as a man's wrist and can be almost as long as the rest of the body.

Cougars kill and eat a wide range of prey, but deer are preferred, and their distribution and migration generally follows that of deer. Cougar hunters mainly use trained dogs to chase and tree the big cats. Pursuit only, a kind of "catch and release" hunting, is popular with some hunters. The hunting season is November to March, but January has the most reliable conditions with fresh, soft snow and the most productive hunting.

Deer

Deer in BC are either white-tailed or black-tailed. Black-tailed deer are further divided into mule deer and coastal (or Columbian) black-tails. The most common in Southwestern BC is the Columbian black-tail. These deer inhabit a thin strip of land and are generally not found more than 200 km (120 mi) inland, preferring to inhabit the dense rainforest found nearer the ocean.

Columbian black-tail deer are relatively small, with a good-sized buck weighing a mere 90 km (200 lbs) and some females as small as 40 kg (90 lbs). But what they lack in size, they make up in cunning – these deer are very elusive. They have almost no rump patch, but have a wide, black tail. When startled, they run with a stiff legged bounce like a mule deer.

Mule deer are not found near the coast, but live farther inland. Mule deer bucks weigh about 100 kg (220 lbs) with does about 2/3 that weight. Both sexes have a grey/brown coat and oversized ears (hence the name) and a light cream coloured rump patch with a narrow, black tipped tail. Mule deer antlers are bifurcated, that is, continuously branched into two as they grow.

Mule deer prefer generally open areas. Hunters should be constantly glassing the hillsides with binoculars when hunting mule deer. Autumn snow forces these animals to lower elevation where they concentrate on south facing slopes for winter. Young mule deer can be brazen regarding humans but big mulie bucks can be shy, although even they become less cautious in the rut (during mid-November).

> *When hunting deer, be extra cautious of noise. Take frequent stops while walking through the bush (up to five minutes at a time), and consider walking in short fast bursts through noisy areas, such as a patch of dry leaves, to imitate the noise of small animals.*

Elk

Elk are one of the most distinguishable members of the deer family, especially the bulls, with their large, sweeping antlers and dark brown heads. Elk are also known as wapiti and are smaller only than moose within the deer family, with bulls weighing up to 450 kg (1,000 lbs) and cows to 270 kg (600 lbs). Bulls challenge each other for possession of cows and the elk is the only member of the deer family in BC that collects a harem.

Elk are found in areas of woodland mixed with grassland. They forage on forbs and grasses in the summer and aspen bark and twigs in the winter.

In the Lower Mainland, the only species of Elk found are Roosevelt Elk, which are slightly larger than Rocky Mountain elk found farther east. Also, the antlers of bulls sometimes terminate in a crown of three or four points.

Elk were extirpated in the Lower Mainland area, but small populations have been re-established on the Sunshine Coast and in the Pitt River and Indian River drainages. While these populations are still small, there is a Limited Entry Hunt on the Sunshine Coast. In the next few years, LEHs may open elsewhere in Region 2, as the herds introduced in the Pitt and Indian drainages are doing quite well.

Moose

Moose are the largest member of the deer family and the largest ungulate in North America. They have long legs, a large, drooping snout and a flap of skin in the shape of a bell under their throats. The have broad hooves and are usually dark brown to black. Male Moose have large, broad antlers that are extremely prized among hunters. A full sized bull moose can stand 2.75 m (9.25 ft) tall.

Moose are usually found in wooded areas next to swamps, lakeshores and streams. They feed on leaves, grass and water plants in the summer. During the winter, moose browse on aspen bark and around the edges of dense forests where there is less snow. In spite of their large size, moose can move through the underbrush quickly and quietly. Moose cannot see very well, but they have an acute sense of smell and hearing.

Moose are not usually found in the thick coastal forests of southern BC. Their main range is the northern interior and the farther northeast you travel, the more likely you are to find moose. There are no openings for moose in the Lower Mainland Region, but there are openings in all the Thompson (Region 3) WMUs.

Mountain Goat

One of most unique mammals in North America, with no close genetic relatives, the mountain goat is known for its sure-footedness and ability to navigate some of the country's steepest terrain. However, while the steep cliffs protect the goats from predators, it makes them extremely vulnerable to poaching and over hunting. Billies can weigh up to 120 km (260 lbs) while nannies average about half that. Other than size, it can be difficult to tell the two apart.

Goats are found in limited numbers in the Coast Mountains, but become more common in the mountains as you head east. There is an extremely Limited Entry Hunt, for hunting mountain goat on Mount Meager (WMU 2–11), as well as more limited alternatives in Regions 3 & 8.

Goats do not migrate more than a few kilometres, usually just moving from the valleys to the alpine as winter turns to spring, then summer. They have low reproductive rates and, since mortality rates can be as high as 50% in the first two years of a goat's life, they do not bounce back very quickly.

Wolves and Coyote

Wolves are the largest wild dogs found anywhere in the world. A full-sized male wolf can get up to 60 kg (130 lbs). Wolves are often grey with dark shading, but fur colour can range from pure black to pure white, and have large feet that help them travel over snow in wintertime.

Coyote are larger than foxes, but smaller than a wolf. An adult coyote weighs between 10 to 23 kg (22 to 50 lb). They are usually grey or reddish grey, with black markings on the back and tail, and lighter colouration underneath. The ears are long and the muzzle is slender and pointed. The bushy tail is usually carried low and close to the hind legs.

Wolves are a pack animal, traveling in groups as small as two or as large as twenty. The primary food of wolves is moose, deer, elk and caribou, but can include beaver, hare, fish and even some plant material. In areas where wolves and ranchers occupy the same territory, there is often some predation.

Coyotes are not pack animals, and usually hunt alone or in pairs, though several may gather at carcasses or other communal feeding sites. They are opportunists, feeding on carrion of livestock, especially in winter. They will also feed on chickens, cats and other small farm animals. In the wild, they feed on hare and mice as well as blueberries and other fruit.

There is a compulsory report of all wolves taken in Region 2.

Game Birds

Ducks

There are, broadly speaking, two types of ducks: dabbling and diving.

Dabbling ducks are typically found in fresh, shallow marshes and rivers. They usually feed by dabbling or tipping, rather than diving underwater, hence the name. The speculum or colored wing patch is generally iridescent and bright. Dabbling Ducks include blacks, mallards and green winged teals and are most commonly found in open wetlands and lakes.

Diving ducks get their name from their feeding habits as well, diving deep below the surface of the water to find food. They feed on fish and aquatic plants, and prefer larger lakes with a lot of underwater vegetation. Diving ducks include canvasbacks, redheads, ring-necked ducks and greater and lesser scaup.

Any ducks feeding on land will likely be a dabbling duck, as these birds are sure-footed and can walk and run well on land. Their diet is mostly vegetables and they are just as likely to be found in a farmer's field as they are in a marsh.

Geese

There are two main species of geese that are hunted in Southwestern BC: snow geese and Canada geese, although there are open seasons for brant, Ross's geese and cackling geese as well.

Canadian geese are one of the most common species of goose in the province. They can be found in agricultural areas, especially where there are lakes and wetlands nearby, particularly in the wetlands around the Fraser River.

Hunting geese in a field is similar to hunting dabbling ducks. Find an area, put out decoys, and get under cover, either with camouflage gear or with netting. Geese like to land near where other geese are feeding, so set your decoys up so that you lead the birds to where you want them. The more decoys you use, the more likely geese are to land, as they find security in numbers.

Feeding geese tend to make lots of noise, especially when they see competition approaching, so a goose call usually helps.

Grouse

Grouse are not known for their cunning, but what they lack in brains they make up for in colouring. You can nearly step on one of these birds before they take off in a chaotic explosion of feathers. Once in the air, grouse are quick, and often fly a random pattern through the forest, making them hard to hit. That's grouse hunting in a nutshell: walk through the woods until you flush a grouse and then try and shoot it down in the two second (at most) window you have.

There are three game species of grouse found in this region. Ruffed grouse have a ruff of black features about their neck and are usually about 43 cm (17 inches) long. Blue grouse are usually a slate gray colour (and not, as you might expect, blue) with a solid black tail and are about 53 cm (21 inches) long. Spruce grouse are smaller, only 38 cm (15 inches) long, and usually mottled grey, brown and black.

VCBC Management Unit Highlights

WMU 2-1 (Maps 6, 7)
This wildlife management unit's bounds are within Manning Provincial Park, which is closed to hunting.

WMU 2-2 (Maps 5, 6, 15, 16)
The Skagit Silver Hope area encompasses the drainage of the Skagit River east of Hope. Here hunters will find a mix of coastal and interior wildlife species. Near Ross Lake, for instance, hunters will find an interior type ecosystem that is more typical of the Cascade. The management unit offers fair hunting for Columbian black-tail deer and mule deer, as well as a hybrid species. The area offers good black bear hunting and fair hunting for cougar and bobcat. The region is not known for its bird hunting, but there are some grouse hunting opportunities towards the dryer eastern section of the area.

Be sure to check the BC Hunting Regulations www.env.gov.bc.ca/fw/wildlife/hunting/ regulations for updated rules and regulations regarding bag limits and season opening and closing dates.

WMU 2-3 (Maps 4, 5, 6, 15)
Encompassing the drainage of the Chilliwack River, this management unit sits on the interface between wilderness and urban areas and between the Cascade Mountains and the lowlands of the Fraser Valley. Hunters need to be aware of private land and not trespass or hunt on these lands without express permission from the landowner. Columbian black-tail deer are tough to find, but they are here. The area also offers good black bear hunting and fair hunting for cougar and bobcat. The region is not known for its bird hunting, although there are some band-tailed pigeons to be found. The northern portion of this area also abuts the Fraser River, where hunters will find some good spots to hunt waterfowl.

WMU 2-4 (Maps 1, 2, 3)
This management unit is made up of the south Fraser Valley, including the cities of Abbottsford, Surrey and Richmond. There are regulations regarding the discharge of firearms in municipal areas, so if you are planning on hunting in this region, make sure you know what the rules are. Also note that there is literally no public land save for some intertidal zones, so if you are planning on hunting, you will need landowners' permission. Here you will find the largest wintering population of waterfowl in Canada. Snow geese have increased in population and are becoming a real nuisance in some areas, feeding on crops and invading public spaces, although most of these areas are closed to hunting. There are plenty of ducks, too. Although very few upland birds exist, there are some private pheasant farms in the region. Being so close to urban development, big game populations are limited to a few deer.

WMU 2-5, 2-12 (Maps 8–11, 18–21, 28–31, 37–39)

These two management units are comprised of the watersheds that drain the Sunshine Coast. There is a fair amount of human habitation along the coastal fringes of these units and hunters need to be wary of private land issues. But there are also vast tracts of land that have no settlement, no roads and some of the most difficult access on the continent. There are relatively good populations of deer, although these are in decline right now, due to a strong population of predators, including coyote, wolves, cougars and bears. This means that there is good hunting for these species as well. Unlike management units with easier access and stronger hunting pressure, there is actually a limited opening for mountain goat. As well, the Roosevelt elk population, re-introduced in the early 1980s, is large enough to support a limited entry hunting season.

WMU 2-6, 2-7 (Maps 11, 12, 21–23, 30–33, 39, 40, 49)

Making up both the eastern and western drainages of the Squamish River, these two management units are part of the coastal ecosystem. Despite the heavy snowpack, there are a couple openings for goat, as well as good black bear and moderate deer population. Although there are a lot of waterfowl in the Squamish area, there is no hunting allowed. Hunters will be happy to note elk have moved into 2-6 from top end of 2-5 and can expect a limited entry season soon.

WMU 2-8 (Maps 1–4, 11–14, 22–24)

Containing the largest human population in the province, finding a place to hunt here is going to be the hardest part of hunting in this management unit. Much of the area is private land and the portions that aren't are generally provincial or regional parks that are closed to hunting, or watersheds that are closed to access. If you can find a place to hunt, opportunities are good. There is a large resident population of Canada geese and other waterfowl, some band-tailed pigeons and even some lager ungulates like deer. Roosevelt elk have been reintroduced into this region over the last decade and will very soon have a small open season, barring any unforeseen circumstances.

WMU 2-9, 2-10, 2-11 (Maps 13, 23, 24, 31–34, 39–42, 48–50)

These three units have good deer populations that include a mix of coastal blacktail, mule, and a hybrid of the two. For mountain goat hunters, there is a limited entry hunt on Mount Meager with a very low success rate. Coastal hunters will be surprised to see some moose here, but it is not a large enough population to support an opening. Wolves are on the increase, as are black bear, which are becoming a nuisance in places. The valley also has some wetlands and hunters will find okay hunting for Canada geese. These regions are also popular areas for cougar and bobcat hunting.

WMU 2-13, 2-14, 2-15 (Maps 28, 37, 38, 39, 46, 47, 48)

These remote management units are boat access only along the mid-Coast and are comprised of the drainages in the area that empty into Toba Inlet and Bute Inlet. And, let's be honest, nobody is going to head go through all the effort of making the trek to this area for a spot of band-tailed pigeon hunting. This is good, because populations of both upland game birds and waterfowl are thin, the latter being found in the marshes and wetlands and the head of these inlets. There is, however, some good big game hunting, including goat, deer and black bear.

WMU 2-16 (Maps 8, 10, 11, 18–20)

Made up of the Howe Sound Islands as well as some of the Northern Gulf Islands, this is a unique area to hunt deer. There are no natural predators and the deer tend to thrive here. In winter, there is a high mortality rate as there is too much competition for food. As a result, this management unit has one of the most liberal open seasons for deer. Hunters who make the trip to Texada Island have a 50-50 chance of going home with a deer, which is the best success rate in the province. However, the three ferries make getting here from Vancouver a hassle. There is no other large game and little in the way of waterfowl or upland bird hunting. Please note it is against the law to discharge a firearm on Bowen, although the island is still open to hunting.

WMU 2-17 (Maps 26, 27)

This management unit is more interior than coast and encompasses the Coquihalla drainage. The area has a lot of deer (mule deer), but heavy snowpack can have a negative impact on populations. There are also lots of black bear, and some good cougar hunting, but the limited number of backroads in this area can make access difficult. The drier interior climate offers better conditions for grouse, too.

WMU 2-18, 2-19 (Maps 4, 5, 13–15, 24–26)

These two management units are comprised of the Harrison Lake drainage, 2-18 on the east side of the lake and 2-19 on the west. This area is far enough inland to not experience the same degree of moderate weather as the west coast, although it still experiences nearly the same amount of precipitation and, as a result, the snowpack is much heavier. This makes it harder for deer to survive, a situation that hasn't been helped by logging in the area that has mostly decimated the deer's winter ranges. There is some human habitation and private land to worry about, but this area is mostly Crown land. The area is best known for its great black bear hunting, while there is some decent cougar hunting, too. Grouse can be found in the eastern portions of 2-18 and some waterfowl hunting along the Harrison River and around the islands in the Fraser River.

WMU 3-13 (Maps 27, 36, 45)

In this area, hunters will find a wide diversity of habitats, from low elevation grasslands through dry forest to alpine. Mule deer, cougar and black bear are abundant. This is a good choice for upland birds, including grouse and ptarmigan, but sharp-tailed grouse are closed for conservation reasons.

WMU 3-14, 3-15 (Maps 16, 24–27, 34–36)

These management units straddle the Fraser River and consist of steep, rugged habitats, from low elevation dry sage-steppe to coastal transition forests and alpine. Access is somewhat limited west of the Fraser. Black bear are abundant and mule deer are common. Elk are present and increasing, but not yet open for hunting.

WMU 3-16 (Maps 34–36, 42–44, 52, 53)

Steep, rocky, forested slopes and bare rocky peaks characterize this area. The terrain and provincial parks limit access, but hunters can find good numbers of mule deer, and some of the best opportunities for mountain goat are in this region.

WMU 3-17 (Maps 36, 44, 45, 53, 54)

This management unit holds a diversity of dry forest types, from low elevation grassland to scattered alpine. This is a good choice for bighorn sheep hunters, because both sub-species are present, while mule deer and cougar are also plentiful. This area also provides a high harvest of black bear.

WMU 3-30 (Map 54)

This management unit includes the dry slopes of the South Thompson and Fraser and the gently rolling forested slopes of the Bonaparte Plateau. Mule deer and moose are abundant, while shot gunners will find good to excellent numbers of virtually every possible game bird. Both upland birds and waterfowl provide good sport.

WMU 3-32, 3-33 (Maps 41–43, 48–53)

These management units consist of the steep forested slopes of the coastal/interior transition. The rugged country rewards experienced hunters with excellent mule deer hunting. Mountain goat and bighorn sheep are also taken through limited entry. These areas are among the best choices in the region for blue grouse and ptarmigan hunting.

WMU 5-4, 5-5 (Maps 48, 49)

The southern tips of these two management units are found on these maps, but very few people are willing to make the trek into these remote areas. Traditionally popular for both alpine deer and California Bighorn sheep, recent populations have been down and the regulations have changed accordingly. There are some moose, mule deer and grouse in the lower valleys, which are a little more popular north of these maps.

WMU 8-04 (Map 7)

With forests of lodgepole pine, Douglas fir and spruce, this area has seen extensive logging and is laced with logging roads. You can find mule deer, moose, black bear, cougar and occasionally elk in the logged openings. The mix of old and young forest also favours ruffed and blue grouse.

WMU 8-05 (Maps 6, 7, 16, 17)

Capturing the pine and spruce forests, there is plenty of logging road access for hunters to pursue mule deer, moose, black bear, cougar, elk and forest grouse. This is a productive area but sees high hunting pressure.

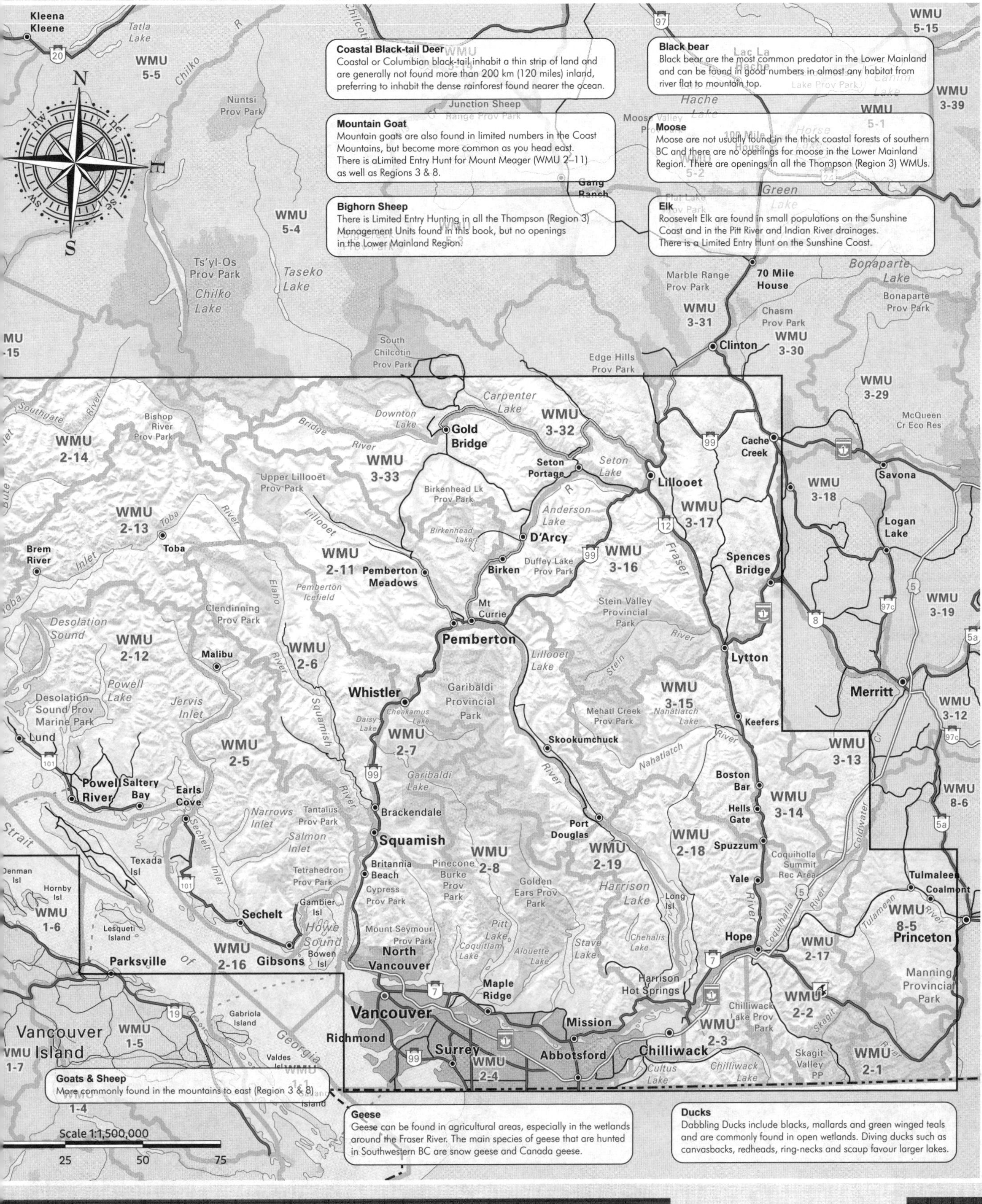

Coastal Black-tail Deer
Coastal or Columbian black-tail inhabit a thin strip of land and are generally not found more than 200 km (120 miles) inland, preferring to inhabit the dense rainforest found nearer the ocean.

Mountain Goat
Mountain goats are also found in limited numbers in the Coast Mountains, but become more common as you head east. There is a Limited Entry Hunt for Mount Meager (WMU 2–11) as well as Regions 3 & 8.

Bighorn Sheep
There is Limited Entry Hunting in all the Thompson (Region 3) Management Units found in this book, but no openings in the Lower Mainland Region.

Black bear
Black bear are the most common predator in the Lower Mainland and can be found in good numbers in almost any habitat from river flat to mountain top.

Moose
Moose are not usually found in the thick coastal forests of southern BC and there are no openings for moose in the Lower Mainland Region. There are openings in all the Thompson (Region 3) WMUs.

Elk
Roosevelt Elk are found in small populations on the Sunshine Coast and in the Pitt River and Indian River drainages. There is a Limited Entry Hunt on the Sunshine Coast.

Goats & Sheep
More commonly found in the mountains to east (Region 3 & 8)

Scale 1:1,500,000

25   50   75

Geese
Geese can be found in agricultural areas, especially in the wetlands around the Fraser River. The main species of geese that are hunted in Southwestern BC are snow geese and Canada geese.

Ducks
Dabbling Ducks include blacks, mallards and green winged teals and are commonly found in open wetlands. Diving ducks such as canvasbacks, redheads, ring-necks and scaup favour larger lakes.

Map labels: Kleena Kleene, Tatla Lake, WMU 5-5, WMU 5-15, Lac La Hache Lake Prov Park, WMU 3-39, Nuntsi Prov Park, Junction Sheep Range Prov Park, WMU 5-1, WMU 5-2, 100 Mile House, Horse Lake, Green Lake, Bonaparte Lake, WMU 5-4, Ts'yl-Os Prov Park, Taseko Lake, Chilko Lake, Gang Ranch, Flat Lake Prov Park, Bonaparte Prov Park, WMU -15, South Chilcotin Prov Park, Marble Range Prov Park, 70 Mile House, WMU 3-31, Chasm Prov Park, Edge Hills Prov Park, Clinton, WMU 3-30, WMU 3-29, McQueen Cr Eco Res, WMU 2-14, Bishop River Prov Park, Downton Lake, Carpenter Lake, Gold Bridge, WMU 3-32, Seton Lake, Cache Creek, Savona, WMU 3-33, Seton Portage, Lillooet, WMU 3-18, Logan Lake, Upper Lilloet Prov Park, Birkenhead Lk Prov Park, Anderson Lake, WMU 3-17, Spences Bridge, WMU 2-13, Toba, D'Arcy, Duffey Lake Prov Park, WMU 3-16, WMU 3-19, Brem River, WMU 2-11, Pemberton Meadows, Birken, Mt Currie, Stein Valley Provincial Park, Lytton, WMU 3-15, Merritt, Desolation Sound, WMU 2-12, Malibu, Clendinning Prov Park, Pemberton Icefield, WMU 2-6, Pemberton, Lillooet Lake, Mehatl Creek Prov Park, Nahatlatch Lake, Keefers, WMU 3-13, WMU 3-12, Powell Lake, Jervis Inlet, Whistler, Garibaldi Provincial Park, Lytton, Boston Bar, WMU 3-14, WMU 8-6, Desolation Sound Prov Marine Park, Lund, WMU 2-5, Daisy Lake, WMU 2-7, Skookumchuck, Hells Gate, Spuzzum, WMU 2-18, Coquihalla Summit Rec Area, Powell River, Saltery Bay, Earls Cove, Narrows Inlet, Tantalus Prov Park, Brackendale, Garibaldi Lake, Port Douglas, Harrison Lake, Yale, Tulmaleen, Coalmont, Texada Isl, Salmon Inlet, Squamish, Sechelt Inlet, WMU 2-8, Golden Ears Prov Park, WMU 2-19, Long Isl, WMU 8-5, Princeton, Denman Isl, Hornby Isl, WMU 1-6, Lasqueti Island, Sechelt, Gambier Isl, Tetrahedron Prov Park, Britannia Beach, Cypress Prov Park, Pinecone Burke Prov Park, Chehalis Lake, Hope, Manning Provincial Park, Parksville, WMU 2-16, Gibsons, Howe Sound, Bowen Isl, Mount Seymour Prov Park, North Vancouver, Pitt Lake, Coquitlam Lake, Alouette Lake, Stave Lake, Harrison Hot Springs, WMU 2-17, WMU 2-2, Vancouver Island, WMU 1-5, Gabriola Island, Georgia, Maple Ridge, Mission, Chilliwack, Chilliwack Lake Prov Park, Skagit Valley PP, WMU 1-7, Richmond, Surrey, WMU 2-4, Abbotsford, WMU 2-3, Cultus Lake, Chilliwack Lake, WMU 2-1, WMU 1-4

PADDLING ADVENTURES

From the rush of whitewater rafting and kayaking to the serenity of sea kayak touring, to just plain cruising around on a lake in a canoe, Southwestern BC provides an endless array of water-based recreational fun. In fact, you will find many of these activities within easy driving distance of Greater Vancouver.

Of course, accessibility often means many other people will be out enjoying themselves. It is true that some of these routes are often busy, but it is not as bad as you might expect. Besides, if you truly want to get away from the crowds, there are places covered by this mapbook where few people ever go. If you want to be alone with your paddle, you only need to travel a little further afield.

Flatwater or Lake Paddling enthusiasts have literally hundreds of lakes and sloughs to choose from in the area. We have selected a good sampling of the small lakes and ponds as well as canoe routes and multi-day destinations. The standout destination is the Powell Forest Canoe Route, but there are a few other fantastic circuit routes on the Sunshine Coast that involve lake and ocean travel. The Parks and Recreation Sites section of this book highlights many of the other smaller lakes that are more easily accessed.

Ocean Paddling along the southwestern coast of the mainland is a mixed blessing. Vancouver Island absorbs the brunt of the wind and waves, and while it certainly can get stormy, it is nothing like on the wild west coast. However, there are other issues. The narrow channels between islands can create strong rip tides, creating whirlpools and other hazards to navigate. And the large population in the Lower Mainland means that there is lots of activity in the area, especially in Burrard Inlet.

River paddlers can pick and choose from a mix of easy floats to hardcore whitewater descents. The variety is fantastic. Serious whitewater paddlers will find the rivers in top form during winter and spring. By the time summer rolls around, many of the smaller volume rivers have lost their spunk.

Below we have listed a few of the best-known areas for all three types of paddling opportunities. Please note that the descriptions given in this book are limited and may not contain enough detail to navigate certain routes safely, especially rivers with higher ratings. Check current conditions with local canoeists/kayakers or local outdoor stores before heading out. It is also essential to scout rivers, since conditions can change daily.

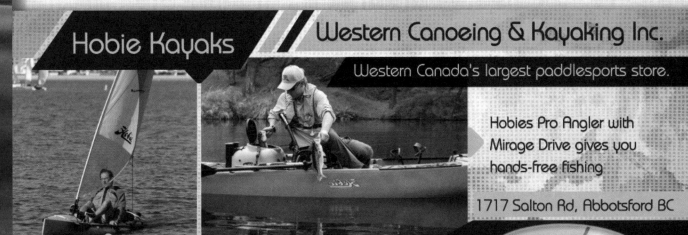

Lake Paddling

Alice Lake (Map 22/D5)
Alice Lake is a small lake north of Squamish and the namesake of Alice Lake Provincial Park. This is a popular vacation spot for families. Because there are no motorized boats permitted and there are rentals available, the lake is a haven for canoeists. Nearby Stump Lake can also be paddled after a portage from the campground.

Alouette Lake (Map 3/A1–13/C6)
A fjord-like lake that runs 17 km (10.5 mi) into the Coast Mountains, Alouette Lake is an extremely popular cruising lake located in Golden Ears Provincial Park. There are a number of destinations to aim for from the boat launch and rental area near the south end of the lake: Campers Beach (4.5 km away), Moyer Creek Campground (9 km away) and the Narrows at 10.5 km. All these are found on the western shore. Gold Creek offers an interesting side trip and is located just past the second vehicle campsite. This lake can be very busy with powerboats during the warmer months.

Birkenhead Lake (Map 42/D3)
Nestled in the mountains north of Pemberton, Birkenhead Lake is a great place to paddle. There is a nice wilderness campsite at the mouth of Sockeye Creek, as well as good fishing. The lake is open to powerboats and can be windy, especially in the afternoon.

Buntzen Lake (Map 12/A7)
It is 9 km (5 mi) around Buntzen Lake, making this a nice afternoon canoe trip. The long, narrow lake offers the illusion of paddling on the ocean, as mountains to the east and west surround it. If you ever do run into trouble, you can put to shore almost anywhere and walk back to your car along the trail that circumnavigates the lake. With a powerboat restriction in place, Buntzen Lake is a peaceful place to ply the paddle.

Burnaby Lake (Map 1/G2)
A return trip from the Still Creek Footbridge at the west end to Cariboo Dam at the east end is 11 km (6.8 mi). This urban lake provides a recluse for a wide variety of wildlife including beavers, muskrats, coyotes, geese, ducks, herons and ospreys.

Chehalis Lake (Map 14/B5)
At 10 km (6 mi) in length, Chehalis Lake is the smallest of the long, narrow lakes that run along the North Shore/Fraser Valley (a series that includes Harrison, Stave, Alouette and Pitt Lakes). The large landslide in 2007 has created a lot of debris on the lake and the three recreation sites were closed making access more difficult. Paddlers should also be wary of sudden winds, the funnelling effect of steep shores and the lack of landing spots. Although the old recreation sites have been abandoned by the province, they are still being used. A new access trail has been created and is accessed via logging roads. Access to the north end of the lake is via the Harrison Lake West Forest Service Road, cutting over the Chehalis-Mystery Creek FSR.

Chilliwack Lake (Map 5/F6)
A big mountain lake, located near the BC/Washington State border at the end the scenic Chilliwack Lake Road. Chilliwack Lake is deep, cold and often windy, but it is fairly remote and quite scenic. The wilderness feel makes this a popular destination with canoeists, most of who are prepared to spend more than a day here. The lake is recommended for experienced paddlers only and they are advised to stay clear of the outflow of Chilliwack Lake as dangerous currents exist both here and for several kilometres downstream.

Green Lake (Map 32/G4)
The biggest of the lakes to be found in Whistler at 6.4 km (4 mi) in length. Highway 99 follows the northwest shores of the lake on its way to Pemberton. There is a boat launch (powerboats are allowed) and some great views of Blackcomb and Whistler Mountains.

Harrison Lake (Maps 4, 14, 24, 25)
Harrison Lake is a big, big lake, at 60 km (37 mi) long and 9 km (5.6 mi) wide in places, with depths up to 279 metres (915 ft). It's not a lake to be taken lightly, especially by canoeists. Still, it is a lovely lake and as long as you paddle in groups, stay close to shore and keep an eye on the weather, you shouldn't have any problems.

Haslam Lake (Map 19/A3–B1)
A fair sized lake, Haslam Lake is much less paddled than the lakes of the Powell Forest Canoe Route that surround it. This is not necessarily a bad thing, especially if you are looking to do something different. If you do not mind carrying a canoe, you can do a mini-circuit. There is a short portage from Haslam to the tiny Giavanno Lake and from there, a rather long portage down to Powell Lake.

Hatzic Lake (Map 3/E4)
Hatzic Lake is a doughnut-shaped lake with an island in the middle. It does not seem like a big lake, but you will travel 9.5 km (5.9 mi) around the outer shore or 5 km around the island. If that's not enough paddling, you can head into Hatzic Slough (at the northern end of the lake) or into nearby Chilqua Slough, both of which attach to the lake.

Hayward Lake (Map 3/C3)
Although Hayward Lake is only 4.3 km long and 1 km wide, you will cover more than 12 km (7.5 mi) if you paddle along the shoreline. This is a lake with lots of nooks and coves to explore. Be warned that the dams at both ends of the lake are off limits.

Inland [Loon] Lake (Map 18/G2)
A popular paddling lake, there are several boat/trail access campsites. The Anthony Island site is by far the most beautiful of the bunch and the most popular with paddlers.

Kawkawa Lake (Map 15/F6)
Located 5 km east of Hope, Kawkawa Lake gives the angler paddler an opportunity to catch both rainbow trout and kokanee. Although a heavily used lake, solitude can be found in the cove near the southeast side or in the northwest bay of the lake. There are some private homes spotted around the lake, but most of the shoreline is wooded and free of civilization.

> As a general rule, big mountain lakes tend to attract wild weather patterns and wind, which funnels down through the narrow valleys. Although you can expect wind at any time, it is often calmer in the morning. Always stay close to shore.

Lightning Lakes (Map 7/C6)
A chain of four lakes (Thunder, Strike, Flask and Lightning Lakes) are threaded together by Lightning Creek. Only the last three, Strike, Flask and Lightning, are reasonably canoeable. There is a 15 minute portage between Lightning and Flask lakes and a 30 minute portage between Flask and Strike Lakes.

Nahatlatch Lakes (Map 25/G1–36/A7)
The most common paddlers out on Nahatlatch Lake are rafters, however, there's nothing to say that canoes or kayaks can't explore the long narrow lake as well. There are three campsites on the lake and two more on Hannah Lake, which is a short stretch of Grade II/III whitewater away. If you decide to head down the river, plan your take-out at the end of Francis Lake. It is not advised to canoe below this point.

Pender Harbour Canoe Route (Map 9/A1)
While Pender Harbour is a popular destination for sea kayakers, some (mostly canoeists) choose to do a 13 km (8 mi) circuit that includes three portages. The portages are: 200 metres (655 ft) from Agamemnon Channel to Sakinaw Lake (please ask for permission to cross the Indian Reserve), 800 metres (2,625 ft) between Sakinaw Lake and Mixal Lake and 700 metres (2,300 ft) from Garden Bay Lake to Pender Harbour. It is also possible to tag the Mixal Lake/Garden Bay leg of this route to the Ruby Lake Circuit (see below).

Pitt Lake (Map 12/F7–E3)
Pitt Lake is the second largest lake in the region, behind Harrison Lake. The end of the Pitt Valley opens up to the Fraser Valley and all the way to the ocean, so the lake can get pretty windy, especially in the afternoon. It is

a couple kilometres longer up the eastern shore (30 km/19 mi in total), but it has more places that a canoe/kayak can pull into if the wind blows up. There are a few wilderness campsites on the lake and a number of bird watching towers along the dikes. Zealous paddlers have been known to bring along bikes to cycle the 15 additional km (9 mi) to the beautiful Pitt River Hot Springs. Rentals are available.

Powell Forest Canoe Route (Maps 18, 19, 28, 29)
Easily one of the best canoe circuits in the province, the Powell Forest Canoe Route can be done in as few as three days, but five days are recommended. Most take up to a week or more to paddle the 57 km (35 mi) route. Although 10.7 km (6.6 mi) of the route is spent carrying your canoe, the portages are clear and comfortable with canoe rests at four to five minute intervals. The 2.4 km (1.5 mi) Windsor Lake to Goat Lake portage descends over 100 metres (330 ft), which can be quite a challenge packing a canoe. This is why most travel this route counter clockwise. This route features great canoeing and some sweet spots to camp. Lois Lake and Powell Lake are both big and can be very windy. It's best to travel these lakes early in the morning. For folks who do not want to canoe the entire circuit, it is possible to double back on your route from Dodd Lake, via the tiny Beaver and Little Horseshoe Lakes.

Ruby Lake Canoe Circuit (Map 9/A1–20/B6)
This is a 31 km (19 mi) circuit route that starts and ends at Earls Cove or at Dan Hosch Park at the south end of Ruby Lake. Expect to take two or three days to finish the route. Starting in Ruby Lake, paddle to the south end, where there is a rustic 750 metre (2,460 ft) portage to Sakinaw Lake. Between Sakinaw Lake and the Agamemnon Channel is a 200 metre (655 ft) portage that crosses Sechelt Indian Band land. Please ask for permission to cross before you set out. Dangers en route include high winds on Sakinaw Lake and strong tidal currents out in the channel. It is best to travel with the tide so check the tide charts. Near the south end of Sakinaw Lake you may see Indian pictographs painted on the rocks. When you get back to Earls Cove, you are only about a kilometre from the starting point. Smart people will have left their car at the cove.

Sakinaw Lake (Map 9/A1–20/B7)
A long, narrow lake, Sakinaw is a popular getaway from Vancouver for a lot of people, many who own cabins on or around the lake. There is no formal camping on the lake, which is part of two canoe circuit routes described above.

Sasamat Lake (Map 2/A1)
Sasamat is an extremely popular lake in the summer and parking can be a challenge. Wiley canoeists have been known to find other places along Bedwell Bay Road to launch from. It's a small lake, which means two things. The first is that it is usually unaffected by wind. The second is that it is one of the warmest lakes in the Lower Mainland. Because of its size, it's great for beginners and kids and the warm water makes a great spot to practice bracing and barrel rolls.

Stave Lake (Map 3/E2–13/E5)
The third-largest lake in the area, you would travel over 70 km (43 mi) circumnavigating the whole lake. The lake does not see much boat traffic but the wind can still kick up without warning. The southern arm of Stave Lake was formed in a very shallow valley and there are numerous stumps, remnants of the heavy logging prior to the flooding of the valley. If you wish to avoid the stumps, follow the red and green channel markers. If you are looking for quiet, avoid the open area on the west side of the lake about 7.5 km from the south. This is a popular off-road enthusiast area on weekends and can be quite loud. The access to this area is from the Davis Lake Road and suitable for four-wheel drive vehicles only. The south end, accessed from Dewdney Truck Road, offers easier access.

Widgeon Slough (Map 12/E7)
This is one of the most popular places for canoeists in the Lower Mainland. It is a spectacular trip from the open floodplains of the Upper Fraser Valley into a mountain valley, with Burke Mountain towering on your left hand side. The scenery is phenomenal, the wildlife plentiful (part of the slough is one of only five National Wildlife Areas in the country), the canoeing easy and the options of exploring the other channels and nearby trails are endless. Crossing the narrow channel from Grant Narrows Park past Siwash Island can be difficult when it is windy. From Grant Narrows to the Widgeon Creek Campground is 4.5 km (2.8 mi).

River Paddling

Alouette River (Map 2/D2–3/A1)
The Alouette River (or South Alouette River) flows 23 km (14 mi) from the BC Hydro Dam on Alouette Lake to its confluence with the Pitt River. While the upper reaches provide some whitewater, it is also very shallow and all but impassable. On the other hand, the lower section is a perfect family style (Grade 1) paddle. Some folks put-in at the 206 Street Bridge, but it is better to put-in 2.5 km below, at the Neaves Road Bridge. Constrained by dykes, the paddling is easy in either direction. For people looking to do an out-and-back trip, it is recommended that they start at the Harris Road Bridge and paddle the 5 km upstream to the Neaves Road Bridge before paddling back down with the slight current. The last stretch of river is 1.6 km from the Harris Road Bridge to the plodding Pitt River.

Ashlu Creek (Map 21/E1–G2)
Located northwest of Squamish, Ashlu Creek travels east to meet the Squamish River. There are three main sections, the Mine Run, Box Canyon and the Bottom Mile. The Mine Run received its name because, yes, there is an abandoned mine at the put-in point. The river here is a Class IV-V at medium levels and features bedrock rapids and many big holes. The best times to run this section are July through early September. The Box Canyon is a Class V run with clean bedrock in a deep box canyon. The river here is dammed so the only real times to run this section are during releases in May, August and September. The Bottom Mile is a Class V run that offers steep boulder piles with difficult but good kayaking. This section can be run whenever water spills over the dam.

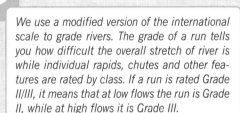

> We use a modified version of the international scale to grade rivers. The grade of a run tells you how difficult the overall stretch of river is while individual rapids, chutes and other features are rated by class. If a run is rated Grade II/III, it means that at low flows the run is Grade II, while at high flows it is Grade III.

Big Silver Creek (Map 14/F2)
An easy river with a couple Class II features, Big Silver Creek is a great place for beginners. Access to the put-in is west from the junction of the Harrison East/Clear Creek roads, along a difficult but short (ten minute) trail. The take-out is just south of the Silver River Logging Camp on Harrison Lake; watch for a small road leading down to the lake off the Harrison East Forest Road. The best time to run this whitewater is from May through July as it is too high during snowmelt and to low later in the season.

Birkenhead River (Map 42/D7–33/D1)
From the put-in where the D'Arcy Road crosses the river north of the Owl Creek Recreation Site, to the take-out north of Mount Currie, this is a 5 km (3 mi) Grade III+ romp along the turquoise waters of the Birkenhead. The river is quite shallow and moves quickly through almost continuous rapids. By late July, the water volume has fallen significantly and it can be a fairly bumpy ride through even shallower water.

Callaghan Creek (Map 32/C5–D6)
Considered one of the classic Whistler runs, it features clean waterfalls, bedrock and boulder gardens. Access is off Highway 99, while the take-out is on the short Daisy Lake Forest Service Road on the Cheakamus River. The river can be run from mid-May through August, but levels change often and if you are unsure, consult a local before attempting the trip. The toughest part of the run is in the first 500 metres as there is a big ledge with a nasty hole. Run as far to the right as possible and if you can't, portaging is recommended. Boulder rapids lead into the waterfalls, a 4 metre (12–15 ft) drop followed by a bigger 6.5 metre (20–25 ft) falls shortly after, then back to boulder rapids, with a few big ones, until the end.

Capilano River (Map 1/C1–11/C7)

The Capilano is one of the most popular rivers in the entire province. Partly due to the location and partly due to the fact that it doesn't freeze in winter. The Cap is a dam controlled drop-and-pool river that flows through North Vancouver in a surprisingly wild valley. At high water levels, the Capilano is rated up to Grade V and sometimes (at very high water levels), unrunnable. At low to medium water, it is a Grade III run. From the fish hatchery just below Cleveland Dam to Ambleside Park, it is 5.6 km (3.5 mi), but there are a number of other take-out points, including Park Royal Mall and Klahanie Park. Watch for people fishing from the riverbanks.

Cayoosh Creek (Map 43/G3–44/A1)

Like most small volume rivers, the difficulty of the Cayoosh changes tremendously with the water – from a Grade III run up to Grade IV at higher water levels. The best time to run this river is July through August. The Cayoosh runs alongside the Duffey Lake Road from Cayoosh Pass to the small town of Lillooet. The most common section for paddlers to run is a 5.8 km (3.6 mi) section between Boulder and Copper Creek. There are two put-ins: one about 2 km south of Boulder Creek and the other about 1 km south of the Cottonwood Recreation Site. The take-out is found at a logging road bridge just before Copper Creek.

Cheakamus River: Upper (Map 32/E6)

This glacier-fed river has many possible put-ins and take-outs and is never far from a road, making this a popular river. There are three main runs, getting progressively easier as you move towards its confluence with the Squamish. The most difficult section is from the Cheakamus West Forest Service Road to the Cheakamus Lake Road Bridge. This is a fast, technical 1.5 km section of river that is popular with Whistler boaters (experts paddle in playboats as there are rodeo holes all over the place). The river is rated Grade IV, with some Class V features at high water levels and there is a more difficult run upstream.

Cheakamus River: Middle (Map 22/C2)

An easier run is from the Highway 99 Bridge south of Daisy Lake to the Highway 99 salt sheds. This is a 4 km (2.5 mi) section of Grade III/III+ whitewater, with a Class IV drop near the mid-point of the run. Despite the fact that this section is below the Daisy Lake Dam, it still acts like a wild river; there is so much water coming down during spring run-off that the gates are usually kept wide open. Please note that the canyon stretch below Daisy Lake is not navigable.

Cheakamus River: Lower (Map 22/C3–C4)

Even easier is the section from the end of Paradise Valley Road to the North Vancouver Outdoor Centre. This Grade II/III route that runs 12 km (7.5 mi) through the forests north of Squamish. There are a number of alternate take-out (or put-in) spots along the way, or you can continue onto the Squamish River. At higher water more of the run is Grade III, making this river appropriate for intermediate kayakers and experienced open boaters. There are plenty of play spots including a great surfing hole right at the put-in and an exciting drop at Culliton Creek. As with all rivers in this region, watch for logjams and sweepers.

Chehalis River (Map 14/C7–4/D2)

The put-in for this Grade III+ river is at about 1.7 km past the Statlu Creek Bridge. More advanced paddlers can put-in at the Statlu Creek Bridge and run Statlu Creek down to the Chehalis (expect Class IV+ boulder gardens). The Chehalis has lively and almost continual drops with rodeo holes and surfing waves. When you have a chance to look around, you will notice that the scenery is pretty spectacular, too. Due to challenging canyons and few places to escape, this river is best left to experienced kayakers.

Chilliwack River: Upper (Map 5/C5–5/A6)

The Chilliwack River Valley offers good fishing, abundant camping sites, easy access and phenomenal scenery. This upper section of the Chilliwack is 9 km (5.6 mi) of steep, non-stop whitewater action. Rated Grade IV at higher water, with some even more difficult features, expect to take about four hours to complete the stretch from Foley Creek Forest Service Road to west of Slesse Creek.

Chilliwack River: Middle (Map 5/A6–4/E6)

The 12 km (7.5 mi) middle stretch of river has Grade III water (with a Class IV drop) and a kilometre stretch that features some challenging whitewater, including the Tamihi, Campground and Sawmill Rapids. Many people choose to portage the rapids, especially in high water, but for expert paddlers, this section is one of the highlights of the four hour plus trip between Slesse Creek Bridge and Chilliwack River Provincial Park.

Chilliwack River: Lower (Map 4/E6–4/C6)

By the time it reaches Vedder Crossing, the Chilliwack has basically run out of steam. From Chilliwack River Provincial Park to Vedder Crossing, this is a 6.5 km (4 mi) run along Grade II waters. A great testing ground for novices or as a warm up before tackling some of the bigger water upstream, the river is medium flow, with lots of braiding and gravel bars. It is runnable from spring to fall. Allow about two hours to run it. Longer if you wish to continue on the Vedder River (see below).

Cogburn Creek (Map 14/G3)

From the Harrison East Forest Service Road Bridge to the Bear Creek Logging Camp, it is a short but wild 3 km (1.9 mi). Rated Grade III/IV with lots of technical manoeuvring, during spring runoff it is almost continual whitewater from the put-in until you hit Harrison Lake. It is a short paddle south on the lake to the camp.

Coldwater River (Map 27/F5–east of maps)

The aptly named river flows beside, and occasionally under, the Coquihalla Highway for 34.5 km (21 mi) from Juliet Creek to Merritt. Access is fairly good along the winding, fast moving Grade II/II+ river with one Class IV drop after the bridge near the 18 km mark. It is possible to break this river up (common put-ins/take-outs are Larson Hill, Coldwater Interchange and Patchet Road) or to do it in one long run. The first section between Juliet Creek and Larson Hill is easy (Grade I) and is often skipped by advanced kayakers. Watch for sweepers.

Coquitlam River (Map 2/C1)

The Coquitlam is more of a winter run than a summer run, when the river all but disappears. It offers an 8 km (5 mi) route through Grade III water during high and medium water levels. This is a great place for intermediate paddlers to practice their skills, as there are lots of places to bail. The put-in is off of Pipeline Road, while the take-out is off Shaughnessy Street.

Dipper Creek (Map 31/E3–F4)

This run, deep in the mountains north of Squamish, features big waterfalls and mandatory Class V knowledge. This is not a trip to be taken lightly. It is very remote and in many places there is nowhere to get out of the water because of canyon walls, making portaging or walking out near impossible. Descending the whole creek takes multiple days and this trip is best done in late fall. Access is decent, with the S 400 accessing the upper reaches and the Squamish Forest Service Road running near the creek's confluence with the Squamish River. Visit www.liquidlore.com for more details.

Elaho River (Map 31/E5–G7)

This fast, silty and ice-cold river flows from the giant Elaho Glacier. The Upper Elaho is a difficult, rarely run river, while, to our knowledge, the far upper reaches of the Elaho has only been run once. Most trips on the Elaho start about 3.5 km (2 mi) upstream from its confluence with the Squamish River and finish their run after the canyon section of the Squamish. The Elaho is Grade III/IV and has some really great surfing waves at moderate water flow. This scenic stretch of river offers some great cliff jumping opportunities and is very popular with the rafting companies. The Elaho is subject to flash flooding, especially during spring rains.

Fraser River (Maps 1–5, 15, 26, 36, 44, 45, 53)

The Fraser Canyon, which begins north of Hope, is a Class IV waterbody that should only be attempted by commercial rafters, while the Fraser's lower reaches, from Hope to Vancouver, are far more placid. Although the lower section does not have any whitewater, it can still be dangerous (up to Grade III) due to the speed and volume of water. Watch out for boils and standing waves between Hope and the Highway 9 Bridge at Bridal Falls. As you get closer to the mouth, watch out for the Pitt River confluence and the commercial traffic that creates wakes often 1.5 metres (4-5 ft) in height.

Furry Creek (Map 11/B2)

This small creek has a tight flow window after rain or during the snowmelt. It features a stout series of waterfalls that are rated Class V-V+ with access found on the logging road a few hundred metres above the golf course. Because this run skirts by the golf course, you will need to keep a low profile so the town doesn't ban access to the creek in the future.

Harrison River (Map 4/D2–F1)
An easy Grade I paddle takes you from Harrison Hot Springs to the Highway 7 Bridge, just before the Harrison flows into the Fraser. This 15 km (9 mi) trip is scenic and enjoyable if it is not too windy and the best time to go is in the fall, when spawning salmon attract a large number of eagles.

Hurley River (Map 51/A4–5)
With an impressive canyon that offers a slightly different feel from the other coastal mountain rivers, this Class V run is best done late in the season (August and September). The put-in is west of the former mining town of Bralorne along the Hurley River Forest Service Road north of Pemberton. The take-out is 10 km (6 mi) downstream at Gold Bridge.

> *Most of the challenging features have portages to help less experienced paddlers negotiate the route more safely.*

Kanaka Creek (Map 2/G3–3/B3)
Kanaka Creek is a mostly slow moving river – hardly more than Grade I, with a couple really slow Grade II sections. There are a handful of places to put-in or take-out along Kanaka Creek Park or the more adventurous can head out onto the Fraser and cross to Derby Reach Park. If you don't want to shuttle, you can put-in at the Highway 7 bridge and paddle upstream for as far as you want, then return. Be careful not to venture above 112 Ave, as there are a pair of waterfalls a few hundred metres upstream.

Lillooet River: Upper (Map 40/E1–F1)
The Lillooet is a long, large, windy and cold river that starts deep in the Coast Mountains before eventually spilling into Harrison Lake. It is faster in its upper reaches. Although the river feels remote, it is paralleled by logging roads for most of its length. As an added bonus, there are a number of hot springs near the river. The section found 2.9 km past the Pebble Creek Bridge to former Meager Creek Bridge is a short (5 km/3 mi) stretch of Grade III/IV whitewater. It features lots of rock gardens and standing waves and one really nice hole to play in. Expect this section to take close to two hours, either on its own or as the start to a longer expedition down the tamer sections of the Lillooet. Note that a huge landslide in 2010 has flooded the Meager Creek/Lillooet River confluence, which will affect the run noted above as well mellowing the ride a fair bit downstream.

Lillooet River: Middle (Map 40/F1–41/F4)
After the Meager Creek confluence, the Lillooet meanders along a broad, flat floodplain with lots of braided channels. While this is a Grade II-III route, picking the right route can be tricky due to the many false channels. Downed trees are common in this river. Expect to take at least 8 hours to do this 35 km (22 mi) section of river between the Meager Creek Bridge and the bridge on the Upper Lillooet River Road.

Lillooet River: Pemberton Section (Map 41/F4–33/C1)
As the Lillooet approaches Pemberton it widens and slows down. The 23 km (14 mi) section between the bridge on the Upper Lillooet River Road to the Highway 99 bridge east of Pemberton is little more than a scenic float, which usually takes about 6 hours to complete.

Lillooet River: Lower (Map 33/G7–24/E5)
Below Little Lillooet Lake, is a 34 km (24 mi) float to the final bridge/take-out before Harrison Lake. Most of this section is Grade II, but there are some Class III features. The hot springs at St. Agnes Well are a popular and relaxing alternate take-out spot about halfway down this run. Most trippers take-out at the last bridge before Harrison Lake.

Mamquam River (22/D6)
A short, interesting Grade II/III route is found just south of Squamish. Easily accessed, the Mamquam is a great river to practice on and short enough to run two or three times in a day. From the put-in off the Mamquam Forest

Service Road (take the side road at about 3.5 km), to the Government Road Bridge (just west of Highway 99), this is a 5.8 km (3.6 mi) stretch.

Further upstream, the Middle Mamquam is accessed from the bridge crossing the river around the 12.7 km mark. The take-out is found between the 7.5 and 8 Mile sign posts at a gated road on the left. Look for the warning signs on the river and take-out river left. It is a short walk up the road to the gate.

Nahatlatch River: Hannah Lake to Francis Lake (Map 36/A7)
The Nahatlatch is a challenging river that flows through a series of canyons on its way from Hannah Lake to the Fraser River. Access is from the Nahatlatch Forest Service Road on the north bank of the river. It is popular during the summer months and is considered one of the premier whitewater rivers in North America. Mid-summer is the best time to paddle this river, when it has passed its peak flow, but has not slowed to a trickle yet. This first section from the Old Ranger Station on Hannah Lake to the west end of Francis Lake is a short warm up route. The shallow 1.5 km (0.9 mi) section is rated Grade II/III, with steady rapids.

Nahatlatch River: Middle (Map 36/A7–C7)
The 8 km (5 mi) section of Grade III whitewater found between the east end of Francis Lake and Apocynum Campground offers a number of Class IV features, including some of the most storied rapids in the province. Some of the names include the Rose Garden, Meat Grinder and Head Wall. This last one is worth noting; if you do not execute a sharp turn, you and your boat will get stuffed under an overhanging ledge. This is not a route for the faint of heart.

Nahatlatch River: Lower (Map 36/C7–26/D1)
This last stretch of river between Apocynum Campground and the former bridge site 500 metres east of Reo Resort is Grade IV, with a number of Class IV+ features. The Canyon is a 5.3 km (3.3 mi) epic section of whitewater, best left for skilled and experienced kayakers. The best time to go is later in summer after the levels dropped substantially.

Norrish Creek (Map 3/G3–G4)
Found just an hour east of Vancouver, near Mission, this half day run offers clean boulder rapids and fine bedrock squeezed between some tight vertical canyons. It is best to run this creek after a heavy rain or spring runoff. At medium water levels you are looking at Class IV-IV+ rapids. Most portaging is easy, but two rapids, including the hardest, cannot be walked.

North Alouette River (Map 2/D2–F2)
While the North Alouette River begins at Jacobs Lake in the UBC Research Forest, you will not be able to put-in until the 232nd Street Bridge in Maple Ridge, and even here it will be difficult. Lining and sometimes carrying the canoe is a must. From 232nd Street to Neaves Road is 7 km (4.3 mi); from Neaves Road to Harris Road is a much nicer 7 km. Those that do travel the river will find a tranquil setting with abundant waterfowl to enjoy.

Pitt River (Map 2/C2–12/E7)
Although this is a flatwater paddle, the Pitt moves a lot of water and sees a fair bit of boat traffic, making it a sometimes dangerous place to be. The Pitt is also a tidal river so it is advised to consult tide charts before setting out. From Grant Narrows to the Port Mann Bridge on the Fraser is a 24 km (15 mi) paddle through mostly farmland.

River of Golden Dreams (Map 32/F5)
Flowing through the heart of Whistler, from Alta Lake to Green Lake, this is a great river for a lazy summer day float. There are two parks on Alta Lake, Wayside and Lakeside, where you can launch your boat. The river winds its way through a marshy area between the two lakes. This is also a popular float trip on inner-tubes and air mattresses.

Rutherford Creek (Map 32/G2–33/A2)
Rutherford Creek is a Class IV-V run that offers boulder rapids and classic bedrock drops. However, due to a hydro dam project, the creek can now only be run at the height of the summer. There are a couple of places to put-in which are accessed from the Rutherford Creek Forest Service Road. The first is at the 3 km mark, at the split between the upper and lower halves of the run. The second is at the 7 km mark if you want to run the whole route. The take-out is at the Highway 99 bridge, just west of Pemberton.

Salmon River (Map 2/F4)

Like many Fraser Delta rivers, the Salmon is difficult to paddle in its upper reaches, because it is narrow and overgrown. The first good launch point comes at McMillian Park on Glover Road near Fort Langley. At low water, the Salmon looks more like a flooded ditch than a river, but does get bigger. Most people take-out at the 96 Avenue bridge about 8 km (5 mi) downstream where there is a pump station/flood box blocking the river.

Seymour River (Map 1/E1–11/F6)

The Seymour flows through some peaceful suburbs and offers a great challenge for novice paddlers. In summer, the Seymour is a little too shallow to paddle, but it is fine the rest of the year. The Seymour is a Grade II/III river, with boulder gardens at low water and lots of play holes at high. From Seymour Park on Riverside Drive to Burrard Inlet it is 4 km (2.5 mi). In summer, contact the GVRD regarding keys for the gate on Riverside Drive. Due to a significant rockslide in late 2014, the upper canyon portion of this river is no longer runnable. The slide damned the river, creating a lake that flooded the first three rapids and extends well past the former Twin Bridges put-in.

Skagit River (Map 6/E3–E7)

A Grade III/IV route through a scenic valley at the base of sheer mountain faces, the Skagit is a beautiful river to run, (though plagued by logjams), particularly from July to October. Most people put-in at 26 Mile Bridge and take-out at Ross Lake. For the most part though, the river follows the Silver Skagit Road and you can put-in and take-out at leisure. The exception is the section from the confluence with the Sumallo River to Silvertip Park, where the Skagit flows through a wild valley.

Soo River (Map 33/A3)

The Soo is a good Class IV river run with lots of rapids from start to finish, following Highway 99 halfway between Whistler and Pemberton. The put-in is at the obvious dirt pull out immediately upstream of the Highway 99 bridge over the river. The take-out is more elusive and is found approximately 3 km back towards Whistler, just as the river bends away from the highway. Look for two small dirt roads between the highway and the river, and take either one. The trick is figuring a way to bash down to the river to mark your take-out on your return.

Squamish River: Upper (Map 31/F5–G6)

The Squamish River is a cold, murky, big volume river that makes its way from the Pemberton Icefield south to Howe Sound at Squamish. The river is never too far from a road but for the most part feels very remote. In late winter, along with salmon, the area is home to thousands of bald eagles. The uppermost section, from the bridge near the 37 km sign to the log sort near the 29 km sign, is an 8.2 km (5 mi) run through the scenic Squamish Canyon. This Grade III/IV section features some great big standing waves including the Steamroller Rapid, which can get as big as 3 metres (10 ft) during high water levels. While this is a river for rafting and advanced kayakers in peak season, at lower levels (April or October), it is a great run for advanced open boaters. Watch for logjams and sweepers. This run is often combined with the Elaho.

Squamish River: Middle (Map 31/G6–21/G2)

The mid-section of the Squamish offers an easy float through a broad valley. Most start at the confluence with the Elaho and take-out at the Steamroller Rapid near the campsite and bridge. This section runs for 12 km (8 mi), avoiding all the really challenging features, and is rated Grade I/II.

Squamish River: Lower (Map 21/G2–22/C5)

The 32 km (20 mi) section between the Powerhouse and Brackendale is mostly a Grade II route. Closer to Brackendale many people like to run the river in January to get an up close view of the Bald Eagles. Be wary of obstacles such as deadheads and logjams as well as braiding channels.

Stein River (Map 34/F3–36/B2)

The North Stein and Stein Rivers make for a remote, multi-day, hike-in Class V + kayak trip. Located in Stein Valley Nlaka'pamux Heritage Park west of Lytton, the North Stein offers the stoutest, steepest runnable mile of whitewater in southwest BC. The best time to complete this trip is July and August. The North Stein starts as a small creek and is infested with logs for the first 10 km (6 mi), making it a slow two to four hour paddle to reach the start of good whitewater. There is also not a lot of good camping at the top of the Stein. A recommended itinerary would be to start early and get the hike (eight hours at a moderate pace) and large portion of the paddle done the first day. The hard section of the North Stein can be done in a day and the main Stein will

take a further two days. Take-out is somewhere with public access to the Fraser River near Lytton. Those who are not into the hike can charter a plane to take them to Stein Lake and the head of the river. Visit www.liquidlore.com for more details.

Sumas River (Map 3/F7–4/A5)

From near the US border (Vye Road Bridge) to Hougan Park (13 km/8 mi from Vye Road), the Sumas is a slow moving river. By the time you reach Hougan Park, almost all forward momentum has stopped and you will have to paddle the remaining 10 km to the Sea Dam, just upstream from the confluence with the Vedder Canal. The Sumas is a nice easy paddle, but a little too close to Highway 1 for some people's tastes.

Thompson River: Goldpan Campground to Nicomen Confluence (Map 45/F7–36/F2)

The southwest reaches of the Thompson River are one of the kayaking and commercial rafting hotspots in the province. This is not an area for the inexperienced, but it is THE place for some whitewater thrills. The 12 km (7.5 mi) Grade II/III route from Goldpan Campground to the Nicomen River confluence has plenty of turbulence and large waves but few rock obstacles. Through this section, the river is fast flowing and offers a scenic paddle through dry ponderosa pine country. The paddling season extends year round except during peak flows.

Thompson River: Lower (Map 36/F2–C2)

As the Thompson River approaches the Fraser River, it becomes more difficult to paddle as the water level and flow of the river increases. Between Nicomen River and Lytton, the river extends 24 km (15 mi) through the dry pine country and is rated as a Grade III-IV expert kayak route. The paddle is not technically difficult but is intimidating due to its large waves, rapids and holes. It is recommended that the route only be tried after a local has shown you the best line to take through the difficult sections. The route is best paddled during late summer and fall.

Tulameen River: West of Tulameen to Tulameen (Map 17/B3–D3)

From the gold mines to the historic Kettle Valley Railway stops, there are many sights to see in the Tulameen area. The Hoodoos and rich red clay banks of the river are another highlight of the trip. The section from the bridge 7 km west of Tulameen flows through the Tulameen Canyon. The first rapid, visible from the put-in, is a Class II+ with rocks, large waves and holes. It is the calling card for the canyon about 200 metres (600 ft) beyond, which is also full of Class II+ features. Past the canyon, the trip to Tulameen mellows to a Grade I or so float.

Tulameen River: Tulameen to Coalmont (Map 17/D3–E3)

Between the famed Coalmont Hotel (B.C.'s oldest operating hotel) and Tulameen, the Tulameen River Road provides good access to the river. But most paddlers choose to run this Grade I–I+ stretch of river from town to town.

Tulameen River: Coalmont to Princeton (Map 17/E3–G4)

This 21 km (5 hours) section of the Tulameen is an easy Grade II paddle, with one major exception: Tulameenie Falls, which should be portaged (through the KVR Tunnel), is a Grade IV+ drop that is particularly dangerous in low water. Below the falls, the river is mostly Grade I, with a few easy Grade II sections. The river is quite variable with many pools, rock and boulder gardens. The best time to paddle the route is in May or June, during spring runoff.

Upper Ryan River (Map 41/D5–E5)

The Upper Ryan River is a Class V boulder run located northwest of Pemberton. Because of bridges being out, once you reach the take-out location (the remains of a bridge where you can drive no further), it's a good two to three hour hike to the put-in. However, it is possible to start earlier. The upper part of the run is very steep, continuous whitewater and you need to scout everything, while the lower section is tamer.

Vedder River (Map 4/A5–C5)

From Vedder Crossing to Number Three Road, the Vedder River is a Grade II run. It is not as challenging as the Chilliwack, but is still lots of fun, especially for open boat canoeists. This section is 8 km (5 mi) long. Beyond Number 3 Road, the Vedder becomes an easy float down to the Sumas confluence along the slow moving Vedder Canal. Not particularly difficult, but a nice family outing, with great views of Sumas Mountain.

Ocean Paddling

Boundary Bay (Map 1/E7–2/A6)
Extensive tidal flats make this a difficult place to explore by boat at low tide. From Boundary Bay Regional Park to Crescent Beach, it is 22 km (14 mi) one-way. It is often windy here, sometimes too windy to safely paddle. The best time is early in the morning.

Copeland Islands Marine Park (Map 28/A7)
Known locally as the Ragged Islands, the Copeland Islands are a fairly easy 8 km (5 mi) paddle north of the boat launch at Lund. The islands are home to colonies of seals and a diverse array of tidal life. The marine park also offers campsites. An easy circuit route for novice kayakers would be to paddle to the Copeland Islands, then around the tip of Malaspina Peninsula and down Okeover Inlet.

Desolation Sound Provincial Marine Park (Map 28/C5)
Desolation Sound is BC's largest and most popular marine park with over 60 km (37 mi) of shoreline to explore. It has warm, sheltered waters, spectacular scenery and lots of nooks and crannies to explore. Marine life flourishes in these waters, which can reach temperatures of 26° Celsius (79°F) in summer. The park is rich in native history as well as natural beauty. Birders will find this area a delight, with loons, kingfishers, eagles, gulls, plovers, murrelets, grebes, herons, oyster catchers and more. It is also possible to explore past the park and all the way into the emerald green Toba Inlet. On route you can visit Homfray Channel, which features the second deepest waters off the coast at 730 metres (2,394 ft).

You can launch from two locations. From Lund, the paddle is more exposed but it takes you past the Copeland Islands Marine Park. If you choose the more sheltered Okeover Inlet route, you will need to paddle during slack tide to avoid tidal currents up to 10 knots in Malaspina Inlet. It can take anywhere for three days to two weeks to explore this area.

English Bay [Burrard Inlet] (Map 1/C2)
English Bay rests inside Burrard Inlet on the Strait of Georgia and offers views of the downtown core and Stanley Park. You can extend your paddling by heading into False Creek, which is a more sheltered inlet with less boat or ship traffic.

Hotham Sound (Map 20/A3)
Located off Jervis Inlet, Hotham Sound is a peaceful destination, easily accessed from Saltery Bay. The Sound offers sheltered paddling, with many coves and bays to explore. On the way from Saltery Bay, you will pass through St. Vincent's Bay, then around Elephant Point. One of the highlights of this trip is the 444 metre (1,456 ft) Freil Falls, which are across from Elephant Point. There is a marine park on Harmony Islands where you can camp and explore the area further. An advantage of camping here is that it is one of the few places in the area that is bear-free.

Howe Sound (Maps 10, 11, 22)
Howe Sound stretches north from Horseshoe Bay to Squamish and is framed by rugged, towering peaks. Before the Sea to Sky Highway went in, the only way to Squamish was by boat. There are a number of great destinations in the Sound, including Gambier Island, which can be circumnavigated in about two days and Anvil Island, a good one-day trip. The most popular places to launch are Porteau Cove, on Highway 99, followed by Port Mellon, on the Sunshine Coast.

Indian Arm (Map 1/G1–12/A5)
The northernmost reaches of Indian Arm are protected inside the boundaries of the Indian Arm Marine Park. This is a gorgeous place to paddle that is well protected from wind, but sees a lot of small boat traffic. There are many sites to see (Silver and Granite Falls), places to camp (Twin Islands, Bishop Creek) and places to just stop and enjoy the stillness of nature. Its 23 km (14 mi) up the west side of Indian Arm, from Deep Cove to the Indian River. Add another kilometre if you travel the east side from Belcarra Park. Deep Cove Kayak (www.deepcovekayak.com) offers a great breakdown of all the points of interest in Indian Arm including great islands to visit.

Jervis Inlet (Maps 19, 20, 30)
There are three good launching points into this undeveloped fjord, which stretches deep into the rugged Coast Mountains and neatly divides the Sunshine Coast into two. Edgemont is one, Earls Cove is the second and Saltery Bay the third. Highlights include the Princess Louisa Inlet and Chatterbox Falls near the head of Jervis Inlet. The inlet can be dangerous if the weather blows up, as the steep cliff lined shore offers no place to shelter. It will take one to two weeks to explore the inlet.

Jedediah Island (Map 8/E4)
Sheltered from all but the most persistent winds by Texada to the north and east and Lasqueti Island to the south and southwest, this 26 hectare (64 ac) island is a favourite of kayakers. The archipelago of islands is often referred to as a string of pearls. This is BC kayaking at its best and, as a result, the campsites can be quite busy in the summer. Near the shoreline around Long Bay is some of the best camping, while the small bays on the east side of the island offer more privacy. However, there is no water available. Jedediah Island is accessible either from Secret Cove on the Sunshine Coast or Texada Island.

Port Moody (Map 2/A1)
Port Moody, the bay, is a large, sheltered finger poking into the Lower Mainland from Burrard Inlet. This is a working harbour, so there is a lot of traffic and not many places to land or launch a boat from.

Redonda Islands (Map 28/B3)
Warm water, secluded coves, BC's tallest island mountain (outside of Vancouver Island) and excellent fishing make West and East Redonda Islands great paddling destinations. These islands are very large and it will take the better part of a week to circumnavigate even one. You can launch from Lund or Okeover Inlet and paddle up Desolation Sound before crossing over. Maybe it is their size or the exposed crossings, but the islands are not popular paddling destinations.

Savary Island (Map 18/B1)
Savary Island has long, curved, dazzling white beaches. It is a summer Shangri-La, attracting kayakers from around the world. This is also where the great tidal currents from the north and south meet, creating a unique warm water environment. If you do not feel comfortable with the 3 km (1.9 mi) crossing, a water taxi at Lund will transport you across. Be warned – there is no fresh water on Savary, so pack what you will need.

Sea to Sky Marine Trail (Map 11/A6–22/B7)
The only saltwater section of the Trans-Canada Trail, the Sea to Sky Marine Trail is a 40 km (25 mi) route between Horseshoe Bay and Squamish. The marine trail officially opened in June of 2015 and features seven public access points on both sides of Howe Sound. There are six recreation sites as well as three provincial parks making it much longer than a 40 km journey if you want to explore all the different inlets and islands, including Bowen, Gambier and Anvil, and camp along the way. The campsites have been designed to be no more than 17 km apart, a distance deemed to be a safe distance for a paddler to travel in a day. The route is also popular destination for humpback and grey whales as well as dolphins and Orcas making it a great canoe or kayak destination.

Sechelt Inlet (Maps 9, 20)
This sheltered is a popular destination and a great place for novice kayakers to get their sea legs. From Porpoise Bay you can travel a few hours or a few weeks into the inlet, exploring its many marine parks and sheltered bays. You can do a round trip or start at Porpoise Bay and arrange for a shuttle at Egmont. There are numerous paddle-in campsites and the area is home to many marine birds and animals; there is even the occasional killer whale spotted by fortunate sea kayakers.

Skookumchuck Narrows (Map 20/C6)
Some people surf the over 2 metre (6 ft) high waves in this narrow bore, which has been clocked at up to 16 knots. This is a great spot for playing, but at anything except slack tide should only be attempted by whitewater kayakers with appropriate skills.

Thornanby Islands (Map 9/B4)
North and South Thornanby Island guard the western entrance to Halfmoon Bay. The two islands are home to a pair of provincial parks and offer secluded campsites overlooking Vancouver Island, some great beaches to explore and lots of marine wildlife. Seals, blue heron, king fishers and a colony of cormorants are some of the more common sightings.

Discover BC Parks

Show your pride in British Columbia's natural beauty. Buy a new BC Parks licence plate and you'll be helping support B.C.'s provincial parks and protected areas.

Get yours today!
icbc.com/bcparksplates

PARK ADVENTURES

Parks and recreation areas are our frontline to the outdoors, and no other region of the country offers the breadth and variety that Southwestern BC does. From dynamic city and regional parks to remote and wild provincial parks, these areas are the best, or at least the easiest, places to experience the Great Outdoors.

There are a number of large wilderness parks in this area, some of which see surprisingly few visitors considering their proximity to the largest urban centre in British Columbia. Then again, these parks have few, if any, facilities and access into these areas can be difficult. Obviously, it is much easier to head for a well-developed park like Cultus Lake than to bushwhack your way deep into the wilds of Pinecone Burke Provincial Park.

This mix of large wilderness areas and popular recreation areas is what makes the park system so great; no matter what it is you love to do outdoors — camp, boat, fish, hike, climb mountains or just lay on a beach all day — you are sure to find a site that will meet your needs.

Provincial and Regional Parks are set aside for a variety of reasons. Two of the biggest reasons are to protect the environment and to provide recreational opportunities for residents and visitors. To make things easier when planning a trip, we have added recreational symbols beside each site name. The symbols will show you some of the more popular activities in the area, while the descriptions will provide you with a good background of the park or recreation site.

In recent years, there have been many changes to the provincial park system. One of the changes was the institution of parking fees at many of the most popular parks and camping fees at the more popular recreation sites. While there was much debate around the parking fees especially, it looks like they're here to stay at parks like Golden Ears, Alice Lake, Brandywine Falls, Cypress and Cultus Lake.

Most campgrounds operate from early spring through to fall. Some stay open all year. Most charge a fee for overnight stays and, as mentioned, the most popular parks have day-use parking fees as well. The camping fees vary according to the facilities and services provided. If you want even more details, the government has put together a fantastic website. Visit www.bcparks.ca. We have noted the parks that currently offer a call-in reservation system through Discover Camping (www.discovercamping.ca).

DID YOU KNOW?

WE CAN PRINT MAPS FROM OUR MAPBOOKS INTO LARGE FORMAT TOPOS

 EASY TO READ

Our large format topo maps have elevation shading with labeled contours to highlight mountains and valleys, along with clearly defined trail systems and trailheads.

 DURABLE

Printed on water and tear resistant material, these maps will tough it out anywhere you do.

 DEPENDABLE

UTM Grids along with latitude and longitude bearings will keep you oriented and on track.

 backroadmapbooks.com/backcountry-maps

Aldergrove Lake Regional Park (Map 3/A7)

This regional park is centred around the man-made Aldergrove Lake, tucked away in the rolling hills beside the US border. The park is 280 hectares (692 ac) and contains both the lake and the surrounding forests and fields. There are 9.5 km (5.9 mi) worth of trails, most of which are open to horseback riding and biking and are dog friendly. During the hot summers, most people come here to swim in the warm waters or lay back on the white sand beach that surrounds the lake.

Alexandra Bridge Provincial Park (Map 26/F6)

A small, 55 hectare (136 ac) day-use park located high above the Fraser River was established in 1984. The original Alexandra Bridge dates back to 1926 and you can still walk across to the other side of the river. A short distance downstream, highway traffic uses a more modern crossing. In addition to the bridge, there is a picnic area just off the highway with a wheelchair accessible pit toilet. Fishing for salmon in season is also possible here.

Alice Lake Provincial Park (Map 22/D5)

Alice Lake is a popular provincial park, 13 km north of Squamish. There are 108 reservable campsites in this 396 hectare (979 ac) park, 55 of which have electrical hook-ups, with 12 walk-in sites. There are also two group campsites that can accommodate 15 to 40 people and a day-use area with picnic tables, a grassy area and sandy beach. Washrooms with showers, a playground and interpretive program and sani-dump are some of the campground amenities here. Alice Lake is one of four lakes that dominate this park and water sports like swimming, fishing and canoeing are the most popular activities here. There are a number of trails in the park, including a stroll around Alice Lake, the 6 km (3.7 mi) Four Lakes Trail and the 3 km (1.9 mi) DeBeck's Hill Trail that offers vistas of Squamish River. Reservations are strongly recommended for camping and there is a daily parking fee.

Anderson Bay Provincial Park (Map 8/F4)

Anderson Bay is an extension of South Texada Island Provincial Park. The 35 hectare (86 ac) parcel of land has no developed facilities but provides a well-protected anchorage, paddling and scuba diving opportunities and access to trails in the area for hiking and wildlife viewing. No-trace backcountry camping is permitted.

Apodaca Marine Park (Map 10/G7)

Apodaca is an 8 hectare (20 ac) marine park located on the eastern shore of Bowen Island. There are no developed facilities, but it is a good place to moor your boat and explore the shore. The park protects the shoreline, which consists of scenic cliffs, rocky knolls, a variety of rare plant species and marine birds and mammals to view.

Arrowstone Provincial Protected Area (Map 54/G3)

Located in the foothills northeast of Cache Creek, this protected area is accessed off the Arrowstone Forest Service Road and Highway 1. The park protects the Arrowstone Creek Drainage as well as the Cache Creek Hills. There are no developed facilities in the park, but it is fairly accessible by foot and the area is popular with hunters. Fishing for brook trout is possible in Tsotin Lake.

Bedard Aspen Provincial Park (Map 54/D7)

Located about 40 km west of Cache Creek, this diverse, trail access only, 173 hectare (427 ac) area is centred around a small lake that contains rainbow trout. ATVs and other motorized vehicles can explore the surrounding area, while backcountry camping is also possible. The park was created because of its unique and rich biodiversity, making it an excellent location for hunting, bird watching and general nature appreciation.

Belcarra Regional Park (Map 1/G1–2/A1)

Protecting the eastern flanks of the entrance to Indian Arm, this 1,116 hectare (2,755 ac) park is the second largest of the Greater Vancouver Regional District parks, second in size only to Lynn Headwaters. Belcarra is a popular recreation destination in summer, with 22 km (14 mi) of trails (only 6 km open to horseback riding and 9.5 km open to mountain bikers). There are two main recreation areas in the park, and a heritage site. The first is Sasamat Lake, a popular beach and swimming lake, looped by a trail. The second area is down at Belcarra Bay, which features a nice picnic site, two shelters, a concession, a playground and a second series of trails. Trails link the two areas and join with nearby Buntzen Lake Park.

Birkenhead Lake Provincial Park (Map 42/B1–D3)

Established in 1963 and expanded in 1996 and again in 2008, this park encompasses the turquoise-coloured Birkenhead Lake, as well as the rugged surrounding mountains. Covering 10,439 hectares (25,795 ac), this beautiful spot is located 55 km northeast of Pemberton along the Blackwater Lake Road. In addition to a popular 91 site campground, 46 of which are reservable, there is also a boat launch, beach, sani-dump and year-round trails. In summer wind surfing is popular. The rustic park is home to many animals, including black bear, bobcat, deer, moose and mountain goat. An additional 4,888 hectares (12,075 ac) have been protected in the Qwalimak/Upper Birkenhead Conservancy that preserves a significant First Nations site, old growth forests as well as moose, salmon and trout habitat. Reservations are recommended for camping and there is a daily parking fee.

Bishop River Provincial Park (Map 47/G1–48/C4)

This provincial park is about as remote a place as you could ask for in this corner of the province. The closest road is a boat access logging road. From here you will have to hike or bike 75 km (46 mi) up the Southgate River. Most people who come here (and there are not a lot of them) get here by helicopter. This is an area of big mountains and glaciers and should be left to experienced mountaineers. Backcountry camping is a possibility along with hunting and wildlife viewing. The use of camp stoves is encouraged to decrease the utilization of wood in the park.

Blackcomb Glacier Provincial Park (Map 33/A5)

This is one of most popular provincial parks in the Whistler area, by sheer virtue of its location, adjacent to both Garibaldi Provincial Park and Whistler Village. The 250 hectare (618 ac) park is a popular hiking destination in summer. In winter, the area is accessed via a series of chair lifts and thousands of people a day pass through the park as they ski Blackcomb Mountain.

Blue Earth Lake Provincial Park (Map 45/D2)

Blue Earth Lake Park is located in a deep valley and offers fishing and rustic camping for up to six groups between two sites. Amenities include a small hand launch and pit toilets. Accessible from the Trans-Canada Highway north of Spences Bridge on Venables Valley Road, this park offers many wildlife viewing opportunities, including chances to see song birds and waterfowl. There are a few small areas of old growth Douglas fir and mature aspen, while spawning trout may be seen in the shallow channel between the lakes in early summer. Hunting is also permitted in the 705 hectare (1,740 ac) park that is bisected by the rough Blue Earth Lake Forest Service Road to the east.

Boundary Bay Regional Park (Map 1/E7)

The biggest draw to this 182 hectare (450 ac) regional park is the sandy beaches and the warm waters of Boundary Bay. When the tide goes out, almost all the water in the bay disappears, leaving a magical intertidal world to explore. The shallow pools fill with marine life and you can walk for miles on the mud flats. The park is also the start of the multi-use 16 km (10 mi) Boundary Bay Regional Trail. Other facilities include a picnic shelter, playground and concession.

Brackendale Eagles Provincial Park (Map 22/C6)

Brackendale Eagles Provincial Park is located within the Squamish River watershed, a large low lying valley in the Coast Mountains. This valley is well known for its significance as a key area for wintering bald eagles in North America. The habitat created by the river is ideal for feeding, perching and roosting. These majestic birds can be seen feasting on the spawned out remains of chum salmon from November to February each year. There are no developed facilities in the 755 hectare (1,866 ac) park and it is recommended that people view the eagles from outside the park boundaries. The park is located on the west side of the Squamish River, so fishing is another option here, but one of the best eagle viewing locations is across the river at the municipal dyke on Government Road in Brackendale.

Brae Island Regional Park (Map 2/F4)

This park was developed in an area previously occupied by a private campground called Fort Camping. In addition to a day-use area, the park features a large campground with over 140 reservable sites (some with 40 amp service), 4 km (2.5 mi) of trails, a group camping area with picnic shelter and three tent cabins, walk-in yurt camping, washrooms with showers and laundry facilities, a café, camp store, heated pool, kid's activity centre, boat rentals and canoe launching facilities. The park is located on

Brae Island, across Bedford Channel from Fort Langley. For reservations call 604-888-3678 or email info@fortcamping.com.

Brandywine Falls Provincial Park (Map 32/D7) ⛺🚶🚵⛷🅿

This park was greatly modified in 2010 which resulted in the loss of the campsite and a tripling of the park in size to 420 hectares (1,038 ac). This expansion was done to provide protected habitat for the rare red-legged frog. Visitors will find a picnic site and washrooms in this day-use park that features the 70 metre (227 ft) high Brandywine Falls. There are a number of trails in the area for mountain biking, hiking and snowshoeing in the winter. The Sea to Sky Trail also runs through the park.

Bridal Veil Falls Provincial Park (Map 4/G4–5/A4) ⛺🚶♿🅿

Bridal Veil Falls Park is a 32 hectare (79 ac) day-use area located just off Highway 1, east of Chilliwack. The landscape encompassing the park is characterized by low elevation valleys and lush, rounded mountains. The falls tumble 60 metres (195 ft) over a smooth rock face and make for a fine hiking destination. Wildlife viewing opportunities include porcupine, song birds, black-tailed deer and black bear. There are picnic facilities with wheelchair accessible flush toilets.

Bridge River Delta Provincial Park (Map 50/B4) 🚤🎣

Found where the Bridge River enters the west end of Downton Lake, this remote park has been left in its natural state. The 992 hectare (2,450 ac) park protects the broad valley and glacial-fed, braided stream complex that is home to large Douglas fir and a rare valley bottom cottonwood stand and riparian zone not typically found in the area.

Buccaneer Bay Provincial Park (Map 9/B4) ⛺⚓🚣🛶🏊🏕🚶🛥🎣

Featuring a broad sandy beach at the southern tip of North Thormanby Island, this 45 hectare (111 ac) park protects both uplands and foreshore areas. The large sheltered bay provides safe anchorage in most summer conditions for small boats or kayaks and a place for saltwater fishing. Scuba diving is popular here, while there is random beach camping (with space for about 5 groups) and a pit toilet. A self-registration system is in place for these first-come, first-served sites. Colonies of sea birds, sea lions and seals may be found on the beaches in the area.

Buntzen Lake Recreation Area (Map 12/A7)
⛺🏊🚣🛶🏕🚶🚵🐕🛥🎣♿🅿

Originally called Lake Beautiful, this very popular recreation area is easily accessed by Sunnyside Road to the north of Port Moody. There is a large beach and picnic area along with a designated area for dogs. Trail enthusiasts will find an elaborate trail system for hikers, bikers and equestrian riders that lead around the lake and up to the scenic vistas on both sides of the lake. Paddlers and anglers can also take advantage of the cartop boat launch, canoe launches and dock.

Burnaby Lake Regional Park (Map 1/F2) ⛺🏊🚶🚵🐎🅿

The majority of this 311 hectare (768 ac) regional park is Burnaby Lake itself, but the really interesting part of the park is where the marshy area meets solid land. It is here where birds and small mammals, like bald eagles, beavers, belted kingfishers, great blue heron, osprey and the rare green-backed heron, tend to hang out. You can explore this area from shore, along the 19 km (12 mi) of trails or from the water in a canoe or kayak.

Burns Bog Regional Park (Map 1/F5) 🚶🚵🅿

For years, Burns Bog was at the centre of a raging debate over development in the area. If Stanley Park is the Lower Mainland's green heart, Burns Bog is its lungs and kidneys. The 2,042 hectare (5,045 ac) domed peat bog is the largest on the west coast of North America and is a designated ecological conservancy area. The bog actually acts like a filter for fresh water and stores carbon dioxide. In 2004, much of the bog was protected as a regional park and is closed to public access. However, the Delta Nature Reserve next door is being developed as the focus of both access and education about the bog and trails. The dog-friendly park features an elaborate boardwalk system and connects with the Delta South Surrey Greenway.

Callaghan Lake Provincial Park (Map 32/B3) 🎿⛺🚣🏕🐕🛥🚤🅿

Callaghan Lake is a high mountain lake at the end of a rough two-wheel drive road. In addition to ten rustic campsites, a pit toilet and rustic boat launch, the lake and nearby Cirque Lake offer fishing for rainbow and lake trout. There are also numerous small wetlands and small lakes, especially in the southern and eastern areas of the park and in the upper headwaters of Callaghan

Creek. Cross-country and backcountry skiing are popular here due to the abundant snow levels. In fact, this was a site for some winter sports during the 2010 Olympics. Canoeing, boating, hiking and hunting are also practiced in the park. Abutting the 2,667 hectare (6,590 ac) park is a new conservation area that protects more of the Callaghan Creek drainage.

Campbell Valley Regional Park (Map 2/E7) ⛺🚶🐎🚵🅿

There are 20 km (12.5 mi) of trails in this 549 hectare (1,356 ac) dog-friendly regional park, 14 km of which are open to horseback riders. The trails are the most prominent feature in the park, winding their way through forest and field, marsh and meadow and are a great place to do some birdwatching from. Campbell Valley is also home to a number of historical sites. The park is accessed at the end of 208th Street south of Langley.

Capilano River Regional Park (Map 11/D7) 🎣⛺🏊🚶🚵🛥🎣🅿

The Capilano River cuts deep into the North Shore. The steep canyon walls, the view from the Cleveland Dam and the few pockets of old growth trees are just some of the highlights of this spectacular area. There are 14 km (8.7 mi) worth of multi-use trails to explore. In the fall, the Capilano Fish Hatchery becomes the centre of attention, as people flock to watch the returning salmon spawn up the river. Anglers also line the banks of the river and more than a few have landed some giant fish. The Cap is a great whitewater river and the odd kayaker has been hooked by errant lures. There are also two reservable dorms for overnight camping groups.

To reserve your campsite, visit Discover Camping at discovercamping.ca or call 1-800-689-9025.

Cascade Falls Regional Park (Map 3/F2) 🚶🚵🛥♿🅿

This 9.5 hectare (23 ac) site is one of the three nature parks in the Fraser Valley Regional District. The park's main feature is a series of waterfalls on Cascade Creek. The largest of which, the upper falls, plunge 28 metres (90 ft) to a large pool. Below the pool a series of smaller falls in a deep, narrow gorge drop the remaining 18 metres (60 ft) to the valley floor. The hike up to the falls is relatively short and easy at 750 metres round-trip. Open April through November, there are stairs to the suspension bridge and a viewing platform. The regional park and falls are found off Ridgeview Road to the east of Sylvester Road on the way to Davis Lake.

Central Park (Map 1/E3) ⛺🏊🚶🚵

Central Park is an 86 hectare (213 ac) patch of green space near the ever-expanding glass and concrete of Metrotown. If you can't get out of the city, this is a good place to go to relax. Only in the heart of the park will the noise of the city fade, but it is easy to ignore the traffic whizzing by on Boundary Road as you relax on the grass beneath the shade of a Douglas fir. The park also hosts 8.5 km (5.3 mi) of multi-use trails winding their way through a small urban forest. There is also an outdoor pool, fitness circuit, playground, ball diamonds, horseshoe pitches, tennis courts and both formal and informal picnic facilities.

Cheam Lake Wetlands Regional Park (Map 4/G3) 🚶🅿

Located just east of Highway 9, this 93 hectare (230 ac) park is mostly lake and wetlands. This is a BC Wildlife Watch site and there are plenty of birds and small mammals in the area. There are a number of trails in the park to explore, some of which are under water in spring and early summer, and there are some floating bridges.

Chilliwack Lake Provincial Park (Map 5/F6)
🎿⛺🚣🛶🏊🚤🏕🚶♿🐕🏍🛥🎣🅿

Chilliwack Lake Provincial Park encompasses 9,258 hectares (22,870 ac) of wilderness around Chilliwack Lake along with a few smaller mountain lakes. At the head of the lake, campers will find 146 drive-in campsites in four separate loops (41 of which are reservable), pit toilets, an adventure playground, boat launch and sani-dump open from early May until mid-October. Day visitors can enjoy the beach, while backcountry campsites are found at Greendrop, Lindeman, Flora and Radium Lakes. There is a trailer on site for rental as well. Chilliwack Lake is ideal for boating, canoeing, kayaking, swimming (although it doesn't get very warm) and fishing. There are over 40 km (25 mi) of established trails, including parts of the Trans Canada Trail and the historic Centennial Trail, as well as some unmaintained routes (please use caution if using unmarked trails and take a compass and map). Hunting is permitted in the park as well. The park is located 64 km southeast of Chilliwack at the end of the paved Chilliwack River Road.

Chilliwack River Provincial Park (Map 4/E6)

A popular spot for anglers and kayakers, this day-use site, established in 1961, is also a nice place for a picnic. It is found a short distance from Vedder Crossing, on the north side of the river. The river is home to some of the best salmon and steelhead fishing in the region.

Clendinning Provincial Park (Maps 31, 39, 40)

Protecting the Clendinning Creek drainage and parts of the Elaho River Valley, the south end of this large 30,330 hectare (74,940 ac) park is accessible by a long, lonely drive up the Squamish Valley Road, then the Elaho Main. There are no facilities or roads, but the deep, forested valleys and rugged glaciated peaks do attract mountaineers looking to explore this dramatic landscape. There is an unmaintained trail through the old growth to Clendinning Lookout, but most access the mountains at the north end of the park by helicopter. Hunting is also permitted in the park.

Cliff Gilker Regional Park (Map 10/B6)

This small regional park is easily accessed off Highway 101 adjacent to the Sunshine Coast Golf and Country Club. It provides a series of popular hiking trails, totalling about 7 km (4.3 mi), through a forested setting with little elevation gain. Amenities include wheelchair accessible pit toilets, a picnic area and a playground. Wooden bridges cross several small streams and Roberts Creek amongst some large second growth timber. There are four well-maintained and easily followed trails within the park.

Colony Farm Regional Park (Map 2/B3)

This is a recently developed 262 hectare (647 ac) parcel of land near the Fraser/Coquitlam River confluence. There are a series of dyke trails with unique bridges to walk (8.7 km/5.4 mi) or bike (6.5 km/4 mi) and viewing platforms for the nature lover. From Highway 7, turn south onto Colony Farm Road and continue to the parking area at the end of the road.

Copeland Islands Marine Park (Map 28/A7)

Located northwest of Lund, this 437 hectare (1,080 ac) provincial park encompasses 180 hectares of land and 257 hectares of foreshore amongst the scenic Copeland Islands. The area is a sanctuary for birds, as well as an excellent spot for scuba diving. The park is often used as a stopover point by sea kayakers heading into Desolation Sound, but the islands also make a nice two or three-day destination themselves. There are pit toilets and 11 designated campsites, each having at least 9 tent pads, throughout the islands. These sites are user maintained, so please pack out what you pack in.

Coquihalla Canyon Provincial Park (Map 15/G6)

This 159 hectare (393 ac) park encompasses the Othello Tunnels, which were built in the early 1900s as part of the historic Kettle Valley Railway. The tunnels are impressive, as are the spectacular views of the canyon, a 93 metre (300 ft) deep gorge of near-vertical granite. The old rail bed is part of the Trans Canada Trail. Picnic tables are available and a daily parking fee applies. Please note that the tunnels are closed in the winter for safety reasons so trail users will have to take a detour along Othello and Kawkawa Lake roads. The park is dog friendly.

Coquihalla Summit Recreation Area (Map 16/E2)

At the summit of the Coquihalla Highway (Hwy 5), is a lovely picnic area for highway travellers. Most visitors will enjoy the incredible views of Zopkius Ridge and Needle Peak before moving on, but the 5,750 hectare (14,200 ac) park offers much more. It is possible to explore the sub-alpine terrain, fish at Falls Lake or challenge the many surrounding peaks along mountain routes best left to experienced mountaineers and backcountry skiers. Backcountry camping is permitted year-round and there are pit and flush toilets located throughout the park. ATV and snowmobile riding are permitted in the area, but only on designated roads. Hunting is also permitted in the park.

Cornwall Hill Provincial Park (Map 54/E7)

To the west of Ashcroft, the Cornwall Hills Lookout Road provides access to this undeveloped park. The summit of Cornwall Hill is a popular launch for hang gliders and offers nice views of the surrounding area. There are also a number of unmarked meadow trails and rare Engelmann Spruce in the 1,188 hectare (2,935 ac) park. The lookout tower itself is in danger of being dismantled in the near future unless a group comes forward to restore it.

Crippen Regional Park (Map 10/F6)

Bowen Island has been a popular getaway for people from the Vancouver area since the early 1900s. People come here to get away from the city and spend a few hours living on island time. The most prominent feature in this 242 hectare (598 ac) park is Killarney Lake. It is possible to walk off the ferry, walk around the lake and return to the ferry in an easy afternoon stroll. There are 12.5 km (7.8 mi) of trail here, 5 km of which are open to horseback riding and biking.

Cultus Lake Provincial Park/International Ridge Recreation Area (Map 4/C6–C7)

This 2,729 hectare (6,740 ac) park, located 13 km south of Chilliwack, sees a lot of water-based activity. There are four well developed campgrounds in the park: Clear Creek (85 sites), Delta Grove (58 sites), Entrance Bay (52 sites) and Maple Bay (106 sites). These sites are open from early April until mid-October and reservations are available. There are also four group campsites that can accommodate parties between 15 and 45 people, two at Westside and two at Honeymoon Bay, and several day use areas with picnic facilities. Amenities include wheelchair accessible washrooms with showers, a playground, interpretive programs and sani-dump. In summer the beaches are often packed and the lake is positively abuzz with powerboats and jet skis. There are canoe rentals, but the lake can be a dangerous place to be in an open craft, as winds can pick up at any time. There are five main trails in the park, ranging from the interpretive stroll along the Maple Bay Trail to a 5 hour hike along the Edmeston Road to Road 918 Trail. The trails also hook up with trails outside the park. A daily parking fee applies.

The International Ridge portion of Cultus Lake Provincial Park is the nearly forgotten backcountry, featuring a couple of lesser known trails. The nearby community of Cultus Lake also provides visitors with local amenities and more family activities.

Cypress Falls Park (Map 11/A7)

The main features of this park, a little known gem of a park near Horseshoe Bay, are a series of waterfalls cutting through old growth trees next to Cypress Creek. There are a number of trails in the park and the most popular route is an easy 3 km (1.9 mi) roundtrip to the falls themselves.

Cypress Provincial Park (Map 11/B6–B4)

Cypress Provincial Park has the distinction of being the most popular provincial park in the province. Most of the visitors to the 2,996 hectare (7,400 ac) park come in the winter, as Cypress is home to a popular downhill ski area, just 15 minutes from downtown Vancouver. Cypress was the site of the Freestyle Skiing and Snowboard Venues for the Vancouver 2010 Olympic Winter Games. On a clear day the views from the top of Mount Strachen (pronounced Strawn) are spectacular. To the south is the sprawling metropolitan area of Vancouver, while to the southeast visitors will see a snow clad Mount Baker in the Cascade Mountain chain. To the west and southwest lie the Gulf Islands and Vancouver Island with Georgia Strait in the foreground. Beyond the ski area, there are many trails in the park including the strenuous but rewarding Howe Sound Crest Trail. Passes are available from the resort to trek the backcountry in the winter months and there is year-round backcountry camping at three sites: Magnesia Meadows, Brunswick Lake and Deeks Lake. A daily parking fee applies.

Dan Bosch Regional Park (Map 20/B6)

This popular day-use park is found on Ruby Lake next to Highway 101. In addition to the nice beach, washrooms and picnic tables, there is boat launch for paddlers and anglers to enjoy. The site is also popular with birders and naturalists looking for painted turtles and even Roosevelt elk, deer and bear that frequent the area.

Daniel Point Regional Park (Map 9/A1)

Daniel Point is a small point that juts out from the Sunshine Coast. This small 1.4 hectare (3 ac) park protects a fragile ecosystem of mosses and lichens.

The main feature for visitors is a short but difficult 2.5 km (1.6 mi) trail to a viewpoint over Malaspina Strait.

Davis Lake Provincial Park (Map 3/E1)
Created in 1963, Davis Lake Provincial Park is located 19 km north of Mission and is in the traditional territory of the Sto:lo Nation. Continue from Sylvester Road past the park boundary and look for a side road that descends south, down the slope to the short trail into Davis Lake. The 192 hectare (474 ac) park surrounds the small, warm water lake with pretty beaches, a scenic waterfall and good fishing. While it is primarily a day-use park, walk-in camping is permitted.

Deas Island Regional Park (Map 1/D5)
A relatively small, 72 hectare (178 ac) park on the Fraser River, Deas Island isn't actually an island, but a peninsula, jutting out into the Fraser. While thousands of commuters pass by here every day, fighting back the road rage that threatens to envelop them, most have no idea that just a few metres away lies a peaceful riverside park. There are 10 km (6 mi) of trails through the park, some of which can be used by horseback riders. The trails will take you along Deas Slough and along the banks of the Fraser and past the heritage buildings. The picnic area with shelter is a fine place to enjoy a sun-set from, while group camping is available for groups up to 40 people. The Inverholme Schoolhouse is a heritage site.

Deer Lake Park (Map 1/F3)
An urban park protecting Deer Lake, an oasis of calm in the midst of the city, Deer Lake Park is home to arts, culture and history, as well as abundant natural beauty. There are canoe rentals for folks who want to get out on the lake for a lazy paddle, as well as well-developed trails, a beach and a surprising amount of wildlife for a park surrounded by city. To get to the park from Highway 1, take the Kensington South turnoff. Turn west on Canada Way and follow the signs to Deer Lake Park.

Derby Reach Regional Park (Map 2/F3)
Edgewater Bar, located in this park, is considered by many to be one of the best, if not the best, fishing bars on the Fraser River. In August and September, this section of the riverbank is choc-a-block with anglers, while the channel just off shore is stuffed with salmon. Besides fishing, this is one of the few regional parks with public camping. There are 38 non-reservable campsites, all of which have access to the river. There is a 9.5 km (5.9 mi) hiking only trail and the 4 km (2.5 mi) Houston Loop trail that skirts Derby Bog that can be used by cyclists and horseback riders. Derby Reach was the original site of Fort Langley. Although the fort is no more, there are a few historical buildings.

Deroche Regional Park (Map 4/B4)
Established in 2004, this small, 4.4 hectare (11 ac) park is located on the north side of the Fraser River east of Mission. There is a boat launch here and fishing is very popular. In the fall and winter, it is a great place to watch bald eagles, while shorebirds and seals can also be seen here.

Desolation Sound Provincial Park (Map 28/B6–D4)
Desolation Sound is one of the most popular yachting and sea kayaking destinations in the world. It is also BC's largest marine provincial park at 8,449 hectares (20,870 ac), encompassing Gifford Peninsula and several small islands. Despite its remote location at the end of the Sunshine Coast, with no access other than by water, it can be busy in the summer. Boat cruisers, sea kayakers and anglers all flock here from Lund or Okeover Inlet. There are several developed backcountry permit-required camping areas throughout the park. As an added bonus, the shallow bays are famous for warm waters, oysters and scuba diving. For more information consult the fishing and paddling sections of the book.

Dewdney Nature Regional Park (Map 3/F4)
This 7 hectare (17 ac) nature park is located outside the dyke on the east side of the south end of River Road South in Dewdney. This is a popular spot for bar fishing along the Fraser River, especially during the fall Coho runs. There is also a concrete boat launch and pit toilets, as well as a chance to see shorebirds, seals and bald eagles in the fall and winter. Swimming and canoeing in the slough is also possible.

Duffey Lake Provincial Park (Map 43/C6–E5)
Located about 35 km east of Pemberton, Duffey Lake is nearly halfway to Lillooet along the Duffey Lake Road (Highway 99). Duffy Lake is a beautiful lake, surrounded by snowcapped mountains and an abundance of wildlife. There is a rough gravel boat launch at the east end of the lake for boaters and anglers. Be wary of afternoon winds.

E.C. Manning Provincial Park (Maps 6, 7)
Adding the Cascade Recreation Area to the northwest has expanded this four season outdoor paradise to 83,671 hectares (206,755 ac) of rugged mountains, valleys, meadows, lakes and rivers. Trails of all shapes and sizes, lakes for canoeing and fishing, wildlife for viewing and slopes for downhill and cross-country skiing in winter are just some of the features of the park.

Highway 3 runs through the park, providing easy access. Campers will find four campgrounds in the park. Lightning Lake Campground is the most popular site with 143 reservable sites and yurts, washrooms with showers, a playground and interpretive programs available from June to early September. There is also a boat launch for non-motorized boats and a sani-dump. Coldspring, Hampton and Mule Deer Campgrounds, with 212 sites between them, are all available on a first-come, first-served basis. There are also two reservable group campsites: Lone Duck I and II in the summer and Cambie Creek and Lone Duck II in the winter.

The camping season is weather dependent, but generally opens in early May (at Mule Deer) and goes to early October (at Coldspring), although the second site at Lone Duck group campsite is open in winter. Trail users will also find 10 designated areas with 55 totals sites for backcountry camping ranging from three to 10 tent pads, with outhouses, bear caches and fire rings usually available. Day visitors will find seven sites around the park including West Gate, Sumallo Grove, Lightning Lake and the popular Sub-Alpine Meadows area. Hunting is also permitted in this park.

> It is ideal to carry a water filter, iodine tablets, or boil water for a minimum of 10 minutes before consuming, as many waterbodies carry the bacteria commonly referred to as Beaver Fever.

Edge Hills Provincial Park (Map 53/D1)
This large 11,850 hectare (29,280 ac) park protects panoramic vistas over the Fraser River canyon as well as ravines, forested valleys and grassy uplands leading to a wide range of wildlife species within Edge Hills. There are unmaintained and unmarked trails in the park, and that's about it for infrastructure. Backcountry camping is allowed within the park, however, check the provincial website for closure information due to mudslide conditions — especially in the Pear Lake area. Hunting is permitted in the park.

Emory Creek Provincial Park (Map 15/F4)
Emory Creek is a roadside park next to the Fraser River, 18 km north of Hope. This historically significant area was a campsite and gold mining hotspot in the mid-1800. Today there are 35 first-come, first-served campsites, three of which are double sites, with pit and flush toilets throughout this 15 hectare (37 ac) park. This is a popular spot for anglers as well.

Epsom Provincial Park (Map 45/G2)
Established in 1997 and located on the west bank of the Thompson River, north of Spences Bridge, this 102 hectare (252 ac) park provides access to the river, mostly for anglers, but visitors can also swim and paddle, being cautious of swift water in the spring months. There is no road access to the park, so anyone wishing to visit must scramble down to the river from Highway 1 along a rough trail. Be careful crossing the railway tracks.

Ferry Island Provincial Park (Map 4/G3)
This 29 hectare (72 ac) Class C provincial park was established in 1963. Located on the south side of the Fraser River, northeast of Rosedale, the park is governed by a local community board. Anglers can access the Fraser River for fishing here.

F.H. Barber Provincial Park (Map 5/B1) ⛲

This small 8.5 hectare (21 ac) day-use area between Highway 1 and the Fraser River is comprised of almost 5 hectares (12 ac) of flood plain. Established in 1978, this provincial park provides public access to the Fraser River — one of only two main access points between Hope and Chilliwack. Gemstone hunters may also find semi-precious stones like jadeite, jasper and agate.

Francis Point Provincial Park (Map 9/A2) ⛲🚣🏊🥾🛶🅿️

Francis Point protects 81 hectares (200 ac) of coastal forest, wetland and open area, as well as about 6 km (3.7 mi) of undeveloped coastline on the Sechelt Peninsula. There is a short walking trail from the end of Merrill Road to a rocky knoll just past the Francis Point Beacon. The area was set aside to protect a number of rare plant species and caution is necessary in this area. This is one of the best diving areas along the Sunshine Coast and is also popular for sea kayaking. There is a day-use picnic area with pit toilets but campfires are not allowed in this park.

> *Help save the fish and other water critters and dispose of soaps and shampoo a good distance from water sources.*

Fraser Foreshore Park (Map 1/E3) ⛲🥾🚴♿🅿️

This picturesque riverside park is located south of Marine Way tucked between an industrial park and the river. The park is long and narrow, and, once you get away from the manicured lawns of the picnic area (off Bryne Road), there are some interesting sites to see and many side trails to explore. Wheelchair accessible washrooms are available.

Fred Antoine Provincial Park (Map 52/F4–53/B2) 🎣🅿️

Combining the Fred Creek and Antoine Creek watersheds, this Class A, 2,230 hectare (5,510 ac) park rests north of the Bridge River Road near Moha. Home to old growth Douglas fir, the area is also an important wildlife wintering range for goats and deer. Grizzly bear, wolves, cougar, California bighorn sheep, fisher, rubber boa and peregrine falcon are all seen here on occasion. BC Parks would like to keep this park free from visitors for conservation reasons, however, hunting is permitted.

Garden Bay Marine Provincial Park (Map 9/B1) ⚓🚣🛥️🚤🥾🛶🅿️

Located around Mount Daniels, this 163 hectare (403 ac) marine park has 200 meters of shoreline for paddling, a dock and picnic area as well as hiking trails. Established in 1969, this park can be accessed by water or by land, off Garden Bay Road. On the rock bluffs next to the ocean is a stand of juniper trees, a rare site on the Sunshine Coast. There is also evidence of Sechelt First Nation use on top of Mount Daniels as well as a First Nations burial site near the dock. Visitors are asked to not disturb these areas.

Garibaldi Provincial Park (Maps 22, 23, 24, 32, 33) 🏕️🥾🚴🎿🏂🏔️🛶🅿️

A large 194,650 hectare (480,990 ac) wilderness park located next to Squamish and Whistler, Garibaldi is a popular destination with outdoor enthusiasts. Day trips are possible (a parking fee applies), but most people who visit plan on spending a few days, or even a few weeks, exploring this alpine paradise. The main access points, from south to north, are the Diamond Head Trail, the Black Tusk Trail, the Cheakamus Lake Trail, the Singing Pass Trail and the Wedgemount Lake Trail. The park has an interesting geological background; volcanic action formed many of the park's peaks. Lava from Clinker Peak created The Barrier, a natural dam that formed the 300 metre (985 ft) deep Garibaldi Lake. The Barrier has been declared a Civil Defense Zone and there is no camping or stopping while travelling through the Zone.

There are 160 first-come, first-served backcountry sites located at 10 different camping areas including Garibaldi Lake, Taylor Meadows, Diamond Head, Singing Pass and Wedgemount Lake throughout the park. During winter there are also several huts or cabins for backcountry skiers and snowshoers to use.

Mountain bikes are only allowed as far as Elfin Lakes on the Diamond Head Trail and dogs are not allowed in the park. For more information check out www.garibaldipark.com.

Glen Valley Regional Park (Map 3/B4) ⛲🚣🛥️🥾🚴🐴🛶🅿️

This park is a thin strip of land along the Fraser River to give access to Two Bit, Poplar and Duncan Bars. Anglers frequent the area and there is a canoe launch, a couple picnic tables and even some short walking, biking and horseback riding trails to enjoy.

Golden Ears Provincial Park (Maps 2, 3, 12, 13, 23, 24) 🎣🏕️⛲🚣🛥️🚤🚴🥾🏊🛶🚣🎿♿🏂🛶🅿️

Golden Ears, at 55,590 hectares (137,310 ac), is one of the largest parks in the province. Most of the recreational usage happens in the southern portion of the park, around Alouette Lake. Here visitors can go boating, canoeing, fishing, swimming, water skiing, windsurfing, or just laze on the beach.

There are three vehicle accessible campgrounds in this park: Alouette, which has 205 sites, 83 of which are reservable, North Beach with 55 sites, 53 of which are reservable and Gold Creek with 148 sites, 74 of which are reservable and complete with showers, an adventure playground and sani-dump. There are also two reservable group camping areas that can accommodate 25 to 50 people, one called Alouette and the other Golden Ears. Backcountry or walk-in camping is allowed at Viewpoint Beach on Alouette Lake, Alder Flats on the West Canyon Trail and Lake Beautiful on the Alouette Mountain Trail.

A number of trails push deeper into the park including the popular Golden Ears Trail and the overnight route to Hector Ferguson Lake. There is a large boat launch at the south end of Alouette Lake along with three day-use areas with nice beaches. A daily parking fee applies.

Goldpan Provincial Park (Map 45/F7) 🎣⛲🚣🛥️🚤🛶🅿️

Located right next to Highway 1 (and between 2 busy railroads), this 5 hectare (12 ac) provincial park is best used as a stopover for travellers on Highway 1. The day-use area is open year-round and is popular with people who wish to explore the Thompson River for fishing and paddling opportunities. In addition, there are 14 rather noisy first-come, first-served campsites with pit toilets. The provincial park is set within the dry sage brush country typical of the Thompson River Valley.

Grant Narrows Regional Park (Map 12/F7) 🚣🚤🛶🥾🚴🅿️

While Grant Narrows Park is a mere 6 hectares (15 ac) in size with little to offer other than a boat launch, it borders a number of interesting ecological areas and low-lying wetlands. The 1,500 hectare (3,705 ac) Pitt Wildlife Management Area lies to the south of Grant Narrows, to the east is the UBC research forest and across the narrows is the Widgeon Slough. All of these areas are prime wildlife habitats and are home to a wide variety of birds and other creatures. From the park visitors can access almost 14 km (8.7 mi) worth of dykes that can be walked or biked, as well as the 4 km (2.5 mi) Mountainside Trail. In addition to viewing platforms, there are canoe rentals available for folks who want to canoe across to Widgeon Creek.

Green Timbers Urban Forest (Map 2/B4) 🥾🚴🛶🅿️

Known as the birthplace of reforestation in British Columbia, Green Timbers Urban Forest is a natural oasis in the middle of Surrey. The area was replanted in 1931 and now offers approximately 5 km (3 mi) of picturesque trails through second growth forests, grasslands, wetlands and around Green Timbers Lake. The lake itself is a very popular fishing hole that has produced some surprisingly big trout. Access is best off 100th Avenue.

Gwyneth Lake Provincial Park (Map 51/A5) 🎣⛲🚤🥾🚴🛶🎣🅿️

Located at the north end of Gwyneth Lake, just off the infamous Hurley River Forest Service Road, this former recreation site offers a user-maintained campsite with space for six groups and a pit toilet. There is a cartop boat launch onto the relatively small marshy lake. This is a good fishing lake and there are hiking and motorized trails to explore in the area. There are also some great mountain views, and hunting is permitted in the park.

Halkett Bay Provincial Park (Map 10/G5) 🏕️⚓⛲🚣🛥️🚤🚣🥾🛶🛶♿🅿️

Located on Gambier Island, this park is only accessible by boat. There are mooring buoys and dingy floats for boaters, ten picnic sites, three boater-access campsites, a pit toilet and a trail leads from here up to Mount Artaban. Scuba diving, paddling and fishing are also popular here.

Hardy Island Marine Provincial Park (Map 19/E6)

Originally called Musket Island Provincial Park, the name of this park was changed in 2004, as the popular anchorage is known as Hardy Island Anchorage. The waters here are clean, green and warm, making it a fine swimming and backcountry camping spot. Fishing, paddling and wildlife viewing for marine life and waterfowl are common here.

Harmony Islands Marine Provincial Park (Map 20/B3)

These small, sheltered islands are just north of the towering Freil Falls in the sheltered Hotham Sound. Swim, snorkel, fish or just appreciate nature, but please respect the privately owned island nearby by not trespassing.

Harry Lake Aspen Provincial Park (Map 54/C4)

This remote 330 hectare (815 ac) park has no developed facilities, but the grasslands are known for a small colourful bloom of wildflowers in summer. Hunting is permitted here.

Hayward Lake Reservoir Recreation Area (Map 3/C3)

Two different BC Hydro recreation sites are found on this popular lake. The Hayward Lake site is found at the north end and offers a nice beach, play areas and picnic site. There is also a boat launch for cartop boats and access to a series of good trails to explore.

Haywire Bay Regional Park (Map 18/G2)

Haywire Bay's main feature is the big campsite that is usually full of drive-in campers. There are 43 sites in the campground, two group sites that can accommodate 10 units, accessible washrooms with showers, a playground and a small boat ramp onto Powell Lake. Canoe route travellers well-schooled in no-trace camping might want to think about staying on the island tucked away in this sheltered bay rather than trying to find a place in the main site.

Homathko Estuary Provincial Park (Map 48/A1)

Because of its location and the fact that water access is hindered by extensive mud flats, this park offers few recreational opportunities. It is possible to explore the beach area at low tide or observe grizzly bears from a distance. There are also paddling opportunities around the park and anglers can do some tidal fishing.

Indian Arm Provincial Park [Say Nuth Khaw Yum Provincial Park] (Maps 2, 11, 12)

Indian Arm is a long, narrow fjord that extends north from Burrard Inlet. The 6,689 hectare (16,525 ac) park protects the upper portion of the inlet and is primarily accessed by water. The landscape is spectacular with rugged, forested mountains, alpine lakes and numerous creeks and waterfalls, including the 50 metre (165 ft) high Granite Falls. The Arm is ideal for boating, canoeing and kayaking, scuba diving and windsurfing, while the Indian River and the lower reaches of some of the creeks are great for fishing. The flat beach areas along the shorelines of Bishop Creek provide good spots for rustic camping or picnicking. Granite Falls is another popular area for camping and picnics, but please note that fires are not permitted in this park. There is a day-use area on the north side of the falls, near a small dock, while tenters will often set up on the south side of the falls. At the south end of the arm, a marine park also protects Raccoon and Twin Islands. There are 5 elevated wooden tent pads and pit toilets on North Twin Island, but be wary of private property on the island. Day moorage for small craft can be found at Granite Falls and North Twin Island.

Inland Lake Provincial Park (Map 18/G1–19/A2)

This popular park north of Powell River features a 13 km (8 mi) wheelchair accessible trail around Inland Lake, along with less developed connecting trails to nearby Powell Lake. The marsh boardwalk on the east side of the lake is a good place to look for birds and other wildlife. The main campsite offers 22 campsites with picnic tables, cabins for disabled people as well as a wharf. Tenting only sites spread around the lake, including 3 scenic, boat access only sites on Anthony Island.

Iona Beach Regional Park (Map 1/B3)

While the park is built around the beach, the most noticeable feature here is the 4 km long jetty, jutting far into the Strait of Georgia. For many years, this out-of-the-way corner of the Lower Mainland was the sewer of the Strait, but in the late 1980s pipes were added to carry the sewage farther out into the strait, well away from this area. Now it is quite a pleasant place to be and a testament to the recovery powers of nature. It is an isolated green space and home to many birds and small mammals. There are tidal flats to explore, as well as marshes, grasslands and the beach, for which this park gets its name. The beach is a great place for a picnic, or to go sunbathing, and some people even go swimming. There are 13 km (8 mi) of trail for walking, 3 km for horseback riding and 4 km for cycling.

Island 22 Regional Park (Map 4/C3)

This is a popular equestrian area, complete with riding ring, corrals, jumps and several equestrian events throughout the year. The park is also a fishing hot spot when the salmon are running. It features a good bar to shore fish from and one of the largest boat launches in the Lower Mainland. The 45 hectare (111 ac) park also has walking trails and is home to migratory birds in late summer and bald eagles in winter. Seals are often seen in the river as well.

Jedediah Island Provincial Park (Map 8/E4)

Jedediah Island Provincial Park, at 253 hectares (625 ac), has long been the destination of boaters and kayakers. It is the largest and most diverse island of a chain of over thirty islands and islets located north and west of Lasqueti Island. Some of the best camping areas are near the shoreline around Long Bay. Small bays on the east side of the island provide campers with a little more privacy, especially during the summer when the island can get quite busy. There are pit toilets available at the most popular anchorages and winter camping is also permitted.

Joffre Lakes Provincial Park (Map 34/A1–43/A7)

This 1,460 hectare (3,605 ac) wilderness park contains the lovely Joffre Lakes and the towering (2,701 m/8,778 ft) Joffre Peak. The trail leading past the three lakes is a fairly rough 5 km (3 mi) mountain route. The terrain beyond the rustic campsite at Upper Joffre Lake is only recommended for mountaineers or backcountry skiers prepared for travelling on glaciers and snowfields. Another popular backcountry destination in the area is the Cerise Creek area where trails and a backcountry hut are located. The Nlhaxten/Cerise Creek Conservancy has been recently established to protect this significant area for local First Nations.

Kanaka Creek Regional Park (Map 2/G3–3/B3)

Kanaka Creek Regional Park follows the valley of Kanaka Creek for 11 km. This is not a popular recreation park, but it does see its fair share of picnickers, trail users, canoeists and nature lovers. There are a couple picnic sites, one just above Cliff Falls and one at the Bell-Irving Fish Hatchery. The hatchery is a fine place to see spawning salmon in fall, while the mouth of the creek is another nice place to watch for wildlife. There are also several walking trails in the 413 hectare (1,020 ac) park totaling 10 km, but these do not all connect.

Katherine Lake Regional Park (Map 9/B1)

Located off Garden Bay Road, Katherine Lake is a pretty lake with sandy beaches and a thickly forested shore. The 37 hectare (91 ac) park has 26 campsites that are large enough for an RV and 10 sites that are tent only, with a small playground and washrooms with showers. These sites are open from the May long weekend to the October Long Weekend. There is also a family friendly beach that makes a nice place to spend a hot afternoon. Call 604-883-9557 to reserve a site.

Kawkawa Park (Map 15/F6)

Formerly a provincial park found just east of Hope off the Kawkawa Lake Road, Kawkawa Park is a day-use park on the west side of the warm lake. In addition to the popular beach, anglers will find excellent fishing for kokanee.

Kilby Provincial Park (Map 4/C2)

Tucked away in a rural pastoral setting, Kilby Provincial Park is located just past the historic Kilby General Store. This provincial park is a great place to watch wintering bald eagles, trumpeter swans, geese and small songbirds. This scenic riverfront park has 35 campsites, 11 of which are reservable, a day-use area with pit toilets and is the main boat launch onto the Harrison River. Waterskiing, swimming and fishing are all popular water activities here.

Lighthouse Park (Map 11/A7)
Lighthouse Park boasts one of the largest stands of remaining old growth in the Lower Mainland. The largest tree here is a Douglas fir, at 77 metres (255 ft) tall. There are numerous attractions at the park including a variety of hiking trails, the lighthouse viewpoint and rock climbing. The park is found in West Vancouver off Marine Drive.

Lost Lake Park (Map 32/G5)
Once a local hideout, Lost Lake Park is now a popular year-round destination in Whistler. The elaborate cross-country trails can be used by everyone from hikers and bikers in summer to skiers and snowshoers in winter. There are also a couple beaches, barbeque pits, picnic tables, washrooms and an off-shore dock to enjoy.

Lower Seymour Conservation Reserve (Map 11/F6)
Formerly known as the Seymour Demonstration Forest, this 5,668 hectare (14,000 ac) site was renamed in 1999. This valley is sandwiched between the ridges of Lynn Headwaters Regional Park and Mount Seymour Provincial Park. The main recreational feature of the park is the new trail that parallels the service road from the parking lot to Seymour Dam. This paved trail leads 10 km (6 mile road) one-way and is a popular walking, biking, and roller blading path.

There are some 65 km (40 mi) of other trails in the park, some official, others not, leading to various spots in the park. Most of the official trails are in the southern corner of the park, including the Fisherman's Trail. This trail runs along the Seymour River providing access for hikers, mountain bikers and, of course, anglers. Another popular, but unofficial, trail is the Temple of Time, which leads to some of the largest old growth trees still standing in the Lower Mainland. No dogs are allowed in the park.

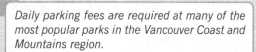

Daily parking fees are required at many of the most popular parks in the Vancouver Coast and Mountains region.

Lynn Canyon Park (Map 1/E1–11/E7)
The majority of visitors to this park are here for one thing: the suspension bridge. It's like a mini version of the Capilano Suspension Bridge and you don't have to pay to use it. Some continue on, but most admire the view into the deep gorge below, then leave. After crossing the suspension bridge, the majority of foot traffic heads north, to a rocky area just below a waterfall through a narrow canyon. In summer, this is a popular destination for families. To the south, a trail follows the canyon for a few kilometres, then crosses over Lynn Creek and returns on the other side, above the canyon.

Lynn Headwaters Regional Park (Map 11/E6)
Lynn Headwaters is the biggest of the regional parks in the Lower Mainland and it helps protect parts of the famed North Shore Mountains. One of the nice things for visitors is that buses stop just a few hundred metres outside the park, making it accessible to everyone. You only have to walk a short way into the park along the access road to have the sounds, smells and sights of the city fade away, replaced with the sensations of this verdant park. There are a number of fabulous hiking trails, 54 km (34 mi) in total, including the Headwater Trail and the Hanes Valley Loop, which takes you over to Grouse Mountain and back on the Baden Powell Trail. The trails in Lynn Headwaters also hook up with trails in the Lower Seymour Conservation Reserve to the east. In winter, when there is snow, the trails are taken over by backcountry skiers.

Malaspina Provincial Park (Map 28/B5)
Located at the north end of the Malaspina Peninsula, this 572 hectare (1,410 ac) park is water accessible only. There are no developed features in the park, but visitors can backcountry camp with a permit. There are kayak rentals and guided tours available.

Manning Provincial Park (Maps 6, 7)
See E.C. Manning

Marble Canyon Provincial Park (Map 53/F3– 54/A4)
A small provincial park just east of Pavilion on Highway 99, Marble Canyon is set at the base of 1,000 metre (3,250 ft) high limestone cliffs. The 335 hectare (825 ac) park contains a trio of lakes, Crown, Pavilion and Turquoise Lakes, with 30 first-come, first-served camping spots found between tiny Turquoise and Crown Lakes. This park is popular with fishers, scuba divers and birders. Visitors should be wary of instability caused by a 2012 forest fire while hiking or ice climbing.

Matsqui Trail Regional Park (Map 3/D5–F5)
Located along the Fraser River beneath the Mission/Abbotsford Bridge, this 117 hectare (289 ac) park is thin and long, stretching 10 km (6 mi) along the south bank of the Fraser. The park is threaded together by a dyke trail, which runs the length of the park. There are six formal campsites, a popular picnic area and plenty of space for bar fishing. But the main feature of the area is the scenic Matsqui Trail. Part of the Trans Canada Trail, this broad multi-use trail can be stretched into a multi-day (or week or month) adventure. Paddling is also popular here.

Mehatl Creek Provincial Park (Maps 25, 34, 35)
The 23,860 hectare (58,940 ac) Mehatl Creek Park is a popular wilderness getaway for backcountry adventurers. During the summer, visitors can trek 3 km (1.9 mi) up the park's only established trail to Mehatl Falls, which is nestled in a sub-alpine bowl. Parking is found adjacent to the bridge at km 48 of the Nahatlatch River Forest Service Road. Other activities include fishing in the lower creek, whitewater paddling and wildlife viewing.

Minnekhada Regional Park (Map 2/D1)
Minnekhada occupies an interesting parcel of land. Part of the park is in the mountains and is forested and rocky. Part of the park is in the lowlands, and is marshy, with dykes providing access to the Addington Lookout. In fall, when the wild berries are ripe, it is common to see black bears around the Minnekhada Farm area. There are over 12 km (7.5 mi) of trails through the park, from easy dyke walks to fairly stiff climbs up to the rocky knolls and pit toilets.

Mount Elphinstone Provincial Park (Map 10/B5–C5)
Three separate parcels of land make up this 139 hectare (343 ac) park. The most notable is the piece on the southwest slopes of Mount Elphinstone, where some of the oldest trees in the province are found. Mount Elphinstone is also home to a prolific number of mushrooms, some of which have yet to be properly identified. Tread carefully and take only photographs. The other sections of the park are found near Roberts Creek and north of Gibsons.

Mount Richardson Provincial Park (Map 9/F3)
Located north of the town of Sechelt, this 1,001 hectare (2,470 ac) park is accessibly by a rough forest service road (four-wheel drive recommended). There is a former recreation site at Richardson Lake, where you will find good fishing and wilderness camping. There are also three backcountry marine campsites at Tuwanek, two to three at Oyster Beach and three larger spots at Nine Mile Point with a pit toilet. There are a number of hiking trails in the area, including a couple routes up the mountain, while scuba diving and swimming are popular in the inlet. Hunting is permitted in the park.

Mount Seymour Provincial Park (Map 1/F1–11/G6)
The 3,508 hectare (8,665 ac) Mount Seymour Provincial Park is located 30 minutes northeast of downtown Vancouver. The park is better known for winter recreation. The downhill ski area is popular with snowboarders and family skiers, while backcountry skiers and snowshoers have many options in the area as well. During summer, Mount Seymour, Mount Elsay and Mount Bishop all make great hiking or backpacking destinations (wilderness camping is permitted in the sub-alpine north of Brockton Point). Reservations can be made for the group campsites and note that a daily parking fee applies.

Mundy Park (Map 2/B2)
This is a suburban park with 12 km (7.5 mi) of multi-use trails weaving their way through the cool, lush forest of the 180 hectare (445 ac) park. The heart of the park is Mundy Lake, but the smaller Lost Lake is also a popular destination. The park is found off Como Lake Road and makes a pleasant year-round destination.

Murrin Provincial Park (Map 11/B1)

This small, 24 hectare (59 ac) park surrounds tiny Browning Lake and is a very popular stop for travellers on the Sea to Sky Highway (Hwy 99). In addition to picnic tables, wheelchair accessible pit toilets and a good fishing hole, rock climbers can be seen testing their skills on six different faces of the bluffs rising above the parking lot. A daily parking fee applies.

Nahatlatch Provincial Park and Protected Area (Map 25/D1–36/A7)

Nahatlatch Provincial Park is a long and narrow 1,695 hectare (4,185 ac) park. The natural beauty of this spot, nestled in the glacier covered mountains with old growth forest and a lake and river system, is like no other in the Lower Mainland. A series of small streams flow into, out of and in between the three lakes in the park. Their waters drain into the Nahatlatch River, one of the best whitewater rivers in the province. For those not interested in these high adrenaline antics, you can canoe in and between the lakes, enjoying the views and looking for wildlife. There are six former Forest Service Recreation Sites that provide camping in the park. From east to west they are: Frances Lake, Hannah Lake, Old Ranger Station, Nahatlatch Lake, Salmon Beach and Squakum. The park entrance is located on the Nahatlatch Forest Service Road (an active logging road) approximately 25 km northwest of Boston Bar. It is identified with a park information shelter.

Nairn Falls Provincial Park (Map 33/B1)

The waterfall for which this park is named plummets 60 metres (195 ft) into the valley below, and is accessible by a short, easy trail. There are 94 campsites, 50 of which can be reserved, next to the Green River, wheelchair accessible pit toilets and a day-use picnic area. In addition to other trails, the river has good fishing for Dolly Varden and rainbow trout.

Neilson Regional Park (Map 3/E4)

A 10 hectare (25 ac) park on the west side of Hatzic Lake, Neilson Park provides public access to the lake. There has been some development, including a cookhouse, picnic tables, washrooms, improved beach area and approximately 2 km of walking trails. The park looks out across the Fraser Valley, with Mount Cheam in the distance. There is also a private campsite on the lake.

Nicolum River Provincial Park (Map 16/A7)

Located east of Hope on Highway 3, the 24 hectare (59 ac) Nicolum River Provincial Park is set in dense forest cover next to a small, fast flowing river. Fishing is really the only pastime here.

Okeover Arm Provincial Park (Map 28/C7)

On the east side of the Malaspina Peninsula, this 4 hectare (10 ac) park is used as a launching point for sea kayakers heading out into Desolation Sound. There are 14 campsites open seasonally and four small sites open all year with wheelchair accessible pit toilets. These sites are usually full and are located close together so there is not much privacy. There is also an undeveloped boat launch and a government wharf here.

Oregon Jack Provincial Park (Map 45/D1)

Easily accessed on the Hat Creek Road, this undeveloped 233 hectare (576 ac) park preserves the Notch (a limestone canyon) and falls on the Oregon Jack Creek drainage. A First Nations Pictograph can be seen in the canyon. No camping or day-use facilities are provided in this park, however, hunting is permitted.

Otter Lake Provincial Park (Map 17/C2)

In the Tulameen Valley northwest of Princeton, Otter Lake provides two separate areas to visit. The 45 site (36 of which are reservable) lakeside camping area is found near the north end of the lake, while the day-use facility, boat launch and developed beach area are found at the south end of the lake. There are wheelchair accessible pit toilets. The lake is certainly the main feature of the park, but the area contains remnants of heavy mining activity as well as the historic Kettle Valley Railway/Trans Canada Trail. Ice fishing is common in the winter.

Pacific Spirit Regional Park (Map 1/B2)

Pacific Spirit has the distinction of being the only clothing optional park in the Lower Mainland, and while most of the nudists hang around Wreck Beach, the entire foreshore area, around the point to Acadia Beach, is clothing optional. It is possible (though difficult in places) to walk the 6 km (3.7 mi)

foreshore at low tide. The biggest part of this 763 hectare (1,885 ac) park is the southeast corner, which has become a haven for mountain bikers. There are over 90 km (55 mi) of trails in the park, 60 km of which are open to mountain bikers and horseback riders.

Peace Arch Provincial Park (Map 2/C7)

The Peace Arch sits on the International Boundary, where BC's Highway 99 and Washington State's Interstate 5 meet at the Canada/United States border. There are 41 picnic tables throughout the day-use park and a wheelchair accessible washroom. This is not a wilderness park, but it is pretty nonetheless — an elegant, well-manicured park with lovely flower gardens.

Pinecone-Burke Provincial Park (Maps 2, 11, 12, 23)

A large, still undeveloped park is tucked in between Pitt Lake and the Coquitlam Lake Watershed. It's a big 38,000 hectare (93,900 ac) park, capturing some of the rugged territory to the west of Pitt Lake and Upper Pitt River Valley. The park protects a number of sites that have been historically popular, but unprotected, like Burke Mountain in Coquitlam, Widgeon Slough and Widgeon Valley (which are accessible only by canoe or kayak from Grant Narrows). Backcountry ski touring and snowshoeing are popular in winter. Most visitors make Widgeon Lake, a pretty lake in a hanging valley, their final destination. But if you keep right instead of heading left to Widgeon Lake, you will follow the Fool's Gold Route north and west to hook up with the Mamquam River Forest Service Road southeast of Squamish. This route is infrequently travelled, but there are first-come, first-served group campsites as well as backcountry camping opportunities. Hunting is permitted in the park.

Plumper Cove Provincial Park (Map 10/D6)

A small marine park on the northwestern shores of Keats Island, this park is accessible by canoe/kayak, by boat or by the infrequent foot ferry from Gibsons (the Dogwood Princess). From Keats Landing, it is 2 km to the park. A good overnight destination for sea kayakers, the park has a developed area with 20 forested walk-in campsites, fire rings, pit toilets and water that can be used year-round. Reservations can be made for the group sites. Marine facilities include a wharf and mooring buoys, while the pebble beach is great for swimming and picnicking.

Porpoise Bay Provincial Park (Map 9/F4)

Located on the shores of Porpoise Bay in Sechelt, this popular 61 hectare (151 ac) provincial park has 84 campsites (62 of which can be reserved) available from mid-April to mid-September. Accessible washrooms with showers, a playground and a separate day-use area are available. The large sandy beach is the main feature in the park, but there are trails that lead to the estuary of Angus Creek, offering great views over the inlet. In the fall, this is a good place to watch spawning salmon. Reservations are recommended for camping and a daily parking fee applies.

Porteau Cove Provincial Park (Map 11/B3)

Howe Sound is the southernmost fjord in North America. Porteau Cove offers 44 scenic reservable campsites stretched out along the shores of the sound, plus a popular walk-in beach area with 16 sites just south of the main campground which are also reservable. The campsites are open from March 1st through October, offering everything from electric hook-ups and showers to interpretive programs and a sani-dump. Mooring buoys, dock facilities and two boat launches are also available for boaters. An old ship has been sunk to attract marine life for scuba divers, making this one of the most popular diving spots in BC. The park is sandwiched between the BC Rail Line and the ocean and many campers have awoken to the rumbling of trains passing by. Be careful around the tracks. Reservations are recommended for camping and a daily parking fee applies for those interested in exploring the beach.

Princess Louisa Provincial Park (Map 28/F3)

Princess Louisa Inlet is located far inland, accessed by way of Jervis Inlet some 48 km from Egmont. The 8 km (5 mi) long inlet is in a magnificent granite-walled gorge; mountains rise sharply from the water's edge to heights in excess of 2,100 metres (7,000 ft). Up to mid-June, the warm sun melting the mountain snowpack creates more than sixty waterfalls that cascade down the steep granite cliffs, straight into the ocean. The most famous of

these, Chatterbox Falls, tumbles 40 metres (120 ft). Beyond the seven to ten knot Malibu Rapids at the entrance, the inlet is as placid as a mountain lake. Wilderness campsites are provided with toilets and picnic shelters nearby. Mooring buoys and docks are provided, while walking trails provide access to nearby scenic features. Scuba divers frequent the park as well.

Richmond Nature Park (Map 1/D4)

The Richmond Nature Park protects a relic example of the raised peat bogs that once covered more than 25 per cent of Richmond. In addition to the bog flora, bog creatures like snakes, turtles, coyotes and deer are often seen. A 5 km (3 mi) network of trails allows you to explore the park.

Roberts Point Regional Park (Map 2/D3)

Located on Barnston Island, this park is accessed by ferry and by foot or bike. There are 2.5 km (1.6 mi) worth of trails in the park, though not all of the trails are open to bikes.

Roberts Creek Provincial Park (Map 9/G5–10/A5)

Located off Highway 101 west of Gibsons, this 14 hectare (35 ac) park has two separate sites built around a cobblestone beach. The campsite is home to 21 first-come, first-served sites with accessible pit toilets and a sani-dump station open from mid-June to mid-September. The day-use area is 1.5 km away at Flume Beach, which is a better destination for picnickers and swimmers. Beachcombers can find an interesting display of marine life at low tides, while orca (killer) whales or harbour seals can often be spotted here.

> *Keep the wilderness wild, and pack out all of your trash!*

Rolley Lake Provincial Park (Map 3/C2)

Less than an hour's drive from Vancouver, Rolley Lake Provincial Park provides a quick escape from urban life. The small, warm lake and sandy beach is great for swimming, fishing and canoeing. For campers, there are 64 popular sites (42 of which are reservable) nestled in the trees with wheelchair accessible washrooms with showers, a playground and sani-dump. There is a trail that circles the lake and leads down to Rolley Falls. Reservations are recommended for camping and a daily parking fee applies for day visitors.

Roscoe Bay Marine Provincial Park (Map 28/B4)

A popular place for boating, kayaking, fishing and camping, Roscoe Bay also features a hiking trail to Black Lake and an annual congregation of Moon Jelly Fish. There is space for four or five tents here and a pit toilet.

Ruskin Dam Recreation Area (Map 3/C3)

This BC Hydro recreation area is found at the south end of Hayward Lake, a popular recreational lake near Mission. The day-use area offers a boat launch and access to a good trail network. Upgrades to the nearby Ruskin Dam have resulted in this site being closed through 2018.

Sabine Channel Provincial Park (Map 8/D4)

Sabine Channel is the channel between Texada and Lasqueti Island. This park protects a chain of small islands and islets that are popular with kayakers and boaters. Backcountry camping is possible year-round.

Saltery Bay Provincial Park (Map 19/E5)

This provincial park is found just west of the Saltery Bay Ferry Terminal. There are 42 campsites (15 of which are reservable) at the east end of the park, wheelchair accessible pit toilets and a sani-dump station. There are also two day-use areas, one adjacent to the camping area and one 2 km west. There is great scuba diving in Saltery Bay, with the famous Emerald Mermaid, a 3 metre (9 ft) bronze statue at 10 fathoms in front of Mermaid Cove and a wheelchair access ramp. From the shore, visitors can sometimes see killer whales and sea lions in the distance. Mounds of seashells, called middens, indicate that this was a traditional gathering area for First Nations.

Sargeant Bay Provincial Park (Map 9/D4)

This tiny park is known for its abundance of intertidal and marine life. In fall, this is a great place to watch fish spawning up a fish ladder. In addition to the picnic area and beach next to the sheltered, undeveloped cove, there is a good trail system. One trail leads through a cedar forest to the tidal pools, another trail leads inland past Triangle Lake and the many swamp creatures found there. Windsurfing is popular here and visitors can also swim and fish.

Sasquatch Provincial Park (Map 14/G7–15/A7)

Sasquatch Provincial Park is 1,217 hectares (3,005 ac) and located north of Harrison Hot Springs, close to Harrison Lake. There are over 175 campsites available in three popular campgrounds: Bench Campground with 64 sites (46 reservable), Hicks Lake with 72 (54 reservable) and Deer Lakes with 42 (most are reservable). Hicks Lake also has a large group campsite that can accommodate 15 to 40 people with a covered shelter. There are also day-use areas (some available year-round) at both of these lakes, and at Green Point, which has wheelchair accessible washrooms, on Harrison Lake. Windsurfing and waterskiing also occur in this part of the park. Amenities range from boat launches and a sani-dump to a playground and interpretive program in summer. Hicks and Deer Lakes are ideal for small motorboats and canoeing while Trout Lake provides a more tranquil fishing experience. Reservations are recommended for camping and a daily parking fee applies.

Sechelt Inlets Provincial Park (Maps 9, 10, 20)

This 140 hectare (346 ac) park is actually made up of nine different marine access sites scattered throughout Sechelt, Salmon and Narrows Inlets. From south to north to east the sites are: Piper Point, Tuwanek Point, Oyster Bay, Skaiakos Point, Nine Mile Point, Halfway Islet, Kunechin Point, Thornhill and Tzoonie Narrows. The inlets are a popular sea kayaking destination and the HMCS Chaudiere was sunk off Kunechin Point to create a wonderful artificial reef for scuba divers. All of the sites, with the exception of Skaiakos, have some development such as tent pads and pit toilets providing up to 60 walk-in campsites and 7 designated day-use areas.

Seton Lake Recreation Area (Map 53/C7)

BC Hydro has created a series of lovely recreational areas just southwest of Lillooet off the Duffey Lake Road (Hwy 99). The Seton Beach Picnic Site provides picnic tables and a viewing platform to watch the salmon spawn. The stand of acacia trees providing shade to the beach area was planted in 1942 by Lillooet residents in memory of World War II casualties. Seton Dam Campsite is a popular 45 site camping area found near the junction of Cayoosh Creek and the Seton River. Part of the Gold Rush in the late 1800s, a Chinese bake oven is located in the campground area and serves as a reminder of these gold miners. Naxwit Picnic Area is a large RV friendly site found 3 km west of Lillooet and is an easy walk from the Seton Dam Campsite. Visitors can find interpretive signs detailing the history and ecology of the area, spectacular mountain scenery and good fishing and wildlife viewing, including mountain goats on the surrounding cliffs.

Seton Portage Historic Park (Map 52/D7)

Now site of Seton Portage Tourist Information Centre, this tiny site commemorates the location of the first railway in British Columbia. The information centre is housed in an old railway caboose. No facilities are provided.

Shannon Falls Provincial Park (Map 22/C7)

Shannon Falls are the third highest falls in the province, at 337 metres (1,105 ft), and are truly an amazing site as they cascade down a steep mountainside. The 87 hectare (215 ac) park offers a small day-use area that allows highway travellers a place to picnic beneath the falls. Many people also explore the trails that lead up and behind the falls or to the top of nearby Stawamus Chief, as well as the new gondola between the falls and the Chief. The park has wheelchair accessible washrooms and a daily parking fee applies.

Shelter Point Regional Park (Map 8/A1)

On Texada Island, this regional park is easily accessed south of Gillies Bay, about 27 km from the Blubber Bay ferry terminal. The campsite has been expanded to 52 non-reservable sites, offering washrooms with showers, a playground and spectacular beach with wonderful views. There are also 2 reservable group campsites, 2 boat ramps and a sani-dump. A scenic 2 km trail leads along the ocean through some large windswept Douglas fir.

Silver Lake Provincial Park (Map 5/F1; 15/F7)

Situated in the scenic Fraser Valley, about 12 km southwest of Hope on the Silver Skagit Road, this small 77 hectare (190 ac) park has a gravel boat launch and plenty of scenery. This area is renowned for its fly-fishing. There is a 25 site first-come, first-served campsite next to the lake, wheelchair accessible pit toilet and day-use area.

Simson Provincial Park (Map 9/B4)

South Thormanby Island is a fairly dry island with a rocky shore and number of small bays. Rising above the ocean is Spyglass Hill. This park is accessed by small boat or kayak, as there are no docking facilities. A trail traverses the island starting at Farm Bay, on the southeast corner of the island. Hunting is permitted in the park.

Skagit Valley Provincial Park (Map 6/D3–F7)

This park is part of a larger protected area complex that includes the US North Cascades National Park and the Ross Lake and Lake Chelan National Recreation Areas. This is a large park, at 27,964 hectares (69,100 ac), in a valley that was carved by glaciers.

The valley is an excellent outdoor recreation destination with 50 km (30 mi) of trails, great fishing and 142 non-reservable campsites (between the Silvertip with 43 sites and Ross Lake Campgrounds and the lesser known Whitworth Meadows Horse Camp with 11 sites). Ross Lake is the biggest with 88 sites, a boat launch, separate day-use area and playground and is open the longest, from early May tomid-October. Visitors should note that Ross Lake fluctuates dramatically and on the Canadian side is empty except for the months of July and August (call 1-604-869-7080 for water level information), creating lake access issues.There is also backcountry camping throughout the area, including more developed sites at Delacey Camp, Large Cedar Camp and Galena Lakes.

> *When exploring the backcountry in a provincial or national park, be sure to look into rules regarding camping, fire and pets be aware that these may vary between areas.*

Skihist Provincial Park (Map 36/D2)

Just northeast of Lytton on Highway 1, this 33 hectare (82 ac) park is mainly used as a stopover for travellers on Highway 1 or by folks heading out rafting on the Thompson. It has 58 first-come, first-served sites with full facilities for camping, including flush toilets, a sani-dump, wheelchair accessible pit toilet and a 12 spot picnic area. The park is located well above the highway and railway tracks in a dry ponderosa pine forest. A loop trail leads to the bench above the campsite and offers fine views of the canyon and the local wildlife, including mountain goats and elk.

Skookumchuck Narrows Provincial Park (Map 20/D6)

Skookumchuck Narrows are an impressive site during tide changes. The water is so constricted that standing waves up to 2 metres (6 ft) high and currents up to 30 km per hour (19 mph) are created. Several unwary vessels have been lost in the whirlpools, yet you often see extreme kayakers surfing the waves. This 123 hectare (304 ac) park is found south of Egmont along an easy 4 km (2.5 mi) one-way trail. The best viewing times are one hour before or after the tide change. There are also scuba diving opportunities, but beware of the aggressive currents.

Smuggler Cove Provincial Park (Map 9/B4)

The name of the cove comes from rumrunners, who in days gone by used this bay as a staging area for trips down into the US. You can still visit the area by boat or kayak, but many people come overland, which requires a 1.3

km hike from Brooks Road to the ocean. Scuba diving is popular here. Along the forested shoreline you will find five tent pads, an accessible pit toilet and a hiking trail. Camping is permitted year-round, but only at the designated sites.

Soames Hill Regional Park (Map 10/D6)

This 39 hectare (96 ac) day-use park is found northeast of Gibsons. To get here, take North Road towards the Langdale Ferry Terminal. Turn right onto Chaberlin Road and then onto Bridgeman Road. It is not a huge park, but there are about 4 km (2.5 mi) of trails leading around and to the top of the titular feature. There are three viewpoints from the top.

South Chilcotin Mountains Provincial Park [Spruce Lake Protected Area] (Map 49/G1–51/B2)

The Spruce Lake area is hiking heaven. It's also biking, horse packing and fishing heaven. There are over 164 km (100 mi) of wilderness trails in the area, which traverse gentle mountain passes and meander through lush alpine grasslands and flowers to destination trout lakes. The park was finally designated in the late 1990s after nearly 60 years of debate and lobbying. There are campsites at the north and south ends of Spruce Lake, Hummingbird Lake, Trigger Lake, Jewel Bridge and Gun Creek Grassland.

The main access points into the area are the Gun Creek Road, Mud Creek-Taylor Creek Forest Service Road and the Slim Creek Forest Service Road. Or, if you prefer, you can always charter a floatplane into Spruce Lake itself. The area is still at the centre of controversy. In 2004, the park boundaries were reduced to 56,796 hectares (140,340 ac) to open up areas for mining exploration. There is a proposal to see the area combined with a number of other parks to create a National Park.

South Texada Island Provincial Park (Map 8/F3)

Essentially a boat access park, the shoreline is steep and rocky with few places boaters can land. Visitors can enjoy the fine hiking, kayaking, fishing and wildlife viewing in the area. A separate parcel of the park is located at Anderson Bay, on the island's southeastern shore. Anderson Bay is a much more protected anchorage for boats and has easier shore access. Hunting is permitted in the park, while hiking on the old roads is also common.

Spipiyus Provincial Park (Map 9/C1–20/C7)

Also known as the Caren Range, the 2,979 hectare (7,360 ac) Spipiyus Park is found north of Halfmoon Bay on the Sechelt Peninsula, about 20 km down the Trout Lake Road. The park protects pockets of old-growth forest and is home to black bear, marbled murrelet, Roosevelt elk, various birds and other small mammals. Hiking trails lead to the restored fire tower on Mount Hallowell with views of Pender Harbour, the Strait of Georgia and Vancouver Island. Please note that motorized access, including vehicles, ATV's, dirt bikes and snowmobiles, is only allowed on the existing logging roads.

Sprockids Regional Park (Map 10/D5)

This park is a popular mountain biking destination; indeed, it was set aside specifically for mountain biking, although hikers will sometimes be seen on the more outlying trails. The 48 hectare (119 ac) park has over 14 km (8.7 mi) of trails featuring jumps, teeterbars and ramps along with a skills area.

Squitty Bay Provincial Park (Map 8/F5)

Located at the southeast end of Lasqueti Island, this small park protects a sheltered anchorage. The entrance to the bay is a little tricky and the small dock is often occupied as the destination is quite popular. There is a small day-use area with two picnic tables and a pit toilet.

Stanley Park (Map 1/C1)

Stanley Park is the life and love of the city of Vancouver, whose reputation is built on the beauty of its natural surroundings. Stanley Park is wilderness light — an introduction to some of the magic of nature without ever having to leave the city. With many developed areas like Lost Lagoon, the Aquarium, the Zoo, the totem poles... it is easy to forget that there are still fragments of wilderness here.

It is impossible to name all the recreational activities — from roller blading the Sea Wall to playing pitch and putt to relaxing on one of the beaches to hiking the trails on the west side of the park to watching the marine life in the Aquarium, Stanley Park is one of the great urban parks in North America and, despite its popularity on a sunny summer Saturday, it is still a wonderful and worthwhile place to visit. You might even spot the odd deer.

Stawamus Chief Provincial Park (Map 22/C7) 🖼️🏕️🚻🥾🧗🎣

The Chief is Canada's rock climbing mecca. After years of climbers sleeping in their VW Vans in the parking lot, BC parks finally developed an actual campground at the base of the Chief. There are 15 vehicle access sites and 47 walk-in sites open from May to mid-October and all are first-come, first-served. There is also a day-use picnic area with pit toilets. There are trails in the park leading up and around the backside of the large granite monolith and over to Shannon Falls. Be sure to check out the new gondola that provides a new vantage point of Shannon Falls and the Chief.

Stein Valley Nlaka'pamux Heritage Park (Maps 31, 32, 43, 44) 🏕️🛖🥾🛶🎣

The Stein Valley area has for centuries had a very special spiritual meaning to the aboriginal people of this region. This is clearly shown by the many unique pictographs and petroglyphs on the rock faces of the valley. As a result, the valley is protected and the provincial government and the Lytton Indian Band jointly manage the park. It is a spectacular 107,191 hectare (264,800 ac) wilderness park, with 150 km (93 mi) of hiking trails, cable crossings, cabins and established backcountry campsites. Although a day hike is possible, most people who visit the area spend a few days. The Stein River is a hardcore white water rafting/ kayaking river. These folks hike in from the west side (off Horlick Creek Road) and arrange for a shuttle on the other side. Be sure to check on the status of the ferry at www.drivebc.ca.

Sumas Mountain Regional Park (Map 3/G5–4/A5) 🥾🚵🐕🛶🎣

Sumas Mountain is the monolith that dominates the eastern part of the Fraser Valley. The park covers 1,445 hectares (3,570 ac) and is best known for its hiking trails leading to the viewpoint overlooking Chilliwack and the eastern Fraser Valley. Fishing and swimming is possible in tiny Chadsey Lake, while biking and wildlife viewing are also popular. The main access is off Batt Road. Although a service road that is used by ATV's and bikers climbs to near the summit, the hiking trails are separate.

Sunnyside Acres Urban Forest (Map 2/B7) 🥾🚵🎣

Found off 24th Avenue near Softball City in south Surrey, this 130 hectare (321 ac) urban forest is being managed to protect valuable wildlife habitat; visitors can see birds, coyotes and black-tailed deer or even the rare orchid and rattlesnake-plantain when visiting the forest. To the north, there are about 4 km (2.5 mi) of trails to explore, while the nearby Semiahmoo Trail to the northeast can also be explored.

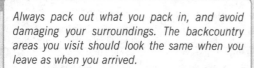

Always pack out what you pack in, and avoid damaging your surroundings. The backcountry areas you visit should look the same when you leave as when you arrived.

Surrey Bend Regional Park (Map 2/C3) 🚻🥾🚵🛶🎣

This park, jointly owned by the City of Surry and the Metro Vancouver Regional District, captures a unique section of relatively untouched, flood plains on the Fraser River. There are a few trails here, used mostly by anglers to access the river, but they are currently under development. Across the waters of Parsons Channel, on Barnston Island, is the Roberts Point Rest Area, which has washrooms and a picnic area. Cyclists often cycle counter clockwise around the island road, stopping at the scenic point for a picnic lunch. From the ferry to Roberts Point is 2 km if you head west and 8 km if you head east (counter clockwise).

Tantalus Provincial Park (Map 21/F3–22/B5) 🏕️🛖🚣🎿🥾🧗🛶🚩

Built around the former Lake Lovely Water Recreation Area, this elaborate 11,351 hectare (28,040 ac) park now includes the Tantalus Range, a popular mountaineering area. Hikers, climbers and backcountry skiers frequent the area and the Alpine Club of Canada Cabin, which can be reserved for a fee, makes the stay that much more enjoyable (visit www.alpineclubofcanada. ca for more information). There are also walk-in backcountry campsites, pit toilets and a couple of canoes to use if you are renting the cabin. Ambitious

anglers will also be rewarded with good fishing in a spectacular setting, while the Este-Tiwilh/Sigurd Creek Conservancy to the north protects the creek and the many wild animals (goats, grizzlies, bald eagles and salmon) that can be seen there on occasion.

Teakerne Arm Provincial Park (Map 28/A3) ⚓🚣🚣🎿🥾🛶🛟🎣

A popular place for boating, kayaking, fishing and camping, Teakerne Arm is home to a 30 metre (95 ft) high waterfall that plunges straight out of Cassel Lake and into the ocean. A 1 km trail leads to Cassel Lake, where visitors can enjoy a swim, and is a highlight of this 128 hectare (316 ac) park. Scuba diving and paddling are also common here.

Tetrahedron Provincial Park (Map 10/A2–C1) 🛖🥾🚵🎿🧗🎣

At 6,000 hectares (14,825 ac), Tetrahedron is the largest provincial park on the Sunshine Coast. It features some dramatic terrain that includes Tetrahedron Peak, Panther Peak and Mount Steele and an extensive trail network that leads to the peaks, with some terrific backcountry huts available year-round on a first-come, first-served basis. These huts are maintained by the Tetrahedron Outdoor Club and donations for maintenance are welcomed. The area also makes a great rock climbing or backcountry skiing destination, and backcountry camping is possible.

Thacker Regional Park (Map 15/F6) 🥾🚵🚣🎣

Found in Hope, this 9 hectare (22 ac) park is home to a spawning channel for Coho, pink and chum salmon. The trail along the channel is part of the Trans Canada Trail and is very popular in fall when the salmon spawn. In summer, there is a popular swimming hole at the confluence of Sucker Creek and the Coquihalla River.

Thompson Regional Park (Map 4/E6) 🚻🥾🎣

Established in 2004, this park provides interpretive panels and maps of the area. It is found 6 km from the Vedder Bridge on Chilliwack River Road. There is a short loop trail around a salmon restoration project.

Ts'yl-os Provincial Park (Map 48/C1–49/D1) 🚻🚣🛶🎿🛟🥾🚵🐕🛶🚩🎣

Ts'yl-os (pronounced "sigh-loss") Park encompasses 233,000 hectares (575,755 ac) of alpine meadows, rugged mountains, glaciers, waterfalls and clear blue lakes. It is bordered by the rugged peaks of the Coast Mountains to the west and the dry Interior Plateau to the east. Due to the Supreme Court ruling that the Tsilhqot'in Nation has aboriginal title in this region, the Gwedat'sih Provincial Campground has been closed and access to this park is by permission from the nation. The heart of the park is the turquoise-coloured Chilko Lake, which is found north of our maps in our Cariboo Chilcotin Coast mapbook.

Tynehead Regional Park (Map 2/C4) 🚻🥾🎣

Located just off Highway 1, Tynehead is a 260 hectare (642 ac) park in the centre of North Surrey. The park contains the headwaters for the Serpentine River and is a popular place to watch salmon spawning in fall. The park is also home to the unique Butterfly Garden. Butterfly attracting plants are grown here, and there are viewing platforms and a pedestrian bridge. There is a fish hatchery here as well, and an off-leash dog park.

Upper Lillooet Provincial Park (Maps 39, 40, 48, 49) 🏕️🥾🚩🎣

This remote 19,996 hectare (49,400 ac) park is not accessible by road or trail. The few visitors that do explore this area usually access base camps in the alpine portions of the park via helicopter. The park was developed to protect the old growth forests, wetlands and high alpine ridges and glaciers around the Lillooet River. Salmon spawn in the many tributaries and wildlife such as black-tailed deer, moose, grizzly and black bears, mountain goat and wolverine are abundant. Backcountry camping and hunting are permitted in the park.

Walsh Cove Provincial Park (Map 28/B2) ⚓🚣🚣🎿🥾🛶🎣

A popular place for boating, kayaking, fishing and diving, visitors to Walsh Cove on the north end of West Redonda Island can see pictographs on the rock faces in the area. There are no developed trails in the 85 hectare (210 ac) park, but people can hike up and down the shoreline.

Welcome Woods Wilderness Regional Park (Map 9/C4) 🥾🚵

This 73 hectare (180 ac) park is a destination for hikers and mountain bikers and the trails here connect up with other hiking and mountain biking trails in the Halfmoon Bay area. The park is accessed from Fullerton Road.

Backcountry
Huts & Cabins

BC's Vancouver Coast region features an extensive network of backcountry huts and cabins, ranging from minimalist shelters that offer little more than protection from the raw elements to fully serviced commercial lodges – outdoorspeople have a lot of options to choose from. Access, setting, size and availability are all things to consider before choosing a shelter to stay in.

Many huts and cabins are used primarily by backcountry skiers and snowboarders. Some are maintained and used by snowmobile clubs, while others are more popular with hikers and mountaineers. A backcountry shelter may be open to the general public on a first-come, first-served basis, or it may require reservations and fee payment months ahead of time. Generally speaking, any backcountry shelter is going to provide a level of comfort and protection that is impossible to pack with you into the wilderness. However, things like cooking supplies and sleeping area are going to vary between each hut and cabin.

For hardcore backcountry adventurers, the most important thing about a particular shelter is going to be the setting. In the Coast Mountains, huts are tucked away in thick stands of evergreen, nestled in multicolored subalpine valleys, perched on barren alpine cliff-faces and everywhere in between. The beauty of these shelters is their extraordinary location. In winter, when thick layers of snow blanket the Coast Mountains, the refuge these huts and cabins provide against the forces of nature is truly remarkable.

While some huts provide gas-powered stoves or lanterns, it is important to bring the correct fuel in with you as many appliances have been ruined through the use of improper fuel. Some huts have wood-fired stoves with firewood provided; it is always good to use this sparingly, as it is no easy task to get firewood to these locations. Many huts are either user-maintained or cared for by groups of volunteers so keeping them tidy and in good order is a basic courtesy. Even if a hut does not charge for an overnight stay there is often a donation box on site and contributing will ensure upkeep and maintenance of the facility for the future (and its good karma, too). Most importantly, enjoy your stay in the backcountry and be sure to make some lasting memories to take home with you!

Black Tusk Hut (Map 22/D1)
Found along the Black Tusk Trail at Taylor Meadows, this hut (really a cooking shelter) is capable of holding 10 people and dozens of mice. The hut is rarely used, except by the aforementioned mice.

Brew Hut (Map 32/B7)
Located at a high col just south of Mount Brew, this hut is used extensively in the winter, but can also be accessed by hikers from the Brew Lake Trail. In winter, the Roe Creek Route is the safest way to the hut. The upstairs loft sleeps 10 people comfortably and 3 more can sleep on the extra wide bench downstairs. There is a wood stove for winter use only and a Coleman stove (using white gas) available for cooking. Drinking water should be taken from the pond on the west side only and grey water should be disposed of on the east side near the outhouse. Contact the Varsity Outdoor Club (VOC), at www.ubc-voc.com to find out about fees and availability.

Brian Waddington [Phelix] Hut (Map 42/D1)
Located in the Tolkien Group of mountains north of Birkenhead, this hut was built in 1998 for backcountry skiers and mountaineers. There is a rough hiking trail to the hut along Phelix Creek. Visitors are asked to avoid this trail between August 15th and October 15th to allow grizzly and black bear undisturbed access to prime feeding areas. The hut sleeps 20 in the three-chambered loft with more downstairs and is equipped with a Coleman stove and lanterns and a cast iron frying pan. Use white gas only in the appliances. The hut is a great place for hiking, skiing, bouldering and climbing. Although the hut is not locked, visitors are asked to contact the VOC to book (www.ubc-voc.com).

Burton Hut (Map 22/F2)
Located in an ecologically sensitive area of Garibaldi Provincial Park, near where Sphinx Creek runs into Garibaldi Lake, access is difficult in summer. There is no trail and no real reason to go there. In winter it's a fairly easy ski across the frozen lake. The A-frame hut can sleep up to a dozen or so comfortably and has been recently re-insulated. It is equipped with a Coleman lantern, catalytic heater and a Coleman stove, all run on white gas. It is still recommended that visitors carry their own stove. Although the hut is not locked, visitors are asked to contact the VOC to book (www.ubc-voc.com).

Connel Creek Cabin (Map 51/F6)
This A-frame cabin is located in the woods at about 1,675 m (5,500 ft), east of Mount Piebiter. Found a good day's trek from the trailhead at Piebiter Creek, the cabin is often used as a first night's stop on a hike to Whitecap Mountain. The cabin is fairly new and a sign on the outside indicates it is associated with Chilcotin Holidays out of Gold Bridge who run guided hiking trips in the area. The cabin sleeps four.

E-Branch Cabin (Map 19/F2)
This cabin, formerly a ski lift hut, was converted for overnight use by the Knuckleheads Winter Recreation Association. It can sleep eight people, and features a full kitchen area with propane stove and an outhouse. A wood pellet stove provides heat in the winter. Visitors can drive up a series of logging roads before they come to a gate – from here it is about an hour and a half hike to the cabin.

Eldorado Creek Cabin (Map 51/A1)
Located in the upper east fork of Eldorado Creek, this is a commercial cabin used by backcountry skiers, mountain bikers and horse outfitters. The cabin sleeps 12 and has a wood stove, sauna, propane cook stove, oven, utensils and pots and pans. Contact Spruce Lake Adventures in Gold Bridge for rental information. They have a number of cabins in the Eldorado Basin, Spruce Lake, the headwaters of Tyaughton Creek and just off Trigger Lake and rent to experienced backcountry skiers.

Elfin Lakes Hut (Map 22/F5)
The largest hut found in Garibaldi Park is at Elfin Lakes along the Diamond Head Trail. It is a very popular destination, but with no reservations the 34 spaces (11 double bunks, 12 single bunks) can fill up quickly on weekends. The hut is well equipped with a heater and propane burners for cooking. There is access to both the main and upper floors from the outside due to the fact that often the lower storey is buried by snow in late winter. There is a fee payable when self-registering in the parking lot. For the hiker, beautiful alpine meadows with good views of Mount Garibaldi and Mamquam Lake, which is 11 km past the cabin, are the main attractions. For those looking for mountaineering, Mount Garibaldi and Atwell Peak are nearby.

Harrison Hut (Map 40/E3)
Built by the Varsity Outdoor Club in 1983, the Harrison Hut is a popular staging area for backcountry skiers and snowmobilers accessing the Pemberton Icefield. The large gothic A-frame hut can sleep up to 15 people, but access on foot is difficult. A new access trail was built recently and is often used to access nearby Meager Creek Hot Springs. A Coleman stove and lantern are provided and run on white gas. Visit www.ubc-voc.com for more information.

Himmelsbach Hut (Map 33/A7)
Found near Russet Lake and Singing Pass in Garibaldi Park, this hut is part of the BC Mountaineering Club network. The hut is available year-round and there is no fee. The hut, which holds 12, makes a great base camp for exploration of the eastern portion of the Fitzsimmons Range. It is a reasonable day's hike from Whistler Village making it a very popular destination. Due to the sheer volume of visitors, many camp outside at night. The hut provides a sheltered cooking area, but visitors are reminded to pack out what you pack in. Visit www.bcmc.ca for more information.

Hollyburn Cabin (Map 11/B7)
Maintained by the Third West Vancouver Scout Troup, this cabin near Cypress Provincial Park is available for rent to large groups, with space for up to thirty people. The cabin is very well outfitted with a commercial propane stove, griddle, ovens and all cooking utensils except personal eating utensils. Hiking trails from the cabin lead to numerous lakes and three mountain peaks. It is only about a kilometre to hike to the cabin, so access is easy.

Jim Haberl Hut (Map 21/G5)

A climbers hut in the Tantalus Range that replaced the old F.J. Green Shelter (aka Red Tit), this hut sits on in the Serratus-Dione Column next to the Serratus Glacier, at 2,075 m (6,800 ft) elevation, just outside the boundary of Tantalus Provincial Park. Access to the hut is by mountaineering routes from Lake Lovely Water or the Squamish River. The hut contains a fully equipped kitchen with propane cook tops, sitting room plus two sleeping rooms that hold 6 each. The hut is open year-round and a propane heater is available. Reservations are required and available through the Alpine Club of Canada (www.aebc.com/acc/huts.asp).

Juliet Creek Cabin (Map 27/D6)

Located off Jenna Peak Trail, access is from the trailhead located at 8.7 km on the Juliet Forest Service Road. The rustic cabin is maintained by Recreation Sites and Trails and is used mainly by ski touring and hiking parties. There is a wood stove and upper loft for sleeping. Please respect this cabin and keep it clean.

Keith Flavelle Hut (Map 43/B7)

Located an easy two hour hike from the nearest road, Keith's Hut is one of the most popular huts in the Coast Mountains. The hut was built in the memory of Keith Flavelle, a great contributor to the BC mountaineering community who was killed during an expedition of Mount Logan. The hut rests north of Anniversary Glacier at the head of Cerise Creek and can hold 8–12. There is a wood burning stove, basic kitchen, loft and outhouse. Access to both the winter and summer trails to the hut originate at the parking pullout on Duffey Lake Road (Hwy 99) and cross a stream immediately after the parking area.

You will need to contact the owners/maintainers of many of the huts listed here to get access.

Lake Lovely Water [Tantalus] Hut (Map 22/A5)

Open from May to October, this hut was built in 1961 as a base for mountaineering in the Tantalus Range. The two storey hut has a large kitchen/dining room on the main floor and a separate sleeping loft above with foam mattresses for 20 people. Access on foot via the Lake Lovely Water Trail does require the crossing of the Squamish River and is about a 6 hour trek. While the Tantalus area offers limited hiking opportunities, the scenery at Lake Lovely Water is fabulous. In good weather, people enjoy swimming, boating and fishing. There are also a wide variety of climbing opportunities of various grades with peaks such as Tantalus at 2,603 m (8,540 ft), Dione at 2,590 m (8,500 ft), Alpha at 2,305m (7,562 ft), Serratus at 2,326 m (7,632 ft) and many others to explore. The hut is kept locked and must be reserved in advance through the Alpine Club of Canada (www.aebc.com/acc/huts.asp).

Lizzie Creek Cabin (Map 34/C5)

Originally a private cabin built by David Nickerson, this cabin is small (room for 8) and in need of repair. It is located a couple hours hike from Lizzie Lake, which is once again a long haul from Lillooet Lake due to washouts on the Lizzie Forest Service Road. Set in a sub-alpine basin below the Stein Divide it is a gorgeous location. Unfortunately, mice and pack rats have claimed the cabin and most people who stay here do so in winter, when the choice between mice and weather favours the rodents.

McGillivray Pass Hut (Map 51/E6)

There are several summer routes to this area, but the only winter route is from the Gold Bridge and Bralorne side. The road past Bralorne is plowed to the Pioneer Mine, where the McGillivray Pass Trail access is found across the bridge on the right. Follow this trail/road for 7 km to a bridge across Piebiter Creek. Take the right fork and follow the road on a long rising traverse into Standard Creek and the McGillivray Pass Valley. The small cabin that sleeps 6–8 people is located to the right as the trail emerges above the tree line. The hut is equipped with a wood stove and utensils and is open year-round except Thanksgiving and Christmas to New Years.

Mountain Lake Hut (Map 11/D2)

Located in an alpine meadow east of Furry Creek, to the south of Squamish, access to this area is via a long hike along a logging road, which slowly turns into a trail. BC Mountaineering Club members can cut off 10 km or so of this hike by getting the gate key. Others can just walk or take a mountain bike. The area hasn't seen much use in the past and the hut is mostly used by mountaineers heading up Sky Pilot, Mount Sheer, Ben Lomond or another local peak. Contact the BCMC at www.bcmc.ca for more information.

Mount Steele & Tetrahedron Provincial Park Cabins (Map 10/B2)

Maintained by the Tetrahedron Outdoor Club, this series of four cabins are located in Tetrahedron Provincial Park. They are located at Bachelor Lake, Edwards Lake, McNair Lake and near the summit of Mount Steele. All the cabins have wood burning stoves and charge a fee. Distances to the cabins are as follows: Parking Lot to Bachelor Lake Cabin is 2.5 km; Parking Lot to Edwards Lake Cabin is 4.5 km; Edwards Lake Cabin to Mount Steele Cabin is 3 km; Edwards Lake Cabin to McNair Lake Cabin is 5 km. You can pay at the Esso Station in Sechelt or online at www.tetoutdoor.ca. They are not reservable and can be busy on weekends and during holidays.

North Creek Cabin (Map 41/A1)

Operated by the BC Mountaineering Club, this hut can sleep up to 18 people and can be reserved with a minimum group size of 10. It sees little use in summer, but is quite popular in winter. The hut contains a 2 burner stove, wood stove and lanterns. The hut is kept locked; contact the BCMC at www.bcmc.ca for more information.

Pebble Creek Hut (Map 50/A6)

This small hut is located in Ash Pass and is booked through a reservation system. In summer it is possible to get to the cabin via McParlon Creek Road. In winter, access is usually by helicopter. The hut sleeps 6 and charges a low nightly fee per person to help cover maintenance and repair costs. Graham Underhill informally offers cabin reservations. His address is PO Box L-17, RR1, Bowen Island, BC V0N 1G0.

Place Glacier Hut (Map 42/E5)

This research hut is open to the public. Although not very big or well equipped, it is a place to keep dry and spend the night, if needed. Getting to the hut is a 12 km round trip, offering a view of a spectacular waterfall that does offer ice climbing during winter if you are equipped and experienced. The huts were originally built at the glacier snout, but global warming has moved the ice into the far distance. You need to add an additional 2 hours to your trip if you want to reach the glacier.

Snowspider Hut (Map 34/C1)

Built in 1993 by the Whistler Ski and Kayak Club, this hut is primarily used in the winter. There is space for 4 in the loft. In the summer, it can be reached by logging roads up Twin One or Van Horlick Creeks.

Sunshine Coast Trail Huts (Maps 18, 19, 46)

True Hut to Hut hiking can now be accomplished thanks to the contributions of Island Economic Coastal Trust, BC Transmission Corporation, Union of BC Municipalities, many smaller donations and thousands of hours of volunteer labour. The trail features 10 huts. Full details are available at www.sunshinecoast-trails.com.

Manzanita Hut:

The Manzanita Hut is located on the Manzanita Bluffs on the Gwendoline Hills trail section at kilometre 16. The location offers great views of the Copeland Islands, Savary Island and the Salish Sea. The hut is partly open and sleeps 8.

Rieveley's Pond Hut:

Named for the pond it sits at the edge of, this hut is an open shelter with a sleeping loft. It is located at kilometre 33 and sleeps 8.

Confederation Lake Hut:

Originally built a number of years ago by the Ministry of Forests, it is now maintained by BC Parks. It sits at the edge of an ancient fir forest at kilometre 74 and sleeps 6.

Fiddlehead Landing Hut:

Being built in 2012, this hut is located on the shore of Powell Lake at kilometre 81. It will sleep 6.

PARK ADVENTURES

Tin Hat Hut:

Located at the halfway point of the Sunshine Coast Trail, this hut offers a panoramic view of the mountains, valleys and lakes that define the Powell River area. The site is a former fire lookout due to its expansive view. Located at kilometre 90, the fully winterized hut is equipped with a pellet stove and sleeps 8.

Elk Lake Hut:

Built in 2011, this hut is nestled in the trees at the edge of Elk Lake. Featuring a swimming dock for summer fun and ice skating in the winter, the partially open hut is located at kilometre 110 and sleeps 8.

Walt Hill Hut:

This fully enclosed hut was finished in the summer of 2012 and overlooks the Horseshoe Valley. Located at kilometre 122, this hut sleeps 8.

Troubridge Hut:

This beautiful Douglas-fir cabin lies in a bowl beside Jocelyn Pond, below the summit of Mount Troubridge. The summit offers views of Jervis Inlet, the Lower Sunshine Coast and the Islands of the Salish Sea. This hut is considered the highlight of a Sunshine Coast Trail Hut to Hut experience and is located at kilometre 158. Fully winterized, it sleeps 8.

Rainy Day Lake Hut:

Sitting atop the Hailstone Bluff, this hut features swimming docks and two picnic areas. The open hut is located at kilometre 169 and sleeps 8.

Fairview Bay Hut:

This open hut offers a magnificent ocean view with nearby sandy beaches for swimming. Located at kilometre 173, it is a two hour hike from Saltery Bay. The hut sleeps 8.

Sentinel Glacier Huts (Map 22/F2)

Found south of Burton Hut, there is a pair of glaciology research huts near Garibaldi Lake that are open to the public when not occupied by researchers. They are smaller, holding only 4 people.

Taylor Basin Cabin (Map 51/A1)

There is an old mining cabin near Taylor Pass that is used year-round by everyone from mountain bikers to snowmobilers. It has 4 bunk beds and despite its exterior, users have maintained it pretty well.

Tenquille Lake Cabin (Map 41/G3)

A cabin was built at Tenquille Lake in the 1940s and was a popular destination for a few decades until it came into disrepair. Luckily, the Pemberton Wildlife Association (www.pembertonwildlifeassociation.com) rebuilt the cabin in 2011. The cabin has a propane stove, kitchen supplies and a wood-burning stove.

Twin Lakes Hut [Haylmore Creek] (Map 43/C4)

This hut is located in the Twin Lakes/Melvin Lake area, about 5 km from the trailhead at the end of the Haylmore Forest Service Road (accessed from Devine on the Pemberton D'Arcy Road). The hut was built by the Cayoosh Recreation Club and makes a great base to explore the surrounding peaks. There is a wood stove and room for 4.

Wedgemount Lake Hut (Map 33/B5)

Part of the Garibaldi Park network of backcountry huts, this BC Mountaineering Club hut isn't far from the trailhead, but the climb is certainly daunting. It is a smaller hut holding 6 or so visitors and available year-round for a small fee. Other than pit toilets, no other amenities are provided. The lake also makes a nice camping area if the hut is full. Visit www.bcmc.ca for more information on the Himmelsbach Hut at Russel Lake.

Wendy Thompson Hut (Map 43/A5)

Located in Marriott Basin northeast of Pemberton, this hut sleeps 16 and is mostly used in the winter. The hut is equipped with a kerosene heater, Coleman stove and lamps and is just over 5 km from the road. It usually takes 2–3 hours to reach, summer or winter. No longer locked, a reservation will get you a key to the heater. Contact the Alpine Club of Canada, Whistler Section at accwhistler.ca.

BACKCOUNTRY TIPS

Heading into the wilderness without a proper plan or the right supplies is never a good idea. Being unprepared can cause you to have an unpleasant backcountry experience, or it can put you into an emergency situation. Always take a bit of extra time and effort to cover all your bases. The following are a few key things to remember before heading out:

Weather

The most predictable thing about backcountry weather patterns is their unpredictability. Even after you have checked the forecast, be ready for unexpected changes in weather.

Terrain

Like the weather, backcountry terrain is consistently variable. Always be ready to encounter loose rocks, streams, waterfalls, snow, ice, crevasses, canyons, and other features.

Know Your Limits

Do not be afraid to turn back. If you are feeling the effects of fatigue, malnutrition or altitude sickness, it is probably best to turn around. The backcountry will be there when you get back.

Bear Aware

BC's backcountry is home to many bears – make lots of noise to avoid startling them and always store food and scented items properly when camping in the backcountry.

Stay on the Trail

Many hiking trails run through sensitive wilderness habitat, and even footsteps can have a serious effect on these environments. Stay on marked trails whenever possible, particularly in softer grasslands or marshy areas.

Check Rules & Regulations

Rules and regulations regarding fires, pets, hunting, fishing, or motorized vehicles may affect where you decide to go and what you bring with you. Be sure to check before you start packing, so you don't set yourself up for a trip that conflicts with regulations.

Navigation

While exploring the backcountry you will not always be able to rely on markings and signage to orient yourself. Some trails and backroads are better marked than others, while some are not marked at all. It is always a good idea to carry a Backroad Mapbook, compass and a GPS device loaded with our Backroad GPS Maps. Don't forget to research your route ahead of time. With the right equipment, research, and a bit of navigation skill you should be able to get wherever you need to go.

B.C.'s Backcounty Playground

With over 1300 sites and 800 trails
for you to explore.

Check out website for information on
locations, activities, and facilities.

www.sitesandtrailsbc.ca

BRITISH
COLUMBIA

Recreation Sites
and Trails BC

RECSITE ADVENTURES

While it is true that you can erect a tent most anywhere that suits your fancy on public land, many of the best sites have already been discovered and at least partially developed.

These sites were originally developed by forestry workers who wanted to be able to access a good fishing lake or interesting hiking trail on their days off. These days, they are looked after by Recreation Sites and Trails BC (a division of the Ministry of Forests, Lands and Natural Resource Operations), although local recreation groups, forest companies, First Nations or private contractors often maintain the sites and some of these sites have been developed to rival provincial parks. While the majority of sites are free; a minimal fee is charged at sites where increased levels of service are provided from May to October. In the off season some sites are gated. In other cases, user groups will look after a site simply because they have a vested interest in keeping the site open and do not charge any fees.

Recreation Sites offer a nice balance between the developed, but often crowded provincial park system and a completely undeveloped patch of Crown land. The sites offer access to some great fishing lakes, paddling routes and scenery that make British Columbia such a beautiful place to explore. Recreation sites are located on Crown land, not inside a protected area, and have been developed to provide recreational opportunities in a forest setting. A site found on the shores of the lake does not usually encompass the lake itself; it merely provides access to that lake. Access to some of the sites can be rough, often leading down active logging roads. Although the remote nature of these sites can be appealing, do take care travelling the backroads and ensure you take necessary precautions.

Most recreation sites have a camping area, although some are day-use only. They usually have toilets and at least one or two picnic tables. Larger sites have trails, firewood and even a caretaker for on-site supervision and maintenance. There are limited sites that allow reservations by calling the local contractor in charge of the site, but most are on a first-come, first-served basis. The more remote sites are user maintained, where users are responsible for collecting their trash, getting their own firewood and even providing their own toilet paper. Please help keep our province beautiful and pack out any garbage you bring in or that was left by inconsiderate visitors. For current conditions, reservation numbers and access details, visit www.sitesandtrailsbc.ca.

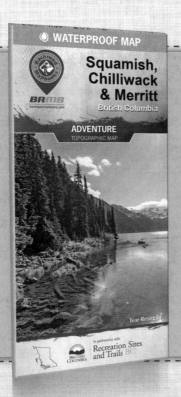

Alexander Falls Rec Site (Map 32/C5)
This is a small, quiet picnic site overlooking the picturesque Alexander Falls. This site is accessed 8 km down the newly paved Callaghan Valley Road. This site is day-use only and fires are prohibited. There are great mountain views and trails leading to the upgraded wheelchair accessible viewing platform overlooking the 43 metre (141 ft) tall Alexander Falls.

Allison Pool Rec Site (Map 4/F6)
Set in a pretty second growth forest next to the Chilliwack River, this 8 unit campsite is accessed by a short gravel road off the Chilliwack Lake Road and is not suitable for RVs. The area is a popular spot for salmon and steelhead fishing and provides access to the Trans Canada Trail. This is a key-accessed site and requires reservations and payment. Call F.H. Forestry Ltd at 604-824-0576 to reserve a site.

Apocynum Rec Site (Map 36/C7)
Recently upgraded and upsized, this popular site is found 16.5 km along the Nahatlatch River Forest Service Road. There is space for 16 groups at the site, which is RV accessible. Whitewater paddling, fishing, hiking and hunting are popular pastimes in the area as the Nahatlatch River and Provincial Park are within close proximity. Like most recreation sites, this campsite is available on a first-come, first-served basis and no firewood is available for sale.

Appleton Creek Rec Site and Trail (Map 18/E1)
A trail access site set in an old growth Douglas-fir stand, there is space for about 3 tenters here. In addition to a unique bridge crossing, there is a network of hiking trails leading to Sliammon Lake and Okeover Inlet that can be accessed from the shores of the creek. From Highway 101 turn onto Wilde Road and follow for about 9 km to get to this site. You will see the trailhead just past Sliammon Lake on your left.

Bain Creek Marine Rec Site (Map 10/E3)
This campsite is frequented mostly by kayakers and canoers. Located in Thornbrough Channel on the western shore of Howe Sound, the closest settlement to the site is Port Mellon. Bain Creek sits along a paddling route connecting the Trans Canada Trail in West Vancouver to the Sea to Sky Trail in Squamish. A stony beach with a mellow grade provides easy landing for paddlers.

Bear Creek Rec Site (Map 14/G5)
Tucked in a nook created by the Harrison East Forest Service Road, Harrison Lake and Bear Creek, visitors will find 40 quiet, shady campsites set into a second growth forest. It is a short hike to nearby Bear Falls and the site is popular with windsurfers. Although is open for the October and April long weekends, the site is gated after the Labour Day long weekend until May 1. It is possible to make reservations for this site in person with the site host.

Beaver Lake Rec Sites (Map 19/D2)
A few canoe access sites are found on Beaver Lake and the portage leading to Dodd Lake. The north site is one of the nicest campsites on the Powell Forest Canoe Route with plenty of space to spread out and a lot of privacy. The southern site is behind the logjam at the lower end of Beaver Lake and has enough space for 1 group to set up. There is also a seldom used site to the southeast that some people portage to.

Big Tree Trail and Picnic Rec Site (Map 9/D4)
Located between Halfmoon Bay and Sechelt this picturesque day-use only site is found at the end of a short, wheelchair accessible trail. The site is located below a number of large old growth fir trees approximately 2 km down the Crowston Lake Forest Service Road.

Blackwater Lake Rec Site (Map 42/F3)
This lake will be the first thing that comes into view (on your left) while travelling on Birkenhead Lake Road, about 45 km from Pemberton. The site itself is a user maintained site with a hand launch for boats. The 6.5 km (4 mi) long, 82 hectare (200 ac) lake provides stocked rainbow trout and there are several trails in the area. When the campsite is not busy, birdwatchers will be able to spot blue herons, bald eagles, and other bird species.

Bob's Lake Rec Site (Map 8/C2)
A small, treed nine unit site used mainly by anglers, hunters and 4wd drive enthusiasts on Texada Island. The recreation site is accessible off Hydro Reactor Road. Please stay on the trails in the area and try not to damage the flora, especially a rare species of orchid found here.

Botanie Lake Rec Site (Map 45/D6)
This small, semi-open three unit recreation site is located next to Botanie Lake, about 17 km up Botanie Creek Road. A favourite spot for winter activity enthusiasts, this site features an enclosed shelter for snowmobilers (although overnight use of the shelter is prohibited). Access to the lake in the summer months is along a decent road which allows small RVs to reach the site. Please note that the lake is on a Reserve and access may be restricted.

Bridge River Picnic Site (Map 52/E6)
Found on the west end of Seton Lake at the Bridge River Powerhouses, this picnic site is located between Seton Portage and Shalalth. Visitors will find a small picnic site and boat launch onto the big lake.

Brohm Lake Day Use Rec Site (Map 22/C4)
This is a popular day-use site that is found just off Highway 99 north of Squamish. In addition to the extensive trail system, there is a place to hand launch small boats. It is a short walk to the lake, where you can swim, fish or picnic. Please note that the lake can be very busy on hot days and parking is limited.

Cabin Lake Rec Site (Map 27/B1)
This is a small, 4 unit site accessed along Miner Forest Service Road by high centered four-wheel drive vehicles only (no off-highway recreational vehicles are allowed at this site). Hikers accessing the Heather Basin Trail frequent the area. This area is also utilized for camping and fishing in the summer and snowmobiling in the winter. It is also a First Nations cultural site used on occasion for tribal gatherings.

Cal-Cheak Rec Site (Map 32/D6)
This is a popular trio of enhanced, heavily used recreation sites, near the confluence of Callaghan Creek and the Cheakamus River. There are 51 campsites divided between the three sites, some of which are walk-in (tenting) only, some of which are big enough for RVs. At the south site, a suspension bridge leads across Callaghan Creek and down to the Brandywine Falls. Visitors will find good fishing in the Callaghan River and the Sea to Sky Trail links to Whistler and the nearby bungee jumping bridge. This site is found on Daisy Lake Forest Service Road, about 3 km north of Brandywine Provincial Park on Highway 99.

Camp Foley Rec Site (Map 5/B5)
This small site is found along the banks of the Chilliwack River, 26.5 km along the Chilliwack Lake Road. The 4 unit campsite is popular for small family groups as it can be reserved as a whole. Key access is required for this site – call F. H. Forestry Ltd at 604-824-0576 to obtain a key. The access road is paved, but not suitable for larger vehicles like RVs.

Carol Lake Rec Site (Map 52/A3)
Carol Lake is a small, popular fishing lake, just north of Carpenter Lake. This site is a great place for a full day of picnicking, nature study, or just relaxing on the wharf. There are 8 campsites large enough for RVs, a cartop boat launch, canoeing, horseback riding, ATVing or if you prefer, there is an extensive trail network to the northwest for the intrepid explorer. This site is located about 75 km from Lillooet, 1 km east of the Marshall Lake Road.

Carpenter Lake Boat Launch Rec Site (Map 52/E5)
Located west of Lillooet along the south shores of Carpenter Lake, this is a small two unit site is a great rest stop for those travelling to and from Seton Portage. Noted more as a boat launch than camping area, picnicking is popular here as the scenery is second to none and it can be quite secluded, too. This site is RV friendly. To access this site from Lillooet, take the Bridge River Road for about 45 km, then left on Mission Mountain Road for another 1.5 km or so.

Cascade Peninsula Rec Site (Map 14/G5)
This medium sized 24 unit forested site is found on the shores of Harrison Lake in a sheltered bay on the eastern side. The site is popular with boaters, anglers and hikers due to its proximity to the lake. This site is run on a first-come, first-served basis only. To get to this site, turn left at the 11 km mark of the Harrison East Forest Service Road and follow the signs.

Cat Lake Rec Site (Map 22/D5)
This site is found 2.5 km down the narrow, winding Cheekye Forest Service Road, which is found about 3.5 km north of the Alice Lake Provincial Park turn-off north of Squamish. The 42 campsites here are all walk-in tenting sites, but they are often busy and a fee is charged to camp here. There is an extensive

network of biking and hiking trails, motorized riding in the area, as well as decent fishing in the small lake. The lake is also a popular swimming destination on hot days.

Cheak Canyon Rec Site (Map 22/C2) △ ⋕ 🖼

This site is a very popular rock climbing area known as the "Chek." The site contains about 100 climbing routes; easy spots for the beginner climber and extremely challenging routes for the expert. This site has three campsites, but be aware that the access road is by four-wheel drive only. You can drive to the site by taking the Conroy Creek Forest Service Road shortly past Brohm Lake on your way out of Squamish. Contact the Squamish Access Society or the Climbers Access Society of BC for more information. Remember to pack out what you pack in.

Chehalis River Rec Sites (Map 4/D1) 🖼 ⋕ 🚤 🏊 🚶 🌊 S

There are actually three separate RV accessible sites on the banks of the Chehalis, one on the left side of the Morris Valley Road, the second on the right before crossing the single lane bridge over the river and the third site is on the far side of the bridge, to your left (to your right is private property). Between the three, there are 56 sites, set in an open forest along the Chehalis River. From the campsite on the north side of the river, a trail runs up the hill and then follows the edge of a spectacular canyon. There is a nice swimming hole and good access to fishing for salmon and steelhead along this trail. Reservations are possible, for more information visit www.westharrisonreservations.com.

Chipmunk Peninsula Rec Site (Map 5/B5) 🖼 ⋕ 🚤 🏊 🚶 🌊 🚵 🛶 (S

Set in a coniferous forest next to the Chilliwack River along the Chilliwack Bench Forest Service Road, visitors will find 21 campsites. There is good access to the river and the site is popular with both ATVers and motorcycles riding the local trails. This site accepts limited reservations through the local contractor; however, most sites are on a first-come, first-serve basis. Visitors can call 604-824-0576 (Monday to Wednesday, 6:00 to 9:00 pm) to make a reservation.

Chipmunk Peninsula on Beaver Lake Rec Site (Map 19/D2) △ ⋕ 🚶 🚤 🌊 🛶

Despite its name, this site is actually on Dodd Lake. Chipmunk Peninsula can be accessed by portaging from Beaver Lake or paddling across from the main Dodd Lake site. This camp features three sites, picnic tables and pit toilets. Dodd Lake is popular for fishing and there are a few nearby hiking trails.

Cinnamon Creek Rec Site (Map 43/G1) 🖼 ⋕ 🚤 🛶 🚻 🏕

There are 11 campsites in this recreation site, located next to the rushing Cayoosh Creek and the scenic Duffey Lake Road (Hwy 99). There are a number of nice spots right on the banks of the creek in this semi-open RV friendly site.

Cogburn Beach Rec Site (Map 14/G4) △ ⋕ 🏊 🚤 🌊 S

This long, open stretch of beach is a popular weekend getaway despite (or because of) the trail access. This is the northern most recreation site on the east side of Harrison and the closest one to Clear Creek Hot Springs. There is space for about 25 groups here.

Cottonwood Creek Rec Site (Map 44/A2) 🖼 ⋕ 🚤 🛶 🚻

This site is located along Cayoosh Creek and the scenic Duffey Lake Road (Hwy 99) between Pemberton and Lillooet. The site has well-spaced campsites giving campers a fair degree of privacy. There are 14 sites with picnic tables that provide good access to the creek.

Dinner Rock Rec Site (Map 18/C1) △ ⋕ 🖼 🚤 🏊 🚶 🚵 🛶 🏕 🦽

Located just off Highway 101, down a steep, but paved access road, the Dinner Rock Recreation Site is a 13 unit, semi-open site located along the Malaspina Strait. There is good salmon fishing in the area, a cartop boat launch and even a popular scuba diving area. This area is wheelchair accessible and makes a fine picnic destination.

Dodd Lake Rec Site (Map 19/C1) 🖼 ⋕ 🚤 🏊 🌊 🚶 🛶 🚻

The 13 unit site on the shores of Dodd Lake is often busy as it is a favourite amongst the locals. Powell Forest canoeists might want to give this one a miss in favour of the much quieter Beaver Lake Recreation Site to the east, which is only accessed by water/portage. This site is easily accessed by two-wheel drive along Goat Lake Main and is suitable for smaller motorhomes.

Driftwood Bay Rec Site (Map 34/A3) △ ⋕ 🖼 🚤 🏊 🚶 🌊 🚶 🛶 🏕 S

There are ten enhanced tent sites on Driftwood Bay, which are often taken up by large parties. The site is found at km 17 on the In-Shuck-Ch Forest Service Road, on a driftwood filled beach next to the jade-green Lillooet Lake. In addition to the typical lake activities, there is a nice even walking trail that runs along the lake.

East Lake Rec Site (Map 19/A4) △ ⋕ 🚤 🏊 🚶 🚶 🚶 🏕

Mainly used for day-use, this is a scenic site found about 4 km down the Duck Lake Forest Service Road. A short trail leads to the lake where a good chance of seeing waterfowl and other wildlife is possible. This site is a favourite for laying down a blanket and taking a dip in the cool refreshing waters.

> Be sure to visit www.sitesandtrailsbc.ca for the latest information on fees, closures and upgrades to the recreation site you plan to visit.

Eaton Creek Rec Site (Map 5/G2) 🖼 ⋕ 🚶 🛶 🌾 🚻 🏕

A small 3 unit site found 16.5 km down the Silver Skagit Road, this site is mainly used by people wishing to hike to nearby Eaton Lake. Two of the sites are set in the forest next to the creek.

Fir Flats Rec Site (Map 36/C7) 🖼 ⋕ 🚶 🚤 🛶 🌾

This 6 unit site is located along the Nahatlatch River, 18 km up the Nahatlatch Forest Service Road northwest of Boston Bar. A great destination for those interested in hiking, fishing and hunting, this site is available on a first-come, first-served basis and is open year-round (weather permitting).

Francis Lake Rec Site (Map 14/E7) △ ⋕ 🚤 🏊 🚶 🚵 🛶

Francis Lake is a small body of water and this 4 unit recreation site is an even smaller. The turn-off to the site is located at the 6.5 km mark of the Sts'ailes (formerly Harrison West) Forest Service Road, 3 km along a four-wheel drive only road. Horseback riding, canoeing, fishing, ATVing and snowmobiling in the winter are all popular activities here.

Friburg Rec Site (Map 51/C2) 🖼 ⋕ 🚤 🏊 🚶 🌊 🚶 🛶 🌾

Friburg is found on the western shore of the picturesque Tyaughton Lake. To drive here take a left at Tyax Junction and continue on Tyaughton Lake Road for 7.5 km. Local First Nations named the lake Tyaughton or 'jumping fish' due to the incredible aerial display the trout in this lake like to perform. The recreation site has room for about 5 campsites along with a cartop boat launch. This is an open site, with space enough to park an RV or two.

Garrison Lakes Rec Site (Map 7/E3) △ ⋕ 🚶 🛶 🌾 🚻 🏕

Found north of Manning Park off the Sunday Summit Forest Service Road, a short 2 km trail leads to the lakes and this tiny, one unit site. Mainly used by anglers, this site is also a favourite for hiking and nature study.

Gillis Lake West Rec Site (Map 27/G2) 🖼 ⋕ 🚤 🚶 🛶 🌾 🚻 🏕

The Murray Lake Road to the west of Kingsvale accesses this site on the western side of the lake. Visitors will find five treed sites as well as a boat launch for anglers testing their luck. This area is known for its wildlife viewing and nature study.

Goat Lake Rec Site (Map 29/D7) △ ⋕ 🚤 🏊 🚶 🚶 🛶

After carrying your canoe down the long portage from Windsor Lake to the south, the Goat Lake Recreation Site is a sight for sore eyes (and shoulders, and back, and legs...). It is one of the prettier spots on the Powell Forest Canoe Route and Goat Lake is much calmer and less travelled than Powell Lake itself. There are eight campsites here.

Gott Creek Rec Site (Map 43/G3) 🖼 ⋕ 🚤 🛶 🌾

This is one of the series of easy access recreation sites found next to the scenic Duffey Lake Road (Hwy 99) between Pemberton and Lillooet. The small, four unit site has 3 picnic tables that appeal more to the day-tripper than campers. Kayakers often run the creek; wildlife is commonly spotted and fantastic mountain views can be enjoyed in the surrounding area.

Grace Lake Rec Site (Map 14/E7)
This is a 10 unit recreation site on the rocky outcrops next to Grace Lake and the busy Sts'ailes (formerly Harrison West) Forest Service Road. Grace Lake has good fishing and a short trail that skirts the shore. Recently, the site has been designated as a staging area for the elaborate ATV/motorized trail system in the area.

Granite Creek Rec Site (Map 17/E4)
This is found just south of Coalmont on the Lodestone Lake Forest Service Road. Its proximity to the Coalmont Road, the scenic Tulameen River and the Kettle Valley Railway makes it a very popular forest service site. There are 21 campsites together with a picnic facility and a canoe launch. The site is often used as a staging area for paddlers as well as the ATV and snowmobile trails in the area.

Gun Creek Campground (Map 51/C4)
This 16 unit campsite is located on the Carpenter Lake, where Gun Creek meets the reservoir. The site is directly adjacent to Highway 40, about 9 km northeast of Gold Bridge. There is good fishing in the area and, at low water; you can explore the old town of Minto, which was flooded in 1954. The RV accessible site is operated by BC Hydro. The reservoir usually fills by late June and remains high until early November.

Gun Lake South Rec Site (Map 50/G3; 51/A4)
Gun Lake is a popular destination lake found just north of Gold Bridge, along Gun Lake Road West. This site is easily accessible, with seven campsites and enough open area to park an RV. There is a boat launch a few kilometres south, near the Lajoie Dam.

Hale Creek Rec Site (Map 14/E4)
This site is currently closed due to wildfire damage resulting in high risk of slide and slope failure, and high numbers of danger trees in the area.

Hope Creek Rec Site (Map 50/F7)
This small site is used mostly as a resting stop in summer for backroad enthusiasts as well as hunters later in the fall. The site offers one campsite and a picnic table and is located about 1 km off the scenic, but often rough Hurley River Road.

Horseshoe Lake Rec Site (Map 19/D3)
Accessed by portage from Lois Lake (and across the Stillwater main at 10 km), this site features four campsites. Enjoy the Powell Forest Canoe Route or simply fish and beetle about Horseshoe Lake.

Ireland Lake Rec Site (Map 19/C2)
This is a tiny, one unit site at the north end of Ireland Lake on the Powell Forest Canoe Route. The site is more functional than pretty; the dock on Ireland Lake itself is an amazing place to watch a sunset, but the actual site is tucked back into the enclosed forest.

Islet View Marine Recreation Site (Map 10/G2)
The most accessible site from Porteau Cove Provincial Park, this site offers a beautiful cleared camping area with no facilities. The beach is a little bit rough, but has a cleared boat run. Be wary of changing conditions in Montagu Channel during your trip in.

Jacobson Lake Rec Site (Map 16/F7)
Found about 50 km down the Tulameen River Forest Service Road, this small five unit site is not accessible to hunters in the fall. There is a horse corral and the site acts as the trailhead for the "Treasures of the Tulameen" complete with information kiosk and map. The Hudson Bay Company Brigade Trail runs nearby and there are snowmobile trails in the area as well.

Jones Lake Recreational Area (Map 5/C2)
Jones Lake is a BC Hydro maintained site located on the shores of Jones (Wahleach) Lake. There are three camping areas on either side of the Wahleach Dam–Jones Lake Main (two sites north and south of Boulder Creek) and Jones Lake West–with a total of 55 sites, most of which are big enough for RVs. However, it is not recommended to bring big units up the steep, rough road into the lake. There are launches for cartop boats and a picnic area at Jones Lake West. Visitors are also advised to bring their own drinking water.

Kenyon Lake Rec Site (Map 13/E6)
The open again, closed again recreation site at Kenyon Lake is open again, with 1 site accessible by 4wd vehicles only. There is also a small island with a site

suitable for overnight camping accessible only by canoe or small boat. Anglers should note the sub-alpine lake is reported barren. To reach Kenyon Lake turn off of Highway 7 onto Sylvester Road, then onto Lost Creek Forest Service Road for about 15 km.

Khartoum Lake Rec Site (Map 19/F3)
Khartoum Lake Recreation Site is a nine unit site found down a well maintained 2wd road, although access is controlled by the logging companies. The treed site is also accessible by canoe from Lois Lake, but few visitors to the Powell Forest Canoe Route venture this far out of the way. There are reports of a washout currently blocking the road in. Call 604-485-3132 for up to date road information.

Kingdom Lake Rec Site (Map 51/B5)
South of Gold Bridge, the short access road to this lake is found just past the 4 km marker on the Kingdom Lake Forest Service Road. The access road can be quite muddy at times so a four-wheel drive vehicle may be necessary. The lovely lakeside site offers nice mountain views and 15 campsites scattered amongst the coniferous trees. The user-maintained site can be used as a base to explore the many lakes and trails in the area. There are several trails and old roads to explore in the area including access to Mount Truax, the highest peak in the area at 2,880 metres (9,450 ft). Remember to pack out what you pack in.

Klein Lake Rec Site (Map 20/B6)
Accessed about 3.6 km down the North Lake Forest Service Road near Earls Cove, this 25 unit site is set in the trees on the northern end of Klein Lake. The campsites are spread out so even on a busy summer weekend you will have at least some privacy. Small RVs can use a couple sites, while there is a wheelchair friendly site as well. There is a day use picnic area, floating dock and the lake makes a nice fishing or canoeing destination. The Suncoaster Trail also runs by the eastern side of the lake, while a population of endangered western painted turtles nests near the shore. Extra care must be taken to protect turtle habitat and dogs are not allowed on the beaches.

Kwotlenemo [Fountain] Lake Rec Sites (Map 53/E6)
In all there are four different sites to choose from on Kwotlenemo Lake. The popular lake is also known as Fountain Lake and is the northern most lake of the scenic Three Lake Valley. Visitors will find good access along Fountain Valley Road into the area and should note that the lake is only open to boats with electric motors. The southern site is the largest of the bunch sporting 17 campsites, while the northern site hosts five sites and a cartop boat launch. The east and west sites are smaller sites situated in the trees.

Lake La Mare Rec Site (Map 52/D2)
Lake La Mare is a popular fishing lake found on a side road off the Yalakom Forest Service Road. Hikers, horseback riders and ATVers have the option of continuing on a trail to Buckholder Lake or along the Hog Creek Trail to Carol Lake. Campers will find room for about 3 units with a small cartop boat launch at Lake La Mare.

Lang Creek Rec Site (Map 19/A4)
Accessed by foot off the Lang Creek Trail, this site is located across from the salmon hatchery. To drive to Lang Creek turn onto Duck Lake Road from Haslam Road and follow for about 3 km. This is a great place to watch salmon spawning in September and October. There is space for about two campsites providing a base camp for exploring the numerous trails and the wildlife found within.

Lewis Lake Rec Site (Map 19/C1)
A little off the beaten path, this recreation site can be accessed by vehicle from Spring Lake Road. This site features four campsites, picnic tables, fire pits, pit toilet, and a boat launch for cartoppers. Activities on the lake include fishing the pristine waters, canoeing and swimming, while Tin Hat Mountain and the surrounding area is used for hiking and motorized vehicles. The access off Spring Lake Road is rough and best left for four-wheel drive vehicles.

Lightning Lake Rec Site (Map 27/C1)
This campsite is found in a heavily forested area along the northern shore of the small mountain lake. There is room for about four units on this site, which is popular for fishing and hunting in the summer and fall or snowmobiling in the winter months. A four-wheel drive vehicle is required to access the lake as the road is very rough as you proceed down Miner Forest Service Road.

Little Horseshoe North Rec Site (Map 19/D2) 🔺⛵️🏊‍♀️🛶

This small two unit site is located on Little Horseshoe Lake along the Powell Forest Canoe Route. This is the start of the portage from Little Horseshoe Lake to Beaver Lake. This quaint little overnight spot can only be accessed by boat or canoe. There is a floating dock allowing for swimming and lazing in the sun while soaking in the surrounding scenery.

Lizzie Bay Rec Site (Map 34/A3) 🚵🏕🏊‍♀️🛶🏊‍♂️🚶🛶🏇🎣🅂

At km 13 on the In-Shuck-Ch Forest Service Road, this is probably the nicest site on Lillooet Lake. However, the access road is a bit rough and only one or two sites are large enough for smaller trailers so the site does not get much use. There is a small beach with 2 campsites that is separate from the rest of the 10 forested campsites on the shore of the lake. The site also features large Douglas-fir and cedar as well as an archeological site where a Native village once existed. The area is used as a base camp for the numerous activities in the surrounding wilderness, while boating, canoeing, fishing, picnicking and swimming are often enjoyed at the site.

Lodestone Creek Rec Site (Map 17/B4) 🚵🏕🛶🏇🐎🏊‍♂️🏊‍♀️🛶🎣

Lodestone Creek can be reached by a series of logging roads near the town of Coalmont. Rice Road, Blakeburn Forest Service Road, and finally Lodestone Forest Service Road will take you to the rec site. Used by fishermen and as a stopover for hikers or horseback riders on the Hope Brigade Trail, there are two sites located in a semi-open forest. There is a boat launch allowing access to the lake.

> ▶ *Each year dozens of forest fires are started by human negligence. Be sure your fire is completely out and cool to the touch before moving on.*

Log Creek Rec Site (Map 36/B7) 🚵🏕🏇🛶🎣🅂

A small recreation site is situated at the Log Creek/Nahatlatch River confluence, about 23.5 km up the Nahatlatch River Forest Service Road. Used mainly by paddlers, anglers and hunters, the site offers six riverside campsites.

Lois Lake Rec Site (Map 19/C4) 🚵🏕🏊‍♀️🛶🏊‍♂️🛶🚶🏇🚴🛶🎣

The starting point of the Powell Forest Canoe Route, this recreation site is used more by RV's and cartop campers than by canoeists. No wonder. The site isn't all that pretty, especially compared to other sites just a short paddle/portage away. There are 12 well used campsites here, most of which are in an open area near the shore, along with 4 walk-in sites. From Highway 1, north of the Salter Bay Ferry, turn onto Canoe Main and follow for around 6 km to get to Lois Lake.

Lois Point Rec Site (Map 19/D4) 🔺🏕🛶🏊‍♂️🚶🏇🛶

Developed to address the issue of Powell Forest canoeists not wanting to share a site with vehicle campers, this site has space for 4 tents. It is also conveniently located for hikers crossing the Sunshine Coast Trail. The site is a short 2 km paddle or walk along the southeast shore of Lois Lake from the start of the canoe route.

Long Island Bay Rec Site (Map 14/F4) 🔺⚓🏕🏊‍♀️🏊‍♂️🛶🚶🛶

Accessible only by boat, this is a popular spot that has two large docks to accommodate large vessels. The sites are secluded and there is ample moorage, a beach and a barbeque shack for cooking dinner. Enjoy the many trails which wind their way through the forest to a lookout over the bay.

Lookout Lake Rec Site (Map 14/D4) 🚵🏊‍♂️🛶

Located at the junction of the West Harrison and the Mystery Creek Forest Service Road, there is only space for one group at this small site. The four-wheel drive access limits visitors here. Current reports indicate this site is closed due to wildfire activity.

Madeley Lake Rec Site (Map 32/C3) 🔺🏕🚶🛶🎣

You will have to walk in about 500 metres to get to this beautiful mountain lake. That is if you can negotiate the 16 km of rough road into the lake. The road does deter some, but the site still remains a popular getaway in summer. In addition to a chance to pitch your tent on the beach there is good fishing on the lake and an often muddy trail leading up to the Rainbow Lake area.

Marshall Creek Rec Site (Map 51/F2) 🚵🏕🏊‍♀️🛶🛶🎣

Located just below where Marshall Creek flows out of Marshall Lake, this is a small, treed site has space enough for three groups. Fishing, boating and hunting in the fall are all popular activities here. There is a cartop boat launch at the site that has good access off the Marshall Lake Road. Due to the size of the sites, small camping units or tents are recommended.

Marshall Lake North Rec Site (Map 51/F2) 🚵🏕🏊‍♀️🏊‍♂️🛶🛶🚶🏇🚴🛶

This is a fairly open site on the northeastern shores of Marshall Lake. There are seven campsites split between two sites; the north shore is suitable for tents or truck campers, while the northwest side has five sites and accommodates small trailers and RV's. Trail enthusiasts (both hikers and ATVers) will be amazed at the number of trails to choose from in the area. To drive to this site take Marshall Lake Road north from Highway 40 until kilometer 89, then turn left for about 1 km.

Middle Point Rec Site (Map 19/C2) 🔺🏕🏊‍♀️🏊‍♂️🚶🛶

An open site carved out of the forest about halfway along the portage trail between Nanton and Dodd Lake on the Powell Forest Canoe Route. Accessed only by foot (usually by people with a canoe on their back), this site is a great place to stop for an evening, with space enough for two tents.

Mission Dam Rec Site (Map 52/E5) 🚵🏕⚓🏊‍♂️🛶🛶🎣🏇

This three unit site is located on the easternmost reaches of Carpenter Lake, a short drive off the Carpenter Lake Road. The Terzaghi Dam is certainly an impressive sight but the busy road detracts from the peaceful nature of the area. Also, swimming in the dam outlet is prohibited due to frequent water release from Carpenter Lake. The site is open, with space for RVs and offers a dock for boaters.

Molson Memorial Rec Site (Map 31/C4) 🏕🚶🛶🎣🏇

This small and rustic site is situated beside the Peaches and Cream Falls on Ponor Creek. Found off G Main from Elaho Main, the remote site has one table and stairs to the waterfall viewing area.

Mosquito Lake Rec Site (Map 42/C7) 🔺🏕🏊‍♀️🏊‍♂️🛶🏊‍♂️🚶🚴🛶

This small, three unit, forested site receives heavy use, especially by anglers. The road is rutted and muddy, but water enthusiasts will brave the conditions to enjoy a day at the beach. There are several little coves accessible only by boat as the lake has an irregular edge. The lake also makes a refreshing stop over for mountain bikers and hikers enjoying the nearby trail system.

Mowson Pond Rec Site (Map 51/C2) 🚵🏕🏊‍♀️🏊‍♂️🛶🏇🏊‍♂️🛶🏇🎣

The Tyaughton Lake Fire in 2009 wreaked havoc on this area and Mowson and nearby Pearson Pond received the brunt of the abuse. The once scenic lake is half its original size and the burned trees create an eerie setting for would be campers. That said; there is space for seven units, a boat launch and good road access for RV's.

Murphy Lakes West Rec Site (Map 17/A3) 🚵🏕🛶🚶🏊‍♂️🚴🛶🎣🏇

There is a recreation site on the western Murphy Lake that offers space for five campers and a cartop boat launch. The lake offers stocked rainbow trout, while trail enthusiasts and hunters can explore the surrounding area. You can drive to Murphy Lakes along Lawless Creek Forest Service Road, Britton Forest Service Road, and Grasshopper Road.

Murray Creek Rec Site (Map 45/D4) 🔺🚴🎣🏇🏇

Located on the Murray Creek Forest Service Road west of Spences Bridge, this is a small four unit semi-open site, which requires a four-wheel drive to reach. The recreation site is next to Murray Creek and is used primarily by hunters in the fall, although the nearby Onion Lake/Monkey Wrench Riding Area does attract dirt bikers in the summer.

Murray Lake Rec Sites (Map 27/F4) 🚵🏊‍♂️🏊‍♂️🏊‍♂️🚴🛶🎣🏇

There are two campgrounds found on Murray Lake, which, in turn, is found on the deteriorating Murray Lake Road north of Exit 240 of the Coquihalla Highway (Hwy 5). In total there are 12 campsites on the scenic lake, nine at the north and three at the south. This site is used primarily by anglers in the spring and summer and hunters in the fall.

Nahatlatch River Rec Site (Map 36/B7) 🚵🏕🏊‍♂️🛶🎣🅂

This is a six unit site on the south side of the Nahatlatch. Recent enhancements have made this a nice campsite to visit. To get to the site, take the Power Puff Road for 3 km, then turn right and follow that road for 4 km to the site.

RECSITE ADVENTURES

Nanton-Ireland North Rec Site (Map 19/C2)
Located on the shores of Ireland Lake at the end of the 2.4 km portage, this four unit site is not as open as others. The shores of the lake are shrubby, and, although the forest is nice, the other two sites on this portage (Nanton-Ireland South, Middle Point) on the Powell Forest Canoe Route are nicer.

Nanton Lake Rec Site (Map 19/C2)
Found on the western shore of Nanton Lake, this recreation site has 16 sites, two of which are right on the lake and 13 of which have picnic tables and are further inland. Visitors come by canoe or vehicle along the Weldwood Goat Lake Main. The site is suitable for smaller RV's and makes a nice picnic site too.

North Dodd Lake Rec Site (Map 19/D1)
Located at the north end of Dodd Lake, well away from the main recreation site at the south end, this is a pretty little site enclosed in the forest. The site is accessible by canoers or by folks willing to do a bit of bushwhacking to get to this remote-feeling recreation site. There is space for two tents and a floating dock.

Owl Creek Rec Sites (Map 42/C7)
There are two enhanced sites here, one on Owl Creek and the other on the Birkenhead River. The best spot is the one next to Owl Creek, which has 15 well spaced campsites. An old apple orchard and maple trees make this a nice site, but watch for bears in fall. The other site is just a big roadside pullout, with space for about 11 vehicles. This site is found along Old Portage Road, 4 km past Mount Currie.

Pearson Pond Rec Site (Map 51/C2)
The Tyaughton Lake Fire in 2009 greatly affected the area around Pearson Pond. The user maintained site sits in an opening next to the stocked pond that once produced decent size brook trout.

Be bear aware. Never bring any food or scented items into your tent - store them in a food cache or hang them at least 5 metres from the ground. Keeping a clean campsite will ensure a fun and bear free camping adventure.

Rainbow Falls Rec Site (Map 14/G6)
Rainbow Falls Recreation Site is a small boat accessed site in a protected bay on Harrison Lake. Formed by Cascade Peninsula, it can also be reached by picking your way down Slollicum Creek. There is space for tenting on the gravel beach, a dock for boaters and a short trail to the beautiful falls.

Ramillies Channel Marine Recreation Site (Map 10/F4)
Located on the eastern shore of Gambier Island, this site is centrally located along the Sea to Sky Marine Trail network. Several picnic tables and tenting sites, as well as an easy to land pebbly beach, make this a popular destination for kayakers. The area is divided into three beaches, with one upland mossy beach ideal for tent camping.

Rapids Rec Site (Map 5/B5)
Situated along the banks of the Chilliwack River, 6.5 km down the Chipmunk Bench Road, this is a newly developed 28 unit campsite. A favourite spot for motorized trail bike riding, this site has a short beginner's dirt bike track (100cc maximum) and hiking trail. Adjacent to this site is the well-known Chipmunk motorcycle trail network for more advanced riders. Rapids recreation site allows a limited number of sites for reservations through the local contractor; however, most sites are on a first-come, first-served basis. Phone 604-824-0576 (Monday to Wednesday, 6:00 to 9:00 pm) to make a reservation.

Riverside Rec Site (Map 5/C6)
Found 28.7 km along the Chilliwack Lake Road, the site is actually alongside a small tributary of the Chilliwack River. The 15 unit site with picnic tables is suitable for RV's and larger groups. Despite its easy access and nice setting, the road traffic does deter some. The Trans Canada Trail also runs through the area, providing excellent hiking and biking opportunities. A limited number of sites are available for reservation by phoning 604-824-0576 (Monday to Wednesday, 6:00 to 9:00 pm).

Roger Creek Rec Site (Map 43/F3)
The Roger Creek Recreation Site is actually a pair of small roadside sites, with 14 campsites in total. The northern site has space for 5 campers and is more open, making this a better place for RVs. The sites are easily accessed off the scenic Duffey Lake Road (Hwy 99), and are connected by a short trail that is often flooded during high water season.

Scuzzy Creek Rec Site (Map 26/D4)
This seven unit site is found on the banks of Scuzzy Creek, in a large mature cottonwood stand. Most two-wheel drive vehicles with enough clearance can make it to this site, which is found 12.5 km up the Scuzzy Creek Forest Service Road. Anglers and hunters are the main visitors to this user maintained site. Remember to pack out what you pack in.

Shingle Beach Rec Site (Map 8/C2)
Located right on the southwestern shore of Texada Island, the open grassy site offers a great ocean view. However, it can also get hammered fairly hard by winds and storms. There is good road access off Mouat Bay Road for RVs and the 30 unit site is home to a music festival every July. Boaters also frequent the site, where salmon fishing and scuba diving can be enjoyed.

Silver Lake Rec Site (Map 27/C1)
Located in a spruce tree stand next to the lake, this site has two campsites and a cartop boat launch. The site is found on a four-wheel drive road off of Spius Creek Road and is a favourite for its hunting, fishing, canoeing and snowmobiling opportunities.

Skwellepil Creek Rec Site (Map 14/B5)
A victim of the massive landslide on Chehalis Lake in 2007, this newly restored site provides 52 campsites and a boat launch on the west side of the popular recreational lake. Boating, fishing, hiking, picnicking and ATVing are all popular activities in the area. There are numerous trails to explore, as well as coves and bays along the shores of 10 km (6 mi) long Chehalis Lake. This area is a favourite for wildlife viewing and nature study, including visiting the landslide area a short drive to the north along the Chehalis Forest Service Road. Reservations are possible, for more information visit www.westharrisonreservations.com.

Sloquet Hot Springs Rec Site (Map 24/D6)
Although very remote, this site attracts all kinds of people due to the small but picturesque hot springs. The area features 20 campsites, and a fee for use of hot springs use is included in the $15.00 a night for camping. Be aware that this area becomes very busy on long weekends despite the 80 km drive down the In-shuck-ch Forest Service Road.

Squamish Riverside Rec Site (Map 21/G2)
Found close to the Ashlu Creek confluence off the Squamish Forest Service Road, this recreation site has recently been upgraded. There are now 10 campsites and a couple new outhouses that are wheelchair accessible. The site is popular with anglers, but is also a destination for swimming, picnicking and kayaking or just hanging out on the beach. Use caution camping here when there is a rainfall warning or high river warning. As of September 2015, flooding damage has caused this site to close until further notice.

Strawberry Point Rec Site (Map 33/G2)
This beautiful sandy beach is found near the 6 km mark on the In-shuck-ch Forest Service Road. A short walk down the hill brings you to a long sandy beach that is littered with driftwood where folks like to make shelters. This site is very popular, especially for dog walkers. There are no defined camping sites due to high water, but there is usually room for six groups to camp here.

Sunrise Lake Rec Site (Map 14/E4)
This isolated site is found at the end of a rough four-wheel drive road off the Sts'ailes (formerly Harrison West) Forest Service Road. Turn left onto the access road at the 24 km mark. The BC Four-Wheel Drive Association has been maintaining the site for years. In addition to having fun bumping their way in, people will find four sites, a cartop boat launch and a nice lake to fish. In the winter months, the area turns into Nirvana for the snowmobiling crowd. Unfortunately, this site is closed until further notice due to wildfire damage.

Sutter Creek Rec Site (Map 16/F5)
This site is found on the Tulameen River Forest Service Road in a quaint little area next to the creek. There are three campsites within a fairly open area not far from nearby Vuich Falls Recreation Site. Hiking to Treasure Mountain, ATVing, wildlife viewing and hunting are popular pastimes.

Tamihi Creek Rec Site (Map 4/E6)

Set in a large open grassy area ideal for RVs, this is one of the bigger recreation sites in the area. There are 116 mostly open campsites as well as some quieter tenting sites in the deciduous forest next to Tamihi Creek. The site is popular with everyone from salmon and steelhead anglers in the fall, to Trans Canada Trail enthusiasts and even ATVers in the spring and summer months. Make sure to check out the beautifully carved log picnic shelter on the eastern side of the site. This site is located about 12 km up Chilliwack Lake Road, near the junction with Liumchen Creek Forest Service Road.

Tantalus Landing Marine Recreation Site (Map 22/B7)

Located at the northern end of Howe Sound this site has a rocky landing area and a tenting site without facilities. The eastern shore is somewhat developed with beach and tent sites, while the western shore is cliffy and less hospitable. This site is within an hour's paddle of Squamish along the Sea to Sky Marine Trail network.

Tenquille Lake Rec Site (Map 41/G3)

A remote, hike in destination, Tenquille Lake is a spectacular backpacking route. The lake is situated in an alpine meadow with mountains that tower across the lake. Numerous hiking trails take you to the lake. The easiest access into the lake is via the 2.5 hour walk from Branch 12, a four-wheel drive road found off the Hurley River Forest Service Road. In addition to a nice camping area, a new cabin was built in 2011 by the Pemberton Wildlife Association, replacing the previous one that was about 60 years old. Remember to pack out what you pack in.

Thornbrough Point Marine Recreation Site (Map 10/F3)

Located on the western shore of Howe Sound, north of Gambier Island, this site features a cleared boat run and a couple of stone beaches. Some tent sites can be found upland from the beaches. The site is part of the Sea to Sky Marine Trail.

Three Sisters Creek Rec Site (Map 45/D1)

This is a small site with one open, grassy campsite and toilet that makes an ideal location for those visiting nearby Cornwall Hills Provincial Park. Hang-gliding is a popular activity in the area. The site can be found about 15 km up Oregon Jack Road. Be aware of extremely slick conditions on this road during wet weather; a four-wheel drive is recommended. Visitors are asked to stay away from the nearby creek as it is the water source for a local community.

Thurston Meadows Rec Site (Map 4/G6)

Thurston Meadows is a large, open, enhanced site that has good access for RVs. The site has a number of day-use picnic sites on the banks of the popular recreational river and space for 52 camping groups. Unlike many of the sites in the Chilliwack Valley, this site is open all year. This site is found about 16 km up the Chilliwack Lake Road. Reservations can be made by calling 604-824-0576 from Monday to Wednesday between 6:00 and 9:00 pm.

Tony Lake Rec Site (Map 19/C3)

Located off the Weldwood Goat Lake Main near Powell River, this is a quiet site that sees little use. There is room for two units and access to the tiny lake for canoeists. Be sure to check out the hiking trails around this serene getaway location.

Twenty Mile Bay Rec Site (Map 14/D3)

Twenty Mile Bay is an enhanced recreation site and features 59 campsites in total. The scenic site sits on a sheltered bay and has a boat launch for those people willing to bump their way 35 km up the often busy Sts'ailes (formerly Harrison West) Forest Service Road. This site is a favourite of the locals and makes a fine base for ATVing as well. Reservations are possible, for more information visit www.westharrisonreservations.com.

Twin One Creek Rec Site (Map 34/B2)

This enhanced site is located about 9 km down the In-Shuck-Ch Forest Service Road on the jade-green Lillooet Lake. There are 15 campsites in a wooded area and a nice beach when the lake level is low. A boat launch is available, but the lake does have a lot of floating wood and deadheads, so use caution when boating. The grassy area next to the lake is popular with picnickers and a creek flows nearby. RV's and trailers may want to use the second entrance to access the site, as it is less steep. Watch for logging trucks and other traffic on the access road.

Tyaughton Creek Rec Site (Map 51/E3)

Another small Carpenter Lake site, this location is close to Gold Bridge and offers room for four camping groups. This site is perfect for those who love horseback riding in the summer and hunting in the fall. Set in a semi-open ponderosa forest, there is also a rough cartop boat launch. Drive to this site along Tyaughton Lake Road, then Mud Creek Forest Service Road.

Vuich Falls Rec Site (Map 16/F5)

Located about 34 km down the Tulameen River Forest Service Road, this three unit site provides access to a lookout over the cascading waters of Vuich Creek. It is a small forested site that is used primarily by hikers in the summer and hunters in fall.

Weaver Lake Rec Site (Map 14/E7)

The short access road to Weaver Lake is suitable for four-wheel drive vehicles only. Weaver Lake is a picturesque lake and the 29 enhanced campsites are set in a lush forest on the lake's shore. There is a separate day-use/picnic area, a gravel boat launch and a great walking trail that circumnavigates the lake. The site is popular with anglers and there is a dock available for boaters with small boats.

Wells Lake Rec Site (Map 17/B6)

Although it is possible to access Wells Lake by an extreme four-wheel drive road off the Tulameen River Forest Service Road, most visitors into the area come by foot, horse or ATV. There are four rustic tenting pads located next to the small fishing lake.

Windsor Lake Rec Site (Map 29/D7)

This site has one of the most unique pit toilets in the entire province – a hollowed out giant stump of a tree. It's worth the trip just to see it, or, if you like, use it. The portage trail down to Goat Lake crosses the Weldwood Goat Lake Main (at the 36 km mark), so it is possible to hike in from here. This is an excellent overnight stop along the Powell River Forest Canoe Route.

Wolf Lake Rec Site (Map 14/E7)

This is a small, three unit recreation site on the shores of Wolf Lake, which is easily accessed off the Sts'ailes (formerly Harrison West) Forest Service Road. A nice dock has been built to allow easier access to the marshy lake. This site is available for exclusive rental by families or small groups; reservations can be made online at www.westharrisonreservations.com.

Wood Lake Rec Site (Map 14/E5)

This popular, enhanced site is set in an opening next to a small lake. The site has been upgraded and now sports 30 campsites spread out between three camping areas around the lake. However, it is gated in the fall and winter. Powerboats are not allowed on the lake, which is found 30.5 km down the Morris Valley and Sts'ailes (formerly Harrison West) Forest Service Road. Reservations are possible, for more information visit www.westharrisonreservations.com.

Yalakom Rec Site (Map 52/E2)

Located next to the Yalakom River, this open, five unit site is easily accessed by RV. Fishing, hunting and exploring the endless trail system throughout the area are the popular pastimes in this dry, often hot landscape. This area is also a hot spot for horseback riders and hiking enthusiasts. Northwest of Lillooet, access is via the Bridge River Road (Hwy 40) and the Yalakom River Forest Service Road.

Zorro Bay Marine Recreation Site (Map 11/A2)

Located near the northern end of Howe Sound, this site is accessed by a choice of easy protected landings. Spacious, well-protected tent sites are located a short hike upland from the water. North and south facing beaches are both composed of gravel and small stones and are excellent places to relax and enjoy views of the Sound.

Zum Peak Rec Site (Map 16/E1)

Although it is possible to camp at the trailhead to Little Douglas Lake, many prefer to camp next to the lake, which is set below the towering Zum Peak. The high elevation lake is a nice summer getaway for anglers or hikers and is a prime spot for cross-country skiing in the winter. Smaller trailers and truck campers should find access relatively easy, but the site is not suitable for large motorhomes or fifth wheels. Take Exit 228 off the Coquihalla Highway (Hwy 5) and continue on Upper Coldwater Road for 7 km to access this rec site.

TRAIL ADVENTURES

The thickly forested Coast Mountains are paradise for lovers of the outdoors. Trails lead up, down and around these rugged mountains. Options range from short interpretative trails to epic treks through places that few people have ever visited.

Many of the trails are destination oriented, leading to fishing lakes, mountain vistas or waterfalls. Because the mountains often start at or near sea level, much of the hiking happens through lush rainforest before eventually breaking out into sub-alpine and alpine territory. The farther away from the coast you get, the higher your starting point (usually) and the easier it is to break out of the trees (again, usually).

To help you select the trail that best suits your abilities, we have included information on elevation gain, return distance and special features wherever possible. Also included in each description is a symbol to indicate what the trail is used for – hiking, mountain biking, horseback riding, ATV, etc. Unless otherwise noted, distances and times are for round trip hikes.

We rate most of the trails with one of the following descriptors: An easy trail has gentle grades and is suitable for family excursions. A moderate trail can involve a long, steep hill, some technical sections (roots, boulders, etc.) and is probably enough to tax most users. Be careful not to overestimate your ability or underestimate the difficulty of the trail. Only experienced trail users should consider difficult trails or routes. These trails are often rough and/or unmarked.

In this region, finding the trailhead is sometimes the toughest part of the adventure. Although we mark most trails on the appropriate map, the actual trailhead is often not marked and easily missed. In urban and rural areas, trails often start side roads too small to mark on our maps.

Trail enthusiasts should also note that higher elevation trails and routes (over 1,000 metres/3,280 feet) might have a limited season due to late season snow. These trails should be left for late summer and early fall (July through October). If you are travelling on unmarked trails, we recommend that you have mountaineering knowledge and are equipped with a topographic map and a compass as well as a GPS receiver. Also, be sure to leave a detailed itinerary of where you are going with family and friends.

Despite the wealth of trails listed below, this still only represents a fraction of opportunities for outdoor adventurers. If you are planning on getting off the beaten path, be careful. The Coast Range is very rugged terrain.

1858 Gold Rush [Gate Mountain] Trail (Map 26/F5)

The trailhead is found nearly 3 km north of the Alexandria Tunnel on Highway 1. This steep trail leads up to the southern ridge of Gate Mountain. At 850 m (2,790 ft) elevation the trail splits into two. Heading south leads to the First Brigade/ 1848 HBC Brigade Trail and to some nice camping spots. Going north leads to the summit of Gate Mountain. This is a 5.5 km (3.4 mi) return trip, with an elevation gain of 560 m (1,840 ft).

Agassiz Trails (Map 4/F2–G3)

The Agassiz Dykes provide a series of gated access roads that run along the Fraser River to the south of Agassiz. These routes can be accessed off of Highway 7 below Mount Woodside, south of Maria Slough or from several of the intersecting rural roads. These peaceful trails are bordered by farmland and offer views along the Fraser River.

Aldergrove Lake Regional Park (Map 3/A7)

Tucked away in the rolling hills beside the US border, this regional park is centred around the man-made lake. There are 9.5 km (5.9 mi) worth of trails, most of which are open to horseback riding, mountain biking, and are dog friendly.

Alice Lake Area (Map 22/D5)

This park and the adjacent area to the east offer good access to several trails in and around the area. The most popular year-round trail is the Four Lakes Walk. This well-developed 6.5 km (4 mi) trail leads past four woodland lakes during a leisurely stroll through a second growth forest. Another option is the 3 km (1.9 mi) DeBeck's Hill Trail that offers views of the Squamish River. The trails also join with trails leading to Cat Lake, the highway and Garibaldi Estates. Bob McIntosh Trail leads out of the park to the northeast and offers access to several trails in that area including the Alice Ridge Trail.

Alice Ridge Trail (Map 22/E4)

Take the right fork when the road splits at the Alice Lake Provincial Park Headquarters and drive up the rough four-wheel drive road as far as you can. From the end of the road, hike uphill to the Little Diamond Head and the base of Mount Garibaldi. If you can get to the end of the road, you will only have to walk 8 km (5 mi) return, gaining 700 m (2,295 ft) along the way. The route, which is best hiked in July to October, provides an alternative route to the Diamond Head Area.

Ambrose Lake Ecological Reserve (Map 20/B6)

To reach the trailhead, follow Timberline Road, which is found about 500 metres from the Earl's Cove Ferry Terminal. The trail leads from the end of the road and follows the powerline to the lake. This is an easy 5 km (3 mi) return hike. The ecological reserve at the lake is home to an abundance of waterfowl.

Ancient Cedars/Showh Lakes (Map 32/F3)

Home to trees estimated at over 1,000 years old, some with diameters of over 3 metres (10 ft), this stand of old growth trees is made up of yellow and red cedar and Douglas fir. The Ancient Cedars Trail is the main trail here, and is an easy 5 km (3 mi) return hike that gains 150 m (490 ft). Also in the area is the Showh Lakes Trail, a loop that rejoins the Ancient Cedars Trail.

Appleton Canyon/Marathon Trails (Map 18/E1)

The trailhead is found only 20 metres north of the Sliammon Lake Trail on the Theodosia Forest Service Road. It is a well-marked trail that leads along Appleton Creek past some nice waterfalls and through an old growth forest. The Marathon Trail continues on past the Appleton Creek Rec Site (at 2 km) and eventually leads to the Southview Road. The trail is 4 km (2.5 mi) one-way. A side trip leads to the Gibraltar viewpoint, which provides a fantastic view of the Strait of Georgia.

Baby Munday Peak Trail (Map 5/C4)

This 6.9 km (4.3 mi) one-way trail provides excellent access to the mountains and alpine along the central park of the Cheam Range. At first the trail is nothing more than an overgrown road, but as you make your way down and across the valley it becomes more defined. After crossing Alpine Creek the trail begins to make its way uphill. And up it goes; there are no switchbacks and at times the grade is 55%, gaining 1,160 m (3,800 ft) in elevation. Eventually, you will come out of the forest and into the alpine meadows of the ridge. At the end of the trail there is a small informal campsite. This site makes a good base camp for those wanting to explore further on the ridges of the area.

Baden Powell Trail (Maps 1, 11)

The main artery to the massive lower elevation trail network of the North Shore Mountains is the Baden Powell Trail. This popular 42 km (25.6 mi) one-way trail leads through the lush second growth forests from Horseshoe Bay all the way to Deep Cove. There are a number of dramatic canyons as well as some great views of Vancouver and the surrounding area. The route is well maintained and marked and can be accessed from at least 12 different roads as well as numerous trails. It would take at least 18 hours to do the whole route, so most people break the trail up over a series of day hikes. There are a couple places where backcountry camping is allowed. Most of the route is open to mountain biking, but riders should expect a very technical route with lots of ups and downs, tree roots and difficult creek crossings.

Barkley Valley Trail (Map 43/C4)

Better known as an ATV trail, the old road becomes impassable to even ATVers after the prospector's cabin. People can continue on foot to Twin Lakes. It is about a 4 km road walk from where the Haylmore Forest Service Road ends to the hiking only trail. The road leads to the abandoned Elliot Creek mining claim, which dates back to the 1950s.

Bear Mountain Trail (Map 14/G7)

To access the Bear Mountain Trailhead turn right at the four-way stop in Harrison and proceed along Lillooet Avenue for 4.9 km, turning at an unmarked gravel road. Look for a sign warning of mining activity– the mining company has long ago left the area and this is your trailhead. From here it is a 9.6 km (6 mi) one-way trail to reach the summit of Bear Mountain, gaining around 1,000 m (3,280 ft) along the way. During the hike you will pass remnants of the former mining operation –turn right after the old mining office. From here you will begin to climb past several small waterfalls and through a few switchbacks before coming to Bear Lake about 6 km into the hike. From here it is another 3.5 km to the summit, where you will be rewarded with spectacular views of the Fraser Valley, Agassiz, and Seabird Island.

Beartooth Mountain Trail (Map 29/C5)

This trailhead is accessed by boat on Powell Lake. The difficult trail begins on the north side of Beartooth Creek and extends 8 km (5 mi) from Powell Lake to the summit of Beartooth Mountain gaining 1,720 m (5,640 ft) along the way. The trail is generally easy to follow and is marked with flagging tape through an old growth forest.

Belcarra Regional Park Trails (Map 1/G1–2/A1)

Accessed by the Bedwell Bay Road off loco Road, this regional park encompasses Bedwell Bay and Burns Point, which juts out into Indian Arm. A 5.5 km (3.4 mi) round trip follows the shoreline past Burns Point to Jug Island. There is a pleasant secluded bay at the end of the trail. Views of Mount Seymour and Second Narrows Bridge are provided along the trail. Another pleasant walk circles around Sasamat Lake. This easy, one hour hike offers a cool, refreshing stroll through the heavy forest around the lake. Other trails include the 5 km (3 mi) Admiralty Point Trail and the 7 km (4.3 mi) Cod Rock Trail. All told, there are 22 km (13.5 mi) of trails with 6 km open to horseback riding and 9.5 km open to mountain bikers. Mountain bikers can also explore the Burrard Thermal Trails, which include the Springboard Trail south of Sasamat Lake, or the Sugar Mountain and Teddy Bear Trails to the east of the lake.

Ben Lomand/Red Mountain Route (Map 11/C–D2)

If you have the key for the gate on the Britannia Creek Forest Service Road, this trail is a difficult 15 km (9.3 mi) loop gaining 1,730 m (5,680 ft). If you don't have the key, a bike will save you the rather uninspiring 13 km (8 mi) return trip along logging roads. Keeping north from Wind Lake, the cairned route leads to BCMC Mountain Lake Hut. Stay right at the far end of Wind Lake to reach a ridge that you can follow southeast along an undefined route. Some scrambling is required to get to the top of the actual mountain. From Ben Lomand you can drop through a saddle and up Red Mountain, a relatively easy scramble compared to Ben Lomand, making this hike a rewarding two-for-one!

Binty's High Trail (Map 32/F4)

A Whistler Mountain Biking Classic, this difficult 7.5 km (4.5 mi) trail climbs 510 m (1,675 ft) from the top of Alpine Meadows (you start on Rick's Roost Trail). Once you reach the top, enjoy the view and then hang on. The trail spills you out on Alta Lake Road, but not before crossing several side trails, which offer similar thrills.

Birkenhead River Trail (Map 42/D5–D7)

Starting from the Owl Creek Recreation Site, the Birkenhead River Trail is a scenic 20 km (12 mi) trail that makes up part of the Sea to Sky Trail. The easy route follows a rolling road along the powerlines on the west side of the river. From the Birkenhead River crossing, it is a further 15 km (9.3 mi) to Birkenhead Lake.

Blackcomb Mountain (Map 32/G5–33/A5)

The expansive sub-alpine terrain of Blackcomb Mountain, frequented by skiers throughout the winter months, gives way to some great hiking trails in the summer. For a fee, take the Solar Coaster Chair and walk up to the Rendezvous Restaurant and the start of the trails. Be sure to pick up the complimentary map that highlights the short alpine walks available. The longest trail is only 2.5 km (1.6 mi) and the elevation gains are minimal (although the Overlord Lookout Trail gains 215 m/705 ft). For mountain bikers, there are guided descents from the top of Solar Coaster, which take about two hours to complete.

Blackcomb Peak, The Spearhead, and Decker Mountain Loop (Map 32/G5–33/A5)

If you are up to the challenge, you can skip the chairlift and start out from Blackcomb Village on a 27 km (17 mi) loop that takes you to three separate peaks. From Blackcomb Peak, it is a short 830 metre trek to The Spearhead, and from The Spearhead to Decker Mountain is another 4 km (2.5 mi), making for a total elevation gain of around 2,740 m (9,000 ft). Be sure to get an early start and pack warm clothing for this loop. The diverse terrain and spectacular scenery will be worth the effort.

Black Tusk Tower Road (Map 32/E6–22/E1)

The Black Tusk Tower Road requires a 1,270 m (4,165 ft) climb over 16 km (9.9 mi) from the Whistler Interpretive Forest trailhead. The steep road offers great views and a fun descent for mountain bikers. A similar road to ride is the Whistler Tower Road, which starts north of Function Junction off Highway 99 and is an 8 km (5 mi) return route.

Blowdown Pass Trail (Map 43/F6–35/C1)

This trail is approximately 25 km (15 mi) in length and is accessed by the rough Blowdown Forest Service Road found past the east end of Duffey Lake Road. This trail is well-marked, but some stretches are prone to overgrowth with shrubs and alder. There are also steep sections of trail and a side trip to the old Silver Queen Mine site is possible (beware of the open pit). The area contains beautiful alpine meadows with great camping and some classic ridge routes.

Bombtram Mountain Trail (Map 16/C2)

A great destination in any season, this mountain is accessed from the Box Canyon parking lot on the Coquihalla Highway (Hwy 5). The route up the mountain is about 3 km (1.9 mi) long with an elevation gain of 980 m (3,215 ft). After a section of forest, the route opens up into a series of alpine bowls. If you are exploring the area in winter or spring be sure to bring your skis as you are sure to find some rewarding lines without having to look too hard.

Botanie Mountain Trail (Map 45/B6)

The length of the hike really depends on how far you can drive along the old lookout road leading from the Botanie Valley Road. If you do not have a four-wheel drive vehicle then you will have to hike about 17.5 km (10.7 mi) over 8 hours, climbing 1,425 m (4,675 ft) to the lookout. Along the way you will pass open meadows with wildflowers (in July) along with great views of the Stein Valley, Thompson River and Fraser River. The hiking season runs from June to October.

Boundary Bay Trail (Map 1/E7–2/A6)

This dyke trail starts from 17A Avenue in Tsawwassen and skirts Boundary Bay all the way to the southern railway tracks (junction of Highway 99 & 91) in Surrey. Along the 25 km (15.5 mi) route, you pass Boundary Bay Airport, Delta Air Park and several access points, which can shorten the route.

Brandywine Falls (Map 32/D7)

Found next to the Sea to Sky Highway (Hwy 99), the 66 m (215 ft) falls are easily accessible at the top, but difficult to access from the base. In addition to the 2 km return hike to the falls, there are a number of trails in the area for mountain biking, hiking and snowshoeing in the winter. The Sea to Sky Trail also runs through the park.

Brandywine Meadows Trail (Map 32/C5)

This 6 km (3.7 mi) trail is steep and short with an elevation gain of 1,000 m (3,280 ft). The trail leads sharply upward from the 6.3 km mark of the Branch 10 logging road, through the dense old growth forest to the alpine meadow with spectacular views and a rustic camping spot. From the meadows, it is possible to gain access to Brandywine Mountain and the Metal Dome.

Brett-Hog Creek Trails (Map 51/G3–52/B2)

Accessed off of Marshall Lake Road, you will find 35 km (22 mi) of trails taking you around Carol Lake along Hog and Brett Creeks and beyond. There really is no limit to the distance you can travel.

Brew Lake Trail (Map 32/C7)

The signed trailhead begins on the BC Rail tracks just south of the Brandywine Falls Provincial Park. It involves a 10 km (6 mi) return hike gaining 1,200 m (3,935 ft) along the way. At the end of the steep trail (best hiked from July to October) is Brew Lake, where you will find a maintained cabin available on a first-come, first-served basis. From the lake, it is possible to explore Mount Brew at 1,740 m (5,710 ft) in elevation or access the Brew Hut 1,620 m (5,35 ft). Brew Lake is 1,430 m (4,690 ft) in elevation and offers reasonably good fishing. In winter, most people head here via Roe Creek.

Bridal Trails (Map 4/G2)

Just east of Harrison Hot Springs, a pair of easy trails can be explored. The Bridal Trail is 3.5 km (2.1 mi) and marked with green markers, while the Mount Streetsidehill Trail is 4 km (2.5 mi) and marked with red markers.

Brimful Lake Trail (Map 44/C6)

From the Texas Creek Trailhead, Brimful Lake is about 6.5 km (4 mi) in. This trail is not marked, but is fairly easy to follow to the beautiful lake. At last report, the Texas Creek Forest Service Road had been deactivated and has 103 water bars to cross in the last 14 km.

> By drinking plenty of water and knowing your limits, heat stroke and exhaustion can be easily avoided.

Brohm Cabin Trail (Map 22/D4)

Brohm Cabin Trail is an 8 km (5 mi) trek which gains 760 m (2,490 ft) in elevation. The cabin is more of a chalet, built in the 1960s in anticipation of ski resort development. The cabin is currently maintained by the Black Tusk Snowmobile Club and requires a nightly fee.

Brohm Lake Interpretive Trails (Map 22/C4)

From the parking lot off Highway 99, an easy 5 km (3 mi) trail with minimal elevation gain circles the lake. The trail provides access to the picnic area next to Brohm Lake and is used for shore fishing as well as wildlife viewing. Around Brohm Lake, you will also find a network of 11 km (6.8 mi) of interconnecting trails used by mountain bikers and hikers. These trails lead away from the lake and through the bluffs and second growth forest typical of the area. There is a second parking lot 1 km south of the main lot.

Brothers Creek Trail (Map 11/C7)

This 7 km (4.3 mi) return hike along Brothers Creek is one of the more popular lower elevation trails in the area. The moderate trail combines longer flat sections with some short, steep grades gaining a total of 435 m (1,425 ft). This is a good year-round hike that follows a fire access road through the forest sporting large old growth Douglas fir and Western Red Cedar and past a scenic canyon with waterfalls to Blue Gentian Lake. Mountain bikers use the road to access some of the steep, difficult trails of the Lower Cypress Area. The trailhead is found on Millstream Road.

Brunswick Mountain Trail (Map 11/B4)

This difficult route climbs 1,550 m (5,085 ft) over 15 km (9.3 mi) return. While there is some minor scrambling near the top, the views over Howe Sound are incredible.

Bug Lake / John Clarke Trail (Map 31/A2–30/G2) ⬛🏃🚵🏊🚴🏕️

Found about 60 km from Highway 99 at the end of the Sims G Main, which is accessed off the Elaho Main, there are reports the road is blocked about 7 km from the trailhead. Be prepared for some extra hiking. Bug Lake itself is not a particularly impressive destination but Mount John Clarke is an excellent challenge for experienced mountaineers. The flat and wide summit is accessed by a narrow ridge with significant exposure on both sides, and panoramic 360 degree views await you at the top. You will be situated at the divide between Sims Creek and Princess Louisa Inlet. This is a 6 km (3.7 mi) one-way trip from the Bug Lake trailhead.

Buntzen Lake Trails (Map 12/A7) 🏃🚵🏊🏕️

Lake Beautiful, as it was originally known, is a popular recreation area that is easily accessed by Sunnyside Road to the north of Port Moody. Within the forest next to Buntzen Lake are a series of multi-use trails that range from gentle family strolls to difficult hikes. The Buntzen Lake Loop is one of the more popular trails, circling around the lake and crossing over a suspension bridge. The Diez Vista is longer with a steep climb, rewarding hikers with excellent views of Indian Arm. Serious hikers can challenge themselves on the ironically named Dilly-Dally Trail as well as the Eagle Peak/Lindsay Lake Loop or the Swan Falls Loop. A variety of easier and more difficult trails surrounds the lake, making this an area for all levels of hikers.

Buntzen Lake Trail:

This popular route is an 8 km (5 mi) loop that circles Buntzen Lake. The best place to start is the South Beach Picnic Area and hike in a counter clockwise direction around the lake. At the north end there is suspension bridge, while at the south end there is a floating bridge to cross. Allow 4-5 hours for this easy trail.

Diez Vista Trail:

This is a moderate 17 km (10.5 mi) return hike with 455 m (1,490 ft) elevation gain. The trail goes up and down a lot and is quite steep and challenging in places. Ultimately, you reach the summit at 600 m (1,970 ft) and will be rewarded with several excellent views of Indian Arm and Buntzen Lake. Although the trail leads from the Pumphouse

Road to the north end of the lake, it is recommended to do this trail north to south.

Dilly-Dally Trail:

You can't Dilly-Dally if you expect to finish this trail in a day. It is a long, steep, difficult 25 km (15.5 mi) trail leading from the South Beach Parking Lot gaining 1,100 m (3,610 ft) to the summit of Dilly-Dally Peak. From the summit, you can continue south on to Eagle Peak by following the ridge. The trail is best tackled in July to October.

Lindsay Lake Loop:

The trail to Lindsay Lake gains 1,020 m (3,345 ft) as it makes a 15 km (9.3 mi) loop to Lindsay Lake, as well as to several viewpoints over Vancouver. Take a left at El Paso Junction and up to the small lake. This is where the loop begins and ends some 6-8 hours later.

Swan Falls Loop:

A difficult 20 km (12 mi) loop gaining 1,150 m (3,775 ft) up through the so-called lakes district (home to ten tarns) of Eagle Ridge. The route continues on to Eagle Peak (Mount Beautiful), then down to Swan Falls and the Powerhouse Road.

Burke Mountain Trails (Map 2/C1–12/D7) 🏃🚵🏊🚴🏕️

Located at the south end of the new Pinecone Burke Provincial Park, most of the trails are reached by the parking lot near the entrance to the Gun Club off Harper Road. The Burke Ridge Trail is quite popular, and features a steady climb leading to views of the Coquitlam Watershed. Village Lake Trail is a good challenge for advanced bikers with difficult, rocky terrain and a lot of climbing en route to Monroe Lake. Most of the other trails are bike trails that are either quite challenging or easy, with little in between.

Burke Ridge Trail:

The Burke Ridge trail begins on the gated old road before breaking off onto a well-marked trail, which climbs steadily uphill to the ridge. The trail is 20 km (12 mi) return gaining 880 m (2,890 ft) to the 1,225 m (4,020 ft) ridge. From the top, you can see into the rarely seen Coquitlam Watershed, as well as the surrounding area.

BUNTZEN LAKE TRAILS	MAP	DIFFICULTY	LENGTH	ELEVATION GAIN	CAMP	BIKE	HIKE	HORSE	SKI	SNOWSHOE	VIEW
Academy Trail	2/A1–12/A7	Easy	4 km (2.5 mi)	Minimal			•	•			
Buntzen Lake Trail	2/A1–12/A7	Easy	8 km (5 mi)	Minimal	•		•				•
Diez Vista Trail	12/A7	Moderate	17 km (10.5 mi)	455 m (1,490 ft)			•				•
Dilly-Dally Trail	12/A7–B7	Difficult	25 km (15.5 mi)	1,100 m (3,610 ft)			•				•
Eagle Peak Trail	12/A7–B7	Difficult	20 km (12 mi)	1,075 m (3,525 ft)			•				•
Energy Trail	12/A7	Easy	1 km (0.6 mi)	Minimal			•				
Halvor Lunden Trail	12/A7–B7	Difficult	Varies	1,100 m (3,610 ft)			•				•
Lakeview Trail	2/A1–12/A7	Moderate	5.8 km (3.6 mi)	150 m (490 ft)jh			•				•
Lindsay Lake Loop	12/A7–B7	Difficult	15 km (9.3 mi)	1,020 m (3,345 ft)			•				•
Nature Trail	12/A7	Easy	1 km (0.6 mi)	Minimal			•				
Swan Falls Loop	12/A7–B7	Difficult	20 km (12 mi)	1,150 m (3,775 ft)			•				•
BURKE MOUNTAIN TRAILS											
Burke Ridge Trail	2/C1–12/D7	Moderate	10 km (6.2 mi)	880 m (2,890 ft)	•	•	•	•	•		
Coquitlam Lake View Trail	2/C1–12/C7	Moderate	5 km (3.1 mi)	570 m (1,870 ft)		•	•				•
Dennett Lake Trail	2/D1–12/D7	Moderate	1.2 km (0.8 mi)	120 m (395 ft)		•	•				•
Galloway Trail	2/C1–12/D7	Moderate	6 km (3.7 mi)			•					•
Munro Lake Trail	2/D1–12/D7	Difficult	4 km (2.5 mi)	940 m (3,080 ft)		•	•				•
Sawblade	2/C1–12/C7	Difficult	11.5 km (7 mi)	400 m (1,300 ft)		•					•
South & North Burke Summit Trail	12/D7	Difficult	3.7 km (2.3 mi)	180 m (590 ft)		•	•				
South Slope Trail	2/C1–12/D7	Difficult	9 km (5.6 mi)	880 m (2,860 ft)		•	•	•			
Triple Crown	2/C1–12/D7	Moderate	15 km (9.3 mi)	550 m (1,805 ft)		•	•				•
Village Lake Trail	2/C1–12/D7	Difficult	7.5 km (4.7 mi)	680 m (2,210 ft)		•	•				•
Woodland Walk	2/C1	Easy	3.5 km (2.2 mi)	200 m (655 ft)		•					

Village Lake Trail:

A 15 km (9.3 mi) hike gaining 680 m (2,210 ft). Mountain bikers should expect difficult, rocky trails and a lot of climbing. The trail will take hikers the better part of a day to complete.

Woodland Walk:

This easy trail bisects the second growth forest at the base of Burke Ridge. The trail gains only 200 m (655 ft) over 7 km (4.3 mi) as it takes you past some spectacular waterfalls, over a moss covered bridge and through remnants of logging from the turn of the century.

Burkholder Lake Trail (Map 52/C2)

From the north end of Lake La Mare Recreation Site off the Yalakom Forest Service Road, this 6 km (3.7 mi) one-way trail takes you to Burkholder Lake. The moderate trail starts out with a fairly stiff 235 m (770 ft) climb before dropping down to the creek draw and the climb back up to Burkholder Lake. Beyond the lake, several trail options are possible including exploring the Shulaps Range to the west or looping back down to the Yalokom River.

Burnaby Lake Regional Park (Map 1/G2)

You can explore the shores of Burnaby Lake along the 19 km (12 mi) of trails that surround it. There is an extra 4 km (2.5 mi) of horse trails, but these run close to the freeway and are not the most pleasant to walk on.

Burnaby Mountain Area (Map 1/G2–2/A2)

The west side of the mountain is now part of an ecological reserve and, outside of the Trans Canada Trail, the trails are hiking-only. The east side trails are designated as multi-use. Although the trails on top do offer the odd vantage point of the city and Burrard Inlet, most of the trails cut through a thickly forested area. You can access these trails from the SFU Campus, Gaglardi Way or North Road.

Burns Bog [Delta Nature Reserve] (Map 1/G4)

A trio of easy looping trails, ranging from a few hundred metres to 1.3 km in length, lead through the ancient Burns Bog. The main trail is a gated service road that can be used by cyclists to join up with the Delta Watershed Trails (see below). Although boardwalks are being added, be prepared for wet trail conditions, especially in winter. Access is from the parking lot of Great Pacific Forum off Nordel Way or from River Road in Delta.

Burrard Thermal Trails (Map 2/A1)

This is a popular mountain biking area. The trail network starts near White Pine Beach at Sasamat Lake. Most of the biking trails are accessed off the 3 km (1.9 mi) BC Hydro access road, which climbs a bit, then descends 165 m (540 ft) towards Bedwell Bay. Hikers will enjoy this short, easy trail, with its views over Burrard Inlet, but mountain bikers tend to get off the main road and onto the more challenging motorbike trails, which range from moderate to extreme.

Cabin Lake Trails (Map 27/B1)

To reach Cabin Lake, you can use a four-wheel drive vehicle, ATV or walk along the rough Cabin Lake Road (7 km/4.3 mi) gaining 215 m (700 ft) to the lake. Hiking time is about four hours. Given the elevation (1,860 m/6,100 ft), the best time to sample the area is in June through September. From the lake, it is possible to access the alpine of Stoyoma Mountain along the moderate 7 km (4.3 mi) trail gaining 420 m (1,375 ft). Another alternative is to access Heather Basin to the west via a 15 km (9.3 mi) hike along an alpine ridge. This difficult route leads past an old aircraft wreck. Another option is to hike to Lightning Lake, which involves a steep 5 km (3 mi) excursion along an old road.

Cal-Cheak Trail (Map 32/D6)

The popular Cal-Cheak or Brandywine Falls Trails lead 4 km (2.5 mi) one-way between Brandywine Falls Provincial Park and the Cal-Cheak Recreation Site. South of the suspension bridge, the trails split with the western trail (under the power lines) being the preferred mountain biking route of the Sea to Sky Trail. Once at the park, be sure to take the side route to look at the spectacular Brandywine Falls.

Camelsfoot Peak Trail (Map 53/C4)

A 3 km (1.9 mi) one-way trail follows an old forestry lookout road to the summit of Camelsfoot Peak, where panoramic views of the Fraser Canyon and surrounding mountain ranges can be found. The trailhead is found 11.5 km up the West Pavilion Forest Service Road, just past the cattle guard.

Campbell Lake Trail (Map 4/F1)

The Campbell Lake Trail is a rugged trail that climbs from the sign on Highway 9 across from Balsam Avenue, south of Harrison Hot Springs, to a remote mountain lake. The average grade of the trail is a steep 16%, climbing 630 m (2,065 ft) over 4.8 km (3 mi). Expect to take about three hours to the lake, with good viewpoints of the Harrison Lake and the Cheam Range along the way. It is possible to arrange for a pick up at the top, via the rough four-wheel drive Mount Woodside Forest Service Road.

Campbell Valley Regional Park (Map 2/E7)

Accessed at the end of 208th Street south of Langley, there are 20 km (12 mi) of trails in this regional park, 14 km of which are open to horseback riders. The trails wind their way through forest and field, marsh and meadow and lead to a number of historical sites.

Capilano Canyon Trails (Map 1/C1–11/D7)

Several parking lots off the Capilano Park and the Capilano Roads provide access to this network of trails. The Capilano Canyon is a deep, narrow gorge surrounded by sheer granite cliffs. The trails are all well maintained so it makes for easy travel under the large Douglas fir. Spawning salmon can be seen in the fall. There are 10 named trails in the park, covering a total of 26 km (16 mi) of distance. The longest trail is the Capilano Pacific Trail, at 7.5 km (4.6 mi).

Capilano Mountain Trail (Map 11/C3)

To access this trail, park at Porteau Provincial Park and walk 100 meters north to the end of the concrete wall. From there, a difficult trail leads 26 km (15.9 mi), or 10 hours, return gaining 1,600 m (5,250 ft) to the summit of Capilano Mountain. The trail initially leads steadily uphill through a second growth forest to a gated logging road. This road leads to Phyllis and Marion Lake if you stay right. From the left branch, the trail eventually takes off to the right and leads past Beth Lake to the summit.

An alternative route is to follow the logging road from just north of Furry Creek Golf Course, until you a reach a gate which may or may not be locked. Be aware that this gate is locked unpredictably, so this will be your best bet for parking. Your trip from here will be 22 km (13.7 mi) return. From the Phyllis/ Marion lakes turnoff, follow the same route described above.

Caren Range Trails (Map 9/E3)

The Halfmoon Forest Service Road provides access to an excellent area for hikers and mountain bikers in the summer and cross-country skiers during the winter. The best place to start is at kilometre 12 junction or at kilometre 15, after the road passes through a stand of old growth timber. The logging roads in the area provide easy backcountry travel with views of the ocean and the Sunshine Coast as well as a chance to explore an ancient forest of yellow cedar, hemlock and balsam, believed to be the oldest forest on the coast.

Carl Creek/Noel Creek Trail (Map 51/B6)

Accessed 2.5 km west of Bralorne along the East Hurley Forest Service Road, the deactivated Carl Creek Road leads to a couple different trail options. Depending on how far you drive, it is about 5.5 km (3.4 mi) and a 425 m (1,400 ft) climb to the ridge. At the ridge, a rough hiking route leads up to a summit and beyond to Mount Noel. Bikers can follow the single-track Carl Creek Trail back down to the East Hurley.

Caswell [Red Mountain] Trails (Map 3/C3)

This series of old logging roads provides an excellent location for those wanting to get outside without motorized vehicles disturbing the peace. There are two main access points: one at Silver Creek Park and another at Shaw Street and Keystone Road. There are three main trails in the system totalling nearly 6 km (3.7 mi). Due to the many side roads/trails it is advised to keep to the marked trails.

Cat Lake Area (Map 22/D5)

Around Cat Lake, a series of motorbike trails offer very challenging routes for the mountain biker. These trails can be accessed off of the Cheekeye River Forest Service Road at the old gondola base area or the Cat Lake Recreation Site. It is possible to cross the Cheekeye River and follow the trails down to Alice Lake or Garibaldi Highlands or continue up the roads to access Brohm Ridge and cabin.

Cayoosh Creek Loop (Map 43/A6–42/G6)

From Highway 99 at the Cayoosh Pass, this 16 km (10 mi) loop requires an elevation gain of 1,260 m (4,130 ft). Be prepared for large boulder fields, loose rocks and a lot of bushwhacking.

Centennial Trail (Map 6/E5–F6)

When it was built in the mid-1960s, the Centennial Trail was one of the most ambitious trail building projects in BC. These days, most of the trail has been incorporated into other trails, including the Trans Canada Trail. In name, the Centennial Trail extends 420 km (260 mi) from The Plaza of Nations in Vancouver to Joe Lake near Keremeos, but in truth, the only section that still survives is from 26 Mile Bridge to the Skyline Trail along the Skagit River.

Central Valley Greenway (Map 1/D1–2/A3)

The Central Valley Greenway is open to foot traffic, bikes, wheelchairs and rollerblades. The 24 km (14.6 mi) long trail links Science World on Vancouver's False Creek with the confluence of the Brunette and Fraser Rivers in New Westminster. While the trail is officially open, there are sections that are temporarily routed along roadways. The route basically follows the Millennium Skytrain line. Most of the trail is paved, though there are some sections that are not.

Cerise Creek Trails (Map 43/B7)

The Cerise Creek trailhead is unmarked, and is located past the Joffre Lakes parking lot on Duffey Lake Road (Hwy 99). The summer trail is located 3.3 km past the green-roofed warehouse, opposite the "end avalanche area" sign. The winter trail is a few hundred metres before this. If you drive to Duffey Lake you will have gone too far. From the trailhead, you hike about 4.5 km (2.8 mi), gaining 550 m (1,805 ft) through the forest along Cerise Creek to some alpine meadows where you will find Keith's Hut. Allow two to three hours for the moderate hike. From the hut, experienced mountaineers can cross over to the Matier Glacier or Joffre Peaks. Another option is the Vantage Peak Trail, an 8.5 km (5.3 mi) one-way hike from the trailhead which gains 980 m (3,300 ft) and provides up-close views of Twin One Glacier.

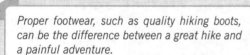

Proper footwear, such as quality hiking boots, can be the difference between a great hike and a painful adventure.

Chapman Falls Trails (Map 9/F5)

A series of trails are found along Lower Chapman Creek. The Chapman Falls Trail is reached by parking at the top of Havies Road and walking along the chain link fence. From there, the trail leads 6 km (3.7 mi) return to the falls. The Hatchery Trail leads to a viewing platform and a series of spawning channels on Chapman Creek. This is a short and easy 500 metre trail. The Lower Chapman Creek Trail is considered one of the premier short hikes on the Sunshine Coast. The trail leads through a nice second growth forest with large red cedar stumps next to the creek. The 2.8 km (1.7 mi) one-way trail also leads to several swimming holes and sandy beaches. The trailhead is located at the parking lot of Brookman Park immediately east of Davis Bay beach on Highway 101.

Cheakamus Canyon Trail (Map 22/B3–C2)

Now a part of the Sea to Sky Trail, this trail starts at the end of Paradise Valley Road. It is 3 km (1.9 mi) to the rather unpleasantly named Starvation Lake climbing 125 m (410 ft) along an old road. Some people turn around here, but the trip doesn't really get interesting until after the lake, as it skirts the edge of the canyon. While you can walk to where the old cattle trail disappears under the new Highway 99, you probably won't want to walk much farther than 1.5 km past the lake. A nice campsite is found at the decent fishing lake.

Cheam Peak Trail (Map 5/A4)

Found at the end of the rough (lots of cross ditching) Chilliwack-Chipmunk Forest Service Road, the Mount Cheam Trail is a beautiful alpine hike. You climb 630 m (2,065 ft) over 9.5 km (5.8 mi). Along the way you will pass

Spoon Lake, rolling sub-alpine meadows dotted with wildflowers, and an old trail down to Bridal Falls. The trail is best hiked from July to September since the area is prone to avalanches in the winter.

Cheam Wetlands (Map 4/G3)

It was only a few years back that Cheam Lake had been drained to harvest lime. Now, an easy network of trails (totalling about 6 km/3.7 mi) meanders around the eastern edge of Cheam Lake and across floating bridges. The highlight here is the abundance of waterfowl and small animals. Some of the trails may be under water in spring and early summer.

China Ridge Ski Trails (Map 17/G4)

This huge multi-use area outside of Princeton offers year-round adventure. There are over 30 km (18.6 mi) of summer trails and over 40 km (25 mi) of winter trails to be found here.

Cliff Gilker Regional Park (Map 10/B6)

Adjacent to the Sunshine Coast Golf & Country Club off Highway 101, there are about 7 km (4.3 mi) of trails leading through the forest in this small regional park. The well-maintained and easily followed trails have wooden bridges crossing the streams and there is a picnic area with accessible pit toilets.

Colony Farm Regional Park (Map 2/B3)

Providing a series of dyke trails with unique bridges and viewing platforms, there are 8.7 km (5.4 mi) of trails here, 6.5 km of which are open to mountain biking. The main trailhead is found south off Highway 7 at the end of Colony Farm Road.

Confederation Lake Trail (Map 18/G1–29/A7)

Part of the Sunshine Coast Trail, the trailhead is found on an old logging road that starts to the east side of Inland Lake. A gate near the Inland Lake Campsite may add an additional 1.5 km one-way to the actual trail. From the trailhead, a well-marked trail leads past Confederation Lake and eventually to Powell Lake. A forest service log cabin is located on the east side of Confederation Lake and provides a wood stove and accommodation for six individuals. It is 8 km (5 mi) one-way to the cabin. Beyond Confederation Lake, the trail continues 7.5 km (4.6 mi) one-way to the old Fiddlehead Farm site on Powell Lake.

Coquihalla Mountain Trail (Map 16/E3)

Access this trail by the Tulameen Forest Service Road. This 14.4 km (9 mi) loop will lead you through forest and colourful alpine meadows, amid many sparkling blue tarns, before the scramble to the top of Coquihalla Mountain. Be careful of loose rocks around the summit. The 1,470 m (4,820 ft) climb will grant spectacular views of Flatiron, Needle, and Jim Kelly Peaks. In season, the area is abundant with blueberries, so be aware of bears looking for a snack.

Coquihalla Summit Recreation Area (Map 16/E1–27/C7)

A series of trails are found near the old tollbooth and Boston Bar Summit Rest Area on the Coquihalla Highway (Hwy 5). These high elevation routes are best travelled from July to October and give experienced hikers a chance to explore the dramatic peaks and fantastic views.

The Falls Lake Trail is found off Exit 221 and offers a nice 1.5 km return walk to the small mountain lake. The Little Douglas Lake Trail is also 1.5 km long and leads from the Zum Peak Recreation Site on the Upper Coldwater Forest Service Road to a small mountain lake. The Thar Peak Route begins from the Boston Bar Rest Area and follows the gas pipeline before heading upwards along a faint trail to the peak providing a phenomenal view. Although you only travel 5 km (3 mi), you should allow five hours return as you climb 1,100 m (3,610 ft) in total to the peak, at 1,920 metres (6,240 ft). The easier Zoa Peak Trail starts from a powerline off of the Falls Lake Trail and is an 8.6 km (5.2 mi) round trip climbing 720 m (2,360 ft). Branching form this trail is a difficult day-long route to Zopikos Ridge, the dramatic rock face seen from the highway. Yak Peak is accessed from the Zupkios Rest Area along a 4.4 km (2.7 mi) trek with an elevation gain of 840 m (2,760 ft). There is a false summit before the true peak, so keep pressing on for the full Yak Peak experience. Also from the Zupkios Rest Area, a 10 km (6 mi) climb leads to Guanaco Peak where a short 1.4 km trek across a saddle takes you to Vicuna peak. Both peaks are impressive in their own right, sitting atop massive rock shelves and towering over their surroundings.

TRAIL ADVENTURES

Coquitlam River Trail (Map 2/B3–C1)
This scenic river trail makes up a good portion of the historic PoCo Trail. From Mary Hill Bypass to Orr Creek Falls this trail stretches 13.5 km (8.2 mi) along the Coquitlam River. In fall, spawning salmon can be seen in the waterway. Several roads (Pitt River Road, Lougheed Highway and Shaughnessy Road) provide alternate access points. All levels of mountain bikers and hikers can enjoy this gentle trail. Beyond the falls, the trail narrows and gets more difficult as it climbs to meet up with the Burke Mountain Trails.

Crumpit Woods (Map 22/D6)
This is a challenging, technical area with little risk, perfect for beginner bikers looking to step up their game. This network of trails is strung together by an easy loop that circumnavigates Mount Crumpit. There are several trails that lead to the northeast that can take you to Powerhouse Plunge, Ring Creek Rip and the Powersmart Trails.

Cultus Lake Provincial Park (Map 4/C6–C7)
In addition to the water based activities and campgrounds, there are five main trails in the park. Trails include the interpretive stroll along the Maple Bay Trail, a 5 hour hike along the Edmeston Road and the Road 918 Trail. The Seven Sisters Trail leads 4 km to a grove of giant Douglas fir trees, some of which have fallen over, while the 2.5 km Teapot Hill climbs to a nice vantage point. For a longer, more challenging route, check out the International Ridge Trail that climbs up to Mount Amadis. A daily parking fee applies.

Seven Sisters Trail (Map 4/C6)
This easy 4 km (2.5 mi) trail is found in Cultus Lake Provincial Park near Windfall Creek. It takes you to a group of seven giant Douglas fir trees, some of which have fallen over.

Teapot Hill Trail (Map 4/C7)
It is only 2.5 km (1.6 mi) and 280 m (920 ft) to the top of Teapot Hill, but the views are surprisingly good making this a popular trail for locals and visitors to Cultus Lake.

Cypress Falls Trail (Map 11/A7)
Despite its natural beauty, Cypress Falls Park is not very well known. The main trail in the park is an easy 3 km (1.9 mi) return trail that loops around Cypress Creek's lower and upper falls. The trail starts out steep, but quickly levels out and becomes easier to hike.

Cypress Mountain Trails (Map 2/B1–12/B7)
Cypress Mountain is located in Coquitlam and has a variety of challenging hiking and mountain biking trails. There are 18 named trails, including trails like Fat Bastard and Decapitator. Some of these trails (Buntzen Connector and White Rock) hook up with the Halvor Lunden Trail in Buntzen Park.

Cypress Park Trails (Map 11/B6)
The Cypress Parkway provides easy access to the sub-alpine area of the provincial park. Within the park are a number of trails as well as the Hollyburn Cross-Country Ski Area and Cypress Bowl Ski Area to explore. For mountaineers, the Howe Sound Crest Trail is a challenging ridge route climbing up and over several mountain peaks before dropping down to Deeks Creek and the northern reaches of the park.

The Black Mountain Loop:
Reached by taking the Baden Powell Trail from the downhill ski area, this loop climbs past a few small lakes to the south summit for a view of the ocean and city. This is a 7.5 km (4.6 mi) trail, gaining 300 m (985 ft) to the summit of Black Mountain. This is the easy way up. A more challenging route is to hike up Black Mountain from Highway 99 at the Whistler/Squamish Exit. From the highway, it's a steep 16 km (9.9 mi) hike gaining 1,140 m (3,705 ft).

Hollyburn Peak Trail:
From the trailhead sign at the cross-country skiing parking lot, this trail leads some 20 km (12 mi) return to the top of Hollyburn Mountain. The trail heads east, past the old Hollyburn Lodge next to First Lake before climbing steadily uphill past the powerline and the Fourth and Fifth Lakes. From the summit, there is a great view of the Gulf Islands and Vancouver Island. An alternate and less strenuous option is to follow the Baden Powell Trail from the downhill skiing parking lot.

Mount Strachan Trail:
From the downhill ski area, this trail climbs 10 km (6 mi) return to the double summit of Mount Strachan (pronounced Strawn) at 1,450 m (4,755 ft). The trail gains 540 m (1,770 ft).

Yew Lake Trail:
A 4 km (2.5 mi) wheelchair accessible trail circles Yew Lake. It is a good choice for a family outing as it involves a generally flat walk (145 m/475 ft in elevation gain) through a sub-alpine forest around a small lake dotted with lily pads. There is some old growth forest in the area as well as a good view of Snug Cove and Deep Bay. The trail becomes accessible in late June with the season ending in October.

Cypress Peak Trail (Map 32/B7)
Found at the end of the Roe Creek Road, this trail climbs steeply to one of the series of peaks found along the Squamish-Cheakamus Divide. The difficult trail is 4.2 km long and climbs close to 975 m (3,200 ft). However, Cypress Peak can also be approached from the north via Mount Fee or from the south via Tricouni Peak and High Falls Creek. There is a small icefield on its west side, which can be skied close to the summit.

Daniel Point Trail (Map 9/A1)
Daniel Point is a small spit of land that sticks out into Malaspina Strait. This moderate 2.5 km (1.6 mi) trail leads to a wonderful viewpoint, while side trails lead to the rocky beach.

Davis Lake Park (Map 3/E1)
Reached by the Lost Creek Forest Service Road off Sylvester Road, this small provincial park offers an easy 5 km (3 mi), flat walk which circles the pretty lake.

Deas Island Regional Park (Map 1/D5)
This riverside park offers 10 km (6 mi) of trails, some of which can be used by horseback riders, and a picnic area. The trails take you along Deas Slough and the banks of the Fraser and past the heritage buildings.

Deeks Lake Trail (Map 11/A4)
There used to be two ways to get to Deeks Lake, but the Sea to Sky improvements have destroyed the more popular (and shorter) trailhead near the Deeks Creek Bridge. Now, the only way up is to start at the north end of the Howe Sound Crest Trail. Watch for the parking lot on the east side of the highway at the new Porteau Overpass. The trail climbs 1,030 m (3,380 ft) as it make its way to the lake. The trail is about 6 km (3.7 mi) to the lake.

Deeks Peak Trail (Map 11/A4)
The general attitude toward this hike is that you do it merely to say you've done it. It is poorly marked, overgrown and hardly worth the effort, save for some outstanding views from the top. It's a 16 km (9.9 mi) round trip gaining 1,615 m (5,300 ft). The trail starts from the new north trailhead for the Howe Sound Crest Trail.

Delta Watershed (Map 1/G5–2/A5)
There are several access points to these trails including 64th Avenue to the north and Highway 10 to the south. As a rule of thumb, the trails to the north of the service road are short and follow well developed trails. To the south, less developed trails offer more of a challenge for cyclists, and feature a lot of custom obstacles for bikers.

Denham's [Weaver Lake] Trail (Map 14/E7)
From the Weaver Lake Recreation Site, a 6.2 km (3.8 mi) trail loops around this picturesque fishing lake. Relatively flat, the trail makes for an easy three hour hike with a number of side trails from which to access the lake.

Deer Lake Park (Map 1/F3)
This urban park provides a well-developed trail system that loops around the lake over a distance of 5 km (3 mi) with little elevation gain. The trails follow mainly access roads through open areas and mixed forests. Access is found off Canada Way; follow the signs to Deer Lake Park.

Derby Reach Regional Park (Map 2/F3)
In addition to fishing and camping, the park offers a couple of trails to explore. There is a 9.5 km (5.9 mi) hiking only trail along with the 4 km (2.5 mi) Houston Loop trail that skirts Derby Bog. This trail can be used by cyclists and horseback riders. Derby Reach was the original site of Fort Langley and there are a few historical buildings to see.

Dewdney Trail (Map 6/F2–17/F7)

Originally constructed in 1860 by Edgar Dewdney, this was one of the first trade routes linking the coast with the interior. These days, most of the route is either grown over or has been covered by roads, but there are some places where the historic route still survives as a trail. The longest surviving section is found in the Cascade Recreation Area, beginning at the parking lot on Highway 3. The trail extends 36 km (22 mi) to the pass, gaining 1,130 m (3,700 ft) along the way. It is possible to trek over the divide into the Whipsaw Creek Forest Service Road. The trail is a popular horseback destination with its panoramic views of the valleys and mountains. There are several side trails and overnight facilities along the well-developed trail system.

Diadem Mountain Trail (Map 20/A1)

This hike is located along a road leading up Lois River Valley. A gate located before the valley may impede travel by vehicle to the trailhead, which is marked by a cairn with flagging tape. The route proceeds through a deep gorge, eventually leading up to a ridge. From there, you cross a creek at the end of a box canyon and proceed up into the sub-alpine past a series of ponds. Eventually, the trail culminates at the 1,283 m (4,210 ft) summit for a total of 8 km (5 mi) return.

Dog Mountain Trail (Map 15/E7)

A few short trails are found around the Devils Lake area off Highway 7. To the north of the highway, the Dog Mountain Trail is a popular mountain biking area, and is a 5 km (3 mi) round trip with minimal elevation gain.

Dorman Point Trail (Map 10/G6)

From the picnic grounds at the ferry in Snug Cove on Bowen Island, this trail leads 4 km (2.5 mi) one-way to a small lookout near Dorman Point. The hike involves a steady uphill climb where you will be rewarded with excellent views of Whytecliff Park and Vancouver.

Downton Alpine [Holly Lake] Trail (Map 43/D3)

Access is found off Branch 2 of the Downton Creek Road. Look for this branch road about 11 km from the Duffey Lake Road (Hwy 99) intersection. The trailhead to the flagged route is another 3 km down Branch 2. The moderate route leads past Holly Lake at 2,080 m (6,825 ft) and requires some route finding, crossing boulder fields and scree slopes as well as open alpine walking. Peaks like Statimcets at 2,631 m (8,630 ft) and Linus at 2,578 m (8,460 ft) can easily be explored in a day.

Duck Lake Area (Map 19/A3)

The Duck Lake Forest Service Road provides access to several hiking/biking trail systems just east of Powell River, all within a conveniently compact area. The longest of these trails is the Duck Lake Loop, stretching for 21 km (13 mi) along logging roads and powerlines. Many of these trails bypass scenic waterfalls, including the 7 km (4.3 mi) Blackwater Trail, the 8 km (5 mi) long Cable Trail, Suicide Creek Loop (also 8 km) and the 7 km (4.3 mi) Sweetwater Creek Loop. Easy options for bikers include the Mud Lake Trails and the 3.7 km (2.3 mi) Blue Trail, while the 10 km (6 mi) round trip Granite Lake Trail is primarily used by hikers.

Duffey Peak Trail (Map 33/G1)

Access this trail directly from Duffey Lake Road (Hwy 99) north of Lillooet Lake. From the parking area, continue on foot about 100 metres up the road before cutting up the hill and beginning to bushwhack. It is a difficult 5.4 km (3.4 mi) trek to the northwest peak of Duffey, gaining 1,425 m (4,675 ft) elevation. Expect to have to navigate deadfall, bluffs and steep sections before reaching the alpine, which will present its own navigational challenges. Tracking your route via GPS on the way up to the peak is recommended in case of limited visibility on the way down.

Eagle Ridge Trail (Map 35/F4)

Located just south of Stein Valley Niakapamux Provincial Park, Eagle Ridge towers above the Kwoiek Creek Valley across from the popular Kwoiek Needle. The challenging trail climbs nearly one vertical metre for every two travelled. All that elevation means plenty of viewpoints towards Chochiwa Lake, Glacier and the surrounding mountains. From the Eagle Ridge itself, you can see the surrounding tableau of mountains, including Skihist Peak, the highest mountain in Southwestern BC. Note that the trail is quite hard to follow.

Eaton Lake Trail (Map 5/G2)

This difficult 4 km (2.5 mi) trail begins at the Eaton Creek Recreation Site on the Silver Skagit Road, south of Hope. Along the way, you will gain 915 m (3,000 ft) in elevation. The rewarding trail begins by approaching Eaton Creek before descending rapidly to a log bridge, where there are great views of the falls and rapids. From here, the hike heads upward towards the popular fishing lake. It is possible to camp at the south end of the lake or continue on to Eaton Peak to the south or Mount Grant to the north. Both routes are best left to experienced mountaineers. Recently three bridges here have been broken, but it is still possible to get across the creek on makeshift crossings.

Eaton Peak Trail (Map 5/G2)

From Eaton Lake this difficult trail gains 840 m (2,760 ft) over 2.4 km before reaching the peak. The distance is relatively short but the terrain is challenging – expect bushwhacking for much of the ascent, including some quite steep sections over krummholz and boulders. You will encounter a steep, exposed crux on the way to the peak, so climbing skills will be essential. The crux has ample foot and hand holds but you may want to consider taking along climbing helmets and rope. The summit offers a fantastic 180 degree view of the surrounding area.

Echo Lake Trail (Map 22/B6)

To access this 4 km (2.5 mi) trail, begin by canoeing across the Squamish River, setting off near where you reach the river dyke from downtown. On the other side, the trail begins near a pile of debris from the old footbridge. The trail is poorly marked at times and passes Jean's Cabin and a series of waterfalls on the way to the impressive lake, climbing 900 m (2,953 ft). There are backcountry campsites at the lake.

Elk-Thurston Trail (Map 4/F5)

This gruelling 14.6 km (8.9 mi) hike starts on the Chilliwack Bench Forest Service Road at a small gravel pit. You climb over 1,000 m/3,280 ft (mostly at the beginning) to the summit of Mount Thurston and breathtaking panoramic views of the Chilliwack Valley and the border peaks. The trail passes through the wildflower carpeted sub-alpine meadows near the base of Elk Mountain and continues onto an exposed ridge.

Emerald Estates Trails (Map 32/G4)

There is a network of mountain biking trails in the Emerald Estates area. The most popular trail in this network is the infamous Shit Happens. This 7.5 km (4.6 mi) trail links Emerald Estates to Alpine Meadows to the south.

Emma Lake Trail (Map 29/F4)

Emma Lake Trail begins off the B-Branch from the Goat Lake Main. The steep trail leads 7 km (4.3 mi) to a forest service cabin set on Emma Lake that has space for eight, but it is often full. If you are planning on spending the night at this beautiful blue lake expect to tent it. If you stay overnight, you can take day trips to Snowy, Thunder Dome and Crossroads Peaks. Also, the South Powell Divide Route leads southward, including a ridge run from Triple Peaks to Center Lakes.

Empetrum Peak Trail (Map 32/F7)

Access this trail from the Cheakamus Lake parking lot, following Helm Creek Trail towards Garibaldi Lake. Just before the Helm Creek Campground, around 1,560 m (5,120 ft) in elevation, turn off the Helm Creek Trail towards Empetrum Peak. From here it will be an 8.5 km (5.3 mi) loop to the peak and back onto Helm Creek Trail, topping out at 2,000 m (6,560 ft) elevation. From the peak you will have a stunning, up-close view of the Black Tusk, so be sure to leave time to soak it in once you reach the summit. Expect some mud and boggy sections on this route late into summer.

Evans Lake Area (Map 22/C4)

North of Evans Lake Camp, a series of trails/logging roads link up with Levette Lake. The wooded trails provide challenging single-track riding or enjoyable hiking in and around the park reserve and the wilderness lakes. There is even a Skyline Trail here. You can access these trails where the road branches to the camp.

First Brigade/1848 HBC Brigade Trail (Map 26/F6)

Access this trail from a pullout 500 meters past the Alexandria Lodge on Highway 1, south of Hells Gate in the Fraser Canyon. This trail has a long history of First Nations and fur trapper use, and you will see historical markers along the way. The first 3 km are steep but after this the trail flattens out, weaving a loop between several small lakes and offering great views of the Fraser River. It is possible to camp near some of these lakes and to continue the hike to the 1858 Gold Rush Trail to Gate Mountain. The return hike covers 12 km (7.5 mi) with an elevation gain of 1,260 m (4,130 ft).

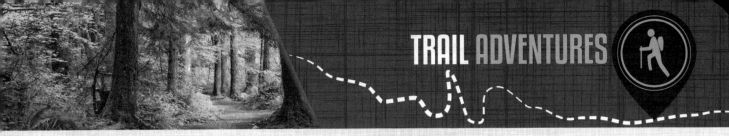

Flora Lake Trail (Map 5/F5)
Be prepared for a steep 1,320 m (4,330 ft) climb on this 8.7 km (5.4 mi) one-way hike. Crest a peak around the 6 km (3.7 mi) mark and the stunning lake will reveal itself to you, some 380 m (1,240 ft) below. Once you descend to the lake you will find a beautiful place to swim during the warm season and an abundant trout population. You can choose to camp here, descend back to the trailhead at Post Creek, or continue on a loop that eventually connects with the Post-Greendrop Trail (20 km/12.5 mi in total). Although some parts of this loop are poorly marked, well prepared hikers with a bit of experience should have no trouble navigating the route.

Fool's Gold Route (Map 12/E7–B1)
Heavy lobbying for conservation of the extensive untouched forest to the west of Pitt Lake resulted in the creation of the Pinecone Burke Provincial Park. Within the park is the rugged and nearly impossible to follow Fool's Gold Route. The route runs some 50 km (31 mi) and will take most backpackers at least a week to complete. The Boise Creek section, a 12 km (7.3 mi) return section to Mamquam Pass is still quite popular, though the first section through a clearcut is quite difficult to follow. Advanced navigation skills are required for this route.

Ford Mountain Trail (Map 5/C5)
From the sign at the end of the Ford Mountain Forest Service Road, a short 1.7 km (1 mi) one-way hike follows the treed ridge to an old forestry lookout with panoramic views. The moderate trail gains 400 m (1,300 ft) in elevation. Experienced hikers can continue along the bare ridge to the base of Williams Peak, which adds an additional 6 km (3.7 mi), climbing 460 m (1,495 ft) along the way. If you do not have a four-wheel drive vehicle, it is possible to hike the road, but this requires an additional climb of 620 m (2,015 ft) over 4.5 km (2.7 mi) one-way.

Freda Mountain Trails (Map 19/F1–29/F7)
To reach the summit of Freda Mountain (1,890 m/6,200 ft), there are three possibilities. The southernmost route is a long trail leading from the Freda Mountain Main just north of the F-Branch. A more direct route is found on the J-Branch at the south end of Freda Lake. This is an 8 km (5 mi) return trip that leads through an old growth forest to the sub-alpine. The third trail begins on the Jenna Branch Road at the east end of Freda Lake. This involves a 12 hour hike on a well-marked (flagged) trail leading through the old growth timber to the sub-alpine.

Frogpond Lake Trail (Map 29/B6)
This steep 5 km (3 mi) trail leads from Powell Lake up to Frogpond Lake. The trailhead is accessed by taking a boat to Cassiar Falls where the trail begins on the east side of the creek. Half way along the trail you reach a bench, which overlooks Powell Lake with a good view of Fiddlehead Farm and Tin Hat Mountain to the south.

Galene Lakes Route (Map 6/E7)
This route begins 55 km down the Silver Skagit Road, at the Chittenden Bridge parking area. It takes you 32 km (20 mi) return to the Galene Lake, climbing 1,250 m (4,100 ft) along the way. The trail crosses a footbridge and then proceeds through meadows along the Skagit River before following Galene Creek up to the lake. The lake offers a rustic campsite, some decent fishing opportunities and great views. The trail is best hiked from July to October.

Gallagher Hills Trail (Map 18/G3)
This trail begins 100 metres along the Inland Lake Road and leads along an old skid trail up to a rock bluff and then on to a radio tower overlooking Powell Lake and the ocean. The total distance of the hike is 5 km (3 mi) return. It is possible to take a side trip off the bluff and walk down to Mowat Bay.

Gambier Island Trails (Map 10/E4)
On Gambier Island, a 16 km (10 mi) return trail starts from Kingston Creek Road at the north end of New Brighton. After crossing Mannion Creek, the trail follows an old road eventually leading to Gambier Lake. The trail gains 220 m (720 ft). Partway up a trail branches off to climb Mount Killam, a distance of 3 Km from the main trail and a gain of 540 m (1,771 ft). From Gambier Lake it is possible to hike to the top of Mount Liddel, a further 4 km (2.5 mi) with a 520 m (1,706 ft) climb. A couple of trails connect Gambier Lake to remote camps on the north end of the island – both 3 km long, to Douglas Bay and Camp Latona. An alternate way to access Gambier Lake is from Camp Artaban on the east end of the island. This trail is almost identical in length and elevation gain as the trail from New Brighton – consider exploring both trails as a way to explore the island from one end to the other.

Garibaldi Highlands (Map 22/D6)
The Highlands are the most popular mountain biking area in Squamish. You can access this area from Alice Lake Park to the north or Perth Drive and Glacierview Road in Garibaldi Highlands to the south. The moderate trails offer easier, smoother terrain than others in the Squamish area.

Garibaldi Provincial Park-Black Tusk (Map 22/D1–F2)
A paved road leads just south of Daisy Lake from Highway 99 to the Rubble Creek parking lot. It is recommended that you either camp at Taylor Meadows or at the Battleship Lakes Camp if you want to explore the surrounding mountains. Taylor Meadows is 7.5 km (4.6 mi) from the parking lot. One of the most popular trails is the Garibaldi Lake Trail, a 9 km (5.5 mi) climb of 940 m (3,055 ft) that leads to spectacular views of the surrounding glaciers. The 13.5 km (8.4 mi) Black Tusk Trail leads to one of the most recognizable natural features in the Coast Mountain climbing 1,735 m (5,690 ft) in total along the way. In the winter, the area turns into a backcountry skiing haven.

Garibaldi Provincial Park-Cheakamus Lake (Map 32/F7–22/F1)
South of Whistler, this popular multi-use trail system begins at the end of the Cheakamus Lake Road, some 8 km from Highway 99. Cheakamus Lake is a turquoise coloured lake surrounded by rugged snow-capped peaks that is truly a delight to fish, canoe or just visit. A moderate 14 km (8.7 mi) return trip takes you to the north end of the lake. The Helm Creek Trail is another popular route, stretching for 14.5 km (8.8 mi) one way with an elevation gain of 600 m (1,970 ft), eventually connecting the trail to Black Tusk.

Garibaldi Provincial Park-Diamond Head (Map 22/E6–G4)
Near Squamish, the Diamond Head parking lot is found at the 16 km mark of the Mamquam Road. The road to the parking lot is open year-round as the road is usually plowed to allow backcountry skiers to access Garibaldi Park. This is one of four main access points into the park. The Diamond Head Trail is an 11 km (6.8 mi) one-way hike that climbs 600 m (1,970 ft) and features a couple of overnight huts to set up base camp at. Little Diamond Head is a 7 km (4.3 mi) return trip through sub-alpine meadows, with a gain of 625 m (2,205 ft). From Elfin Lakes, you can also take a 6.5 km (4 mi) trek to the volcanic outcropping of Opal Cone, and from here continue to Mamquam Lake.

Ghost Pass Trail (Map 6/D2)
This trail begins at the West Gate of Manning Park and leads along an old engineering road to a signed trailhead. You must climb to Ghost Pass, which is 11 km (6.8 mi) one-way from the trailhead, before reaching Ghost Pass Lake. Beyond the lake, the trail disappears.

Goat II Access Trail (Map 29/F6)
At the end of Goat 2 Road is the Goat II Access Trail, a difficult hike to a beautiful alpine area with wildflowers in July. If you proceed south you will see a trailhead marked by flagging tape. From here, you must do some bushwhacking past two small creeks, across a rockslide before reaching the ridge and ultimately the traverse down to Skwim Lake. If you proceed in a northern direction, you will have to walk along the deactivated road to an old trail heading up to the base of Triple Peaks. From the alpine area, you can continue on the South Powell Divide Trail leading to Emma Lake and beyond.

Goat Ridge Trail (Map 11/C1)
From Petgill Lake this difficult trail climbs 1,110 m (3,640 ft) over 5.6 km (3.5 mi) to Goat Ridge, a long alpine plateau extending towards Sky Pilot Mountain. Hitting alpine on the Coast Mountains means starting near sea level, so be prepared for some serious elevation gain. The trail is well marked through the difficult and varied terrain, including deadfall and steep rock bluffs. Once you reach the sub-alpine the incline diminishes and the landscape opens up to reveal Garibaldi and Tantalus Mountains in the background. You will pass a series of tarns on your way to the alpine ridge which will offer stunning views of the Sky Pilot and Mount Habrich, among others.

Golden Ears Provincial Park Trails (Maps 2, 3, 12, 13)

There are a number of trails in this wilderness park, some multi-use, some hiking only. The highlights include an abundance of wildlife, the scenic Alouette Lake and the mountains that glow like golden ears in the sun.

Alouette Mountain Trail (Map 2/G2–13/A7)

This difficult 22 km (13.5 mi) return trip climbs 1,100 m (3,610 ft) to the summit. Along the way, you will pass some scenic meadows and ponds. There are a couple variations on how to start this trail, either along the Incline Trail, Mike Lake Trail or the old fire access road. The latter is the easiest (but longest) and is open to mountain bikers and equestrians, who are able to follow the fire access road to the hitching post at Lake Beautiful.

East Canyon Trail (Map 3/B1–13/B7)

A rocky, 11 km (6.8 mi) trail follows the banks of Gold Creek north to the Lower Falls. This trail is open to mountain bikers, but expect a difficult trail with rough sections and a 320 m (1,050 ft) elevation gain. Past here, the Hector Ferguson Trail continues deep into the heart of the park.

Golden Ears Trail (Map 3/A1–13/A7)

This popular 24 km (14.6 mi) trip gains 1,500 m (4,920 ft) to the popular peak. The hike begins at the West Canyon Parking Lot and follows Gold Creek and the West Canyon Trail to Alder Flats. Most people heading for the peak set up camp here and hike the remaining distance to the peak without a pack. This is a good idea, as most of the elevation gain happens in the last few kilometres. The trail heads steeply up the ridge past a rustic mountain shelter to the summit of Panorama Ridge.

Hector Ferguson Trail (Map 13/B6)

A 22 km (13.5 mi) hike along the east side of Gold Creek. The trail leads to a tiny lake that forms the headwaters of the creek, deep in the heart of Golden Ears. This is the farthest north you can hike into the park by land (there are a couple lake access routes that head farther in). Expect to take at least a day to get to the lake and back.

West Canyon Trail (Map 3/A1–A7)

Beginning at the West Canyon parking lot, this trail heads north, following the western banks of Gold Creek. If you want to loop back along the East Canyon Trail, you will need to ford the creek near Lower Falls. This makes for a nice 9 km (5.5 mi) return hike with minimal elevation gain.

Gotcha Peak Trail (Map 43/F7)

A short hike following a 15 km (9.3 mi) drive up Blowdown Creek Forest Service Road will bring you to this unique peak. The drive up the steep four-wheel drive road is enough to attract visitors to this area, as the alpine is accessible without having to leave your vehicle. Once you get to Blowdown Pass, park your car, and from here it is a short 1.2 km hike to Gotcha Peak, gaining 380 m (1,250 ft) elevation. The trail runs along a ridge to the peak, providing an alpine experience within minutes of leaving your car. The dry, barren landscape will have you feeling like you are deep in the mountains. Nearby Gott Peak is equally as accessible from the parking area.

Great Blue Heron Nature Reserve (Map 4/B5)

The Chilliwack Rotary Club has built an Interpretive Centre and trail system next to the Great Blue Heron nesting ground. There are 5 km (3 mi) of easy trails here. As you might expect, most trail users come to see the birds.

Great Blue Heron Way Trail (Map 1/D6)

This multi-use trail links the communities of Ladner and Tsawwassen along a scenic path that follows the shoreline through the Tsawwassen First Nation Lands. From the trail's southern end, off Tsawwassen Drive North just north of the Ferry Causeway (Hwy 17), it is possible to link over to the Boundary Bay Side to extend a trip. This is a 4 km (2.5 mi) one-way trail with minimal elevation gain.

Green Lake Trails (Map 32/G5–33/A4)

Within the Green Lake area there are several trails. The 15 km (9.3 mi) Green Lake Loop goes along hydro line road on the eastern side of Green Lake. This trail can be used to access the Wedgemont Creek Forest Service Road and the Comfortably Numb/Secret Trail. The Comfortably Numb/Secret Trail is a 23 km (14 mi) advanced trail that goes from the Wedgemont area towards Lost Lake. Once at Lost Lake it is possible to head back towards Green Lake.

Green Mountain Trail (Map 50/G5)

The Branch 6 Road is a rough four-wheel drive road that starts from km 6 on the Hurley River Forest Service Road and leads to an old Forest Service fire lookout on Green Mountain. Continue past the first switch back and two other branch roads to the trail leading to the bowl and ridge area. Hikers can follow the ridge to the southwest, while mountaineers often use the cabin as a staging area before tackling Mount Sloan to the west. Snowmobiler and backcountry skiers should avoid the main bowl area in winter. Hikers should also note that the old Green Mountain Trail found at the 8 km mark on the Hurley River Road is not recommended due to blowdowns on the trail.

Green Mountain Trails (Map 4/G2)

This moderate series of mountain biking trails is found off the Agassiz bypass, just north of the railway tracks (on the west side). A tough climb takes you 455 m (1,490 ft) up the access road to the network of trails at the top of Green Mountain. The access road eventually turns into a single-track trail and will take you down to the farmer's field on the other side.

Grouse Mountain Trails (Map 11/D7)

Starting at the base of Grouse Mountain at the end of Nancy Green Way is a series of popular trails, including the infamous Grouse Grind. Hikers wishing to explore the alpine areas often prefer to ride the gondola to the top. Either way, the views can be fabulous. Due to snow, hikes up the surrounding mountain are best left until July to early November, including the climbs up Crown and Goat Mountains.

Crown Mountain Route:

This route involves making your way along a difficult, exposed route where one misstep could be disastrous. With this in mind, Crown Mountain is best left to folks who know what they're doing. It is 9.6 km (6 mi) from the top of the gondola to the peak, climbing 695 m (2,280 ft).

Grouse Grind:

The Grind is not a trail – it's a social phenomenon. On evenings after work and on weekends, this trail, which heads straight up the mountainside just east of the gondola, sees hundreds of walkers, looking for a good burn as the trail climbs 853 m (2,800 ft) in 2.9 km (1.8 mi). If you do the math, that's about 1 metre up for every 3.4 metres travelled, which makes this a good cardio-workout. This partially explains the high traffic the trail sees. Another important element in the Grind's popularity is the fact that there is a restaurant at the top and you take the gondola (for a fee) back down. The trail has seen lots of recent improvements and is literally one long wooden and rock staircase. It is also closed in winter.

Goat Mountain Trail:

From the top of the gondola, this hike is 8 km (5 mi) return gaining 275 m (900 ft) to the summit at 1,400 m (4,600 ft). The hike starts on an old road before the trail heads up Goat Ridge. You can include the Dam Mountain Loop in your hike and maybe even a side trip to Little Goat Mountain. The views of the Lower Mainland are great...on days you can actually see Greater Vancouver.

Hanging Lake Trail (Map 5/F7)

This is a moderate 8 km (5 mi) round trip hike to a gorgeous lake, at the base of Mount Lindeman. Hanging Lake provides good fishing and Lindeman is a fine rock-climbing destination.

Harrison Lookout Trail (Map 14/E4)

Located off the Sts'ailes (formerly Harrison West) Forest Service Road, this short but steep 4 km (2.5 mi) trail leads to an old forest service lookout on a hill above Harrison Lake. You hike along an old road to a beautifully wooded trail past mossy knolls to the vantage point from the lookout some 350 m (1,150 ft) later.

Hat Mountain Trail (Map 11/B4)

There are two different trailheads to Hat Mountain. The first is located at Lions Bay next to The Lions/Mount Harvey trailhead. The second is at a new tourist turnoff about 3 km past Lions Bay. This trail is more popular for its shorter distance and scenery and is a 19 km (12 mi) round trip, gaining 1,400 m (4,600 ft). The trail winds through mystical coastal forest before reaching a breathtaking viewpoint of the Howe Sound area. A hard-to-find warming hut/overnight shelter is reported to exist in the area.

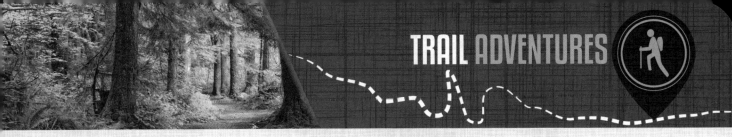

Hayward Lake Trails (Map 3/C3)

In and around Hayward Lake are a series of easy trails to explore. The Pond Interpretative Trail is a short 1.5 km stroll around a small beaver pond. The Railway Trail can be accessed either near Ruskin Dam from Wilson Road or off of the parking lot just south of the Dewdney Trunk Road. This easy trail leads 12 km (7.3 mi) return along an old rail bed, which was used in the early part of the century while building Stave Falls Dam. The Reservoir Trail follows the east shores of the reservoir for 9 km past Steelhead Falls, a floating bridge and old growth and second growth forests.

Haywire Bay Regional Park Trails (Map 18/G2)

There is a pair of trails here. The Lost Lake Trail is 6 km (3.7 mi) in length and leads through old growth forest past Lost Lake to Inland Lake. There are several steep sections along the trail. Tony's Trail leads along the eastern banks of Powell Lake in a southward direction. This trail is 8 km (5 mi) one-way and culminates at Mowat Bay.

H.B.C. Brigade Trail 1849 (Map 16/A6–17/B5)

This historic trail east of Hope is seeing some significant upgrades by the Back Country Horsemen Society of BC. The 48 km (30 mi) trail makes its way from the Peers Creek Forest Service Road over towards the Whatcom Trail. Due to the distance and elevation gain of almost 1,570 m (5,155 ft), this trail is best travelled on horse. Along the way there are several designated campsites complete with food caches and toilets.

High Falls Creek Trail (Map 21/G2–22/A2)

The High Falls Creek Trail was the first trail that local legend Halvor Lunden built, although parts of the trail have been clear cut. From the 24 mile mark on the Squamish Forest Service Road, the steep trail gains 622 metres (2,040 ft) in just over 4 km (2.5 mi) to a view of the impressive falls that cascade 100 m (325 ft) into a narrow canyon. There are some short chain assisted areas to climb. Past the falls, the trail continues a short distance up to a vista overlooking the Squamish River Valley. The trail also hooks up with a nearby logging road where it is possible to head back along the road or work your way up Cloudburst Mountain or Tricouni Meadows.

Hillside Demonstration Forest (Map 10/D4)

Located along McNair Creek, this demonstration forest illustrates different silviculture practices of the Sunshine Coast and provides a view of the Port Mellon Mill as well as Howe Sound. The forest is on the west side of McNair Creek and it is best to park on the west side of the McNair Creek Bridge and hike up the hill. The trail is 4 km (2.5 mi) return and has a number of interpretative signs along the way.

Hollyburn Heritage Trails (Map 11/C7)

From the west side of Lawson Creek Bridge on Pinecrest Drive, an extensive trail network leads through the second growth forest typical of the North Shore. The main trail leads 6.7 km (4.2 mi) return to the Hollyburn Giant, an 1100-year-old Douglas fir that is 3 m (9.7 ft) in diameter. The trail crosses the Crossover and Baden Powell Trails. Another possible access point is at the junction of Eyremount, Crestwell and Millstream Roads.

Hoover Lake Trail (Map 3/D2)

Give yourself about an hour to reach the lake as you hike through a heavy forest east of Stave Falls Dam. This trail starts out along an old road as it climbs steadily to the lake. The trail is 7.4 km (4.5 mi) return with an elevation gain of 250 m (820 ft).

Hope Lookout Trail (Map 15/F7)

You have a choice of a short 2 km (1.2 mi) loop around the base of Hope Mountain or a 5 km (3 mi) hike to the lookout. The latter hike involves a 500 m (1,640 ft) climb as you switchback up the talus slopes to the lookout. The trailhead is found off Highway 1 near Exit 173, across from the Rainbow Inn.

Hope Mountain Trail (Map 15/G7)

The trailhead is found opposite Nicolum Provincial Park on Highway 3 along a four-wheel drive road. The road climbs 8 km (5 mi) over many waterbars to the parking lot. The difficult trail leading to the right (left leads to Wells Peak) will take about 5 hours to climb Hope Mountain. After climbing 800 m (2,625 ft), you will be rewarded with panoramic views (on clear days).

Hope-Nicola Valley Trail (Map 15/G6)

Found near the popular Othello (Quintette) Tunnels next to the Coquihalla Canyon, the Hope-Nicola Valley Trail continues north from the old Kettle Valley Railway/Trans Canada Trail up and over the mountain and back to the parking lot. This trail makes a nice 8 km (5 mi) loop.

Hope Pass Trail (Map 6/G3–7/C1)

This trail leads 26 km (16 mi) one-way from Cayuse Flats on Highway 3 to a branch road off the Whipsaw Creek Forest Service Road. The first 4 km (2.5 mi) of the trail follows an old fire access road before heading in a north-eastern direction along the banks of the Skagit River. At around the two hour mark, watch for the Grainger Creek Trail, which departs to the right. As an alternate, you could loop back along this route and camp at Nicomen Lake. The trail reaches Hope Pass at the 21 km mark (13 mi) before descending to the Whipsaw Creek Forest Service Road. Some people turn around at the pass and hoof it back to Cayuse Flats for a very long (12-14 hour) day hike. From Highway 3 to Hope Pass, there is an elevation gain of 1,050 m (3,445 ft). There is an interesting side route to Dick's Cabin on top of Skaist Mountain.

Howe Sound Bluffs (Map 11/A4)

Unlike the other trails in the Deeks area, this trail doesn't climb past the 450 m (1,475 ft) mark, making this a good intermediate route. Even better, when the higher trails to Deeks Lake and Deeks Peak are snowed under, the trail to the bluffs is still navigable. This trail is 8.4 km (5.2 mi) return and should take about 5 hours to hike. This trail hooks up with the Deeks Lake Trail.

Howe Sound Crest Trail (Map 11/B6–A4)

Linking the northern and southern portions of Cypress Provincial Park, the trail is 29 km (17.7 mi) one-way and is clearly marked with orange markers. It links a number of North Shore Mountain hikes and is best hiked between mid-July to the first snowfall. This is a difficult but rewarding hike. From Cypress Bowl, the trail climbs up to St. Marks Summit and drops a few hundred metres before heading up to Unnecessary Ridge. The highest point on the trail at 1,525 m (5,000 ft). From here, the trail follows an undulating ridge before dropping down to Deeks Creek.

Hut Lake Trail (Map 22/B4)

With a four-wheel drive vehicle, you can park at the north end of Levette Lake and follow the overgrown, washed out logging road part way to Hut Lake. It is a 5 km (3 mi) trek that should take about 1.5 hours. The lake offers good fishing for small rainbow.

Inland Lake Trail (Map 18/G2)

Inland Lake Trail is a wheelchair accessible area, complete with a cabin, picnic tables and a dock. The trail leads 13 km (8 mi) around the lake. From the west side of the lake, it is possible to connect with the Lost Lake Trail, which culminates at the Haywire Bay Regional Park. At the north end of Inland Lake, you may wish to hike 700 metres along the portage route to Powell Lake. This is a well-marked and popular family trail enjoyed by both hikers and bikers.

International Ridge/Mount Amadis Trail (Map 4/D7)

Accessed off the gated Edmesten Road, this 16 km (9.9 mi) ridge route leads to the 1,525 m (5,000 ft) high summit of Mount Amadis. You will climb 1,325 m (4,345 ft) over about eight hours. From the summit, you get a good view of the Fraser Valley and over the border into Washington State.

Iona Jetty (Map 1/B3)

Located in Richmond, just north of the airport, the Iona Jetty juts 4 km into the into the Strait of Georgia creating an 8 km (5 mi) return trip starting and returning to Iona Beach Park. Many bikers combine this with the dyke and road to create a 24 km (15 mi) return bike trip. There are also 13 km (8 mi) of trail for walking, 3 km for horseback riding and 4 km for cycling at the park. Explore the tidal flats and marshes, enjoy the ocean views or watch jets taking off and landing.

Isolillock Peak Trail (Map 5/E1)

Access this trail from the Sowerby Creek Forest Service Road. You can park close to the trailhead just past the bridge over Sowerby Creek, about 6.5 km up the road. The first part of the trail passes through dense second growth forest, before opening up into old growth grove and an area of burnt trees, making for much easier hiking and excellent views. Around the 1,700 m (5,560 ft) level you will reach the false summit, providing a view of your route up to Isolillock Peak. From here it is another 370 metre climb, or rather scramble, to the top where you can enjoy a view far up the Fraser River and of Cheam and Outram Mountains. This 9.5 km (5.9 mi) round trip gains 1,550 m (5,085 ft) in elevation.

Jenna Peak Trail (Map 27/D6)
Accessed from the trailhead at the 8.7 km mark on the Juliet Forest Service Road, this trail leads to the peak between the Anderson River and July Mountain. Used mainly by backcountry skiers and hikers, the trail is 4.8 km (3 mi) one-way, climbing about 500 m (1,640 ft). The Juliet Creek Cabin provides shelter with a wood stove for overnight use.

Joffre Lake Trail (Map 43/A7)
The trailhead is located approximately 23 km east of Mount Currie on Highway 99. The very popular trail is well marked and leads from the parking lot past two smaller lakes on your way to the picturesque Upper Joffre Lake. The upper lake, which offers wilderness camping, is simply spectacular as it lies directly below the icefields of Matier Glacier. The trail is 11 km (6.8 mi) gaining 400 m (1,300 ft). Some mountaineers hike to the glacier edge or climb Joffre or Matier Peaks (see Twin Goat Ridge Route below).

July Mountain Trail (Map 27/E6)
A nice trail leads from a branch road off of Juliet Creek Forest Service Road, following North July Creek up to Drum Lake. More ambitious hikers can continue onto the top of July Mountain along the northern ridge, making for a 9.5 km (6 mi) return trip and an elevation gain of 715 m (2,345 ft). Camping is possible at Drum Lake.

Kanaka Creek Regional Park (Map 2/G3–3/B3)
Following the valley of Kanaka Creek, there are about 10 km (6 mi) of trails in this regional park. Some of the highlights include Cliff Falls and the Bell-Irving Fish Hatchery where you can see spawning salmon in fall. There are also a couple picnic sites.

Keats Island (Map 10/D6)
Keats Island is a small island accessed by foot ferry from Gibsons. From the landing, it is a 2 km (1.2 mi) jaunt to Plumper Cove Marine Park. At the park, a handful of trails weave their way through the woods, taking you to viewpoints and along oceanfront trails.

Killarney Creek/Lake Trail (Map 10/F6)
On Bowen Island, the Killarney Creek Trail follows the north side of Killarney Creek past the small set of falls at the head of the lagoon. You also pass a fish-spawning channel before circling lovely Killarney Lake. The best place to find the trailhead is at the Union Steamship Co. Store in Snug Cove or at St. Gerard's Catholic Church. The trail is about an 8 km (5 mi) hike from the ferry landing around the lake. Allow about 2.5 hours. There are also about 12.5 km (7.8 mi) of trail at Crippen Regional Park (where the lake sites), 5 km of which are open to horseback riding and biking.

Kingdom Lake Trail (Map 51/B5)
The Kingdom Lake Trail is a multi-use trail that connects three beautiful lakes on the plateau above Bralorne. Mountain bikers prefer riding south to north, from Kingdom at the far end of the recreation site, to Lost Lake. The trail links to the Mount Truax Trail as well as back to Bralorne for a nice loop. Closer to town, the Bradian Trail Network can also be explored.

Knuckleheads Recreation Area (Map 19/F2)
This is a popular winter recreation area, accessed on the E Branch Road off of the Stillwater Mainline. In the summer, the area is popular for hiking, bicycling and ATVing, but is better known as a winter destination with a cabin and a variety of old roads/trails to explore. Beta Lake is accessed from the end of Branch E-100 via a short, 1.5 km trail to the small sub-alpine lake. The trail is not well marked and often has snow into summer. Black bears are common to the area so be cautious. It is possible to continue on to the Knuckleheads, which is an excellent alpine climbing area with views of the surrounding lakes, or to Walt Lake Ridge. The Knuckleheads Trail is steep and unmarked and will take 6-8 hours to complete.

Kwotlenemo Trails (Map 53/F7)
This popular recreation lake is home to a series of multi-use trails. In winter the 12 km (6.7 mi) system is used by cross-country skiers, while in the spring through fall, mountain bikers and hikers frequent the trails. The lake is accessed by the Fountain Valley Road.

Lake Lovely Water Trail (Map 22/B5)
The hike into this scenic sub-alpine area, now part of the Tantalus Provincial Park, is difficult but rewarding. It involves crossing an Indian Reserve to the Squamish River and then paddling a canoe across the river. From the west banks of the Squamish River, the trail follows the creek draw leading to the lake. The trail is 15 km (9.3 mi) return gaining over 1,200 m (3,935 ft). While it is a difficult climb, the trail is in good condition. The Alpine Club maintains a cabin at the lake, which can be rented. The area also offers good fishing, wilderness camping areas and climbing opportunities.

Landstrom Ridge [Crack Mountain] Trail (Map 15/E7)
A short, stiff trail climbs to a series of four lookouts on Landstrom Ridge including Crack Mountain. Although fairly easy, expect to climb 150 m (490 ft) over the 3 km (1.9 mi) round trip. Accessing the Landstrom Ridge Trail is tricky as it has been blocked by highway construction debris. Look for the weigh scale west of the junction with Highway 1. At the western side of the scale you will see the debris – climb over to find the trail.

Lighthouse Park (Map 11/A7)
From the parking lot at Lighthouse Park, an extensive year-round trail network leads through old growth forest to the rocky shoreline of Point Atkinson. If you hike around the perimeter of the park, the 5 km (3 mi) should take about two hours, but there are many other trails snaking through the forest. Make sure you visit the lighthouse, which was erected in 1912.

Lillooet River Dyke Trails (Map 33/C1–B7)
Starting from Highway 99 on the east side of the Lillooet River Bridge, a gentle trail follows the river in a northwest direction for about 5 km (3 mi). At the end of the dyke road, a moderate single-track loops around MacKenzie Lake. From here, it is possible to return along the steep (1,000 m/3,280 ft) MacKenzie Basin Road. The Dyke Trail also extends for several kilometres in the opposite direction. This easy route cuts through the Indian Reserve, marshland and offers fine views of Mount Currie.

Ling Lake Trail (Map 5/D4)
The trailhead for the Ling Lake Trail is found at the end of Foley Creek Road. Unfortunately, there is a gate located near the Foley Creek Recreation Site so you will have to hike or bike up the logging road before actually starting the trail. From the gate, the trail is about 18 km (11 mi) long. Give yourself at least a day to the alpine lake. The principle users of the trail are fishermen.

Lions Trail (Map 11/B5)
The trailhead to this popular hike is found at Lions Bay by taking the Oceanside Road exit off Highway 99 and driving to the gate at the end of Mountain Drive (parking is limited). The difficult trail follows an old road upward until there is a fork in the road. The right fork leads to the Lions Trail, while the left fork accesses the Brunswick Mountain Trail. You will climb down to Harvey Creek, then head up through an old growth forest. The last part of the 15 km (9.3 mi) hike climbs steeply to a small summit to the south of the West Lion, where it is possible to pitch a tent and enjoy the view of the Howe Sound. You will climb 1,280 m (4,200 ft). The hike is best done in late summer or early fall.

Little Spearhead Trail (Map 32/G5)
From the Upper Village, follow the signs to the Singing Pass Parking Lot. Here you cross Fitzsimmons Creek (be careful, there's no bridge) and descend on Blackcomb Mountain. This 13 km (8 mi) round trip climbs 325 m (1,065 ft) and is a moderate ride.

Liumchen Lake Trail (Map 4/E7)
This is a beautiful alpine hike that starts at the end of the very rough Liumchen East Forest Service Road (about 9.5 km along this four-wheel drive road). From the trailhead you climb sharply uphill to a ridge, which offers great views of the Chilliwack Valley. From the ridge, the trail drops 280 m (910 ft) into the lovely Liumchen Lake bowl. It will take about five hours to hike 9.4 km (5.8 mi) return. Many continue on to Church Mountain, which is an additional 1.5 km along the ridge. Alternatively, Liumchen Mountain is south from the alpine meadows. You will climb 455 m (1,490 ft) over 2.5 km (1.6 mi) one-way to this great vantage point that overlooks Washington State. The hike is best done in late summer (for the flowers) or in early autumn.

Lizzie Creek [Stein Divide] Trail (Map 34/C5)
Although it used to be possible to drive to Lizzie Lake and start hiking from there, a bridge washout has lengthened the hike by 10 km (6 mi). The extra hiking means you have a much better chance of having Lizzie Creek Cabin (a 15 km/ 9.3 mi hike from the trailhead with a 1,500 m/4,920 ft elevation gain) to yourself. From here you have numerous options for exploring the surrounding lakes and mountains. To reach the Stein Divide requires scrambling

up a rockslide, hiking past several small alpine lakes to Cherry Pip Pass and then skirting over to Caltha Lake, which is about an 8-10 hour one-way hike from the cabin and an 870 m (2,850 ft) elevation gain. Further along the route are Stein Lake and Elton Lake. This area provides exceptional hiking in the alpine with endless backpacking and backcountry skiing options. The remote area is best left to experienced hikers.

Locomotive Peak Trail (Map 41/E2)

Access the trailhead from the Hurley River Forest Service Road. The trail climbs about 250 metres over 1.5 km before flattening out in the alpine, running past several small lakes and tarns. The trail swings behind the main Locomotive ridge to the gentler inclined hind ridge, which faces the Pemberton Valley. Here you will pass through a mixture of rock and snowfields before reaching the scrambling section to the peak. It will be a steep climb but there are a variety of routes to choose from. From the peak you will have a prime view of the rest of Gouty Ridge, Face Mountain and Goat Peak among others. In total, the trail climbs 1,030 m (3,380 ft) over a one-way distance of 6 km (3.8 mi).

Loquilts Lake Trail (Map 30/F3)

This trailhead is access by boat from Princess Louisa Inlet at Chatterbox Falls. From here ascend the east side of Loquilts Creek to Loquilts Lake, a steep 6.9 km (4.3 mi) one-way trail climbing over 1,300 m (4,265 ft). It is possible to camp at the gorgeous lake amid the huge rock formations, and set out from here to the open alpine of Contact Lakes and Mount John Clarke. Alternately, it is possible to reach the Elaho-Jervis divide by heading south from Loquilts Lake. This scenic route requires some glacier travel.

Lost Lake Ski Trails (Map 32/G5)

30 km (18.3 mi) of well-maintained cross-country ski trails leads from the parking lot adjacent to the municipal hall in Whistler or from the parking lot next to the Chateau Whistler. When the snow is gone, the trail network is heavily used by hikers, joggers and mountain bikers. Periodically, you will find maps and signs to help mark the way. The main trail leads around Lost Lake with easy access to the north end where you will find a nice wharf and a doggie beach.

Lower Seymour Conservation Reserve (Map 11/E7–F6)

Formerly known as the Seymour Demonstration Forest, this 5,668 hectare (14,000 ac) area was created in 1987 to educate the public about forest ecosystems and logging practices. Within the reserve there are some 65 km (40 mi) of trails, some official, others not, leading to various spots in the park including Rice Lake, Seymour Falls Dam and Twin Bridges. The main trailhead is found at the end of Lillooet Road. No dogs are allowed in the reserve.

Fisherman Trail & Twin Bridges Trail:
A popular trail with anglers and mountain bikers, the Fisherman Trail is a moderate 7 km (4.3 mi) route along the scenic Seymour River. Follow the Twin Bridges Trail 2.6 km to the bottom of the hill, then head north (left) before the bridge. Other trails in the area can extend both trails.

Rice Lake Trail:
A gravel road connects the Rice Lake loop trail with the main parking area. In total it is about 4 km (2.5 mi) along an easy grade and is open to mountain biking.

Seymour Valley Trailway:
From the main parking lot, this popular paved route leads 10 km (6 mi) one-way to the Seymour Falls Dam and takes about three hours. The rolling track is used by walkers, bikers and inline skaters and can be busy. The trail offers great views of the Fannin Range, Lynn Ridge Peaks, the Needles and cliffs of Jack's Burn and Paton's Lookout. At the end of the trail, there are boardwalks and a salmon hatchery.

Lucky Four Mine Trail (Map 5/C4)

This moderate trail climbs 650 m (2,130 ft) over 4 km (2.5 mi) one-way as it makes its way along an old access road to the site of an old mine. From the mine, a difficult route heads up and onto the glacier below Foley Peak, an additional 2.5 km (1.6 mi) and 400 m (1,300 ft).

Lynn Canyon Park (Map 1/E1–11/E7)

While it's much bigger brother, Lynn Headwaters, gets all the press, Lynn Canyon is arguably a nicer place to be. A suspension bridge, just a few steps from the parking lot, is the main feature of the park. To the north are a rocky

beach and waterfall that are often busy on a hot summer day. A second bridge spans the creek there, making an easy loop. More energetic hikers can continue straight and connect up with the Baden Powell Trail, which can be used as the second leg in an 8 km (5 mi) loop (the third leg is along the Fisherman/Homestead Trails, back to Lynn Canyon).

Lynn Headwaters Regional Park (Map 11/E7–E5)

This popular park offers a wide variety of trails ranging from easy creek walks to strenuous wilderness treks. The heavily wooded trails make for good wet weather walking. All told, there are about 54 km (34 mi) of trails, as well as links to the Lower Seymour Conservation Reserve to the east. In winter the trails are taken over by backcountry skiers. The park is accessed off the Lynn Valley Road past Dempsey Road. Some of the more popular trails include the Lynn Loop and the scenic Norvan Falls Trail. Hikers can access Grouse Mountain along the steep Hanes Valley Loop, or take the challenging hike up Coliseum Mountain. Lynn Peak offers a moderate summit to conquer, while Lynn Lake is a challenging hike along a lengthy, ragged trail.

Coliseum Mountain Route:
Certainly not one of the easier routes in the area, this difficult hike is best left for the drier weather of late summer and early fall. It is a steep 25 km (15.5 mi) return hike that follows a sometimes indistinct route. The route is marked with orange flagging as you pass through the steep forested area and enter the Norvan Meadows on your way to Norvan Pass, gaining 1,245 m (4,085 ft). Although there is no camping allowed in the park, the Coliseum is the type of destination that makes a perfect overnight trip.

Hanes Valley Loop:
Linking hikers with Grouse Mountain is a steep 17 km (10.5 mi) hike along Hanes Creek. The trail gains 900 m (2,950 ft), mostly as you climb up the steep scree slope out of the valley to Crown Pass. The trail leaves the trail to Lynn Lake at Norvan Creek and has some difficult creek crossings. Good route finding skills are a must.

Norvan Falls:
This trail follows the same path as the Lynn Loop, but when the loop doubles back, keep heading north. From the parking lot it is 16.4 km (10. 2 mi) return gaining over 235 m (770 ft) in elevation to the scenic falls.

Lynn Lake:
Since there is no camping allowed, you will really have to leg it to hike the 25 km (15.5 mi) to the lake and back. Even better, the trail is ragged and rough and sometimes not even a trail at all. This route is best left for experienced (and fast) hikers.

Lynn Peak:
At 1,000 m (3,280 ft), this peak is the runt of the North Shore Mountains. But the only way to the top of Lynn is with your own two feet. It will take about four hours to hike the 7 km (4.3 mi) moderate return trip. You can continue past Lynn Peak to the Needles.

Mackenzie Trails (Map 33/C1–42/C7)

The Mackenzie Trails stretch for more than 40 km (25 mi) and are generally rougher, steeper and more challenging than the nearby Mosquito Lake Trails. Most of the trails are accessed off the Cell Tower Road, which leads up to the paraglide launch. For people looking for less aggressive riding, it is possible to ride up past the launch (and trails with names like Blood, Sweat and Fear and Cop Killer, named after a local mountain biking policeman who wasn't quite up to the trail) and back down into the valley along the main road, creating the Mackenzie Basin Loop.

Madely Lake Trail (Map 32/D4)

While access is much improved now that the Callaghan Road is paved, the spur road to the lake still calls for a high clearance vehicle. From the trailhead, the trail leads 6 km (3.7 mi) one-way to Rainbow Lake gaining 500 m (1,640 ft). This is a shorter alternative for hiking to Rainbow Lake although, like the other trail, the approach is through an unremarkable forest. Once you exit the woods, the scenery is spectacular and you climb through beautiful meadows with the possibility of scrambling some rocky peaks. There is a bridge out and the trail can be hard to follow as it crosses a boulder field. Watch for flagging tape.

Manning Park (Maps 6, 7)

Trails cut through rugged mountains, meadows, lakes and rivers in this spectacular park. The park has designated areas for backcountry camping, while closer to the highway there are many short loop trails to explore. A number of trails run through Manning's picturesque sub-alpine meadows, including Bonnevier, Grainger Creek and Heather/Three Brothers Trails. Monument 78 and 83 Trails go right up to the Washington border and the start of the Pacific Crest Trail. The highest peak in Manning Park is accessed along the Frosty Mountain Trail, which passes Windy Joe Mountain on the way up. A number of lakes, with some decent fishing, are accessible along the Lightning Lakes Chain Trail and the Poland Lake Route. From Lightning Lakes, Skyline I and II Trails provide access to Camp Mowich and the Skagit Valley.

Frosty Mountain Trail (Map 7/C6–C7)

Frosty Mountain is the highest peak in Manning Park. From the Windy Joe Trailhead it is a 29 km (17.7 mi) return trek, while from Lightning Lakes it is a 22 km (13.5 mi) route. It is possible to combine the two into a 27.5 km (16.8 mi) loop. Although this trip can be done in a long, strenuous day, there are campsites on either route. The best times to visit Frosty Mountain are in late July/early August when the meadows are full of wildflowers or mid-September when the larch trees turn a brilliant gold colour. For folks not wanting to make the entire trip, Larch Plateau at 9 km (5.5 mi) is a worthy destination. Some of these trees are estimated to be 2,000 years old.

Heather/Three Brothers Trail (Map 7/D5–B2)

This is the main trail through Manning Park's vast sub-alpine meadows. In mid-July to August, the sub-alpine are notorious for their amazing display of colourful wildflowers. To get here, you will have to drive up to the trailhead. Fortunately, the road leads all the way up to the sub-alpine, meaning you will only gain 290 m (950 ft) to the Nicomen Ridge overlooking Nicomen Lake. The trail is 21 km (13 mi) one-way, but it is possible to add the steep, 1 km side trail up to the top of the First Brother to the venture. Please remember that these sub-alpine meadows are extremely fragile.

Lightning Lakes Chain Trail (Map 7/B7)

This trail begins at Spruce Bay or at the day-use area and leads 12 km (7.3 mi) one-way past a series of good fishing lakes. This is an easy walk through a pleasant forest. Wilderness camping is offered at Stake Lake and fishing can be excellent. Alternately, it is a 9 km loop around Lightning Lake itself.

Monument 83 Trail (Map 7/E6–F7)

From the Monument 78/83 parking lot, this is a 16 km (9.9 mi) one-way hike along an old fire access road to the US Forest Service tower. Along the trail, you will pass by an old cabin built in the 1920s by the US Forest Service as well as Pasayten Pete's grave. It is possible to head east out of the park on the Pasayten River Trail, which is part of the historic Centennial Trail. You will gain 850 m (2,790 ft) to the tower.

Skyline Trails (Map 6/G6–7/C6)

From Lightning Lake, the Skyline I Trail runs 17 km (10.5 mi) one-way to Camp Mowich. From the camp, it is possible to hike 8.5 km (5.3 mi) into the Skagit Valley via the Skyline II Trail.

Windy Joe Mountain (Map 7/D6)

Beginning at the Beaver Pond parking lot, this trail leads 15 km (9.3 mi) return along an old fire access road to the summit of Windy Joe Mountain, with an elevation gain of 655 m (2,150 ft). A fire lookout serves as a shelter at the end of the trail. The Windy Joe Mountain trail also provides access to Frosty Mountain, a 28 km (17 mi) return trip which gains 1,205 m (3,950 ft) in elevation.

Marion & Phyllis Lakes Route (Map 11/B3)

A long bike ride takes you along the gated access road north of the Furry Creek Golf Course past Marion Lake to Phyllis Lake. The 450 m (1,475 ft) climb over 16 km (9.9 mi) return brings you to some nice vantage points across Howe Sound as well as good fishing holes. The area beyond Phyllis Lake (the Greater Vancouver Watershed) is closed to the public.

Marriott Basin Trail (Map 43/A6)

From the Duffy Lake Road, this trail heads high into the sub-alpine at the foot of Mount Marriott along an old road. Keep left as you hike up the road and left again where the trail splits (the right trail heads to Rohr Lake). Marriott Basin is an explorer's paradise; once you get up to the basin, you can wander almost anywhere you want to, but please avoid treading on the fragile plant life. You will hike about 16 km (9.9 mi) and climb 370 m (1,210 ft).

Marshall Lake Trails (Map 51/E2)

The 10 km (6 mi) long Marshall Lake Trail takes you up the hill from the east side of Marshall Lake down to Carpenter Lake. From here, you can arrange for a pick up or retrace your path. Also in the area are a variety of other trails that follow old roads and tracks to a variety of vantage points.

Matsqui Trail (Map 3/D5–F5)

Since this dyke system is part of the Trans Canada Trail, you can virtually walk, bike or ride as long as you like. Most visitors start from the picnic area in this popular Regional Park (found at the end of Riverside Road below the Mission Bridge) and walk towards the Page Road trailhead. This portion of the dyke is about 17 km (10.5 mi) return and offers several vantage points of the Fraser River.

MANNING PARK TRAILS	MAP	DIFFICULTY	LENGTH	ELEVATION GAIN	CAMP	BIKE	HIKE	HORSE	SKI	SNOWSHOE	VIEW
Bonnevier Trail	7/D4-F4	Difficult	25 km (15.5 mi)	950 m (3,115 ft)			•				•
Frosty Mountain Trail	7/C6-C7	Difficult	27.5 km (17 mi)	1,205 m (3,950 ft)	•		•		•	•	•
Grainger Creek Trail	7/B2	Difficult	11 km (6.8 mi)	800 m (2,625 ft)	•		•				•
Heather/Three Brothers Trail	7/D5-B2	Moderate	21 km (13 mi)	290 m (950 ft)	•		•				•
Lightning Lakes Chain Trail	7/B7	Easy	12 km (7.3 mi)	25 m (80 ft)	•	•	•		•	•	•
Memaloose Trail	7/A5	Moderate	9 km (5.5 mi)	420 m (1,380 ft)			•				•
Monument 78 Trail	7/D6-D7	Moderate	12 km (6.7 mi)	200 m (655 ft)	•	•	•	•			•
Monument 83 Trail	7/E6-F7	Difficult	16 km (9.9 mi)	850 m (2,790 ft)	•	•	•	•			•
North and South Gibson Trails	7/B6	Easy	7.6 km (4.6 mi)	125 m (650 ft)			•	•			•
Pacific Crest Trail	7/D6-D7	Difficult	4,300 km (2,700 mi)	4,010 m (13,155 ft)	•		•	•			•
Poland Lake Trail	7/A5	Easy	8 km (5 mi)	435 m (1,425 ft)	•	•	•	•	•	•	•
Skagit Bluffs	6/F3	Easy	5.6 km (3.5 mi)	80 m (260 ft)			•				•
Skyline I Trail	6/G6-7/C6	Moderate	17 km (10.5 mi)	560 m (1,840 ft)	•		•				•
Skyline II Trail	6/F6-G6	Difficult	8.5 km (5.3 mi)	1,080 m (3,545 ft)	•		•				•
Three Falls/Strawberry Flats Trail	7/A6	Moderate	4.5 km (2.8 mi)	125 m (410 ft)		•	•				•
Windy Joe Mountain	7/D6	Moderate	7.5 km (4.7 mi)	655 m (2,150 ft)	•	•	•	•	•	•	•

McGillivray Pass Trail (Map 43/A1–51/E1)

Best accessed in the winter on skis or a snowmobile, the Kingdom Lake Forest Service Road beyond Bralorne is washed out and becoming overgrown. It is a better idea to climb to the scenic pass from the Anderson Lake side. Depending on how far you park up the old road, expect at least a 15 km (9.3 mi) one-way trek along McGillivray Creek. Along the way you will pass many historical buildings and mines and other remnants of the area's mining past. The route is challenging and takes you through grizzly bear country.

Mehatl Falls Trail (Map 25/C2)

Nestled in a sub-alpine bowl, it is a 3 km (1.9 mi) hike to Mehatl Falls. Parking is available adjacent to the 48 km bridge of the Nahatlatch River Forest Service Road.

Melvin Creek Trail (Map 43/E4)

From the Cayoosh Creek Recreation Site on Duffey Lake Road, this 6 km (3.7 mi) one-way trail crosses Cayoosh Creek and accesses a large alpine basin containing several small lakes. The trail was built by hunting guides, but hikers and horseback riders can enjoy the route in the spring and summer.

Minnekhada Park Trails (Map 2/D1)

This regional park is located on Quarry Road northeast of Port Coquitlam. Within the park, there are 12 km (7.3 mi) of interconnecting trails through a thick canopy of second growth forest. The main trail leads from the large parking lot on the west side of the park past a marshy lake to a picnic site. Eventually, you reach a viewpoint overlooking the Addington Marsh next to Pitt River. Another trail circles the perimeter of the park in a clockwise direction. A further option is to cross the floating bridge in the middle of the marshy lake and head west to the viewpoint. If you are interested in a dyke walk, take Oliver Drive off the Quarry Road and park at a convenient point after the gates. From there, you can explore the Addington Marsh for a return distance of up to 14 km (8.7 mi).

Mission Ridge Trail (Map 52/F5)

Access to this trail is along Mission Mountain Road (four-wheel drive required), past the Terzaghi dam. This is a steep hike and should take about two hours to reach the summit, where you will have a clear view of the communities of Seton Portage and Shalath, as well as Seton and Anderson Lakes. A couple of old, derelict geodesic domes sit at the summit.

Moon Lake Trail (Map 53/B6)

Located off Bridge River Road, this is an 8 km (5 mi) 3 hour hike along an old four-wheel drive road/trail to Moon Lake. Extreme cyclists can continue on to Mount McLean.

Mosquito Creek Trails (Map 11/D7)

Mosquito Creek Trail is a great choice if you want to sample the North Shore Mountains without the usual elevation gain. This one only gains 320 m (1,050 ft). From the bottom of the Grouse Mountain Gondola, head east along the Baden Powell Trail. The Mosquito Creek Trail departs the Baden Powell only after passing the Grouse Mountain Trails. About 25 m (75 ft) past the Village Chair Trail, the Mosquito Creek Trail finally breaks free of the Baden Powell and heads east to Mosquito Creek. The trail follows the east banks of Mosquito Creek to the Mosquito Creek Cascades (they aren't quite big enough to be called falls). The hike is 8 km (5 mi) return.

Mosquito Lake Area (Map 33/C1–42/C7)

A challenging network of mountain bike trails that offer fast, undulating single-track trails with extreme descents. The trails are accessed from Ivey Road (at the crest near the sub-station), the recreation site or along the MacKenzie Basin Road. There are over 80 km (50 mi) of trails here, ranging from intermediate to expert.

Mount Artaban Trail (Map 10/F5)

The trailhead to this Gambier Island hike is accessed by boat to the south end of Halkett Bay Park (near the scout camp). The hike involves a 600 m (1,970 ft) elevation gain beginning on an old road before passing by a couple of streams and continuing uphill through the forest and some open meadows. As a rule of thumb, stay to your right along the rough trail until you reach the summit, a round trip of 10 km (6 mi).

Mount Cook Trail (Map 33/B4)

From the Wedgemont Lake Hut it is a 5.3 km (3.3 mi) round trip to the peak Mount Cook, with an elevation gain of 840 m (2,750 ft). This is a relatively short trek but gets to be difficult near the top due to expansive scree slopes, so be prepared for variations in trail surface. From the peak you will get an up-close view of the Armchair Glacier to the southeast, with glaciers surrounding Mount Cook from three directions.

Mount Corriveau Trail (Map 5/E6)

The most direct access to Mount Corriveau is from Centre Creek Forest Service Road. This route involves some serious bushwhacking straight up the mountainside through heavily forested and mossy terrain. Expect this to be a slow, challenging hike, but once you hit snowline the going will get easier. At the summit you will find a couple of flat rock platforms on which to relax and enjoy the view of countless surrounding peaks. This route climbs 1,300 m (4,265 ft) over 4 km (2.5 mi). Once at Corriveau, many continue onto MacDonald Peak.

Mount Crickmer Trail (Map 3/C1)

From the Florence Lake Forest Service Road, this difficult 8.8 km (5.5 mi) one-way hike follows an old gated road and then a trail to the top of Mount Crickmer. The route gains 1,310 m (4,300 ft) as you cross several gullies and creeks on your way to the open meadows below the rocky summit. From the top, there are fantastic views of Stave Lake, Mount Blanshard and Mount Robbie Reid to the north.

Mount Currie Trail (Map 33/A2)

Mount Currie is the prominent peak found south of Pemberton. A new trail leads up the west flank to a lookout overlooking the Pemberton Valley and beyond. Currently the trail is about 6.3 km (3.9 mi) and takes three to four hours to climb. Expect about a 1,000 m (3,280 ft) elevation gain to the lookout. The first 4 km of the trail is easy to navigate, but the route beyond to the alpine is much more challenging. The trail starts 3.5 km from Highway 99 along a rough forest service road requiring a four-wheel drive.

Mount Daniel Trail (Map 9/B1)

The parking area for this easy but steep trail is located 3.4 km down the Garden Bay Road north of Pender Harbour. Follow the old road and take the first left, which eventually turns to a trail. Allow 1.5 hours to climb 385 m (1,265 ft) in the short 1.2 km (0.7 mi) trek up to the great vantage point. This sacred area also boasts Indian rock formations near the top.

Mount Drew Trail (Map 20/E5)

To reach the 1,885 metre high (6,185 ft) summit of Mount Drew is a difficult trek. Your first obstacle is getting across Sechelt Inlet to the mouth of Earle Creek from Egmont. Boat is the preferred method of travel. From there, hike or mountain bike up the network of logging roads and then scramble to the top of the summit. Given the distance, it is best to make the hike across in two days. The 36 km (22.5 mi) return trip climbs 1,885 m (6,185 ft) in elevation.

Mount Elphinstone Trails (Maps 9/G5, 10/A4–D5)

Over 150 km (90 mi) of multi-use trails stretch up the Sunshine Coast between Gibsons and Sechelt. Many of these trails follow old roads or short connectors between the three parcels of Mount Elphinstone Provincial Park. Mountain biking is popular on many of these trails, as is hiking and snowshoeing in the winter. The trails can be accessed right from Gibsons or from various points off Highway 101. The South Elphinstone Heritage Trails are a popular section, featuring many short trails that cover significant elevation change, while long distance hikers and trekkers can challenge themselves on the 42 km (27 mi) Mount Elphinstone Bike Loop, which starts right at the Langdale ferry terminal. Other popular trails include the Brodie and Clack Creek trails, while mountain bikers will be challenged by trails such as the Black Tower, 1st, 2nd and 3rd Step and many, many more.

Mount Fromme Trail (Map 11/E7)

A series of trails access Mount Fromme. The main trail is a 15 km (9.3 mi) route that begins off Prospect Road near Mosquito Creek. It is a difficult, steep trail that gains 870 m (2,850 ft) to the summit. The trail begins on the Baden Powell Trail and shortly turns onto a trail labelled "To the Old Mountain Highway." From there, follow the steep Old Mountain Highway, a popular biking route, past Meech Lake to the summit. Once you reach the top, it is best to descend through Pipeline Pass back to the Old Mountain Highway and walk down the road to St. George's Trail, an alternate trail up. Eventually, you meet up with the Baden Powell Trail and a return to the start. Another alternative is to follow the Per Gynt Trail to the peak of Mount Fromme. This is one of the trails built by legendary trail builder Halvor Lunden.

Mount Gardner Trails (Map 10/F6)

The trailhead to this popular network is found on the road between poles 490 and 491 off the Mount Gardner Road. The main trail climbs 725 m (2,380 ft) to the summit along paved, gravel and forested paths. From the top, you will be rewarded with a great view of Bowen Island and Howe Sound. The main trail is 10 km (6 mi) long, but there are many side trails (mostly old logging roads) to explore. Most of the exploring is done by mountain bikers, not hikers. From the ferry landing it is a long 17.5 km (10.7 mi) hike/bike.

Mount Gillespie Trail (Map 12/A1)

This challenging route is best left to experienced mountaineers as you gain 1,040 m (3,410 ft) over 5.6 km (3.5 mi). Accessed off the E110 branch of the Mamquam Forest Service Road, the trek begins by heading east through the forest. You will soon reach a peak which offers a good view of Mount Gillespie ahead of you, and November Lake below. From here it will be a scramble over rocks, around tarns and a glacier to get to the steep scramble to the peak. You may choose to cross the glacier, but be extremely careful of crevasses; a safer route is to cut a C-shape around the lake. From the peak, enjoy views of the Garibaldi and North Shore areas. The Five Finger group will also be visible from here.

Mount Grant Trail (Map 5/G2)

The difficult trail to Mount Grant branches off of the Eaton Lake Trail around the 1,290 m (4,230 ft) elevation level, right around where a pile of deadfall creates a crossing across Eaton Creek. This route follows a steady incline and, without a well-defined trail, you should be extra observant for flagging as you bushwhack up to the junction. From the trail turnoff to the peak is about 2.5 km (1.6 mi), gaining close to 870 m (2,850 ft).

Mount Hallowell Trail (Map 20/C7)

From the Halfmoon-Carlson Forest Service Road, this trail begins at the abandoned red cable spool, about 19.5 km from Highway 101. The trail leads through a clearcut and some old growth timber to the summit and a newly restored forest service fire lookout tower. It is about 1 km to the summit. From the top, you will get an excellent view of the Sechelt Peninsula and the ocean.

Mount Harvey Trail (Map 11/B5)

The trail up Mount Harvey is quite steep, gaining 1,465 m (4,800 ft) in 12.5 km (7.8 mi). There are old ropes along the first part of the trail to help with the elevation gain. There are a few points near the top where you may need to use your hands to scramble up, but it isn't too technical. The trail will take most people about 8 hours.

Mount Henning Trail (Map 16/G1–27/G6)

This area is easily accessed from the Britton Creek Rest Area off the Coquihalla Highway (Hwy 5). An 8 km (5 mi) hike/bike leads along an old road to a viewpoint and then along a faint trail through some alpine meadows to the base of Mount Henning. Overall, the elevation gain is 550 m (1,805 ft) to the summit at 1,818 m (5,965 ft). Most hikers return to the parking lot by way of another faint trail passing by an old mining camp and then leading along the old road. Another option is to hike the 7.5 km (4.6 mi) trail that leads through the sub-alpine between Thynne Mountain and Mount Henning. In the winter, the area becomes an extensive series of snowmobile trails.

Mount Jimmy Jimmy/Coin Lake (Map 21/E2)

Access this trail from the Ashlu Forest Service Road. The first 4 km will be an easy jaunt along the road with minimal elevation gain. Be sure to look for flagging on your right around 910 m (2,990 ft) in elevation – this will indicate the start of a bushwhacking ascent up to Coin Lake. Following a 570 m (1,870 ft) ascent over 2.8 km you will find yourself at Coin Lake, where you will have a clear view of the peak of Mount Jimmy Jimmy protruding in the near distance. To reach the peak you will have to gain 920 m (3,020 ft) over a distance of 5.8 km (3.6 mi). You may want to break this up into an overnight trip if you choose to summit Jimmy Jimmy as there is some glacier travel en route. A large cairn sits atop the summit, and from here, you will have a far reaching 360 degree view of your surroundings.

Mount Klaudt Trail (Map 14/E6)

Mount Klaudt is one of the two mountains that frame Hemlock Valley. In summer, a trail climbs to the saddle below Mount Klaudt, before switchbacking its way up to a viewpoint over Harrison Lake. This moderate trail is 11.5 km (7 mi) return. While it doesn't climb to the top, it gets close enough.

Mount Laughington Trail (Map 5/B5)

A four-wheel drive vehicle is recommended to access this trail as the overgrown road is very rough in some spots. From the trailhead, it is a 6.2 km (3.9 mi) trek to the top of Mount Laughington, with a 900 m (2,950 ft) elevation gain. In season, huckleberries and blueberries along the trail make delicious treats for both hikers and bears. Early on, the trail opens up into alpine heather meadows and equally delicious views of the surrounding peaks.

Mount Lincoln Trail (Map 15/F2)

Mount Lincoln towers above Highway 1 just east of Yale. A rough, sometimes sketchy 1.8 km trail leads up to the 655 m (2,150 ft) summit from near sea level. This difficult climb sometimes resembles rock climbing more than hiking and there are a few spots with fixed ropes to help you ascend. Although not as tall as other mountains in the area, there are still some great views of the Fraser Canyon.

Mount McGuire Trails (Map 4/G7–5/A7)

This prominent 2,020 m (6,625 ft) peak southeast of Chilliwack has several trails/routes that lead to its summit and alpine area. The main trail is found off of Sleese-Borden Forest Service Road, however this road has several bridges out and must be walked. Once you gain the trail you will pass through forest into the alpine meadows and eventually onto the ridge. Summiting is possible, but there is some exposed scrambling to do. Both the northwest and northeast ridges also offer ways up this mountain. The northeast approach might seem like an easier route, but the 7.8 km (4.9 mi) trail is not clearly marked and the surrounding cliffs make GPS navigation difficult. With a 1,315 m (4,310 ft) ascent, be ready for a challenge.

Mount McLean Trails (Map 53/A6)

Picture yourself descending from a high alpine meadow 2,100 vertical m (6,825 ft) down to the sagebrush in the valley below. En route you will cover 14 km (8.7 mi) of spectacular single-track trail. Now, keep that image in mind as you grunt 14 km (8.7 mi) and 2,100 m (6,890 ft) to the top of Mount McLean from Moon Lake. Luckier (and richer) folks have been known to catch a helicopter to the top.

Mount Mercer Trail (Map 5/A5)

Mount Mercer is found at the east end of the Elk Thurston Ridge and marks the highest point along the ridge at 1,705 m (5,595 ft). Access to this trail is from as high as you can get along the Thurston Forest Service Road (an extremely rough and dangerous road past the 2.2 km mark). The official trail begins at the pass around the 1,525 metre elevation mark and climbs towards the summit. The trail starts in a forested area and leads into the alpine meadows of the ridge line where hikers will be rewarded with fantastic views of the surrounding area.

Mount Mulligan/Anif Peak Loop (Map 22/E7)

A four-wheel drive vehicle is recommended to access these peaks from the Mamquam Forest Service Road. The trek to Mount Mulligan is only 2 km, climbing 440 m (1,440 ft), while the hike across the saddle to Anif Peak is an additional 1.7 km. Enjoy the impressive views of the Sky Pilot area and Mount Habrich before the 3.4 km descent back to the trailhead. Combined this is a 7.3 km (4.5 mi) loop.

Mount Outram Trail (Map 6/D2)

This trail begins at the West Gate of Manning Park and leads along the old engineering road to a signed trailhead marking the route to Mount Outram. This moderate trail is 18 km (10.9 mi) return and is best hiked from July to September. The total elevation gain is 1,760 m (5,720 ft). The trail begins in a forested setting before crossing the creek and then continuing through a series of meadows to a steep, rocky ridge and eventually up to the summit of the mountain. You get a spectacular view of the surrounding mountain peaks from the top.

Mount Rexford Trail (Map 5/D6)

The trail to Mount Rexford is an access trail for climbers and is not well maintained, although a crew went up in 2008 to do some work and it is in much better condition now. There are still places where it is difficult to follow. The trail is only 3 km (1.9 mi) one-way, but will take most people about three hours climbing up, as the trail gains nearly 1,000 m (3,280 ft) in that distance. It is relentlessly steep, with no place where the trail levels out for more than a few feet. However, the views back over Slesse are terrific.

Mount Richardson Trail (Map 9/F2)

The best place to access Mount Richardson is from Richardson Lake, which is four-wheel drive vehicle accessible. From the lake, proceed in a southwestern direction by bushwhacking 2 km (1.2 mi) one-way to the summit along an old road. From the summit at 986 m (3,235 ft), you will get a great view of the Sechelt Peninsula and Inlet.

Mount Roderick Trail (Map 22/A7–21/G7)

This long day trip requires you to take the ferry to the Woodfibre Pulp Mill before biking or hiking to the trailhead several kilometres up the main logging road. Here you cross a footbridge to join the trail that passes a helipad before narrowing. Continuing north, the trail climbs up the open ridge to the sub-alpine for a great view of Howe Sound. This is a 20 km (12 mi) difficult hike gaining 1,475 m (4,840 ft). The trail is best hiked in June through October.

Mount Rohr Trail (Map 43/B6)

This 16 km (9.9 mi) return trip starts from Duffey Lake Road (Hwy 99), near the Cayoosh Creek Bridge, and gains 1,500 m (4,920 ft) in elevation. This is an ideal peak for beginner scramblers, and round trip shouldn't take more than five hours. The trail is well defined and easy to follow, eventually running out amid boulder fields below the peak. From here it is pretty straightforward to follow a series of cairns to the summit, just make sure to follow the same route on your way down. Rohr Lake is 9 km (5.5 mi) return climbing 430 m (1,410 ft) along the way. Most of the route is along an old logging road that climbs quickly into a lovely sub-alpine meadow.

Mount Sampson Trail (Map 41/D1)

Be prepared for serious bushwhacking on this 13 km (8 mi) one-way route. Thick alder interspersed with relatively easy forest passages will make up the terrain for your 1,610 m (5,280 ft) ascent. From the end of this trail it is possible to continue on through rock and snowfields to the Sampson Summit, but be sure to start early in the morning if you plan on taking this trail to the peak.

Mount Seymour Provincial Park (Map 11/F7–G6)

Easily reached by way of the Mount Seymour Parkway, this park contains a variety of trails from easy strolls to rough backcountry excursions. The trails are very popular given their scenic surroundings, views of Vancouver and proximity to the city. One of the more popular trails is the namesake Mount Seymour Trail (also known as Three Pumps) which takes you to the summit for fantastic views of metro Vancouver. Easy options in the area include Dog Mountain, Goldie and Mystery Trails, while Old Buck and Three-Chop Trails are more challenging lower elevation options. Hikers looking for a challenge can try the Elsay Lake Trail, which is a rugged trek with a lot of climbs and descents. From here a bushwhack leads to the top of Mount Elsay. Due to snow accumulations at higher levels, the best time to hike is from July thru November. In winter, the hills remain busy with snowshoers and backcountry skiers. Note that the Old Buck Trail is the only trail where horseback riding and mountain biking are allowed.

Dog Mountain Trail:

This easy 6 km (3.7 mi) return hike from the north end of the upper parking lot is more popular in winter with snowshoers. There is little elevation gain as it leads through an old growth sub-alpine fir stand to the bluff overlooking the Seymour River and Greater Vancouver. The trail follows the First Lake Trail for 30 minutes, before heading to the west from the lake. On the return trip, complete the First Lake Loop by taking the north branch of the trail at First Lake and connecting with the Mount Seymour Trail. A further option is to hike the short distance (less than a kilometre) to Dinky Peak for another great view.

Elsay Lake Trail:

A difficult 20 km (12 mi) hike leads through Canadian Pass and some rugged alpine country. The total elevation gain is 885 m (2,900 ft), but there are a couple ups and downs along the way. The hike begins at the north end of the upper parking lot, initially following the Mount Seymour Trail. Take the branch trail just before the First Pump that leads northwest to tiny Gopher Lake. Beyond here, the trail narrows and is occasionally marked. A small backcountry shelter marks the end of the trail at the north end of the lake. Most people stay overnight. Be wary, it is a steeper trek on the return trip.

Mount Elsay Trail:

Little more than a bushwhack from the Elsay Lake Trail, this is a 16 km (9.9 mi) return trek from the upper parking lot. It involves climbing 1,050 m (3,445 ft) along a difficult route with some rock scrambling. From the summit at 1,422 m (4,665 ft), you are rewarded with an excellent view and most likely will have the peak all to yourself (something that can't be said for most other trails in the park). The hike is best left to experienced backpackers.

Mount Seymour Trail:

Also known as the Three Pumps Trail, this is the main trail leading from the north end of the upper parking lot. The moderate hike is 9 km (5.5 mi) return, with an elevation gain to 450 m (1,475 ft) to the Third (and final) Pump. The popular trail climbs steadily through a fairly open sub-alpine forest before breaking out into the alpine meadows. The trail gets more challenging as you dip and climb to the Second Pump and dip and climb again to the Third Pump, which is the actual 1,450 m (4,755 ft) summit of Mount Seymour. Since views of Greater Vancouver are offered from any of the three pumps, most people do not bother climbing beyond the First Pump. Those that make it to the Third Pump will enjoy even better views and a more peaceful setting.

Mystery Lake Loop:

This trail follows the Mystery Ski Lift before connecting with the Mount Seymour Trail and the return to the parking lot. It will take about 1.5 hours to complete this 3 km (1.9 mi) loop, with an elevation gain of 180 m (585 ft). The beautiful sub-alpine lake is a good spot to swim during a hot summer day.

Mount Shadowfax Trail (Map 42/D2)

This 25 km (15.5 mi) round trip gains 1,810 m (5,940 ft) in elevation from the trailhead near the Birkenhead Park boundary. Most hikers choose to use the Brian Waddington Hut (10.5 km/6.5 mi from trailhead) as an overnight shelter and summit Shadowfax or one of the other nearby peaks from here. Mount Gandalf and Mount Aragorn are two popular Tolkien-themed destinations close to the hut. Some loose scree and snowfields will have to be navigated on your way to the top of Shadowfax, but the view of the surrounding area will be worth it.

Mount St Benedict Trail (Map 3/F1)

The trail leads from the Davis Lake Provincial Park and is 15 km (9.3 mi) return gaining 1,000 m (3,280 ft) to the summit. The hike involves traversing a mixture of old road and trails along Mundro Creek past tiny McKay Lake to the summit. Good views of Mount Judge Howay and Robbie Reid are offered from the top, but the hike up is unremarkable (unless you like clear cuts). Snow limits the hiking season to July through October.

Mount Steele Trail (Map 10/B2)

This popular year-round trail in Tetrahedron Park begins by traversing some old growth timber past Edwards and Gilbert Lakes. Eventually, you reach the open sub-alpine terrain and the Mount Steele Cabin, climbing 540 m (1,770 ft) across the 9 km (5.5 mi) one-way trail. Mount Steele is an additional 2 km and 265 m (870 ft). From the summit, enjoy the views of Tetrahedron and Panther Mountains, and look for the North Shore Mountains and the Vancouver Coast on a clear day.

Mount Truax Trail (Map 51/C4)

Mount Truax is the highest peak in the Gold Bridge area at 2,880 m (9,450 ft). The main trail follows the old road from Lost Lake along Fergusson Creek before climbing towards the summit. The difficult trail climbs about 1,525 m (5,000 ft). Alternatively, the unmaintained Why-Not Trail starts from Noel Lake and climbs steeply to join the Mount Truax Trail at the creek. This alternative is 5.7 km (3.5 mi) long.

Mount Varley Trail (Map 10/D2)

To reach the summit of Mount Varley, you must bushwhack off the end of Rainy Forest Service Road. It is about 3 km (1.9 mi) one-way to the summit. In order to reach the end of the Rainy Forest Service Road, it is necessary to use a four-wheel drive vehicle.

Mount Weart Trail (Map 33/B4)

This peak is 5.4 km (3.4 mi) round trip from the end of the Wedgemont Lake Trail, following along the Wedgemont Glacier for much of the 870 m (2,850 ft) climb. The terrain consists of lots of loose jagged rocks and scree slope, so consider this a challenging climb despite the relatively short distance. The view at the top of the glacier will explain why this is such a popular peak. Rocky peaks, glaciers, lakes, and forest stretch in every direction.

Mount Wrottesley Trail (Map 10/F2) 🚶🚴🥾

To reach the prominent peak, boat to McNab Creek or to Camp Potlatch in Howe Sound. From Camp Potlatch, a well-established trail leads along the creek to the Potlatch Road. Continue up the road to where a small creek drains off the southern side of the mountain. From there, bushwhack through the timber to the sub-alpine and then to the summit. From McNab Creek, you must hike/bike up the main haul road and cross over to the Potlatch Road. It is a full day trip (including the boat crossing) involving an elevation gain of 1,625 m (5,330 ft) and a 13 km (8 mi) return distance.

Mowat Bay Trail (Map 18/F3) 🚶🥾

From the Powell Lake Bridge on Highway 101, a 2.3 km (1.4 mi) trail leads to Mowat Bay where you can enjoy a nice swim in Powell Lake. The hike switchbacks (100 m/325 ft) up the northern side of Valentine Mountain before descending to the bay. From the bay, Tony's Trail leads up the eastern shores of Powell Lake.

Mundy Park (Map 2/B2) 🚶🚴🐎🌲

Found off Como Lake Road, this suburban park offers 12 km (7.3 mi) of multi-use trails weaving their way through the cool, lush forest. The heart of the park is Mundy Lake, but the smaller Lost Lake is also a popular destination.

Munro-Dennett Lake Trail (Map 2/D1–12/D7) 🚶🌲🥾

From the signed trailhead on Quarry Road, the hike begins along an old road for a few hundred metres before the trail climbs relentlessly straight up the hillside through a thick, mature Douglas fir forest. It is a 4 km (2.5 mi) climb to Munro Lake, or at least what is left of the lake since the dam is no longer. Expect a stiff 940 m (3,080 ft) climb. Since Dennett Lake requires another

short, but steep grunt up an ill-defined trail, many people stop at Munro. To Dennett, the hike is 10 km (6 mi) return gaining 860 m (2,820 ft), but route finders can join up with the Burke Ridge Trail. Due to snow and wet trail conditions (on top), this hike is best left until late June through October.

Musical Bumps Trail (Map 32/G6) 🚶🚴🥾🌲

This fabled 19 km (12 mi) hike starts from the top of the Whistler Village Gondola and leads to Singing Pass. The trail is so named, as it crosses Piccolo, Flute and Oboe summits on its way to Singing Pass, where it hooks up with the Singing Pass Trail. Along the way, you get great views of Cheakamus Lake and Glacier.

Myrtle Springs Trail (Map 18/G3) 🚶🚴

This 5 km (3 mi) trail begins approximately 200 metres along the Haslam Lake Road. It follows an old road network eventually leading to Duck Lake Road near the Haslam Slough. You can either return along the logging road or the way you came.

North Shore Trails

Located right next to metro Vancouver, these trails are easily accessed from the city and provide a welcome respite from the hustle and bustle of urban life. You will be amazed how quickly you find yourself in stunning wilderness settings once you get on the trail. Some trails do get quite busy, but the further you go, the more secluded your adventure will be.

North Shore Trails:
GROUSE MOUNTAIN TRAILS

	MAP	DIFFICULTY	LENGTH	ELEVATION GAIN	CAMP	BIKE	HIKE	HORSE	SKI	SNOWSHOE	VIEW
BCMC Trail	11/D7	Difficult	3.5 km (2.2 mi)	805 m (2,640 ft)			•				•
Crown Mountain Route	11/D7	Difficult	9.6 km (6 mi)	695 m (2,280 ft)			•				•
Grouse Grind	11/D7	Difficult	2.9 km (1.8 mi)	855 m (2,800 ft)			•				
Goat Mountain Trail	11/D7	Moderate	4 km (2.5 mi)	275 m (900 ft)			•			•	•
Peak View Trail	11/D7	Easy	0.5 km (0.3 mi)	Minimal			•			•	•

LOWER SEYMOUR CONSERVATION RESERVE

	MAP	DIFFICULTY	LENGTH	ELEVATION GAIN	CAMP	BIKE	HIKE	HORSE	SKI	SNOWSHOE	VIEW
Fisherman Trail	11/E7–F6	Moderate	7 km (4.3 mi)	270 m (885 ft)		•	•				
Rice Lake Trail	11/E7–F6	Easy	4 km (2.5 mi)	Minimal		•	•	•		•	
Seymour Valley Trailway	11/E7–F6	Easy	10 km (6.2 mi)	300 m (985 ft)		•	•				•
Twin Bridges Trail	11/E7–F6	Moderate	2.6 km (1.6 mi)	110 m (360 ft)		•	•				

LYNN HEADWATERS REGIONAL PARK

	MAP	DIFFICULTY	LENGTH	ELEVATION GAIN	CAMP	BIKE	HIKE	HORSE	SKI	SNOWSHOE	VIEW
Coliseum Mountain Route	11/E7–F6	Difficult	12.5 km (7.8 mi)	1,245 m (4,085 ft)	•		•			•	•
Hanes Valley Loop	11/E7–D6	Difficult	17 km (10.5 mi)	900 m (2,950 ft)			•			•	•
Lynn Loop	11/E7	Moderate	9.5 km (5.8 mi)	350 m (1,150 ft)			•			•	•
Lynn Lake Trail	11/E7–E5	Difficult	12.5 km (7.8 mi)	600 m (1,970 ft)			•			•	
Lynn Peak Trail	11/E7–E6	Moderate	3.5 km (2.5 mi)	720 m (2,360 ft)			•				•
Norvan Falls	11/E7–E6	Moderate	8.2 km (5.1 mi)	235 m (770 ft)		•	•			•	•

MOUNT SEYMOUR PROVINCIAL PARK

	MAP	DIFFICULTY	LENGTH	ELEVATION GAIN	CAMP	BIKE	HIKE	HORSE	SKI	SNOWSHOE	VIEW
Dog Mountain Trail	11/F7	Easy	3 km (1.9 mi)	40 m (130 ft)			•			•	•
Elsay Lake Trail	11/F7–G6	Difficult	10 km (6.2 mi)	885 m (2,900 ft)	•		•			•	•
Goldie Lake Loop	11/F7	Easy	2 km (1.2 mi)	220 m (720 ft)			•			•	•
Flower Lake Loop	11/F7	Easy	1.5 km (0.9 mi)	150 m (490 ft)			•			•	•
Perimeter Trail	11/F7	Moderate	1.5 km (0.9 mi)	240 m (790 ft)			•			•	•
Mount Elsay Trail	11/F7–G6	Difficult	8 km (5 mi)	1,050 m (3,445 ft)			•			•	•
Mount Seymour Trail	11/F7–G6	Moderate	4.5 km (2.8 mi)	450 m (1,475 ft)			•			•	•
Mystery Lake Loop	11/F7	Easy	3 km (1.9 mi)	180 m (585 ft)			•			•	•
Old Buck Trail	11/F7	Moderate	5.5 km (3.4 mi)	670 m (2,200 ft)			•			•	•
Three-Chop Trail	11/F7	Moderate	6.5 km (4 mi)	550 m (1,805 ft)			•			•	•

TRAIL ADVENTURES

Nairn Falls Trail (Map 33/B1) 🚶🚴📷

Made up of a series of falls, Nairn Falls are found north of Whistler within Nairn Falls Provincial Park. An easy 2.4 km (1.5 mi) return hike along the Green River follows a well-worn trail to the 60 m (200 ft) high falls. Other trails extend north to One Mile Lake and along the river.

Nicomen Island (Map 3/G4–4/A4) 🚶🚴🛶📷

Nicomen is a quiet little island that has a 5 km (3 mi) scenic riverside dyke trail. From December to February, Bald Eagles are common in the area.

Northwest Passage (Map 32/F6) 🚴📷

Found at the top of Nordic Estates off of Whistler Road, a dirt access road climbs under the Quicksilver Chairlift on the bottom of Whistler Mountain. At the crest of this steep climb (420 m/1,375 ft), you head left for some downhill roller coaster thrills. The difficult 7 km (4.3 mi) route will spit you out at Whistler Village.

Ogilvie Peak Trail (Map 16/A6–15/G6) 🚶📷

This trail climbs steeply from the Kawkawa Lake Road for about 4 km (2.5 mi), until it breaks out into the sub-alpine of Ogilvie Peak. From here you can pick your route to a series of peaks and ridges.

Okeover Trail (Map 18/D1–28/D7) 🚶🚴📷

This well-marked and scenic trail begins at the south end of Okeover Inlet off the Southview Road. It heads 8 km (5 mi) to the Theodosia Forest Service Road. Rather than proceeding back the way you came, you can follow the forestry road along the eastern shores of the inlet.

One Mile Lake Trails (Map 33/B1) 🚶🚴

The popular One Mile Lake picnic area found south of Pemberton offers some enjoyable trails that can be used by mountain bikers or hikers. The One Mile Loop is an easy 1.5 km loop around the lake. The most popular trail is the Nairn Falls Trail, which runs for 2 km to the provincial campground. This moderate trail has a few sections that require dismounting (if you are on a bike) as you climb over roots and descend along a rocky trail. Side trails also lead to more challenging biking terrain, including Tour de Soo.

Othello Tunnels [Coquihalla Canyon] Trail (Map 15/G6) 🚶🚴📷

This popular trail is part of the Kettle Valley Railway, which is in turn a part of the Trans Canada Trail. Most people only hike through the canyon itself, an easy walk through a dramatic gorge and the equally impressive Othello (Quintette) Tunnels. This short trail is less than a kilometre return, but it is possible to stretch this into a 12 km (7.3 mi) trek along the north side of the Coquihalla River all the way to the Hope Cemetery.

Owl Lake Trail (Map 42/B6) 🔺🚶🛶📷

The trailhead to this hike is found off the Owl Creek Forest Service Road, which is four-wheel drive accessible. From the trailhead, it is a 7 km (4.3 mi) return trip, gaining 140 m (455 ft) along the way. The trail leads through the Owl Creek Valley to the lake where you will find a rustic campsite on the western shores. As of 2012 the trail was closed due to large mud holes.

Pacific Spirit Park [UBC Endowment Lands] (Map 1/B2) 🚶🚴

This large urban park offers an enjoyable place to walk, jog, horseback ride or mountain bike. There are over 90 km (55 mi) of trails in the park, 60 km (37 mi) of which are open to mountain bikers and horseback riders. Please obey the signs. With easy access from a variety of locations (4th Avenue, 16th Avenue or SW Marine Drive), these trails are popular year-round as they dissect the lush vegetation and old growth forests.

Pender Hill Trail (Map 9/A1) 🚶📷

Allow half an hour to climb about 170 m (555 ft) in just under 1 km to the hilltop offering panoramic views of Pender Harbour. The trail begins about 60 metres east of Lee's Road near Coastview Drive.

Penticton Maze Trail Network (Map 18/G4) 🚴

Easily accessed from Penticton Street in Powell River, this group of mountain bike trails make up close to 30 km (19 mi) of rideable terrain. Most of the trails are single track and suitable for intermediate riders, with little elevation change but a lot of flow.

Petgill Lake Trail (Map 11/C1) 🔺🚶🏍📷

The hike begins on the marked trail north of the parking lot of Murrin Provincial Park (on the opposite side of Highway 99). This 11.5 km (7 mi)

trail begins by climbing steeply through the bluffs before entering a second growth forest. It soon meets an old logging road and heads south. Eventually, the road becomes completely overgrown at which time the trail departs the road and leads up a ridge to the lake. The trail can be hiked from March through November and gains 640 m (2,080 ft) in elevation. From the lake, it is possible to access the Goat Ridge Route and several climbing opportunities.

Phelix Creek Trail (Map 42/E1) 🔺🚶🚴🏍📷

A flagged 3.5+ km (2.2+ mi) trail leads from the end of Phelix Creek Road up to the Brian Waddington Hut. If you do not have a high clearance vehicle you might need to add 6 km to your hike. You will gain 435 m (1,425 ft) along the steep trail. There is a voluntary trail closure between August 15th and October 15th to allow grizzly and black bear undisturbed access to prime feeding areas. See www.ubc-voc.com for more information on the trail, hut and activities in the area.

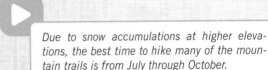

Due to snow accumulations at higher elevations, the best time to hike many of the mountain trails is from July through October.

Pierce Lake/Mount McFarlane Trail (Map 5/B6) 🔺🚶🏍🛶📷

A rough, steep trail climbs steadily from the Pierce Creek Trailhead to the south end of Mount MacFarlane. It begins by rising sharply through a second growth forest before breaking out onto a scree slope. From here, the trail crosses Pierce Creek and begins to deteriorate before reaching the lake. On the way, you will pass two lakes, alpine meadows and some spectacular viewpoints. Take a breather and try your luck fishing for small trout at the lake, which is a 6.7 km (4.2 mi) one-way hike that climbs 1,340 m (4,400 ft). The trail to MacFarlane is 10 km (6 mi) one-way and gains almost 2,100 m (6,890 ft) in elevation, so be prepared for a steep climb. For your efforts, you be rewarded with wide-open view of jagged rocky peaks scraping the sky in every direction.

Pioneer [Bear Mountain] Trail (Map 3/D3) 🚶🚴📷

Found to the east of the Dewdney Trunk Road are a series of trails that are best accessed from Saunders Road (off Richards Ave.) to the south. Saunders Trail is a short 600 metre interpretive trail at the foot of Bear Mountain. The Pioneer Trail follows an old forestry road to the top of the hill, where the Bear Mountain Challenge Downhill Mountain Bike Race is held. From the top, you descend along single-track to the Mill Pond, some 3.2 km (2 mi) later. Also in the area is the Carral Loop.

Pitt Polder Wildlife Area (Map 12/F7–2/F1) 🚶🚴📷

The extensive dyke network begins at the end of Rannie Road in Grant Narrows Park. The dykes are flat, wide cart paths perfect for mountain biking, horseback riding and hiking. The distance of the route really depends on how far you want to travel, as there are 20 km (12 mi) of interconnected dykes and side trails in the area. Waterfowl is abundant in the marshy wetland.

Pitt River Dyke Trail (Map 2/D2) 🚶🚴🐴🏍🚶📷

As part of the Trans Canada Trail and the historic PoCo Trail, this series of interconnected dyke trails has seen some recent improvements. Still sections remain overgrown, mostly with nasty brambles. The main dyke trail runs from the end of Kingsway north to the Debouville Slough Lookout Trail in Port Coquitlam. This is an 11 km (6.8 mi) trip and leads to a wildlife viewing tower.

Pitt River Regional Greenway (Map 2/D3) 🚶🚴📷

The first phase of the Pitt River Regional Greenway, from Harris Landing at the south end of Harris Road to Ferry Slip Road near the Highway 7 crossing of the Pitt River, is now open. The trail follows a series of dykes along the Fraser, then Pitt River allowing for good bird watching opportunities. Over the next ten years, additional sections will be added to the route, ultimately stretching about 30 km (18 mi) to Grant Narrows Regional Park. For now, the trail is 10 km (6 mi) long.

Place Glacier Trail (Map 42/E5) 🏕️🚶🏃🚴🎿🚡

Access this trail from a small cul-de-sac called Anson Place, off of Portage Road. This steep trail gains 1,500 m (4,920 ft) over 6.5 km (4 mi). Early on in the hike you will pass the impressive 412 m (1,375 ft) high Place Creek Falls. The falls alone make for a rewarding short hike. When you reach the glacier you will find a lake and two shelters – plan on spending the night in one of these. Make sure to leave yourself time to explore the glacier and the scattered remains of scientific research stations.

Post-Greendrop Trail (Map 5/F5) 🏕️🚶🏃🎿🚡

The popular trail starts at the Post Creek Recreation Site and climbs 320 m (1,050 ft) over 6.3 km (3.9 mi) to the south end of Greendrop Lake, taking you past Lindeman Lake. This moderate trail will lead you in and out of forest and boulder fields. There is rustic camping at Greendrop Lake and good fishing in both lakes. The Centennial Trail continues along a logging road, but most people just spend the night at Greendrop Lake, then return. For the more adventurous, an unmarked route runs northeast to Flora Lake.

Powersmart Trails (Map 22/D6) 🚶🚴

Located near Garibaldi Park Road, the Powersmart Trails are divided into upper, middle and lower sections offering over 4.5 km (2.8 mi) of mostly moderate trails between them. Also in the area are several other trails such as Flat Alley, P-Nuts Wild Ride, Mrs. Wigglesbottom and Skookum that interconnect with each other to make this area one of the most popular mountain biking areas in the Squamish area.

Pushki Trail (Map 43/D7) 🚶🚡

This 5.8 km (3.5 mi) trail follows an overgrown logging spur for most of its length, while the last 1 km is along a well-flagged and worn path. Some deadfall and thick vegetation may slow your progress. This trail branches off the Van Horlick Road and ascends the first major valley to the east.

Radium Lake Trail (Map 5/E6) 🏕️🚶🚴🐾🚡

BC Parks has closed the trailhead and suspension bridge over the Chilliwack River, but the Trans Canada Trail runs past the new start to this moderate trail. That means the trail is now over 15 km (9.3 mi) return. It is a stiff climb that gains 880 m (2,860 ft) to tiny Radium Lake nestled below two towering peaks. A forestry cabin can be used as a base to explore nearby peaks, including challenging routes to MacDonald Peak or Mount Webb.

Rainbow Lake Trail (Map 32/E4) 🚶🚴🐾🚡

This alpine trail starts from the wooden map located on the west side of Alta Lake Road. The trail to Rainbow Lake is 18 km (11 mi) return, gaining 800 m (2,625 ft). Near the start, look for the glimpses of Rainbow Falls. Trails lead to Beverly and Gin and Tonic Lakes as well as Rainbow Mountain and Mount Sproatt. No camping is allowed at the lake, but there is a campsite near Hanging Lake just over the ridge on the other side of the lake. The trail is open from March through December, but dogs are not permitted on the trail.

Rainbow Mountain Skywalk Trail (Map 32/E4) 🚶🚡

This is a continuation of the Rainbow Lake Trail or, at least, you can't start this trail until you hike the 9 km (5.5 mi) to Rainbow Lake. From there, the trail climbs 850 m (2,790 ft) to the top of Rainbow in just over 3 km (1.2 mi). That's a wickedly steep climb, but people still somehow drag their bikes to the top. An alternate route cuts to the northwest, providing an easier approach to the summit before the inevitable scramble up. The alternate trail makes a 6.5 km (4 mi) loop from where it diverges from the main trail.

Red Rock Trail (Map 53/C7) 🚶🚡

Red Rock is a familiar landmark in Lillooet. To access the moderate trail leading to this landmark, follow Victoria Street to the end of the pavement and the parking area. When you reach the water tank turn right and follow flag markings for 3.5 km (2.2 mi) for a great view of the townsite and Fraser Canyon. Red Rock gets its distinctive red colour from the oxidized iron on the outside of the rock.

Richmond Dyke Trails (Map 1/B4–C5) 🚶🚴🚡

This is an extremely popular place for hikers, bikers, joggers and families looking for an easy walk together. The most popular section is the West Dyke Path, which runs 10 km (6 mi) from north of Westminster Highway to Steveston. The wide gravel path takes you past radio receivers as you peer out on the Strait of Georgia. The South Dyke is found between Gilbert Road and No. 5 Road. The Richmond Nature Park also offers a 5 km (3 mi) network of trails to explore.

Ring Creek Rip & Powerhouse Plunge (Map 22/E6) 🚴

Ring Creek Rip is a difficult mountain bike trail that is found just after the bridge over the Mamquam River on the Mamquam River Forest Service Road. It begins on an old railbed and heads downhill for about 9 km (5.6 mi) to the Ring Creek crossing and onto the Diamond Head Road. Further to the east, the trail hooks up with the Powerhouse Plunge Trail where you can link back up with the Mamquam Forest Service Road via other trails. Other options can take you north towards the Powersmart area. The entire loop covers about 30 km (18.5 mi) in distance; be prepared for a long haul.

Roberts Bank Dyke Trail (Map 1/C6) 🚶🚴🚡

This 5.8 km (3.6 mi) dyke trail leads from River Road and 34th Street to Deltaport Way, which services the busy port area south of Vancouver. The trail provides great ocean views and a chance to see ferries, large ocean liners and even whales. The Great Blue Heron Way Trail continues south to the Ferry Causeway in Tsawwassen.

Rolley Lake & Falls Trail (Map 3/C2) 🚶🚡

Rolley Lake is a popular family day-use area during the summer, so visit in the off-season if you are looking for a relaxing escape into nature. The trail is easily accessed from the main parking lot, and spans 5.1 km (3.2 mi) in total, with minimal elevation gain. Turn left after the bridge over Rolley Creek to access the falls area, and look for a small viewing platform which offers the best views of the falls. From the Florence Lake Forest Service Road, a short 2 km (1.2 mi) loop leads past two sets of falls providing a great view of Stave Lake along the way. The well-developed trail climbs 130 m (420 ft) as it meanders through a thick second-growth forest. Allow one hour to do the loop or continue around Rolley Lake, which adds another 1.5 km (.9 mi) and 45 minutes to your trip.

Ruby Creek Trail (Map 15/B7) 🚶🚴🚡

The Deer Lake Forest Service Road continues past Deer Lake as a four-wheel drive road. This route is a fairly easy 14 km (8.7 mi) return trip to a viewpoint over the Fraser River. While the road connects to Highway 7, it crosses private property, so turn around at the viewpoint about halfway down into the valley.

Ruby Lake-Klein Lake Traverse (Map 20/C6) 🚶🚡

This trail traverses the saddle between Klein and Ruby lakes, a 4 km (2.5 mi) one-way trip. It is easier to start at Klein Lake (if you start from the south end, you must climb a steep stretch of the trail to the saddle). The highlight of the trail is the excellent views from the rocky bluffs along the route. The southern access is found off an old road 50 metres south of Dan Bosch Park.

Salal Creek/Athelney Pass Trail (Map 49/D7) 🏕️🚶🎿🚴🚡

Mountaineers will find a 15 km (9.3 mi) trail to Athelney Pass, which climbs 800 m (2,625 ft). Although the trip can be done overnight, allow a few days to explore the surrounding peaks, including Ochre Peak, the Black Molar, the Icemaker and Guthrum Mountain. The trail leads from the end of the water-barred road past an old mining exploration camp, small lakes, pumice meadows and glaciers.

Saltery Bay Park Trails (Map 19/E5) 🚶🚡

Saltery Bay Provincial Park has a network of trails worth exploring. The main trail leads 10 km (6 mi) along an overgrown road and then a well-defined trail. There is a steep climb at the beginning of the trail, but you get a good view of Nelson and Hardy Islands from the summit. A much easier option is to walk 2 km (1.2 mi) one-way from the campsite at the provincial park to the beach.

Sasquatch Provincial Park Trails (Map 15/A7) 🚶🚴🐾🚡

The roads into and around Sasquatch Park offer enjoyable mountain biking or hiking. The Deer Lake Trail is an easy route along the north side of Deer Lake. It is possible to continue east on the Ruby Creek Trail. The 6 km (3.7 mi) Hicks Lake Loop takes about 3 hours to complete. It is also possible to follow an old logging road along the Seabird Island Overlook Trail at the south end of the lake. The Moss Lake Trail is the most difficult route in the park as it follows the steep and rocky access road past Moss Lake to several unnamed lakes.

Sea to Sky Trail (Maps 22, 32, 33, 42, 43) 🚶🚴🏕️🚡

This ambitious trail, intended to link Squamish to the tiny hamlet of D'Arcy, is an ongoing project, but there are a number of sections already on the ground. From Squamish the route follows the Corridor Trail, then the Ray Peters Trail along Squamish Valley Road up to the Paradise Valley Road to

the historic PGE Railway road from the Cheakamus River to Highway 99. Follow the highway north for 4.5 km (2.8 mi) to the Chance Creek Bridge over the Cheakamus River. Dirt roads and trails will take you up to the Pinecrest/Black Tusk entrance to Highway 99. Follow Highway 99 again for another 3.5 km (2.2 mi) to Brandywine Provincial Park where 20 km (12 mi) of trail will take you to Whistler Village. North of Whistler the route is still being determined and existing sections lack connections to each other. Until this happens it is mainly along the highway or secondary roads, with existing sections around Pemberton and Birken. For up-to-date information visit the website at www.SeaToSkyTrail.ca.

Seaton Highline Road (Map 43/A3–52/D7) 🚴🚵🚶

A scenic but gruelling four hour mountain bike ride follows the road next to the hydro lines high above Anderson Lake. The roller coaster route stretches 32 km (19 mi) from D'Arcy (and the end of the Sea to Sky Trail) to Seton Portage. The route gains 200 m (655 ft) in the first 1.5 km, with a total elevation change of 1,650 m (5,410 ft). The road is open to four-wheel drive vehicles as well.

Secret Lake Trail (Map 14/E7–4/F1) 🚶🚵🚴

Branching south from the Sts'ailes (formerly Harrison West) Forest Service Road, about 2 km after Grace Lake, this trail leads to a pretty little lake. Foolish off roaders have been known to drive down this rough, rocky path, but it is better hiked. It is about 3.3 km (2 mi) one-way to the lake.

Seed Peak Trail (Map 12/A1) 🚶🚵🚴

Access this trail from Mamquam Forest Service Road. This 5.3 km trail gains 950 m (3,120 ft) in elevation. The first 50 metres of this trail are an intense bushwhack, but are probably the most difficult part of the hike. Past this you will enter into fairly easygoing old growth forests, before opening up into the alpine. Be prepared for snow and steep terrain on you way to the peak.

Seton Ridge Trail (Map 43/G1) 🚶🚵🚴

From a switchback on the Seton Ridge Logging Road, this is an 11 km (6.8 mi) route taking you along the ridge between Cayoosh Creek and Seton Lake. Once you are in the alpine, you can access the surrounding mountains for even better views.

Shadow Lake Interpretive Trails (Map 33/A3) 🚶🚵🚴

Shadow Lake Trails are located north of Whistler near the Soo River, right off Highway 99. There are a number of short trails totalling 6 km (3.7 mi) providing examples of the various forest practices. This trail network is a good choice if you want to get away from the crowds of Whistler and enjoy an easy stroll through a forested setting.

Shannon Falls Trail (Map 22/C7) 🚶🚴

Although many view the impressive 337 m (1,105 ft) falls from their base, those looking for a nice hike can take the Stawamus Chief Trail to the Upper Shannon Falls Trail (now called the Sea to Summit Trail). The 3.5 km (2.2 mi) hike gains 450 m (1,475 ft). Enjoy the falls and the views from Squamish to Howe Sound.

Shulaps Basin Trail (Map 51/G3–52/C2) 🚶🚵🐎🚴🏕️🚣‍♂️🚴

Part a series of trails in the Shulaps Range, this trail leads to the divide between the eastern and western parts of the Shulaps Range. The scenic trail stretches almost 19 km (12 mi) from the trailhead found west of the Lake la Mare Recreation Site to the Marshall Creek Forest Service Road near Brett Creek. Serpentine Lake makes a nice 2.5 km (1.6 mi) one-way side trip. Please note this trail is not ATV friendly.

Sigurd Creek Trail (Map 21/G3–F3) 🚶🚴

The trailhead is found at the end of Branch A251 off the Ashlu Forest Service Road (past the second bridge). The trail climbs 1,065 m (3,490 ft) over a one-way distance of 8.2 km (5 mi), passing through forest and waterfalls, to an area of several granite-lined lakes. Add three or more hours of hiking to explore the lakes from the peak of the trail. Alternately, Ossa Mountain can be hiked from a trail branching off around the 5.9 km mark. The side trail to Ossa is another 7.2 km (4.5 mi), so consider doing this as an overnight trip. In the summer, you can stop for refreshing a swim in a glacial tarn, and enjoy the excellent views of Mount Jimmy Jimmy, Tantalus and Pelion. This difficult route climbs 2,290 m (7,510 ft) and is best hiked in mid-July to October.

Silver Daisy Mountain Trail (Map 6/F3) 🚶🚴

It is possible to do this 20 km (12 mi) trail up to the summit of Silver Daisy Mountain in about 9 hours. The trail starts at the Sumallo Grove Picnic Area off Highway 3, crosses the Skagit River and switchbacks its way up a steep hill to a saddle, which offers great views of the Skagit Valley. From here, the trail continues through a meadow to the 2,040 m (6,630 ft) summit, gaining 1,435 m (4,700 ft) along the way. Part of the trail follows an old mining tram. The trail is best left for late summer/early fall.

Singing Pass Trail (Map 32/G7–33/B7) 🏕️🚶🚵🚴🚴🚴

The Singing Pass Trail is probably the most popular alpine trail in the Whistler Area. This beautiful hike starts from the end of the well-signed Singing Pass Road and follows Fitzsimmons Creek, then Melody Creek, to the pass. The area has alpine flowers in late summer along with spectacular glacier and mountain views. Allow 7 hours to complete the moderate 12 km (7.3 mi) hike, which gains 600 m (1,970 ft). The cabin at Russet Lake is another 2 km beyond and 250 m (820 ft) up, offering a good base for mountain climbers looking to explore the area's summits. A popular destination among these is Overlord Mountain, a 5.4 km (3.4 mi) trek from Russet Lake with a total gain of 1,040 m (3,410 ft) through majestic glacial terrain. Whirlwind Peak must be climbed before traversing across to Overlord. Given it is 15 hours or so from the Whistler Village to hike to Overlord, it is best to plan to camp at Russet.

Skagit River Trail (Map 6/E3–D5) 🏕️🚶🚴🐎🚣‍♂️🚴

This trail begins at the Sumallo Grove Picnic Area and leads 13 km (8 mi) one-way along the east side of the Skagit River. Along the route, you pass through an ecological reserve, which has a nice grove of old growth cedar, fir and cottonwood. The trail is best hiked in mid-June when the wild Rhododendrons start blooming at Sumallo Grove. The adventurous can hike all the way to the 26 Mile Bridge on the Silver Skagit Road, but the last part covers a poor, often indistinct trail. It is 20 km (12 mi) one-way to the road.

> ▶️
>
> *The mountainous landscape can be very difficult to navigate and hikers should carry a map, compass and GPS and know how to use all three.*

Skookumchuck Narrows [Brown Lake Trail] (Map 20/C6) 🚶🚴

From Egmont Road, an easy 4 km (2.5 mi) one-way trail leads along a well maintained trail past Brown Lake to the narrows, one of the most popular areas on the coast. You can explore the tidal pools at low tide or watch the tide rip through a narrow, shallow channel during high tide. Consult the tide tables for the best viewing times.

Skyline Trail (Map 11/C7) 🚶🚴🐎🚵🚴🚴

Not to be confused with the epic hike in Manning Park, this Skyline Trail is actually an old service road for the powerline that gains 375 m (1,230 ft) over 7 km (4.3 mi). This trail is an easy, surprisingly scenic hike, but a difficult mountain bike ride that forms part of the Trans Canada Trail hiking route. There are several technically demanding and steep mountain bike trails that depart from this trail.

Skyline II Trail (Map 6/F6–G6) 🏕️🚶🚴🐎🚵🚴🚴

The western trailhead to the Skyline Trail is accessed off the Silver Skagit Road at the parking lot north of Ross Lake. The trail leads 26 km (16 mi) return from the valley bottom to an alpine ridge at Camp Mowich. Along the way, the trail climbs steeply, gaining 1,310 m (4,300 ft) to the ridge. The hike initially begins in a forest and then crosses several creeks before proceeding into some sub-alpine meadows and then along the ridge. Part of the historic Centennial Trail, it is possible to continue on to Lightning Lake via the Skyline I Trail.

Sky Pilot Mountain Trail (Map 11/D1) 🚶🚴🚴

Given the difficult road access from the Stawamus Indian Forest Service Road, you may want to bring a mountain bike to ride along the last bit of road before the trailhead. The actual trail gains 610 m (2,000 ft) in elevation over 2.8 km (1.7 mi) and requires some serious rock climbing to get to the summit. Make sure to bring proper gear and safety equipment. From the top you will have breathtaking views of the Tantalus range and Garibaldi Park.

Slesse Memorial Trail (Map 5/C6) 🏕️🥾🚴🧗🅿️

This trail climbs about 300 m (985 ft) along the old Nesakwatch Creek Forest Service Road to a monument built to acknowledge a plane crash. The hike takes about three hours to cover the 8.5 km (5.3 mi) return distance and has spectacular views of the mountains all around. Beyond the monument at the old logging landing, turn left uphill through the blueberry bushes to a ridge and then follow the trail and ribbons to the old glacier. A propeller in a crevasse indicates the end of the hike, but mountain climbers can continue from this point.

Slesse Mountain Trail (Map 5/C7) 🏕️🥾🧗🅿️

This trail will take you right into the heart of the Slesse Mountain Ridge. Access is made more difficult due to locked gates on the Slesse Creek Forest Service Road; expect to make a long approach hike or bike just to get to the trailhead. At about the 7.5 km mark, look for the trailhead; be sure to maintain your elevation and do not cross Slesse Creek. The first part of the trail follows old logging roads, but once you get to the trail portion expect a gruelling uphill climb (1,200 m/3,935 ft elevation gain) with no switchbacks. Your hard work will be rewarded with fantastic views of the alpine ridges in this remote area. It is possible to camp in the alpine and save the knee crunching descent for the next day.

Sliammon Lakes Trail (Map 18/F2) 🥾🚶🅿️

The trail begins at the end of Sutherland Street and proceeds northward eventually leading to the Theodosia Forest Service Road. The well-marked trail leads through second growth timber and up some steep sections. The hike takes you past Little Sliammon Lake, where there is a nice beach for swimming and on to Sliammon Lake. The trail connects with Appleton Canyon/Marathon Trails so it is possible to walk up to 18 km (11 mi) if you so choose. Other alternatives include a side trail to Three Mile Bay and an old mine site. This trail is 5 km (3 mi) return. It is also possible to hike up Scout Mountain. This trail offers views of Powell Lake and Wildwood Heights before dropping to the Kinsman Park near the Powell Lake Marina.

Smoke Bluffs Trails (Map 22/C6) 🥾🚴🧗🅿️

These multi-use trails are located in Squamish around the Smoke Bluffs Climbing Area. From the parking area on Loggers Lane you wind your way through the Smoke Bluffs to the top of Plateau Drive where a good variety of trails that will suit all levels of mountain bikers can be found. The single-track trails are generally quite technical and twisty. As an added challenge, there is occasionally climbing rope strung across the trail to dodge.

Smugglers Cove Provincial Park (Map 9/B4) 🥾🅿️

Smugglers Cove has a fascinating history of illegal Chinese labourer smuggling a century ago. Today, tiny Smugglers Cove is a beautiful marine park and one of the most popular and best summer anchorages on the Sunshine Coast. The park provides easy hiking on a number of short trails totalling about 3.5 km (2.1 mi). A forested trail leads to the secluded anchorage of Smugglers Cove. A little further on, the main trail ends at a small bay off Welcome Pass, with views across to south Thormanby Island and north to Texada Island. This park is accessed by Brooks Road northwest of Sechelt.

Snowcap Lake Route (Map 23/F3–24/A1) 🥾🅿️

The east side of Garibaldi is far less travelled than the west side. In fact, this route, accessed off logging roads west of Skookumchuck, is about the only viable entry point into this vast wilderness. Even so, you will probably have to bushwhack your way up from the end of the road to the ridge. Its 20 km (12 mi) from the end of the road to the lake, or more, depending on how far you can drive up the logging road, found along the In-Shuck-Ch Forest Service Road.

Snowspider Hut Trail (Map 34/C1) 👤🥾🎿🅿️

This trail follows Van Horlick Road for most of its length, but the pulling of the bridge over Morris Creek means you have to ford this deep but narrow creek early on. A second, easier fording of Van Horlick Creek is required about 5 km after Morris Creek. From here, a 1.5 km ascent takes you past some large, dry grassy meadows to a small lake, at the far end of which sits the cabin.

Soames Hill Park (Map 10/D6) 🥾🅿️

This popular 4 km (2.5 mi) trail network is found to the northeast of Gibsons. The trails can be accessed off Bridgeman or Esperanza Roads, which are side streets off Chamberlin Road. From either trailhead, it takes about half an hour to hike the several hundred stairs cut out of fallen logs to the top of the hill. The view from the top (at 240 m/785 ft) is worth the effort. It is also possible to walk the short wooded trails around the southern slope of the hill.

South Elphinstone Heritage Trails (Map 10/C5) 🥾🚴🅿️

Mount Elphinstone has been preserved into a provincial park. The southern slopes of the mountain have a long history of logging and many of the access routes have been turned into fine multi-use trails. Although relatively short, they gain significant elevation, such as the 1.5 hour hike up the K2 Summit Trail, which gains 640 m (2,080 ft). Cablevision Trail offers a 1.5 hour climb to the B&K Logging Road and access to an old ski hut and the Elphinstone summit. The Langdale Creek Waterfall Trail is a little easier as it runs for 2.5 km one-way to the namesake falls through stands of second growth Douglas fir. Alternatively, Mountain Trail leads to a series of old logging camps while Shaker Trail is a short climb connecting to B&K Logging Road. There are many different access points from side roads north of Gibsons.

South Powell Divide Trail (Map 29/F4–F6) 🏕️👤🥾🚴🏃🅿️

This high ridge route extends 20 km (12 mi) from the Goat Access II Trail north to the B Branch Road. Only experienced hikers with the appropriate maps and route finding skills should consider this route, which usually takes a couple days to complete. Along the way you can enjoy the splendid views of the surrounding lakes and mountain peaks. The popular Emma Lake Cabin makes for a good overnight destination (if it isn't full).

Spirit Caves Trail (Map 15/E2) 🥾🅿️

The trailhead is located off Highway 1, across from the Pioneer Cemetery at the south end of Yale. This 5 km (3 mi) trail gains 500 m (1,640 ft) to the caves and has several vantage points of the Fraser River and Yale.

Sprockids Mountain Bike Park (Map 10/C5) 🥾🚴

A popular mountain bike area containing 14 km (8.7 mi) of trails for all skill levels that feature jumps, steep downhill, teeter-bars and ramps. The bike to the top of the trails is fairly steep but the payoff will be worth it. The trails are built and maintained by volunteers. To access these trails drive uphill from the Langdale Ferry Terminal and turn right – the parking lot will be on your left after 200 metres.

Spruce Lake Trails (Maps 50, 51) 🏕️👤🥾🚴🎿🏃⛵🚶🅿️

The Spruce Lake area offers world-class hiking and backpacking, horse packing, fishing, cross-country skiing and mountain biking. There are 164 km (100 mi) of wilderness trails in the area, which traverse over gentle mountain passes and meander through lush alpine grasslands and flowers to destination trout lakes. The main access points into the area are the Gun Creek Road, Mud Creek-Taylor Creek Forest Service Road and the Slim Creek Forest Service Road. Most of the trails have few or no signs and there are a number of rough routes that are only for experienced route finders. Also, due to snow accumulations the trails are best hiked or biked in late summer/early fall.

Gun Creek Trail (Map 50/G2–F1)

From the signed trailhead off Slim Creek Forest Service Road, this is the main trail into the heart of the Spruce Lake area. The trail crosses a footbridge (Jewel Bridge) and follows the north side of Gun Creek eventually breaking from the pine forest to the open grasslands and aspen trees. The mountain views are tremendous. Around 11.5 km (7 mi), at Cowboy Camp, the trail branches. Heading north is the popular trail that climbs 200 m (655 ft) to Spruce Lake, where campsites and a beach are found. The lake has excellent rainbow fishing. Continuing west the Gun Creek Trail passes Hummingbird Lake and Trigger Lake before climbing south to Taylor Pass along the Gun Creek Valley. The northern section beyond Trigger Lake doesn't see a lot of use and is suffering from blow down. Most people heading for the Taseko Lakes area take the Warner Pass Trail.

Taylor Basin Trail (Map 51/B1)

This is one of the gentlest mountain routes you will ever encounter. Depending on how far you can drive up the Mud Creek-Taylor Creek Forest Service Road, it may take you a few hours to walk to the cabin at Taylor Basin. The route follows an old road beyond the footbridge and it slowly climbs through a scenic valley with wildflowers, wildlife and fantastic mountain views. The route is extremely popular with mountain bikers and snowmobilers. This 23 km (14 mi) round trip climbs 700 m (2,295 ft).

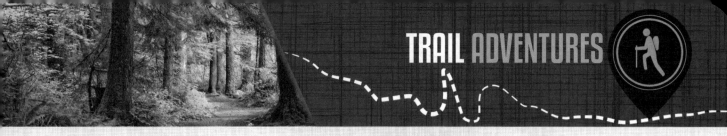

Stanley Park (Map 1/C1)

We dare you to find another trail in Southwestern BC that sees as much traffic (foot, bike and inline skating) as the Stanley Park Seawall. This 8.8 km (5.5 mi) seawall is part of a much longer seawall system that forms part of the Trans Canada Trail. Besides the Seawall, there are 35 km (22 mi) of trails in the park, although only one other (a combo of Bridle Path, Lake Trail and part of Beaver Lake Trail) is open to bikers. The trails are mostly short, interconnected trails that can be joined together into a number of combinations. The trails on the western side of the park are, in general, longer and wider than the trails on the eastern side of the park.

Statlu Lake Trail (Map 14/B4)

Found off the Chehalis-Mystery Forest Service Road, this 4.5 km (2.8 mi) hike leads to the east end of Statlu Lake, gaining 220 m (720 ft). Small campsites can be found all around the lake, which is a pristine body perfect for swimming and fishing. Past the western end of the lake, a short hike will take you to a viewpoint overlooking a steep gorge with two waterfalls descending into it. Determined climbers can bushwhack up the Brotherhood Trail to the Upper Lake or on to the Mount Ratney climbing area.

Stave Dam Interpretive Trails (Map 3/C3)

Just east of Stave Falls Dam are a series of short trails. The Stave Dam Interpretive Trail is a short (1.7 km/1 mi) trail that cuts through a second growth forest with an elevation gain of 150 m (490 ft). Further east, the Steelhead Mountain Trail is a 2 km (1.2 mi) trail that climbs from the south end of Campbell Street (off Johnson, off Cardinal) along an old forest service road.

Stawamus Chief Trails (Map 22/C7)

The dramatic 652 m (2,140 ft) granite monolith is one of the most popular climbing destinations in Canada and considered to be the second largest free-standing granite outcropping in the world. There are a series of very popular trails that head from the parking lot (off Highway 99 south of Squamish) up the back of The Chief. There are three peaks to reach on the Chief, the first being a 7 km (4.5 mi) round trip with an elevation gain of about 500 m (1,640 ft). The second peak is a 9 km (5.5 mi) round trip with around 550 m (1,800 ft) elevation gain, and the third peak is a 12 km (7.5 mi) hike with 605 m (1,985 ft) of gain. The Stawamus Squaw is a 14.5 km (8.8 mi) trail gaining 540 m (1,770 ft). For rock climbers, there is a choice of over 600 routes between The Chief and the Smoke Bluffs. Regardless of which hike you choose, you should expect a steep uphill climb that is rewarded with great views from the top. The trails are best hiked in March to November.

Sunshine Coast Trails – Gibsons to Pender Harbour

The lower Sunshine Coast offers a variety of trail and old road systems to explore. Many of the trails are quite short but lead to scenic areas overlooking the ocean, old growth forests and waterfalls. Others are part of elaborate mountain bike networks. The following trail chart includes some of the more popular trails or trail systems as well as a few of the notable bike loops.

Sunshine Coast Trails:
CHAPMAN CREEK FALLS TRAILS

	MAP	DIFFICULTY	LENGTH	ELEVATION GAIN	BIKE	HIKE	HORSE	SNOWSHOE	VIEW	WHEELCHAIR
Chapman Creek Falls Trail	9/F5	Moderate	3 km (1.9 mi)	90 m (295 ft)	•	•	•		•	
Cliff Gilker Regional Park	10/B6	Easy	7 km (4.3 mi)	Minimal	•	•				•
Daniel Point Trail	9/A1	Moderate	1.3 km (0.8 mi)	Minimal		•			•	
Francis Point Trail	9/A2	Easy	1.4 km (0.9 mi)	Minimal		•			•	
Homesite Caves Trail	9/C3	Easy	1.0 km (0.6 mi)	Minimal		•			•	
Kinnikinnick Trails	9/E5	Varies	6 km (3.7 mi)	Varies	•	•	•		•	
Langdale Creek Waterfall Trail	10/C5	Moderate	2.5 km (1.6 mi)	760 m (2,490 ft)	•	•				
Mount Daniel Trail	9/B1	Moderate	1.2 km (0.7 mi)	385 m (1,265 ft)		•			•	
Mount Elphinstone Trails	Map 10/A5–C6	Varies	164 km (102 mi)	Varies	•	•	•	•	•	
Pender Hill Trail	Map 9/A1	Moderate	1 km (0.6 mi)	170 m (555 ft)		•			•	
Smugglers Cove Provincial Park	Map 9/B4	Easy	3.5 km (2.1 mi)	Minimal		•			•	
Soames Hill Park	Map 10/D6	Moderate	4 km (2.5 mi)	200 m (655 ft)		•			•	
Sprockids Mountain Bike Park	Map 10/C5	Varies	14 km (8.7 mi)	Varies	•	•			•	
Suncoaster Trail	Map 9–20	Moderate	33 km (20 mi)	320 m (1,050 ft)	•	•			•	
Triangle Lake Trail	Map 9/D4	Easy	4 km (2.5 mi)	165 m (540 ft)		•			•	
Tuwanek Point Beach Trail	Map 9/F3	Moderate	2 km (1.2 mi)	Minimal		•			•	
Welcome Woods/Sargeant Bay Trails	Map 9/D4	Varies	43 km (27 mi)	Varies	•	•			•	
Wilson Creek Trail	Map 9/G5	Easy	2 km (1.2 mi)	Minimal		•			•	

SUNSHINE COAST BIKE LOOPS

	MAP	DIFFICULTY	LENGTH	ELEVATION GAIN	BIKE	HIKE	HORSE	SNOWSHOE	VIEW	WHEELCHAIR
Angus Creek Bike Loop	Map 9/F4	Moderate	22 km (13.5 mi)	280 m (920 ft)	•				•	
Carlson Lake Bike Loop	Map 9/D2	Moderate	21 km (13 mi)	390 m (1,280 ft)	•				•	
Clack Creek Bike Loop	Map 10/A5	Moderate	12 km (7.5 mi)	420 m (1380 ft)	•				•	
Halfmoon Creek Bike Loop	Map 9/C4	Easy	8.5 km (5.2 mi)	80 m (260 ft)	•				•	
Homesite Creek Bike Loop	Map 9/C3	Moderate	8 km (5 mi)	200 m (565 ft)	•				•	
Lyon Lake Bike Loop	Map 9/D1–C7	Difficult	17 km (10.5 mi)	200 m (565 ft)	•				•	
Mount Elphinstone Bike Loop	Map 10/C4–B6	Difficult	42 km (26 mi)	820 m (2,690 ft)	•				•	
Redroof Bike Loop	Map 9/C4	Easy	15 km (9.3 mi)	100 m (330 ft)	•				•	
Roberts Creek Bike Loop	Map 10/B5–C4	Difficult	30 km (18 mi)	800 m (2,625 ft)	•				•	
Trout Lake Bike Loop	Map 9/D4	Moderate	15 km (9.3 mi)	140 m (460 ft)	•				•	

Stein River Trail (Map 36/B2–34/F4)

This 58 km (35.4 mi) backpacking route leads through the heart of a magnificent wilderness park. To reach the trailhead, cross the Fraser River north of Lytton and proceed 4.5 km north along the Westside Road to the short side road leading to the trailhead. From here, the trail follows the Stein River to the park boundary at Tundra Lake. The trail begins as a moderate riverside route and leads through lush old growth forests to spectacular alpine ridges. In addition to campsites, there are cable car crossings and numerous Indian Pictograph sites along the trail. Many people allow a week to explore the area, but it is possible to do an overnight trip to the first river crossing. Be prepared for fallen trees, bears and snow in the alpine.

Stein Valley Trails (Maps 34, 35, 36, 43, 44)

In the late 1980s, environmentalists fought long and hard to see the Stein Valley preserved in a park. Today, the provincial park boasts a number of impressive hiking and backpacking trails, about 150 km (93 mi) in total, featuring cable crossings, cabins and established backcountry campsites. Although a day hike is possible, most people who visit the area spend a few days. It is possible, utilizing a shuttle system, to create some interesting one-way trips, although most of the roads leading to the park are very rough. The main access is from the Westside Road, just north of Lytton.

One of the main hikes in the area is along the Stein River Trail, a 58 km (35.4 mi) journey that is divided into lower, mid and uppers sections and features backcountry camping along the way. A couple of beautiful lakes require a much shorter hike, including Brimful Lake (6.5 km/4 mi from Texas Creek Trailhead) and Elton Lake (a 4 km/2.5 mi unmarked route). Pictographs can be seen along the Stryen Creek Trail, 6.5 km (4 mi) from West Side Road. Blowdown Pass Trail stretches for 25 km (15 mi) along an often overgrown route, past Silver Queen Mine.

> To protect against wood ticks, wear slippery finished clothes with elastic cuffs to protect the body.

Stoltmann Wilderness Route (Map 40/C6–D3)

Also known as the Elaho-Meager Trail since it joins the two valleys, the 29 km (17.7 mi) one-way trail will take at least a couple days to hike. Although marked with orange blazes, the pole and rope bridges are subject to washouts (see our online updates). The chance to encounter moose, cougars and grizzly bears and the remote nature of the trail makes this an area for experienced, well-equipped backpackers. The route takes you past the Elaho Giant near Sundown Creek and the Grizzly Fir, another large Douglas fir next to Last Chance Creek. After a day and a half, you will reach the Thousand Lakes Plateau, which offers panoramic views of glacier-clad mountains amidst the meadows and ponds. By day three, you will be overlooking the Meager Creek Valley and the half-day journey to the hot springs, the perfect end to a difficult trek. The trailhead is found at kilometre 99 on the E1000 Road (off the Elaho Main). It is best to arrange for a second vehicle to pick you up at the Meager Creek.

Sugar Mountain Trail (Map 2/A1)

Accessed from the White Pine Beach parking area at Sasamat Lake, this trail is part of the popular mountain biking area that also includes the Teddy Bear Trail. The Sugar Mountain Trail is a 6.1 km (3.8 mi) loop that climbs 380 m (1,245 ft) to a viewpoint over Sasamat and Buntzen Lakes. It is possible to link with the Diez Vista Trail or link with the Teddy Bear Trail, an easier 2.5 km (1.6 mi) loop that follows the powerline south to link back up with the White Pine Beach Road and Sasamat Lake Trail.

Sumas Mountain Trails (Map 3/F5–4/A5)

There are a few alternatives up this scenic mountain. From the west the original trail begins up the Sumas Mountain Road (at the tiny sign marked Centennial Trail), while the new trailhead is found at the end of Carlyle Road. Expect to hike through thick underbrush and cross Wades Creek along the way past Chadsey Lake to the summit. The hike is about 12 km (7.3 mi) return gaining about 700 m (2,295 ft) in elevation. From the top are great views of Sumas

Prairie and Vedder Mountain. Some hikers prefer to forgo the last 280 metre climb to the summit and instead stop at the peaceful Chadsey Lake. The eastern access off Quadling Road is no longer accessible due to the rock quarry.

Suncoaster Trail (Map 9–20)

This 33 km (20 mi) multi-use trail starts at Homesite Creek near Halfmoon Bay and passes through the Caren Range to Klein Lake. The trail follows roads in some places, including a stretch along Highway 101. The highlight of the trail is its north end, with views over Ruby and Sakinaw Lake and a waterfall, viewed from a bridge over Sakinaw Creek. Portions of the route are wheelchair accessible.

Suncoast Trails (Map 19/A5)

Also known as the Airport Reserve, this group of 30 or so mountain bike trails cover a lot of terrain suitable for beginners. Easily accessed by the Duck Lake Main Forest Service Road off the Sunshine Coast Highway (Hwy 101), a few trails connect with the Hammil Lake and Duck Lake trail areas to the north.

Sun God – Seven O'Clock Loop (Map 42/B4)

Expect a mixture of scree/loose rock, snowfields, and scrambles on this 13 km (8 mi) loop. With a cumulative elevation gain of 1,680 m (5,510 ft), this is a challenging but reasonable two-peak day hike. Waterfalls, lakes, and glaciers add to the rich scenery and diverse terrain on this loop. The trailhead is found near the end of the Tenas Creek Forest Service Road.

Sunnyside Acres Urban Forest (Map 2/B7)

There are about 4 km (2.5 mi) of trails, along with the nearby Semiahmoo Trail to the northeast, to explore in this urban forest. Access is found off 24th Avenue near Softball City in south Surrey.

Sunset Trail (Map 11/B6)

Found opposite the Sunset Marina on Highway 99, the Sunset Trail leads up (and up and up) past a gate on the second road (ignore the no trespassing sign), all the way to Yew Lake and Cypress Bowl. You will have hiked 7 km one-way and climbed 855 m (2,800 ft) by the time you are finished. If you still have energy, why not hike to the 1,455 m (4,775 ft) summit of Mount Strachan? This second alternative is 22 km (13.5 mi), climbing 1,400 m (4,600 ft) along the way.

Sunshine Coast Trail (Map 19/F5–28/A6)

The Sunshine Coast Trail is located on the Upper Sunshine Coast and stretches 180 km (112 mi) from Saltery Bay in the south to Sarah Point in Desolation Sound. As a general rule, the closer you get to Sarah Point, the tougher the route gets. Mount Troutbridge is just a few kilometres before the end and is the highest point on the trail, at 1,260 m (4,130 ft). One of the interesting aspects of this trail is the fact that there are a couple of Bed and Breakfasts located en route. Along the trail you can find great ocean views, occasional waterfront access, old growth forests, ocean vistas, an oceanfront campsite and a lakeside campsite with swimming and freshwater fishing. If you are planning on beginning (or ending) at Sarah Point, you will have to arrange for a water taxi from Lund, unless you want to hike in. You will also have to arrange for boat transportation to get across Powell Lake. To do the whole trail from end to end will take a week to ten days, but most sections are doable as one or two day hikes.

Sunshine Mountain Trails (Map 51/B6)

Found south of Bralorne, this moderate trail starts from about the 2 km mark on the Noel Creek Forest Service Road. Look for the old mining road that climbs about 395 m (1,300 ft) to the old Bralorne Ski Hill and Cabin on Sunshine Mountain. Beyond the recently refurbished cabin, mountain bikers can follow the Alfigetti Trail back down to the road, while hikers and ATVers can continue up the trail to the alpine areas of the Cadwallader Range. From here mountaineering routes abound.

Taggart Peak Trail (Map 3/G6)

Proximity to the city and a relative absence of snow makes this a popular trail for locals. The summit offers nice views of the Fraser Valley and the lush greenery of the trail makes for a satisfying, moderate 5.4 km (3.4 mi) hike. The trail gains 890 m (2,920 ft) and is accessed from Lakemount Road, close to the Gun Club.

Tenquille Lake Trails (Map 41/F3–42/A3)

Tenquille Lake is a beautiful alpine lake set in meadows surrounded by rugged mountain peaks. At the lake is a newly refurbished cabin together with an area for camping. The area is extremely popular with backpackers, mountaineers, snowmobilers and even extreme mountain bikers. The lake can be accessed several ways. For more information on the lake, cabin and trails should contact the Pemberton Wildlife Association (www.pembertonwildlifeassociation.com).

Branch 12/Hurley River Access:

This is the easiest route if you have a four-wheel drive vehicle. It starts near the end of the Tenquille Lake West Road, which is accessed from Branch 12 off the Hurley River Forest Service Road. Depending on how far you can drive, the trail gains about 440 m (1,440 ft) over a 13.8 km (8.6 mi) return route. The trail begins in an old cut block and then crosses a creek before joining with the other trail leading from the Lillooet River.

Pemberton Valley Access:

An alternative and more challenging route is to climb from the Lillooet River valley 10.6 km (6.6 mi) one-way gaining 1,460 m (4,745 ft). The trailhead is accessed from the parking lot at the bridge crossing the Lillooet River. Although the hike is extremely strenuous, you will be rewarded with excellent vistas of the valley below and the opportunity to walk through beautiful meadows filled with wildflowers. Part of this trail goes through a burn area from a forest fire in 2009.

Tenquille Creek/Birkenhead Lake Access:

This trail leads from the end (or as far as you can go) of the Tenquille Creek Forest Service Road and heads directly up to the lake. From the furthest point possible to drive to, it is 4.5 km (2.8 mi) to the lake, climbing around 200 m (655 ft). Access to this forest service road is from the Birkenhead Forest Service Road off the Pemberton Portage Road, on the opposite side of the range as the previous two trails.

Tenquille Mountain Trail (Map 41/F3) 🚶🚵📷

One of several rugged mountain peaks surrounding Tenquille Lake, Tenquille Mountain begs to be climbed. From the cabin, it is a difficult 4 km (2.5 mi) return trip climbing 730 m (2,395 ft).

Tetrahedron Provincial Park Trails (Map 10/B2) 🚶🏕️🚵⛷️🎿📷

This provincial park is home to an extensive network of alpine hiking, biking and backcountry ski trails. The main area is reached off the Sechelt Forest Service Road. A popular trail is the 10 km (6 mi) long Five Lake Circuit, which provides access to cabins along Edwards and Bachelor Lakes. Chapman Lake Trail is 10 km long and provides access to McNair Cabin. This cabin is also accessed by the 3 km long McNair Lake Trail. From here it is possible to ascend into the alpine to Panther Peak, making for a 14 km (8.7 mi) trip and an elevation gain of 745 m (2,450 ft). Another prominent peak is at Mount Steele, accessed along an 11 km (6.8 mi) trail that passes Mount Steele Cabin and climbs 805 m (2,640 ft).

Tetrahedron Peak Trail (Map 10/D4) 🚶🚵📷

Access to this challenging trail is from the Rainy Forest Service Road, approximately 9 km from the Rainy River Bridge. Cross the Rainy River again, this time on a wire foot bridge, and follow an overgrown logging road. Make sure to pay attention to the trail flagging, particularly at the several creeks you cross once you get off the road. It is a 6 km hike to the base of the highest peak on the Sunshine Coast. In total, it is over 8.5 km (5.3 mi) climbing over 1,260 m (4,130 ft) as you scramble up the open slopes beneath the peak. Allow a full day to reach the summit where spectacular panoramic views are your reward.

Texada Island Bike Loop (Maps 8, 18, 19) 🏕️🚵🚗📷

From the Blubber Bay Ferry Terminal, this is a long, moderate 73 km (45 mi) return bike ride that should take a day to complete. Cycling in a clockwise direction from Vananda, you follow Central (High) Road to Bell Road and down to the hydro lines. Here a steep downhill will bring you to the Davie Bay Road, where you head north to Gillies Bay and back to Vananda and the ferry. It is possible to take side trips to Bob's Lake Recreation Site or Shingle Beach Recreation Site to camp.

Thacker Mountain Trail (Map 15/F6) 🚶🚵📷

In the heart of Hope, this trail leads 5 km (3 mi) along an old road to the summit of Thacker. You gain 160 m (520 ft) and are rewarded with a good view of the Fraser Valley and Hope.

Theodosia Trails (Map 18/E2) 🚵

This group of mountain bike trails is located northwest of Powell River, near Sliammon Lake, and has a wide range of length and difficulty, including a couple of black diamond runs. The Theodosia Forest Service Road provides easy access to most of the trails.

Tin Hat Mountain Trail (Map 19/B1) 🚶🚵🏕️🚴📷

This trail starts just north of Spring Lake, along an old road. While it is possible to drive part of the way, it is best to park your vehicle and walk the old road northward. Eventually, you will pick up a well maintained, but difficult trail that leads to the summit some 13 km (8 mi) return gaining 1,600 m (5,250 ft) along the way. Alpine flowers, bunchberries and great views of the Powell Lake area are offered. The hike is best left for late summer and early fall.

Tommy Creek Trail (Map 51/G4) 🚶📷

This remote 10 km (6 mi) hike leads along an old mining exploration road and then along an overgrown trail to the sub-alpine. The trailhead is accessed by boat to the south side of Carpenter Lake. This is seldom visited grizzly bear country so come prepared.

Toquenatch Trail (Map 18/D1) 🚶📷

This well-marked trail begins approximately 3.5 km along the Southview Road, from where it leaves Highway 101. The hike extends in a northwest direction 5 km (3 mi) one-way. It leads past two large Douglas fir trees and follows the creek where salmon spawn in the fall to the south end of Okeover Inlet.

Tour de Soo (Map 32/G4–33/B1) 🚵📷

30 km (18 mi) of logging roads and 10 km (6 mi) of single-track make up this difficult ride, which will take good riders about three hours including a few mandatory hike-a-bike sections. From the Cougar Mountain Road, you climb over to the Soo River Valley and onto Echo Lakes, Rutherford Creek and eventually out to the Highway. From here, make your way north to Pemberton along trails found around and above the railway.

Traboulay PoCo Trail (Map 2/B3–C1) 🚶🚵

This 25 km (15.5 mi) trail encircles the City of Port Coquitlam and helps form a portion of the Trans Canada Trail. The PoCo Trail was renamed in 2001 to honour former mayor Len Traboulay who helped establish the trail.

Train Glacier - 5 Peaks Loop (Map 41/E2) 🚶🚵📷

Expect some glacier travel, route finding and advanced scrambling on this trail. If you are up for the challenge, a five peak day with spectacular views will be your reward. Advanced hikers can make an additional summit of Handcar Mountain for a six peak adventure. The entire loop will gain 2,500 m (8,200 ft) in elevation over a distance of 18 km (11 mi). The trail is accessed from the Hurley River Forest Service Road.

Trans Canada Trail (Maps 1, 2, 3, 4, 5, 6, 15, 16, 27) 🚶🚵🏕️🚴⛷️📷

The Trans Canada trail weaves its way from Horseshoe Bay to Hope and into the Okanagan as it ultimately makes its way across the province and the country. Many people have hiked on the TCT without knowing it, as the trail incorporates many pre-existing trails into the route. Included in the TCT are parts of the Centennial Trail, the Baden Powell Trail, Burnaby Mountain Trails, the Pitt River Dykes, the Matsqui Trail, the Kettle Valley Railway and more. While some parts of the trail in BC are yet to be completed, the trail is essentially in place in the Lower Mainland.

Tricouni Meadows & Peak Trail (Map 22/A1–32/A7) 🚶🚵🚴📷

From the Branch 200 road system off the Squamish Forest Service Road, this trail climbs steeply past the meadows to Tricouni Peak. Depending on how far you can drive, the trail is roughly 6.4 km (4 mi) long, climbing 1,205 m (3,955 ft) next to the creek draw. It takes about two hours to access the open meadow and sub-alpine lakes. From here, it is a more difficult climb to the peak, which is the highest peak along the south end of the Squamish-Cheakamus Divide.

Trout Lake Trails (Map 9/D4) 🚵🚴🏕️🚗📷

Located about 10 km west of Sechelt on Highway 101, Trout Lake is a popular destination for hiking, mountain biking, off-roading, horseback riding and swimming. The Trout Lake Loop is a 15 km (9.3 mi) moderate mountain bike loop that will take you clockwise along a series of roads back to the highway. Allow 1.5 hours to enjoy the many viewpoints. Between Trout Lake and Redrooffs Road another series of moderate trails can be explored. The powerlines above Trout Lake also offer moderate riding that turns quite difficult the further you head west.

TRAIL ADVENTURES

Tszil Mountain Trail (Map 43/A7)
Access this trail from the Lower Joffre Lake parking lot. From here it is a 1,360 m (4,460 ft) climb to the peak of Tszil Mountain, over a distance of 8.5 km (5.3 mi) one-way. Along the way you will pass Middle and Upper Joffre lakes, as well as many smaller tarns and creeks. The trail will get fairly steep past Upper Joffre Lake and, as you get closer to the peak, be prepared for snow and ice. Backcountry skiers will be able to find some tasty lines in the area.

Tuwanek Point Beach Trail (Map 9/F3)
The trailhead to this ocean front walk is found off Upland Road just before the gravel pit. The trail leads 2 km (1.2 mi) to the ocean following the shore of Sechelt Inlet to the point.

Twin Goat Ridge Route (Map 34/A2–43/A7)
This difficult bit of ridge walking traverses 22 km (13.5 mi) one-way from Upper Joffre Lake all the way to Lillooet Lake Road just north of the Twin One Recreation Site. Give yourself a full day to get from one to the other. Initially, you ascend from Upper Joffre Lake at 1,280 m (4,200 ft) all the way to 2,380 m (7,800 ft) at the foot of the Matier Glacier. From here you descend steadily to Lillooet Lake, at 200 m (655 ft) in elevation. It can only be hiked after the snow melts, which is usually July to September.

Tyaughton Lake Trails (Map 51/C2)
An elaborate system of old roads and trails is found on the east side of Tyaughton Lake. This multi-use system can be accessed from Tyax Mountain Resort at the north end of the lake (hiking, biking, horseback riding only), or off the Tyaughton Lake Road, which is the better option for motorized users. One nice hiking trail is the Black Forest Trail, which leads to a viewpoint over the lake. The trail branches from the old road and is 5.2 km (3.2 mi) return climbing 200 m (655 ft).

U.B.C. Research Forest (Map 2/F2–12/G7)
There are a number of trails and old roads in this large research forest, just north of Maple Ridge. The routes range from 1.4 km to 6.5 km (4 mi) in length, with elevation gains of up to 610 m (2,000 ft). The trails weave their way through a mixed second growth forest and some of the high points offer good views over the Fraser Valley. Take 232nd Street north of Haney and park at the gate near the forestry headquarters. You must register at the office before heading out. No mountain bikes are allowed.

Unnecessary Mountain Trail (Map 11/B5)
Unnecessary Mountain gets its name from the obstacle it forms on the Howe Sound Crest Trail. As a destination, the mountain does offer a rewarding view. Unfortunately, the unmaintained trail is rough, rugged and steep. From the gate on Oceanview Road (right before the Harvey Creek Bridge in Lions Bay), follow the road to the trailhead marked by orange markers. In all, it is a difficult 9.5 km (5.9 mi) return hike gaining 1,310 m (4,300 ft) to the summit at 1,510 m (4,955 ft).

Upper Chilliwack River Trail (Map 5/G7)
From Depot Creek at the south end of Chilliwack Lake, the trail starts along the shores of the lake to the estuary of the Chilliwack River. Where the trail splits, follow the right branch leading south to the US border along the east side of Chilliwack River. This is a rewarding trail that meanders among an ecological reserve with old growth cedar, majestic Douglas fir and Amabilis fir next to the Upper Chilliwack River. It is also an easy trail covering 5.4 km (3.3 mi) return. The more adventurous can continue on into Washington State, along a difficult two-day trail, which ultimately leads to Mount Baker.

Valley Trail System (Map 32/F5)
Within the Whistler Valley is an extensive 20 km (12 mi) network of well-maintained gravel and paved trails. The trail network extends from Alta Lake along the River of Dreams to Green Lake. At most intersections, there are signs marking the various routes. The trail system is heavily used throughout the summer months by mountain bikers, joggers, hikers and in-line skaters and by cross-country skiers in the winter. The easy trails will take you through the heart of the Whistler Valley past creeks and lakes, forested areas and golf courses.

Vedder Mountain Trails (Map 4/B6)
An excellent hiking trail is found off an old spur road on the Vedder Mountain Forest Service Road. This is a well-developed, moderate 11.5 km (7 mi) trail

gaining 365 m (1,195 ft) to the summit. Once you break out of the dense hemlock forest you will be rewarded with views of Sumas Prairie, Vedder Canal and area. Spring flowers brighten the way. Once on the summit, you can follow an old trail down to return along the road. Alternatively, you can use the old trail from the Yarrow side to access the top.

For mountain bikers, this is one of the best places to ride in the Chilliwack area. The main route follows the forestry road from Parmenter Road, 21.5 km (13 mi) around the ridge. This moderate ride offers great views of the surrounding valley while climbing 490 m (1,610 ft). Several side trails in the area have been developed by motorcyclists and provide experienced mountain bikers with fast and twisty thrills. A popular option follows the Vedder Mountain Classic Route. This route heads south (left) from the main road and follows several trails and old roads back to the main road and the start some 17 km (10.5 mi) and 340 m (1,115 ft) later.

Vedder River Trail (Map 4/A5–C6)
The scenic dyke system along the north side of the Vedder River has benefited from extensive work by the Chilliwack Rotary Club. This trail is open to hikers, bikers and horseback riders and is part of the Trans Canada Trail. The main access points are the Keith Wilson Bridge to the west and Vedder Crossing to the east. While there are many places to access the trail, the longest you can hike here is about 15.5 km (9.6 mi).

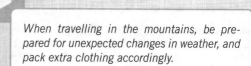

When travelling in the mountains, be prepared for unexpected changes in weather, and pack extra clothing accordingly.

Viera Creek Trail (Map 52/E5)
This is an 8 km (5 mi) trail along a series of mining exploration tote roads and old hunting trails. The trailhead begins a few kilometres west of Mission Dam off the Carpenter Lake Road.

Walt Lake Ridge Route (Map 19/F2)
A four-wheel drive spur road leads to the Beta Lake/Khartoum Lake trailhead. From there, a difficult and unmarked route leads to the alpine. The route cuts south around Beta Lake and past the Knuckleheads Cabin before a crescent shaped meander along the ridge overlooking Walt Lake. Total distance from the trailhead and back is 21 km (13 mi), with most of the 660 m (2,160 ft) elevation gained by the time you reach the cabin. This area is particularly popular in the winter for snowmobiling, snowshoeing and skiing.

Waterloo [Mt. Fergusson] Trail (Map 51/C5)
Just before the 7 km mark of the Kingdom Lake Forest Service Road, look for the old road that accesses an old limestone kiln and Mount Fergusson. The road leads through a forested area for about a kilometer to a fork. Here, the difficult Waterloo Trail follows the right fork along an old road that climbs to an avalanche chute (the left fork continues to the old kiln site). Climb the avalanche path to the treeline where a route continues up the ridge towards the summit of Mount Fergusson. It is about a 1,370 m (4,500 ft) climb; to actually summit requires mountaineering gear.

Wedgemount Lake Trail (Map 33/B4)
A short, but steep trail climbs to a beautiful lake set at the foot of a glacier below cascading peaks. From the end of the Wedgemount Creek Forest Service Road, you climb a gruelling 1,220 m (4,000 ft) through the heavy forest, past a rockslide with a view of the falls on Wedgemount Creek, to the rocky sub-alpine meadows around the lake. At the lake, it is possible to camp or use the cabin as a base for further exploration. The 12 km (7.3 mi) return trail is best tackled in July to September. From the cabin, it is possible to climb to nearby Mount Cook, Mount Weart and Wedge Mountain. This steep trail climbs 765 m (2,510 ft) over 2 km.

Wedge Mountain Trail (Map 33/B4) 🏕️🥾🚴🎿⛷️🚻

Wedge Mountain is the highest peak in Garibaldi, rising some 2,905 metres (9,530 feet) above sea level. Although the mountain can be scrambled up, the real appeal of this trip is the series of glaciers (Weart, Needle and Chaos) north and east of the peak. Give yourself at least two days to explore the area. The BC Mountaineering Club maintains a cabin at Wedgemount Lake. It is also possible to access this area from Blackcomb Mountain to the south via Wedge Pass. From the end of the Wedgemount Lake Trail, it is a 3.4 km hike to the peak, gaining some 1,030 m (3,380 ft).

Wednesday Lake Trail (Map 28/B7) 🥾🚴🚻

This 8 km (5 mi) hike leads along an old road from Malaspina Forest Service Road to tiny Wednesday Lake, which drains into Trevenen Bay of Okeover Inlet.

Welcome Woods/Sergeant Bay Trails (Map 9/D4) 🥾🚴🚻

This series of trails is located west of Sechelt, near Halfmoon Bay, and encompasses the area between Sargeant Bay Provincial Park and Trout Lake. Some of these trails are designated as hiking only, but mountain bikers and equestrians riders still have a lot of terrain to explore in the area as there are over 40 km (25 mi) of named trails here. Many of these trails can be accessed from Redroofs Road or right from Highway 101. Popular trails in the area include the Redroofs Loop and the 3.5 km (2.2 mi) Triangle Lake Trail.

Wells Peak Trail (Map 15/G7–5/G1) 🥾🚻

The access road is found opposite Nicomen Park on Highway 3 and is marked by the Hope Mountain Trail sign. Once up the rough waterbared road, the trail to the left leads to Wells Peak some 8 km (5 mi) later. Allow five hours as it is a steep 700 m (2,295 ft) climb to the summit.

> *Never feed wild animals while hiking. They will become accustomed to human feeding and this will put them in serious danger.*

Whatcom Trail (Map 6/F2–17/B5) 🥾🚻

From the Cascade Recreation Area parking lot off of Highway 3, this trail follows the Dewdney Trail for 2.5 km (1.6 mi) before splitting off to the right. From there, the trail climbs steeply through second growth forest to the sub-alpine meadows of Whatcom Pass and the Punch Bowl. The trail then descends into the Paradise Valley and the Tulameen River near Wells Lake where a variety of trails continue on. You will gain 650 m (2,130 ft) over 17 km (10.5 mi) one-way to the ridge. Unless you are on horseback, you will probably want to arrange for a shuttle at the far end. The hike is best done in late summer or early fall.

Whippoorwill Point/Sandy Cove Trail (Map 4/F1) 🥾🚻

Most visitors to Harrison Hot Springs enjoy the easy stroll to the source of the hot springs. However, few take in the scenic trail that leads to Whippoorwill Point. This 5 km (2.4 mi) trail climbs quickly from the hot springs to its high point, which is only about 40 m (130 ft) above the lake. From here it descends to Sandy Cove, which is a great place for a picnic and on to Whippoorwill Point. Although the trail is regarded as easy, there are tricky sections to negotiate.

Whistler Interpretative Forest (Map 32/E6) 🥾🚴🎿⛷️🚣‍♂️⛵🚻

The Whistler Interpretative Forest is easily accessed by the Westside Main Cheakamus Lake Roads. It is a total of 3,500 hectares (8,645 ac) and ranges from the valley bottom all the way to the sub-alpine at 1,600 m (5,250 ft). Through the interpretative forest are numerous short trails exploring the various silviculture practices and ecosystems of the Cheakamus Valley. There are stands of old growth timber along the western banks of the Cheakamus River, scenic vistas and access to a good fishing lake. The Ridge Trail, Lower Riverside Trail, Highline Trail and the Logger's Lake Access Trail are open to everyone, while the Crater Rim Trail, Riverside Interpretative Trail and Whistler West Ridge Trail are closed to mountain bikes. Several signs within the interpretative forest allow you to decide on which route to travel.

Whistler Mountain Trails (Map 32/G6) 🥾🚴🎿⛷️🚻

After the ski season ends and the snow melts, Whistler Mountain becomes a spectacular hiking and biking destination. The glacier covered peaks and the rugged treeless terrain makes the area a gorgeous place to visit. During the off-season, the Whistler Village Gondola runs to the Roundhouse Lookout for a fee. There are four different guided bike routes that lead from the Roundhouse Lodge to the Whistler Village. For hikers, options include Glacier Trail, Harmony Lake Trail, Little Whistler Trail, Musical Bumps and Ridge Lookout Trail. Outside of the Musical Bumps Trail, the trails are short (up to 3.5 km long), but do require a bit more climbing than the nearby Blackcomb Mountain Trails. The Highnote Trail, which leads to a spectacular viewpoint overlooking Cheakamus Lake, returns to the lodge via the Singing Pass Trail.

Whyte Lake Trail (Map 11/A6) 🥾🚴🏇🚻

This short but beautiful trail leads to a nice loop around Whyte Lake making a 5 km (3 mi) round trip with an elevation gain of 240m (790 ft). The trail can either be accessed from the Trans Canada Trail or the Baden Powell Trail. An outhouse is located at the lake.

Widgeon Bowl Lookout Trail (Map 12/E7) 🥾🚻

This is a very stiff climb up 700 m (2,295 ft) over a mere 2 km — that's just about one metre up for every two metres you hike. Overall the trail gains just over 900 m (2,950 ft) in 5 km (3 mi). The trailhead is difficult to find from the water accessible Widgeon Lake Recreation Site or from Burke Mountain along a poorly marked trail. Although the views of Pitt Lake from the bowl below Widgeon Peak are spectacular, this climb is only for folks in really good shape.

Widgeon Falls Trail (Map 12/E6) 🥾🚻

A popular boat access hike is found across from Grant Narrows Park at the south end of Pitt Lake. From the end of the slough at the Widgeon Lake Recreation Site, it is an easy 2.7 km (1.7 mi) walk along an old logging road (note that the old trail along the creek is now closed). Allow one hour to reach the falls, gaining 40 m (130 ft) along the way.

Widgeon Lake Trail (Map 12/E6) 🥾🚴🛶🚻

The first part of this trail from the Widgeon Lake Recreation Site is along an old logging road. It is possible (some would even argue preferable) to bring a mountain bike along in your canoe and cycle the first leg of the trail. The second stretch of this 18.5 km (11 mi) trail climbs steeply up into the cirque where Widgeon Lake is located, getting progressively steeper the closer you get. The lake is at found at the 815 m (2,675 ft) mark and most of that is gained in the last couple kilometres.

Wildwood Hill Trail (Map 18/F3) 🥾🚴🚻

The trail begins on the west side of the Powell Lake Bridge off Highway 101. This trail switchbacks twice before it connects with the powerline to the south. It eventually leads back to the Petro Canada Service Station. The trail is easily followed and is wide enough for both mountain bikers and hikers.

Williams Ridge Trail (Map 5/D5) 🥾🚻

A gruelling 11 km (6.8 mi) trail is found near the 32 km mark of the Chilliwack Lake Road. Orange markers indicate the steep, undeveloped trail as it rises through a second growth forest past a clearing with a good view of the valley. From here, the trail continues along a forested ridge to connect with the Ford Mountain Trail (see above). This is a tough hike, gaining 1,440 m (4,725 ft) including a lung-busting 900 m (2,950 ft) in the first 1.5 km to the ridge that runs between the lookout and Williams Peak. It is also possible to scramble up to the prominent Williams Peak.

Williamson Lake Trail (Map 5/C5) 🥾🚻

Beginning at the Foley Lake Recreation Site, the trail is a difficult 13 km (8 mi) hike gaining 1,200 m (3,935 ft) to the lake. Not only will you feel like a mountain goat as you scramble up (and up), you might actually see one. The trail begins by crossing Foley Creek and then it rises sharply along the ridge above Williamson Creek to the lake. In spring, runoff makes creek crossings difficult and, if there is snow left, there is a good chance that there will be an avalanche. Leave this one until late summer and early fall.

Wilson Creek Trail (Map 9/G5) 🥾🚴🚻

The trail is found by parking on Jack Road and then crossing Highway 101. The scenic trail leads through a second growth forest along Wilson Creek before crossing a bridge. The trail continues on to the powerlines for a 2 km (1.2 mi) round trip. This route can be ridden by experienced mountain bikers.

ATV [OHV] ADVENTURES

British Columbia offers a massive network of logging roads, trails and decommissioned railroad beds to explore. In fact, it is estimated that there are over 550,000 kilometres (341,754 mi) of trails and old forestry roads in the province, with the majority of them being open to responsible off-road use.

These roads lead to remote lakes, mountain peaks, river valleys and sometimes dead ends. The vast network of forestry roads often loop together and intersect, or stretch on seemingly forever. As you venture deeper into the wilderness it is always a good bet that the roads and trails get rougher and tougher.

Within the southwestern part of the province, riding experiences vary from dense temperate rain forests with muddy forest trails to drier mountainous regions. Beginners can ride the open forest service roads, while expert riders can ride the many challenging mountain roads and trails that seem to lead up every peak in the area. However, only a select few trails are open to ATVs due to the steep, narrow trails and sensitive alpine terrain.

Make sure you know before you head out that motorized riders are always under heavy scrutiny, so tread lightly. ATVers have got a bad reputation in some areas due to irresponsible riding by a notable minority. As a result, some of the riding areas near the populated areas of the Vancouver Coast are at risk of being closed.

Although there are fewer trails in the more populated areas immediately around the Lower Mainland, there are still some excellent systems to explore here. Heading up the Chilliwack River Valley, the Sea to Sky Corridor or as far as Gold Bridge opens up some fine possibilities. Other popular areas include Powell River and the Sunshine Coast.

For more information check with one of the many riding clubs in the area, like the Fraser Valley Dirt Riders Association (www.fvdra.com), the Squamish Dirt Bike Association (www.squamishdirtbikeassociation.com) or the Lower Mainland ATV club (www.lmatv.com). But that's just the first step; ATVs and motorbikes can have a dramatic effect on trails, so pitch in and help with trail maintenance. Noise is the number one cause of complaints in popular areas, so keep your machine running efficiently, at 96db or less. And for heaven's sake, don't go riding in areas that are not open to motorized vehicles, especially wet areas and in the alpine where the damage is obvious.

JOIN A CLUB, JOIN THE FUN!
Become a member and join local community clubs

See BC ATV on an ATV

QUAD RIDERS ASSOCIATION
ATVBC
OF BRITISH COLUMBIA

✉ tourism@atvbc.ca atvbc.ca

ATV [OHV] ADVENTURES

Ashcroft Motorcycle Route (Maps 45, 54)
If you are feeling adventurous you can try to reclaim some of the old trail system around Ashcroft. Once well maintained and marked, this system had over 400 km (240 mi) of trails. Unfortunately, extensive sections of the old trails have been logged over the years and it may be difficult to locate some of the routes. But if you are up to the task, grab your GPS and mapbook and go exploring.

Barkley Valley/Twin Lakes Trail (Map 43/C4)
The Barkley Valley Trail is cross country riding at its best. You can ride in and camp or do a loop that takes about five hours. The ATV trail begins where the Haylmore Forest Service Road becomes impassable on a normal vehicle, about 14 km southeast of Devine. Some cars can make it to the 16 km mark, where a steep narrow ATV track continues along an old pack trail that was upgraded to a road in the 60's before being left to the elements. It follows a constant grade until leveling off 4 km from the trailhead, when you reach the sub-alpine. The road leads to the abandoned Elliot Creek mining claim, which dates back to the 1950s. Later, a counter culture group tried to make a commune in the area, but was beaten by the massive snowfalls common to the area. There is a campsite approximately 5 km (3 mi) in with access to Twin Lakes.

BC Nickel Mine Road Riding Area (Map 15/E4)
Found about 12 km north of Hope on Highway 1, then west on Nickel Mine Road, is a loading area with free camping and day parking. There are approximately 100 km (60 mi) of trails here, maintained by FVDRA (Fraser Valley Dirt Riders Association) volunteers that offer everything from family friendly riding to very challenging off-road riding. The main family friendly area is located along the powerline corridor. There are large flat areas for beginners adjacent to the campsite. There is also a mini MX track. More experienced riders will find nearly three-dozen named trails in this area, including the difficult Yahoo Hill and Sesame Street. Some of the trails are too narrow for quads.

Bear Mountain Trail (Map 4/G1–15/A7)
Only 5 km from the main intersection of Lillooet Avenue and Rockwell Drive in Harrison Hot Springs is the turn off to Bear Mountain Trail. The trip is about 20 km (12 mi) return to the tiny lake tucked in a pretty valley. Past the lake, the old roads continue to the top of Bear Mountain. If you reach the top, you will have climbed over a 1,000 metres (3,280 feet). Look for a "Mining Act" warning sign as the trailhead — the mining company has long ago vacated the area. Follow the road and take a right at the fork. You will pass many small waterfalls and see some great views.

Bible Camp Trail (Map 9/F2)
This trail continues from the north end of the Sechelt-Gray Forest Service Road to a seaside youth church camp that has been abandoned for many, many years. Most of the buildings are in very poor condition and so is the road in. The ride leads through a creek where the bridge has been washed out and includes challenging hill climbs and boulders. For ATVers, this is a pretty easy trail with lots of cross ditches to slow down for. The camp is a place frozen in time and is worth checking out if you are in the area.

Blue Mountain Area (Map 3/B2)
Once featuring over 100 km (60 mi) of off-road riding, this area still has some fine terrain to explore. With mostly intermediate to advanced terrain, Blue Mountain should be avoided by novice riders. This area can be very muddy and may be gated at any time. Further, some trails are motorcycle, single track only and riders should pay attention to signage. Access can be found off 256th Street in north Maple Ridge.

Blue Trail (Map 19/A4)
Built by the forest service in the mid-1980s this trail is still used today as an interpretive trail. The trailhead is just south of the Duck Lake bridge junction and goes into what is known as the Washout Trail. This is a fairly popular multi-use area close to Powell River, and there have been some bridge improvements completed recently.

Britannia Mines Area (Map 11/B2)
A turn off from the Sea to Sky Highway (Hwy 99) is found about 4 km south of the Britannia Mine site. As you head up to the old mining area there is lots of loose rock and good mud at times. You can easily spend a day and put on 30 km (18 mi) or more as you explore the old mine sites, equipment and core samples. The terrain is not too difficult but you can find some more challenging off shoots to explore, as well.

Cabin Lake Trails (Map 27/B1–D1)
There are multiple ways to access this site, as it sits between three different highways. You can head east on the Anderson River/Spius Creek Forest Service Roads from Boston Bar and Highway 1 or head west from the Coquihalla Highway (Hwy 5) along the Patchett Road/Spius Creek Forest Service Road. The easiest access is probably out of the north (see our Thompson Okanagan Backroad Mapbook), heading south of Highway 8 on the Prospect Creek Forest Service Road. Once in the area, several routes can be explored.

The Cabin Lake Road climbs roughly 7 km (4.3 mi) along a rough four-wheel drive/ATV route, gaining 215 m (700 feet) to the lake and recreation site. Beyond the lake several routes continue including the Heather Basin Trail, which is a steep 5 km (3 mi) long trail that most people walk. En route, a side trail leads to an old plane crash site. Once at the top you are rewarded with a beautiful view of the Heather Basin. The road up is quite steep and coming down may be the most difficult part.

Another option is to head to Lightning Lake. This route involves a steep 5 km (3 mi) excursion along an old road. Just south of Lightning Lake you can accesses a series of trails to Silver Lake and the Silver Lake Road, which is an alternate route into the area.

ATVs and motorbikes can have a dramatic effect on trails, so pitch in and help with trail maintenance.

Carpenter Lake Area (Maps 51, 52, 53)
In the summer months the man-made lake is a popular destination for ATVers. The area consists of many lakes connected by a network of roads and trails. Popular routes include the Mission Mountain Road, which climbs from the Terzaghi Dam over Mission Mountain and then descends into Shalalth and Seton Portage. Further west, the Yalakom and Marshall Creek Forest Service Roads provide good access to trail systems around Lake la Mare, Marshall Lake and into the Shulaps Range. Other popular points include the steep Jim Creek Road near Marshall Lake, the easier La Rochelle Creek/Verbenkov Forest Service Road loop from the Yalakom Recreation Site and the Lake la Mare Road. Be wary of other trail users, as well as vehicles and loaded logging trucks when riding the main roads.

Capilano Mountain Area (Map 11/C2)
Located just east of Furry Creek off the Tanac Connector Road, this area has multiple spur roads to explore. Riding here can be challenging, with elevation gains of up to 1,250m (4,100 ft), narrow tracks and hiking-only trails. There are no official trails so make sure you have your map and GPS handy.

Cat Lake/Brohm Riding Area (Map 22/D5)
Around Cat Lake is a series of challenging trails. These trails can be accessed off of the Cheekeye/Brohm Forest Service Road 11 km north of Squamish. There is a parking area just 100 metres off the highway and another staging area about 1.4 km in. Several trails lead out from the staging areas, including some trails for beginners. The entire area is a network of criss-crossing trails and roads, including some that are technical and single track. Although the trails are unsigned, please refrain from riding your ATV on single track trails. It is possible to cross the Cheekeye River and follow the trails down to Alice Lake or Garibaldi Highlands.

Cheakamus Canyon Area (Map 22/C3)
The access to this trail is directly across from the old roadhouse entrance north of Brackendale and runs parallel to the Sea to Sky Highway (Hwy 99) for a few metres before it cuts into the forest and goes into a hill climb. At the top you will get a nice view of the surrounding area. The road down is challenging near the bottom as there are some large rock steps and jagged boulders to maneuver around. You can explore around Starvation Lake or you can head north to access the Cheakamus Canyon. The trail ends at the old lookout at the side of the highway, where highway access is currently blocked.

Chehalis Lake Riding Area (Map 14/B7–C4)

There are many ways to access Chehalis Lake from the West Harrison Riding Area. The Hemlock Valley and Cartmell Creek Forest Service Roads lead north of the ski area to the south side of the lake. Further north, the Mystery Creek Forest Service Road has long been a popular four-wheel drive route to the north end of Chehalis Lake. Once at the lake, there is no shortage of roads to explore. The massive landslide area at the north end of the lake is worth visiting, while a nice loop takes you southwest around Dickson Lake.

Chilliwack River Valley (Map 4/E7–5/D7)

Many of the area's best riding trails are accessed off the paved Chilliwack Lake Road, which runs through the Chilliwack River Valley. This is an area that is well suited for all levels of riders, however, due to close proximity to urban centres this area can get quite busy. Further up the valley, forest service roads like the Tamihi and Nesakwatch offer easy riding to some very scenic areas. Other popular rides include the Chipmunk Creek Trails, the DND Powerline Road and the many trails and roads around Tamihi Creek Recreation Site. Riders must note that some areas are single track or hiking only and are not open to ATVs, no matter how tracked out they look. The fragile alpine has been heavily damaged in the past and the area is constantly at risk of being shut down completely.

Chipmunk Creek Riding Area (Map 5/A5)

Accessed from either the Chipmunk Peninsula or Rapids Recreation Sites, there are about 60 km (37 mi) of tight trails available year round. In the summer, an additional 40 km (25 mi) of higher elevation trails become available. Originally created by off-road dirt bikers, technical ATV riders looking for a challenge will enjoy this area, although most trails remain too narrow to navigate on a quad. In 2010, the BCORMA created the Bear Cub beginner and kids loop. It is located at the east end of the Rapids Recreation Site and has marked entrances and a trail map. The Rapids Staging area has large campsites available and was built for off-loading with a great dirt ramp to back up to.

Coalmont/Tulameen Area (Map 17)

The discovery of gold in 1885 helped develop this area. Most of the activity occurred around Granite City near present-day Coalmont. Today, the Granite Creek Recreation Site is a popular base for exploring the Lodestone Mountain area. Here countless roads (new and old) make for some exciting riding leading into the mountains. Across the river and Coalmont Road, riders can also explore a mix of roads that lead into the ATV friendly town of Tulameen. From here, routes continue west and north up into the Coquihalla Lakes and Mount Henning area. There are way too many routes to list in this area, but a popular long distance route follows the Whatcom Trail south past Lodestone Lake, creating a nice loop for a full day of riding.

Dakota Ridge Area (Map 10/B4)

Best accessed from Sechelt Chapman Forest Service Road from Wilson Creek's Field Road, there is a fork in the logging road that points to Dakota Ridge or to the Dakota Bowl. A series of interconnected trails allows riders to explore a few different options on any given ride. You could follow the Dakota Creek Loop Trail over to the Port Mellon Highway or explore the areas around Mount Elphinstone Provincial Park, including Dave's Bypass – a wet, muddy, but otherwise easy track that runs through Wilson Creek.

DND Powerline Road (Map 4/G5)

Further west on the Chilliwack-Bench Forest Service Road is another popular route. Take the steep descent from the main road down to the powerline road and start exploring. The trail loops around and there are numerous branches to check out. Be mindful of the hill climbs as some are very steep, and once you commit you will have to keep the throttle on.

East Harrison Riding Area (Maps 14, 25)

North of Harrison Hot Springs, off Rockwell Drive, this area opens up to tons of logging roads and endless spur roads. Some areas are private property, some are regulated, but there is no shortage of terrain. In fact, it is possible to ride all the way to Boston Bar in the Fraser Canyon.

Goat Lake Route (Map 19/C5–29/E3)

Found 18 km south of Powell River, head north on Dixon Road, then along the west side of Lois Lake before joining the Goat Lake Mainline Road. The route then passes Nanton, Ireland and Dodd Lakes up to the south side of the Ironface and Vision Peaks. It is about 138 km (86 mi) total and creates a nice day trip.

Gold Bridge Trails (Maps 50, 51)

Offering some of the best riding alternatives in BC, this expansive area links east to Lillooet or north towards the Gang Ranch and 100 Mile House. The scenic trails lead alongside dramatic cliffs, high above the big lakes that define the valley and up towards snow-capped mountains. South of Gold Bridge, the gravel road network allows you to explore around the abandoned mine sites like Bralorne or the Pioneer Mine, while others lead up creek draws like Truax and Jamie Creeks and even the head of the Bridge River. The trails in this area are too numerous to list; the best thing to do is set up basecamp at one of the many recreation sites and go exploring.

Green Mountain Trail (Map 50/G5)

Located south of Gold Bridge, the Green Mountain Trail is a rocky, twisting route up the mountain. It can be difficult for ATVs and most people hike or mountain bike up. The route leads up Branch 6, which is found 6 km down the infamous Hurley River Forest Service Road.

Greyrock/Truax Creek Riding Area (Map 51/B4–D4)

The Truax Creek Forest Service Road is a deactivated logging road that climbs into the mountains above Carpenter Lake. You can ascend up to 1,700m (5,580 ft) in under 14 km (8.6 mi) as you climb between the imposing figures of Mount Williams and Mount Truax towards the abandoned Greyrock Mine. There are a pair of bridges that are slowly degenerating, so don't be surprised if this route becomes impassable. Closer to Carpenter Lake, the Greyrock Forest Service Road and its many side routes also offer some good riding and fine vistas.

Hale Creek Area (Map 14/E4)

Found approximately 36 km from the highway along the Sts'ailes (formerly Harrison West) Forest Service Road, the Hale Creek area offers camping at multiple spots such as Wood Lake, Hale Creek, Sunrise Lake, Lookout Lake and, just up the road, the Twenty Mile Bay Recreation Site. ATV trails are abundant in the area, and there is a very small trail network to check out near the beach.

Liability insurance is now required in order to ride on any forest service road in BC.

Jane Lake Area (Map 32/E6)

Access is south of the Sea to Sky Highway (Hwy 99) at Function Junction. Head down the Cheakamus West Forest Service Road (Westside Main) to an old washed out road suitable for mountain bikes, foot traffic, and ATVs. This is a rugged 18 km (11 mi) return trip leading to Jane Lakes at 930 metres (3,025 ft) in elevation.

Lava Flow Riding Area (Map 22/D6)

Featuring over 20 km (12 mi) of trails, this riding area is accessible from Squamish off Mamquam Road, a few kilometres past the Quest University campus. The terrain is varied, with riding for novice to advanced riders, but pay attention to signage as some trails are single track and not to be used by ATVs, and some are one-way. There is a spur road that can be used for parking, and this is the trailhead for the Ring Creek Rip Trail.

Mamquam/Stawamus-Indian Forest Service Roads
(Map 22/D7–12/A5)

Some long road riding routes are found in the Mamquam Valley as well as up and over to Indian Arm. There are a few side routes and the occasional single track trail tossed in for good measure. Note that the Stawamus-Indian Forest Service Road is a seasonally deactivated four-wheel drive only road — some sections may be impassable and washouts are frequent. There is a trailhead located immediately north of the Stawamus Chief overflow lot. From here follow the forest service road and explore the many branches and forks in the area.

Mount Mulligan Area (Map 22/E7)

This popular hiking area also has many ATV trails that branch off the Mamquam and Ray Basin Forest Service Roads. Trails reach elevations of 1,820 metres (5,970 ft) and can be quite challenging. The multi-use Crumpit Woods Recreation Area is nearby, just north of the Mamquam Forest Service Road.

Mystery Creek Area (Map 14)

This area runs around the backside of Lookout Lake and down into the Mystery Valley. There are some creek crossings combined with tight treed sections. Another trail connects at the end of Mystery Creek Forest Service Road where, at a bridge, you can turn south towards Chehalis Lake or head the opposite direction for a 12 km (7 mi) one-way ride. After the second bridge (the first one is decommissioned and you have to ride through a creek) you can follow another route to Statlu Lake and Falls.

Onion Lake/Monkey Wrench Riding Area (Map 45/B4)

This area is considered one of the most challenging riding areas in Canada and is located about 20 km north of Lytton on Highway 12. The trails are rocky, steep and slimy, but very popular. A series of trails and old roads are found around Onion and Turnip Lakes, with some easy and some highly technical riding. The high elevation of 1,525 metres (5,000 ft) can limit the riding days to late spring and early fall. One camping and staging area is found at the 4.5 km mark and gives access to the lower trails, and another at the 14 km mark, both on the Laluwissin Creek Forest Service Road. There is a kid's loop here and spectacular views in all directions, as the area is surrounded by 2,130+ metre (7,000+ foot) mountain peaks.

When off-roading in the region it is always wise to have a well prepared trip plan and good equipment. The weather has been known to change quickly on people while exploring the wilderness. Further, floods have washed out bridges, active logging has altered road patterns and fallen trees from wind storms have blocked roads in and out.

Peg Leg Bar (Map 4/D3)

This is an area along the Fraser River's edge that can fluctuate greatly with water levels. At times the trails can be dry and other times they may be completely under water. Due to the mud and potential to get really stuck, it is best to not ride this area alone. The area is suitable for intermediate to advanced riders.

Powell River Riding Area (Maps 18, 19, 28, 29)

The Powell River ATV Club has built bridges and maintained a high environmental standard in this area. Instead of riding through creeks and mud bogs the club has built over 50 structures, all through volunteer efforts. With 300-400 km (185-250 mi) of trails, the club is always expanding and builds an average of 7-11 km of new trail per year. Unlike other areas that have a lot of private land breaking up the riding area, this area is quite open, and the club and its partners work hard to keep it this way. Trails and routes to explore include the easy Blue Trail near town or the extended Goat Lake and Theodosia Inlet Routes.

Sea to Sky Corridor (Maps 11, 22, 32)

This area is a world renowned tourism destination that has an international reputation for exceptional outdoor recreation. With a network of over 700 km (435 mi) of trails, there is no shortage of terrain to explore. However, some trails are not for motorized use, so plan your route ahead of time. We have listed a few alternatives for ATV riders in this section, including trails around Britannia Mines, Cat Lake, Cheakamus Canyon, Jane Lakes, Showh Lakes and more.

Showh Lakes Loop (Map 32/G4)

Access to this 21 km (13 mi) loop is off Cougar Mountain Road/Sixteen Mile Creek Forest Service Road, just north of Whistler. This route has a few off shoots to explore and can create a nice little loop on the west side of Cougar Mountain and up to Showh Lake if you take the north turn off about 4 km in.

Stave Lake West Riding Area (Maps 3, 13)

Entrance to Stave Lake is off Burma Road at the Stave Falls Hydro Dam. There is a gravel parking lot and a boat launch at the south end of the lake, but to hit the ATV trails you will want to head north down the Florence Lake Forest Service Road. There are many trails to explore and some fine loop rides to be found. These routes range from beginner to advanced, depending on where you go. This area is muddy in the summer and snowy in the winter, which makes for some fun riding (winch recommended!). The Stave Lake area can get very busy on the weekends so watch out for other riders and vehicles on the main roads.

Stave Lake East Riding Area (Maps 3, 13)

Found at the far north end of Sylvester Road in Mission this side of the lake does not have mud flats but does have some steep trails and rocky sections. There are lots of old trails and shelf roads and you can even find your way to the Hemlock Valley. Please note that although it was once quite common to ride in Davis Lake Provincial Park, riding there is currently not permitted.

Tamihi Riding Area (Map 4/E6)

This popular location is found just past the first bridge over the Chilliwack River near the Tamihi Creek Recreation Site. The Tamihi Staging Area is new and improved and includes a kids riding area, outhouses, picnic tables and access to many trails and old roads. Some of the more popular routes to follow include the Liumchen Lake or Liumchen East Forest Service Roads that switchback their way up to Church Mountain for fantastic views over the Chilliwack River Valley. The Tamihi Creek Forest Service Road is also a nice ride.

Theodosia Inlet Route (Map 18/E2–29/A5)

North of Powell River riders can explore the Theodosia Inlet, including Olsen Lake, Olsen Landing and a waterfall. The route is about 95 km (59 mi) long and starts off the Southview Road, directly off the Sunshine Coast Highway about 15 km north of town.

Vedder Mountain Trails (Map 4/B6)

With over 200 km (125 mi) of varied trails, including 70 named trails, this area offers excellent variety for motorized users, hikers, bikers and equestrian riders. Access is found off Parmenter Road on the west side of Cultus Lake. The main route follows the forest service road 21.5 km (13 mi) around the ridge, but there are several side trails to explore that offer more challenging riding. Caution must be exercised in this area due to the many narrow side hills, switchbacks and tight trails combined with heavy rain and occasional snow cover.

Weaver Lake Area (Map 14/E7–B6)

Accessed off the Weaver Forest Service Road, this area offers some good rocky steps to climb and some steep hills. This area includes homemade bridges to cross and plenty of washouts. With routes leading behind the Hemlock Valley Ski Resort, it is possible to link to the West Harrison Lake and Chehalis Lake areas. There are multiple camping spots in the region, including the main staging area at Grace Lake.

West Harrison Riding Area (Map 4/E1–25/C7)

Just north of the Lougheed Highway (Hwy 7) at Harrison Mills are the Chehalis River and Grace Lake Recreation Sites. Both rec sites have great staging areas. It is possible to follow the Sts'ailes (formerly Harrison West) Forest Service Road all the way to Mount Currie, passing by First Nations villages, logging camps, recreation sites and viewpoints over the big lake. The best thing to do is to set up a basecamp and explore from there. Popular destinations en route include Hale Creek, Sunrise Lake, Twenty Mile Bay and the area around the 61 km (38 mi) mark of the deteriorating main road. The Sts'ailes Forest Service Road is an active logging area, so be careful.

ATV [OHV] ADVENTURES

ATV Safety Tips

ATVing is a blast, whether you are covering serious distance in the backcountry or just out for a fun rip on the trails. In order to keep your ride fun and carefree, you need to be prepared and take all necessary precautions. The following are some things to consider before heading out.

EQUIPMENT

Helmet
This is the most basic and most important piece of equipment for ATVing. ATVs are prone to tipping, hazards can come from overhead or below and it is pretty easy to get flung off of your ride. Wearing a proper full-face helmet is always the right choice.

Gloves
Good riding gloves will protect your hands from flying gravel and rocks, branches, and wear and callouses. They also absorb a lot of vibration from your ATV, making your ride a lot more comfortable.

Boots
A good pair of riding boots will give you crucial grip and support, absorb shock, and protect your feet and legs in a crash. They will also absorb the heat that comes off the motor while you ride.

Goggles
Flying debris is inevitable while ATVing, and bugs and branches are a constant threat to your eyes. Proper riding goggles that fit around your helmet are the best way to keep your eyes protected and keep you moving on the right track.

Chest Protector
A chest protector will shield you from large debris and stationary objects, and will give you crucial protection in case you roll over and your ATV lands on top of you.

Long Sleeves
A long sleeved shirt and pants will protect you from scrapes, cuts and abrasion, and shield you from the elements.

ETIQUETTE

Look Around
If you are riding near a campground or public space, be aware of dust and noise. Slow down and travel through public areas quietly.

Trails
Only ride your ATV on designated ATV or multi-use trails. ATVs can leave a serious impact on the environment, and it is your responsibility to ensure the viability of future ATV areas by complying with all rules and regulations. Be a good steward for the sport and keep away from sensitive areas, private property, and non-ATV-friendly trails.

Yielding
Yield to other ATVers by pulling over to the right and letting them pass, whether they are approaching head-on or from behind. If you are the one passing, do not pressure the other rider by riding too close. Extra care must be taken when meeting a horse on the trail — pull over, get off the ATV, and take off your helmet so the horse can recognize you as a person. Additionally, warn the horseback rider if there are other ATVers in your group. If you encounter hikers or mountain bikers, stop and allow them to pass you to avoid spraying them with mud and debris.

GENERAL SAFETY

▶ **Take a Course**
Taking a basic ATV safety course is the best way to get acquainted with safe riding techniques. A good course will also teach you about local laws and regulations surrounding ATV use.

▶ **Inspect Your Ride**
Always check tire pressure, fuel level, oil level, chain slack and lube and tightness of all nuts and bolts before going out riding.

▶ **Be Alert**
ATV trails do not have a uniform surface and are not as well kept as normal roads, so keep a constant eye out for hazards.

▶ **Check the Weather**
Rain and wind can be serious hazards while ATVing, so check the forecast and avoid riding in inclement conditions.

▶ **Slow Brake**
Avoid sudden braking. You could be flung forward off your ATV.

▶ **Hills**
Avoid sudden braking or acceleration when travelling up or down a hill. Keep your weight toward the front while ascending, and towards the back when heading downhill.

▶ **Passengers**
Never carry a passenger on a single ATV.

▶ **Tell a Friend**
Let a responsible party know where you are going riding and when you expect to be back, so they can take the appropriate action if you get into trouble.

▶ **Turning**
When turning the ATV, decrease your speed and shift your body weight towards the inside of your turn. Always make turns as wide as possible.

▶ **Keep it Off-Road**
ATVs can be very dangerous when riding on concrete, as they tip very easily. Keep any travel on solid surfaces to a minimum.

▶ **Stay Sober**
Never operate an ATV under the influence of alcohol or drugs.

SNOWMOBILE ADVENTURES

Southwestern BC has plenty of places for snowmobilers to play in the snow. The sledding areas in this region encompass a wide variety of terrains that range from easy snow covered roads and groomed trails to challenging hillside routes climbing to wide open glaciers.

For most of the population of the Vancouver Coast snowmobiling may seem to be a foreign concept, but outside of the Fraser Valley snowmobiling is quite popular. In fact, places like Pemberton and Gold Bridge have a well-deserved reputation for sledding fun.

Families and beginners can travel along established routes through forests and open fields, while advanced sledders will revel in steep and remote riding areas. Snowfall is generous in many regions of this part of the province, resulting in lots of powder and a long season. Generally, the season lasts from December to April in most areas.

With beautiful vistas, historical destinations, abundant wildlife and never a dull kilometre, there are plenty of reasons to explore this area. In particular the trails around the community of Gold Bridge combine industrial history with natural beauty. Not to be outdone, there are several good riding areas a short drive from Whistler and Pemberton on the Sea to Sky Highway (Hwy 99) offering equally rugged and beautiful terrain.

As in most popular winter recreation regions of British Columbia, representatives of the snowmobile community have worked for years with the outdoor recreation sectors of government to reach balanced recreation land use agreements. Remember, it is your responsibility to be familiar with the winter activities allowed in various parts of the area before you visit. Please obey and respect closed areas as every snowmobile rider must be an ambassador for the sport. Also give careful consideration to your effect on the trails, the environment and on other recreationists.

BC has more than 70 local snowmobile clubs that maintain extensive trail networks and sledding areas throughout the province. Visitors new to an area can find knowledgeable guides or club members in many snowmobile-friendly communities throughout the province. For more detailed season and route information contact the BC Snowmobile Federation at 1-877-537-8716 or www.bcsf.org or www.abcsnow.ca.

Before heading out pay careful attention to the conditions out there. The website www.avalanche.ca/sled is a good starting point. Additionally, always check the weather forecast, ice and/or snow conditions and carry the necessary safety equipment along with the knowledge on how to use it.

Allen Creek Snowmobile Trails (Map 54/C1)

Located 13 km south of Clinton or 26 km north of Cache Creek, access is just off Highway 97 near the Carquile Rest Area. Experienced snowmobilers can ride the popular route into a vast alpine area which opens up to large bowls and untouched areas. Riders must use caution and be fully prepared for emergency situations as this is a remote area.

Brandywine Mountain Snowmobile Area (Map 32/B5)

Located just 10 minutes south of Whistler, this is the most popular snowmobile destination in the region. The Brandywine Bowl is a great starting point for all levels of rider as there are groomed trails and some loops throughout the bowl. The main trail is about 40 km (25 mi) long. For a greater challenge, check out the north side of the bowl, where tougher terrain and some deep alpine riding can be found. You can also find access to the Pemberton Icefield and the Powder Mountain area, as well as the Around the World Trail. South of Whistler look for signs to the Callaghan Valley, drive past the transfer station to the booth and parking area. Passes can be purchased at the Brandywine Trailhead booth starting as early as late November (depending on snow levels). In total there are three spacious parking lots located on the Brandywine Forest Service Road.

Avalanche Alley (Map 32/A5)

From the fork along the main access trail at km 5 head straight through Avalanche Alley. When the groomed trail ends, the alley starts and from this point the trail can get pretty challenging. The reward is access to some incredible open terrain and the trail eventually wraps around to Grizzly Lake. Some side hilling may be required in the area where large avalanches come down in the spring.

Brandywine Bowl (Map 32/B5)

Access the main parking lot off the Sea to Sky Highway (Hwy 99) and follow the well-groomed trail until a fork in the road around km 5. Take the trail to the right to access the Brandywine Bowl. The main area here is Brandywine Meadows, which is one of the more popular destinations. From the meadows you can take the S Chute or the Gauntlet to access Grizzly Lake and the Ice Cap. Alternatively you can access Grizzly Lake via an easier hill climb at the Chocolate Bowl, although this route should be avoided when avalanche danger is high as it passes through Avalanche Alley. You can also access some fun trails that run through the trees, such as the Metal Dome Trail.

Brohm Ridge (Map 22/D4)

Found 10 minutes north of Squamish, Brohm Ridge sits at the rim of an ancient volcano about 1,615 metres (5,300 ft) above sea level. The ridge offers a wide variety of terrain; there are large bowls for hill climbing, challenging creek and treed routes, breathtaking peaks, endless powder and amazing meadows with groomed trails for novice riders and children. Although snowmobilers are not allowed into Garibaldi Provincial Park, this ridge just outside the park is a good approximation of the terrain and scenery inside the boundaries. Due to the close location to Squamish this can be a busy area. There is a proposal to develop the area into an all season resort which could displace the club and public from riding here. However, the Black Tusk Snowmobile Club is working hard to keep things as they are. A fee is required to ride here.

Callaghan Country Wilderness Area (Map 32/C4)

Located about 90 minutes north of Vancouver or 15 minutes from Whistler, the Callaghan Country Wilderness Area offers powdered mountain bowls and convenient access to a full range of amenities and experiences. Snowmobiles are not allowed in the Callaghan Lake Provincial Park, however, there are trails to a series of bowls outside the park and on to the Pemberton Icefield. Access is near the Alexander Falls Recreation Site off Callaghan Valley Road.

Camelsfoot Range Trails (Map 53/C3–A1)

Another in a series of long ridges stretching north from the Bridge River, the Camelsfoot Range is a semi-arid range. Most of the range is covered in open pine forest, but there are some alpine areas, especially north of Hogsback Mountain. The southern part of the range is more mountainous with decent access from the road systems leading west from the West Pavilion Forest Service Road.

Chance Creek Snowmobile Area (Map 22/B2–32/B5)

This difficult route follows the Chance Creek Forest Service Road in behind Tricouni Peak to the Seagram Creek area. The first section is mostly road riding and is not too difficult. The difficult part is heading up Roe Creek, past Mount Fee to connect up with the Brandywine Mountain Area. To access this area, turn off the Sea to Sky Highway (Hwy 99) onto Chance Creek Forest Service Road about 1 km south of Garibaldi Lake turn-off. Chance Creek and Roe Creek Forest Service Roads are also used for access to snowcat skiing in winter, so expect to see some snowcat traffic on the main road.

Chipmunk Creek Area (Map 5/A5)

This area see a lot of use during the summer months as a dirt biking/ATV destination, and snowmobilers take over once the snow hits. The Chilliwack Snowmobile Club looks after a good combination of backroads and trails in the area. Access Chipmunk Creek at the 26.8 km (16.6 mi) mark down the Chilliwack Lake Road. Turn left after the bridge on Foley Lake Road and look for Chipmunk Creek on your right.

Coquihalla Summit Snowmobile Area (Map 16/G1–17/D3; 27/G7)

There are endless opportunities for snowmobiling in the Coquihalla Summit region between Highway 5 and Tulameen. Maintained by the Coquihalla Summit Snowmobile Club, access is found at the Britton Creek Rest Area off the Coquihalla Highway (Hwy 5). Park at the lot 200 metres down the Tulameen Forest Service Road. There is access to several different riding areas that offer varying terrain for beginners and experts alike. The club grooms over 60 km (37 mi) of trails to make for easy access to the alpine. The Henning alpine is 6 km (3.7 mi) from the parking lot and the 10-K alpine is 15 km (9 mi) in. Some trails also follow unplowed forest service roads southeast from the lakes and can be easily ridden all the way to Tulameen and beyond. The Coquihalla Lake Lodge is found right next to the trailhead, while the club also has two cabins in the alpine stocked with firewood. The parking lot has lots of room for any size rig, as well as a loading dock and a heated changing room. There is a fee to ride here.

10-K Snowmobile Trails (Map 16/G1–27/G7)

The Coquihalla Summit and the 10-K Snowmobile Trails are both found at the Britton Creek Rest Area off the Coquihalla Highway (Hwy 5). The 10-K riding area is for advanced riders only, as there are many ridges and a few nice but challenging bowls found about 15 km (9 mi) from the trailhead. There is also a cabin in the area. Access this area by keeping south on the Tulameen Forest Service Road to where the Britton Creek FSR branches off, and heading further south from there.

Cypress Bowl (Map 11/B6–B7)

Although Cypress bowl is best known as a ski area in winter, there are a trio of trails, totalling over 15 km (9 mi), for snowmobilers. The riding area is below the ski area, so when ski conditions are good on top, it does not necessarily mean good riding below. A parking area can be found at the end of the Cypress Parkway near the chairlifts.

Contact the BC Snowmobile Federation at 1-877-537-8716 or www.bcsf.org or www.abcsnow.ca for updates and current route information.

Gold Bridge Area Trails (Map 51)

Offering seemingly endless riding, amazing mountain and lake views and relatively few riders, the trails in this area are too numerous to list. The Hurley River Forest Service Road, Lone Goat and Slim Creek Roads are groomed monthly by the Bridge River Valley Snowmobile Club (BRV). The East Hurley Forest Service Road and other backroads around Bralorne are groomed by the Mineshaft Pub, and the Hurley from Pemberton to Hope Creek is groomed by Backcountry Snowcats. These are just some of the places to start. Please help support the local clubs by purchasing a membership at the Mineshaft Pub, Morrow Chalets or Gold Bridge Hotel.

Bralorne Area (Map 51/B5)

The Bralorne area can be accessed from Lillooet or by sled from the Hurley Pass, just north of Whistler. You can unload your sled in Bralorne and reach most trails directly from town, while the Backcountry Snowcats keep the Hurley groomed for easy access to Bralorne from Pemberton. In addition, the Bridge River Valley Snowmobile Club grooms and maintains the East Hurley, Kingdom Lake and Noel Forest Service Roads. The Kingdom Lake Road allows for easy riding past the small lakes in the area and over to the old Pioneer Mine. Those looking for a greater challenge can find it at Sunshine Mountain.

Gun Lake Area (Map 51/A3)

Gun Lake offers family friendly riding at the north end of the lake, by the airport, along trails that that lead around the Plateau Ponds area. For more of a challenge, the Slim Creek Forest Service Road provides access to the Slim Creek Snowmobile zone and the South Chilcotin Mountains Provincial Park. The trailhead is at the Jewel Creek Bridge. Another option is to ride up the east side of Gun Lake to the top of Mount Penrose for a great view of the surrounding area.

Hope Creek Area (Map 51/F7–41/G2)

Maintained by Backcountry Snowcats, this trail system takes you beyond their 485 hectare (1,200 ac) tenure, towards Tenquille Glacier. The route mostly follows logging roads, but eventually you will need to blaze your way through the trees to find the alpine areas. Other popular areas to explore here are the Canine and Chipmunk Bowls. These bowls and high alpine meadows are accessed off the Hope Creek Road/Trail by following the side road, through the cut blocks, to the avalanche path leading into the alpine and bowl area.

Hurley River Forest Service Road (Map 41/E3–51/B4)

The Hurley River Forest Service Road is not plowed during the winter, but the Backcountry Snowcats and Bridge River Valley Snowmobile Club do groom it and maintain a parking lot on the Pemberton side. From the 4 km mark on the Upper Lillooet Forest Service Road, the road rises dramatically out of the Lillooet River Valley and climbs the pass before dropping back down to Gold Bridge. This easy 50 km (31 mi) route has always been used to access some of BC's best snowmobiling areas, including Lone Goat, Face Mountain, Hope Creek, Green Mountain and Noel.

Knuckleheads Recreation Area (Map 19/F2)

Snowmobilers do not have many official options in the Powell River area, however there is the Knuckleheads Recreation Area off the Weyerhauser Stillwater Main road, north of Lois Lake. At about 1,645 m (5,400 ft) the ridge extends west with gently sloping terrain. There are clear-cut areas and old logging roads great for snowmobiling. There are also two cabins in the area. The sub-alpine area gets snow from the coastal snowbelt beginning in November and can be good until May, or even June on the north slope. Be wary of backcountry skiers in the area.

Lodestone Snowmobile Trails (Map 17/D3–C7)

The Lodestone Snowmobile Trails are accessed about a kilometre northeast of Blakeburn near the town of Coalmont. From here, the trails head up to Mount Jackson near Tulameen, Tanglewood Hill or over to Lodestone Lake. There is close to 100 km (60 mi) of trails in the area. Further south, a well-used side trail leads to Wells Lake.

Lone Goat Snowmobile Area (Map 50/F6–C5)

This is a sprawling area, known for alpine bowls, snow caves and light, fluffy powder, with about 115 km (70 mi) of trails to explore. The trails are best left to intermediate and expert riders, and are not safe on low visibility days. A trail starts across the bridge from the East Hurley Forest Service Road junction, which is about 17 km south of Gold Bridge. The trail follows the creek through the forest for about 15 km (9 mi) before breaking out onto a network of glaciers and ice caves. The Bridge River Snowmobile Club maintains an emergency shelter in the area.

Mount Crucil Snowmobile Area (Map 9/G2–10/A2)

North of Sechelt, the Gray Creek Forest Service Road heads up to Tetrahedron Provincial Park. About three quarters of the way to the park, an old road leads southeast towards the Mount Crucil area. This area usually offers the best and most consistent riding on the Sunshine Coast. While it is not huge, it is the Sunshine Coast Snowseekers main riding area, and boasts a new cabin. There are lakes, hill climbs, tree riding and road riding and only a small amount of regular users.

Mount Henning Area (Map 16/G1–27/G7)

Access to the Coquihalla Summit Snowmobile Club Trails, including Mount Henning, are off the Coquihalla Highway (Hwy 5) at the Britton Creek Rest Area. There are fees to ride the Coquihalla Summit Snowmobile Trails, whereas the Timberline Cruisers Snowmobile Club Trails have no fees. The Timberline Trails link directly to Tulameen via Riddell Creek Forest Service Road. There are no less than 50 km (30 mi) of trails around Mount Henning plus a 7.5 km (4.6 mi) trail that links this system with the 55 km (34 mi) of trails around Thynne Mountain. This extensive series of snowmobile trails provides a good mix of moderate to challenging riding along with some amazing scenery.

> Note that when travelling in the backcountry, avalanches are always a danger. Visit www.avalanche.ca for current conditions, and be prepared with both avalanche knowledge and safety equipment to help make your visit to the mountains safe.

Noel Creek Snowmobile Area (Map 50/G6–51/B6)

In Upper Noel Creek you will find a rolling alpine country with a beautiful 46 metre (150 ft) high glacier. This terrain is recommended for intermediate and advanced riders. In all, there are about 80 km (50 mi) of trails to explore. An easier loop takes you south from Bralorne around Mount Noel and over to the Hurley River Forest Service Road before returning on the East Hurley. This loop follows mostly ungroomed logging roads except for the section around the Mount Noel pass. The Noel Forest Service Road is also groomed for easy access to Pemberton and Bralorne.

North Air Mine/Sproatt Mountain Snowmobile Area (Map 32/D5)

This is a small, but fun area around the North Air Mine Road. It is only about 10 km (6 mi) from the road to Sproatt Mountain, which provides a fabulous introduction to backcountry sledding. This location is ideal for first time snowmobilers and families.

Follow wide, winding trails to an open play area and experience the perfect mix of easy riding and spectacular scenery. Access is found just before the Callaghan Valley at the U-Turn area, where there is a short rough road up to the parking area. The abandoned mine here has become a surreal little world of colourful murals on the abandoned cement foundations. Since there are no fees to ride here and only a small parking area, it is best to arrive early. Be careful not to enter the watershed area for Whistler while keeping an eye out for those long untracked lines in the rolling alpine terrain.

Pavilion Mountain Trail (Map 53/F1)

A short ride up to the top of Pavilion Mountain can be found north off Highway 99 on Pavilion-Clinton Road. There are a number of viewpoints along the 10 km (6 mi) ride to the microwave tower at the summit. Views project out in all directions and include the Marble Range to the north, Clear Range to the south, Coast Mountains to west and Dunn Peak/Wells Gray to east and northeast.

Pemberton Icefield (Maps 31, 32, 40, 41)

The Icefield offers vast, wide open, treeless riding with spectacular views of the Coast Mountains and beyond. Stretching over 300 km2 (185 mi2) and boasting of an average snowfall of 12 metres (39 ft), the riding can be amazing here. However, riders should be experienced and avoid low visibility days. Good snow conditions are usually found between December and April, but riding can last well into summer. The main access point can be found at the Rutherford Creek Bridge off the Sea to Sky Highway (Hwy 99), 6 km south of Pemberton. Other, more challenging, access points are found just south of Whistler via the Brandywine Mountain or Callaghan Lake systems. Access from the north from the Meager Creek area has been cut off by the washed out bridge over the Lillooet River.

SNOWMOBILE ADVENTURES

Powder Mountain Icefield (Map 32/A5)

This large icefield sits above Grizzly Lake, which is accessed from the Brandywine Mountain trailhead via Brandywine Bowl or Avalanche Alley. From the lake it is a simple loop to access the Ice Cap, which is a huge area with lots of natural halfpipes and open zones to play around in. Follow the snowmobile trails away from the lake and continue on the glacier. An easy grade will take you to the summit, but watch for crevices and ice caves.

Rutherford Snowmobile Trail (Map 33/A2–32/D1)

Probably the best way to access the Pemberton Icefields, this 23 km (14 mi) trail follows the Rutherford Creek Valley and is groomed regularly. There is a staging area near the Rutherford Creek Bridge, and from here it is a 16 km (10 mi) ride to the alpine. The access to and from the ice cap allows a circuit route and long distance route via the Rutherford and Meager Creek Valleys. Trail use can be heavy at times but the season does run into early summer depending on snow conditions.

> When riding in a group, safety is a shared responsibility. Make sure your riding companions are experienced and knowledgeable

Shulaps Range Trails (Map 51/E1–52/E3)

The Shulaps Range is a high narrow range of mountains running northwest between the Yalakom River and Carpenter Lake. Stretching almost 60 km (37 mi) long and 8 km (5 mi) wide, this area is rich in mining history. The dry, windblown mountains can be scarce of snow, but there are some nice bowls for snowmobilers to play in. Popular access points include the steep Jim Creek Road near Marshall Lake, the easier La Rochelle Creek or the Verbenkov Forest Service Road from the Yalakom Recreation Site or from the Lake la Mare Recreation Site.

Slim Creek Snowmobile Area (Map 50/A2–51/A3)

Found near Gold Bridge to the west of Gun Lake, Slim Creek offers access to the high alpine, climbing as high as 2,700 metres (9,000 ft). Bring extra gas as you can easily cover up to 200 km (125 mi) or more in a day. Be wary, this is an area for experienced riders only. It is also a terrible place to be in a snowstorm since it is easy to get lost in the wide open terrain, especially if you cannot follow your tracks back. From the north end of Gun Lake, 30 km (19 mi) of road riding will get you to the trailhead with a sign-in box. The bridge over Slim Creek is blocked but ATVs and snowmobiles can still pass. From here, a trail follows Slim Creek for another 15 km (9 mi) or so until you get to the glaciers of the Lillooet Icefield. Make sure you have good visibility to travel the glaciers.

Stave Lake Area (Map 3/C1)

One of the closest riding areas to Greater Vancouver, this is a popular destination. The terrain is limited for sledding, but there is a cabin and room to spend a day exploring. Most of the riding follows the roads up the Kearsley Creek drainage and southern slopes of Mount Crickmer. Snow is typically found at the 400 metre (1,300 ft) level from November through May. Access is found off of the Florence Lake Forest Service Road at the end of Burma Road.

Sunshine Coast Snowmobiling (Maps 9, 10, 20)

Although the Sunshine Coast is better known for its temperate winters than mecca snowfalls, there are a few areas that locals can get out and play in. Notably, the mountainous terrain between Sechelt Inlet and Gibsons offers the best snow conditions and a few popular areas to ride. The Sunshine Coast Snowseekers operate a groomer and maintain some trails in the Sechelt area. Mount Crucil is the biggest area and offers a blend of lakes, hill climbs, tree riding and road riding. Other popular areas include Dakota Ridge, Gray Creek West and Spipiyus Park along the Caren Range which stretches between Sechelt inlet and the Georgia Strait, offering stunning ocean views. The Dakota Ridge Winter Recreation Area, near Wilson Creek, has sledding trails

that are named and marked. The Sunshine Coast Regional District maintains the road to the Dakota Ridge Trail system, however a four-wheel drive vehicle with chains may still be necessary.

Dakota Ridge Area (Map 10/B4)

This popular area can be a bit challenging to get to in winter but offers a great winter playground, as there is no shortage of places to explore. It offers one of the most reliable locations for snow in the area and has great views over the Georgia Strait, the North Shore, Vancouver Island and Mount Baker. To get here follow Field Road north, turn right on the Wilson Creek Forest Service Road and follow the signs for approximately 14 km to Dakota Ridge. The Snowseekers Snowmobile Club provides a single trail, passing through the middle of the ski trail system, to access the trails in the backcountry. Snowmobilers are asked to stay off the cross-country and snowshoe trails.

Gray Creek Area (Map 9/F3–10/A2)

Snowmobilers can drive up the Gray Creek Forest Service Road to the Tetrahedron Provincial Park parking lot. Snowmobiles are not allowed in the park itself, but heading left takes riders away from the park, along the 600 Road and into some good riding that skirts the edge of the park. If the snow is not good here, check out the Mount Crucil area to the south.

Spipiyus Provincial Park (Map 9/C1–20/C7)

Located just before Halfmoon Bay, approximately 11 km north of Sechelt, turn north off Highway 101 onto Trout Lake Road to reach this park. While most provincial parks do not allow snowmobilers, they are allowed on the logging roads here. It is possible to make a nice loop north towards Mount Hallowell and back. It is not a long ride, and remember, you are not allowed off the road. Running along the Caren Range provides views of the islands and fjords of Pender Harbour, the Strait of Georgia and Vancouver Island.

Taylor Basin (Map 51/A1)

Taylor Basin is an excellent alpine area to play in. In addition to a warming cabin at the 2,000 metre (6,600 ft) level, there are two mountain slopes that climb up to 2,460 metres (8,000 ft) in elevation. This area is open to all skill levels, but the higher slopes are best left to intermediate and expert riders. Access starts 5 km north past the Tyax Lodge, on Tyaughton Lake Forest Service Road. There is a fork at which you should take the western most turn. From the cabin you can explore the countless peaks and ridges throughout the valley. Expect to put on up to 100 km (60 mi) as you play around on these open slopes.

Thynne Mountain Trails (Map 27/G6)

Part of the Merritt Snowmobile Club, the staging area for the Thynne Mountain Trails is found near Brookmere, where the Thynne Mountain Forest Service Road starts. There are 55 km (34 mi) of trails to explore here, and the majority of them are groomed and signed. The club also maintains two shelters known as the Tin Shed and Andy's Lake Emergency Shelter. Andy's Lake Shelter is on the north shore of Andy's Lake. All fees go directly to the maintenance of these shelters and trails.

Upper Lillooet River Area (Map 41/F3–49/E7)

When the snow falls and the roads remain unplowed, there are seemingly endless places to ride here. In particular, the 45 km (28 mi) trip along the Upper Lillooet Forest Service Road north of Pemberton is a popular route for beginners. There are a number of alternate routes or side roads in this area for snowmobilers to explore. Unfortunately, one of the most popular was the trip to the Meager Creek Hot Springs, but the bridge over the Lillooet River was washed out in 2010 and there are no plans to repair this given the high risk of landslides and avalanches in that area. Riders looking for hot springs to soak in are better off looking for the Keyhole Falls Hot Springs further up the Lillooet River Valley. Closer to the start of the forest road, the Hurley River Forest Service Road also provides access to many good riding areas. The Hurley is also a very scenic road that makes a fine ride itself.

Safety Tips

Snowmobiling allows you to cover a lot of ground and cross some difficult terrain, but this increased mobility comes with increased dangers. It is important to exercise caution while snowmobiling in order to keep things fun. Here are some pointers to keep in mind while sledding.

Avalanche Safety

First Thing
The number one way to prevent avalanche deaths is by taking proper safety courses and carrying the right gear (beacon, shovel, and probe). Always keep your safety gear on your person and not on your sled, in case you get separated from it.

Wait Your Turn
Always ride a slope (in any direction) one person at a time. Wait until the person on the slope is completely clear of it to proceed.

Parking
Never park at the bottom of a steep slope. Park to the sides of the slope with snowmobiles side by side (never single file) and pointed away from the slope.

Lending a Hand
Never go up a steep slope on your sled to help someone who has become stuck. Adding the weight of you and your snowmobile to the snow could trigger an avalanche.

Terrain Traps
Avoid gullies, creek beds and slopes that end in depressions. These pose a high probability for deep burial.

Stay on the Scene
In the event of an avalanche, do not leave to get help. You only have around 15 minutes to get the buried person out, so you have to perform the rescue. This is why proper training and gear is essential.

Group Riding Safety

Single File
Always ride single file on trails, in case you meet oncoming traffic or encounter an unexpected obstacle.

Three Seconds Rule
When following another snowmobiler, mark an object that they pass and count the time it takes you to reach it. If it is under three seconds, you are following too close.

Open Areas
When travelling side by side in the open, always leave plenty of side-to-side room in case your fellow sledders need to maneuver around unexpected obstacles.

Ice Crossings
Never ride across ice single file. If the first rider falls into the ice, you may not have enough time to avoid following them into the same hole.

BEFORE YOU GO OUT
▶ Check the weather forecast and trail conditions before you go out. In some areas, you may need to assess whether there is danger of an avalanche.

▶ Let a responsible party know where you are going riding and when you expect to be back, so they can take the appropriate action if you get into trouble.

▶ It's helpful to know basic first aid including the signs of hypothermia and what to do if it happens.

HAVE THE RIGHT EQUIPMENT
▶ Wear well-insulated protective clothing including goggles, waterproof snowmobile suits and gloves, and rubber-bottomed boots.

▶ All drivers and passengers should wear helmets approved for snowmobiles (DOT or similar approved – not a bicycle helmet).

▶ Snowmobiles should have brightly coloured antenna flags mounted on rods that are 1.2 to 2.4 metres long located on the back of the snowmobile. This is especially important if you're driving in a hilly area so that others can see you.

▶ Carry a first-aid kit, an emergency tool kit (with spark plugs, and drive and fan belts), an extra key, and a survival kit that includes flares. A cellular phone is helpful if you're in an area with service.

DRIVE SAFELY
▶ Beginners should stick to groomed trails and drive during the day.

▶ Travel at safe speeds, especially on unfamiliar or rugged terrain where you might run into hazards you can't see, such as barbed wire or overhanging trees.

▶ Keep the headlights and tail lights on at all times to improve the visibility of your snowmobile to other vehicle operators.

▶ Travel in groups of two or more, and only on designated, marked trails away from roads, waterways, railroads and pedestrians. Do not carry more than one passenger.

▶ Don't pull people on saucers, skis, tubes, or toboggans behind a snowmobile.

▶ Never drink alcohol or use drugs before or while you're operating a snowmobile.

WILDLIFE ADVENTURES

One of the greatest things about being in the wilderness is spotting the local residents in their natural environments. Wildlife watching has always been a popular pursuit, but in the last few decades, the sub-genre of bird watching has gone from the fringe to the mainstream — birdwatchers used to be portrayed in movies as a poorly dressed guys in coke-bottle glasses and ties stumbling about the bushes with overly large pairs of binoculars.

Avid birdwatchers are always looking for new and unusual species to add to their lists, and Southwestern BC is a great place to watch birds. In fact, the internationally famous George C. Reifel Bird Sanctuary is one of the best birding locations in the province, if not the country.

Some wildlife is easy to spot. Salmon viewing, for instance, is a matter of getting down to the right stream at the right time. On the other hand, many birds and animals tend to flee when they hear, see or smell humans. In order to improve your chances of spotting these more elusive creatures, wear natural colours and unscented lotions. Bring along binoculars or scopes so you can observe from a distance and move slowly but steadily. Keep pets on a leash, or better yet, leave them at home, as they will only decrease your chances of spotting wildlife. Early mornings and late evenings are usually the best time to see most birds and animals.

Never approach an animal directly and, for heaven's sake, do not feed wild animals. Animals can become conditioned to handouts, which may put both of you in harm's way. Rather, figure out what natural foods they prefer and situate yourself near where these animals will feed.

This list is certainly far from complete. Black bear are a common site around the berry farms near Minnehkada in fall, for instance, and there are many other rivers and streams where eagles congregate in fall besides the Squamish. It is, however, a fairly good start. Not all wildlife watching sites are created equal. Some of the sites listed cater to birders; others are good places to see salmon spawning. Most wildlife watching is seasonal. Eagles congregate in Squamish in winter, while spring is the time to visit the Reifel Bird Sanctuary. As you discover the joys of watching wildlife, you will learn the rhythms of the seasons.

Anne Murray's series of books are valuable resources for wildlife watching. Visit natureguidesbc.com for more information on those.

WILDLIFE ADVENTURES

Agassiz Farmlands (Map 4/G2–5/A2)
The farmlands around Agassiz are wintering grounds for waterfowl. During the winter months, this area is home to trumpeter and tundra swans, while large flocks of ducks may be seen on flooded fields. Maria Slough, although surrounded by privately owned land, is an excellent place to see spawning salmon and trumpeter and tundra swans from the water.

Alouette River Dykes (Map 2/E2)
Great blue heron and hawks are common throughout the year, while in winter there are bald eagles and occasionally trumpeter swans. A great blue heronry is located on private property across the Alouette River from a small parking lot off 210th Street, where the road turns right. The best viewing time is from March to late July. Bring binoculars.

Apodaca Marine Park (Map 10/G7)
Apodaca is an 8 hectare (20 ac) marine park located on the eastern shore of Bowen Island. The park protects the shoreline, which consists of scenic cliffs and rocky knolls, with the offshore waters providing habitat for marine birds and mammals. Species include harbour seals, killer whales and marbled murrelets. Intertidal species include ochre starfish, pacific octopus and rockfish. Some land dwelling species include black-tailed deer and a variety of birds.

Bell-Irving Hatchery (Map 3/G3)
Located in Kanaka Creek Regional Park, this hatchery is open to visitors year-round. There are ponds, tanks and troughs which contain Coho and chum; the latter are released with great fanfare in late April every year. There are trails along the creek itself where visitors can watch spawning salmon in the fall.

Birkenhead Lake Provincial Park (Map 42/B1–D3)
Nestled in the Coast Mountains, Birkenhead Provincial Park is home to Phelix Creek. In September and October watch for spawning kokanee in the Sockeye Creek watershed. During the rest of the year, spotted owl, mountain goats, bobcat, deer and even grizzly and black bear can be seen on occasion.

Bishop River Provincial Park (Map 49/C2)
Accessible only by boat or helicopter, this large remote park provides habitat for grizzly bear, mountain goat and wolverine.

Blue Earth Lake Provincial Park (Map 45/D2)
Located north of Spences Bridge off Venables Valley Road, Blue Earth Lake Park is located in a deep valley and offers many wildlife viewing opportunities, including chances to see song birds and waterfowl. Spawning trout may also be seen in the shallow channel between the lakes in early summer.

Boundary Bay Regional Park (Map 1/E7)
Boundary Bay is an area of international significance to migrating and wintering birds. There are several trails, a boardwalk and two viewing structures located in the park. Many bird species nest on the ground in the grassland and sandy areas, so please stay on the designated trails. Crescent Beach is home to the Birds on the Bay display from late January to May.

Brackendale Eagles Provincial Park (Map 22/C6)
The Squamish River hosts thousands of bald eagles every winter. These majestic birds can be seen feasting on the remains of spawning chum salmon from late November to January. The area on the west side of the Squamish River has been designated as special eagle habitat by BC Parks. Other wildlife species in the park include black bear, bobcat, cougar, coyote, Columbian black-tailed deer, gray wolf and mink. Smaller mammals include the Northern flying-squirrel, the snowshoe hare, and the yellow-pine chipmunk. Reptiles and amphibians in the park include three species of garter snake, the tailed frog and the northwestern salamander. Visitors will also discover about 148 bird species that use the park at various times throughout the year.

Burnaby Lake Regional Park (Map 1/G2)
Located in the heart of Burnaby, this park is an oasis for wildlife and humans alike. The marshy edges of the lake are an important feeding and nesting habitat for waterfowl, shorebirds and small mammals. Species include beaver, bald eagles, belted kingfishers, great blue herons, osprey and rare birds such as the small green-backed heron.

Callaghan Lake Provincial Park (Map 32/B3)
Callaghan Lake is a high mountain lake at the end of a rough two-wheel drive road. It is home to a variety of wildlife, such as bobcat, cougar, coyote, mink, squirrel and weasel. Other large mammal species include black bear, black-tailed deer, grizzly bear, moose, mountain goat, wolf and wolverine.

Capilano River Hatchery (Map 11/D7)
The Capilano River Hatchery is located just below Cleveland Dam in North Vancouver. The hatchery is open every day, but the hours of operation change throughout the year. The best viewing time is October through November to see returning adult salmon and March to May to see juveniles.

Cascade Recreation Area (Maps 6, 16, 17)
This large, 11,858 hectare (29,290 ac) recreation area was incorporated into E.C. Manning Provincial Park in 2013. Visitors can access the area from either the Cascade Recreation Area Parking Area or along the Whipsaw Creek Road. This pristine backcountry wilderness area has seen very little development over the years and is the seasonal home to a Rocky Mountain elk herd. Other wildlife in the park includes bear, beaver, chipmunk, cougar, coyote, deer, moose and wolf. Birders will find great blue heron, eagle, kingfisher and owl.

Chapman Creek Hatchery (Map 9/G5)
A number of fish species are reared at Chapman Creek Hatchery, including Chinook, Coho, chum and pink salmon as well as cutthroat trout. From August through December adult salmon use Chapman Creek to spawn. Pink are present in August and September, while Coho and chum are present beginning in mid-October. A viewing platform provides good views of the creek and a trail leads upstream along Chapman Creek.

Cheam Lake Wetlands Regional Park (Map 4/G3)
Located near Bridal Falls, Cheam Lake is a fine example of habitat restoration. The original lake was drained in the 1950s to mine marl, but a water control structure with a fish ladder was installed in 1992 to allow the lake to flood. Changes are occurring as the lake re-establishes and new wildlife species are beginning to visit the park. A wide variety of birds are already present. There are beaver and muskrats, and from late March through August, the park is a good place to look for butterflies.

Chehalis River Hatchery (Map 4/D2)
The Chehalis River Hatchery is responsible for rearing and for releasing a wide range of fish species, including Coho, Chinook and chum salmon as well as steelhead and cutthroat trout. The hatchery compound is open to visitors year-round and there are self-guiding interpretive signs on site. The best viewing time is November when salmon spawn in the hatchery outflow channel and in the small stream near the parking lot.

Chilliwack Lake Provincial Park (Map 5/F6)
There are good salmon viewing opportunities near where the Chilliwack River flows out of the northern end of Chilliwack Lake. October to mid-November is the best time to view pink (odd years only), sockeye and Coho salmon. In April look for steelhead trout spawning.

Chilliwack River Hatchery (Map 5/A6)
The Chilliwack River Hatchery is situated just upstream of the junction of Slesse Creek and the Chilliwack River. It is open daily from 8:00 am to 3:30 pm. A summer run of Chinook begins to arrive in August and the hatchery is busy through to December with other species of salmon returning. Steelhead trout return in March and April.

Colony Farm Regional Park (Map 2/B3)
Located along the Coquitlam River, this park provides nesting and feeding habitats for a wide range of birds, especially raptors and songbirds. The wooded areas are good places to look for woodpeckers and chickadees, while the old fields are frequented by Short Eared Owls. From Highway 7, turn south onto Colony Farm Road and continue to the parking area at the end of the road.

Copeland Islands Marine Park (Map 28/A7)
The Copeland Islands are a small chain of islands, islets and rocks off the northern corner of the Sunshine Coast. It is an excellent place to explore by kayak or canoe and is home to marine mammals like seal and sea lion as well as numerous species of waterfowl, bald eagles and the odd deer.

Coquihalla Canyon Provincial Park (Map 15/G6)
Better known for its impressive scenery and equally impressive series of old railway bridges and tunnels, the area is also a great place to watch steelhead spawning up the river. The bridges give a great perspective on the fish as they lay in deep pools of water.

Cornwall Hills Provincial Park (Map 54/E7)
To the west of Ashcroft, the Cornwall Lookout Road provides access to this 1,188 hectare (2,935 ac), undeveloped park with spectacular valley views,

meadows and rare Engelmann Spruce. The park also protects habitat for black bear, blue grouse, cougar, mule deer and a variety of upland mammal and bird species.

Cypress Provincial Park (Map 11/A7–B4)
Established in 1975, this 2,996 hectare (7,400 ac) park is made up of several types of old growth forests, some mixed second growth forests, sub-alpine wetlands, rocky bluffs and mountaintop plateaus. Black bear, cougar, coyote and deer frequent the park and may be encountered on trails and in open areas. Smaller animals include hare, squirrel and weasels and there are a variety of birds like chickadee, gray jay, grouse, hawk, owl, raven, warbler and woodpecker.

Duck Lake Protected Area (Map 19/A3)
Located east of Powell River and south of Haslam Lake, this protected area is an important nesting area for a variety of bird species. Bird watching is a popular pursuit in the 768 hectare (1,898 ac) park as it is an important nesting area for both migratory and non-migratory birds. There are a series of trails to help explore the area.

Duffey Lake Provincial Park (Map 43/C6–E4)
Located about 35 km east of Pemberton, Duffey Lake is nearly halfway to Lillooet along the Duffey Lake Road (Highway 99). The park itself is very beautiful, providing habitat for grizzly and bear, deer and mountain goat as well as great blue heron and osprey.

Fee Creek Spawning Channel (Map 42/D7)
Located about 11 km from Mount Currie along Highway 99, Fee Creek runs into the Birkenhead River. The man-made channels in this area provide important, year-round habitat to young salmon. Watch for fry darting about the channels.

Fred Antoine Provincial Park (Map 52/F4–53/B2)
Combining the Fred Creek and Antoine Creek watersheds, this Class A, 2,230 hectare (5,510 ac) park rests north of the Bridge River Road near Moha. Home to old growth Douglas fir, the area is also an important wildlife wintering range for goats and deer. California bighorn sheep, cougar, fisher, grizzly bear, peregrine falcon, rubber boa and wolf are all seen here on occasion.

A good set of binoculars or spotting scope will allow you to observe birds and animals more easily and from further distances.

Garibaldi Provincial Park (Maps 22, 23, 24, 32, 33)
Garibaldi is a big, spectacular park, containing all kinds of animals and birds. In particular, watch for Hoary Marmots and pika in or near the alpine meadows or in talus slopes. Access into Garibaldi is mainly on foot.

Gates River Spawning Channel (Map 43/A3)
The spawning channel at Gates River is an excellent place to observe spawning sockeye salmon in late summer and early fall. There is a large fish ladder that provides fish with access from Gates River into the channel. The spawning channel is located in Devine, just south of D'Arcy.

George C. Reifel Migratory Bird Sanctuary (Map 1/B5)
This sanctuary is ground zero for Lower Mainland birders. Located on Westham Island in Delta, it contains habitats important for migrating birds, including tidal saltwater mudflats, freshwater, brackish and salt marshes and upland fields. All types of birds, including raptors, shorebirds and woodpeckers are found here year-round. But during the late fall and early winter months the island comes alive with over 25,000 lesser snow geese visiting the area. Winter visitors often encounter the small Saw-Whet Owl roosting and the sanctuary provides winter shelter for many types of eagles, hawks and owls, while spring is the perfect time to view eagles, hawks and seals. The sanctuary is open from 9:00 am to 4:00 pm daily. Additional details can be found on their website at www.reifelbirdsanctuary.com.

Golden Ears Provincial Park (Maps 2, 3, 12, 13, 23, 24)
Golden Ears is another big, spectacular park that is home to all sorts of birds and mammals. From chipmunks to black bear and cougars to cowbirds and ospreys, you never know what you may encounter next. In the high country, you may even see mountain goats on the rocky mountain cliffs.

Grant Narrows Regional Park (Map 12/F7)
Grant Narrows Park has interesting ecological areas including low-lying wetlands. There are viewing platforms and trails from which to see plenty of shorebirds and waterfowl, including the sandhill crane, along with muskrat and other small mammals.

Great Blue Heron Nature Reserve (Map 4/B5)
Located in the Wet Bridge training area of the old Chilliwack Armed Forces Base, the Great Blue Heron Nature Reserve is one of the few nesting sites for herons in the Lower Mainland. Look for the colony nests west of the parking area and along the dyke off Sinclair Road. Things start to happen here in March, when adults begin claiming nests.

Harrison Bay/Chehalis Flats (Map 4/C2)
In winter, bald eagles hang out around the Chehalis Flats in great numbers (some years, there are over 1,000 eagles here). The eagles arrive in November and stay until January, attracted by dead and dying spawning salmon. As an added bonus, this is also a winter feeding ground for trumpeter swans.

Hayward Lake Reservoir (Map 3/C3)
While wildlife can be seen throughout the Hayward Lake area, the Pond Trail is where you will see most of the action. Birds (waterfowl, woodpeckers and assorted songbirds) and beavers…or at least, signs of beavers (lodges, felled trees, etc.) are seen from the trail. Nearby Ruskin Dam features a spawning channel where chum salmon may be observed from early October through late November.

Hell's Gate Fishways (Map 26/E5)
More than 31 million sockeye were harvested from the 1913 run on the Fraser River. When the remaining fish reached Hell's Gate, they ran into an almost impenetrable obstacle caused by the construction of what is now the Canadian National Railway. All but the hardiest fish were blocked by a rockslide that shrank the already narrow channel and created a five metre high waterfall. By 1915, the removal of 45,000 cubic metres of rock from the channel had eased the problem; this remains one of the toughest obstacles on the river. There are now specially designed fishways to aid the spawning salmon.

Hope Slough/Camp Slough (Map 4/E3)
While most of these sloughs are on private land, the drive though this area will reveal plenty of great roadside stops to pull over and observe waterfowl and other birds.

Inch Creek Fish Hatchery (Map 3/G4)
Throughout the year, you can see and learn about young salmon in various stages of development in the tanks and troughs. On site, there is a large pond, which is home to several large white sturgeons, the largest of which weighs over 91 kg (200 lb). The hatchery compound is open to visitors every day (except Christmas Day) from 9:00 am to 3:00 pm.

Indian Arm Provincial Park (Maps 2, 11, 12)
Indian Arm Provincial Park plays host to a number of large mammals, including black bear, black-tailed deer, cougar, coyote and red fox as well as amphibians, 79 species of birds and smaller mammals including harbour seal. But most visitors here are interested in the marine life. The sandy isthmus connecting Twin Islands is home to a variety of clams and other shellfish like prawn and crab, while tidal pools along the rocky shoreline abound with sea life. The river itself supports no less than five species of salmon, steelhead and sea-run cutthroat populations.

Inland Lake Provincial Park (Map 18/G2)
Best known for its wheelchair accessible trail that circles the lake, there are a number of places to view wildlife–primarily avian–at the lake. One of the best places is along the marsh boardwalk on the east side of the lake.

Iona Beach Regional Park (Map 1/B3)
This area has long been recognized across North America as one of the best places to study shorebirds. The riverbank, Fraser River tidal flat, marsh, grassland and beach habitats attract over 280 species of birds, including many rare and vagrant species.

Joffre Lakes Provincial Park (Map 34/A1–43/A7)
Located off of Duffey Lake Road (highway 99) just east of Pemberton, this park provides habitat for black bear and grizzly bear, deer and mountain goat. Hikers may also be able to see pikas near the third lake.

Jones Creek Spawning Channel (Map 5/B1)
This spawning channel is located west of Hope near Laidlaw. Chum, Coho and, on odd-numbered years, pink salmon spawn here during October. Access is from Jones Creek Road east off Highway 1.

Kanaka Creek Regional Park (Map 2/G3–3/B3)
This park stretches along Kanaka Cree. Just off 256th Street, a fish fence was built in conjunction with the Bell-Irving Hatchery. Every October, this location plays host to the annual Return of the Salmon event, during the heart of the chum and Coho spawn. Farther upstream, a hatchery is open to visitors year-round. The chum salmon release in late April is worth catching. The riverfront area of the park is located along the estuary and is a great place to watch birds.

Khartoum Lake Recreation Site (Map 19/F3)
The rocky bluffs found around the lake and further up the Lois River Valley are home to mountain goat. They are best seen in the spring and fall.

Kilby Provincial Park (Map 4/C2)
About 15 km west of Agassiz at Harrison Mills, Kilby Provincial Park is a hot bed for bald eagle viewing during late fall and winter, and has been designated as a British Columbia Wildlife Watch area. The park is also home to migrating trumpeter swan, raven, finch, geese and other birds.

Lang Creek (Map 19/B4)
Where the fresh water of Lang Creek enters the salt water of Malaspina Strait is a great place to see waterfowl and shorebirds. November to January is the best time to see the eagles, attracted by the salmon carcasses. Also in the area are Lang Creek Falls and the Lang Creek Hatchery, both of which offer a chance to watch salmon in a spawning channel from mid-August to late November.

Mamquam Spawning Channel (Map 22/C6)
This series of spawning channels is located on the north side of the Mamquam River just east of the bridge over the river on Highway 99. Coho and chum salmon can be seen in November and December.

Manning Provincial Park (Maps 6, 7)
Manning Park is a big, beautiful park with more than 200 resident species of bird. In addition to birds, the park is a wonderful place to view a wide range of small and larger mammals, including black bear and mule deer. Be sure to check out the Manning Park Bird Blitz in mid-June each year.

Maplewood Flats (Map 1/F1)
Maplewood Flats is about 2 km east of the Second Narrows Bridge. This 96 hectare (237 ac) area is made up of mudflats and some salt marsh, which make ideal waterfowl and bird habitat. Log pilings provide perching and nesting habitat for osprey, while Maplewood Farm gives visitors a hands-on up close experience with over 200 animals and birds.

Maria Slough (Map 4/G2)
While much of the land surrounding the slough is private, there are several places where the road crosses or approaches the slough. The shallows off Chaplin Road are a great place to watch salmon spawning in the fall, while fall and winter are a good time to watch for birds. Trumpeter and tundra swans can be seen here.

Mehatl Creek Provincial Park (Maps 25, 34, 35)
This park, combined with the Nahatlatch and Stein protected areas, provides habitat for species that are dependent on old-growth ecosystems. The Mehatl Creek valley is prime habitat for black bear, cougar and grizzly bear. Other species include lynx, mountain goat, mule deer, spotted owl and wolf.

Nanton Lake Recreation Site (Map 19/C2)
There is a small herd of Roosevelt elk, which have been transplanted to this area. The best viewing times are in the early morning and before dusk.

Nairn Falls Provincial Park (Map 33/B1)
Located in Pemberton just north of Whistler, Nairn Falls Provincial Park provides habitat for some very different and special wildlife. Included in this menagerie is the smallest member of the boa constrictor family — the rubber boa. This species is one that is more tolerant to cold and rather small in size compared to its cousins, at a length of only 45 cm (18 inches). This brown or gray snake is nocturnal and is rarely seen.

Nahatlatch Provincial Park and Protected Area (Map 25/D1–36/A7)
The natural beauty of this park, nestled in glacier covered mountains with old growth forest and a lake and river system, stands alone in the Lower Mainland. In combination with the Mehatl and Stein protected areas, Nahatlatch offers a home for species that are dependent on old growth ecosystems and a high degree of wilderness. A variety of wildlife can be found in the park, including black bear, coyote, cougar, deer, grizzly bear, lynx and wolf. Smaller species and birds include bald eagle, beaver, osprey and spotted owl.

Nicomen Slough (Map 3/G5–4/A4)
Nicomen Slough contains habitat that is important to many species, including bald eagles and spawning salmon. Most notably, the slough provides important wintering habitat for between 100 and 200 trumpeter swans, from late November through January.

Noons Creek Hatchery (Map 2/B2)
Started by a handful of area residents who wanted to see salmon reintroduced to Noon Creek, the Noon Creek Hatchery now releases thousands of Coho and chum salmon every year. The best viewing times are in May, when fingerlings are released, and in fall, when salmon return to spawn. The hatchery is located on the west side of the Port Moody Recreation Centre on Ioco Road.

Oregon Jack Provincial Park (Map 45/D1)
Easily accessed on Hat Creek Road, this park preserves 233 hectares (576 ac) of habitat for black bear, moose and waterfowl. The marsh area is the focal point of most wildlife activity.

Pinecone-Burke Provincial Park (Maps 2, 11, 12, 23)
This park located near both Maple Ridge and Coquitlam is a sister park to Garibaldi Provincial Park, and extends south to include Burke Mountain. Anglers will be happy to find all five species of Pacific salmon here, as well as steelhead and cutthroat trout and migratory Dolly Varden. The park also provides habitat for grizzly and black bear, mountain goat and black-tailed deer. Visitors may also note that the park is home to six vulnerable species that include the great blue heron, Vaux's swift, the tailed frog, Huttons' vireo, the Pacific jumping mouse and the shrew mole. In addition, the park contains Widgeon Valley — a nationally recognized wetland.

Pitt-Addington Marsh Wildlife Area (Map 2/E1–12/F7)
The Pitt-Addington Marsh Wildlife Management Area encompasses 2,972 hectares (7,340 ac) south of Pitt Lake that includes Grant Narrows Regional Park, Addington Marsh, Pitt Polder and MacIntyre Creek. The tidal freshwater mudflats, marshes and wetlands are viewable along a network of dykes, as well as a number of viewing platforms and towers. Viewing highlights include great blue herons, trumpeter swans, ospreys and other raptors, sandhill cranes and a wide variety of songbirds.

Pitt Meadows/Pitt Polder (Map 2/D2–12/F7)
The open farmlands around Pitt Meadows provide great wildlife watching opportunities. During winter, waterfowl and hawks can be seen in the flooded fields around Pitt Meadows Airport. In the summer, short-eared owls are seen hunting, often during the day. Coyote are also frequently seen in the fields.

Pitt River Dykes (Map 2/E2)
To prevent flooding, dykes have been built along the Pitt River. These dykes provide great access along the rivers for birders. Look for osprey who build their nests on top of old pilings along the river.

Porpoise Bay Provincial Park (Map 9/F4)
This 61 hectare (151 ac) park is found on the east side of the Sechelt Inlet. Angus Creek, which flows through the park, is a popular place to watch salmon, but the site is best known as a destination for birders. There are plenty of waterfowl that overwinter here and in the spring there are migratory songbirds. The estuary is a place to spot bald eagle and other birds.

Roscoe Bay Marine Provincial Park (Map 28/B4)
This marine provincial park is the site of the unusual, yet beautiful annual congregations of Moon Jellies or jellyfish. Located on the Sunshine Coast just northwest of Desolation Sound, this park is also home to a variety of other marine life.

WILDLIFE ADVENTURES

Ruby Creek and Lake (Map 20/B6)
Ruby Creek is a short creek that connects Ruby Lake to Sakinaw Lake. Through habitat enhancement projects, new gravel beds and covers have been added over portions of the creek. These features will help protect the spawning habitat for a rare population of coastal cutthroat trout and for kokanee in fall. Ruby Lake and its lagoon also have 82 species of birds, 150 species of trees and shrubs, painted turtles, Roosevelt elk, deer & bear in a coastal rainforest setting protected by a 99 acre wildlife and bird sanctuary area. Only 1 km from the lake is the Iris Griffith Field Studies and Interpretive Centre, where an innovative nature school program is taught.

Ruskin Dam Recreation Area (Map 3/B3)
Located just south of Hayward Lake, below the Ruskin Dam, a small spawning channel has been built next to the Stave River. Here chum salmon can be seen spawning from early October through late November. Bald eagle and other birds that feed on salmon can also be seen at this time.

Saltery Bay Provincial Park (Map 19/E5)
Established in 1962, this park is found south of Powell River and is home to mink, otter, seal and bald eagle. Visitors can comb the ocean shore to view the abundant sea life, and at low tide spot star fish, urchin, crab and small fish. Sea lions and killer whales can also be seen in the area. Please remember not to disturb this sensitive habitat.

Sargeant Bay Provincial Park (Map 9/D4)
This park contains a shingle beach, a small lake with a cattail marsh and an upland area of second growth forest. The park is noted for its beautiful bay and excellent bird watching. A fish ladder is also provided here for spawning fish.

Sasquatch Provincial Park (Map 15/A7)
There are three main viewing areas in Sasquatch Provincial Park. The most active site is the Beaver Pond area where beaver, or signs of beaver activity, can be seen. The best times to observe this Canadian icon is at dawn or just before sunset. Bird life also abounds in this area. Another place to watch wildlife is at the outlet of Hicks Lake, which features a small dam and fish ladder. A trail leads along the creek and across the dam. In March and April, look for spawning cutthroat trout. They are best seen early in the morning or at sunset. Finally, watch for spawning chum salmon in October and November in the lower reaches of the Trout Lake Creek.

Sechelt Inlets Provincial Park (Maps 9, 10, 20)
Only accessible by boat, the marine environment protected by this park provides a pristine habitat for nesting shore birds and sea birds alike. Seals are also common in the inlet and can often be seen sunning themselves around Kunechin Islets. The sea bird colonies are very sensitive to disturbances so visitors are asked to be respectful and watch from a distance.

Sechelt Marsh (Map 9/F4)
This marsh is located across the street from the head of Sechelt Inlet. Together the freshwater marsh and the saltwater inlet provide important wildlife habitat, mostly for waterfowl and shorebirds. You will also see woodpeckers and songbirds in the upland areas. Further north, Porpoise Bay Park is also a good birding area.

Serpentine Wildlife Area (Map 2/B6)
The Serpentine Wildlife Area contains 71 hectares (175 ac) of extensive marshes, which can be accessed along the many trails in the area. There are three covered viewing towers but please note that many of the dykes are closed to public access. While birds are the big attraction here (from herons to raptors to waterfowls), you will also find small mammals (like muskrats), coyote and harbour seal in the Serpentine River.

Seton Lake Recreation Area (Map 53/C7)
Southwest of Lillooet off the Duffey Lake Road (Highway 99), BC Hydro has created a series of recreational sites. Wildlife enthusiasts can watch salmon spawn from the Seton Beach Picnic Site or look for other wildlife, including mountain goats, on the surrounding cliffs at the Naxwit Picnic Area.

Shelter Point Regional Park (Map 8/A1)
On Texada Island, this regional park is easily accessed south of Gillies Bay, about 27 km from the Blubber Bay ferry terminal. The park is home to crows, ducks, eagles, osprey and ravens, while deer, raccoon and squirrel are often seen scurrying around the park.

Skagit Valley Provincial Park (Map 6)
The Skagit Valley is home to diverse wildlife habitat, and, not surprisingly, diverse wildlife. Nearly 200 species of bird have been recorded in the area and commonly seen mammals include Columbian black-tailed deer, mule deer, snowshoe hare, beaver and common pika. The open meadows near Ross Lake are home to many butterfly species.

Skookumchuk Narrows Provincial Park (Map 20/D6)
Chickadees, nuthatches and woodpeckers are common along the forest trail to the viewpoint over the narrows. At the viewpoint, many diving ducks are visible, including mergansers and grebes. Harbour seal are also common along the inlet.

In order to improve your chances of spotting birds and animals, wear natural colours and unscented lotions.

Sliammon Creek Hatchery (Map 18/E2)
Located alongside Sliammon Creek, the best time to watch spawning chum salmon is during October and November. The hatchery is north of Powell River along Highway 101.

South Arm Marshes Wildlife Area (Map 1/C5)
The Fraser River estuary is the single most important area of aquatic bird and raptor migration and wintering habitat in British Columbia. The 937 hectare (2,315 ac) South Arm Marshes Wildlife Management Area provides critical wintering, migration and breeding habitats for waterfowl, shorebirds, raptors and many passerine species. The management area contains a series of islands surrounded by both freshwater and intertidal marshes, including Ladner Marsh and Ladner Lagoon. There are more species of birds here than you could shake a spotting scope at, plus seal, sea lion, beaver, mink and other species of mammals.

South Texada Island Provincial Park (Map 8/F3)
Essentially a boat access park, the shoreline is steep and rocky with rich tidal life. The park, along with nearby Anderson Bay Park, is also home to black-tailed deer and a variety of bird species.

Spences Bridge (Map 45/G5)
Large herds of bighorn sheep are visible in and around the community of Spences Bridge throughout the year. Although the sight of the sheep excites visitors, they do cause the local residents grief by eating laundry hanging to dry. A patient wildlife observer may also see elk, deer, coyote, black bear, cougar, bobcat, lynx, bald eagles, ospreys and many other wildlife species.

Sweltzer River (Map 4/C6)
Draining Cultus Lake into the Chilliwack River, this is a popular salmon viewing spot. Chum return from mid-October to mid-December. Other species are seen less frequently, though around the same general timeframe.

Tenderfoot Creek Hatchery (Map 22/C4)
Located off Paradise Valley Road, the hatchery contains tanks and troughs holding young fish most of the year. During November and December spawning Coho and chum salmon may be observed next to the hatchery.

Thacker Regional Park (Map 15/F6)
A spawning channel and boardwalk has been built on Sucker or Kawkawa Creek at this park found in Hope. This is a good place to view spawning Coho, pink and chum salmon in the fall (Coho and chum return here from early October to mid-November). Visitors can also find plenty of marsh habitat species and birds.

Weaver Creek Spawning Channel (Map 4/E1)
Weaver Creek spawning channel is one of the biggest in the area. An average of 32,000 sockeye salmon and 2,500 chum salmon use the channel, depositing an estimated 76 million eggs. Next to the Adams River, this is the best site in British Columbia to see sockeye spawning in September. In winter, the channel and surrounding streams are terrific places to look for American Dippers, a small slate-grey songbird that walks under water.

WINTER ADVENTURES

The winter storms that bring endless rain to Vancouver in January bring snow — tons of snow — to the mountains. While never ending snow might sound like a good thing, it can make touring the mountains dangerous — not just for avalanche hazards, but simply for navigation purposes. Mid-winter trips tend to contain extended periods of time stuck in a tent or at home.

But, come April, the sun comes out and there are a few weeks—and in higher elevation snowfields, months—of perfect touring weather. Sunny, warm and snow everywhere.

Snowshoeing is a sport that has been rapidly gaining popularity for snowbound hikers. Part of its newfound appeal can be attributed to the radical design innovations that have taken place over the last few years. Snowshoes have gone from unwieldy racquets attached to the feet, to devices that are only slightly larger than a pair of boots and are just as easy to walk in.

Whatever the reason, you will now find people snowshoeing all sorts of snow-covered trails in winter. They tie in well with the few cross-country areas that exist in Southwestern BC. The Coast Mountains are also a ski touring paradise. Routes range from easy (cross-country skiers will find that they don't need special touring skis to do some of these routes) to extremely precipitous. We could only list a few of the more popular routes, but there are more out there…many more.

Finding places near the Lower Mainland to ride a snowmobile is a challenge, as the lower valleys usually have no snow and the higher mountains are mostly protected behind park boundaries, all of which are snowmobile-free zones. But snowmobiling is actually quite popular once you start to head a bit farther out of the city. Even around Chilliwack, you will start to find areas that are good snowmobiling territory. The heartland of snowmobiling, at least in this mapbook, is the region around Pemberton, Bralorne and Gold Bridge. There are dozens of places to snowmobile that are accessed off (and sometimes on) the Hurley River Forest Service Road and the Upper Lillooet Forest Service Road.

It is important to remember that backcountry travel comes with a degree of risk that, while manageable, is never non-existent. If you don't know what you're doing, don't do it! Travel with someone who has more experience, take an avalanche safety training course and always carry an avalanche transceiver.

Atwell Peak (Map 22/E4)

This one is for the ski mountaineers in the crowd. Atwell Peak is one of many destinations accessed from the Elfin Lakes Hut in Garibaldi Provincial Park. The first few kilometres of the route past the hut are accessed along the Garibaldi Neve Traverse, but just past where the trail heads to Mamquam Lake, turn left (west) instead of right (east) and head up, up, up to the top. It is a stiff climb to the top with plenty of avalanche slopes to be wary of. The rock on the mountain is loose and rotten so climbing should only be attempted when the mountain has a hard snow or ice coating. While the north and south ridges are the most visible routes, the east face often offers the easier route.

Birkenhead Peak Route (Map 42/E4)

A microwave tower road leaves the Blackwater Lake Road just before it crosses under the power lines. This is the usual access up to Birkenhead Peak, a solitary massive with two officially named peaks — Birkenhead and the secondary Mount McDonald. It is 14.6 km (9 mi) to the actual peak and back, but most people spend a day or two exploring.

> Head wear, like a balaclava or wool toque, are essential on a winter trip since most of your body's heat loss is from your head.

Black Tusk/Garibaldi Lake (Map 22/E2)

This area is an advanced backcountry ski touring area. There are huts (Burton and Sentinel Glacier Huts) on the east side of Garibaldi Lake, and people ski across Garibaldi Lake during January and February to spend the night. The day-use shelters at Garibaldi Lake can be used for sleeping in during the winter months only. The road to the parking lot is not ploughed during the winter. Parking is along the Sea to Sky Highway (Hwy 99).

Bombtram Mountain (Map 16/B4)

A good spring skiing destination, this mountain is accessed from the Box Canyon parking lot on the Coquihalla Highway (Hwy 5). The route involves skinning about 3 km (1.9 mi) with an elevation gain of 980 m (3,215 ft) up through the trees and into alpine bowls that can offer some wonderful late season powder. And, if you come back via the canyon (downhill all the way), it's only about a 1 km traverse back to the vehicle. It is possible to get a couple or three runs on a good day.

Brandywine & Metal Dome (Map 32/B5)

This is a popular summer destination that loses none of its beauty and appeal in winter. The only complaint could be its popularity, both with snowmobilers and heli-skiers. It is still possible to find some areas that are not tracked out. From the Brandywine Forest Service Road, follow the snowmobile tracks most of the way to the summit of Metal Dome, a distance of 7.8 km (4.9 mi) with an elevation gain of 1,330 m (4,250 ft). From the summit you will have a breathtaking view of the surrounding peaks and glacier as you follow the ridge over to Brandywine Mountain. There is a snowmobile warming hut near Metal Dome, maintained by the Powder Mountain Snowmobile Club.

Brohm Ridge (Map 22/E4)

Because it is located outside of Garibaldi Park, anything goes on Brohm Ridge. Depending on when you show up and where you go, you might see ski tourists, snowmobilers and even snowboarders working on some backcountry jumps. There is a warming hut and lots of great skiing that is easily done in a day. The snowmobile trails and cabin are maintained by the Black Tusk Snowmobile Club.

Callaghan Country Wilderness Adventure (Map 32/C4)

Located 13 km west of Whistler, this area (formerly Mad River Ski Area) is often used as a staging area for trips to the Callaghan Lake Lodge, 12.5 km up trail from Alexander Falls. There are a total of 47 km (29 mi) of groomed trails in the area, plus lots of great backcountry skiing, especially around the lodge found at an elevation of 1,370 metres/4,500 feet. Most people who travel this way stay at the five-room backcountry lodge, but this is by no means

a requirement for using this area. You do have to pay the trail fees, though. In addition to cross-country and backcountry skiing, there is also 15 km (9.3 mi) of backcountry snowshoeing. In particular, the old growth forests and sub-alpine meadows of the Upper Callaghan Valley make a fine destination on snowshoe. Full details, maps, fees and more can be found on the Callaghan Country website, www.callaghancountry.com.

Callaghan Lake Provincial Park (Map 32/C3)

An average of 275 centimetres (108 inches) of snow falls in the Callaghan Lake area, making it one of the most reliable areas for skiing in the Lower Mainland. While there are no developed trails here, there are many informal trails that can be followed. There are also opportunities for alpine touring on the surrounding mountains. Those skiing here do so at their own risk; the area is prone to avalanches as well as unsafe ice and snow layers on Callaghan Lake. Proper planning and the right equipment will make all the difference here.

Cambie Creek Cross-Country Ski Trails (Map 7/C5)

Located in Manning Provincial Park, this series of cross-country ski trails have also become a popular snowshoeing destination. The trails range from the easy Cambie Loop, which is a 2.5 km loop trail through the meadows and over a bridge, to the difficult Fat Dog Trail, a 15 km (9.3 mi) return trip that climbs all the way up into the sub-alpine. These trails are not groomed, but are usually well tracked.

Cayoosh Range (Map 42/G6–43/B6)

This is a phenomenal ski area. It's so good, in fact, that plans have been underway for about a decade to turn this area into a ski hill. It may take even longer than that to see these plans come to fruition, if they happen at all, but this is still a prime skiing destination. Without the lifts, plan on spending at least two days here, more if you want to explore the Northern part of this range. Most of the skiing happens on Mount Rohr and Cayoosh Mountain, which are more easily accessed of the Duffey Lake Road (Highway 99). The Alpine Club of Canada maintains the Wendy Thompson Hut near Marriott Basin — contact accwhistler.ca for more information.

Cheam Peak (Map 5/A3)

Cheam is one of the most prominent peaks in the Fraser Valley, offering a 360-degree panoramic view at the top. How far you have to ski depends on how high you can get a vehicle up the Chipmunk Creek Forest Service Road to the south; a high clearance four-wheel drive vehicle is recommended. At the base of Cheam Peak is a lovely open meadow and the ascent, while stiff, is not too difficult. Nearby Knight Peak is another popular ski destination.

Cloudburst Mountain Route (Map 22/B2)

Turn off of Highway 99 onto the Chance Creek Forest Service Road and continue on this road for about 6.5 km. Expect a lot of bushwhacking on this difficult 5.8 km (3.6 mi) one-way trip, which is a popular winter route with skis or snowshoes, as the bushwhacking sections become much easier to cross once covered by a layer of snow. Expect to pass through forest, sub-alpine, alpine, and snowfield terrain on this 1,190 m (3,900 ft) climb that requires some wayfinding skills.

Cypress Mountain Ski Area (Map 11/B6)

Cypress Mountain is the closest place to Vancouver for cross-country skiers to get their fix; Cypress Bowl has 19 km (12 mi) of trails groomed for skate and classic. 7.5 km (4.7 mi) of the trails are lit for night skiing. There are some challenging up and down hill sections, but novices will be able to find some interesting loops, too. Cypress is also home to several kilometres of snowshoeing trails with, about 10 km (6 mi) of these marked. For downhill skiers, the mountain offers eight lifts (two of which are high speed quads), servicing 600 skiable acres and 53 named runs, including a number that are lit for night skiing. It is considered the most challenging local Vancouver ski hill. Full details regarding the ski area can be found on their website, www.cypressmountain.com.

Dakota Ridge Area (Map 10/B4)

This popular area on the Sunshine Coast is a bit difficult to get to, but offers a bunch of recreation options. From cross-country and backcountry skiing to snowshoeing and even snowmobiling, there is no shortage of places to explore. It offers one of the most reliable locations for snow in the area and has great views over the Georgia Strait, the North Shore, Vancouver Island and Mount Baker. Currently, there are about 17 km (10 mi) of cross-country ski trails and 8 km (5 mi) of snowshoe trails. Access is north on Field Road

— turn right at the T junction on the Wilson Creek Forest Service Road and follow the signs for approximately 13 km (8 mi) to Dakota Ridge. This route can be treacherous in the winter so carry chains and ensure you have a four-wheel drive vehicle.

Dam Mountain (Map 11/D6)
A popular hiking route in the summer, Dam Mountain is gaining popularity as a winter snowshoeing route. The 3 km (1.9 mi) trail is groomed and patrolled, making it a great place for beginners to practice their snowshoeing chops. The route heads to the left of the lifts from the lodge and climbs stiffly up to the peak of Dam Mountain. On a clear day, stop here and admire the view. On a stormy, foggy, nasty day, continue on the trail, which loops around Dam Mountain, then back to the Grouse Mountain Lodge for a little après-snowshoe.

Diamond Head (Map 22/F4)
Diamond Head is an intermediate backcountry ski touring area that follows the main trail to Elfin Lakes and beyond. In summer the alpine area is a fragile environment and hikers are bound to the main trail. In winter the whole area is a playground and some great skiing can be found right near Red Heather Shelter. The Rangers mark the route past the shelter with orange snow poles (below the shelter the trail is fairly obvious through the forest). Snow removal is periodic on the road to the Diamond Head parking lot and you may require a four-wheel drive. This touring area is the most popular ski touring destination in Southwestern BC, with the exception of Hollyburn in Cypress.

Garibaldi Neve Traverse (Map 22/F3)
This moderate route is one of the most popular multi-day skiing trips in the area. The climbs are gentle and there is little in the way of avalanche hazards. The trip crosses a number of glaciers and in times of low snow there are some dangerous crevasses near the Sharkfin. From The Black Tusk Trailhead to the Diamond Head Trailhead is just over 30 km. The trip takes most groups take two or three days.

Grouse Mountain Ski Area (Map 11/E6)
Grouse Mountain is becoming less about the skiing and more about the experience, what with Vancouver's first and only wind turbine (complete with view pod), sleigh rides, ice skating, a sno limo, ziplines, Heli jets, a wildlife rescue area, and of course, skiing and snowshoeing, too. There are 10 km (6 mi) of snowshoeing trails, 26 alpine runs for skiers and snowboarders (14 runs are lit for night skiing), along with two terrain parks serviced by four lifts. Additional details can be found on the resort website, www.grousemountain.com.

Helm Creek Trail (Map 22/E1–32/F7)
This trail is used to access the alpine meadows east of Black Tusk. Although it is longer than the Black Tusk Trail, it is less crowded. Expect to take at least two days to do a return trip, though a day trip to the Black Tusk Trailhead is possible if you can arrange a shuttle pick-up.

Hemlock Valley Ski Area (Map 14/D6)
Best known for its small but interesting family downhill area, Hemlock Mountain was closed for a couple years and has re-opened. The 35 runs are serviced by three chairlifts and one surface lift. In addition, there is a terrain park and a snow tubing park. For cross-country skiers, there are 9 km (5.6 mi) of trails, while random snowshoeing is possible. The trails wander around and sometimes through the village at the base of the hill. There are also old logging roads in the area for folks looking to do some easy backcountry exploration. The ski trails are not groomed or track-set, but there still is a trail fee. Visit the resort website at www.hemlockvalley.com for more information.

Hollyburn Mountain Cross-Country Trails (Map 11/B6)
In the winter, this popular hiking area becomes a popular ski destination for all types of skiers. Cypress maintains a popular cross-country ski area (see above), but for folks wanting to learn the basics of ski touring, this is also a popular destination. Trips in this area don't usually last more than a day and there are many routes to choose from.

Knuckleheads Recreation Area (Map 19/F2)
East of Powell River, this is a popular winter recreation area that is accessed from the gate on the E Branch Road off of the Stillwater Mainline. A four-wheel drive vehicle is required to get to the trailhead. Snow can start in November and last through May for those looking for an extended winter season. The Knuckles sit and an elevation of 1,676 metres (5,500 ft), while the old Mount Diadem Ski Club Cabin sits at around 975 metres (3,200 ft). With room for eight, the cabin makes a nice base to explore the many old roads/trails in the area that lead to Alpha Lake, MOM (Mount of Moon), Walt Lake Ridge and some old logging clearcuts. Both backcountry skiers and snowshoers can enjoy the trail system in winter.

Lost Lake Cross-Country Area (Map 32/G5)
Nestled amongst the trees at the base of Blackcomb Mountain, this 32 km (19.5 mi) series of trails are some of the best cross-country skiing in the province. The amenities are pure Whistler—water stations, a warming hut, lessons and of course, rentals—the views of the surrounding mountains (at times, the trails break out into flat, wide, open areas, which in summer are golf courses) are breathtaking and the (daily) grooming impeccable. The trails are well signed and rated from novice to expert. There's even 4 km (2.5 mi) of trail around Lost Lake lit for night skiing. There are also snowshoe trails located in the same area.

Magnesia Meadows (Map 11/B4)
One of the few open alpine meadows this close to the highway, the route to Magnesia Meadows is mostly along old logging roads. The meadows are tucked in behind Mount Harvey. There is a shelter at the head of Magnesia Creek, but this is best used for emergencies only as it only provides basic shelter for three to four people.

Manning Park Resort (Map 7/C6)
Located between the Manning Park Lodge and the downhill area, the Manning Park Cross-Country Ski Trails are a favourite getaway for many Vancouver cross-country skiers. The trails weave in and out and up and down the rolling forested hills around Lightening Lake. The 30 km (19 mi) of groomed trails include 17 km (10.5 mi) groomed for skating. There are also many backcountry routes in the area, including a 3 km (1.9 mi) ski to the end of Lightning Lake, and some serious climbs up to the ridge of the Three Brothers (to the north of the highway). There are over 13 km (8 mi) of snowshoe trails, but those wishing to explore further can head into the backcountry. The family orientated downhill area at Gibson Pass features 140 skiable acres, with thirty four marked trails and four lifts. If you plan to make a weekend trip and stay at the resort, it is best to plan early. Additional details about the resort can be found on their website, www.manningpark.com.

Be sure to dress in layers, in order to enable you to peel off or add clothing as needed to adjust your comfort level.

McGillivray Pass/Whitecap Alpine (Map 51/F7)
Whitecap Alpine is now operating out of the classic McGillivray Pass Hut, one of the most popular ski touring destinations in the mountains south of Gold Bridge. The area started gaining popularity in the 1950s, but really became popular once the lodge was built in 1972. For the past twenty years, the Andrews Family has operated Whitecap Alpine out of the lodge, offering heli-skiing adventures to the local peaks. Do it yourselves can still ski in from Bralorne along the Kingdom Lake Forest Service Road and stay at the lodge, making trips to Whitecap Mountain, Mount McGillivray, Mount Piebiter and Prospector Ridge, among others. Most people who tour this area, however, do so with Whitecap Alpine. Learn more about the cabin and the heli-skiing opportunities at www.whitecapalpine.ca.

Meslillooet Mountain (Map 12/B3)
The Meslillooet Icefield is the closest glacier to Vancouver, just north of Indian Arm. However, getting to the icefield is a bit of an adventure, as there is no easy road access. Rather, it is a long trip north up Highway 99, then back-tracking southeast along the Mamquam and Stawamus-Indian Forest Service Roads. An alternate approach would be via boat up Indian Arm and then hike/ski in along the Hixon Creek Forest Service Road. Give yourself at least three days for either option.

Mount Bishop (Map 11/G5)

Mount Elsay and Mount Bishop are the two big summits behind Mount Seymour. These mountains are accessed from the Mount Seymour Trail at Brocton Point. Many people just stay in the Mount Elsay area, but it is possible, in good snow conditions, to make it to Mount Bishop. There is a cabin near Elsay Lake, and this intermediate trip can be done in a day. The normal summer route travels through avalanche areas and is not recommended.

> Visit www.avalanche.ca for current avalanche conditions when visiting the mountains. Go prepared with both avalanche knowledge and safety equipment to help make your adventure safe.

Mount Sedgewick (Map 21/G6)

Mount Sedgewick is located on the west side of Howe Sound, past Mount Roderick on the Mount Roderick Trail. Give yourselves at least two days to explore this moderately difficult area. Access to the area is via the Woodfibre Ferry, just south of Squamish.

Mount Sproatt Trail (Map 32/E5)

Turn off the Rainbow Lake Trail around 1,140 m (3,740 ft) elevation to access the Mount Sproatt Trail. This 3.3 km (2.1 mi) trail gains 720 m (2,360 ft) in elevation, and is most popular in the winter. Rolling alpine snowfields will make up the terrain on your way to the summit to view the spectacular vistas surrounding this wonderland.

Needle Peak Trail (Map 16/D2)

This challenging route climbs over 2,000 metres (6,560 ft) to its summit. There are a couple exposed areas near the top, which might prove too much for some, but there is an alternate route to a small lake just below the peak for those not comfortable with the exposure. Much of the climbing happens near the beginning of this 13 km (8 mi) route.

Pemberton Icefield (Maps 31, 32, 40, 41)

This huge icefield north of Whistler and east of Pemberton is a backcountry winter sport mecca. The ascents and descents are gentle and a backcountry ski trip here dovetails nicely into the Squamish-Cheakamus Divide, making a good weeklong trip. To ski from the north trailhead to the south trailhead can take as little as three days, but most people take a few more days to explore.

Phelix Creek Trail (Map 42/E2–D1)

Accessing the Brian Waddington Hut requires a challenging climb up the Phelix Creek Road and then a flagged route from the Blackwater Creek Road near Birkenhead Lake. The route is about 10 km (6 mi) one-way and leads to a popular backcountry ski area surrounded by Mount Aragorn, Shadowfax, Gandalf and Peregrine. If the weather is bad, there is also good tree skiing available. Visit www.ubc-voc.com for more information on the hut and trails.

Post Creek Cross-Country Trails (Map 5/E5)

A 7.3 km (4.5 mi) cross-country ski trail system with easy and moderate trails, it is recommended to ski these trails in a counter clockwise direction since this is the way the trails are signed. The trails are found adjacent to the Post Creek Recreation Site across from the Chilliwack Lake Road.

Railroad Pass/Icemaker Mountain Area (Map 41/E2–49/F5)

The old fashioned way to do this trip was to ski in and ski out. These days, most people catch a helicopter or bush plane in to Icemaker, stay at the Pebble Creek Hut for a few days and then ski out. Which is not a bad plan as far as things go. While most people can ski the 40 km (25 mi) down from Icemaker to Railroad Pass in a day, getting up takes most people at least two. The whole area is full of ski touring options, from hardcore mountain skiing to some easy skiing along ungroomed forest service roads.

Roe Creek Ski Route (Map 32/B7)

Roe Creek is the safest and most popular access to the Brew Hut and skiing in the Mount Brew area. The route follows Change Creek and Roe Creek Forest Service Roads to the south, which can be driven or skied, depending

on how much snow there is. When the route is not driveable, snowcats often travel part of the route, making most of the route easier than if you had to cut your own trail. If you have to ski, it adds nearly 10 km to the 3.6 km route to Brew Lake. The full length of the trail is 13 km (8 mi) with an elevation gain of 1,120 m (3,670 ft). The low, gentle summit of Mount Brew is perfect for ski touring, but most people stay a few days to explore the terrain of the Squamish/Cheakamus Divide. Contact the Varsity Outdoor Club, at www.ubc-voc.com to find out about fees and availability of the Brew Hut.

Seymour Mountain (Map 11/G7)

For alpine skiers and snowboarders, there are 39 named runs and 200 skiable acres. The area is serviced by five lifts and considered by many to be the premier snowboarding area out of the three local hills. The mountain features four terrain parks, four snow tubing lanes and eight toboggan runs.

The official Seymour snowshoeing trails lay to the east of the parking lot, between the Mystery Peak Chairlift and the Goldie Rope Tow. There are ten short trails, ranging from 100 metres to 1 km long. These add up to 5.5 km (3.4 mi) of trails, mostly in the beginner to intermediate range. But there are other, more challenging, places you can go on snowshoes and backcountry skis. For instance, you can follow a trail from the parking lot, along the left-hand edge of the ski area boundary, all the way to the top of the mountain. It is a 10 km (6 mi) return trek with a fairly stiff uphill climb all the way to the top. Expect to take about four hours to the top; another two if you want to follow zthe ridge along the three pump routes. On a clear day, the views are worth the effort. An easier trail runs up the mountain to the right of the ski lifts. This route is also popular with backcountry skiers. Full details can be found on their website, www.mountseymour.com.

Singing Pass Trail (Map 32/G6–33/A6)

Access to Singing Pass is via Fitzsimmons Creek, which flows between Whistler and Blackcomb Mountains. This is a moderate route, with a good cabin at the north end of Russet Lake, maintained by the BC Mountaineering Club. This trip can easily be done in a day, but the whole joy of this area is exploring the slopes behind Whistler Mountain. Avid skiers spend days on end up here enjoying the wide variety of terrain. Visit www.bcmc.ca for more information on the Himmelsbach Hut at Russel Lake.

Sky Pilot (Map 11/D1)

At the base of Sky Pilot Mountain (the highest summit in the area at 2,025 metres (6,645 ft) is an area of rolling basins and fine subalpine skiing. This area is well suited for easy day trips, although the BC Mountaineering Club maintains a locked cabin near Mountain Lake for overnight excursions. This area is reached fairly easily off the Stawamus-Indian Forest Service Road. Those interested in going beyond the base and up the climber's route to the summit of Sky Pilot need advanced mountaineering skills. Visit www.bcmc.ca for more information on the Mountain Lake Hut.

Snowcap Lake Route (Map 24/A4–23/E3)

Most of the terrain in Garibaldi Park is accessed from the west side, which means that those people willing to take the extra effort will find more peace and solitude on the east side of the big park. Snowcap Lake is one such location. Allow about three days from logging roads off the Lillooet Lake Road to access the lake. The route isn't as high as some and so it must be done in late winter/early spring. The route does cross over the Icemantle Glacier and the 2,370 metre (7,775 ft) Greenmantle Mountain. From here longer, more difficult trips can be made to Thunderclap Glacier, Misty Glacier and Stave Glacier, deep in the untrammelled heart of Garibaldi Park.

Snowspider Mountain Area (Map 34/C2–43/B6)

Located in the high mountains above Lillooet Lake, Snowspider Mountain is a great weekend trip. Although the trip can be done in two or three days from the Van Horlick Creek Road, arguably the best approach is to ski up Cerise Creek from the Duffy Lake Road (Highway 99). When the snow is high, an alternate route is up the logging road along Twin One Creek from Lillooet Lake. There is a hut that holds four on Snowspider.

Squamish-Ashlu Divide (Map 31/C6–21/E1)

Also known as the Ashlu-Elaho Divide, this area is heavily glaciated and has great ski touring terrain. The divide is best accessed from the southwest, along an unnamed creek west and slightly south of Porterhouse Peak, though the road is not usually passable until early May. Expect to take about three days to reach the south trailhead on logging roads just off Branch A-700.

Squamish-Cheakamus Divide (Map 32/A3–22/B1)

One of the most popular multi-day trips in the area, the Squamish-Cheakamus Divide was built for ski touring, with easy climbs and some great descents. The moderate trip is generally best done from Callaghan Lake south to Tricouni Meadows. The four day route hooks up with other trails, including the Brandywine and Metal Dome Route as well as Brew Mountain and Roe Creek. These other access points allow people to shorten the trip.

Spearhead Traverse (Map 32/G6–33/B7)

This route follows the string of glaciers behind Blackcomb Mountain deep into the heart of Garibaldi Provincial Park. The area is a popular heli-skiing destination and you may even see snowshoers in the area. The traverse is best done clockwise, starting at the Blackcomb Ski Area, along the Blackcomb, Decker, Trorey, Tremor, Platform and Fitzsimmons Glaciers, then south to Overlord Mountain. The loop takes you back to Whistler Mountain, either via the Singing Pass Trail or over the Musical Bumps. This moderate route will take most parties three days, although bad weather can extend the length of this trip. In good conditions there are numerous peaks offering great short side trips.

Stein Divide (Map 34/A3–35/F6)

Give yourself at least a week to ski this route, which is as challenging as it is rewarding. The route starts from Lizzie Creek Forest Service Road, most likely where it meets the In-Shuck-Ch Forest Service Road. The route follows the road and then the hiking route to Cherry Pip Pass. Once in the alpine, experienced route finders can head farther south, past Figure Eight Lake and onto Mount Skook Jim. From here, the route heads east onto the Rutledge Glacier, past Longslog Mountain, eventually meeting logging roads that head up Log Creek.

> *Our ski touring or backcountry skiing destinations are only a fraction of the places the intrepid explorer can get to in winter. If you're looking for more adventurous trips, there are groups out there, like the Federation of Mountain Clubs, who can help.*

Sunshine Mountain Area (Map 51/B6)

Home to the former Bralorne Ski Hill, this is still a popular family ski area that is accessible by snowmobile in winter. Adding to the appeal of the area is the old cabin that was built in the 1940s and has recently been renovated. The access route is found about 2 km up the Noel Creek Forest Service Road on an old mining road. The road leads right to the old ski runs. It is possible to continue into the alpine areas to access backcountry ski lines. Avalanche training and mountain travel experience is recommended for anyone venturing beyond the old ski area. No snowmobiles are allowed above the cabin in winter — only self-propelled travel is permitted. Winter updates from the valley can be found on www.southchilcotin.ca/winter.

Tantalus Range (Map 22/A4)

The Tantalus Range does not offer good winter ski routes, as the mostly up and down landscape makes it more appealing to mountaineers. However, from the Alpine Club of Canada hut at Lake Lovely Water there are a couple of good destinations, including Mount Pelops and Mount Niobe. These trips are fairly strenuous and should not be undertaken by the inexperienced. Visit www.aebc.com/acc/huts.asp for more details on the Jim Harerl Hut.

Tetrahedron Plateau/Mount Steele Area (Map 10/B2)

At 1,738 metres (5,700 ft), Tetrahedron Peak is the highest on the Sunshine Coast. The surrounding area makes for an easy to moderate ski touring destination with lots of gentle, rolling terrain and some good downhill skiing from either Mount Steele or Panther Peak. The popular area has a well-established trail system and four cabins to set up base camp at. The cabins are maintained by the Tetrahedron Outdoor Club (www.tetoutdoor.ca) and were built to accommodate 12 people. They are not reservable and often very busy during weekends and holidays in the winter; plan to get there early. It should also be noted that the road in requires a four-wheel drive vehicle with good winter tires and chains as the roads are not plowed in winter.

Tyaughton Lake Trails (Map 51/C2)

Best accessed from Tyax Mountain Resort, there is a series of old roads and trails to explore on skis or snowshoes on the east side of Tyaughton Lake. This multi-use system is also popular with snowmobilers.

Wedge Mountain (Map 33/B4)

Wedge Mountain is the highest peak in Garibaldi, rising some 2,905 metres (9,530 ft) above sea level. Although the mountain can be scrambled up, the real appeal of this trip is the series of glaciers (Weart, Needle and Chaos) north and east of the peak. Give yourself at least two days to explore this area. The BC Mountaineering Club maintains a cabin at Wedgemount Lake; visit www.bcmc.ca for more information. It is also possible to access this area from Blackcomb Mountain to the south via Wedge Pass.

Wedge-Currie Traverse (Map 33/B4–D2)

This difficult route follows the Weart Glacier north onto the Hibachi Ridge, which straddles the Garibaldi Park border. From here, experienced route finders can make their way to Mount Currie and out along Gravell Creek.

Whistler Blackcomb Ski Area (Map 32/F6)

With over 8,000 skiable acres, one vertical mile of elevation and more than 200 trails, Whistler Blackcomb is the embodiment of everything that is best and worst in BC skiing. When the snow is right, there is no better place to be anywhere. And when you're out on the mountain, you can ignore the tourist trappings that have built up around the resort. Or you can embrace them, if that's your style. One thing you can't ignore, though, is the people. The 39 lifts shared between the two mountains (including the Peak to Peak Gondola between the two mountains) can move over 65,500 people an hour and there are days when it seems the lifts are at capacity.

In addition to downhill skiing and boarding, the resort offers five terrain parks, a super pipe, a snow cross track, 17 on-mountain restaurants and one of the best nightlife scenes in the country. If the ski hill gets too much, there are also heli-skiing options, with access to 175,000 hectares (432,000 ac) of terrain, featuring 173 glaciers and 475 runs. Full resort details can be found at www.whistlerblackcomb.com.

Whistler Olympic Park (Map 32/C4)

This new Olympic venue opened to the public in 2009 and has over 95 km (59 mi) of trails, 30 km (19 mi) of which are dog friendly. Well, not quite. Only 55 km (34 mi) are in the Olympic Park. The rest are located in Callaghan Country Wilderness Adventure next door, although the trail systems do interlock. The trails are groomed for both classic and skate, and trails rate from beginner-friendly to routes that are designed for Olympic-level athletes. This venue is decked out with all the bells and whistles, including one of the nicest cross-country skiing day lodges around. There are some easy snowshoe trails, but the longer trails are found in Callaghan Country, along with 6 km (3.7 mi) of trails lit for night skiing. The park also offers baseboarding, tobogganing, ski jumping and more. Check out everything the park offers at www.whistlersportlegacies.com.

Zoa Peak Trail (Map 16/E1)

Zoa Peak is a popular destination in both summer and winter, and probably the most popular in the Coquihalla Summit area. It offers a relatively little amount of climbing (635 m/2,085 ft) across its 11 km (6.8 mi) return distance. The trail passes through a gradually thinning forest onto the ridge up to Zoa.

Zupjok-Alpaca Ridge (Map 16/D1)

Offering some gorgeous scenery and the occasional unexploded avalanche control shell, this route is not travelled very often. The trip to Alpaca Peak is 18 km (11 mi) return, gaining 1,220 metres (4,000 ft) as it makes its way up to the top. The route is challenging, and involves a fair bit of climbing, with an average grade of just over 9 percent. A shorter, easier route would be to turn around at Zupjok Peak, which cuts the distance and elevation gained in half. The route starts along the old Ottormite Mountain Road, but you will have to head off-trail to follow the obvious ridge up the peak. The trail is usually well flagged.

THE FRASER VALLEY

BRITISH COLUMBIA

Abbotsford Panoramic

Chilliwack River

Fraser River

The Fraser Valley is a lush and fertile stretch of land around the lower reaches of the mighty Fraser River, where this waterway bisects the towering mountains of BC's Coast Mountain and North Cascade ranges before emptying into the Strait of Georgia and the vast Pacific Ocean. Emerald green farmland pushes against the feet of giant mountains in either direction of the Fraser, BC's longest river and the wellspring of abundance for inhabitants of the Fraser Valley for thousands of years.

The Fraser Valley is a hotspot for outdoor recreation, with sport fishing being one of the main draws for thrill seekers from all over the world. All six species of Pacific salmon travel the voluminous waters of the Fraser, as does the prehistoric, giant White Sturgeon, the largest freshwater fish in the Americas. These behemoths can exceed 4 m (13 ft) in length and live well over 150 years old, making for the catch of a lifetime for those lucky enough to reel in one of these ancient river monsters. The Fraser, its many tributaries and the surrounding freshwater lakes also provide world-class terrain for kayakers and canoers, who flock to the Valley for both whitewater excitement and tranquil, silent glides along remote halcyon waterbodies.

For those looking for an elevated outdoor experience, the mountains on either side of the valley offer complex networks of hiking and mountain biking trails. Trail riders can rip through stands of giant cedar before catching some air off of expertly-built obstacles, while hikers can test their mettle while accessing some of the Coast and Cascade ranges' most spectacular viewpoints. The beauty of the Fraser Valley shines even more brightly when viewed from above, and the list of stunning locations to hike to is endless. For accessing the truly hard-to-reach

SUPER, NATURAL BRITISH COLUMBIA ♦ CANADA

areas, many ATV and snowmobile-friendly trails extend deep into the mountains, and are just waiting to be explored. In winter, a thick blanket of snow transforms the area into an alabaster-shrouded dream world, with resilient evergreens bending under the weight of winter's bounty like melting candles.

Hemlock Resort and nearby Manning Park provide downhill skiers and snowboarders with top-quality riding, while cross-country skiers and snowshoers can chart their own course through the backcountry.

Following a long day of playing outside, what better way to recharge than to have a taste of the Fraser Valley's impeccable culinary culture? With over fifty percent of BC's total agricultural production occurring in the Valley, there is no better place to eat local. Numerous outstanding wineries and craft breweries are sure to quench your thirst and satisfy even the most discerning palettes. There is no shortage of things to taste, see, catch, or climb in the Fraser Valley!

EXPLORE THE FRASER VALLEY
The Trans-Canada Highway takes you through the Fraser Valley. It can also be accessed via Highway 7 and 11.

WELCOME TO Abbotsford

YOUR COUNTRY PLAYGROUND

Nestled among rural farmland and towering mountains, Abbotsford is a community often referred to as a city in the country. With a population of over 133,000 and more than 200 annual festivals and events, Abbotsford's natural wilderness surroundings set the perfect backdrop for its rich culture and history. The bounty of Abbotsford's fertile soils attracted pioneer settlers from around the world establishing the heritage and multicultural nature of the community. Sites such as Trethewey House were built by master craftsmen from India, immigrants who went on to construct Canada's oldest Gurdwara Temple, now a National Historic Site.

Abbotsford is the heart of the Fraser Valley where visitors can enjoy a wide range of urban and outdoor recreation opportunities in close proximity. Just a 15 minute drive from downtown Abbotsford, mountain bikers will find dual-wheeled bliss on the Sumas Trail System, offering incredible views and top-quality trails that weave through stands of huge cedar. Nearby, Chadsey Lake provides a great place to swim, fish, and picnic, along with a large network of hiking trails to be explored.

If you find yourself searching for a truly high-altitude adventure, take to the air with Coastal Air Tours for a scenic flight over the rolling valley, or take a leap of faith at the Abbotsford Skydive Centre, which offers lessons and guided jumps. Alternately, a variety of equestrian and hiking opportunities are available in the area for those wishing to stay grounded.

With more than 90% of land area dedicated to agricultural use, an abundance of locally produced products including poultry, wine, craft beer and cheese are waiting to be enjoyed. A great way to sample some of Abbotsford's outstanding harvest is to take the Circle Farm Tour, a self-guided driving tour of local farms, eateries and other attractions for an insightful and delicious taste of country living. Whether you are looking for adventure, culture, or cuisine, Abbotsford has something new and unique to offer!

" Welcome to our playground, feel free to set your own limits "

TO LEARN MORE, CONTACT

Abbotsford Visitor Centre
34561 Delair Road, Abbotsford, BC
Ph: 604-859-1721
www.tourismabbotsford.ca

MAP

From top to bottom: Skydiving - Tourism Abbotsford; Biking Sumas Mountain - Tourism Abbotsford; Wakeboarding at Albert Dyke Park - Tourism Abbotsford; Mt.Lehman Winery - Tourism Abbotsford

WELCOME TO Chilliwack

#SHARECHILLIWACK

Overflowing with natural beauty and a rich heritage, Chilliwack offers numerous outdoor recreational opportunities throughout its neighbouring mountains and mighty rivers. This expanding city is known for its bountiful corn harvest, but also as an exciting place to visit and explore. It truly is "The Great Outside."

Although there is a concentrated downtown core, situated along Highway 1, Chilliwack can be described as an amalgamated group of villages and communities, bordered by the Fraser River to the north and the US-Canada border to the south. Multiple townsites and shifting boundaries have been a part of Chilliwack's unique history since its very beginning, when the terrain along the Fraser River prevented the township from expanding in its original location.

Become immersed in Mother Nature and discover her hidden gems around every bend and turn, such as the spectacular Bridal Veil Falls, tumbling for a colossal 122 m (400 ft) over a wide rock face. Head the opposite direction where, on the Chilliwack River, lies the Great Blue Heron Nature Reserve - an abundant 130 hectare (321 ac) birdwatcher's paradise. Find solitude among the 90 Great Blue Heron nests, along with numerous other rare species of plants and animals that inhabits this flood plain.

> **Our rugged roads meander up valleys where recreational options are almost as limitless as the sky.**

Let adventure become a family affair and visit Cultus Lake Provincial Park, one of BC's most popular outdoor escapes. Located just 16 km from downtown Chilliwack, this large, warm freshwater lake sees over one million visitors each year, and plays host to numerous attractions including a waterpark, amusement rides, golf course, boat rentals and much more. In addition to the campgrounds located on the northwest and southeast sides of the lake, several cozy and centrally located cabins are ready to take in tired explorers after a long day of excitement.

Surrounded by mountains, Chilliwack offers hikers an extensive network of trails to explore and peaks to conquer. Discover the crown jewel of these trails on the trek to Lindeman and Greendrop lakes. These brilliant blue lakes are set amongst lush landscape, rich with various flora and fauna. Lindeman is easily accessed with a friendly hike of just 3.4 km (2 mi). The area also offers mountain bikers a whole universe of trails to explore for a faster paced journey around Chilliwack's backcountry. Vedder Mountain sports one of the most popular trail systems, containing nearly 100 km (62 mi) of trails, offering adventure for riders of every skill level.

From top to bottom: Rafting on the Chilliwack River – Chilliwack River Rafting, Camping in Elk Mountain – Inmist Media House, Hiking Elk Mountain – Inmist Media House, Snowshoeing Elk Mountain – Roxanna Froese.

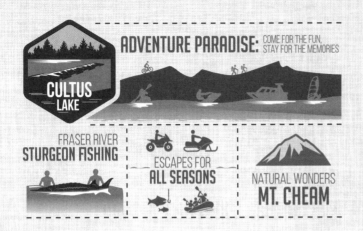

ADVENTURE PARADISE: COME FOR THE FUN, STAY FOR THE MEMORIES

CULTUS LAKE

FRASER RIVER STURGEON FISHING

ESCAPES FOR ALL SEASONS

NATURAL WONDERS MT. CHEAM

For the thrill seeker at heart, Chilliwack is home to the world-renowned Tamihi rapids; the Chilliwack River draws a steady stream of rafters and kayakers wanting to test their skills in these adrenaline pumping waters. This dynamic section of river plays host to national whitewater championships and has produced Olympian kayakers. The nearby recreational area and campsites make it the perfect destination for an adventure-filled paddling vacation.

Home to all five Pacific species of salmon, anglers will find a lifetime of world-class fishing opportunities on the mighty Fraser River. For sport fishermen, the exhilarating fight for one of the river's massive sturgeon can make for sensational photos and lifelong memories. These river monsters can reach 4 m (13 ft) in length, weigh up to 680 kg (1,500 lb) and live well over 100 years, attracting big game anglers from all over the world.

Relax, restore and recharge on one of Chilliwack's spectacular golf courses, set beneath the prolific peaks of the Coast and Cascade Mountains. Providing the perfect mix of beauty and challenge, these well-maintained courses accommodate all levels of play. Between tree-lined fairways novice golfers can practice their swing technique, while seasoned vets maneuver the more demanding technical terrain.

Alternatively, a relaxing day-trip in Chilliwack could lead to a stop at one of the vibrant local artisan businesses. Local dairy products, soap, flowers, beer, honey, fruit and vegetables are available at a variety of Chilliwack owned and operated establishments – fill up on delicious food and drink with a truly local flavour, or find the perfect gift for someone special. Chilliwack is also home to an ever-expanding variety of fine and casual dining restaurants, delis and bistros. In the fall, stroll through the Chilliwack Corn Maze and Pumpkin Farm for a taste of farming life and an assortment of family-friendly activities. Whether you are looking for outdoor adventure or a taste of local culture, Chilliwack has plenty to go around.

MAP

TO LEARN MORE, CONTACT

Chilliwack Visitor Centre
44150 Luckakuck Way, Chilliwack, BC
Ph: 604-858-8121
www.tourismchilliwack.com

 From top to bottom: Sturgeon Fishing on the Fraser River – Lang's Fishing Adventures & Carl and Alex Fishing; View of the Cheam Mountain Range – Inmist Media House; Vedder Mountain - James Lissimore; Tamahi Rapids – Inmist Media House.

WELCOME TO Harrison

Hot Springs

FIND NATURE... JUST UP THE ROAD

Located at the southern shore of Harrison Lake, this welcoming village of 1,500 people is one of the best places to see and appreciate nature in all its glory. Extending north towards a backdrop of snow-capped coastal mountains, Harrison Hot Springs offers world-class accommodation, outdoor recreation, cultural events and, of course, the hot springs themselves. While small in size, Harrison has a lot to offer, from its healing mineral waters to the stunning scenery of the surrounding forests and trails. The hot springs were originally established as a resort destination in 1886, after the opening of the Canadian Pacific Railway, and before that had been used and treasured by the Sts'ailes First Nation for innumerable generations.

The legendary, naturally heated mineral water sprouts from two sources in Harrison – the Potash (40° C) and Sulphur (65° C) springs – and has some of the highest concentration of dissolved mineral solids of any known spring. The hot water is cooled and pumped into a public indoor pool, as well as a number of pools at Harrison Hot Springs Resort and Spa. The warm waters offer a welcome contrast to the usually frigid temperature of the glacial-fed Harrison Lake. The therapeutic waters and lavish resort opportunities surrounded by a truly wild and awe-inspiring landscape are some of the reasons why Harrison is so popular amongst visitors.

On foot, by bicycle or ATV, exploring Harrison's river carved valleys and dense forests can be as adventurous or as leisurely as you like. Several easy foot trails start right in town, with minimal elevation gain and some great scenery. For a greater challenge, the Harrison Grind takes you up Aggasiz Mountain to a stunning mountain lake and breathtaking views of Harrison Lake below. Biking around Harrison can be considered a leisurely activity, with flat country roads being the primary attraction for cyclists, meandering through picturesque farmland and allowing stops for farm tours. For a more high-octane adventure, explore the rugged and scenic terrain around Harrison by ATV. The onset of winter in the surrounding mountains turns this year round playground into a magical winter wonderland, waiting to be explored by ski, snowshoe or snowmobile.

" Whether you seek an adventure with the kids, a romantic getaway or a fun-filled trip with friends, Harrison Hot Springs has what you are after. "

 From top to bottom: Campbell Lake Trail aka the Harrison Grind - Graham Osborne; Kayaking Harrison Lake - Graham Osborne; Windsurfing Harrison Lake - Graham Osborne; Green Point - Graham Osborne

HOME TO THE SASQUATCH

SALMON RUN

WATER ADVENTURES MAKE A SPLASH!

FIND YOUR INNER BEAST

The sandy beaches and cool waters of Harrison Lake offer visitors of all ages a diverse range of activities to indulge in. The sandy southern shoreline gives this small village its resort holiday atmosphere during the summer months, with families swimming, building sand castles, flying kites or enjoying the array of water-sports. All manner of watercraft can be rented in town, and powered boat tours are available as well. A floating waterpark, featuring Harrison's home game version of "Wipeout," is located on the lake in front of Harrison Hot Springs Resort and Spa, offering additional adventure and fun for the whole family.

Paddlers will enjoy the challenge of Harrison Lake and the tranquility of the Harrison River. For those looking for something to paddle toward, there are a couple of islands and a beautiful waterfall that make terrific destinations on the lake. In the fall, paddle from Harrison West down the river to Harrison Mills and witness thousands of bald eagles on their migratory route, attracted by the annual salmon run. Celebrate this natural spectacle at the Fraser Valley Bald Eagle Festival, in nearby Harrison Mills. Additionally, the neighbouring Hicks, Trout, and Deer Lakes, surrounded by the magnificence of Sasquatch Provincial Park, offer unprecedented paddling experiences.

Avid anglers will appreciate Harrison River as the first river in Canada to be designated as a Salmon Stronghold. Home to all five species of salmon, plus steelhead trout, and with fly-fishing hot spots aplenty, a day on Harrison River makes for a fishing expedition to remember. For a more serene fishing experience, opt for the tranquil lakes of Sasquatch Provincial Park. For those seeking an adrenaline infused experience, the nearby Fraser River provides big game fishing enthusiasts with phenomenal battles of man versus fish as they reel in a giant white sturgeon, the largest freshwater fish in North America.

Wildlife enthusiasts and Bigfoot hunters alike will revel in the second-growth and birch forest of Sasquatch Provincial Park. The series of pocket lakes and campgrounds surrounded by forested green mountain slopes offer great hiking, wildlife viewing and picnicking opportunities. The name of the park harkens to a rich mythology surrounding the Sasquatch in the Harrison area, dating back to Sts'ailes legend of a vanishing "hairy man." These days, Harrison is home base for some of the world's leading Sasquatch experts, who offer guided tours deep into remote Sasquatch territory.

TO LEARN MORE, CONTACT

Harrison Hot Springs Visitor Centre
499 Hot Springs Rd, Harrison Hot Springs, BC
Ph: 604-796-5581
www.tourismharrison.com

 From top to bottom: Mt. Breckenridge- Graham Osborne; Backroads above Harrison Lake - Graham Osborne; Canoeing Hicks Lake - Graham Osborne; Hiking in Sasquatch Provincial Park - Graham Osborne.

WELCOME TO Hope

EMBRACE THE JOURNEY

A beautiful and dramatic wilderness destination nestled at the confluence of the Coquihalla and Fraser Rivers, Hope has long been a site of First Nations settlement and a logical stopping point for anyone travelling between the coast and the interior. The natural bounty of the rivers, the beauty of the surrounding area and the advantageous geographic location have sustained Hope for countless generations and make it a marvelous place to visit to this day.

Hope's soaring mountains, deep canyon ravines and peaceful lakes offer a multitude of outdoor recreation opportunities. Mountain bikers can explore a network of trails stretching deep into the surrounding forests, or test out techniques at the brand new Hope Bike Skills Park. Hiking enthusiasts can check out the short trip to beautiful Flood Falls, or tackle one of the imposing local peaks, such as Mount Outram, which offers panoramic views of the Cascade mountain range.

While the surrounding Coquihalla and the Fraser are popular with paddlers and fishers, the nearby Thompson, Nahatlatch, and Chilliwack Rivers also offer plenty of reactional opportunities. Thrill seekers will find that dynamic rapid runs and multi-day adventures await the ambitious paddler. Anglers can set up at one of the many hot-spots and test their luck for some of the area's famous salmon. The Fraser is also home to the giant prehistoric Sturgeon, attracting sport fishers from all over the world. Fishing opportunities abound at glistening Kawkwa Lake, home to more than 10 species of fish, and at the beautiful Skagit River, regarded as having the best fly fishing in BC.

Southeast of Hope, Skagit Valley Provincial Park is an outdoor playground of lush meadows, pristine lakes and rivers and towering mountains. Environmentalists fought tooth and nail to preserve this magical area, and a visit to the park will make it clear why. Nearby Othello Tunnels showcase an engineering feat, having been blasted through solid granite cliffs in the early 1900s. Winter snowfalls turn the area into a magical wonderland – skiing, snowshoeing and snowmobiling become popular ways to explore the Hope area, while the nearby Manning Park Resort offers top-grade terrain for downhill skiers and snowboarders.

There is just too much to write about Hope – come and see for yourself!

❝ Our sky scraping mountains, deep canyon ravines, raging rivers and serene lakes are the perfect playground for outdoor enthusiasts. ❞

MAP

TO LEARN MORE, CONTACT

Hope Visitor Centre
919 Water Avenue, Hope, BC
Ph: 604-869-2021
www.hopebc.ca

 From top to bottom: Kettle Valley Trail - AdvantageHOPE; Flood Falls - AdvantageHOPE; Nickel Mine - AdvantageHOPE; Needle Peak - AdvantageHOPE;

SEA TO SKY COUNTRY
BRITISH COLUMBIA

Garibaldi Lake

Sea to Sky Highway

Seton Lake

Beginning in Horseshoe Bay, just 30 minutes north of downtown Vancouver, Sea to Sky Country stretches along Highway 99 all the way up to Lillooet. Consisting of traditional Coast Salish territory, this immaculate stretch of BC's coast presents a stunning contrast between the glittering waters of Howe Sound and the giant mountains that rise right out of the aqueous depths, their glacial summits reaching into the sky. Inland and to the north, the Sea to Sky continues into the very heart of BC's Coast Mountains.

Outdoor recreation abounds in this region, with Whistler and Blackcomb Mountains offering arguably the best downhill skiing and snowboarding in the world, and Squamish proudly identifying as the "Outdoor Recreation Capital of Canada," known in particular for its unbeatable rock-climbing terrain. Sea to Sky Country also offers premiere opportunities for water sports, fishing, hunting, wildlife viewing, horseback riding, hiking, snowmobiling and more, making it a top recreation destination in any season.

While Squamish and Whistler make up the larger urban centers of the Sea to Sky, the region is peppered with quaint communities steeped in a rich history of logging, mining and ranching. Despite the close proximity to Vancouver, you might feel like you have stepped backwards in time as you wander the quiet streets of Pemberton or explore

the interactive exhibits of the Britannia Mine Museum. With untamed wilderness surrounding you in every direction, the Sea to Sky is an easy-to-access portal into a different reality.

Sea to Sky Country is home to 10 stunning provincial parks which protect the natural landscape for the enjoyment of outdoor enthusiasts. Mountain goats, deer, cougars and bears are some of the local residents who enjoy the parks' protected status, having adapted to these specific landscapes over

tens of thousands of years. A diverse array of fauna paints these wildlands in a kaleidoscope of colours, and shimmering alpine lakes complement the almost hallucinatory views. The beauty of Sea to Sky Country has to be seen to be believed.

From countless generations of First Nations, to throngs of gold miners, to modern recreationists, the Sea to Sky has been providing a natural bounty for diverse groups of people since time immemorial. Why not come and sample these unparalleled natural riches for yourself?

SUPER, NATURAL BRITISH COLUMBIA ♦ CANADA

EXPLORE SEA TO SKY COUNTRY
Travel Highway 99 from Horseshoe Bay through Whistler all the way to the historic Pemberton Valley

WELCOME TO Squamish
CANADA'S OUTDOOR RECREATION CAPITAL

In the traditional language of the Squamish People, the word "Squamish" can be translated as "Mother of the Wind". Sitting at the northern tip of Howe Sound, the small city gets its fair share of gusts and gales, but that does not hinder a thriving recreational and cultural scene in this coastal mountain paradise. Nestled below the imposing granite massif of the Stawamus Chief, Squamish embodies the fluid boundary between relaxation and adventure.

The massive "Chief", as it is fondly known, is an impressive solid granite formation and makes for a stunning backdrop to the community. As one of the world's foremost rock climbing destinations, the variety of routes available is staggering and the sticky granite affords climbers a sure grip. The Chief and the surrounding area contain over 3,500 climbing routes and bouldering problems. For those that don't wish to climb the Chief's rocky face, this monolith can be hiked from the back side, through a network of easily accessible hiking trails. Sensational views of Squamish and Howe Sound await those who visit this rocky giant's three peaks.

Right next door and accessible by trail is the thunderous Shannon Falls – BC's third tallest falls. The 335 m (1,100 ft) drop is the perfect setting for a picnic surrounded by towering trees, old growth stumps, and the swirling mist from the roaring falls above.

Squamish is one of the wildest and most exotic places to ride in the world and sports some of BC's top wilderness biking. With sites throughout the Squamish area, endless kilometers of singletrack offer action and challenges for all skill levels throughout the surrounding mountains. The Crumpit Woods and Valleycliffe areas offer expansive networks of narrow trails that take cross-country riders through stream beds, lush woodlands and granite features of Squamish's West Coast forests.

Water sport enthusiasts can plunge into Squamish's arterial network of rivers, perfect for kayaking and whitewater rafting, as well as a multitude of pristine freshwater lakes. Kiteboarders, windsurfers and sailors will enjoy harnessing the natural power of windy Howe Sound, while canoers and stand-up paddleboarders can enjoy the calm waters of Alice and Brohm Lakes. Under the water, divers of all experience levels can explore the sunken park at Porteau Cove. Home to a colourful host of marine life such as the plumose anemone, harbour seals, and giant lingcod, this is a diver's paradise.

> **The world's most epic outdoor adventures - from Sea to Sky - all within 10 minutes of one another.**

189

From top to bottom: Downtown Squamish - Ian Robertson; Squamish River - Chris Christie; West Coast Railway Heritage Park - Tourism Squamish; Howe Sound - Chris Christie.

THE STAWAMUS CHIEF

SEA TO SKY
VERTICAL RISE
885 METERS

BIRD WATCHERS
PARADISE

HARDWIRED FOR ADVENTURES

335 METERS:
SHANNON FALLS

Freshwater lakes and rivers and the salty waters of Howe Sound provide ample fishing opportunities. Glistening Mamquam, Cheakamus, Squamish and Elaho rivers are crowded with a selection of different Pacific Salmon as well as Bull and Cutthroat Trout. Brohm and Browning lakes are also a relaxing way to land a fair sized Rainbow or Cutthroat Trout.

An unparalleled way to take in the best of Squamish year-round is a trip on the Sea-to-Sky Gondola. This gateway to outdoor adventure features numerous hiking trails, interpretive walks, panoramic views of gorgeous Howe Sound and the surrounding coastal mountains, as well as fresh, local dining experiences. A 10-minute ride to the top takes you 885 m above sea level, and in winter becomes a sparkling snowy utopia with access to over 3,000 acres of backcountry terrain and winter activities for every age and ability, including front and backcountry skiing, snowshoeing and tubing.

Squamish offers copious backcountry riding opportunities for those willing to put in a little bit of extra effort. Immensely beautiful, Garibaldi Provincial Park is a popular destination for skiers and snowboarders, while Brohm Ridge is one of the top snowmobiling areas in Canada. At night, refuge can be found in one of the well-maintained huts in the park. For wildlife viewers, winter means the return of thousands of majestic bald eagles to the Squamish Valley – a designated viewing area is located in Brackendale Eagles Provincial Park.

The opportunities for adventure in the Squamish area are endless. Why not come and take a closer look?

TO LEARN MORE, CONTACT
Squamish Visitor Centre
38551 Loggers Lane, Squamish, BC
Ph: 604-815-4994
www.exploresquamish.com
#exploresquamish

From top to bottom: Sea to Sky Gondola - Paul Bride; Climbing the Stawamus Chief - Chris Christie; Squamish Alpine - Chris Christie; Bald Eagle - Garry Broeckling.

WELCOME TO Pemberton

ADVENTURE BEGINS HERE

Situated in a fertile valley below the majestic, snow-capped Mount Currie, Pemberton enjoyed the title of Canada's fastest growing rural community and boasts a rich history of First Nations activity, agriculture and forestry. Until 1964, Pemberton was accessible only by train, and with its stunning surroundings of verdant forests, sparkling rivers and lakes, towering mountain peaks and glacial ice fields, it is easy to imagine why the locals may have wanted to keep this spectacular outdoor playground all to themselves. Today, Pemberton still retains the sleepy, tranquil charm of an old fashioned mountain town, due in no small part to its humbling natural setting.

Pemberton and the surrounding communities of Mount Currie, Birken and D'Arcy are truly an outdoor recreationist's paradise. Think of virtually any outdoor activity, and the Pemberton area will provide a world-class option. The numerous pristine lakes and rivers that surround Pemberton are unbeatable destinations for kayakers, canoers, boaters and fishers alike. Anglers can try their luck for trout, Dolly Varden, whitefish and all five species of salmon. Local heli-fishing outfitters provide access to virgin rainbow trout in little to zero pressure lakes for an unforgettable fishing experience, while ice fishing in the winter offers a more rustic, laid back option. Take in the winter landscape while you drop a line at one of the many cutthroat trout hotspots in the area – the fish are plentiful and aggressive.

For a more adrenaline-charged activity, Pemberton offers an intricate network of mountain bike trails, and is quickly becoming one of BC's premiere mountain biking destinations. Pemberton's location on the border between two climate zones – the coastal temperate rainforest and the dry interior plateau – make for a longer riding season and drier trails than Whistler to the south. This allows for prime hiking terrain as well, and a number of trails lead right from the village to breathtaking mountaintop viewpoints.

Why not try a time-honoured method of exploring the wilderness around Pemberton and head out on an equestrian adventure? The dedicated members of the local chapter of the Backcountry Horsemen of BC work hard to preserve historic horse trails in the area. If you don't have your own horse, a number of local outfitters offer guided tours, including to the Li-Lik-Hel Mine, which is officially designated as a Signature Canadian Experience. Shorter day trips are also available for booking, making an unforgettable horseback riding adventure possible for explorers of all levels.

❝ Hailed as a 'mountain biking mecca' with some of BC's top wilderness biking. ❞

 From top to bottom: Duffey Lake - Brad Knowles; Sockeye Creek Trail - Brenda Williams; Fescues Restaurant - Big Sky Golf; Upper Lillooet River - Brad Knowles.

MT. CURRIE 2,591 M (8,500 FT)

SIGNATURE CANADIAN EXPERIENCE: **LI-LIK-HEL MINE TOURS**

ADRENALINE SEEKERS: **HELI ASSISTED SKI TOURING**

MOUNTAIN **VIEWS**

NAIRN FALLS

If you are looking for an overnight adventure, two nearby Provincial Parks are excellent places to camp and to set up a base for exploring the surrounding area. Located just 3 km south of Pemberton, Nairn Falls Provincial Park offers a wheelchair accessible day-use area and dazzling views of the namesake falls. There is also an incredibly refreshing swimming hole near the falls, which you won't be able to help yourself from dipping in on a hot summer day. North of Pemberton, near D'Arcy, lies Birkenhead Provincial Park, which features a number of amenities including walk-in campsites, wheelchair access, drinking water, pit toilets, sani-station, fire pits, a sandy beach area, concrete boat launch and numerous recreation opportunities. For campers, these parks are just too splendid to not take advantage of. There are also a number of Forestry Recreation Sites scattered throughout the area, particularly along Lillooet Lake and Duffey Lake Roads, perfect for those looking for more of a wilderness camping experience.

In winter, the area around Pemberton becomes a utopia for snowmobilers, backcountry and cross-country skiers and snowshoers. The Pemberton Icefields are one of Western Canada's top snowmobiling destinations, offering vast treeless areas with unobstructed views of the Coast Mountains and beyond. The Duffey Lake area, located just east of Pemberton, offers some of the best backcountry skiing in BC, and there are a number of ski huts scattered throughout the mountains to make overnight trips easy. There is definitely something special about warming up by the roaring woodstove of a remote backcountry cabin after a day of epic powder lines. For that extra special backcountry adventure, consider hiring one of Pemberton's heli assisted ski touring outfits for that run of a lifetime.

For a more refined recreational activity, golfers can take a swing at either of Pemberton's two 18-hole courses. The golfing experience can be either technically challenging or casual and is suited to golfers of all abilities. At the end of the day one can enjoy the brilliant settings below the looming Mount Currie and relax in either of the courses restaurants and outdoor patios.

Several hot springs in the Pemberton area create year-round attractions for locals and visitors, including Keyhole (or Pebble Creek), Skookumchuck (or St Agnes Well) and Sloquet. Some of these springs have changerooms, outhouses and manmade pools, while others offer a more rustic, wild setting, with each providing their own unique charm or appeal.

We could go on forever writing about things to do in and around Pemberton. Come and see for yourself why this small village is making big impressions!

MAP

TO LEARN MORE, CONTACT
Pemberton Visitor Centre
Hwy 99 & Pemberton Portage Rd, Pemberton, BC
Ph: 604-894-6175
www.tourismpembertonbc.com

From top to bottom: Bridge River Valley - Andy Meeker, Blackcomb Helicopters; Mackenzie Area - "Blood, Sweat, Fear" Trail - Dave Steers; Joffre Lake - Jason McClean; Zippermouth Creek - Julie-ann Chapman, She Shreds Mountain Adventures

WELCOME TO Lillooet

GUARANTEED RUGGED

The town of Lillooet appears about 240 km (150 mi) up the British Columbia Railway line from Vancouver. Carved into the rugged, rocky and mountainous terrain of the South Chilcotin, Lillooet graces the shores of the Fraser River and bursts with opportunities for outdoor adventure. Once a gold rush era town, the community now bustles with activity. With a number of restaurants, bed and breakfasts, campsites and other lodging options, Lillooet opens a welcoming door to visitors.

The culture here pulses with appreciation for the great outdoors. Over a hundred geocaches lie hidden within the landscape. Every July, the Lillooet Apricot Tsaqwen Festival celebrates local culture with live music and delicious local eats. Experience the St'át'imc First Nations culture with a Xwísten Experience Tour, and appreciate the ancient customs of the region's first inhabitants. You will find Lillooet's Museum and Visitor Centre housed in an old Anglican church.

Stroll along the Jade Walk on Main Street and behold the beautiful jade sculptures. Follow the tracks of the Rocky Mountaineer and ride the Kaoham rail along the shores of Seton Lake. Dip your feet into the majestic Fraser River as you comb the rocks, or hit the trails and discover a world of mountain biking, hiking and snowmobiling opportunities. Rivers and lakes gleam with boating spots, and Lillooet's trademark steep mountains create an ice climber's delight during winter months.

When the snow falls, embrace the outdoors with heli-skiing and snowmobiling. In warmer months, indulge in a round of golf at the Lillooet Sheep Pasture Golf Course. Kick back and savour a taste at the Fort Berens Estate Winery, where vineyards sprawl across a sagebrush-covered bench at the foot of the mountains in the Fraser Canyon. The sandy soil of Lillooet lends itself to premium grapes.

From scenic road trips winding along the Fraser, to music-filled parks in the heart of the community, to rugged backcountry expeditions, there is something for everyone in Lillooet!

" The culture here pulses with appreciation for the great outdoors. "

TO LEARN MORE, CONTACT
Lillooet Museum and Visitor Centre
790 Main Street, Lillooet, BC
Ph: 250-256-4308
www.lillooetbc.ca

 From top to bottom: Pavilion Lake – Brad Kasselman; Pavilion Lake – Brad Kasselman; Gun Lake Trails - Brad Kasselman; Tyaughton Lake Trails – Brad Kasselman.

SUNSHINE COAST
BRITISH COLUMBIA

BC Ferries - Sunshine Coast Tourism

Coastal Aerial - Sunshine Coast Tourism

Patricia Theatre - Sunshine Coast Tourism

The Sunshine Coast comprises 180 km of picturesque coastline on the Strait of Georgia, stretching from Howe Sound to Desolation Sound. The region is characterized by deep inlets, sandy beaches and an interconnected patchwork of brilliant lakes. While the Sunshine Coast is only accessible by ferry, boat or floatplane it is still a very popular tourist destination, and is home to a growing number of internationally renowned artists, musicians and artisans. The majestic landscape is nothing short of inspiring.

With stately mountain peaks towering over deep ocean waters, the Sunshine Coast offers a wide range of outdoor recreation opportunities. Hikers can liberate themselves from the trappings of modern life on a multi-day trek across the Sunshine Coast Trail, which stretches across 180 km of serene coastal shoreline, meandering mountain creeks, pristine lakes, ancient old growth forest and sky-scraping mountains. Paddlers can take on the Powell Forest Canoe Route, a 57 km long journey across eight immaculate lakes that usually takes five days to complete. If these options are any indication, the Sunshine Coast is a place to escape your routine and disappear for a little while into a slower-paced, secluded microcosm of civilization.

Some of the communities that inhabit the Sunshine Coast include Gibsons, Sechelt, Powell River, Lund and Pender Harbour. Though each community is

comprised of unique characteristics shaped by cultural and historical roots as well as its natural setting, many share common roots in fishing and forestry, while tourism has more recently become an economic mainstay of the region. The

SUPER, NATURAL BRITISH COLUMBIA
❦ CANADA

natural resources of the region sustained a vibrant population of Squamish, Sechelt and Sliam on Squamish Nation, shíshálh Nation, Tla'amin Nation for countless generations. These cultures maintain prominence on the Sunshine Coast, and the area resonates with a deep history of these first peoples.

The pristine natural environment of Sunshine Coast make its waters, mountains and forests the perfect home to a rich variety of wildlife. Deer and elk graze the forests, providing an occasional meal for the stealthy and ruthless cougar. Shaggy mountain goats roam across treacherous high alpine terrain. Beavers navigate the web of waterways, while otters and seals frolic in the open waters of the Strait. Dolphins, porpoises, orcas and baleen and grey whales all pass through the Strait, providing spectacular wildlife viewing opportunities. This region is bristling with life of all kinds.

Although it is located close to Vancouver, the Sunshine Coast offers a radical change of pace from the hustle and bustle of city life. Slow it down a bit and come for a visit.

EXPLORE
THE SUNSHINE COAST
Take a ferry from Horseshoe Bay or Comox. Fly from YVR, Victoria & Nanaimo via scheduled or charter flight.

WELCOME TO
Gibsons

GATEWAY TO THE SUNSHINE COAST

Gibsons is a charming seaside paradise, perched on a steep hillside, located at the south end of the Sunshine Coast. Accessed by an easy 40 minute ferry ride from Horseshoe Bay, this picturesque community overlooks the beautiful Howe Sound and the many islands that protrude out of its azure waters. Gibsons is situated comfortably in the rain shadow of the Vancouver Island Ranges and sees relatively mild rainfall while still benefitting from the warm climate of a temperate rainforest zone. This makes it a popular destination for outdoor enthusiasts year-round, as well as an inviting climate for a variety of wildlife.

Fishing is deeply ingrained in the town's history, and continues to be an economic and recreational anchor for the community. For the leisurely angler, fish can be caught right off the docks of the Gibsons marina, while those looking for more action can chose to charter a fishing boat for prime salmon fishing throughout the year.

Divers can delight in checking out the newly sunken HMCS Annapolis, which makes up the eighth artificial reef in BC. The former helicopter-carrying destroyer now lies in the bottom of Howe Sound, in an inlet off Gambier Island, and serves as a habitat for many marine species and a world-class attraction for underwater explorers.

Relaxation on the water can also be found locally in the form of sailing, kayaking, canoeing or even swimming. Head out for a day of leisurely exploring among the numerous sandy beaches of Gibsons, or stray to the surrounding islands. Peaceful Gambier Island has an excellent network of hiking trails, and a population of under 200 full time residents. Take an opportunity to meet the locals a get a feel for the relaxed pace of island life at the Gambier Community Hall which hosts a variety of events and dinners. Keats Island is smaller than Gambier and hosts excellent camping, swimming, hiking and fishing, with a population of just a few dozen full-time residents.

Recreational opportunities around Gibsons are not limited to the water. Get your adrenaline pumping with an extensive mountain bike trail system, or visit nearby Dakota Ridge for unbeatable Nordic skiing and snowshoeing during winter. A bright array of local eateries, artisan shops and art studios offer a taste of authentic Gibsons culture. Come and discover Gibsons' unique charm for yourself!

" There is no lack of outdoor activities in the Gibsons area, many of them year-round. "

TO LEARN MORE, CONTACT

Gibsons Visitor Centre
417 Marine Dr, Gibsons, BC
Ph: 604-886-2374
www.gibsonsvisitorinfo.com
www.sunshinecoastcanada.ca

From top to bottom: Gibsons Landing - Sunshine Coast Tourism; Persephone tugboat - Sunshine Coast Tourism; Windsurfing - Sunshine Coast Tourism; Dakota Ridge - Sunshine Coast Tourism.

WELCOME TO
Powell River
COASTAL BY NATURE

Powell River is a piece of pacific paradise and an escape into the wilds of nature, located in the heart of the Malaspina Peninsula. Surrounded by a stunning array of fjords, islands, mountains and lakes, this laid-back community offers plenty of scenic hiking trails, water courses to navigate and panoramic vistas to take in.

Powell River occupies a unique geography separated by an additional ferry ride from the southern part of the Sunshine Coast. This remote location blesses Powell River with an unusually intact natural beauty, which the local Tla'amin (or Sliammon) First Nations have been enjoying for thousands of years. A historically rich community, Powell River officially started off as an industrial centre. In the early 20th century, Powell River became home to the world's largest newsprint mill, ensuring the lasting establishment of a modern town.

Anglers will delight in Powell River's abundant fishing opportunities, with all five species of salmon present at various times of the year, while the many nearby lakes offer fantastic freshwater trout fishing. Hikers can tackle parts (or all) of the Sunshine Coast Trail, which wind for 180 km through breathtaking mountain landscapes surrounding Powell River. Hunters can try for the abundant blacktail deer population, with prime territory being opened up by logging over the last few years. Mountain bikers have an extensive trail system through the lush mossy forests of Powell River to pick and choose from, including the popular multi-use 48 km Duck Lake network to the south of town.

Unsurpassed scenery can be found to the north of Powell River in Desolation Sound, BC's largest marine park, containing endless opportunities for swimming, paddling, boating, sailing, diving, fishing and more. Lund, a charming village of around 300 year-round residents, serves as the gateway to this outdoor paradise and marks the end of Highway 101. Protected from harsh currents and winds, the waters of Desolation Sound are unusually warm, making it a haven for recreationists and a hospitable environment for many types of plants and wildlife. A multicoloured array of huge starfish and vibrant anemones cover the ocean floor, while Orcas glide through the waters above under the watchful eyes of soaring eagles.

No matter your choice of outdoor activity, Powell River offers up shining adventure opportunities in a brilliant setting!

> **This area is home to some of the best hiking trails in the world. Trails feature unlimited variety for hikers of all skill sets, from scenic oceanfront strolls to backcountry treks.**

MAP

TO LEARN MORE, CONTACT
Powell River Visitor Centre
4760 Joyce Ave, Powell River, BC
Ph: 604-485-4701
www.powellriver.info
www.sunshinecoastcanada.ca

 From top to bottom: Powell River Marina - Sunshine Coast Tourism; Tinhat Hut - Sunshine Coast Tourism; Kayaking in Desolation Sound - Sunshine Coast Tourism; BC Bike Race - Sunshine Coast Tourism.

WELCOME TO Sechelt

BLESSED BY SUN AND SEAS

Discover the authenticity of the charming coastal community of Sechelt, perched on the isthmus between the Strait of Georgia and the Sechelt Inlet. Famous for its pristine beaches, vibrant arts culture, ochre-red arbutus trees, sprawling coastline and dense green forests, this remarkable stretch of Sunshine Coast is truly blessed by mother nature. Home to the shíshálh Nation, the many totem poles that grace the area attest to a rich First Nations history.

Outdoor enthusiasts will find a multitude of breathtaking views and fascinating wildlife in and around Sechelt. Just north of town is Hidden Grove, a protected area of maple wetlands containing many old growth cedars and Douglas firs. Hikers can explore the well-maintained trail system winding through this abundant forest, admiring these resolute ancient giants. To the east of Sechelt lie Chapman Falls, an enchanting series of three waterfalls that seem to plummet right out of the thick forest canopy.

Truly an angler's paradise, the plentiful fishing options around Sechelt offer all five species of salmon, in addition to snapper and cod. Fly-fishing enthusiasts will enjoy the surface-feeding trout at Trout Lake, just north of Sechelt. For those opting to relax along the shorelines, there are plenty of pebble and sand beaches to choose from right around town. If the itinerary calls for even quieter outing, take a trip to the secluded Thormanby Island and its sprawling sandy shoreline. Near Sechelt, the sunken HMCS Chaudière serves as a vibrant artificial reef, offering a world-class diving destination teeming with aquatic life. The numerous water-access only campsites along the shoreline are the ultimate peaceful getaway for paddling enthusiasts.

Mountain bikers will find that top quality trails run throughout Sechelt. Or, for a more leisurely outdoor pursuit, golfing is an option. Sechelt also boasts a number of cultural and culinary attractions within the town, including the Sunshine Coast Arts Centre. With so much to explore, why not come and see the bright shine of Sechelt for yourself?

> **With over 500 km of inner and outer coastline, and plenty of mountains, lakes and rivers, the Sunshine Coast is an outdoor lover's paradise.**

MAP

TO LEARN MORE, CONTACT

Sechelt Visitor Centre
5790 Teredo St, Sechelt, BC
Ph:604-885-1036
www.secheltvisitorcentre.com
www.sunshinecoastcanada.ca

From top to bottom: Sechelt Aerial - Sunshine Coast Tourism; Totems - Sunshine Coast Tourism; Stand up paddle boarding in Sechelt Inlet - Sunshine Coast Tourism; Tuwanek Dive Site - Sunshine Coast Tourism.

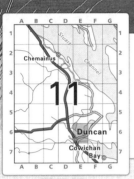

The **Map Index** listings consist of: listing name, page number/coordinates. In the example found on the left, Duncan is found on page 11/E6.

For the **Adventure Index**, the listing also consists of the Reference Page number, where the description of the listing is found. In the example below, the Stuart Channel listing description is found on page 89.

Stuart Channel..........11/B1-G4;**89** ──────► **Reference Page**

Name   **Map Page/Coordinate**

The grid lines found in the example are used for illustration purposes only. The blue grid lines found on the maps refer to UTM coordinates.

ADVENTURE INDEX

BACKROAD ADVENTURES

FISHING ADVENTURES

VIEW OF VANCOUVER FROM GROUSE MOUNTAIN, BC

HUNTING ADVENTURES

FISHING IN ENGLISH BAY, BC

PADDLING ADVENTURES

PARK ADVENTURES

LOWER FALLS IN GOLDEN EARS PROVINCIAL PARK, BC

GARIBALDI LAKE, GARIBALDI PROVINCIAL PARK, BC

MOUNT SEYMOUR PROVINCIAL PARK, BC

ADVENTURE INDEX

SNOWSHOEING NEAR WHISTLER, BC

MAP INDEX
(Name, Page/Coordinates)

BUNTZEN LAKE, BELCARRA REGIONAL PARK, BC

KAYAKING NEAR DEEP COVE, BC

VIEW OF HOWE SOUND FROM THE SEA TO SKY GONDOLA IN SQUAMISH, BC

PITT LAKE AREA NEAR MAPLE RIDGE, BC

GREEN LAKE, WHISTLER, BC

WHISTLER
32/F5

AREA (TOTAL)
10.63 km²

ELEVATION
670 m (2,200 ft)

POPULATION (2011)
TOTAL: 9,824

AREA CODE(S)
604, 778, 326

BRITISH COLUMBIA / ALBERTA

How to use this Distance Chart

The distance from Camrose to Dawson Creek is 687 Kilometres

1 Kilometre = 0.621 Mile

1 Mile = 1.6 Kilometres

Speed Conversion Chart

Contacts

IMPORTANT NUMBERS

Avalanche Conditions .... www.avalanche.ca
.... 1-800-667-1105
BC Ferries .... www.bcferries.com
.... 1-888-223-3779
Highways Report .... www.drivebc.ca
.... 1-800-550-4997
Destination BC .... www.hellobc.com
.... 1-800-435-5622
Updates .... www.backroadmapbooks.com
Weather Conditions..... www.weatheroffice.ec.gc.ca
Wildfire Information Line............ 1-888-336-7378
To Report Forest Fires (Emergency Only) ....
.... 1-800-663-5555
.... *5555 (cellular phones)

B.C. FOREST SERVICES

Ministry of Forests .... www.gov.bc.ca/for
Northern Interior Forest Region... www.for.gov.bc.ca/rsi
.... 250-565-6100
Southern Interior Forest Region ....
.... www.for.gov.bc.ca/rsi
.... 250-828-4131

Fish and Wildlife

BC Fishing Regs ....
.... www.env.gov.bc.ca/fw/fish/regulations
BC Hunting Regulations ....
www.env.gov.bc.ca/fw/wildlife/hunting/regulations
BC Wildlife Federation............ www.bcwf.bc.ca
Freshwater Fisheries Society of BC ....
.... www.gofishbc.com
Observe, Record and Report ....www.RAPP.bc.ca
.... 1-877-952-7277 or *7277
Salmon and Steelhead Regulations ....
.... www.pac.dfo-mpo.gc.ca

PARKS & RECREATION SITES

BC Parks........................www.bcparks.ca
BC Recreation Sites & Trails...........................
.... www.sitesandtrailsbc.ca
Park Reservations........... www.discovercamping.ca
.... 1-800-689-9025

CLUBS & ASSOCIATIONS

ATV BC .... www.atvbc.ca
BC Fishing Resorts & Outfitters Assoc...www.bcfroa.ca
BC Lodging & Campground Assoc. ....
.... www.travel-british-columbia.com
BC Snowmobile Federation ....www.bcsf.org
Camping & RV BC Coalition.www.rvcampingbc.com
Canoe Kayak BC .... www.canoekayakbc.ca
Horse Council BC......................www.hcbc.ca
Trails BC...........................www.trailsbc.ca

212

TRIP PLANNING

TRAILS

PARKS

SNOWMOBILE

CHOOSE YOUR
ADVENTURE

BACKROADS

ATV [OHV]

FISHING

PADDLING

HUNTING

WINTER

RECSITES

WILDLIFE

BRMB
backroadmapbooks.com

For a complete list of our products

Backroad Mapbooks

GPS Maps

Fishing Maps

BRMB Navigator

Waterproof Maps

TOPO Maps

Digital Maps

visit us at backroadmapbooks.com